D0161569

# American Women in Science

## 1950 to the Present

# American Women in Science

## 1950 to the Present

### A Biographical Dictionary

Martha J. Bailey

ABC-CLIO

Santa Barbara, California
Denver, Colorado
Oxford, England

Library of Congress Cataloging-in-Publication Data
Bailey, Martha J.
American women in science, 1950 to the present : a biographical dictionary / Martha J. Bailey
p. cm.
Includes bibliographical references and index.
ISBN 0-87436-921-5 (alk. paper)
1. Women scientists—United States—Biography—Dictionaries.
2. Women in science—United States—Biography—Dictionaries.
I. Title.
Q141.B254 1998
500'.82'092273—dc21
[B] 98-22433
CIP

04 03 02 01 00 99 10 9 8 7 6 5 4 3

ABC-CLIO, Inc.
130 Cremona Drive, P.O. Box 1911
Santa Barbara, California 93116-1911

This book is printed on acid-free paper. 

Manufactured in the United States of America

# Contents

# NAMES

Farquhar, Marilyn (Gist)
Fausto-Sterling, Anne
Fedoroff, Nina Vsevolod
Ferguson, Angela Dorothea
Fischer, Irene (Kaminka)
Fisher, Anna L.
Fitzroy, Nancy (Deloye)
Flanigen, Edith Marie
Fossey, Dian
Fox, Marye Anne
Free, Helen (Murray)
Friedl, Ernestine
Friend, Charlotte
Fromkin, Victoria Alexandria (Landish)
Fuchs, Elaine V.
Futter, Ellen Victoria
Gaillard, Mary Katharine
Galdikas, Birute Marija Filomend
Gantt, Elisabeth
Garmire, Elsa (Meints)
Gayle, Helene Doris
Geller, Margaret Joan
Gerber, Judianne. *See* Densen-Gerber, Judianne
Giblett, Eloise Rosalie
Glusker, Jenny (Pickworth)
Goldberg, Adele
Good, Mary (Lowe)
Graham, Frances (Keesler)
Graham, Susan Lois
Grandin, Temple
Granville, Evelyn (Boyd)
Grasselli, Jeanette (Gecsy)
Greer, Sandra Charlene
Greibach, Sheila Adele
Gross, Carol A. (Polinsky)
Gross, Elizabeth Louise
Guttman, Helene Augusta (Nathan)
Haas, Mary Rosamond
Hamilton, Margaret
Hammel, Heidi
Harris, Jean Louise
Harris, Mary (Styles)
Harrison, Faye Venetia
Harrison-Ross, Phyllis Ann
Haschemeyer, Audrey Elizabeth Veazie
Hatfield, Elaine Catherine
Hay, Elizabeth Dexter
Healy, Bernadine Patricia
Helm, June
Herzenberg, Caroline Stuart (Littlejohn)
Hewlett, Sylvia Ann
Hite, Shere
Hoffman, Darleane (Christian)
Hollinshead, Ariel Cahill
Horner, Matina (Souretis)
Horning, Marjorie G.
Hoy, Marjorie Ann (Wolf)
Hrdy, Sarah C. (Blaffer)
Huang, Alice Shih-Hou
Hubbard, Ruth (Hoffman)
Hubbell, Sue (Gilbert)
Hunt, Eva (Verbitsky)
Hutchins, Sandra Elaine
Intriligator, Devrie (Shapiro)
Jackson, Jacquelyne Mary (Johnson)
Jackson, Shirley Ann
Jemison, Mae Carol
Johnson, Barbara Crawford
Johnson, Betsy. *See* Ancker-Johnson, Betsy
Johnson, Virginia (Eshelman)
Johnston, Mary Helen
Jones, Anita Katherine
Kanter, Rosabeth (Moss)
Karp, Carol Ruth (Vander Velde)
Kaufman, Joyce (Jacobson)
Keller, Evelyn (Fox)
Kempf, Martine
Kidwell, Margaret Gale
Kieffer, Susan Werner
Kimble, Judith
King, Mary-Claire
Klinman, Judith (Pollock)
Komaroff, Lydia. *See* Villa-Komaroff, Lydia
Kreps, Juanita (Morris)
Krim, Mathilde (Galland)
Krueger, Anne (Osborn)
Kubler-Ross, Elisabeth
Kuhlmann-Wilsdorf, Doris
Kurtzig, Sandra L. (Brody)
Kwolek, Stephanie Louise
LaBastille, Anne
Lancaster, Cleo
Laurie, Georgia. *See* Lesh-Laurie, Georgia Elizabeth
Leacock, Eleanor (Burke)
Ledley, Tamara (Shapiro)
Leeman, Susan (Epstein)
Leopold, Estella Bergere
Lesh-Laurie, Georgia Elizabeth
Levelt-Sengers, Johanna Maria Henrica
Linares, Olga Frances
Lippincott, Sarah Lee
Liskov, Barbara Huberman
Long, Irene (Duhart)
Long, Sharon (Rugel)

Shipman, Pat
Shockley, Dolores Cooper
Shoemaker, Carolyn (Spellmann)
Shreeve, Jean'ne Marie
Simpson, Joanne Malkus (Gerould)
Singer, Maxine (Frank)
Sinkford, Jeanne Frances (Craig)
Smith, Elske (Van Panhuys)
Solomon, Susan
Spaeth, Mary Dietrich
Spurlock, Jeanne
Steitz, Joan (Argetsinger)
Sterling, Anne. *See* Fausto-Sterling, Anne
Stubbe, Joanne
Sudarkasa, Niara
Sullivan, Kathryn D.
Taylor, Kathleen Christine
Tharp, Marie
Thomas, Martha Jane (Bergin)
Thornton, Kathryn (Cordell)
Tinsley, Beatrice Muriel (Hill)
Tolbert, Margaret Ellen (Mayo)
Townsend, Marjorie Rhodes
Turkle, Sherry
Tyson, Laura (D'Andrea)
Tzanakou, Evangelia. *See* Micheli-Tzanakou, Evangelia
Uhlenbeck, Karen (Keskulla)
Underhill, Anne Barbara
Vaughan, Martha
Villa-Komaroff, Lydia
Vitetta, Ellen Shapiro
Walbot, Virginia Elizabeth
Wallace, Joan (Scott)
Wallace, Phyllis Ann
Walster, Elaine. *See* Hatfield, Elaine Catherine
Watson, Patty Jo (Anderson)
Wattleton, (Alyce) Faye
Weertman, Julia (Randall)
Weisburger, Elizabeth Amy (Kreiser)
Weisstein, Naomi
West-Eberhard, Mary Jane
Westheimer, (Karola) Ruth (Siegel)
Wexler, Nancy Sabin
Whitman, Marina (von Neumann)
Widnall, Sheila (Evans)
Williams, Roberta
Wilsdorf, Doris. *See* Kuhlmann-Wilsdorf, Doris
Witt, Cecile. *See* DeWitt-Morette, Cecile Andrée Paule
Woods, Geraldine (Pittman)
Wu, Ying-Chu (Lin) Susan
Yeboah, Jennie. *See* Patrick-Yeboah, Jennie R.

# Professions

***Anatomy***
Hay, Elizabeth D.

***Animal science***
Grandin, Temple

***Anthropology***
Archambault, JoAllyn
Bateson, Mary C.
Beall, Cynthia
Bricker, Victoria
Buikstra, Jane E.
Cole, Johnnetta
Douglas, Mary
Fossey, Dian
Friedl, Ernestine
Galdikas, Birute
Haas, Mary R.
Harrison, Faye V.
Helm, June
Hunt, Eva
Leacock, Eleanor
Linares, Olga F.
Lubic, Ruth
Lurie, Nancy
McClellan, Catharine
Medicine, Beatrice A.
Nader, Laura
Partee, Barbara
Rose, Wendy
Shipman, Pat
Sudarkasa, Niara
Watson, Patty Jo

***Archaeology***
Buikstra, Jane E.
Mertz, Barbara
Watson, Patty Jo

***Astronaut***
Cleave, Mary L.
Cobb, Geraldyne M.
Dunbar, Bonnie J.
Fisher, Anna L.
Jemison, Mae C.
Lucid, Shannon
Ochoa, Ellen
Resnik, Judith A.
Ride, Sally K.
Seddon, Margaret R.
Sullivan, Kathryn D.
Thornton, Kathryn

***Astronomy***
Burbidge, Eleanor Margaret
Cordova, France A.-D.
Elmegreen, Debra M.
Faber, Sandra
Geller, Margaret J.
Hammel, Heidi
Lippincott, Sarah L.
McFadden, Lucy-Ann A.
Roemer, Elizabeth
Roman, Nancy G.
Rubin, Vera
Shoemaker, Carolyn
Smith, Elske
Tinsley, Beatrice M.

***Astrophysics***
Burbidge, Eleanor Margaret
Cordova, France A.-D.
Geller, Margaret J.
Intriligator, Devrie
Underhill, Anne B.

***Aviator***
Cobb, Geraldyne M.

***Bacteriology***
Gross, Carol A.

***Biochemistry***
Benesch, Ruth E.
Chilton, Mary-Dell
Daly, Marie M.
Edwards, Cecile H.
Fuchs, Elaine V.

Gross, Elizabeth L.
Guttman, Helene A.
Haschemeyer, Audrey E. V.
Horning, Marjorie G.
Hubbard, Ruth
Klinman, Judith
Low, Barbara W.
Lucid, Shannon
Neufeld, Elizabeth
Osborn, Mary J.
Richardson, Jane S.
Rolf, Ida P.
Singer, Maxine
Steitz, Joan
Tolbert, Margaret E.
Vaughan, Martha

### *Biology*

Cobb, Jewel P. (cell)
Cox, Geraldine A.
Farquhar, Marilyn (cell)
Fuchs, Elaine V. (cell)
Gantt, Elisabeth
Hay, Elizabeth D. (cell)
Hrdy, Sarah C. (evolutionary)
Hubbard, Ruth
Lesh-Laurie, Georgia E. (developmental)
Long, Sharon (developmental)
Lubchenco, Jane (conservation)
McCammon, Helen M. (marine)
Margulis, Lynn (cell)
Moss, Cynthia J. (wildlife)
Murray, Sandra A. (cell)
Owens, Joan M. (marine)
Pardue, Mary Lou (developmental, cell)
Poole, Joyce (wildlife)
Profet, Margie (evolutionary)
Ramaley, Judith (reproductive)
Scott, Juanita (developmental)
Sedlak, Bonnie J. (developmental, cell)
Walbot, Virginia E.
Wattleton, (Alyce) Faye

### *Biophysics*

Micheli-Tzanakou, Evangelia
Mielczarek, Eugenie V.

### *Botany*

Davis, Margaret B
Earle, Sylvia A. (marine)
Gantt, Elisabeth
Rissler, Jane F. (plant pathology)

### *Cancer*

Bertell, Rosalie
Glusker, Jenny
Hollinshead, Ariel C.
Krim, Mathilde
Osborn, Mary J.
Weisburger, Elizabeth A.

### *Chemistry*

Anderson, Gloria
Berkowitz, Joan B. (physical)
Brill, Yvonne
Caserio, Marjorie C. (organic)
Flanigen, Edith M. (inorganic)
Fox, Marye A. (physical, organic)
Free, Helen (clinical)
Good, Mary (inorganic, radiation)
Grasselli, Jeanette (analytical)
Greer, Sandra C. (physical)
Hoffman, Darleane (nuclear)
Kaufman, Joyce (quantum)
Klinman, Judith (physical organic)
Kwolek, Stephanie L. (polymer)
Michel, Helen (nuclear)
Reichmanis, Elsa (organic)
Savitz, Maxine (organic, electrochemistry)
Shreeve, Jean'ne M. (inorganic)
Solomon, Susan (atmospheric)
Stubbe, Joanne
Taylor, Kathleen C. (physical)
Thomas, Martha J. (analytical, physical)

### *Climatology*

Ledley, Tamara

### *Computers*

Bell, Gwen
Berezin, Evelyn
Butler, Margaret K.
Conway, Lynn A.
Davis, Ruth M.
Estrin, Thelma A.
Goldberg, Adele
Graham, Susan L.
Granville, Evelyn
Greibach, Sheila A.
Hamilton, Margaret
Hutchins, Sandra
Jones, Anita K.
Kempf, Martine
Kurtzig, Sandra L.
Liskov, Barbara H.
McSherry, Diana H.

Pfeiffer, Jane
Pickett, Mary S.
Pour-El, Marian B.
Reichmanis, Elsa
Sammet, Jean E.
Shaw, Mary M.
Turkle, Sherry
Williams, Roberta

### *Conservation*
Beattie, Mollie H.
Matola, Sharon R.

### *Cosmology*
Faber, Sandra
Geller, Margaret J.
Rubin, Vera

### *Crystallography*
Glusker, Jenny

### *Cultural History*
Hite, Shere

### *Cytology*
Rowley, Janet D.

### *Demography*
Menken, Jane A.

### *Ecology*
Beattie, Mollie H.
Berenbaum, May R.
Davis, Margaret B.
LaBastille, Anne
Leopold, Estella B.
Lubchenco, Jane (marine)

### *Economics*
Adelman, Irma G.
Hewlett, Sylvia A.
Kreps, Juanita
Krueger, Anne
McWhinney, Madeline
Rivlin, Alice
Tyson, Laura
Wallace, Phyllis A.
Whitman, Marina

### *Embryology*
Fausto-Sterling, Anne
Hay, Elizabeth D.
Woods, Geraldine

### *Endocrinology*
Elders, (Minnie) Joycelyn
Leeman, Susan
Ramaley, Judith

### *Engineering*
Benmark, Leslie A. F. (industrial)
Brill, Yvonne (aerospace)
Cleave, Mary L. (environmental)
Colmenares, Margarita H. (environmental)
Conway, Lynn A. (electrical)
Darden, Christine V. (aeronautical)
Dicciani, Nance K. (chemical)
Drake, Elisabeth (chemical)
Dresselhaus, Mildred (electrical)
Dunbar, Bonnie J. (biomedical, ceramic)
Estrin, Thelma A. (biomedical, electrical)
Fitzroy, Nancy
Garmire, Elsa (electrical)
Hamilton, Margaret (systems)
Hutchins, Sandra (communications)
Johnson, Barbara C. (aerospace)
Johnston, Mary H. (metallurgic, materials)
Kurtzig, Sandra L. (aeronautical)
Matthews, Alva T.
Micheli-Tzanakou, Evangelia (biomedical)
Napadensky, Hyla S. (combustion)
Nichols, Roberta J. (environmental)
Ochoa, Ellen (electrical)
Paté-Cornell, (Marie) Elisabeth L. (industrial)
Patrick-Yeboah, Jennie R. (chemical)
Peden, Irene (electrical)
Pressman, Ada I. (systems)
Resnik, Judith A. (electrical)
Townsend, Marjorie R. (electronics, aerospace)
Widnall, Sheila (aeronautical)
Wu, Ying-Chu (Lin) Susan (aerospace)

### *Entomology*
Berenbaum, May R.
Hoy, Marjorie A.
West-Eberhard, Mary J.

### *Environment*
Berkowitz, Joan B.
Caldicott, Helen M.
Cleave, Mary L.
Colmenores, Margarita H.
Cox, Geraldine A.
Earle, Sylvia A.
Ehrlich, Anne

Matson, Pamela A.
Smith, Elske

### Enzymology
Neufeld, Elizabeth

### Epidemiology
Broome, Claire V.
Gayle, Helene D.
Harris, Mary
King, Mary-Claire

### Ethnology
Bricker, Victoria
Friedl, Ernestine
Helm, June

### Forestry
Beattie, Mollie H.

### Genetics
Fuchs, Elaine V.
Giblett, Eloise R.
Harris, Mary
Hoy, Marjorie A.
Kidwell, Margaret G. (evolutionary)
Kimble, Judith
King, Mary-Claire
Krim, Mathilde
Rowley, Janet D.
Singer, Maxine
Walbot, Virginia E. (plant)

### Geochemistry
Navrotsky, Alexandra A. S.
Roy, Della M.

### Geodesy
Fischer, Irene

### Geography
Bell, Gwen

### Geology
Kieffer, Susan W.
McCammon, Helen M.
Ocampo, Adriana C.
Schwarzer, Theresa F.
Sullivan, Kathryn D.
Tharp, Marie

### Geophysics
Dreschhoff, Gisela A.-M.
McFadden, Lucy-Ann A.
McNutt, Marcia K.
Navrotsky, Alexandra A. S.

### Immunology
Marrack, Philippa C.
Vitetta, Ellen S.

### Information Technology
Davis, Ruth
Goldberg, Adele
Hutchins, Sandra

### Inventor
Bryenton, Elisabeth
Spaeth, Mary D.

### Law
Densen-Gerber, Judianne
Futter, Ellen V.

### Linguistics
Bateson, Mary C.
Fromkin, Victoria A.
Haas, Mary R.
Partee, Barbara

### Management Consultant
Kanter, Rosabeth
Pfeiffer, Jane

### Materials Science
Roy, Della M.

### Mathematics
Bertell, Rosalie
Butler, Margaret K.
Davis, Ruth M.
Fischer, Irene
Granville, Evelyn
Greibach, Sheila A.
Karp, Carol R.
Keller, Evelyn
Morawetz, Cathleen
Pour-El, Marian B.
Rosenblatt, Joan
Rudin, Mary E.
Uhlenbeck, Karen

### Medicine
Avery, Mary E. (pediatrics)
Broome, Claire V. (epidemiology)
Caldicott, Helen M. (pediatrics)

Densen-Gerber, Judianne (psychiatry)
Elders, (Minnie) Joycelyn (pediatrics)
Estrin, Thelma A. (computer)
Farquhar, Marilyn (pathology)
Ferguson, Angela D. (pediatrics)
Fisher, Anna L. (physician)
Free, Helen
Gayle, Helene D. (pediatrics)
Giblett, Eloise R. (hematology)
Harris, Jean L. (internal medicine, allergy)
Harris, Mary (epidemiology)
Harrison-Ross, Phyllis A. (pediatrics)
Hay, Elizabeth D. (anatomy)
Healy, Bernadine P. (cardiology)
Jemison, Mae C. (physician)
Kubler-Ross, Elisabeth
Long, Irene (aerospace)
Lubic, Ruth (nurse-midwife)
New, Maria I. (pediatrics)
Novello, Antonia (pediatrics)
Profet, Margie (biomedicine)
Ranney, Helen M. (hematology)
Seddon, Margaret R. (physician)

## *Metallurgy*
Johnston, Mary H.
Kuhlmann-Wilsdorf, Doris
Weertman, Julia

## *Meteorology*
Simpson, Joanne M.

## *Microbiology*
Brooks, Carolyn
Colwell, Rita (marine)
Friend, Charlotte (medical)
Guttman, Helene A.
Huang, Alice S.-H.
Margulis, Lynn
Vitetta, Ellen S.

## *Molecular Biology*
Chilton, Mary-Dell
Fedoroff, Nina V.
Fuchs, Elaine V.
Keller, Evelyn
Long, Sharon
Murray, Sandra A.
Osborn, Mary J.
Shapiro, Lucille
Steitz, Joan
Villa-Komaroff, Lydia

## *Natural Science*
Ackerman, Diane
Bonta, Marcia
Futter, Ellen V.
Hubbell, Sue

## *Neurobiology*
Villa-Komaroff, Lydia

## *Neurophysiology*
Brown, Barbara B.
Pert, Candace D.

## *Nutrition*
Brody, Jane E.
Calloway, Doris
Edwards, Cecile H.
Seddon, Margaret R.

## *Oceanography*
Earle, Sylvia A.

## *Paleontology*
Davis, Margaret B.
Leopold, Estella B.
Shipman, Pat

## *Pathology*
Farquhar, Marilyn

## *Pharmacology*
Brown, Barbara B.
Hollinshead, Ariel C.
Horning, Marjorie G.
Kaufman, Joyce
Shaw, Jane E.
Shockley, Dolores C.

## *Physics*
Ajzenberg-Selove, Fay (nuclear)
Ancker-Johnson, Betsy (solid state)
Berezin, Evelyn
Chasman, Renate (nuclear)
De Planque, E. Gail
Dewitt-Morette, Cecile Andrée Paule (theoretical)
Dreschhoff, Gisela A.-M. (radiation)
Dresselhaus, Mildred (solid state)
Edwards, Helen T. (accelerator)
Gaillard, Mary K. (theoretical)
Garmire, Elsa
Herzenberg, Caroline S.
Intriligator, Devrie (space)

Jackson, Shirley A. (elementary particle)
Kaufman, Joyce
Keller, Evelyn
Kieffer, Susan W. (mineral)
Kuhlmann-Wilsdorf, Doris
Levelt-Sengers, Johanna M. H.
Lubkin, Gloria
McSherry, Diana H. (medical)
Micheli-Tzanakou, Evangelia (neuro)
Mielczarek, Eugenie V. (solid-state)
Prichard, Diana (chemical)
Prinz, Dianne K. (solar)
Ride, Sally K.
Sarachik, Myriam P. (solid-state)
Spaeth, Mary D. (nuclear)
Thornton, Kathryn
Weertman, Julia (solid-state)

### Physiology
Cowings, Patricia S.
Graham, Frances
Haschemeyer, Audrey E. V.
Lancaster, Cleo
Leeman, Susan
Rolf, Ida P.
Shaw, Jane E.
Sinkford, Jeanne F.

### Plant Physiology
Bryenton, Elisabeth

### Political Science
Shalala, Donna E.

### Primatology
Fossey, Dian
Galdikas, Birute M. F.
Hrdy, Sarah C.

### Psychiatry
Densen-Gerber, Judianne
Harrison-Ross, Phyllis A.
Kubler-Ross, Elisabeth
Spurlock, Jeanne

### Psychology
Attneave, Carolyn
Brothers, Joyce D.
Chesler, Phyllis
Cowings, Patricia S.
Delgado, Jane L.
Estes, Clarissa P.
Eyer, Diane E.
Graham, Frances
Hatfield, Elaine C.
Horner, Matina
Johnson, Virginia
Maccoby, Eleanor
Mitchell, Mildred B.
Payton, Carolyn
Reinisch, June M.
Scarr, Sandra
Turkle, Sherry
Wallace, Joan
Weisstein, Naomi
Westheimer, (Karola) Ruth
Wexler, Nancy S.

### Science Writer
Brody, Jane E.

### Social and Political Critic
Sheehy, Gail

### Sociology
Baca Zinn, Maxine
Deer, Ada E.
Jackson, Jacquelyne M.
Kanter, Rosabeth
Nelkin, Dorothy
Riley, Matilda
Turkle, Sherry
Wallace, Joan

### Soil Science
Matson, Pamela A.

### Spectroscopy
Grasselli, Jeanette

### Statistics
Rosenblatt, Joan

### Toxicology
Weisburger, Elizabeth A.

### Virology
Krim, Mathilde

### Volcanology
Kieffer, Susan W.

### Zoology
Fossey, Dian

# PREFACE

Volume 2 of *American Women in Science* focuses on American women scientists in all areas of science. Although volume 1 stressed the physical and natural sciences, this one includes more people in the social and behavioral sciences.[1] It concentrates on women who were born in or after 1920 and/or started their careers after 1950, or after World War II, but it does include a few women who were elected to the National Academy of Sciences or the National Academy of Engineering late in their careers or who were inadvertently omitted from the previous volume.

As a guideline, I used the professions represented in the memberships of the National Academy of Sciences and the National Academy of Engineering.[2] There was no attempt to establish an exact percentage of either professions or minorities in each profession because women scientists tend to be concentrated in the biomedical, social, and behavioral sciences. Also, although the number of reference books concerning women has exploded since the late 1980s, many minority groups are underrepresented in those sources. There are many sources for African Americans and a few for Native Americans, but there are fewer for Chicanos/Latinos/Hispanics and Asian Americans.

Several women are included who are popularly considered to be scientists. Joyce Brothers and Ruth Westheimer have standard credentials in psychology, but they are known as media personalities. Shere Hite has conducted some unique studies that have brought her prominence, and the author Barbara Mertz was identified as an Egyptologist in a documentary that aired on cable television.

## *Researching American Women in Science, 1950 to the Present: A Biographical Dictionary*

The breaking point for the two volumes was designated as 1950 because after World War II, science changed drastically. The second 50 years of the century ushered in the era of "big science" with innovations such as the development of computers, the determination of DNA structure, an increase in military weapons programs, and the development of the space program. Research increasingly was funded by the federal government until the early 1990s, and the discoveries of research teams increasingly replaced those of individuals as new research methodologies were developed.

In the 1950s, women still had difficulty being accepted in some curricula although in general they could attend the university of their choice. For example, Gail Sheehy was not allowed to enroll in the business school as an undergraduate and enrolled instead in home economics, which she considered the next best thing. Even when women completed advanced degrees they had difficulty finding suitable employment. Positions were not advertised at that time, and one obtained information about employment opportunities through a network of personal contacts. Women, especially married women, had difficulty securing full-time positions of any type as professionals. This situation was somewhat relieved by later federal and state legislation that governed equal opportunity in employment.

In spite of these barriers, women embarked on significant careers that brought them national and international recognition. This fact is reflected in the amount of biographical information that is available. I used standard biographical sources to choose names. Caroline Herzenberg's *Women Scientists from Antiquity to the Present*[3] provided a starting point. In addition, the supplement to Norma Ireland's *Index to Women of the World*[4] supplied some names, and others were gleaned from the lists of members the National Academy of Sciences and the National Academy of Engineering publish each year. I also searched other biographies and sources listed in the Bibliography for suitable candidates.

Starting in the 1980s, several authors wrote books listing the contributions of women, such as Ethlie Vare and Greg Ptacek's *Mothers of Invention*[5] and Autumn Stanley's *Mothers and Daughters of Invention.*[6] During the 1980s and 1990s, there was an explosion of books about notable women in mathematics, anthropology, physics, chemistry, life sciences, etc. More women could be located in *American Men and Women of Science*[7] and in *Who's Who in Science and Engineering*[8] than in previous volumes, and women scientists were also included in larger numbers in *Who's Who in America*[9] and *Who's Who of American Women.*[10] Although there are numerous reference books concerning African-American women and a few about Native Americans, other minorities have been sadly neglected.

One unexpected resource was the number of articles about women scientists being published in journals and magazines. In addition to the articles women have published in the professional journals and the notices of the awards they have received, there are reviews, interviews, biographical sketches, and autobiographies available. The popular magazines *Time, Life, People Weekly, Working Woman,* and *Scientific American* and the business magazines *Fortune* and *Business Week* proved to be good sources, and *Ebony* has articles and photographs of many of the African-American women included in this volume. These articles are accessible through databases such as "Infotrac." Several of the professional magazines, for example, *Chemical & Engineering News,* have issues devoted to women scientists, and *Scientific American* has published one or two biographies of women each year since 1990. Women scientists are even endorsing products—oceanographer Sylvia Earle appeared in an ad for Rolex watches that was published in *National Geographic* in September 1997.

The criteria for inclusion were:

- Born 1920 or after and/or started work after 1950 (exceptions are noted above)
- Member of National Academy of Sciences or National Academy of Engineering
- Recipient of major award, such as the Garvan or Lasker Award
- Worked primarily in the United States although not necessarily born there (exceptions are people like Dian Fossey who conducted research in a habitat overseas)
- Engaged in a profession represented by members of the National Academy of Sciences or the National Academy of Engineering such as chemistry, mathematics, physics, biology, anthropology, computer science, archaeology, ecology and environment, demography, sociology, engineering, paleontology, psychology, medicine, and statistics
- Made significant contributions to science in sometimes nontraditional ways or are considered by the general public to be a scientist

I wish to thank the many library employees who assisted me in obtaining information for this book. Particular thanks go to the librarians and staff members of Purdue University Libraries in West Lafayette, Indiana, and to those of Indiana University–Purdue University at Indianapolis (IUPUI) library. My research was supported partially by the Purdue University Libraries.

## Notes

1. Martha J. Bailey. *American Women in Science: A Biographical Dictionary.* Santa Barbara, CA: ABC-CLIO, 1994.

2. National Academy of Sciences. *Membership and Organization.* Washington, DC, 1995.

3. Caroline L. Herzenberg. *Women Scientists from Antiquity to the Present.* West Cornwall, CT: Locust Hill Press, 1986.

4. Norma O. Ireland. *Index to Women of the World from Ancient to Modern Times, a Supplement.* Metuchen, NJ: Scarecrow Press, 1988.

5. Ethlie Ann Vare and Greg Ptacek. *Mothers of Invention: From the Bra to the Bomb; Forgotten Women and Their Unforgettable Ideas.* New York: Morrow, 1988.

6. Autumn Stanley. *Mothers and Daughters of Invention: Notes for a Revised History of Technology.* Metuchen, NJ: Scarecrow Press, 1993.

7. *American Men and Women of Science.* New York: Bowker, 1906– .

8. *Who's Who in Science and Engineering.* Chicago: Marquis Who's Who, 1992–1993.

9. *Who's Who in America.* Chicago: Marquis Who's Who, 1976–1977.

10. *Who's Who of American Women.* 6th ed. Chicago: Marquis Who's Who, 1970–1971.

# INTRODUCTION

After World War II, the picture of science changed completely. Owing to the upheaval in Europe prior to the war, scientists poured into the United States seeking sanctuary. This movement continued for decades after the war as scientists moved to the United States from France, England, Yugoslavia, China, etc., seeking better employment opportunities, and the trend continues today, thus opening U.S. science to people with diverse ethnic backgrounds. Research was heavily funded by the federal government in both academe and corporations until the early 1990s, and the emphasis was on team research rather than individual work. During the war, many women had been able to complete their education and obtain significant assignments as substitutes for the men who were in military service, but when the men returned to civilian life, the women were expected to return home. The universities were burgeoning with students as men took advantage of the GI Bill to obtain or to complete degree programs. Although there was a high demand for instructors, women often were not hired; even though women were admitted to the universities or programs of their choice, they were not welcome. The male students were embarrassed to sit next to them in class, and several women who are profiled in this volume said the general feeling was that women were not serious about being scientists or engineers. In many universities, some people believed that women attended graduate school in all disciplines only to find a husband and possibly to work for a year or two after graduation. Women students at the graduate level were told they were not intelligent enough to understand physics or advanced mathematics, and they were told by department heads that they did not belong in graduate schools.

Even women who graduated from prestigious universities had difficulty securing tenure-track permanent employment in those same universities, and it was often next to impossible to find a position in industry or government. The equal employment legislation in the 1970s alleviated some of the discrimination, but it still exists in many areas. Mary Catherine Bateson gave a vivid description of the problems at Amherst College. Although the university was hiring women faculty members in many departments, the faculty burdened the women with large undergraduate classes and many committee assignments, which left them little time for either research or family. Finally, the women would just give up in disgust and leave. Psychologist Naomi Weisstein was an outspoken critic of the situation in education in the 1970s.

If women were hired in industry, they might work in the laboratories for a few years and then be shunted to an office position or appointed a technical librarian. Stephanie Kwolek, the inventor of Kevlar, escaped this fate at Du Pont because she started working in a significant research area and made several important discoveries early in her career. However, for many years her name in publications, patents, and awards was listed as "S. Kwolek." In later years, Du Pont changed its policies and hired a large number of women scientists including the wives of employees to work in research and administrative positions. Many corporations instituted a separate ranking for research positions, and both men and women became research associates, senior research associates, and corporation research associates—positions that were comparable to university professorial ranks. Women were gradually appointed to administrative-level positions in corporations up to the level of vice president—for instance, Betsy Ancker-Johnson and Marina Whitman were both vice presidents of General Motors Corporation for a time—but few women became president or chief executive officer. Some women founded their own companies. Adele Goldberg of ParcPlace Systems, Evelyn Berezin of Redactron, and Sandra Kurtzig of ASK Computer Systems were presidents of their own companies (ASK is the largest private company in the United States that was founded by a woman).

Although women scientists worked for the federal government for many years in "women and family" related departments, there was not a significant number in research activities until World War II. Many women who secured positions during the war were able to continue in the same departments after it, and many advanced in rank, although often their salaries and classifications were lower than those of men who performed the same work. Many women later received high-level appointments, such as Sheila Widnall, secretary of the U.S. Air Force; Antonia Novello, the first female surgeon general; Bernadine Healy, the first woman to head the National Institutes of Health; Alice Rivlin, the first director of the Congressional Budget Office; and Ada Deer, a Native American, the first woman to direct the Bureau of Indian Affairs.

In the 1950s and 1960s, it was common practice for single women to be asked in employment interviews if they planned to marry, and wives were asked when they planned to start a family. Also in those years, women who became pregnant had to quit their jobs at six months—there was no general practice of paid maternity leave—and some states had laws requiring that women quit at six months. One woman found she could not even enter a laboratory building to attend a seminar or borrow a book from the library after six months. Some women who wanted to work longer would lie about when the baby was due, but Betsy Ancker-Johnson's boss hired her as a consultant even though she was six months pregnant; she worked until a few days before the baby was born and returned in a few weeks. Universities, companies, and government agencies had nepotism rules, sometimes unwritten, under which husbands and wives could not work in the same department, for the same employer, or at the same installation. These rules were gradually abandoned in the 1970s.

Two factors influenced the acceptance of women scientists and engineers in the workplace: the development of the computer and the space program. Many women started working and assuming responsibility in the computer industry and government agencies during the early stages of computer development, especially in the areas of the personal computer, programming languages, and software. Long before women were accepted in the astronaut program, women engineers and scientists were computing orbits for missiles, rockets, and space vehicles and developing new materials needed to withstand the extremes of heat and cold in space. Female physiologists and psychologists were analyzing the physical and mental problems associated with weightlessness, motion sickness, and the gravity (G) forces experienced by pilots flying at high altitudes and reentering the earth's atmosphere. Women astronomers and astrophysicists were providing data on the distance to the moon and planets and the composition of those planets.

In addition to working in new fields of research, women scientists and engineers have revised the direction and methods of research. Some research now focuses on women's concerns, especially on factors concerning women's health and medical treatment. While president of the American Heart Association, Bernadine Healy emphasized that heart disease was a leading cause of death in women as well as men; when she was director of the National Institutes of Health, she brought about reforms in the clinical testing of drugs for women and children—the drugs could no longer be tested only on men, they had to be tested on women as well.

Just as Margaret Mead and Gregory Bateson revolutionized anthropology by using photography and recorders in their field studies, Jane Goodall and her American colleagues, Dian Fossey and Birute Galdikas, revised the direction of research in primatology. These three women have often been referred to as "Leakey's ladies" because the archaeologist Louis S. B. Leakey started them on their studies of the chimpanzee, the mountain gorilla, and the orangutan so he could compare their results with his lifelong study of early humans. Virginia Morell called them "the trimates" because they revolutionized primatology.[1] Goodall restructured research methodology when she started naming her chimpanzee subjects in Tanzania instead of identifying them merely as female or male as other scientists did. She followed the pattern of naming the mother Susan, the daughter Sally, and the son Sam in order to identify the family structure. She saw the chimpanzees as individuals whose life histories influenced the structure of the group. "Only three months into her study, she observed behaviors no researcher had ever reported: chimpanzees feasting on a wild piglet they had killed; chimpanzees hunting monkeys; chimpanzees using tools made from twigs to extract termites from their nests."[2] The last discovery discredited the previous scientific assumption that toolmaking distinguished humans from primates. Fossey and Galdikas also used Goodall's methods of observation and reported findings that no male primatologist had observed using the standard scientific methods. The three women changed the entire focus of research in primatology. Prior to their work, the field was almost exclusively dominated by male scientists; today, more than 50 percent of the primatologists are women. Other wildlife biologists have also adopted the methods used by Goodall, Fossey, and Galdikas. For example, Cynthia Moss and Joyce Poole name the elephants they study according to family groups and also use the same methods of observation.

## The Professions

A problem one encounters is how to designate a person's profession. Why does a woman list herself as a biologist in one biographical source and as a geneticist or a molecular biologist in another? One answer probably is that the editor of a particular volume has decided to use the generic terms of "biologist" or "physicist" for people. However, research moves forward rapidly, and at each stage, the researchers included in volumes such as *American Men and Women of Science* try to describe their work by changing the designation.[3] It is obvious that Sally K. Ride (1951– ) is a physicist, a former astronaut, and a researcher. In recent years, some of the granting agencies have emphasized interdisciplinary studies, and many require not only economic but also social impact studies as part of the proposals that are submitted to them. These interdisciplinary studies influence the job titles people give themselves in order to slant a proposal to fit the agencies' requirements, and resulting publications are included in a variety of journals. For example, a chemist might publish a paper analyzing shards from an archaeological site in a journal for archaeologists rather than in a chemistry journal.

In searching for information about scientists, and women in particular, one must be a detective. It is best when checking one reference title, such as *American Men and Women of Science* or *Who's Who of American Women*,[4] to check several editions and to even check volumes for five or ten years earlier. Some scientists who have long careers and many accomplishments tend to condense their biographies, and an inexperienced searcher may miss pertinent information the person provided in earlier years. Also, people are not listed in each and every edition of a reference work, their names may not be spelled correctly, or the information may not be correct.

There is always the problem of how an editor has listed the "Mc" and "Mac" names or the hyphenated names. Some female scientists might be listed under their family name or under a previous husband's name in a specific edition or reference book, and people sometimes omit parts of their names. Eleanor Margaret Burbidge is listed also as "Margaret" and as "E. Margaret," and some sources list her under "Burbridge." Former surgeon general Joycelyn Elders is listed as (Minnie) Joycelyn Elders; one edition of *American Men and Women of Science* includes two biographical sketches of the same person, one under Anne Sterling and the other under Anne Fausto-Sterling; and another listed one person as both Johanna Sengers and Johanna Levelt-Sengers. Sylvia Earle was listed as Sylvia Mead until she divorced her husband and resumed her family name. Some readers question why one should include the dates of marriages or divorces, but the dates can provide a clue to a possible name change in the reference books. It is sometimes difficult to determine the gender of a scientist by the name. A few reference books handily include a note about "son of" or "daughter of" and give the parents' names; *Notable Twentieth-Century Scientists* includes a gender index.[5]

## Discrimination

Women have been admitted to more schools and to more programs since World War II than previously, but that fact does not imply they have been treated equally with men. When men returned from service after the war and obtained undergraduate and/or graduate degrees, most women scientists were shunted into undergraduate teaching, research assistantships, or library assignments, which had a long-term effect on their careers. These positions often were not tenure-track appointments, and the first two could be paid from grant funds rather than from the university payroll. In the early 1970s, when the crush of postwar enrollments was reduced, many universities required that people be promoted to associate professor in order to receive tenure—previously, people could be tenured at a lower level or could work on a contract basis. At the same time, the universities began giving tenured faculty members a formal letter of tenure, and many of those letters specified that tenure was in effect only if funds were available in the particular department. During this period of formalizing appointments, Fay Ajzenberg-Selove had to file a grievance on the basis of age discrimination with federal and state equal opportunity agencies in order to transfer from a research position to a professorship with tenure; the University of Pennsylvania had not yet established its own formal grievance procedure. Many women were able to take advantage of increased funding for science education after Sputnik. However, people would tell them they were selected only to fill quotas, as opposed to being chosen for their capabilities. The same was said when they received appointments to choice jobs, especially if they were minorities.

Even very prominent women face bias. The first American woman to receive a Nobel Prize in Science, Gerty Cori (1896–1957),[6] was subjected to questions about how much of what she contributed to her husband's work resulted in the award. Another Nobel winner, Rita Levi Montalcini (1909– ),[7] was accused of fraud by a European newspaper in 1995. The charge was that her Italian company had "purchased" the prize for her; she was proved innocent of the charge.

Women also have had difficulty receiving credit for their work, partly because there is a limit to the number of people who can receive credit for some of the prizes. Nobel awards are limited to three people in each category; the Lasker awards in medicine are limited to five. Jenny T. L. Chuang[8] was one of four people who developed programs for Wang computers, but she was never credited for her work. Candace Pert did not receive the Lasker Award in 1978 for her contribution to work on endorphins, and Annie C. Y. Chang[9] was not included in a 1986 Nobel Prize for her work on gene splicing. Herman Goldstine omitted Thelma Estrin from the list of the research team at Johns Hopkins in his book *The Computer from Pascal to Von Neumann* (1972); her name is in the index to the book but does not appear on the page cited.

In the competitions for credit and grants, women as well as men have been accused of misconduct. There was a long, drawn out case in which Margot O'Toole charged in 1989 that the immunologist Theresa Imanishi-Kari had committed scientific misconduct in a paper published in the journal *Cell* in 1986—O'Toole had a postdoctoral appointment in Imanishi-Kari's lab. There was a book about the case,[10] and the scientist was finally cleared of the charges in 1996.[11] There has been a controversy about whether or not genes should be patented. The National Institutes of Health endorsed this practice when Bernadine Healy was director in the early 1990s, but the anthropologist Carol Jenkins was later accused of patenting the genes of a remote native tribe.[12] She and the National Institutes of Health had patented a virus-infected cell line taken from blood of the natives but had not patented the gene.

## Success in a Professional Career

In glancing through the biographies, the interviews, and other articles in this volume, there seems to be general agreement that several factors contribute to success in women's careers. These include:

- A strong technical background in a subject
- The ability to be a good team member
- Excellent communication skills, both oral and written
- A childhood interest in science and mathematics supported by parents
- If married, strong support from her husband for her technical career

## Specific Areas of Research

Among the significant developments in the last half of the twentieth century are the development of the computer, the determination of DNA structure, developments in the science of plate tectonics and in mapping the earth, theories about the disappearance of the dinosaurs, the space program, environmental and ecological concerns, and the development of new instrumentation and methodologies other than the computer. In the 1950s, solid-state physics was in its infancy. Transistors, which had been introduced in about 1948, were followed by research on semiconductors, and the integrated circuits that were used later in computers, automobile electronics, and the entertainment industry were developed, as were lasers in about 1955–1960. The advent of acquired immune deficiency syndrome (AIDS) led to new areas of medical research, and there is still a problem in the medical field as to the interjection of politics in the diagnosis and treatment of that disease and others. For example, Is there a Gulf War Syndrome? Do synthetic breast implants cause various illnesses? Should tobacco companies compensate people who have smoking-related illnesses? And even though birth-control pills have been marketed since the 1960s, their long-term physical effects are still being questioned.

One positive situation is that in universities, women are no longer routinely assigned to home economics departments to teach household physics or household chemistry. Most of the women surveyed are members of specific subject departments—and, in fact, in 1994 the American Home Economics Association changed its name to the American Association of Family and Consumer Sciences. There have been many changes in the overall social structure, both through legislation, such as equal opportunity in employment, and through access to services concerning the structure of family and society. More women are combining careers with marriage and family, and there have been revisions in attitudes toward sex as a result of the research by Alfred Kinsey and of the research on sexual therapy by William Masters and Virginia Johnson. Shere Hite has presented some interesting and sometimes controversial insights on human sexuality, and Ruth Westheimer has offered sex counseling to the general public via radio, television, and print sources.

One problem women still face is gender stereotyping, including statements such as, Boys are better at mathematics than girls, and Girls are more social than boys. Psychologist Sandra Scarr has conducted extensive studies of gender differences in addition to studying the effects of day care and adoption on the child/parent bond. Diane Eyer is dispelling the myths of mother guilt and of the mother/infant bond.

There are also concerted efforts to reexamine and record the histories and contributions of African Americans, Hispanics, and Native Americans. Psychologist Jane Delgado is working with various agencies to improve services, especially medical and educational services, to Hispanics, and sociologist Maxine Baca Zinn is conducting research to dispel many myths about Mexicans and Latinos, especially the role of women in those societies. A number of women are conducting research on African Americans: psychologist Jeanne Spurlock is studying black families; anthropologist Niara Sudarkasa is examining the role of black women in Africa and the United States; economist Phyllis Wallace researches the economics of discrimination; sociologist Jacquelyne Jackson is studying aging, particularly in minority groups; and anthropologist Faye Harrison is researching blacks of African descent, including those in the Caribbean. A number of anthropologists are conducting research on Native Americans in both Canada and the United States. Eleanor Leacock has studied the natives of Labrador; Nancy Lurie, North American natives; Catharine McClellan, the Yukon and Canadian Indians; and June Helm, the Déné Indians. Beatrice Medicine and Wendy Rose, both Native Americans, are studying their respective tribal groups, and Helm is an authority on Native American linguistics.

Although it is not possible to treat all of the topics just mentioned, there are several in which women scientists have played a prominent role.

## Computers

A great many people contributed to the development of computers before Bill Gates and Steve Jobs were born. In the nineteenth century, Charles Babbage designed his analytical engine, which is credited with being the forerunner of the computer. Although he did not build a model of his design, his work was supported financially by Augusta Ada King, Lady Lovelace, the daughter of the poet Lord Byron. It is significant that she was credited in the twentieth century for her contribution when one of the first programs developed for the modern computer was named "Ada" in her honor.[13] Numerous women were involved in software and hardware development during World War II, a notable one being Grace Murray Hopper (1906–1992),[14] who designed software for the digital computer. This work continued during the Cold War and the years of the space program, and the development of the personal computer brought a new impetus to developing newer, faster machines that could outperform the mainframes and to developing software that could be used by the general public as well as by computer experts. One of the intriguing developments has been the use of computers in designing aircraft, cars, trucks, etc., and the combination of the laser and the computer is used by the entertainment industry to develop computer games and to draw animated cartoons. One book that describes the participation of women in the development of the computer is Autumn Stanley's *Mothers and Daughters of Invention*.[15] Gwen Bell founded the Computer Museum in Boston to gather together the computers and components developed throughout the world. Many of the personal computers on display are loaded with the original software, and Bell has produced a video on the history of the computer that is available for sale from the museum.

One of the primary developments of the twentieth century is the invention of the word processor. Many people contributed to this effort, but Evelyn Berezin is often called the mother of word processing. Although computers had been used for number crunching and calculating for years, few were capable of handling word processing easily. Today, we are accustomed to seeing a word processor on every desk and counter in academe, government, and business; approximately 40 percent of the homes in the United States have personal computers; and it seems that laptop computers are everywhere. The first commercially available word processor was not developed until the 1970s, but within a few years, it had overtaken the editing typewriter in many areas that required repetitive typing such as legal forms, proposals for grants, business reports, etc., and by the 1980s, word processors were standard equipment in any work situation. Berezin founded her own company, Redactron Corporation, in 1969 to manufacture and sell them, and Adele Goldberg helped to develop a personal computer at Xerox's laboratory in Palo Alto, California, a facility that is familiarly called PARC. The computer used a very simple programming language called Smalltalk, which was also the name of the computer. When Xerox delayed introducing the computer, Goldberg persuaded the company to allow her and several colleagues to establish ParcPlace Systems (first as a subsidiary in about 1980 and later as a separate company) to produce the computer. It was what is called an "object oriented" computer, and it had many of the features that had been developed by Xerox but not used, including icons, windows, and the mouse. Margaret Butler helped develop one of the first digital computers for science as a staff mathematician at Argonne National Laboratory in the early 1950s, Lynn Conway is known for designing and fabricating integrated computer circuit chips, and Elsa Reichmanis helped develop new materials that are used in integrated circuits.

Many women have been involved in the development of computer programming languages and software. Martine Kempf and Sandra Hutchins have worked on voice recognition software, Sandra Kurtzig founded her own company to produce software (called ASK Computer Systems, it is the largest public company founded by a woman), and Ruth Davis helped establish international standards for data encryption of computers. Davis also developed the bibliographic information system for the National Library of Medicine, which is recognized as a superior system. Several women have done research on computer applications in brain research, including Thelma Estrin and Evangelia Micheli-Tzanakou. Mary Pickett was involved in programming industrial robots for use in manufacturing at General Motors Corporation in 1984. Previously, robots had had to be programmed individually, but she and a colleague developed the software that made it possible to automate an entire production line. Although she did not develop the program, Jean Sammet was instrumental in introducing and refining the high-level programming language called COBOL, which was one of the most widely used programming languages in the world from the late 1960s through the 1970s. She also assisted in introducing the programming language called "Ada" for the Department of Defense. She was in charge of programming languages at International Business Machines Corporation (IBM) for many years, and in 1969, she published a history of programming languages entitled *Programming Languages: History and Fundamentals*.[16] Mary Shaw is an expert on software and is leading an effort to establish software engineering as a profession. Roberta Williams is considered to be queen of the adventure computer game. When she thought the available computer games too tame, she started designing her own adventure games, and she and her husband founded their own company, Sierra On-Line, which was valued at $1 billion when they sold it in 1996. A psychologist, Sherry Turkle, is the authority on the psychological and sociological effects of computers on humans. Her research centers on how people interact with computers, and one of her theories is that computers can change our very identities. She is especially concerned about the immersion of young people into computer games until the games become more real than reality.

### *The Space Program*

Probably the most important influence on the careers of many women scientists and engineers is the U.S. space program following the Russian launching of Sputnik in 1957. Not only have women shared in the increased funding for mathematics, science, and engineering education in schools and colleges, they have also worked on projects of the National Aeronautics and Space Administration (NASA). A large number have worked for NASA itself, but an even larger number have worked for companies and universities under NASA contracts. The U.S. Air Force also participated in the program from the first and continues to work with NASA on many projects.

The women who are involved are mathematicians, computer scientists, nutritionists, astronomers, metallurgists, ceramic engineers, psychologists, medical personnel, etc. Alice Hamilton at the Massachusetts Institute of Technology was the assistant director of a contract to design the computer systems for the Apollo command module and the lunar excursion vehicle. Heidi Hammel, also of the Massachusetts Institute of Technology, and Margaret Burbidge of the University of California, San Diego, are among the astronomers who were involved in the design of the Hubble space telescope and in correcting its flawed lens several years later.

Although NASA was slow to accept woman as astronauts, numerous women worked at various NASA laboratories. When Marjorie Townsend was in charge of the program for designing and launching astronomical and meteorological satellites, she was the only woman in the world to be in charge of a satellite program. Mary Johnston designed metals that could withstand the extreme heat and cold in space, and Patricia Cowings worked with astronauts on their problems with motion sickness and the physiological effects of weightlessness and taught the astronauts how to use biofeedback to control motion sickness. Several women joined NASA with the hope of joining the astronaut program; Bonnie Dunbar was one of the few who succeeded. Psychologist Mildred Mitchell worked for the U.S. Air Force and helped select the male astronauts for the Mercury project. Devrie Intriligator, a physicist at the California Institute of Technology, analyzed data from the Pioneer spacecraft in orbit around the sun; Barbara Johnson of Rockwell International Space Division was a systems engineering manager for the Apollo project; and Caroline Herzenberg, then at ITT Research Institute, had a grant from NASA to test Apollo lunar samples. Christine Darden, an engineer at NASA's Langley Research Center, created the computer software program used across the United States for simulating a sonic boom in a wind tunnel. She was also involved in redesigning aircraft to minimize the sonic boom because military aircraft sometimes reach supersonic speeds as they fly across populated areas.

NASA's astronaut program is another area in which women have done pioneering work. Since the space exploration program was spearheaded by U.S. Air Force personnel, it was natural for them to specify that the astronauts should have combat flying experience, as that would have given them experience in facing unknowns in flying. Another requirement was that the men should have experience flying at high altitudes, because pilots tend to lose consciousness during some maneuvers at high altitude; it was thought that such men would be able to work with researchers in overcoming the problem. Both of these requirements barred women from the astronaut program because none of the armed services had women pilots at that time and the only supersonic aircraft were owned by the armed services. However, barring women from participation was part of a general pattern of "protecting" women from hazardous situations, such as working in mines or in the ocean or conducting research in Antarctica. For many years, there were the myths that women caused mines and tunnels to collapse and that they were bad luck in oil fields. Women were barred from research in Antarctica because the research facility at McMurdo Sound was operated by the U.S. Navy, which provided the only transportation and housing—and barred women from that facility.

Opening the astronaut program to women was a long struggle. In the 1960s, Jerrie Cobb, one of the foremost women pilots of the day, was asked to help modify the physical and psychological tests that were used to screen the male astronauts. After she proved that women could equal or exceed the performance of men in many tests, she was asked to select 12 women to validate the tests. However, NASA refused to continue the tests, and Congress supported that decision even though Cobb testified before Congress on the question. At the end of the Apollo program, when NASA was starting the orbital space program, the jet pilot requirement was eliminated, and NASA started selecting the first six female astronauts. The criteria for both women and men were that they should be scientists and engineers with college degrees in a variety of disciplines. The women were not required to be pilots, but most of them trained as such anyway in case they might have to fly the shuttle in an emergency. One woman, Air Force Lieutenant Colonel Eileen Collins,[17] was copilot on *Discovery* in a launch in 1995 and was assigned to be the commander and pilot of *Columbia* in December 1998. She is one of the few living women pilots to have her portrait in the National Air and Space Museum in Washington, D.C.

One reason the astronaut program was finally opened to women is that, gradually, the barriers to women working in oceanography, mines, tunnels, oil fields, and similar "hazardous" situations have been eliminated. The armed services allowed women to be jet pilots in the late 1970s, and the U.S. Navy even allowed women access to the research facility in Antarctica in 1969/1970.[18] In 1978, six women were chosen for the astronaut program: Sally Ride, Kathryn Sullivan, Anna Fisher, Rhea Seddon, Judy Resnik, and Shannon Lucid. Two more women joined in 1980, Mary Cleave and Bonnie Dunbar. Ride was the first of the women to fly in outer space in 1983, Sullivan was the first American woman to walk in space, Fisher was the first mother in orbit, Seddon's pregnancy barred her from being first in space but she had her shuttle ride later, Resnik died in the *Challenger* disaster in 1986, and Lucid spent 188 days aboard the space station *Mir* in 1996. During the 1980s, these women received a great deal of publicity; in addition to several books about them, there were articles in *Time, Life,* and all of the news magazines. Unfortunately, their scientific accomplishments were not much publicized, and very little information about them was readily available until Shannon Lucid's adventures on *Mir.* The women want to be recognized for their work, but they also want to be considered as part of the team. Those who are mothers say they are just working mothers who have interesting jobs. However, NASA is missing an opportunity to attract young women into careers in science and engineering by not having them included in *American Men and Women of Science, Who's Who of American Women,* and other standard reference sources.

NASA continues to add both women and men to the astronaut program, but at the same time, there has been a steady stream of nonastronaut scientists who also fly into space. They are designated as payload specialists who are "career scientists or engineers selected by their employer or country for their expertise in conducting a specific experiment or commercial venture on a space shuttle mission."[19] It is sometimes difficult when reading about specific missions to determine who is an astronaut and who is not. Also, astronauts assigned to a mission may not actually fly on it; they might be the backup people for the mission or some of the people who work at Mission Control during the flight.

## DNA Structure

DNA (deoxyribonucleic acid) is the genetic substance of all living cells and many viruses, and hereditary information that is transmitted from each generation to the next is encoded in the structure of the DNA molecules. DNA was first discovered by the Swiss biochemist Friedrich Miescher in 1869, but the actual structure of the DNA molecules was finally announced in *Nature* in 1953. This work was done in great part by the American biochemist James D. Watson, British molecular biologist Francis Crick, and British biophysicist Maurice Wilkins. British crystallographer Rosalind Franklin (1920–1958) discovered that the molecule was a double helix. Without her permission, Wilkins gave Watson the photograph of the helix, from which Watson and Crick built the model. Although she received credit for her discovery, she died four years before the three men were awarded the Nobel Prize in Physiology or Medicine for their research.[20]

One American researcher who worked for more than 40 years on maize (corn) genetics was Barbara McClintock (1902–1992).[21] Her work included mutation in kernels of maize, transposable genetic elements, and molecular and microbial genetics, but it was only after other scientists working on DNA realized the significance of her work that she was awarded a Nobel Prize in 1983. Virginia Walbot met McClintock while the latter was still actively involved in research, was able to work with her for several summers, and used what she learned in her own work on transposons in maize. Other women who have conducted research on plants are Jane Rissler (engineered plants), Sharon Long (genetics research on legumes), Nina Fedoroff (maize transposable elements), and Mary-Dell Chilton (genetic engineering of agricultural crops).

Other women scientists include Mary Lou Pardue, who is known for her work in insect genetics, and Margaret Kidwell, who studied the transfer of genes in fruit flies. Maxine Singer is a leading figure in human genetics, and her laboratory helped to decipher the genetic code. Elizabeth Neufeld is an international authority on human genetic diseases, and Mary-Claire King is renowned for her research on breast cancer in which she theorized the existence of the gene BRCA1, which, if damaged, can predispose women to breast and ovarian cancer.

The Human Genome Project is a worldwide effort to identify each of the millions of genes for research purposes, and the social implications of this research are many. When the genes for a specific disease, such as breast cancer, are identified, can a person be denied employment because of a potential illness and/or denied insurance because of the potential expense for treatment? Psychologist Nancy Wexler has led the search to identify the gene that causes Huntington's Disease, an inherited debilitating disease that strikes in middle age. After an intense international effort, the gene has been identified, but there is not yet a cure for the disease. Wexler's own mother died from it, and one of its more famous victims was the musician Woody Guthrie; both the Guthrie and the Wexler families have been leading proponents of this research. However, members of some families refuse to be tested because if one member does not carry the gene, that means one of his or her siblings could. In each generation, each family member has a 50 percent chance of carrying the gene.

### *Plate Tectonics*

Marie Tharp is the geologist who pioneered charting the ocean floor, and her particular contribution was her discovery of the valley that divides the Mid-Atlantic Ridge. Although the theory current at the time was that the earth was in the process of cooling and shrinking, other scientists finally agreed that the ocean floor was being created at these ridges and spreading outward. This "seafloor spreading" led to acceptance of the theory of continental drift, which is now called plate tectonics.

Marcia McNutt is renowned for her research on plate tectonics, particularly mapping the ocean floor and measuring the depth of the ocean. She has been working on mapping areas of the oceans of the Southern Hemisphere, which have remained uncharted because they are far from shipping lanes and are in areas that are not of military importance. However, they are potential sites for new fishing grounds, which is important because the fishing grounds near the continents are becoming depleted.

### *Disappearance of the Dinosaurs*

One question that puzzled scientists for years was why the dinosaurs disappeared from the earth about 65 million years ago. For a number of years, geologists had noticed a layer of iridium at the Cretaceous-Tertiary (KT) boundary in areas of Italy, Scandinavia, the western United States, and other parts of the world. Iridium is not normally found on earth, but it does exist on other planets. In about 1979, the Nobel physicist Luis Alvarez developed the theory that a giant asteroid had struck the earth. The resulting cloud of smoke and dust circled the earth, blotting out the sun, killing the vegetation on which the dinosaurs and large mammals fed, and eventually killing them also. His son, geologist Walter Alvarez, joined him in looking for the impact crater. An international team also joined the search, and eventually the crater was located in the 1990s on the coast of Yucatán. The crater had escaped earlier detection because it was under water.

Several women were heavily involved in this research project. Nuclear chemist Helen Michel at the University of California, Berkeley, conducted the analyses of samples for the Alvarez team, and it was the planetary geologist Adriana Ocampo of NASA's Jet Propulsion Laboratory who contributed to confirming the location of the crater. Susan Kieffer, a geologist who is now at the University of British Columbia and studied impact craters on planets, advised the team on the characteristics of a crater site and on the possible trajectory of the asteroid.

Although the possibility that another huge asteroid will hit earth seems to be only a subject for science fiction books and movies, that possibility does exist. In March 1998, press releases indicated that an asteroid had been identified which may come close enough to earth in 2028 to impact it, but the theory is not generally accepted. For many years, astronomers have been tracking "earth approachers" each month for two weeks during the dark of the moon at the Mt. Palomar Observatory, and it was during one of these scheduled observations that Carolyn and Eugene Shoemaker identified Shoemaker-Levy 9, the comet that impacted Jupiter.

Astronomer Lucy-Ann McFadden at the University of California, San Diego, was the principal investigator for NASA's planetary geology program and oversaw that program. Elizabeth Roemer of the University of Arizona had the unique research project of recovering "lost" comets, that is, comets whose planned rediscovery is based on predictions from previous returns. The efforts of these researchers are helping to keep track of the myriad number of earth approachers.

## *Astronomy and Astrophysics*

The development of powerful telescopes in various observatories around the world and the orbiting observatories such as the Hubble space telescope have resulted in increased knowledge of the universe. There have been great strides in cosmology, which is the branch of astronomy concerned with the origin of the universe, and many women are doing significant research in this field.

Sandra Faber and Margaret Geller are known for their research on galaxies, and in the 1970s, Vera Rubin, in her work on galaxies, demonstrated that the universe is made up of large areas of dark matter that is invisible to the naked eye. Margaret Burbidge collaborated in developing the theory of the origin of chemical elements, Anne Underhill used orbiting observatories to observe stars at ultraviolet wavelengths, and Nancy Roman designed NASA's satellite observatories to explore the universe from a vantage point that is free from atmospheric interference. Astronomer Sarah Lippincott specialized in identifying the planetlike companions, or extrasolar planets, to nearby stars.

## *Environment and Ecology*

The terms *ecology* and *environment* are interpreted in many different ways. One popular topic is the preservation of endangered species, and Mollie Beattie, as director of the U.S. Fish and Wildlife Service, had responsibility for enforcing the Endangered Species Act in the United States. Cynthia Moss and Joyce Poole were active in having the African elephant declared endangered when the illegal trade in elephant tusks was decimating the herds, and Anne LaBastille worked to preserve the wildlife habitat of many bird species. Sharon Matola established the Belize Zoo and Tropical Education Center to preserve not only the animals that were native to that area but also the land itself.

Helen Caldicott resigned her position as a physician to campaign against the use of nuclear energy—for peaceful as well as for military uses—and Anne Ehrlich and her husband have published several books on topics related to the future of the world's population and the earth. Several women have been active in industrial situations. In the 1970s, Maxine Savitz, who was working in the U.S. Department of Energy at the time, developed energy standards for heating and lighting buildings, new batteries, fuel-efficient cars, and all manner of methods to preserve the fossil fuels and reduce pollution. Kathleen Taylor is an expert on catalytic converters to reduce emissions from General Motors vehicles, and Roberta Nichols, at Ford Motor Company, leads the industry in developing alternate fuels for vehicles as well as designing vehicles that are more energy efficient. Elizabeth Gross has researched photovoltaic cells, or "living batteries," to convert sunlight directly into electricity to preserve fossil fuels and reduce pollution.

While Geraldine Cox was the technical director of the Chemical Manufacturers Association, she was instrumental in developing chemical safety standards in the United States after the explosion at the Union Carbide Corporation plant in Bhopal, India, in 1984. Joan Berkowitz is an internationally known expert on environmental hazards and the co-owner of a consulting service. Susan Solomon confirmed that the chlorofluorocarbons (CFC) in air conditioners, aerosol sprays, and refrigerators were contributing to the hole in the ozone layer over Antarctica, and most countries have since reduced their use of those products. Pamela Matson researches the role of land-use changes on global warming.

## *Medicine*

The advances in medicine are so extensive that one cannot discuss the topic in a few short paragraphs. The research includes new instruments, new methodologies, new diseases, new cures, and nonconventional medicine and treatment. It also includes AIDS, cancer, Huntington's Disease, and sickle-cell anemia. One new profession, actually a reemphasis of an old one, is an increase in the use of nurse-midwives in childbirth, possibly the result of the 1960s and 1970s emphasis on alternative lifestyles and alternative medicines. Genetics research that identifies a specific gene as the cause of a disease leads to ethical and social questions.

## *Awards and Prizes*

Two indications of success in a career are to be elected to prestigious societies and to receive awards. In the sciences, the prestigious associations in the United States are the National Academy of Sciences and the National Academy of Engineering. The former is a nongovernmental organization of scientists and engineers that was established in 1863 by Congress to be an official adviser to the government in all matters related to science and technology. New members are elected by the membership on the basis of their distinguished contributions to research. In 1964, the National Academy of Engineering was organized under its own charter.[22] Several people, including at least two women in this volume, currently are members of both organizations.

Another prestigious society, one that has a more interdisciplinary membership, is the American Academy of Arts and Sciences. Founded in 1780, it is an honorary society that includes scholars and national leaders from four areas: mathematical and physical sciences, biological sciences, social arts and sciences, and humanities. The society "conducts interdisciplinary studies of current social and intellectual issues. Seeks to bring together scholars and leaders whose research, experience, or knowledge can help to clarify contemporary problems and place them in perspective."[23]

Each professional group also has its own set of professional organizations. Many of these societies designate selected members as "fellows" to recognize outstanding contributions to the field, and each awards various prizes. There are also many prizes awarded by other groups, some of which include substantial funds, such as the five-year awards of the MacArthur Foundation, the five-year Presidential Young Investigator Award of the National Science Foundation, and the Lasker Award in medicine. Two other awards of the National Science Foundation are the National Medal of Science and the National Medal of Technology; recipients are selected from among all disciplines and receive the award in an annual White House ceremony from the president of the United States.

## *Brief Survey*

Although the National Academy of Sciences and the National Academy of Engineering are among the most distinguished scientific societies, very little is known about them by the general public. Two women listed in this volume are members of both academies: Mildred Dresselhaus and Johanna Levelt-Sengers. As part of my research, I contacted a number of the female members for further information on their careers and their views on the two academies.

My impression while preparing these biographies is that the members of the National Academy of Sciences are correcting past neglect by electing a few people quite late in their careers, for instance, women in their seventies and eighties. Most of the members I corresponded with, however, agreed that more women and more minorities should be included. They felt the organizations were each doing an adequate job but that selection should be stepped up. Some said the National Academy of Sciences was still an old boys' club. The National Academy of Engineering seems to be selecting women at a younger age than men, women in their forties as opposed to fifties for the men. Several women mentioned that women need the boost that membership gives them earlier in their careers instead of a reward prior to retirement. They mentioned that one advantage of election is that other people then pay attention to what they say; they cannot be ignored. Some said they had received more invitations to attend seminars, to speak, to participate on prestigious committees, and to write and edit after election to one or the other society.

## *Notes*

1. Virginia Morell. "Called 'Trimates': Three Bold Women Shaped Their Field." *Science* 260 (April 16, 1993): 420–425.
2. Ibid.
3. *American Men and Women of Science.* New York: Bowker, 1906– .
4. *Who's Who of American Women.* 6th ed. Chicago: Marquis Who's Who, 1970–1971.
5. *Notable Twentieth-Century Scientists.* Edited by E. J. McMurray. Detroit: Gale Research, 1995.
6. Martha J. Bailey. *American Women in Science: A Biographical Dictionary.* Santa Barbara, CA: ABC-CLIO, 1994, pp. 70–71.
7. Ibid, pp. 209–211.
8. Autumn Stanley. *Mothers and Daughters of Invention: Notes for a Revised History of Technology.* Metuchen NJ: Scarecrow Press, 1993, pp. 700–701.
9. Ibid.
10. Judy Sarasohn. *Science on Trial: The Whistle-Blower, the Accused, and the Nobel Laureate.* New York: St. Martins Press, 1993.
11. "Imanishi-Kari Ruling Slams ORI." *Science* 272 (June 28, 1996): 1864–1865.
12. "Anthropologist Exonerated." *Science* 272 (April 12, 1996): 203.
13. J. A. N. Lee. *Computer Pioneers.* Los Alamitos, CA: IEEE Computer Society Press, 1995.
14. Bailey, op. cit., pp 168–169.
15. Stanley, op. cit.
16. Jean Sammet. *Programming Languages: History and Fundamentals.* Englewood NJ: Prentice-Hall, 1969.
17. "Ms. in Control." *People Weekly* (March 23, 1998): 151.
18. Barbara Land. *The New Explorers: Women in Antarctica.* New York: Dodd, Mead & Company, 1981.
19. U.S. National Aeronautics and Space Administration. *Astronaut Fact Book.* May 5, 1996.
20. *Notable Twentieth-Century Scientists.* Op. cit., pp. 689–692; Lisa Yount. *Twentieth-Century Women Scientists.* New York: Facts on File, 1996, pp. 60–73.
21. Bailey, op. cit., pp. 221–222.
22. *Encyclopaedia Britannica 1990.* Chicago: Encyclopaedia Britannica, 1990.
23. *Encyclopedia of Associations.* Detroit: Gale Research, 1996.

# American Women in Science

## 1950 to the Present

# A

## *Ackerman, Diane (Fink)*
(1948– )
***naturalist, poet***

***Education:*** Student, Boston University, 1966–1967; B.A., Pennsylvania State University, 1970; M.F.A., Cornell University, 1973, M.A. in English, 1976, Ph.D., 1978

***Professional Experience:*** Social worker, New York City, 1967; government researcher, Pennsylvania State University, 1968; editorial assistant, *Library Journal,* 1970; teaching fellow, Cornell University, 1971–1978; assistant professor, University of Pittsburgh, 1980– ; visiting writer in residence, College of William and Mary, 1982–1983 and Ohio University, 1983; director of writing program, Washington University, St. Louis, 1982– , writer in residence, Washington University, 1984– ; visiting writer, Columbia University, 1986

***Diane Ackerman*** has been combining her interest in natural science with her background in poetry in a series of publications that have earned her national recognition. She lists herself as a poet, pilot, scuba diver, explorer, naturalist, and journalist. An essay on bats, in which she tried to debunk the various vampire superstitions and health fears about the night creatures, was published in the *New Yorker* in 1988 and earned her a staff writing position at that magazine. A collection of her essays on bats, whales, crocodiles and alligators, and penguins was published in the book *The Moon by Whale Light* (1991). In that work, she describes sitting astride an alligator in Florida, raising baby penguins in quarantine at Sea World in San Diego, visiting penguins in the wild in the Antarctic, playing among the spotted dolphins in the Bahamas, facing an active volcano on a remote island to see the last remaining short-tailed albatross, and accompanying a National Zoo expedition to a Brazilian rain forest to turn loose some golden lion tamarins.

Her interest in pure science as well as her lifelong interest in the animal world is reflected in her second book of poetry *Wife of Light* (1978). After three visits to a ranch in New Mexico, where she assisted in branding cattle and birthing calves, she recorded her experiences in her first book of prose *Twilight of the Tenderfoot* (1980). After earning a pilot's license, she wrote a memoir of her romance with flight in her second prose work, *On Extended Wings* (1985). During the 1980s and 1990s, she continued writing while teaching writing at a number of colleges and universities and also wrote articles based on science and nature for publications such as *Life, National Geographic,* and the *New Yorker.*

The book that brought her national attention was *A Natural History of the Senses* (1990). This collection of essays, observations, and anecdotes relates to and analyzes the five senses, not in the scientific manner, but in the poetic. *A Slender Thread: Rediscovering Hope at the Heart of Crisis* (1997) is based on her experiences during the years she spent answering phones in a clinic in upstate New York. In this work, she shares with her readers a naturalist's perspective on the origins and purpose of some of our most troubling emotions, for example, anxiety, dread, panic, aversion, and depression. The "thread" refers to the telephone wires that reached invisibly between Ackerman and the often desperate person at the other end. Her most recent book of poetry is *I Praise My Destroyer* (1998). As part of the Public Broadcasting System (PBS) *Nova* series, she hosted *Mystery of the Senses . . . with Diane Ackerman* in 1995.

Reviewers sometimes criticize Ackerman's work as being too effusive, too wordy, too imaginative. They forget that she is writing as a poet, not as a scientist, on scientific subjects. She also has a large group of loyal readers. Her photograph was published in *Current Biography* (1997), *People Magazine* (March 10, 1997), and *Vogue* (September 1991).

***Bibliography:*** *Contemporary Authors* v. 57–60; *Current Biography* 1997; *Who's Who of American Women,* 20th ed., 1997–1998.

# *Adelman, Irma Glicman*

(1930– )

***economist***

***Education:*** B.S., University of California, Berkeley, 1950, M.A., 1951, Ph.D. in economics, 1955

***Professional Experience:*** Instructor, University of California, 1956–1957, lecturer with rank of assistant professor, 1957–1958; visiting assistant professor, Mills College, 1958–1959; acting assistant professor, Stanford University, 1959–1961, assistant professor, 1961–1962; associate professor, Johns Hopkins University, 1962–1965; professor of economics, Northwestern University, 1966–1972, University of Maryland, 1972–1978; professor of economics and agricultural economics, University of California, Berkeley, 1979–1994, professor emeritus, 1994–

***Concurrent Positions:*** Consultant, Division of Industrial Development, United Nations, 1962–1963; Consultant, Agency for International Development, U.S. Department of Agriculture, 1963–1972; Consultant, World Bank, 1968–

***Married:*** Frank L. Adelman, 1950, divorced 1979

***Children:*** 1

***Irma Adelman*** is an internationally renowned economist who was born in Romania and emigrated to the United States with her family in 1949; she became a naturalized citizen in 1955. Her father had the foresight to leave Romania in 1939 for Palestine, so the family escaped the fate of many Jews during that period. She finished high school in Palestine and participated in the Israeli war of independence. After completing her graduate work at Berkeley, she was amazed that a woman who had graduated in the top of her class at an outstanding university could not find a permanent position. She held a series of short appointments at several schools, and when her physicist husband accepted an appointment in the Washington, D.C., area, she obtained a position at Johns Hopkins University and began working on summer research projects at the Brookings Institution. She was invited to join the faculty at Northwestern University in 1966, and her husband followed her to the Chicago area. She returned to the East Coast in 1972 when she accepted a professorship at the University of Maryland. In 1979, she returned to the University of California, Berkeley, as a professor. During her career she continued to conduct research at the United Nations, the Agency for International Development, and other places.

In an autobiographical sketch published in the fall 1990 issue of *American Economist,* Adelman describes how the problems encountered by professional women—discrimination and handling the multiple demands of home, child, and career—impinged on her life and career. Although there was a high demand for college instructors in the 1950s, there was discrimination against women faculty members. At the time, job openings were not advertised; they were "publicized" only through a network of personal contacts. She herself finally was able to secure a professorship at Johns Hopkins through personal contacts. However, when she asked for a raise after three years, the department head told her to solicit alternative offers as an indication of her professional reputation. The University of Maryland offered a salary that was 60 percent higher than her present one, and Northwestern offered one that was 80 percent more. She accepted the latter offer. After several years, she and her husband looked unsuccessfully for joint appointments at a university before returning to the East Coast where Irma received a faculty appointment at the University of Maryland and Frank wrote a book. She commuted to the Maryland campus from Washington, D.C., and expended so much energy on teaching, research, and child care that she and her husband separated and later divorced. She found that combining child-rearing and a career requires tremendous physical stamina.

Adelman has received numerous appointments and awards for her work internationally, including awards in Korea and Vietnam. In 1977, she was invited to hold the Cleringa Chair at Leiden University in the Netherlands, a one-year appointment that rotates between a Dutch professor and a foreign professor. She was the fourth holder of the chair and only the second economist. She has published more than 130 papers and books, was elected a fellow of the American Academy of Arts and Sciences, and is a member of the Econometric Society and the American Economic Association. Her areas of research are how the economic growth of nations is affected by and, in turn, affects economics and political institutions; how institutions and economic structure and choices affect the diffusion of benefits from economic and institutional change; and examining income distribution and poverty, both descriptively and from a policy viewpoint.

***Bibliography:*** *American Men and Women of Science* 11–13; *Contemporary Authors* v. CANR-3; *Who's Who in America,* 51st ed., 1997; *Who's Who of American Women,* 20th ed., 1997–1998.

# *Ajzenberg-Selove, Fay*
(1926– )
### *nuclear physicist*

***Education:*** B.S.E., University of Michigan, 1946; M.S., University of Wisconsin, 1949, Ph.D. in physics, 1952

***Professional Experience:*** Assistant professor and then associate professor of physics, Boston University, 1952–1957; associate professor to professor, Haverford College, 1957–1970, acting department chair, 1960–1961 and 1967–1969; research professor, University of Pennsylvania, 1970–1973, professor of physics, 1973– , associate department chair, 1989–1993

***Concurrent Positions:*** Smith-Mundt fellow, U.S. State Department, 1955; visiting assistant professor, Columbia University, 1955; visiting professor, National University of Mexico, 1955; visiting associate physicist, Brookhaven National Laboratory, 1956; lecturer, University of Pennsylvania, 1957; Guggenheim fellow, Lawrence Radiation Laboratory, 1965–1966; consultant, California Institute of Technology, 1970–1972

***Married:*** Walter Selove, 1955

***Fay Ajzenberg-Selove*** is an internationally recognized authority on nuclear structure. She was born in Berlin of Russian parents, but because of financial problems the family moved to Paris in 1930. The family was forced to flee that city in 1940 because some family members were Russian Jews who had supported the Communist Party. Fortunately, her family believed in education for women, and they allowed her to study any subjects she chose. She completed her high school education after arriving in the United States in 1941 and enrolled in the Engineering School at the University of Michigan, the only woman in a class of 100. After spending a year in the graduate school at Columbia University, she taught college-level mathematics at the University of Illinois at Chicago. She then entered the graduate school at the University of Wisconsin and received her degree in physics in 1952.

When she was offered a position in the Physics Department at Boston University, she understood that she was to receive the standard salary for that position. However, when the dean decided that her salary would be 15 percent less than the standard, she declined to take the lower amount and promptly received a contract with the appropriate salary. She met Walter Selove, a physicist at Harvard University, in 1954, and they married in 1955. The immediate problem was to find appointments for both at the same institution. Walter received an associate professorship at the University of Pennsylvania and Fay an associate professorship at nearby Haverford College. She received an appointment at the University of Pennsylvania as a research professor in the Physics Department in 1970 and in 1972 applied for a transfer to a full professorship with tenure. Although she was internationally recognized as an authority on nuclear structure, had been publishing extensively, and had had many appointments to professional committees of the American Physical Society and the American Institute of Physics, the physics faculty voted to reject her request, citing that she was not active enough in the field and that she was too old. Since the University of Pennsylvania had no formal grievance procedure at that time, she filed a complaint with the equal opportunity agencies of the federal and state governments. By this time legislation was in place barring discrimination on the basis of age, and the state ordered the university to grant her full professorship with tenure.

She was a joint editor of *Energy Levels of Light Nuclei* for the fourth edition (1952) and the fifth edition (1955); she has been solely responsible for the sixth edition (1973) and all subsequent editions. In addition to numerous other scientific publications, she has been active in encouraging women to pursue careers in physics. Her autobiography, *A Matter of Choice: Memoirs of a Female Physicist* (1994), describes many of the professional problems she faced, problems that still, unfortunately, plague women today. She is a fellow of the American Association for the Advancement of Science and of the American Physical Society. Her areas of research are neutron spectra and nuclear structure.

***Bibliography:*** *American Men and Women of Science* 11–19; Herzenberg, C., *Women Scientists from Antiquity to the Present;* Rossiter, M., *Women Scientists in America; Who's Who in America*, 51st ed., 1997; *Women in Chemistry and Physics; World Who's Who in Science.*

# *Ancker-Johnson, Betsy*
## (1929– )
## *solid-state physicist*

***Education:*** B.A., Wellesley College, 1949; Ph.D. in physics, Tübingen University, 1953; honorary degrees: D.Sc., New York Polytechnic Institute, 1979, University of Southern California, 1984; LL.D., Bates College, 1980

***Professional Experience:*** Junior research physicist and lecturer in physics, University of California, Berkeley, 1953–1954; staff member, Inter-Varsity Christian Fellowship, 1954–1956; senior research physicist, Microwave Physics Laboratory, Sylvania Electric Products, Inc., 1956–1958; member of technical staff, David Sarnoff Research Center, Radio Corporation of America, 1958–1961; research specialist, Electronic Scientific Laboratory, Boeing Scientific Research Laboratories, 1961–1970, supervisor of solid-state and plasma electronics, 1970–1971, manager of advanced energy systems, Boeing Aerospace Company, 1971–1973; assistant secretary for science and technology, U.S. Department of Commerce, 1973–1977; associate laboratory director for physics research, Argonne National Laboratory, 1977–1979; vice president of Environmental Activity Staff, GM Technical Center, General Motors Corporation, 1979–1992; retired 1992

***Married:*** Harold H. Johnson, 1958

***Children:*** 4

***Betsy Ancker-Johnson*** is an internationally known solid-state physicist who was elected to membership in the National Academy of Engineering in 1975. She has had a distinguished career working for several corporations, reaching the level of a vice president at General Motors Corporation. In 1973, she was the first woman scientist to be appointed assistant secretary for science and technology at the U.S. Department of Commerce. However, as a young woman she faced discrimination even before she secured permanent employment. She decided to attend graduate school at Tübingen in Germany because she was interested in other cultures and people as well as physics. Psychologically, she was not prepared for comments from fellow students at the university that women cannot think analytically and therefore she must be hunting a husband. She found herself excluded from the students' informal study groups at first, but later she developed friendships with many of them. She decided that she must select the difficult subject of solid-state physics in order to prove she was at least twice as determined as a man with the same competencies in order to succeed as a physicist.

When she returned to the United States, she searched without success for a position in industrial research. Instead, she secured an appointment as a lecturer at the University of California, Berkeley, and it was there that she met her future husband, Harold Johnson, a mathematics professor. When her husband accepted a position at Princeton University, she found a job at Boeing Corporation. At that time, employers routinely asked married women if they planned to start a family, and she told her employer that she planned to have children but that she had already arranged to have live-in help for their care. During her first pregnancy she was not allowed to enter the laboratory building for three months before delivery—not even to attend a lecture or borrow a book. She did not receive a salary until she returned to work even though a male colleague received a week's leave with pay when his wife had their child. When Ancker-Johnson worked for another company, the state law stipulated that she again had to stop working three months prior to delivery. This time, her boss immediately hired her as a consultant, and she worked until a few days before delivery.

After working several years in research, she requested that she be transferred to a management position. The Boeing executives were shocked by the request, but they complied, and she performed marvelously as a manager. While she worked at Boeing she received at least four electrical or related patents, of which she was the sole inventor of three. Other patents were for a solid density probe, a solid signal generator, and a solid-state amplifier and phase detector. For four years she was assistant secretary for science and technology at the Department of Commerce, and after leaving there, she worked as associate laboratory director for physics research at Argonne National Laboratory. She then moved to the General Motors Corporation as vice president in charge of environmental policy. In this capacity she headed a staff of over 200 and was responsible for automobile safety, fuel economy, and noise and auto emissions as well as for all waste from GM plants worldwide. She retired in 1992, but she continues to be active as a member of committees and commissions on a national level.

She has been very active in promoting the role of women scientists, especially through her memberships in professional organizations. She wrote the book *Nobel Prize Women in Science: Their Lives, Struggles, and Momentous Discoveries* (1993). She is a fellow of the American Physical Society and of the Institute of Electrical and Electronics Engineers and a member of the Society of Automotive Engineers. An early autobiography was published in Ruth B. Kundsin's "Successful Women in the Sciences," and her photograph can be found in *Working Woman* (February 1980) and *Newsweek* (September 14, 1981).

***Bibliography:*** *American Men and Women of Science* 11–19; Kundsin, R., "Successful Women in the Sciences"; Stanley, A., *Mothers and Daughters of Invention;* Vare, E., *Mothers of Invention; Who's Who in Engineering,* 9th ed., 1995; *Who's Who in Technology Today,* 2d ed., v. 5; *Who's Who of American Women,* 20th ed., 1997–1998; *World Who's Who in Science.*

# *Anderson, Gloria (Long)*

(1938– )

## ***chemist***

***Education:*** B.S., Arkansas Agricultural, Mechanical and Normal College (now the University of Arkansas, Pine Bluff), 1958; M.S., Atlanta University, 1961; Ph.D. in organic chemistry, University of Chicago, 1968

***Professional Experience:*** Instructor in chemistry, South Carolina State College, 1961–1962; instructor in chemistry, Morehouse College, 1962–1964; professor in summer school, South Carolina State College, 1967; Calloway Associate Professor and chair of the Chemistry Department, Morris Brown College, 1968–1973, professor and chair of the Chemistry Department, 1973–1984, chair of the Natural Science Division and dean of academic affairs, 1984–

***Married:*** Leonard S. Anderson, 1960

***Children:*** 1

***Gloria Anderson*** is an authority on the industrial, medical, and military applications of fluorine-19 chemistry. In addition, she is a distinguished college administrator at Morris Brown College in Atlanta, Georgia. Fluorine-19 chemistry began to be an important field of research prior to World War II when many commercial applications were discovered. Anderson chose fluorine-19 as her thesis topic and has retained it as her major interest in research. Her research has involved the use of nuclear magnetic resonance (NMR) spectroscopy, a procedure that enables an extremely sophisticated analysis of the molecular structures and interactions of various materials.

Anderson has conducted research in a variety of fields, and starting in 1971, the National Institutes of Health, the National Science Foundation, and the Office of Naval Research have funded her investigation of fluorine-19. She conducted research on amantadines, a drug used to prevent viral infection, under the sponsorship of the National Institutes of Health, and she held a faculty industrial research fellowship with the National Science Foundation in 1981 and with the Air Force Office of Scientific Research in 1984. In 1985, she conducted research on the synthesis of solid rocket propellants under the auspices of the Air Force Office of Scientific Research. She has been a research consultant for BioSPECS of the Hague, Netherlands, since 1990.

She has been very much involved in education on the national level. She was appointed to the board for the Corporation for Public Broadcasting in 1972 for a six-year term, and while there, she chaired committees on minority training, minorities and women, and human resources development and served as vice chair of the board from 1977 to 1979. She has also served on the review panel for the National Science Foundation's Women in Science Program. In addition to her heavy schedule of research and professional activities, she has served as chair of the Chemistry Department at Morris Brown College and as dean of academic affairs since 1984. She is a member of the American Association for the Advancement of Science and of the American Chemical Society. Her research includes synthetic organic fluorine chemistry, fluorine-19 nuclear magnetic resonance spectroscopy, mechanism of transmission of substituent effects, and synthetic organic chemistry. Her photograph is included in *Notable Twentieth-Century Scientists.*

***Bibliography:*** *American Men and Women of Science* 12–19; *Blacks in Science and Medicine; Notable Twentieth-Century Scientists; Who's Who in Science and Engineering,* 3d ed., 1996–1997.

# *Archambault, JoAllyn*
(1942– )
## *anthropologist, museum program director*

***Education:*** B.A., University of California, Berkeley, 1970, M.A., 1974, Ph.D. in anthropology, 1984

***Professional Experience:*** Lecturer in Native American studies, University of California, Berkeley, 1976–1979; chair of Ethnic Studies Department, California College of Arts and Crafts, 1979–1980; part-time research associate, Center for the Study of Race, Crime and Social Policy, Cornell University, 1980–1982; assistant professor of anthropology, University of Wisconsin, Milwaukee, 1983–1986; director of the American Indian Program at the National Museum of Natural History, Smithsonian Institution, 1986–

***JoAllyn Archambault*** is a prominent anthropologist and the program director for Native American culture at the Smithsonian Institution in Washington, D.C. She was born into a mixed-blood Standing Rock Dakota, Creek, Irish, and French family in Claremore, Oklahoma. Her responsibilities at the museum consist of preserving and promoting Native American art and culture and political anthropology. She functions as an ethnic liaison, supervises Native American fellowship interns, and manages a $110,000 annual program budget. She was responsible for the redesign of the North American Indian Ethnology Halls for the "Changing Culture in a Changing World" exhibit. She has curated and implemented four major exhibits: "Plains Indian Arts: Change and Continuity" (1987), "100 Years of Plains Indian Painting" (1989), "Indian Basketry and Their Makers" (1990), and "Seminole!" (1990). She contributed to the Los Angeles Southwest Museum's quincentennial exhibit "Grandfather, Hear Our Voices" in 1992.

Her research for her doctorate centered on the Gallup ceremonial, an annual tourist event held in Gallup, New Mexico, to display Native American arts of that region. Originally the ceremonial was sponsored by white people as a business venture, but by the 1980s, the Native Americans had established their own dealer contacts. Since that time, her interests have included research in several urban and reservation communities, including reservation land use, health evaluation, expressive art, material culture, contemporary native culture, and the sun dance ceremony of eight different Plains groups. She has provided a great deal of assistance with respect to conservation, architecture, public programming, and research projects to tribes and to Indian-controlled museums, archives, and other types of cultural projects. She has lectured at several colleges both before and after joining the Smithsonian.

One of the controversies in Native American anthropology involves the number of skeletal remains that are housed in museums and laboratories across the United States. The problem continues to escalate because federal regulations require an anthropological analysis of any potentially historical material that is discovered. Although many people agree that the Native American skeletal remains should be returned to the tribes, it is often difficult to establish which tribe is involved or whether an established tribe still exists. Archambault has served on the Commission on Native American Reburial of the American Anthropological Association as well as on the University of California Joint Academic-Senate-Administration Committee on Human Skeletal Remains. She is a member of the American Ethnological Society as well as of several similar associations.

As a working artist herself, she received many awards between 1969 and 1980, and her work can be found in the permanent collections of several museums that specialize in Native American art. She has published one book, *An Annotated Bibliography of Sources on Plains Indian Art* (ca. 1995).

***Bibliography:*** Bataille, G., *Native American Women; Native North American Almanac; Notable Native Americans.*

# *Attneave, Carolyn (Lewis)*
(1920–1992)
## *psychologist*

***Education:*** Student, Occidental College and California College of Arts and Crafts; A.A., Yuba College, 1939; B.A., Chico State College (now California State University, Chico), 1940; M.A., Stanford University, 1947, Ph.D. in psychology, 1952; postdoctoral study University of Chicago and University of Oklahoma Medical School

***Professional Experience:*** Elementary school teacher, 1940–1942; director of student personnel, Texas Woman's University, 1956–1957; assistant professor of psychology and human development, Texas Technological College (now Texas Tech University), 1957–1961; coordinator, Oklahoma State Department of Health, 1962–1969; senior psychologist, Philadelphia Child Guidance Clinic, 1969–1971; assistant professor of clinical psychology, Tufts University School of Medicine, 1971; coordinator of public service careers programs, Massachusetts Department of Mental Health, 1971–1972; supervisor of family therapy, Boston University, 1972–1975; research associate and lecturer, Harvard University School of Public Health, 1973–1975; professor of psychology and adjunct professor of behavioral sciences, University of Washington, Seattle, 1975–1987, director of American Indian studies, 1975–1977; retired 1977

***Concurrent Positions:*** Consulting psychologist and family therapist in private practice; U.S. Coast Guard Women's Auxiliary (SPARS), 1942–1946

***Married:*** Fred Attneave II, 1949, divorced 1956

***Children:*** 2

***Carolyn Attneave*** was the founder of network therapy and probably the best-known Native American psychologist. She was internationally renowned for her expertise in cross-cultural topics in counseling and psychotherapy and for her pioneering work to extend family therapy to include the social network of the identified client. Her book *Family Networks: Retribalization and Healing* (1973) is considered the most comprehensive and significant presentation of social network therapy for families. Instead of merely assisting the client and family to solve an immediate problem, the therapist convenes a group as large as 40 people who are related to the identified client by blood, friendship, need, or physical proximity. The members of this large, diverse group bring their strengths to help the client cope with the problem and to prepare the client to handle the next crisis of living.

Attneave started developing her theory of network therapy while teaching elementary school as she began to focus on working with troubled children within the larger context of family and community. However, her own experiences as a child visiting her grandparents during the summer on the Delaware Indian tribal lands in Oklahoma impressed on her the need to retain contact with her Indian heritage. Her mother was descended from the Delaware Indian tribes but had grown up with little knowledge of the customs and traditions of the community. While working for the Oklahoma State Department of Health, Attneave was able to develop the idea further. There, she collaborated with physicians, civic organizations, tribal and federal agencies, tribal leaders, and medicine men in providing mental health services to the seven Native American tribes in the region.

She became a founding member of the Boston Indian Council, one of the largest Native American centers in the country, and she started a newsletter, *Network of Indian Psychologists,* to exchange information about services available to the American Indian community. The subscribers to the newsletter eventually evolved into a formal organization, the Society of Indian Psychologists. In 1981, she directed a project sponsored by the National Institute of Mental Health to compile a computerized bibliography of American Indian mental health research. The bibliography is housed at the National Center for American Indian and Alaska Native Mental Health Research at the University of Colorado, Denver.

Although Attneave grew up in two worlds—white and Indian—she did not experience conflicts between the two cultures. She spent her childhood in northern California where there were few tribes; instead, the minority groups were the Japanese and the Basques. The first time she lived among Indians as an adult was when she worked in Oklahoma, where she was gradually accepted by the local tribes because, as she said, she did not pretend to be anything that she wasn't. When writing up case studies, she asked Indians to read them to assure that what she wrote was fair or that it was not too personal or embarrassing. She found in her work in Philadelphia that the lack of understanding between the black and white communities was owing to the same problems that existed between Indian and white communities in Oklahoma. In many tribal groups she was regarded as "the wise mother of the tribe."

There is a biography and an extensive interview with Attneave in the May–June 1990 issue of *Journal of Counseling and Development;* this includes several photographs. There is an obituary in the May 1996 issue of *American Psychologist,* and there is also a photograph in the *Native North American Almanac.*

***Bibliography:*** *American Men and Women of Science* 13; *Contemporary Authors* v. CANR-1 and 45–48; *Native North American Almanac.*

# *Avery, Mary Ellen*
(1927– )
***pediatrician***

***Education:*** B.A., Wheaton College, 1948; M.D., Johns Hopkins University, 1952; honorary degrees: M.A., Harvard University, 1974; D.Sc., Wheaton College, 1974, University of Michigan, 1975, Medical College of Pennsylvania and Trinity College, 1975, Albany Medical College, 1977, Medical College of Wisconsin and Radcliffe College, 1978, Russell Sage College, 1983, Memorial University of Newfoundland, 1993; LHD, Emmanuel College, 1979

***Professional Experience:*** House staff in pediatrics, Johns Hopkins Hospital, 1952–1957; research fellow in pediatrics, Harvard University Medical School, 1957–1959; fellow in medicine, Johns Hopkins University, 1959–1960, assistant professor, 1961–1964, associate professor of pediatrics, 1964–1969, pediatrician in charge of newborn nurseries at Johns Hopkins Hospital, 1962–1969; professor of pediatrics, McGill University Children's Hospital, 1969–1974; Thomas Morgan Rotch Professor of Pediatrics, Harvard University Medical School, 1974–

*Mary Ellen Avery* discovered the medical condition called infant respiratory distress syndrome (RDS) and participated in developing treatments for the condition. Her work also instigated a discipline she calls a study of the metabolism of the lung. One experience that led to her focus on diseases of the lung was that in 1952, just after she had completed her medical school studies, she was diagnosed with tuberculosis. The standard treatment at the time was bed rest for one year, and medications to treat the disease were just being developed. After spending two days in a sanatorium, she decided to return home to complete her required year's rest.

In her research, she found that RDS resulted from the lack of a fluid called pulmonary surfactant, which normally coats the internal surface of the lungs. This soapy fluid enables the lungs to retain some air after exhalation, which makes it easier for the lungs to expand with the next breath. One factor that had previously puzzled physicians was why some newborn infants breathed for several hours after birth and then suddenly stopped breathing. Avery's research indicated that the surfactant is essential to keep air in the lungs and that a deficiency of it is responsible for RDS in infants. Prior to her studies, it was thought that the hyaline membranes were the cause of the infant deaths.

She also pioneered the discipline of the metabolism of the lung as her work on the surfactant led to the study of the nature of lung tissue. The prevailing view had been that the lung was a large surface area, but the work of molecular biologists led to a better understanding of the function of the proteins that make up the surfactant.

She has received numerous awards, the most prestigious of which is the National Medal of Science (1991). She was elected to membership in the National Academy of Sciences in 1994. In a letter to the author dated May 28, 1997, Avery commented that she had never thought a pediatrician would be elected to the academy and was taken by surprise when she received the announcement. In response to the author's questions, she said that she remains concerned about the current situation of women scientists. "Not enough recognition has been given to the special demands on women whose scientific productivity may be delayed during childbearing years."

In addition to numerous journal publications, Avery has written several books: *The Lung and Its Disorders in the Newborn Infant* (4th ed., 1981), *Diseases of the Newborn* (6th ed., 1991), *Born Early* (1984), and *Pediatric Medicine* (2d ed., 1994). She is a fellow of the American Association for the Advancement of Science and of the American Academy of Arts and Sciences. She is a member of the American

Academy of Pediatrics, the American Physiological Society, the Society of Pediatric Research (president, 1972–1973), and the American Pediatric Society (president, 1990) as well as other associations. Her photograph is included in *Notable Women in the Life Sciences.*

***Bibliography:*** *American Men and Women of Science* 11–19; *Contemporary Authors* v. 118; *Notable Women in the Life Sciences; Who's Who in America,* 51st ed., 1997; *Who's Who in Science and Engineering,* 3d ed., 1996–1997; *Who's Who of American Women,* 20th ed., 1997–1998.

# B

## Baca Zinn, Maxine
(1942– )
***sociologist***

***Education:*** B.A., California State College, Long Beach (now California State University, Long Beach), 1966; M.A., University of New Mexico, 1970; Ph.D. in sociology, University of Oregon, 1978
***Professional Experience:*** Faculty member, University of Michigan, Flint, 1975–1990; senior research associate, Julian Samora Research Institute, Michigan State University, 1990–
***Concurrent Positions:*** Visiting professor of sociology, University of California, Berkeley; guest professor of sociology, University of Connecticut; distinguished visiting professor in women's studies, University of Delaware
***Married:*** Alan Zinn
***Children:*** 1

M*axine Baca Zinn* is credited with being one of the first people to conduct sociological work on Latino families and Mexican-American women. She is a pioneer in the field of family, race, and ethnic relations, and some of her colleagues refer to her as one of the mothers of Chicana feminism. As an undergraduate sitting in sociology classes, she could not identify with what her professors were saying when they were discussing minorities, for the discussions in no way reflected the Chicana she knew.

She feels that Mexican-American women have been especially maligned because of erroneous assumptions and limited empirical research. In a paper in the winter 1982 issue of *Signs,* she states that the portrayal of Chicanas in the social sciences has been narrow and biased. "They have been portrayed as long-suffering mothers who are subject to the brutality of insecure husbands and whose only function is to produce children—as women who themselves are childlike, simple, and completely dependent on fathers, brothers, and husbands. Machismo and its counterpart of female submissiveness are assumed to be rooted in a native cultural heritage." Her research has focused on examining the true role of the Chicana in society, and she compares the role of Chicanas to that of all minority women—black, Asian, etc.—and feels that an important source of minority women's subordination lies in their exclusion from the public life of the society at large.

One of her contributions was to define the cultures of Hispanic, Mexican, Chicano, and Latino women. The terms often are used interchangeably, but in general, Chicano means Mexican American; Mexican means a person from Mexico; for Latin Americans, Hispanic means persons from the United States or that country's Hispanic neighbors, and Latino means a person of Latin-American or Spanish-speaking descent. Baca Zinn's goal is to make sociology more minority inclusive, and in the paper mentioned above, she discusses the work of other scholars who are also revising the past and presenting new interpretations of the sociological framework of minorities and their families. Currently, she is working on how Chicana/Latina feminism differs from other forms, such as black feminism. In her book *Women of Color in U.S. Society* (1995), she and other scholars explore race, class, and gender as systems of oppression against women of color in the United States.

She has received several awards for her research, including the Outstanding Alumnus Award from California State University, Long Beach (1990), and the Cheryl Miller Lecturer Award on Women and Social Change (1989). She has also received a special recognition award for contributions to the Western Social Science Association, of which she was president in 1985–1986. Her photograph is included in the book *Notable Hispanic American Women.*

***Bibliography:*** *Notable Hispanic American Women.*

# *Bateson, Mary Catherine*

(1939– )

## *anthropologist, linguist*

***Education:*** B.A., Radcliffe College, 1960; Ph.D. in Arabic languages, Harvard University, 1963

***Professional Experience:*** Associate professor of anthropology, Ateneo de Manila University, 1966–1968; senior research fellow in psychology and philosophy, Brandeis University, 1968–1969; research staff member, Massachusetts Institute of Technology, 1969–1971; visiting professor of anthropology, Northeastern University 1969–1971 and 1974–1975; researcher, University of Tehran, 1972–1974; professor of anthropology and dean of graduate studies, Damavand College, Tehran, 1975–1977; professor of anthropology and dean of social science and humanities, University of Northern Iran, 1977–1979; visiting scholar in anthropology, Harvard University, 1979–1980; professor of anthropology, Amherst College, 1980–1987, dean of faculty, 1980–1983; Clarence Robinson Professor of Anthropology and English, George Mason University, 1987–

***Concurrent Positions:*** President, Institute for Intercultural Studies, New York City, 1979–

***Married:*** J. Barkev Kassarjian, 1960

***Children:*** 1

M*ary Catherine Bateson,* a distinguished anthropologist, is the daughter of two famous persons: the pioneer anthropologists Margaret Mead and her third husband, Gregory Bateson. Margaret Mead was famous as an anthropologist even before Catherine was born. During Margaret's first two marriages, physicians had told her that she was unable to have children, but when she did have a child, she was a devoted mother and, later, grandmother. As the only child of older, educated parents, Catherine had a somewhat unusual childhood. For instance, her parents, and especially her mother, used her for studies of the mother-child interaction and reported the results in published papers. Catherine reveals much about her own life in her biography of her parents, *With a Daughter's Eye* (1984), as well as in two autobiographies.

Her parents had progressive ideas about rearing and educating children and sent her to what were considered to be progressive schools. Her mother adapted the practices of mother-child interaction she had observed in primitive societies in rearing her own child. For example, she breast-fed her baby, which was not common in the 1940s in the United States, and established an on-demand feeding and sleeping schedule for the baby. She also selected Dr. Benjamin Spock as her daughter's pediatrician early in his career.

Margaret Mead and Gregory Bateson separated when Catherine was six years old, but they continued to work together professionally for the rest of their lives. After they divorced in 1949, Catherine spent her summers with her father. As a single mother who worked and traveled, Margaret shared living quarters with various friends so that Catherine would have a stable family life while her mother continued her career. Margaret did not take her daughter on any of her fieldtrips, but when Catherine did accompany her mother to a conference in Israel, she decided to enroll there for her final year of high school to learn Hebrew, the first of her many languages. Her mother permitted her to stay with a local Israeli family for the school term but insisted that she return to the United States to enroll in college. While she was attending Radcliffe, she met J. Barkev Kassarjian, an Armenian student at Harvard, and they married in 1960, before either one of them had completed their doctorate.

After graduation, the couple moved to the Philippines where they both taught at universities. While there, Catherine expanded her subject area, adding anthropology and psychology to linguistics in order to secure employment. The couple then moved to Iran where both taught in universities until the political situation became unstable. During this period, their daughter was born, an event that was soon followed by the illness of both of Catherine's parents. She returned to California for a short time to help her father complete his book *Mind and Nature* (1979). Margaret died in 1978 and Gregory in 1980. Meanwhile, Catherine and Barkev, along with all other Americans, were evicted from Iran during the revolution.

After several interim appointments, she secured a position in 1980 as professor of anthropology and, later, dean of the faculty at Amherst College. In her book *Composing a Life* (1989), she gives a detailed account of her efforts to open the curricula to new areas of study, to encourage collaboration with other universities in the area, and to retain more women faculty members. Although the Amherst departments were hiring women faculty, the women tended not to stay because they were thrown into situations that undermined their confidence and aspirations. Catherine herself was treated badly by the college administrators. She was not appointed acting president when the president died, and when the new president replaced her as dean, she was notified by letter. She then returned to the teaching faculty at Amherst but left in 1987, with dignity and on her own terms, for a position at George Mason University.

She has written extensively about the need for women to take control of their lives. In her autobiography *Composing a Life,* she compares her life to that of four of her women friends, one of whom is Johnnetta Cole. She describes how each of the five women approached or handled a problem and talks of the need to have a capacity for change and for new learning. She suggests that women should view themselves as composing a life rather than juggling career, family, and marriage. Juggling implies a precarious position while composing implies bringing diverse elements to a whole. Her later book *Peripheral Visions: Learning Along the Way* (1994) arose from reactions to *Composing a Life* indicating that change applies to both men and women. She says both men and women must make changes in their lives because of the downsizing of companies, losing the family farm, business failures, etc. She talks of encounters with other cultures to develop communication and empathy.

She has published numerous scientific papers and books in addition to those mentioned above and is a member of the American Anthropological Association. Her photograph is included in *Whole Earth Review* (winter 1988), *Working Women* (May 1990), and *Publishers' Weekly* (May 30, 1994).

***Bibliography:*** *Contemporary Authors* v. 137; *Who's Who in America,* 51st ed., 1997; *Who's Who in Science and Engineering,* 3d ed., 1996–1997.

# *Beall, Cynthia*
## (1949– )
## *anthropologist*

***Education:*** B.A., University of Pennsylvania, 1970; M.A., Pennsylvania State University, 1972, Ph.D. in anthropology, 1976

***Professional Experience:*** Assistant professor of anthropology, Case Western Reserve University, 1976–1982, associate professor, 1982–1987, professor of anthropology, 1987–

*Cynthia Beall* is a renowned anthropologist and an authority on how people live at high altitudes. Usually when one thinks of high-altitude research, one thinks of aviation or space research, but Beall has examined both the physical and the social aspects of people in Tibet, Mongolia, Peru, Bolivia, Nepal, and Ethiopia. Her studies have included such diverse topics as China's birth-control policy in Tibet, the impact of China's reform policy on the nomads, the hemoglobin concentration in people at high altitudes, age differences and sensory and cognitive functions in elderly Nepalese, and the physical fitness of elderly Nepalese farmers.

In a telephone conversation with the author on August 29, 1997, she said that the high point of her career to that point was that she had established a solid scientific footing for the study of population differences in the reaction to high-altitude hypoxia, or inadequate oxygenation of the blood. When she talked of the opportunities for women in the field of anthropology, she said she would definitely encourage women to enter the field. Women anthropologists are very well trained, and there are many women in the profession. There would not be barriers to obtaining a position when one applied for it.

She was elected a member of the National Academy of Sciences in 1996. She said her reaction when she was notified of her election was one of surprise, for she had not given a moment's thought to the possibility of being elected. If she had not known well the person who telephoned, she would have thought it a joke. She said that the election quickly made somewhat of a difference in her career in that she began receiving invitations to participate in symposia that might not have been forthcoming otherwise.

In *Nomads of Western Tibet: The Survival of a Way of Life* (1990), she and M. C. Goldstein present an overview of the life of Tibetan nomads in the years since the Chinese invaded the country in 1950. It is a collection of photographs with a short, nontechnical text, and an article in *National Geographic* (June 1989) summarizes their 16-month project. Theirs was the first research team to receive permission to conduct a long-term study of the area since the Chinese invasion. In *The Changing World of Mongolian Nomads* (1994), the same authors describe a three-year study of Mongolia after the death of communism led to the privatization of the nomads' collective farming system. An overview of that study is also given in an article in *National Geographic* (May 1993).

Beall was a founding coeditor of *Journal of Cross-Cultural Gerontology* from 1986 to 1995. Her research has been sponsored by grants from the National Science Foundation, the National Geographic Society, and the American Federation for Aging Research. She is a member of the American Association for the Advancement of Science, American Anthropological Association, American Association of Physical Anthropology, Human Biology Council (president, 1991–1994), Society for the Study of Human Biology, Association for Anthropology and Gerontology, Council for Nutritional Anthropology, and

Gerontological Society of America. Her photograph is included in *National Geographic* (June 1989 and January 1998).

***Bibliography:*** *Who's Who in America,* 51st ed., 1997.

# *Beattie, Mollie Hanna*
## (1947–1996)
## *forester, government official*

***Education:*** B.A. in philosophy, Marymount College, 1968; M.S. in forestry, University of Vermont, 1979; M.A. in public administration, Kennedy School of Government, Harvard University, 1991

***Professional Experience:*** Newspaper reporter; tour guide for Outward Bound, 1974–1976; program director, Windham Foundation, 1983–1985; commissioner of forests and parks, Vermont, 1985–1989; deputy secretary, Vermont Agency of Natural Resources, 1989–1990; executive director, Richard A. Snelling Center for Government, 1991–1993; director, U.S. Fish and Wildlife Service, 1993–1996

***Married:*** Rick Schwolsky

***Mollie Beattie*** was the first woman to head the U.S. Fish and Wildlife Service, but unfortunately, she served only three years before she died of a brain tumor. She had an eclectic life, working as a newspaper reporter after college and becoming interested in the outdoors after being involved in Outward Bound activities. As a child, she had been introduced to nature studies by her grandmother Harriet Hanna, who was a self-trained botanist in upstate New York. Mollie truly was an outdoors person. For example, when she was being interviewed by Governor Madeleine Kunin for the commissioner's position in Vermont, Mollie had to purchase a dress because she had none suitable to wear. Most photographs of her show her in jeans and boots out in the field.

She was well qualified for her position with the Fish and Wildlife Service because she had one degree in forestry and another in public administration. Her previous assignment had been with the Richard A. Snelling Center for Government, a public policy institute that is now affiliated with the University of Vermont. Its aims are to educate citizens about state and local governments. Her experiences with the Vermont natural resources, forests, and parks agencies prepared her for similar activities on a national level. The Fish and Wildlife Service enforces wildlife laws, administers the Endangered Species Act, and carries out wetland protection and management.

She was known as an ardent supporter of the Endangered Species Act and the National Wildlife Refuge System. She oversaw the reintroduction of the gray wolf into the northern Rocky Mountains and won the support of the environmental community when she served as vice chair of a 1991 commission created by the Defenders of Wildlife organization to study the condition and future of the 91-million-acre National Wildlife Refuge System. During her confirmation hearings for that position, some of the senators asked her if she did any hunting. She replied that although she did not hunt, she valued hunters as a major conservation support group and did not see hunting or fishing as incompatible with biodiversity goals. She used the culling of deer in the national parks to prevent the overgrazing of vegetation as an example and said she found biodiversity concepts a good strategy for maintaining wildlife. Her plan to conserve species was to manage the entire ecosystem instead of waiting until individual species became endangered.

The move to Washington, D.C., was especially trying for her. She and her husband, a contractor, had lived in a house in the Green Mountains where they had utilized solar power for their energy requirements, and the noise of the urban environment was very disturbing for her. When questioned about the number of women employed in the service, she said that the number was increasing but that unfortunately, women were concentrated in administrative and clerical positions rather than in the higher grades. After her death in 1996, a wilderness area in the Arctic National Wildlife Refuge in Alaska was named in her honor.

She was the lead author of the book *Working with Your Woodland: A Landowner's Guide* (rev. ed., 1993). Her obituary was published in the *New York Times* (June 29, 1996), and there are photographs of her in *Audubon Magazine* (March–April 1994), *Endangered Species Bulletin* (July–August 1996), and *American Forests* (May–June 1994).

# *Bell, Gwen (Dru'yor)*
(1934– )
## *geographer, computer museum founder*

***Education:*** B.A., University of Wisconsin, Madison, 1955; Master of City and Regional Planning, Harvard University, 1957; Ph.D. in geography, Clark University, 1967
***Professional Experience:*** Faculty member, Graduate School of Public and International Affairs, University of Pittsburgh, 1966–1973; founder and director, Computer Museum, Boston, 1980–
***Married:*** Gordon Bell, 1959
***Children:*** 2

***Gwen Bell*** has made a unique contribution to the computer industry by founding and directing a museum to house a wide array of computers and components, even including a number of computer games. In addition, she was the first person credited with developing a geographic information system on a computer and with producing a variety of maps. She was first introduced to computers while on Fulbright scholarship in Australia and then used the TX-O at the Massachusetts Institute of Technology to analyze a redevelopment area of Boston. After receiving her doctorate, she taught in the Graduate School of Public and International Affairs at the University of Pittsburgh. In the 1970s, she worked as a United Nations consultant on planning and edited a journal and three books. She is a member of the Association for Computing Machinery (president, 1992–1994).

In 1978, Ken Olsen, president of Digital Equipment Corporation (DEC), asked her if the TX-O computer could possibly be rebuilt in DEC headquarters at Marlboro, Massachusetts. This request started her on her project to establish a computer museum, which she did in 1980. She received grant funds in 1982 and moved the museum to a renovated warehouse that overlooks Boston harbor in 1984.

The idea of a museum had started years before. Her father, a newspaper owner in Prairie du Chien, Wisconsin, had long championed the historic preservation efforts in that community. Her husband, Gordon Bell, an engineering executive at DEC, was a computer junkie who, along with his wife, had long been collecting computing and calculating artifacts. They met while both were scholarship students in Australia, and he proposed via a visual display terminal. Although DEC was the original sponsor of the museum, there was a concerted effort to collect representative pieces throughout the world. As in any burgeoning field, there are disputes about who should be credited with discoveries, and the museum staff has attempted to display the work of as many contenders as possible.

One of the oldest exhibits is a set of John Napier's calculating bones that dates back to the sixteenth century. As computers have shrunk in size, the museum has been able to include entire machines, like the PDP-1, DEC's first computer, and the Altair of the Massachusetts Institute of Technology. There are many displays of components such as transistors. Many of the display items are in working order, especially the personal computers, and older models are loaded with the software that was developed for them. Many of the major exhibits have been designed by local students using their own time and energy to develop lively presentations.

The museum sponsors a number of lectures by computer pioneers each year, and these have been videotaped for use by scholars in the future. A video by Bell entitled "Computer Pioneers and Pioneer Computers" (1996) is available commercially. In addition, there is a series of seminars on diverse topics, such as demonstrations of computer music and discussions about old machines such as the ENIAC.

A photograph of Bell is included in J. Lee's *Computer Pioneers* (1995), and articles about the museum are included in *Datamation* (May 1983 and March 1, 1985), *PC Magazine* (February 5, 1985), and *Business Journal* (February 28, 1994).

***Bibliography:*** Lee, J., *Computer Pioneers.*

# *Benesch, Ruth Erica (Leroi)*
(1925– )
### *biochemist*

***Education:*** B.S., University of London, 1946; Ph.D. in biochemistry, Northwestern University, 1951

***Professional Experience:*** Demonstrator in chemistry, University of Reading, 1945–1947; research associate in chemistry, Johns Hopkins University, 1947–1948; fellow, University of Iowa, 1952, Enzyme Institute, University of Wisconsin, 1955; independent investigator, Marine Biological Laboratory, Woods Hole, 1956–1960; research associate, College of Physicians and Surgeons, Columbia University, 1960–1964, assistant professor, 1964–1972, associate professor, 1972–1980, professor of biochemistry, 1980–

***Married:*** Reinhold Benesch, 1946, died 1986

***Children:*** 2

***Ruth Erica Benesch*** is considered an equal contributor to the work that she and her husband conducted, primarily on hemoglobin. Although she was born in Paris, the family returned to their home in Berlin shortly after she was born. In 1939, she and her sister were removed by storm troopers and sent to England while their mother survived the war by hiding under the protection of non-Jewish comrades. Since money was in short supply and she needed to support herself at the University of London, Ruth worked at a rubber factory where Reinhold Benesch was a consultant. After their marriage in 1946, they moved to the United States where both became citizens and received doctorates from Northwestern University.

Their research for 40 years at various institutions centered on oxygen transport and other aspects of hemoglobin chemistry. Their earliest work was involved with sulfur in proteins, and they developed analytical and synthetic methods that allowed the introduction of the thiol groups and an accurate determination of their number in proteins. All but 13 of their 125 papers deal with hemoglobin, with special emphasis on its oxygen-carrying capacity. Nearly all the oxygen needed by cells is transported by hemoglobin; and although the normal pressure of oxygen in the lungs ensures complete saturation, or loading, of the hemoglobin, unloading depends not only on oxygen pressure and hemoglobin saturation but also on the oxygen affinity of the hemoglobin. This attractiveness of hemoglobin for oxygen has been studied extensively by the Benesches and others. If carbon dioxide accumulates, the affinity decreases and more oxygen is released. In 1967, the Benesches established that D-2,3-diphosphoglycerate is the third substance necessary for the proper functioning of the oxygen-hemoglobin system. They determined both the site at which diphosphoglycerate and related compounds bind to the protein and the nature of those bonds, and their discoveries resulted in a dramatic change in the way such systems are viewed and studied.

Beginning in 1960, they conducted a long and productive series of studies concerning the importance of the two different types of protein chains found in hemoglobin. Each chain differs in its amino acid composition, and they have been able to show that both types of protein chains are essential for the proper action of hemoglobin. They have also been able to show the exact differences among the various hemoglobin mutants.

This research led to their research on the cause of sickle-shaped cells in the deadly blood disease sickle-cell anemia. Although other scientists had used x-ray diffraction to study the disease with limited success, the Benesches used electron micron microscopic studies. These have given significant results concerning the formation of sickle cells. Just before Reinhold Benesch's death, the couple investigated a new class of compounds that might inhibit the polymerization of hemoglobin associated with sickle-cell anemia.

Ruth is a member of the American Chemical Society, the American Society of Biological Chemists, Biophysical Society, and the American Society of Hematology. Her research interests include physical biochemistry, protein chemistry, enzymology, structure-function relationship in hemoglobin, sickle-cell anemia, and hematology.

***Bibliography:*** *American Men and Women of Science* 11–19; Stanley, A., *Mothers and Daughters of Invention; Women in Chemistry and Physics.*

# *Benmark, Leslie Ann (Freeman)*

(1944– )

***industrial engineer***

***Education:*** B.S., University of Tennessee, 1967, M.S., 1970; Ph.D. in information systems, Vanderbilt University, 1976; J.D., University of Delaware, 1984

***Professional Experience:*** Systems analyst, Monsanto Company, St. Louis, 1967–1968; systems analyst, E. I. Du Pont de Nemours and Company, 1968–1970, systems analysis supervisor, 1970–1975, design supervisor, 1975–1976, planning and industrial engineering supervisor, 1976–1979, business analysis manager, 1979–1987, business strategy manager, 1987–1990, management systems consultant, 1990–1993, global planning manager for integrated processes and systems, 1993–

***Concurrent Positions:*** Computer science instructor, University of Tennessee, 1973–1975; assistant to dean of engineering and director of women engineers program, Vanderbilt University, 1975–1979

***Married:*** Gary N. Benmark, 1969

***Leslie Benmark*** is known nationally and internationally for her work on the accrediting boards for engineering curricula. Since 1993, she has been the global planning manager for integrated processes and systems for the international Du Pont Company, work that involves long-range strategic planning for global systems. Not all scientists and engineers who work for industrial concerns are engaged in research, as the corporations need people with scientific and technical expertise to work in the entire range of corporate operations. Benmark has always been involved in industrial systems, and she acquired a law degree when she was a business manager for Du Pont.

She has been a member of the accrediting boards for engineering curricula for a number of years, and she works with similar boards in several countries. For example, she is a fellow of the Institute of Industrial Engineers of Ireland. She is also a member of the National Society of Professional Engineers, the organization that prescribes the curricula for granting professional engineering licenses in the United States. Graduating from an accredited engineering school does not automatically make a person a professional engineer. The person must pass additional course work and have a specified number of years of experience. In addition to working on the national and international levels, Benmark serves on advisory boards for engineering programs such as those at the Georgia Institute of Technology, New Jersey Institute of Technology, and West Virginia University. She is particularly interested in working with curricula for women engineers. She is also the former chair of the Total Quality Engineering Committee of the Union of Pan-American Associations of Engineering.

Benmark was elected to membership in the National Academy of Engineering in 1993. In a telephone conversation on June 23, 1997, the author asked her what her reaction was when she received the notice of her election. She replied it was not entirely a surprise because she was aware that she was being nominated for some sort of an award, but she did not realize how difficult it was to be nominated until she became involved in academy activities. She is a member of the nominating committee for the industry, manufacturing, and systems engineering section, and she said the academy is making an active effort to increase the balance between members in industry and those in academia and to increase the number of women and minorities. When asked if she would encourage women to pursue a career in engineering, she said she definitely would. She herself is still heavily involved in making speeches, participating in high school career days, and serving on advisory boards to encourage women to pursue an engineering career.

Among other committee appointments, she has been a member of the Board of Directors of Manufacturing Studies of the National Research Council since 1993, and she is a fellow of the Institute of Industrial Engineers and a member of the American Society for Engineering Education.

***Bibliography:*** *American Men and Women of Science* 19; *Who's Who in Engineering,* 9th ed., 1995; *Who's Who in Science and Engineering,* 2d ed., 1994–1995.

# *Berenbaum, May Roberta*

(1953– )

***entomologist***

***Education:*** B.S., Yale University, 1975; Ph.D. in ecology, Cornell University, 1980

***Professional Experience:*** Assistant professor of entomology, University of Illinois, Urbana-Champaign, 1980–1985, associate professor, 1985–

***Concurrent Position:*** Affiliate, Institute of Environmental Studies, 1983–

May ***Berenbaum*** is that rare scientist who writes equally well whether she is writing scientific texts or a popular treatment of her subject. She had a childhood fear of insects that she finally overcame after taking an introductory course in entomology while a freshman at Yale University. She then decided to make them part of her life's work and specialized in insect ecology and evolutionary biology. Her professional success was evident when she received a National Science Foundation's Presidential Young Investigator Award (1984). She was also elected to membership in the National Academy of Sciences (1994) at a comparatively young age, received the Founders Award of the Entomological Society of America in the same year, and has been a University Scholar at the University of Illinois since 1985. In some sources she lists herself as a chemical ecologist.

In the books that she has written for the general public she stresses how insects affect our daily lives. As part of her efforts to improve the image of insects among the students and visitors to the university, she hosts an annual Insect Fear Film Festival. In her book *Bugs in the System: Insects and Their Impact on Human Affairs* (1995), she presents startling information about how insects affect our lives, stating that in wartime, the creatures cause more deaths than bombs or bullets for both the troops and the civilian population. For example, Napoleon's troops were defeated by lice, which are carriers of typhus; mosquitoes that carry malaria and fleas that spread the plague have taken a heavy toll on human populations through the centuries; and the French wine industry was nearly wiped out by a gall in 1860. However, insects have also contributed to society. At least a third of the food grown in the world is the direct result of insect pollination, and scale insects have been the sources of varnishes and dyes. Other books that Berenbaum has written for the general public are *Ninety-Nine Gnats, Nits, and Nibblers* (1989) and *Ninety-Nine More Maggots, Mites, and Munchers* (1993).

She discusses careers in the field of entomology in an article in *Illinois Research* (fall/winter 1994). In outlining the past, present, and future of entomology, she points out that both basic and applied entomology are multidisciplinary. Such scientists work with soil scientists, plant pathologists, agricultural economists, microbiologists, animal scientists, and epidemiologists, to name a few, as well as collaborating with colleagues in every area of life sciences. Her scientific works include the book *Herbivores, Their Interactions with Secondary Plant Metabolites,* vol. 1 (2d ed., 1992) and *Insect-Plant Interactions* (1986). From 1982 to 1985, she served as associate editor of the journal *American Midland Naturalist,* a primary journal on ecology.

In her research, she specializes in chemical aspects of insect-plant interaction, evolutionary ecology of insects, phototoxicity of plant products, and host-plant resistance. She is a member of the American Association for the Advancement of Science, American Genetics Association, Entomological Society of America, Ecological Society of America, and International Society of Chemical Ecology.

***Bibliography:*** *American Men and Women of Science* 16–19; *Who's Who in America,* 51st ed., 1997; *Who's Who in Science and Engineering,* 3d ed., 1996–1997.

# *Berezin, Evelyn*

(1925– )

***computer scientist, physicist***

***Education:*** B.S. in physics, New York University, 1951

***Professional Experience:*** Design engineer, Electronic Computer Corporation and Underwood Corporation; head of logic design section, Teleregister Corporation; manager of logic design, Digitronics Corporation, ca. 1960–1969; founded Redactron Corporation, 1969; sold Redactron to Burroughs Corporation, 1978; president of Burroughs office products group, 1978; consultant for automation industry, 1979– ; founded Greenhouse Management Corporation, 1980–

***Married:*** Israel Wilenitz

***Evelyn Berezin*** has been called the mother of word processing, a designation she declines to accept. She thinks of herself as a pioneer in word processing. One of the finest business machines of the twentieth century is the word processor. The development started with the memory typewriters of the 1960s and progressed through dedicated systems to emerge at the end of the century in personal computers. She was a business major in college until an unexpected job offer prompted her to switch to physics. When an Atomic Energy Commission fellowship expired, she could not find a job in her field. The new area of electronic data processing looked interesting, and she obtained a job with Electronic Computer Corporation. Her first assignment was to design a computer; this was the Elecom 200. Although the computer was not patented, some of its components were. In 1953, she designed the first office computer for Underwood Corporation, but this computer was never marketed because Underwood was sold to the Olivetti Corporation.

She moved to Teleregister Corporation as head of the logic design section in the late 1950s and led a team that designed, among other things, on-line systems for three major banks. The design she is the proudest of was United Airlines' nationwide on-line computer-reservation system in the early 1960s. This was a major achievement because it was the first nonmilitary on-line interactive system. It worked reliably for about 11 years after its installation and was the forerunner of similar systems for other airlines.

She moved to Digitronics Corporation in the 1960s and became manager of logic design. She designed the first high-speed commercial digital communications terminal, a machine that sent information from one place to another, like the Telex only faster and with fewer errors. Another major design was a 1962 digital on-line race track system, installed in 1965 at Roosevelt Raceway. This machine, now common at most race tracks, continuously computes the odds prior to a race and then immediately computes the winnings when the first horse crosses the finish line.

She and two male colleagues formed their own firm, Redactron, in 1969 to design a competitor for IBM's editing typewriter. Since she was the president and not the chief design engineer for the product, called Data Secretary, she demurs about her role in its development. She already was moving from design to management, but she admits she had a lot to say about the design. The Data Secretary had new capabilities, such as allowing more changes in recorded text than IBM's editors; it also undersold the IBM model by $2,000. Surveys published at the time estimated that installing a word processor to replace a memory typewriter could double an office's productivity. Redactron went public in 1971 and grew from 9 employees to 900 in 1976. After selling Redactron to Burroughs Corporation in 1978, Berezin became the president of that company's office products group. However, she left in 1979 to form her own firm again, this time a consultant firm for the automation industry. Later she formed Greenhouse Management Corporation, a venture capital group that invests in high-technology companies.

In an article in the February 1983 issue of *Working Woman,* she advised women to start their own businesses if they feel they have something to market. She says there is not job security anywhere. "The only security is the strength of a new industry like office automation plus your knowledge of your own abilities." She notes that most women start small companies rather than large ones. Her photograph is included in *Business Week* (December 2, 1972).

***Bibliography:*** Stanley, A., *Mothers and Daughters of Invention.*

# *Berkowitz, Joan B.*
(1931– )
## *physical chemist*

***Education:*** B.A., Swarthmore College, 1952; Ph.D. in physical chemistry, University of Illinois, 1955; certificate, Senior Executive Program, Sloan School, 1977
***Professional Experience:*** National Science Foundation fellow, Yale University, 1955–1957; physical chemist, Arthur D. Little, Inc., 1957–1980, vice president and section head of Environmental Business World Wide, 1980–1986; chief executive officer (CEO), Risk Science International, 1986–1989; founder and managing director, Farkas, Berkowitz & Company, Inc., 1989–
***Concurrent Position:*** Adjunct professor of physical chemistry, Boston University, 1965–1970
***Married:*** Arthur P. Mattuck, 1959, divorced 1977
***Children:*** 1

***Joan Berkowitz*** is internationally known as an authority on environmental hazards. Her interest in science started with science projects that she designed as a child, and when she decided she would always earn a living, the opportunities to work part time and to combine work with marriage and family seemed better in the sciences than in many other fields. After receiving her undergraduate degree from Swarthmore, she decided to pursue studies in physical chemistry at Princeton University, where her future husband was studying. However, the Princeton Chemistry Department would not accept women graduate students, so she completed her graduate studies at the University of Illinois in three years and then held a National Science Foundation fellowship at Yale University.

She accepted a position as a physical chemist at Arthur D. Little, Inc., an international management and technology consulting firm, while Arthur Mattuck joined the mathematics faculty at the Massachusetts Institute of Technology. They married in 1959, and she managed to bend the rules to continue to work until the day before her daughter was born and returned to work within two weeks. At Little she was very successful with high-temperature oxidation studies and those led to opportunities for projects in hazardous waste disposal. After she had worked for about 20 years, the company funded her participation in the Senior Executive Program of the Sloan School. In 1980, she became a vice president of Little and was further promoted to head the section Environmental Business World Wide. In 1986, she became the CEO of Risk Science International, a consulting firm in Washington, D.C. In 1989, she teamed with Allen Farkas to form Farkas, Berkowitz and Company to consult on waste treatment and disposal, remediation technologies, and market potential assessment.

At the beginning of her career, the technology of research was changing with the development of sophisticated scientific instruments, especially the computer. Versatility in adapting to new instrumentation and in moving into emerging fields enabled her to participate in many important areas of research. She has been able to develop research programs in electrochemistry, high-temperature chemistry, solar energy, and environmental science.

Because of the requirements of the space program, there was a need for research into the behavior of materials at high temperatures such as molybdenum, tungsten, and some of the other transition metals that had been used to provide alloys that maintained tensile strength and hardness at elevated temperatures. She developed a major research program in high-temperature oxidation of transition metals that showed molybdenum disilicide had the greatest oxidation resistance at all temperatures. It also was corrosion resistant. The plating techniques using molybdenum disilicide that the National Aeronautics and Space Administration (NASA) developed were used in industry also. Other related projects involved mechanisms of oxidation reactions in gas streams, studies of radiation shields, and the use of electrical fields to retard high-temperature oxidation of metals and alloys.

As Berkowitz became more involved in investigating potential environmental hazards, she headed a team that produced a multivolume catalog of all possible manufactured products with any potential to cause pollution problems. She headed another team that cataloged the potential techniques of treating hazardous wastes, and she also investigated the problem of "scrubbing," a technique in which sulfur dioxide is removed from the air to improve air quality.

She used the expertise she had gained from her environmental studies in her positions at Risk Science International and at Farkas, Berkowitz. In addition to scientific papers, she has published several brief articles on environmental problems in the journals *Environmental Science and Technology* and *ENR*. She was the first woman president of the Electrochemical Society (1979–1980), and she is also a member of the American Chemical Society and the American Physical Society. She received the Achievement Award of the Society of Women Engineers (1983) for her pioneering contributions in the field of hazardous waste management. Her photograph is included in *Environmental Science and Technology* (February 1992) and in the *Journal of the Electrochemical Society* (September 1978).

***Bibliography:*** *American Men and Women of Science* 11–19; Herzenberg, C., *Women Scientists from Antiquity to the Present;* Ireland, N., *Index to Women of the World . . . Suppl.; Notable Twentieth-Century Scientists;* O'Neill, L., *Women's Book of World Records and Achievements; Women in Chemistry and Physics.*

# *Bertell, Rosalie*
(1929– )
## *biomathematics*

***Education:*** B.A., D'Youville College, 1951; M.A., Catholic University, 1959, Ph.D. in mathematics, 1966; honorary degree, Mount St. Vincent University, 1985

***Professional Experience:*** Assistant in mathematics, Catholic University, 1957–1958; instructor, Sacred Heart Junior College, 1958–1962, associate professor, 1965–1968; coordinator and teacher, D'Youville Academy, 1968–1969; associate professor of mathematics, D'Youville College, 1969–1973; assistant research professor, State University of New York at Buffalo, 1974–1980; consultant, 1980–

***Concurrent Positions:*** Senior research scientist, Roswell Park Memorial Institute, 1970–1978; cancer research scientist and cancer research consultant, 1975–1980

***Rosalie Bertell*** has studied the hazards of low-level radiation of nuclear energy for a number of years. Although she has a doctorate in mathematics and is a former senior cancer research scientist at a prominent laboratory, the Roswell Park Memorial Institute in Buffalo, New York, she has had difficulty getting her theories accepted. The former nun has consulted for the Environmental Protection Agency, the Energy Task Force of the National Council of Churches, and the Citizens' Advisory Committee to the President's Commission on Three Mile Island.

She states that there are no peaceful uses of atomic energy because it leads to either a quick death from atomic weapons or a slow death from the pollution emanated by atomic production. She feels that health risks do not stop with increased cancer rates. Radiation also increases susceptibility to infectious diseases and causes an earlier onset of heart disease, diabetes, arthritis, coronary-renal disease, and other chronic health problems.

She has proposed several statistical methods for measuring the population at risk from radiation hazard and argues that the current methods are employed to convince people that low-level radiation is harmless. She proposes a sophisticated health-monitoring system using as health indicators the average age at diagnosis of chronic diseases, cancer occurrences grouped together for a common cause, and survival rates for immature infants. She suggests using state-of-the-art techniques in epidemiology to apportion responsibility for harmful radiation effects. For example, if a 20 percent increase in lung cancer in a geographic area is attributed to the careless handling of uranium mine tailings, then the persons or government agencies responsible for the carelessness should be liable for 20 percent of the medical costs for all lung cancer victims in that area. Such an apportionment would make individual lawsuits unnecessary.

There is still a great deal of controversy over the hazards of atomic energy, particularly the health hazards. The data about secret experiments conducted during World War II are gradually being declassified, with many startling revelations. At the time the experiments were being conducted, many scientists did not have sufficient data to anticipate what some of the results would be. However, there still is not a consensus on how the data should be interpreted. Bertell presents one interpretation.

She is a member of the Health Physics Society, American Academy of Political and Social Science, American Public Health Association, and International Biometric Society. Her research involves mathematical statistics, analysis, measure theory, the aging effect in humans associated with exposure to ionizing radiation, updating relative risk methodology for biomedical applications, and lifestyle and chronic diseases.

***Bibliography:*** *American Men and Women of Science* 12–19; Stanley, A., *Mothers and Daughters of Invention.*

# *Bonta, Marcia (Myers)*
(1940– )
## *nature writer*

***Education:*** B.A., Bucknell University, 1962
***Professional Experience:*** Nature writer
***Married:*** Bruce D. Bonta, 1962
***Children:*** 3

***Marcia Bonta*** is renowned as a writer on nature subjects, primarily in the state of Pennsylvania. She has contributed greatly to the history of nature writing with her books *Women in the Field: America's Pioneering Women Naturalists* (1991) and *American Women Afield: Writings by Pioneering Women Naturalists* (1995). In the late nineteenth and early twentieth centuries, women were not admitted to many colleges and often had difficulty finding jobs even if they did have science degrees, and they had to resort to publishing their own observations in newspapers, magazines, or pamphlets. Many women contributed greatly to the dissemination of scientific knowledge by writing on scientific subjects for the general public. In the field of natural history many people would recognize the names of John Muir or Aldo Leopold, but few people would recognize the names of the women Bonta includes in her two books.

She said that since she enjoys walking and observing in the woods, she began looking for women in past generations who were obsessed with the natural world. She traveled to archives all over the United States and read all she could find written by women. Much of this material is not readily available to the general public and her hope is that her books will be used in high school and college classrooms to inspire new generations of women.

She has written several books about her native Pennsylvania, including *Outbound Journeys in Pennsylvania* (1988), *Appalachian*

*Spring* (1991), *Appalachian Autumn* (1994), and *More Outbound Journeys in Pennsylvania* (1995). She has also published more than 200 articles in state and national magazines.

She says she is first a naturalist and second a writer. She began writing to educate people about the wonders of the natural world, especially about the wonders in their own backyards. She hopes that her Appalachian series will inspire people to look at the natural world wherever they live. She wrote her outbound journeys books and a long-standing magazine column to bring the people's attention the beauties of Pennsylvania. People think of Pennsylvania as a large state with a large city, Philadelphia, on the East Coast, rusted-out steel mills in Pittsburgh, and coal mines in the mountains. The national media has overlooked it as a state full of natural beauty. She also wants people to think of the outdoors as more than a place to play sports. She calls herself a missionary for the natural world, and she protests the proliferation of malls and creeping suburbanization.

***Bibliography:*** *Contemporary Authors* v. 148.

# *Bricker, Victoria (Reifler)*

(1940– )

## *anthropologist, ethnologist*

***Education:*** B.A., Stanford University, 1962; M.A., Harvard University, 1963, Ph.D. in anthropology, 1968

***Professional Experience:*** Visiting lecturer of anthropology, Tulane University, 1969–1970, assistant professor, 1970–1973, associate professor, 1973–1978, professor, 1978– , department chair, 1988–1991

***Concurrent Positions:*** Book review editor, *American Anthropologist,* 1971–1973; editor, *American Ethnologist,* 1973–1976

***Married:*** Harvey M. Bricker, 1964

**Victoria Bricker** is known as an ethnologist and anthropologist who specializes in comparing the oral tradition with the written history of Mexico. She was born in Hong Kong and moved to the United States in 1947, becoming a citizen as a teenager in 1953. She has had an impressive career: editing a major journal, receiving promotions in rank at Tulane University at short intervals, and being elected to membership in the National Academy of Sciences (1991).

She has prepared several publications relating to the Dresden Codex and the Madrid Codex, original Mayan manuscripts that describe the history and culture of the Maya (the names of these particular records result from their being housed in archives in Dresden, Germany, and Madrid, Spain, respectively). The Maya developed a type of pictogram called glyphs in which they recorded events on buildings, monuments, and tree bark. When the Spaniards conquered the Maya, they melted the gold and silver ornaments, and the Spanish priests destroyed many written records, although much writing remained on buildings and monuments. Often buildings were razed so that churches and government buildings could be built in centralized locations, but some of the manuscripts written on tree bark were saved and eventually ended up in archives in several European countries. The Dresden Codex contains astronomical calculations, and the Madrid Codex contains information on astrology and divination practices.

One area in which Bricker specializes is the astronomical portions of the codices. Among the ancient civilizations, the Maya are known to have been particularly astute astronomers. They used their data to predict the seasons for planting and harvesting crops as well as to determine the dates for various religious ceremonies, which sometimes related to guaranteeing successful harvests. It is generally accepted that many of their monuments and buildings were designed as observatories to provide the best possible view in that geographic region of specific stars and constellations.

Bricker has published numerous papers and journal articles deciphering the glyphs and contents of various manuscripts. She has published several books, including *The Indian Christ, the Indian King: The Historical Substrate of Maya Myth and Ritual* (1981) and *A Grammar of Mayan Hieroglyphs* (1986). Since 1977, she has served as the general editor of *Supplement to Handbook of Middle American Indians.* She is a fellow of the American Anthropological Association and a member of the American Society for Ethnohistory, Linguistic Society of America, and Société des Americanistes.

***Bibliography:*** *American Men and Women of Science* 13; *Contemporary Authors* v. 53–56; *Who's Who in America,* 51st ed., 1997; *Who's Who of American Women,* 20th ed., 1997–1998.

# *Brill, Yvonne (Claeys)*
(1924– )
## *aerospace engineer, chemist*

***Education:*** B.Sc., University of Manitoba, 1945; M.S., University of Southern California, 1951
***Professional Experience:*** Mathematician in aircraft design, Douglas Aircraft Company, 1945–1946; research analyst for propulsion and propellants, Rand Corporation, 1946–1949; group leader, igniters and fuels, Marquardt Corporation, 1949–1952; staff engineer, combustion, United Technology Corporation, 1952–1955; project engineer, preliminary design, Wright Aeronautical Division of Curtiss-Wright Corporation, 1955–1958; consultant, propulsion and propellants, FMC Corporation, 1958–1966; manager, propulsion, RCA Astro-Electronics, 1966–1981, staff engineer, preliminary design, 1983–1986; manager, solid rocket motor, National Aeronautics and Space Administration (NASA) headquarters, 1981–1983; staff member and space engineer, International Maritime Satellite Organization, 1986–1991; consultant, 1991–
***Married:*** William F. Brill, 1951
***Children:*** 3

***Yvonne Brill*** has been involved in the aerospace industry both in the United States and England during her entire professional career, specializing in both liquid and solid rocket propulsion. She developed new rocket propulsion systems for communication satellites; the single propellant rocket system, the hydrazine/hydrazine resistojet, which she developed in 1974 and for which she holds the patent, is still in use today. She served with the National Aeronautics and Space Administration (NASA) space shuttle program office from 1981 to 1983, and she was involved in developing the propulsion system design for the International Maritime Satellite Organization (INMARSAT). She was elected to membership in the National Academy of Engineering in 1987.

She was born in Canada and attended undergraduate school there but became a U.S. citizen. After receiving her undergraduate degree in mathematics, she was unable to find work in Canada and accepted a position at Douglas Aircraft as a mathematician assisting with studies of aircraft propeller noise. She began graduate studies in chemistry in order to obtain more challenging work and transferred to Douglas's Aerodynamics Department. She then obtained a position as a research analyst in the Propellant Department at Rand where she researched rocket and missile designs and propellant formulas. She moved to Marquardt as a group leader on super propellants and experimental ramjets.

She received her master's degree in chemistry in 1951, the same year that she met and married William F. Brill. In 1952, they moved to Connecticut, where she obtained a position as a staff engineer with United Technology Research Laboratory to study rocket and ramjet engines. In 1955, she joined Curtiss-Wright where, as a project engineer, she directed the corporate development of high energy fuels and studied turbojet and turbofan engines adapted for advanced aircraft. After the birth of their first child in 1957 she worked as a part-time consultant on rocket propellants for FMC Corporation. The couple had two more children before Yvonne Brill returned to work full-time in 1966.

At RCA Astro-Electronics (now GE Astro), she was hired as a senior engineer but was named manager of NOVA propulsion in 1978. It was at RCA that she developed a hydrazine/hydrazine resistojet thruster, which was a monumental advance for single propellant rockets. The thruster augments the performance of the propellant with electrically applied heat; it also enables satellites to change orbits in space. She performed preliminary work on the Mars Observer spacecraft that was launched in 1992, and she also tracked launch vehicle performance on the Scout, Delta, Atlas, and Titan spacecraft. RCA awarded her the Astro-Electronics Engineering Excellence Award in 1970.

In 1981, she joined NASA as a director of the solid rocket motor program in the Office of Space Flight (shuttle program). Although she missed having hands-on responsibilities for design, she enjoyed her work with NASA. She returned to RCA in 1983 but found herself merely writing proposals. She then joined INMARSAT in London as a space segment engineer until retiring in 1991. Later she worked for Telespace, Ltd., to monitor propulsion system activities for all of the INMARSAT-2 spacecraft; these were communication satellites that were in orbit in 1994.

Yvonne Brill has received many awards and honors. She received the Resnik Challenger Medal of the Society of Women Engineers in 1993 (the award was named for the astronaut Judith Resnik) and the SWE Achievement Award in 1986. She is a fellow of the American Institute of Aeronautics and Astronautics and of the Society of Women Engineers and is a member of the British Interplanetary Society and the International Astronautical Union. In addition to her patents, she is the author of more than 40 publications. Her photograph is included in *Notable Twentieth-Century Scientists.*

***Bibliography:*** *American Men and Women of Science* 17–19; *Notable Twentieth-Century Scientists;* Stanley, A., *Mothers and Daughters of Invention; Who's Who in America,* 51st ed., 1997; *Who's Who of American Women,* 20th ed., 1997–1998.

# *Brody, Jane Ellen*

(1941– )

***science writer, nutritionist***

***Education:*** B.S. in biochemistry, New York State College of Agriculture at Cornell University, 1962; M.S. in journalism, University of Wisconsin, Madison, 1963; honorary degrees: HHD, Princeton University, 1987; LHD, Hamline University, 1993
***Professional Experience:*** Reporter, *Minneapolis Tribune,* 1963–1965; science writer, *New York Times,* 1965– , author of column "Popular Health," 1976–
***Concurrent Positions:*** Columnist, *Family Circle* magazine; author; lecturer
***Married:*** Richard Engquist, 1966
***Children:*** 2

***Jane Brody*** currently is perhaps the most well-known author of articles and books on science and medicine written for the general public. Although she has an undergraduate degree in biochemistry, she considers herself a science writer, not a scientist. She is following the tradition of many women at the turn of the twentieth century who, barred from securing a university education, wrote articles and books to explain science to the general public. For, example Fannie Farmer (1857–1915) opened a cooking school to teach wives and mothers how to cook nutritious meals and published in book form the recipes she used in the classes. Brody does not have a cooking school, but she has presented demonstrations on sensible nutrition on public television programs in addition to publishing books and articles.

She developed a special interest in nutrition and disease at an early age, for she lost both her mother and her grandmother to cancer while she was in her teens. She enrolled in the biochemistry curriculum at the New York State College of Agriculture at Cornell University and planned to become a research scientist. When she spent a summer in a research laboratory under a National Science Foundation fellowship at the New York State Agricultural Experiment Station at Geneva, New York, however, she decided laboratory research did not appeal to her as a career. In her senior year, after joining the staff of the *Cornell Countryman,* a school magazine dealing with scientific and agricultural research, she enrolled in a few journalism courses as electives. She received a science writing fellowship for a one-year graduate program in journalism at the University of Wisconsin, Madison, where she received a master's degree in 1963.

She obtained a position as a general reporter for the *Minneapolis Tribune* and worked there for two years before securing a job as a full-time science writer, specializing in medicine and biology, at the *New York Times.* She brings a wealth of information to her columns, spending hours researching her subject and consulting experts in the field in order to present all sides of controversial subjects. In 1976, she was asked to write the "Personal Health" column. She urges her readers to adopt a healthy diet that features a high intake of complex carbohydrates, a moderate intake of proteins, and a reduction in the consumption of fat, sugar, and salt. She also advises some exercise daily rather than being a "weekend athlete." She warns against making a radical change in lifestyle. Her philosophy is one of moderation, a concept foreign to many Americans. She warns people that a healthy lifestyle does not mean one may eat a low calorie salad and then "reward" oneself with a dessert rich in calories and fats. She speaks from her own experience. Although she is only five feet tall, in graduate school she weighed 140 pounds. She lost 40 pounds over a period of two years.

Her first book to gain national attention was *Jane Brody's Nutrition Book* (1981) in which she expanded the information she had been giving in her columns. The companion volume, *Jane Brody's Good Food Book* (1985), is a collection of her recipes and also has been a best-seller. Other books include gourmet recipes, recipes for children, and seafood recipes. Her most recent volume is *Jane Brody's Allergy Fighter* (1997). In an interview published in volume CANR-23 of *Contemporary Authors,* she explains that she tests all of the recipes she recommends. When she is conducting her tasting parties, her husband and sons help to prepare the rating forms with pencils attached to them, set the tables in a certain way, label the foods, and prepare the foods.

She has received numerous awards, including one from the American Heart Association (1971), a science writers' award from the American Dental Association (1978), and a lifetime award from the American Health Foundation (1978). Her photograph is included in *Current Biography* (1986).

***Bibliography:*** *Contemporary Authors* CANR-23; *Current Biography* 1986; *Who's Who in America,* 51st ed., 1997; *Who's Who of American Women,* 20th ed., 1997–1998.

# *Brooks, Carolyn (Branch)*
## (1946– )
## *microbiologist*

***Education:*** B.S., Tuskegee University, 1968, M.S., 1971; Ph.D., in microbiology, Ohio State University, 1977
***Professional Experience:*** Researcher, community health studies, Kentucky State University, 1977–1980; research associate professor, University of Maryland, Eastern Shore, 1981–
***Married:*** Henry Brooks, 1966
***Children:*** 3

***Carolyn Brooks*** is a microbiologist who has received recognition for her research on legumes. Legumes, which are plants such as soybeans, peas, and beans, enrich the soil and require little or no fertilizer. Legumes welcome the presence of certain microbes in the outer layer of their roots, for the microbes form colonies or make nodules that absorb nitrogen from the air. The nitrogen is then transformed by the microbes into compounds the plant can absorb and use to construct amino acids in its cells. The amino acids are used to build plant protein and consequently make the plant more nutritious and at the same time enrich rather than deplete the soil. Since crops such as corn and wheat do not attract the nitrogen-gathering microbes, farmers often alternate crops of corn and legumes in order to use less fertilizer and to protect the soil. Brooks has visited several West African countries to study a legume called the groundnut in order to help researchers in those countries increase the food value of that plant.

Another area of her research is the creation of crop plant species that have built-in resistance to insects and other predators. If a naturally resistant plant is the same species as a valuable crop plant, selective breeding can sometimes provide the desired results; if the pest-resistant plant is a different species, the same results may be accomplished with genetic engineering by selectively transferring genes with the desired trait to the valuable crop plant.

Brooks was born in Richmond, Virginia, and first attended segregated schools until the public schools were integrated. Fortunately, her teachers realized that with the changes in the social climate, educated African Americans would have many opportunities. The teachers encouraged her to do well in her classes and to attend special summer sessions for science students. After graduation she received offers of scholarships at six different colleges. She chose Tuskegee Institute, which had a strong science program, probably because of the prestige of its founder, George Washington Carver. She married at the end of her second year of undergraduate school but stayed in school until she received her master's degree in 1971, her two boys and daughter being born during that time. She enrolled at Ohio State for her doctorate. Although there were no black faculty members and few black students in the Microbiology Department at that university, she found the faculty to be very supportive of her work.

Her first position after graduation was at Kentucky State University in a community health studies program that combined the resources of the university and statewide social services to improve the lives of rural residents. In her work on nutritional needs of the elderly, she found that the subjects' hair indicated the amount of mineral intake in their diets, which meant that medical problems caused by improper diet could be diagnosed. Unfortunately, other important medical problems of the elderly cannot be detected by this method.

In her position at University of Maryland, Eastern Shore, she guides the research of students in addition to conducting her own research. To her, the most significant awards she has received recognize her ability as an outstanding mentor to her students. In 1988, she received such an award at the first annual White House Initiative on Historically

Black Colleges and Universities. Her photograph is included in *Distinguished African American Scientists of the 20th Century.*

***Bibliography:*** *Distinguished African American Scientists of the 20th Century.*

# *Broome, Claire Veronica*
(1949– )
## *epidemiologist, physician*

***Education:*** B.A., Harvard University, 1970; M.D., Harvard Medical School, 1975; diplomate, American Board of Internal Medicine, 1981
***Professional Experience:*** Deputy chief in pathogens, Bacterial Disease Division, Centers for Disease Control and Prevention, 1979–1980, chief in pathogens, 1981–1990, associate director, 1991–
***Concurrent Positions:*** Clinical assistant, School of Medicine, Emory University, 1977– ; consultant, World Health Organization (WHO)
***Married:*** John F. Head, 1988
***Children:*** 2

***Claire Broome*** has performed significant research on the health aspects of pneumonia, meningitis, toxic shock syndrome, and Legionnaires' disease. Born in England, she emigrated to the United States with her family in 1951. After completing her education, she joined the Centers for Disease Control and Prevention in 1979 and has remained there ever since. One of her significant achievements is her novel approach to estimate the effectiveness of a pneumococcal vaccine by comparing the distribution of stereotypes (organisms distinguished by different surface antigens) in vaccinated and unvaccinated persons who have had the disease. Her method has proved essential in defining the appropriate use of the vaccine in the United States.

Another area of study has been the incidence of cerebrospinal meningitis epidemics. Meningitis is comparatively rare in the United States and other industrialized countries (the last epidemic in the United States was in the 1940s), but the disease still reaches epidemic levels in underdeveloped countries. In an article published in *Scientific American* in November 1994, Broome reports that people living in central Africa are uniquely susceptible to repeated outbreaks of meningitis. The cycles of epidemics may correspond to environmental changes, to unusual patterns of immunity, or to association with still other infectious diseases. The bacterium causing meningococcal meningitis is called *Neisseria meningitidis,* or "meningococcus." It is a very common organism that many people carry without being infected.

The disease starts when the organism invades the bloodstream and causes the membranes that surround the brain and spinal cord to infiltrate the cerebrospinal fluid that bathes the central nervous system. This fluid becomes a culture medium for the rapid growth of bacteria in the brain and spinal cord. Epidemics are difficult to study because outbreaks are generally unpredictable and infrequent. In the United States, people born with a rare genetic deficiency are unusually susceptible to the disease and, therefore, may account for the few cases that occur in that country. Another factor to consider is that antibody levels against the organism might change in a population over time. After an epidemic, those who had been infected develop an immunity that may decrease in 5 or 10 years, but epidemics in Africa occur about every 12 years. Another factor is that in Africa, it seems that high temperature and low humidity make people more prone to the disease once they have been infected. Still another factor is that an upper respiratory infection may be followed by the onset of the disease. Even in industrial nations, meningococcal disease is prevalent during midwinter months when cold viruses are common.

Broome received the meritorious service award from the U.S. Public Health Service in 1986 and was named one of the 100 outstanding young scientists by *Science Digest* in December 1984. She is a fellow of the Infectious Diseases Society of America and a member of the American Epidemiology Society, American College of Physicians, American Society for Microbiology, and American College of Epidemiology. Her research involves pneumococcal vaccines, toxic shock syndrome, and bacterial meningitis.

***Bibliography:*** *American Men and Women of Science* 15–19; Ireland, N., *Index to Women of the World . . . Suppl.;* Stanley, A., *Mothers and Daughters of Invention; Who's Who in America,* 51st ed., 1997; *Who's Who of American Women,* 19th ed., 1995–1996.

# *Brothers, Joyce Diane (Bauer)*
(1929– )
## *psychologist, television and radio personality*

***Education:*** B.S., Cornell University, 1947; M.A., Columbia University, 1950, Ph.D. in psychology, 1953; honorary degrees: LHD, Franklin Pierce College (1969) and Gettysburg College

***Professional Experience:*** Teaching fellow, Hunter College, 1948–1950, instructor, 1950–1952, research fellow, 1952–1953; independent psychologist and writer, 1952– ; television and radio personality, 1958–

***Married:*** Milton Brothers 1949, died 1989

***Children:*** 1

***Joyce Diane Brothers*** has been the psychologist for the people since she first conducted her own radio show in 1958. Although the program initially was broadcast only locally in New York City, it became so popular that it was soon aired on a national network. This was the start of her career as a writer of books and magazine and radio columns as well as appearances on call-in talk shows and interviews.

She had attracted the attention of broadcast executives when she appeared on the television program *$64,000 Question* as an expert on boxing in 1955. At that time, her husband still was in medical school, and she was not yet established in her practice as a psychologist because she was staying home with her new daughter. She was one of only two people appearing on the program to win the top prize of $64,000. In 1957, the television producer started the *$64,000 Challenge,* which pitted some of the winners on the previous show against experts in each field. Since she had memorized an encyclopedia on boxing, she easily defeated the boxing experts, all of whom were former fighters. Her total winnings from the two shows was $134,000. In 1959, when hearings were held on corruption in quiz shows, she successfully demonstrated that no one had supplied her with answers prior to the broadcasts, as was the case with some of the other contestants.

Although Brothers has been held in high esteem by members of the general public, who consider her a mental health professional, she has faced constant criticism from other psychologists. They complain that her advice is facile and shallow and that she often does not suggest that people should seek professional treatment. Many complain she does not treat men fairly in her advice. However, her fans say that in her written and spoken advice, she uses simple language and avoids professional jargon. She gives correspondents specific directions to take specific action and often quotes authorities to support her case. The problems she deals with are family problems, male-female relationships, and marital problems. She says she will not undertake mental problems, although on one or two occasions she has encountered disturbed people who threatened suicide while on the air.

She has written numerous books that have enjoyed high sales. These include *The Brothers System for Liberated Love and Marriage* (1975), *How to Get Whatever You Want Out of Life* (1978), *What Women Should Know about Men* (1982), *What Every Woman Ought to Know about Love and Marriage* (1988), *The Successful Woman* (1989), *Widowed* (1990), and *Positive Plus: The Practical Plan to Liking Yourself Better* (1994).

There are few recent photographs, but some are available in *Current Biography* (1971), *The 100 Greatest American Women*, and *Psychology Today* (July–August 1993). The various sources do not agree on her date of birth: estimates are 1927, 1928, 1929, and 1949, and probably one of the first three is correct. Her name appears frequently on lists of America's most respected women.

***Bibliography:*** Blashfield, J., *Hellraisers, Heroines, and Holy Women; Contemporary Authors* CANR-13 and v. 21–24R; *Current Biography* 1971; *The 100 Greatest American Women; Who's Who in America,* 51st ed., 1997; *Who's Who of American Women,* 20th ed. 1997–1998.

# *Brown, Barbara B.*
## (1917– )
## *neurophysiologist, pharmacologist*

***Education:*** B.A., Ohio State University, 1938; Ph.D. in pharmacology, University of Cincinnati, 1950

***Professional Experience:*** Head of Division of Pharmacology, William S. Merrell Company, 1953–1957; research neuropharmacologist, Riker Labs, Inc., 1957–1962; consulting neurophysiologist, Veterans Administration Hospital, Sepulveda, California, 1963–1965; associate professor of pharmacology, University of California, Irvine, 1965–1973; chief experimental physiologist, Veterans Administration Hospital, 1967–

***Concurrent Positions:*** Pharmacologist, Center for Health Science, University of California, Los Angeles, 1957–1962; lecturer, Department of Psychiatry, UCLA Medical School, 1973

***Barbara Brown*** is known as a pioneer in the science of biofeedback, which is a method of learning to control one's bodily functions by monitoring one's own brain waves, blood pressure, degree of muscle tension, etc. In the 1970s, she found that the brain emits at least four distinct kinds of waves, depending on its activity at the time. These are delta, the sleep pattern; theta, linked to creativity; beta, connected with mental concentration; and alpha, reflecting a relaxed state. The brain's constant electrical activity produces wave patterns, and these patterns can be measured and recorded using an electroencephalograph (EEG) attached to the scalp. Brown hypothesized that if people could connect physical sensations with each emission, they could perhaps learn to achieve the various states at will.

Not only did she discover biofeedback, but she made innovative applications of its findings to human health. She also invented two toys to make alpha waves more vivid and memorable to patients and research subjects—the Alpha train and the Alpha wave racetrack. The Alpha train records the signals that reveal brain or body activity by starting when the alpha waves appear in a subject and stopping when they disappear. For the Alpha wave racetrack, she invented another toy consisting of a race-car set operated by brain waves. Two people can be wired up at once and race their cars against each other, competing for alpha wave control.

At the time the theory of biofeedback was developed, it was considered mind-boggling that a tone or light activated by the EEG could tell people being trained when they were producing alpha waves. The implications for medicine have been profound—from reeducation of damaged muscles to slowing the heart and reducing blood pressure, controlling otherwise intractable pain, and managing stress. With practice, people may learn to switch alpha on and off at will without resorting to the EEG.

After receiving her doctorate, Brown was employed as a pharmacologist with two corporations, William S. Merrell Company and Riker Labs, Inc. She then was appointed an associate professor of pharmacology at the University of California, Irvine, for several years before securing an overlapping position as the chief physiologist at the Veterans Administration Hospital, Sepulveda. In addition to numerous papers, she has published three books on biofeedback: *New Mind, New Body: Bio-Feedback, New Directions for the Mind* (1974), *Stress and the Art of Biofeedback* (1977), and *Supermind, the Ultimate Energy* (1980). She is a member of the Biofeedback Research Society (chair, 1969–1970).

***Bibliography:*** *American Men and Women of Science* 11–13; Levin, B., *Women and Medicine;* Stanley, A., *Mothers and Daughters of Invention.*

# *Bryenton, Elisabeth*
## (1961– )
## *plant physiologist*

***Education:*** B.A., Princeton University, 1983

***Elisabeth Bryenton*** has achieved success in developing a product that grew out of a school science project. In the seventh grade, she became intrigued with the nutrient requirements of plants when she was searching for possible projects to undertake. In the library at Case Western Reserve University she came across an "old" article about using algae as a nutrient. She spent several years in her home laboratory creating mixtures of green and blue-green algae that provide plants with as much nitrogen as synthetic fertilizers. She found that plants grown in algal-inoculated soil have a much lower rate of disease than those utilizing commercial fertilizers, and germination and growth rates also seem to be faster. Algal inoculation is not really new. For example, researchers in Rothamstead, England, began experimenting with blue-green algal nutrients in the 1850s, with positive results, and seaweed, which is a giant alga, has been used as a fertilizer for millennia in many cultures.

Bryenton's parents had always rewarded her creativity and achievements, and when she was a sophomore in high school, her biology teacher encouraged her to submit the idea to the local science fair. She received several prizes for her idea, including a prize at the International Science Fair in 1979, which meant a trip to Japan to receive a medal. Although she has received numerous solicitations to market the product, she has decided not to patent it. However, she will not reveal the formula, and since there are at least 2,000 possible strains of algae from which she chose the approximately 12 for use, others may have difficulty duplicating the formula.

Bryenton's major contribution has been to combine several species in the most effective proportions for varying conditions. When applied to the soil around plants, the algae can fix nitrogen from the air, just as the Rhizobium bacteria associated with legumes do, except her inoculant works for any kind of plant. She has successfully tested it with wheat and soybeans and has found that the fertilizing effect lasts a whole growing season and that the best-adapted algae survive and reproduce in a given location. Therefore, after two or three years of applications, the algae produce a renewable fertilizer when the healthy populations of nitrogen fixers become established. The inoculant can be marketed as a liquid concentrate to be diluted with water when applied to the soil, requiring only about a gallon per acre. She says it does everything synthetic fertilizers do, only naturally and at a fraction of the cost.

Although she received offers from several corporations to join their research laboratories after high school graduation, she decided to obtain a liberal arts degree instead of a science degree at Princeton. After receiving her undergraduate degree, she decided to follow her artistic interests in both painting and sculpture to attend an art school, although she also talks about obtaining a doctorate in neuroscience. She says that women are natural inventors and that she considers herself an inventor. Her photograph is included in the July 1982 issue of *Working Woman.*

***Bibliography:*** Stanley, A., *Mothers and Daughters of Invention.*

# *Buikstra, Jane Ellen*
(1945– )
## *anthropologist, archaeologist*

***Education:*** B.A., DePauw University, 1967; M.A., University of Chicago, 1969, Ph.D. in anthropology, 1972

***Professional Experience:*** Instructor, Northwestern University, 1970–1972, assistant professor, 1972–1976, associate professor, 1976–1986, professor, 1986, associate dean, College of Arts and Science, 1981–1984; professor, University of Chicago, 1986–

***Concurrent Positions:*** Associate editor, *American Journal of Physical Anthropology,* 1978–1981; resident scholar, School of American Research, 1984–1985; adjunct professor of anthropology, Washington University, 1986–

***Jane Buikstra*** is renowned for her research on prehistoric skeletal populations of the Americas and was elected to membership in the National Academy of Sciences in 1987. Her area of research is called paleodemography, which is the study of vital rates, population distribution, and density in extinct human groups, especially those for which there are no written records. This is a composite field involving forensic anthropology, physical anthropology, archaeology, and demography.

Earlier scientists did not have today's sophisticated research tools to aid them in their studies, as ethnographic data and sophisticated mathematical models are relatively recent when compared to the history of paleodemography. There are several flaws in studies that have been conducted in the past. The age at death distributions often are not supported by the skeletally based mortality profiles. The age classes are not evenly represented, which affects the age at death data, and many studies omit older people and do not separate people by sex. The methods that are currently available for estimating age at death for skeletal remains are not precise, so it is not possible to identify significant, biologically informative variations among human groups.

Expertise in dating skeletal remains cannot be regarded as an esoteric study. Archaeologists and forensic scientists today are asked to identify remains at possible crime scenes, and Native American tribes are increasingly interested in documenting their histories. Some of the latter have demanded that skeletal remains and artifacts currently housed in museums, archives, and galleries should be returned to the tribes under the American Graves Protection and Repatriation Act. Federal regulations specify that artifacts which are encountered in construction projects should be examined by trained archaeologists before a decision can be made regarding their disposal, which means that construction projects sometimes are delayed for months while the various parties argue about disposal of the artifacts. At times, the decision becomes complicated when several tribes claim an artifact or the tribe that should do so no longer exists.

In addition to her many scientific publications, Buikstra has published the books *Standards for Data Collection from Human Skeletal Remains* (1994), *The Archaic and Woodland Cemeteries at the Elizabeth Site in the Lower Illinois Valley* (1990), and *Prehistoric Tuberculosis in the Americas* (1981) and is coeditor of *Human Identification: Case Studies in Forensic Anthropology* (1984). Her research has been supported by grants from the National Science Foundation and the Wenner-Gren Foundation. She is a fellow of the American Academy of Forensic Sciences and the American Association for the Advancement of Science and a member of the American Anthropological Association, the American Association for Physical Anthropologists (president, 1985–1987), and the Society of Professional Archaeologists. Her research involves an intensive regional approach to the study of prehistoric skeletal populations and emphasizes microevolutionary change and biological response to environmental stress.

***Bibliography:*** *American Men and Women of Science* 13–19.

# *Burbidge, (Eleanor) Margaret (Peachey)*

(1919– )

***astrophysicist, astronomer***

***Education:*** B.Sc., University of London, 1939, Ph.D. in astrophysics, 1943; honorary degrees: more than 14

***Professional Experience:*** Acting director, University of London Observatory, 1943–1951; research associate in astronomy, Yerkes Observatory, 1951–1953; research fellow in astrophysics, California Institute of Technology, 1955–1957; Shirley Farr fellow in astronomy, Yerkes Observatory, 1957–1959; associate professor, University of Chicago, 1959–1962; associate research professor, University of California, San Diego, 1962–1964, professor, 1964–1990, director of Center for Astrophysics and Space Science, 1979–1988, university professor, 1984–1990, research physicist, 1990– , emeritus professor of physics, 1990–

***Concurrent Position:*** Director, Royal Greenwich Observatory, 1972–1973

***Married:*** Geoffrey Burbidge, 1948

***Children:*** 1

***Margaret Burbidge*** is considered the premier woman astrophysicist today. She was elected to membership in the National Academy of Sciences in 1978 and was the first woman president of the American Astronomical Society (1976–1978). She was also the first woman to serve as director of the Royal Greenwich Observatory in England (1972–1973). The tradition was that the director should be named the Astronomer Royal and serve as the chief astronomer of the country, but since Margaret was a woman, the honor of being Astronomer Royal was given to a male astronomer. Margaret and her husband divided their time between the United States and England for a number of years before becoming U.S. citizens in 1977.

Born in England, she became interested in science at an early age because of the influence of her father, who was a chemistry professor. Her first job was with the University of London Observatory, but unfortunately, London is subject to fog and air pollution, which limits the use of that university's telescopes. In order to find better telescopes and viewing conditions, she obtained a Carnegie fellowship, which allowed young astronomers access to the Mt. Wilson Observatory near Los Angeles, but only men were allowed to use that observatory at that time. She then obtained a grant to conduct research at Yerkes Observatory while her husband studied at Harvard University Observatory.

About 1953, the Burbidges became interested in the origin of chemical elements. Although some astronomers thought all elements had been created when the universe was born, the Burbidges were among those who believed that elements are constantly being made inside stars. The couple returned to England in 1953 to work with astronomer Fred Hoyle and nuclear physicist William Fowler to refine Hoyle's theory that elements are created by fusion reactions, each fusion reaction creating heavier elements than the one before. The four scientists called the theory "the B2HF theory," based on the initials of the four participants—the Burbidges jokingly were called by fellow astronomers "B2" or "B squared." When the couple returned to the United States in 1955 to gather more experimental data, they resorted to a subterfuge to work at Mt. Wilson Observatory. Geoffrey applied for observation time, and Margaret pretended to be his assistant. However, she had to give up her observations prior to her daughter's birth in 1956 because of the steep stairways in the observatory. The couple received the Warner Prize of the American Astronomical Society in 1959 for a paper on B2HF.

Geoff was offered an associate professorship at the University of Chicago, which operates the Yerkes Observatory, and because of nepotism rules, Margaret could only be given a research fellowship. After the nepotism rules were changed, she was appointed an associate professor. The two were offered positions at the new University of California, San Diego, in 1962 where Margaret was appointed a full professor of astronomy. There they conducted research on quasars. She was invited to be director of the Royal Greenwich Observatory, and her husband was offered a position as an astronomer. They took leaves from the university and accepted the offers. When Geoff complained in a letter to *Nature* about the poor viewing conditions at Greenwich and supported building a new observatory, the couple became embroiled in a controversy with the staff astronomers and returned to California.

In the 1970s, Margaret served on the Space Science Board, which advises the National Aeronautics and Space Administration (NASA) on programs in space. After the decision was made to launch a telescope in space, the University of California, San Diego, was assigned to oversee building the spectrograph, and the project was named the Center for Astrophysics and Space Science. Margaret served as its director, and the Hubble telescope was launched in 1990.

Although Margaret has retired, she continues to work as a research professor. In addition to numerous papers, the couple published a book *Quasi-Stellar Objects* (1967). She has received many awards, including the National Medal of Science (1985) and the Albert Einstein World Award of Science Medal (1988). She was elected a fellow of the American Academy of Arts and Sciences, the American Association for the Advancement of Science (president, 1982), and the Royal Society of London. She is a member of the American Astronomical Society (president, 1976–1978), Royal Astronomical Society, International Astronomical Union, American Philosophical Society, and New York Academy of Sciences.

She published an autobiographical sketch, "Watcher of the Skies," in *Annual Review of Astronomy and Astrophysics* (1994). Her photograph is included in Lisa Yount's *Twentieth-Century Women Scientists* and in *Science* (May 14, 1982). Some of the sources list her name in error with an extra "r" (Burbridge); some list her as "(Eleanor) Margaret Burbidge" or "E. Margaret Burbidge."

***Bibliography:*** *American Men and Women of Science* 14–19; Fins, A., *Women in Science;* Golemba, B., *Lesser-known Women;* Ireland, N., *Index to Women of the World . . . Suppl.;* Rossiter, R., *Women Scientists in America; Who's Who in America,* 51st ed., 1997; *Who's Who in Science and Engineering,* 3d ed., 1996–1997; *Who's Who of American Women,* 20th ed., 1997–1998; Yount, L., *Twentieth-Century Women Scientists.*

# *Butler, Margaret K.*
(1924– )
## *mathematician, computer scientist*

***Education:*** B.A., Indiana University, 1944
***Professional Experience:*** Statistician, U.S. Bureau of Labor Statistics, 1945–1946 and U.S. Air Force in Europe, 1946–1948; mathematician, Argonne National Laboratory, 1948–1949; statistician, U.S. Bureau of Labor Statistics, 1949–1951; mathematician, National Energy Software Center, Argonne National Laboratory, 1951–1980, director, 1960–1993, senior computer scientist, 1980–1993; retired 1993
***Married:*** James W. Butler, 1951
***Children:*** 1

*Margaret Butler* helped to develop one of the first digital computers for science as a staff mathematician at Argonne National Laboratory in the early 1950s, participated in the evaluation and selection of the first commercial digital computer for scientific computation in 1956–1957, and prepared and implemented programs for certain reactor equations, diffusion-theory equations, reactor kinetics, spherical harmonics problems, etc., for both the UNIVAC and the AVIDAC computers. In addition, she worked on the logical design of Argonne's GEORGE computer and designed computer programs to solve engineering problems and to aid in the design of nuclear reactors. She did important early work in software in the 1940s. As a junior mathematician in the Naval Reactor Division at Argonne, she performed some of the computation work underlying the *Nautilus* submarine prototype.

Between 1959 and 1965, as head of the applications programming section of the Applied Mathematics Division (AMD) at Argonne, she directed the development of the AMD Program Library and Argonne's first computer operating system. She participated in preparing an operating system for the IBM 704, the documentation of the CDC 3600 subroutine library, and the design and development of many computer programs in the reactor and high-energy physics areas, such as one-dimensional multigroup diffusion, the Monte Carlo spark chamber analysis, and accelerator design studies.

During the late 1960s and early 1970s, she researched computers for image processing and reactor physics computation. As a senior computer scientist in the 1980s, she conducted benchmark studies for evaluating laboratory computers. She researched computing technology forecasting, measuring and evaluating computer performance, computer history, and applying computers to scientific and engineering problems, and she was involved in preparing standards for computers and information processing.

She feels her primary contribution was to create and direct the National Energy Software Center (also called the Argonne Code Center). This is a clearinghouse for the worldwide exchange of computer programs for peaceful uses of nuclear energy and develops world standards for computer technology.

She was elected a fellow of the American Nuclear Society in 1972. She also is a member of the Association for Computing Machinery, American Association for the Advancement of Science, Institute of Electrical and Electronics Engineers, Association of Women in Science, and Association for Women in Computing. Her research interests are information systems, computer program interchange, computer system performance, documentation standards, and scientific and engineering applications.

***Bibliography:*** *American Men and Women of Science* 11–19; Herzenberg, C., *Women Scientists from Antiquity to the Present;* Ireland, N., *Index to Women of the World . . . Suppl.;* Stanley, A., *Mothers and Daughters of Invention;* Vare, E., *Mothers of Invention; Who's Who in America,* 51st ed., 1997; *Who's Who in Engineering,* 9th ed., 1995; *Who's Who in Technology Today* v. 1

# C

## *Caldicott, Helen Mary (Broinowski)*
(1938– )
### *pediatrician, antinuclear activist, environmentalist*

***Education:*** B.S. in surgery, University of Adelaide, M.B. in medicine, 1961
***Professional Experience:*** Intern, Royal Adelaide Hospital, South Australia, 1961; general practice of medicine in South Australia, 1963–1965; fellow in nutrition, Children's Hospital Medical Center, Boston, 1967–1968; intern, Adelaide Children's Hospital, 1972, resident, 1973–1974, founder and head of cystic fibrosis clinic, 1975–1976; fellow in cystic fibrosis, Children's Hospital Medical Center, 1975–1976, associate, 1977–1980; activist and writer, 1980–
***Concurrent Positions:*** Fellow in nutrition, Harvard University Medical School, 1966–1968, instructor in pediatrics, 1977–1980
***Married:*** William Caldicott, 1962
***Children:*** 3

***Helen Caldicott*** quit her position as a physician at the Children's Hospital Medical Center in Boston, Massachusetts, in 1980 to devote all of her time to her campaign against the use of nuclear energy, including an attempt to ban the mining of uranium in the western part of the United States. She was a six-year-old child living in Australia when the atomic bomb was dropped on several cities in Japan, and she first became concerned about nuclear energy when, as a teenager, she read Nevil Shute's book *On the Beach*, a chilling story set in Australia about a nuclear holocaust. She was a practicing physician in Australia when she received a fellowship for further study at Children's Hospital Medical Center and her husband, also a physician, received a fellowship from Harvard. On her return to Australia for further training in pediatrics, she worked with children who had cystic fibrosis and became head of the cystic fibrosis unit in 1975.

She had a devastating experience in 1969 when she caught hepatitis from a patient by accidentally pricking her finger. She felt that her life had been saved because she was meant to make a commitment to human survival. She became incensed that the French government, ignoring an international ban, was conducting atmospheric nuclear tests on islands in the Pacific in 1971 (underground tests were still permitted at that time), for the fallout was drifting toward the state of South Australia. She started gathering reports on the amount of radioactive matter in drinking water and cow's milk in Australia and sent the reports to medical groups, newspapers, news organizations, and other sources and was interviewed on radio and television programs. She gained so much public support that in 1973, the Australian and New Zealand governments took the French government before the International Court of Justice in The Hague in an effort to get the French to discontinue the tests. The French government complied with the court's ruling and stopped the tests.

When Caldicott and her family returned to Boston in 1975, she tried to rally the American public to ban all military and peaceful uses of nuclear energy. Since this was the period of the Cold War between the United States and Russia, she had little success with her campaign, particularly with regard to the military nuclear programs. She produced several documentary films; some were broadcast on public television stations, but others never were aired. She published a book *Nuclear Madness: What You Can Do* (1970), which was revised as *Nuclear Madness: What You Can Do, with a New Chapter on Three Mile Island* (1980). It was not until the failure at the nuclear power plant at Three Mile Island in Pennsylvania that she started receiving some popular support. That accident had brought so much pollution to the community involved that the town was razed and the site abandoned. She had felt that America was such a democratic nation that she could stop the nuclear energy industry as quickly as she had stopped the French government in 1973. Unfortunately, this did not happen.

The organization Physicians for Social Responsibility was founded in 1962, but its membership had dwindled over the years. She revived the organization in 1978 and was president until 1983. However, the members became more conservative during those years, and many members thought she was too strident to bring about the reforms they were advocating. She founded the groups Medical Campaign Against Nuclear War, Women's Action for Nuclear Disarmament, and Women's Party for Survival. She wrote *Missile Envy* (1986) and *If You Love This Planet: A Plan to Heal the Earth* (1991). Her autobiography is *A Desperate Passion* (1996). At present, the Cold War between the United States and Russia is over, and nuclear weapons are banned.

Several references to her describe her as an attractive woman with a compelling personality. She articulates her views in a slight Australian accent. There are photographs in *Current Biography* (1983), *Parents Magazine* (June 1982), *Vogue* (July 1982), and *Life* (June 1982).

***Bibliography:*** *Contemporary Authors* v. 114 and 124; *Current Biography* 1983.

# *Calloway, Doris (Howes)*
(1923– )
## *nutritionist*

***Education:*** B.S., Ohio State University, 1943; Ph.D. in nutrition, University of Chicago, 1947; diplomate, American Board of Nutrition, 1951; honorary degree: D.Sc., Tufts University, 1992

***Professional Experience:*** Intern in dietetics, Johns Hopkins University Hospital, 1944; research dietitian, Department of Medicine, University of Illinois, 1945; consulting nutritionist, Medical Associates of Chicago, 1948–1951; nutritionist, QM [Quartermaster] Food and Container Institute, 1951–1958, head of metabolism laboratory, 1958–1959, chief of nutrition branch, 1959–1961; chair, Department of Food Science and Nutrition, Stanford Research Institute, 1961–1964; professor of nutrition, University of California, Berkeley, 1963–1991, provost and professor, 1981–1987, professor emeritus, 1991–

***Married:*** Nathaniel O. Calloway 1946, divorced 1956; Robert O. Nesheim, 1981

***Children:*** 2

***Doris Calloway*** is a renowned nutritionist and has had a wide range of experience working in several areas of her profession. She was employed for about ten years by the QM Food and Container Institute, which is affiliated with or at least funded by the U.S. Army Quartermaster Corps. She then moved to the Stanford Research Institute as chair of the Department of Food Science and Nutrition. She received an appointment as professor of nutrition at the University of California, Berkeley, a school that has an international reputation in nutrition. During her tenure there, she also served as provost of the professional schools for six years; she retired in 1991.

She has served on numerous committees and panels ranging from United Nations groups to the National Institutes of Health and its National Institute of Aging and National Institute of Arthritis, Metabolic and Digestive Diseases. She also was involved in work with the International Maize and Wheat Improvement Center, a renowned research facility located in Mexico City, and the National Research Council. In addition to her journal publications she served as editor of the book *Nutrition and Physical Fitness* for the eighth to the eleventh editions (1966–1984). She also wrote *Nutrition and Health* (1981) and *Human Ecology in Space Flight* (1967). She was associate editor of *Nutrition Reviews* from 1962 to 1968, and she was a member of the editorial boards of *Journal of Nutrition, Environmental Biology and Medicine, American Dietetic Association Journal,* and *Interdisciplinary Science Review.*

She was elected a fellow of the American Institute of Nutrition (president, 1982–1983) and a fellow of the International Union of Nutritional Science. She is also a member of the Human Biology Council. Her research involves human nutrition, protein and energy requirements, and international nutrition issues.

***Bibliography:*** *American Men and Women of Science* 11–19; *Contemporary Authors* v. 21–24; *Who's Who in America,* 51st ed., 1997; *Who's Who of American Women,* 20th ed., 1997–1998; *World Who's Who in Science.*

# *Caserio, Marjorie Constance (Beckett)*

(1929– )

***organic chemist***

***Education:*** B.Sc., Chelsea College, University of London, 1950; M.A., Bryn Mawr College, 1951, Ph.D. in chemistry, 1956

***Professional Experience:*** Associate chemist, Fulmer Research Institute, England, 1952–1953; from assistant to instructor in chemistry, Bryn Mawr College, 1953–1956; fellow, California Institute of Technology, 1956–1964; assistant professor, University of California, Irvine, 1965–1967, associate professor, 1967–1971, professor, 1971–1990, chair of Chemistry Department, 1987–1990; professor of chemistry and vice chancellor of academic affairs, University of California, San Diego, 1990–

***Married:*** Frederick Caserio, 1957

***Children:*** 2

**Marjorie Caserio** is recognized as a leading physical organic chemist in the United States. She was born in England, but her family had early ties to America. Her grandparents had emigrated to the United States but had returned to England after a few years because her grandmother did not adjust to the life in America. Marjorie's senior year in high school was the last year of World War II, and she spent most of the school year in a bomb shelter. She entered Chelsea College, University of London, at age 15 to study podiatry, but she soon found her science classes were more interesting than her medical classes, so she switched to chemistry and completed her undergraduate degree. She obtained a fellowship from the English Speaking Union to do graduate work at Bryn Mawr College. She returned to England and obtained a position at the Fulmer Research Institute, but she found the work to be routine.

After World War II, former service personnel in both England and the United States were obtaining college degrees or advanced degrees and were first in line for job openings, and she realized that as a woman, she could not hope to obtain a research position without further graduate studies. After searching without success for acceptance in a graduate program in England, she was able to obtain one plus financial aid at Bryn Mawr. She then applied for a postdoctoral appointment at California Institute of Technology, where she stayed for nine years. While there she met another postdoctoral appointee, Fred Caserio; they married in 1957, the same year she became a citizen of the United States.

After her husband completed his postdoctoral work, the couple moved to Laguna Beach where her husband worked for an industrial firm. Although she had to commute 50 miles each way, she continued working at Caltech in Pasadena several days each week. By this time, the couple had two children. The new campus at the University of California, Irvine, started hiring in the mid 1960s, and she was the second faculty member to be hired in the Chemistry Department. She rose steadily through the academic ranks because she proved she could maintain her own research group, work on her own ideas, and publish papers. With the growth of the women's movement in the 1970s, this prominent woman chemist found herself involved more and more in regional and national activities. She moved to the University of California, San Diego, in 1990 as vice chancellor of academic affairs and professor of chemistry.

Her significant contributions to research have been recognized by the award of the Garvan Medal of the American Chemical Society (1975), a medal given annually to an American woman chemist. She received the award for her work in physical organic chemistry, and she has also made important contributions to chemistry education by her innovative teaching methods. In the early 1960s, she coauthored the book *Basic Principles of Organic Chemistry* (lst ed., 1964; 2d ed., 1977). This text had a large impact on the teaching of organic chemistry, and its emphasis on spectroscopic methods has been copied by many other authors. Her expertise was recognized by her appointment as a member and then chair of the Committee on Professional Training of the American Chemical Society. This group establishes accreditation standards and curricula for professional accreditation in the chemical sciences—not every college and university that teaches chemical sciences has an accredited program.

She has achieved excellence in governance and administration. She served as department head at U.C. Irvine, chair of the academic senates of both U.C. Irvine and the University of California system, and vice chancellor at U.C. San Diego. In her professional association activities she is a member of the American Chemical Society and various committees. Her research centers on reaction mechanisms in organic chemistry. Her photograph is included in *Notable Women in the Physical Sciences* and in *Chemical & Engineering News* (May 1, 1989, and September 4, 1974).

**Bibliography:** *American Men and Women of Science* 11–19; Ireland, N., *Index to Women of the World . . . Suppl.; Notable Women in the Physical Sciences;* O'Neill, L., *The Women's Book of World Records and Achievements;* Rossiter, M., *Women Scientists in America; Women in Chemistry and Physics.*

# Chasman, Renate (Wiener)
(1932–1977)
***nuclear physicist***

***Education:*** M.Sc., Hebrew University, Jerusalem, 1955, Ph.D. in physics, 1959
***Professional Experience:*** Research associate, Columbia University, 1959–1962; research associate in physics, Yale University, 1962; assistant physicist, Brookhaven National Laboratory, 1963–1967, associate physicist, 1967–1969, physicist, 1969–1977
***Married:*** Chellis Chasman, 1962
***Children:*** 2

***Renate Chasman*** was known for her work in the development of particle accelerators. She and her twin sister, Edith, were born in Berlin; in 1938, the family was forced to flee as refugees first to Holland and then to Sweden. After the sisters graduated from high school in Sweden, they went to Israel to continue their education. After receiving her doctorate in experimental physics, Renate moved to New York to work as a research associate for the prominent woman physicist Chien-Shiung Wu at Columbia University. There she worked on research on a unique type of positron emission from radioactive nuclei. She met Chellis Chasman at Columbia, and they married in 1962. She was scheduled to join him at Yale University when she was notified that since she still held Swedish citizenship, she had to leave the country for two years and then reapply for entrance. Her husband planned to leave the country with her, but the administrators at Yale convinced the U.S. Immigration Service that the Chasmans were working on critical research in nuclear spectroscopy, and the deportation notice was canceled.

In 1963, the couple moved to the Brookhaven National Laboratory where Renate compiled and systematized neutron cross-sections. This was fairly routine work, but in 1965, she was able to switch to a new field, accelerator physics, and became one of the key participants in the development of particle accelerators. She was the only woman physicist in her department, but she was the chief theorist for the group. The Alternating-Gradient Synchrotron (AGS) at Brookhaven was the world's highest-energy particle accelerator at that time, and Renate was responsible for the theoretical aspects of the design for this device. She created and used computer programs for exploring the behavior of the beam during the acceleration process, and when the device was put into operation, it was found to behave in excellent agreement with her theoretical predictions. She then joined the group that explored the concept and design of superconducting storage rings for protons in the range of several hundred GeV (a GeV is defined as a giga-electron volt; a giga means a billion; thus, several hundred billion electron volts).

As her reputation grew, she was invited to serve on review committees at the Fermi National Accelerator Laboratory in Illinois and at the European Laboratory for Particle Physics in Switzerland; both are also accelerator facilities. In the 1970s, she investigated the radiation from several electron synchrotrons and storage rings; the goal was to use them as a source of ultraviolet, or X-rays, in numerous studies in solid-state physics, chemistry, and biology. She also assisted in designing storage rings especially for the production of synchrotron radiation.

In 1972, she was diagnosed as having malignant melanoma, but she continued to work while receiving treatment. The construction of the last project on which she worked, the National Synchrotron Light Source, was approved in the fall of 1977, but she never saw its completion. In 1985, the Brookhaven National Laboratory established a Renate W. Chasman Scholarship awarded annually to a woman who plans to resume her scientific studies after an interruption. Her obituary and photograph are included in *Physics Today* (February 1978).

***Bibliography:*** *Women in Chemistry and Physics.*

# Chesler, Phyllis
(1940– )
***psychologist***

***Education:*** B.A., Bard College, 1963; M.A., New School for Social Research, 1967, Ph.D. in psychology, 1969

***Professional Experience:*** Instructor in psychology, Institute for Development Studies, 1965–1966; fellow in neuropsychology, New York Medical College, 1967–1968; clinical research associate, Metropolitan Hospital, New York City, 1968–1969; from assistant professor to professor of psychology, sociology, anthropology, and women's studies, College of Staten Island, 1969–

***Married:*** Nachmy Bronstien, 1973

***Children:*** 1

***Phyllis Chesler*** calls herself a feminist activist who is still fighting for women's causes. Her book *Women and Madness* (1972), which traces the psychological enslavement of women and details the damage traditional psychiatry has done, is still a topic of discussion. She has been extremely involved with a range of concerns but focuses on custody, abortion, rape, equal pay, health care, incest, battery, pornography, motherhood, spirituality, and mental health. She has taught at the College of Staten Island since 1969 and says that she has had to fight for each level of promotion in rank: each time, the dean has overruled the negative votes of the promotion and tenure committee. An outspoken person, she is committed to supporting the causes she endorses.

*Women and Madness* is still considered a groundbreaking book. More than 2 million copies have been sold, and it was reissued in 1989. The main thesis of the book is that women are controlled by a patriarchal mental health system that labels them "mad" whether they act out the stereotypical female role of overconforming and being too feminine or whether they reject it by underconforming or being too masculine.

Her book *Women, Money, and Power* (1976) discusses sexual abuse of women, including a chapter on the beauty myth; *About Men* (1978) summarizes the feminist viewpoint on men; and *With Child: A Diary of Motherhood* (1979) describes her reactions when she herself became a mother. One reviewer called the last work an informal, very personal narrative that is marked by the ambivalence toward motherhood that grew out of the feminist movement. *Mothers on Trial: The Battle for Children and Custody* (1986) and *Sacred Bond: The Legacy of Baby M* (1988) each deal with the problems surrounding mothers and custody. Her most recent book, *Patriarchy: Notes of an Expert Witness* (1994), is a collection of her essays and papers on a variety of feminist issues and covers patriarchy, psychiatric treatment of women, custody battles, child abuse, and the criminal justice system. Most of her books still are in print and are also available in editions in Europe.

She is a member of the American Association for the Advancement of Science, American Psychological Association, Association for Women in Psychology, and National Organization for Women.

***Bibliography:*** *Contemporary Authors* v. 49–52 and CANR-4; Ireland, N., *Index to Women of the World . . . Suppl.; The 100 Greatest American Women; Who's Who of American Women*, 20th ed., 1997–1998.

# Chilton, Mary-Dell (Matchett)
(1939– )
## molecular biologist, biochemist

***Education:*** B.Sc., University of Illinois, 1960, Ph.D. in chemistry, 1967; honorary degree: Dr. Honoris Causa, University of Louvain, Belgium, 1983
***Professional Experience:*** Fellow in microbiology, University of Washington, Seattle, 1967–1969, fellow in biochemistry, 1969–1970, assistant biologist, 1971–1973, research assistant professor of biology, 1973–1977, research associate professor, 1977–1979; associate professor of biology, Washington University, St. Louis, 1979–1983; executive director of agricultural biotechnology, Ciba-Geigy Biotechnology Facility, 1983–1991, vice president of biotechnology, 1991–
***Married:*** 1966
***Children:*** 2

***Mary-Dell Chilton*** is renowned for her research on the genetic engineering of agricultural crops. She was a member of a team of university and industry scientists who developed the first method to introduce foreign genes into plant cells and reliably produce normal fertile plants. They utilized the natural form of genetic engineering (a bacterium invades a plant and sometimes destroys it) to inject a bacterium into a crop plant to modify it genetically. Chilton and her colleagues moved a gene from a yeast into tobacco plant cells, using the bacterium that causes crown gall disease as the carrier of the alien genetic material. Their innovation was to alter the bacterial DNA to keep it from causing tumors in the tobacco plant cells. Crown gall disease can afflict a wide range of broad-leaved plants, and it causes considerable loss in certain crops, notably grapes, stone fruits, and ornamental plants. She published a paper in the June 1983 issue of *Scientific American* that outlines the process the team announced in 1983. She continues her research on other crop plants, such as maize.

Genetic engineering of plants is on the front line of research in both academic and industrial institutions, and millions of dollars are invested each year to improve crop plants. Although there has been much controversy about genetic engineering in animal research, especially the cloning of animals, there is also criticism of plant research. The fear is that agriculture will become too dependent on specific strains of plants, so if that strain were wiped out by disease, the world food bank could be in trouble.

As a child, Chilton was encouraged by her parents to achieve; there was a strong work ethic and success orientation. After receiving her doctorate, she held both research and teaching posts at the University of Washington, Seattle, and Washington University, St. Louis. She continued her research as an executive at Ciba-Geigy Corporation, located at Research Triangle Park in North Carolina, and became vice president of biotechnology.

She was elected a member of the National Academy of Sciences in 1985, just two years after the successful genetic engineering of plants was announced. She has received the Bronze Medal from the American Institute of Chemists (1960). She is a member of the American Society for Microbiology. Her research involves crown gall tumorigenesis, bacterial plasmids, plant genome organization, satellite DNA, DNA and RNA hybridization, and bacterial genetics.

***Bibliography:*** *American Men and Women of Science* 14–19; Stanley, A., *Mothers and Daughters of Invention.*

# *Cleave, Mary L.*
## (1947– )
### *environmental engineer, astronaut*

***Education:*** B.S. in biological sciences, Colorado State University, 1969; M.S. in microbiological ecology, Utah State University, 1975, Ph.D. in civil and environmental engineering, 1979

***Professional Experience:*** Research staff, Utah State University, 1971–1980; astronaut, National Aeronautics and Space Administration (NASA), 1980–1990, deputy project manager, NASA Ocean Color Satellite Program, 1991–

***Mary Cleave*** was one of eight women astronauts selected between 1978 and 1980—six women were selected in 1978 and two in 1980. The United States was very slow in permitting women to participate in space flight, although numerous women, some of whom are included in the present volume and some in the previous one, worked behind the scenes for NASA and its predecessor, the National Advisory Committee on Aeronautics (NACA). By the mid 1970s, however, the experimental flight programs were winding down, and the orbital space station project was getting under way. NASA modified the requirements so that astronauts no longer had to have jet pilot experience and began to emphasize scientific expertise.

Women had to be very persistent and possess science or engineering degrees to be accepted into the program. Although she is only five feet two inches in height, Cleave tried, without success, to enter the astronaut program through aviation. After taking flying lessons and earning two doctoral degrees, she was accepted in 1980. She said she was chosen in case NASA had a job for a midget.

She was a mission specialist on STS 61-B in 1985 and on STS-30 in 1989. The former mission lasted from November 26 to December 3; the latter, from May 4 to May 8. Most astronauts have been members of the program at least five years before going into space. Although Cleave left the astronaut program in 1990, she continued to work for NASA at Greenbelt, Maryland, in the Ocean Color Satellite Program, specializing in environmental problems. She is a member of the Water Pollution Control Federation, and her research is on ocean color satellites.

There was a great deal of publicity about the women astronauts in the 1980s, particularly after Sally Ride made her first flight in June 1983. There were articles and photographs in most of the news magazines, and two books in particular contain much background information: A. R. Oberg's *Spacefarers of the '80s and '90s* (1985) and Karen O'Connor's *Sally Ride and the New Astronauts* (1983). There are photographs of Mary Cleave in these two books and in *U.S. News and World Report* (February 21, 1981), among other publications.

***Bibliography:*** *American Men and Women of Science* 19; Ireland, N., *Index to Women of the World . . . Suppl.;* Oberg, A. R., *Spacefarers of the '80s and '90s;* O'Connor, K., *Sally Ride and the New Astronauts;* U.S. National Aeronautics and Space Administration, *Astronaut Fact Book; Who's Who in Science and Engineering,* 2d ed., 1994–1995.

# *Cobb, Geraldyne M.*
(1931– )
## *aviator, astronaut consultant*

***Education:*** student, Oklahoma College for Women, 1948
***Professional Experience:*** Teacher, aviation school, 1949; self-employed charter pilot, 1950; charter pilot of commercial and military planes, Fleetway, Inc., chief pilot in charge of South American operations, 1951–1955; chief pilot, Executive Aircraft, Inc.; executive pilot and advertising and sales promotion manager, Aero Design & Engineering Company, 1958–1964; consultant on astronaut qualifying tests, National Aeronautics and Space Administration (NASA), 1960–1961, consultant 1961–1962; owner, air cargo business, 1983–

***Geraldyne M. (Jerrie) Cobb*** is a pioneer woman astronaut who never made a space flight. More than 20 years before astronaut Sally Ride made her historic launch in 1983, Jerrie Cobb was invited by the National Aeronautics and Space Administration (NASA) to assist in modifying the physical and mental tests used for male astronauts for use by women. Since 1957, she had established international records for speed, altitude, and distance in the twin-engine class of airplanes, piloting Aero Commander planes, and was considered one of the premier women pilots of that era. Although numerous women had ferried military planes overseas during World War II, the military services had no data on the physical capabilities of women pilots. None of the military services had women pilots in the 1960s.

Cobb worked with NASA to modify for women astronauts the 87 tests that potentially could be used. She passed all of the tests herself and surpassed the performance of men in several of them. The results indicated that women are more capable than men of withstanding the physical demands of space travel because they have a lower body mass, require less oxygen and food, and have a greater tolerance to radiation levels. NASA then requested her to select a group of women to be tested, but after the first 12 women passed the first phase, NASA would not permit them to take the second phase because NASA executives could not agree on hiring women astronauts, and those who endorsed the program lost the argument. Although Cobb participated in congressional hearings on funding for the program to select women astronauts, the project was dropped. However, the Russians had several women in their astronaut program, and Valentina Tershkova orbited the earth for three days in 1963. Cobb briefly remained with NASA as a general consultant.

She became interested in flying early, and when she was 12 years old, her father installed pedal blocks and seat cushions so she could fly his biplane. As a teenager, she paid for her flying lessons by working on a horse farm and waxing planes at the local airport. She earned her private pilot's rating when she was only 16 years old, and leaving college after one year, she received her commercial pilot and flight instructor's license and obtained a job teaching in an aviation school. For three years, she played on a women's softball team to help pay for her own plane. One of the most dangerous jobs she had was ferrying World War II fighter planes that the Navy had sold to the Peruvian air force. Flying in the Andes is considered one of the most challenging experiences for any pilot, and she made solo trips there for several years when she worked for Fleetway, Inc. She also tested reconditioned commercial and military planes and flew them throughout the world for the same company. She became engaged to her boss, Jack Ford, but after they broke their engagement, she left the company in 1955.

When she was competing for the flight records mentioned above, she used planes supplied by the Aero Design & Engineering Company. In 1958, she joined the company as executive pilot, and the company generously gave her the time she needed to participate in the NASA testing program intermittently between 1960 and 1962. Very little information can be found about her career after 1964, although one news article indicates that she operated an air cargo service in Florida between 1983 and 1991. Her autobiography is *Women in Space, the Jerrie Cobb Story* (1963).

***Bibliography:*** Blashfield, J., *Hellraisers, Heroines, and Holy Women; Current Biography* 1961; Ireland, N., *Index to Women of the World . . . Suppl.;* May, C., *Women in Aeronautics;* Read, P., *Book of Women's Firsts;* Rossiter, M., *Women Scientists in America.*

# *Cobb, Jewel Plummer*

(1924– )

***cell biologist***

***Education:*** Student, University of Michigan, 1941–1942; B.A., Talladega College, 1944; M.S., New York University, 1947, Ph.D. in cell biology, 1950; honorary degrees: 18

***Professional Experience:*** Instructor, Anatomy Department, and director, Tissue Culture Laboratory, University of Illinois, 1952–1954; research instructor in surgery, New York University, 1955–1956, assistant professor, 1956–1960; professor, Biology Department, Sarah Lawrence College, 1960–1969; dean and professor of zoology, Connecticut College, 1969–1976; dean and professor of biological science, Douglass College, 1976–1981; president and professor of biological sciences, California State University, Fullerton, 1981–1990, president emeritus, 1990– , trustee professor, 1990–

***Concurrent Positions:*** Member of the corporation, Marine Biological Institute, Woods Hole, 1972– ; member, U.S. Department of State Advisory Committee on Oceans and International Environment and Science Affairs, 1980–1990; chair, Committee on Women in Science and Engineering, National Research Council, 1993–

***Married:*** Roy R. Cobb, 1954, divorced 1967

***Children:*** 1

*Jewel Plummer Cobb* is known as a researcher in cell biology, an educator who develops programs to encourage ethnic minorities and women in the sciences, and an administrator who has headed several colleges and universities. Her research in cell biology has focused on melanin, a brown or black skin pigment; she also studies the causes and growth of normal and cancerous pigment cells. In addition, she has studied the effects of newly discovered cancer chemotherapy drugs on human cancer cells.

She became interested in science at an early age owing to the example of her physician father. She selected a career in biology in her sophomore year in high school when she first looked through a microscope. Despite being from an upper-middle-class family, she faced segregation in the Chicago public schools because of her race. She selected the University of Michigan because some of her friends were enrolling there and she admired the football team, but she left after three semesters because the dormitories were segregated: all black students, undergraduate and graduate students alike, had to live in one house. She transferred to Talladega College in Alabama and graduated from there and received a fellowship at New York University where she completed her education. Instead of choosing a medical career, she elected to work in biology because she preferred the theoretical approach of biology to the pathological approach of medicine.

All of her investigative work is in some way related to melanin, preferably melanoma, which is usually a malignant tumor of the skin. One of her first accomplishments was establishing and directing the Tissue Culture Laboratory at the University of Illinois, and she managed to continue her research during appointments at Sarah Lawrence, Connecticut College, and Douglass College even though her positions there required heavy administrative responsibilities. When she was selected to be president of California State University, Fullerton, however, she had to reduce her involvement in research. As president, she established the first privately funded gerontology center in Orange County, lobbied the state legislature to approve the construction of a new engineering and computer science building and a new science building, installed the first president's opportunity program for students from ethnic groups that were not fully represented on campus, and changed the campus from being a strictly commuter one to a campus with an apartment complex for student residences. The apartment complex was named in her honor.

Cobb has received honors and awards too numerous to mention. She was elected to membership in the Institute of Medicine of the National Academy of Sciences and is a fellow of the New York Academy of Sciences and of the American Association for the Advancement of Science. She is a member of the Association of Women in Science and the Tissue Culture Association. Her photograph is included in a number of publications listed in the Bibliography plus *Ebony* (fall 1986 and August 1982). Some references spell her name "Jewel" and others "Jewell"; the former seems to be the preferred spelling.

***Bibliography:*** *American Men and Women of Science* 11–19; *Black Women in America; Blacks in Science and Medicine; Distinguished African American Scientists of the 20th Century;* Ehrhart-Morrison, D., *No Mountain High Enough;* Herzenberg, C., *Women Scientists from Antiquity to the Present;* Ireland, N., *Index to Women of the World . . . Suppl.; Journeys of Women in Science and Engineering; Notable Black American Women; Notable Twentieth-Century Scientists; Notable Women in the Life Sciences; Who's Who in America,* 51st ed., 1997.

# *Cole, Johnnetta (Betsch)*

(1936– )

***anthropologist***

***Education:*** Student, Fisk University, 1953; B.A. in sociology, Oberlin College, 1957; M.A., Northwestern University, 1959, Ph.D. in anthropology, 1967

***Professional Experience:*** Instructor, University of California, Los Angeles, 1964; director of black studies, Washington State University, Pullman, 1969–1970; professor of anthropology, University of Massachusetts, 1970–1983, associate provost of undergraduate education, 1981–1983; visiting professor, Hunter College, 1983–1984, professor of anthropology, 1983–1987, director of Inter-American Affairs Program, 1984–1987; president of Spelman College, Atlanta, 1987–

***Married:*** Robert Cole 1960, divorced 1982; Arthur J. Robinson, Jr., 1988

***Children:*** 3

***Johnnetta Cole*** is an anthropologist and, since 1987, the president of Spelman College in Atlanta, Georgia. Spelman is the premier college for black women in the United States and is often compared to Wellesley College and Smith College in academic excellence. She was born into a prominent middle-class family in segregated Jacksonville, Florida. Her great-grandfather had helped to found an African-American insurance company in 1901—a local library and a YMCA were named for him—but even though her family was a prominent one, she attended segregated public schools. At the age of 15 she was accepted at the predominantly black Fisk University in Nashville, Tennessee, under its early admissions program. A year later she transferred to Oberlin College in Ohio, where she first experienced the culture shock of being in a predominantly white institution.

At Oberlin, she switched her major to sociology in order to enroll in graduate school at Northwestern University to study anthropology. After receiving her master's degree in 1959, she married fellow student Robert Cole in 1960. In interviews in Mary Catherine Bateson's *Composing a Life* (1989), Johnnetta describes the tensions when Robert, who is white, visited her family prior to the wedding. However, Robert's family members and hers were equally opposed to the marriage.

The couple departed for Liberia to gather data for their doctoral projects, his in economics and hers in anthropology. She comments that the marriage succeeded probably because they were living and working in a mixed society instead of in the United States, which still was segregated at that time. They were equal colleagues while in Liberia. When they returned to the United States, her husband completed his doctorate and secured a position at Washington State University, Pullman. Johnnetta taught part time at the same institution and received her doctorate from Northwestern in 1967. She also conducted fieldwork in Cuba, Haiti, and Grenada and was involved in a Peace Corps training project at San Francisco State University in 1965. One son was born in Liberia and the second in Pullman.

She was appointed assistant professor of anthropology and director of the black studies program at Washington State and was then invited to join the anthropology faculty at the University of Massachusetts, where she later developed a black studies program and served as associate provost for undergraduate education. Her husband taught at Amherst College in Massachusetts, and the couple had a third son in 1970. After a new provost was appointed at Massachusetts, Johnnetta returned to full-time teaching. She accepted a visiting professorship at Hunter College in 1983, which resulted in her receiving an appointment as professor of anthropology and director of the Inter-American Affairs Program at Hunter. She was selected president of Spelman in 1987. She and her husband divorced in 1982, and she married Art Robinson, a childhood friend, in 1988. He is an administrator with the Centers for Disease Control and Prevention in Atlanta.

Spelman College is a private school founded in 1881 to educate the daughters of former slaves. Johnnetta, the seventh president, is the first black woman to serve as president and the first to be considered a "scholar." Shortly after arriving on the campus she called herself "sister president" in articles in *Ms Magazine* and *Ebony* to indicate her perspectives. In 1988, the college received a gift of $20 million from Bill Cosby and Camille Cosby, the largest personal gift to a historically black college and one that attracted nationwide attention.

Cole's scholarship focuses on cultural anthropology, African-American studies, and women's studies. Her fieldwork has included studies of a Chicago black church, labor in Liberia, racial and gender inequality in Cuba, Caribbean women, female-headed households, the way women age, and the Cape Verdean culture in the United States. In a recent book, *Conversations: Straight Talk with America's Sister President* (1993), she discusses some of the problems faced by African-American women, such as racism and sexism, as well as ways to deal with those problems. In addition, she has edited three textbooks on anthropology: *Anthropology for the Eighties* (1982), *All American Women: Lines That Divide, Ties That Bind* (1986), and *Anthropology for the Nineties: Introductory Readings* (1988).

In 1992, she was considered for an appointment as secretary of education in the Clinton administration, but she did not receive the appointment because of rumors that she was a left-wing extremist. The perception that she is a radical is at odds with her professional ties to several corporations. She is the first woman elected to the board of Coca-Cola Enterprises and the first black women to become a member of the Atlanta Chamber of Commerce. She is a fellow of the American Anthropological Association and a member of the Association of Black Anthropologists. There are numerous photographs of her in *Ebony* (February 1988 and July 1996), *Current Biography* (1994), *Notable Black American Women*, and *Black Women in America.*

***Bibliography:*** *Black Women in America; Current Biography* 1994; *Notable Black American Women; Who's Who among Black Americans* 1991–1993; *Who's Who in America*, 51st ed., 1997; *Who's Who of American Women*, 20th ed., 1997–1998.

# *Colmenares, Margarita H.*
(1957– )
## *environmental engineer*

***Education:*** Business major, California State University, Sacramento; student, Sacramento City College; B.Sc. in civil engineering, Stanford University, 1981

***Professional Experience:*** Field construction engineer, Chevron Corporation, 1981, recruiting coordinator for San Francisco office, field construction engineer in Salt Lake City, foreign training representative, 1983–1986, compliance representative and lead engineer in environmental cleanup at Chevron refinery at El Segundo, 1986, air quality specialist at El Segundo plant, 1989–1996; director of corporate liaison, U.S. Department of Education, 1996–

***Concurrent Positions:*** White House fellow 1991–1992

*Margarita Colmenares* is the first Hispanic engineer to be selected as a White House fellow since the program was established in 1964, and during her 1991–1992 fellowship years, she served as special assistant to the deputy secretary of education in Washington, D.C. She was also the first woman president of the Society of Hispanic Professional Engineers.

She was born in Sacramento of parents who had emigrated from Mexico. Her parents sent her and her siblings to parochial schools in order to provide the best education for them, and she was selected in high school for a program for inner-city youth to work at Xerox Corporation. However, in high school, she was trapped in typing and shorthand classes and was not encouraged to prepare for college. She entered California State University, Sacramento, to study business courses. In her freshman year, she discovered engineering but found that she lacked the prerequisites to be admitted to the Engineering School, so she took chemistry, physics, and calculus at Sacramento City College before entering the Engineering School at Stanford University. While attending Sacramento City College, she secured a part-time job with the California Department of Water Resources inspecting the structural conditions of dams and water-purifying plants. She won five scholarships to attend Stanford; while in school there, she worked for the Chevron Corporation in Texas and California in that company's cooperative education program.

Colmenares obtained a position as a field construction engineer at Chevron when she completed her undergraduate degree in 1981. Already a member of the Society of Hispanic Professional Engineers (SHPE), she founded the San Francisco chapter in 1982 and served as national president in 1984. When she was a field construction engineer in Salt Lake City, she was the first female engineer contractors had ever dealt with, and they found her to be very capable in handling her job. In 1983, she received a post as a foreign training representative, a position that involved planning training programs lasting from two days to two years for Chevron's international visitors.

She received her first assignment specifically involved in environmental protection when she was named the compliance specialist at Houston. Her responsibilities were ensuring compliance with federal, state, and local environmental, safety, fire, and health regulations at Chevron's facilities. In 1986, she was assigned to direct an environmental cleanup project at the Chevron refinery in El Segundo and was promoted to air quality specialist at El Segundo in 1989. At this time she also was national president of SHPE and persuaded Chevron to give her a one-year paid leave while she was president. During her term of office, she promoted education, especially engineering education, for Hispanics. In 1989, she also participated in the National Hispana Leadership Initiative, a program for women that included training sessions in public policy at Harvard's John F. Kennedy School of Government.

She received a White House fellowship for the years 1991–1992, and at her request, she was assigned to the Department of Education. Chevron gave her a paid leave for this assignment also. In 1996, she accepted a position as director of corporate liaison, U.S. Department of Education, where she works with business leaders and organizations around the country to engage their support for education. She has received recognition for her commitment to the Hispanic community. In 1990 and 1992, *Hispanic Business* recognized her as one of the 100 most influential Hispanics in the country. Her photograph is included in *Journeys of Women in Science and Engineering* and in *Notable Hispanic American Women.*

***Bibliography:*** *Journeys of Women in Science and Engineering; Notable Hispanic American Women; Notable Twentieth-Century Scientists.*

# *Colwell, Rita (Rossi)*
(1934– )
### *microbiologist, marine microbiologist*

***Education:*** B.S., Purdue University, 1956, M.S. in genetics, 1958; Ph.D. in marine microbiology, University of Washington, Seattle, 1961; Honorary degrees: D.Sc., Heriot-Watt University, 1987, Purdue University, 1993

***Professional Experience:*** Research assistant professor, University of Washington, 1961–1964; visiting assistant professor, Georgetown University, 1963–1964, assistant professor of biology, 1964–1966, associate professor, 1966–1972; professor of microbiology, University of Maryland, 1972–, director, Center for Marine Biotechnology in Maryland, 1987–1991

***Concurrent Positions:*** Consultant, Environmental Protection Agency, 1975– ; director, Maryland Sea Grant Program, 1978–1983; vice president of academic affairs, University of Maryland, 1983–1987

***Married:*** Jack Colwell, 1956

***Children:*** 2

R***ita Colwell*** is a leader in marine biotechnology, a field that involves the application of molecular techniques to marine biology for harvesting medical, industrial, and aquaculture products from the sea. She investigates the ecology, physiology, and evolutionary relationships of marine bacteria and was one of the first people in the United States to use computers to identify microorganisms.

She was the seventh of eight children, but her parents emphasized that all should have a good education. When she was in the sixth grade, she scored higher on the IQ exam than anyone in the school's history, and she obtained a full scholarship to Purdue. Although she received a solid education as a scientist, she still experienced discrimination. She married in her senior year of college and planned to continue in the master's program in bacteriology while her husband completed his degree in physical chemistry. However, the head of the Bacteriology Department told her it would be a waste of fellowship money to give it to a woman. She then applied for and was accepted into the program in genetics and completed her master's degree. After she and her husband received their doctorates from the University of Washington, her husband accepted a fellowship from the National Research Council of Canada. Since that organization had rules that prohibited a husband and wife working for the same employer, Rita obtained a grant from the National Science Foundation, requested a leave from the University of Washington, and joined her husband in Canada to conduct her research.

Colwell accepted a research and teaching position at Georgetown University and later moved to the University of Maryland. While in graduate school, she had become interested in the field of marine biotechnology, a new field at the time. Based on her expertise, she was appointed director of the University of Maryland Sea Grant Program between 1978 and 1983 and director of the Center for Marine Biotechnology in Maryland between 1987 and 1991. She believes the future of marine biotechnology lies in new drugs made from marine sources, new methods of cost-effective fish culture, seaweed genetics, and improved biotechnological waste recycling. She advocates using genetic engineering in the marine sciences, especially in the area of marine pharmaceuticals. However, the greatest opportunity is applying genetic engineering to pursue the untapped gene pool representing transport systems for minerals, metal concentration, novel photosynthetic systems, and marine pheromones by marine animals.

In addition to numerous scientific papers, she is the author of *Estuarine Microbial Ecology* (1973) and *The Global Challenge of Marine Biotechnology* (1996). She edited *Biomolecular Data: A Resource in Transition* (1989), *Biotechnology of Marine Polysaccharides* (1985), and *Microbial Diversity in Time and Space* (1996). In 1998 she was nominated to be director of the National Science Foundation.

She has received many awards and honors. From 1983 to 1990, she was a member of the National Science Board, which advises the federal government on science policy. She is a fellow of the American Association for the Advancement of Science, the Society for Industrial Microbiology, and the American Academy of Microbiology. She is a member of the American Society for Microbiology (president, 1984–1985) and the Society for Invertebrate Pathology. Her photograph is included in *Notable Twentieth-Century Scientists* and *Science* (February 20, 1998).

***Bibliography:*** *American Men and Women of Science* 11–19; Fins, A., *Women in Science;* Herzenberg, C., *Women Scientists from Antiquity to the Present; Notable Twentieth-Century Scientists; Notable Women in the Life Sciences; Who's Who in America,* 51st ed., 1997; *Who's Who in Science and Engineering,* 3d ed., 1996–1997; *Who's Who of American Women,* 20th ed., 1997–1998.

## *Conway, Lynn Ann*
(1938– )
***computer scientist, electrical engineer***

***Education:*** Student, Massachusetts Institute of Technology; B.S., Columbia University, 1962, M.S. in electrical engineering, 1963

***Professional Experience:*** Member of research staff, IBM Corporation, 1964–1969; senior staff engineer, Memorex Corporation, 1969–1973; research engineer, Xerox Corporation, 1973–1983; chief scientist and assistant director of strategic computing, Defense Advisory Research Projects Agency (DARPA), 1983–1985; professor of electrical engineering and computer science and associate dean of the College of Engineering, University of Michigan, 1985–

***Lynn Conway*** is famous for two major developments in computer circuitry, the first being the invention of a new approach to the design of integrated computer circuit chips. She demystified the design process by creating a unified structural methodology that allowed computer engineers with general backgrounds to design chips. Her second major achievement was a new method of chip fabrication that enabled designers to rapidly obtain prototypes with which to test their hardware and software designs. The latter development is reported in the textbook *Introduction to VLSI Systems* (1980). She is known as an innovator who seeks challenging projects, but she prefers to concentrate on new ideas once a project is completed. Although she is capable of fine-tuning designs, she prefers to delegate the finishing touches to others. She was elected to membership in the National Academy of Engineering in 1989.

Since she excelled in physics and mathematics in high school, she enrolled as a physics major at the Massachusetts Institute of Technology (MIT). After three years she became restless, left school, and traveled and worked around the United States. She returned to school in the early 1960s, this time at Columbia University, to complete her undergraduate degree and obtain her master's degree. While at Columbia she prepared a software system project for a course; the project impressed a visiting professor and led to a job with IBM's research facility in Yorktown Heights, New York. She later transferred to California where she was a member of a project team for the Advanced Computing Systems (ACS). Unfortunately, ACS was not compatible with IBM's 360 product line, and the project was canceled.

In 1969, she accepted a position with Memorex Corporation where she was assigned to a project to develop an inexpensive office computer; she headed the team that designed the system's processor. Memorex decided to drop its computer business, and in 1973, she joined Xerox Corporation on a project to superimpose an optical character recognition over a facsimile system. The prototype was a mammoth machine that filled a room, and Xerox dropped the project. She next formed a group to design computer chips, which resulted in the major accomplishment of simplifying computer chip design mentioned above. The group prepared the textbook to send around the country to computer experts for their comments, and Conway taught a successful one-semester course on chip design at MIT. The students in her class designed the chips, she sent the designs over ARPAnet (an early version of the Internet) to Xerox, and Hewlett-Packard Research fabricated the chips and sent the finished chips to the students within six weeks. In the early 1980s, Xerox was losing interest in continuing the chip service and arranged for the University of Southern California to take over the project.

Conway's next project was knowledge engineering, or the work of designing and building expert systems. In 1983, she had the opportunity to work for the Defense Advisory Research Projects Agency (DARPA) in Washington, D.C., the agency that developed ARPAnet. Part of her job was to oversee the preparation of an advanced computing program to secure funding from Congress. After the money was budgeted, she was ready to leave Washington and accepted the position of associate dean of the College of Engineering at the University of Michigan in 1985. There she has been involved in keeping the university and the college at the forefront of computer research and technology.

Conway is truly a pioneer in computer technology, and many of the projects she worked on seem rather simplistic today in view of the advances that have been made in the past few years. She has worked at the forefront of artificial intelligence (AI), robotics, telecommunications, etc. She is a fellow of the Institute for Electrical and Electronics Engineers and a member of the American Association for the Advancement of Science and of the American Association for Artificial Intelligence. She has received many awards, such as the Wetherill Medal from the Franklin Institute (1985), the Meritorious Civilian Service Award given by the secretary of defense (1985), and the National Achievement Award of the Society of Women Engineers (1990). Her photograph is included in *IEEE Spectrum* (December 1987) and *Datamation* (October 1993).

***Bibliography:*** *American Men and Women of Science* 13–19; Lee, J., *Computer Pioneers; Notable Twentieth-Century Scientists;* Stanley, A., *Mothers and Daughters of Invention.*

# *Cordova, France Anne-Dominic*
(1947– )
## *astronomer, astrophysicist*

***Education:*** B.A., Stanford University, 1969; Ph.D. in physics, California Institute of Technology, 1979
***Professional Experience:*** High school teacher, 1969–1971; research assistant in astrophysics, California Institute of Technology, 1975–1979, fellow, 1979; staff member and department group leader in astrophysics, Los Alamos National Laboratory, 1979–1989; professor and head, Department of Astronomy and Astrophysics, Pennsylvania State University, 1989–1993; chief scientist, National Aeronautics and Space Administration (NASA), 1993–1996; vice chancellor for research, University of California, Santa Barbara, 1996–
***Married:*** Christian J. Foster, 1985
***Children:*** 2

***France Cordova,*** an observational astronomer and high-energy astrophysicist, was considered by the scientific community to be a top choice when she was selected for the position of chief scientist of the National Aeronautics and Space Administration (NASA) in 1993. Her credentials are staggering, and her scientific work covers a wide range of subjects: observational and experimental astrophysics, multispectral research on x-ray and gamma-ray sources, ultraviolet spectroscopy of nearby binary stars, thermal emissions from neutron stars, and spaceborne instrumentation.

She has strong connections with the astronomical community, having served on the board of the Associate Universities for Research, which directs such places as the Kitt Peak Observatory and the Hubble Space Telescope Institute. She served on NASA's Space Science and Applications Advisory Committee and has been a member of astronomy or space science advisory groups at the National Science Foundation and the National Research Council. Since she was on a paid leave from Pennsylvania State University, she was not an employee of the federal government while she worked for NASA. In 1996, she accepted a position as vice chancellor for research at the University of California, Santa Barbara.

Strangely enough, science was not her first choice as a career. After receiving an undergraduate degree from Stanford University, she considered studying anthropology but instead taught physics and math in several high schools and worked for the *Los Angeles Times.* She decided to study physics and astronomy after viewing a television special on cosmology, and she received her Ph.D. in physics in 1979. At the Los Alamos National Laboratory between 1979 and 1989, she studied white dwarfs, neutron stars, and black holes. She theorized that white dwarfs should emit x-rays but at lower intensities than neutron stars. She looked at more than 200 white dwarf close binaries with x-ray satellites to prove this theory and, with colleagues, described mathematically the low-energy pulsations in these systems. She moved to Pennsylvania State University in 1989 as professor and head of the Department of Astronomy and Astrophysics. Her husband heads a Ph.D. program in cognitive science and education at the same university.

Cordova has served on numerous prestigious committees, including the President's National Medal of Science Committee (1991–1993), the committee that selects the persons to receive the National Medal of Science, one of the top awards in the nation.

She is a member of the American Astronomical Society and the International Astronomical Union. She was named one of the top 100 young scientists by *Science Digest* in December 1984; that issue includes her photograph. She has found that one advantage of visiting observatories throughout the world is that she can indulge in her favorite pastimes of mountaineering and rock climbing. She appeared on a television program on pulsars in the PBS series *Science in America* on April 8, 1996.

***Bibliography:*** *American Men and Women of Science* 16–19; *Who's Who in America,* 51st ed., 1997; *Who's Who in Science and Engineering,* 2d ed., 1994–1995; *Who's Who of American Women,* 20th ed., 1997–1998.

# *Cowings, Patricia Suzanne*
## (1948– )
## *psychologist, physiologist*

***Education:*** B.A. in psychology, State University of New York at Stony Brook, 1970; M.A. and Ph.D. in psychology, University of California, Davis, 1973
***Professional Experience:*** National Research Council Postdoctoral Associate, National Aeronautics and Space Administration (NASA) Ames Research Center, 1973–1975; research specialist, San Jose State University Foundation, 1975–1977; research psychologist and principal investigator, Psychophysiological Research Laboratory, NASA Ames Research Center, 1977–
***Concurrent Position:*** Adjunct associate professor of psychology, University of Nevada, Reno, 1987
***Married:*** William B. Tiscano
***Children:*** 1

***Patricia Cowings*** is known for her work in the specialized field of psychophysiology, which is the study of the relationship between the mind, behavior, and bodily mechanisms. The specific area in which she is working is developing a treatment for the motion sickness commonly experienced by astronauts during manned space flights. An article in *Psychology Today* (May 1984) describes the physiology of this condition, and she has pioneered the use of biofeedback coupled with autogenic training to help the astronauts suppress the problem. Biofeedback is a method of learning to control one's bodily functions by monitoring one's own brain waves, blood pressure, degree of muscle tension, etc.; autogenic training is a series of self-suggestion exercises, or a method for getting people to focus attention on a part of the body. The results of her research were first tested in space during the September 1992 Spacelab-J mission, an eight-day flight of the space shuttle *Endeavour.* The test was a success.

In her research, she replicated the conditions that cause motion sickness, such as zero gravity, to deliberately make the subjects sick and then recorded the physiological and psychological changes that occurred. The astronauts affectionately called her "the Baroness of Barf." In autogenic training, she teaches a subject to mentally evoke a sensation, like warmth in a limb or relaxation of muscles, to bring about desired physiological changes such as increased skin temperature or relaxed muscles. In biofeedback, she teaches people to control as many as 20 physiological functions related to motion sickness. These include heart rate, skin conductance, depth and rate of respiration, and flow of blood to the hands. Subjects learn to regulate these functions by watching as they are displayed numerically and on an oscilloscope. The subjects learn in later sessions how to manage the symptoms without feedback data and under distracting conditions. During the first test in space, the astronauts had biofeedback units strapped to their wrists.

Another area in which Cowings has worked is therapy to exercise the veins in the astronauts' legs so the veins will remain as taut as when they are on the earth. When people are exposed to weightlessness in space for long periods of time, the veins in the lower extremities lose their tautness, which causes difficulty in walking when back on earth. Her research has been the subject of several television programs of the Public Broadcasting System.

Cowings had become interested in science, particularly in space, by the age of 11, and she knew she wanted to become a psychologist by the time she was in high school. After receiving her doctorate, she received a postdoctoral appointment at NASA's Ames Research Center and has continued working there during most of her career.

In Dorothy Ehrhart-Morrison's book *No Mountain High Enough* (1997), Cowings says that she did not experience prejudice until she completed her education. One problem was that she received her doctorate at age 23 and no one took her seriously. Early in her career she was supervising people who were much older than she; now that she herself is older, that problem no longer exists. As a second problem, she says that affirmative action actually placed her at a disadvantage because people assumed she was chosen only because she is black, not because she is a "serious" scientist. Some of her peers, both in graduate school and in the workplace, have assumed that she is less qualified than they are. Third, she says that some individuals at another NASA space center attempted to remove her as a principal investigator because she was not the right type to interact with astronauts and that sexism and the old-boy network are just part of the challenge women have to fight and overcome. She has not felt prejudice because her husband is white; he is a colleague at NASA. Although they planned to delay parenthood, their son was born in 1987, part of "the baby boom" at NASA after the *Challenger* accident in 1986.

She has received several awards, such as the NASA Individual Achievement Award (1993). She is a member of the Society for Psychophysiological Research, American Association for the Advancement of Science, and New York Academy of Sciences. Her photograph is included in *Notable Twentieth-Century Scientists; Blacks in Science, Ancient and Modern;* D. Ehrhart-Morrison's *No Mountain High Enough;* and *Psychology Today* (May 1984).

***Bibliography:*** *Blacks in Science, Ancient and Modern; Blacks in Science and Medicine;* Ehrhart-Morrison, D., *No Mountain High Enough;* Ireland, N., *Index to Women of the World . . . Suppl.; Notable Twentieth-Century Scientists;* Oberg, A. R., *Spacefarers of the '80s and '90s.*

# *Cox, Geraldine Anne (Vang)*
(1944– )
## *environmental scientist, biologist*

***Education:*** B.S., Drexel University, 1966, M.S., 1967, Ph.D. in environmental science, 1970
***Professional Experience:*** Technical coordinator of environmental programs, Raytheon Company, 1970–1976; White House fellow, special assistant to secretary, U.S. Department of Labor, 1976–1977; environmental scientist, American Petroleum Institute, 1977–1979; vice president and technical director, Chemical Manufacturers Association, 1979–1991; vice president, Fluor Daniel, subsidiary of Fluor Corporation, 1991–
***Married:*** 1965

***Geraldine Cox*** is known for her work in establishing the chemical industry's guidelines for community emergencies following the accidental release of methyl isocyanate gas at a plant in Bhopal, India, late in 1984. At the time, she was vice president and technical director of the Chemical Manufacturers Association, a professional organization whose members represent 90 percent of the chemical companies in the United States. The explosion was devastating to the owner of the plant, Union Carbide Corporation, because of the contamination of the area around the plant and the adverse publicity about safety procedures at that location. In the United States, the Chemical Manufacturers Association's guidelines established the Community Awareness and Emergency Response (CAER), which led to the adoption of a federal and later an international standard drafted by the United States, both based on Cox's model.

Before the cause of the accident could be determined, chemical companies began rigid inspections of operating procedures in plants worldwide and assured that the safeguards built into the processing units were still running smoothly. The industry experts gathered at the Chemical Manufacturers Association to plan to expand services that protect public health and safety and to work with Congress on drafting effective legislation. Two major programs evolved: CAER and the National Chemical Response and Information Center (NCRIC).

The CAER program expands the industry's involvement in local emergency response planning and helps communities protect public health and safeguard against potential chemical hazards. NCRIC improves the industry's ability to respond to emergencies and to provide hazard information to the public. The industry view is that it is responsible for the safe manufacture and transportation of its products and that it must provide information about the hazards associated with the manufacture, storage, use, and disposal of its products to employees, neighbors, and customers. The group emphasizes that it must demystify chemical manufacturing, which is often shrouded in secrecy partially because, as a high-tech industry, it is difficult to understand. Also, the news media focus on disasters, or threats of danger, which heightens the public's fear of the unknown.

Cox left the association in 1991 to join Fluor Daniel as a vice president. She has held many significant committee assignments such as chair of the Marine Water Quality Committee (1975–1980), member of the Transportation Advisory Committee of the U.S. Coast Guard (1980– ), and member of the Engineering Affairs Council of the Association of American Engineering Societies (1987–; chair, 1991– ). She has received the Achievement Award of the Society of Women Engineers (1984) and is a member of the American Society for Testing and Materials, Water Pollution Control Federation, American Chemical Society, American National Standards Institute, and Society of Women Engineers. Her research includes oil pollution, marine pollution, freshwater pollution, ecological damage assessment, and environmental health.

***Bibliography:*** *American Men and Women of Science* 14–19; *Notable Twentieth-Century Scientists; Who's Who in America,* 51st ed., 1997.

# Daly, Marie Maynard
(1921– )
***biochemist***

***Education:*** B.S., Queens College, 1942; M.S., New York University, 1943; Ph.D. in chemistry, Columbia University, 1947

***Professional Experience:*** Instructor, Howard University, 1947–1948; assistant, Rockefeller Institute, 1951–1955; associate, Columbia University Goldwater Memorial Hospital, 1955–1959; assistant professor of biochemistry, Albert Einstein College of Medicine, 1960–1971, associate professor of biochemistry and medicine, 1971–1986; retired 1986

***Concurrent Positions:*** American Cancer Society fellow, Rockefeller Institute, 1948–1951; established investigator, American Heart Association, 1958–1963; career scientist, Health Research Council of New York, 1962–1972, Commission on Science and Technology, 1986–1989

***Married:*** Vincent Clark, 1961

***Marie Daly*** was the first African-American woman to receive a doctorate in chemistry from Columbia University (in 1947; some sources say 1948), and she is known for her research on the chemistry of the cell nucleus. She taught at Howard University for one year while she sought an American Cancer Society fellowship to conduct research at Rockefeller Institute. At the institute, she examined the ways in which proteins are constructed within the cells of the body, in particular the cell nucleus. In 1952, James Watson and Francis Crick described the structure of DNA, the spiral molecules that carry the genetic code of every living thing. Daly was fortunate that this breakthrough led to an immediate increase in the scientific study of the chemistry of the cell nucleus. When her research team moved to Columbia University, they undertook a long series of studies related to the underlying causes of heart attacks. She focused on the blockage of arteries that supply oxygen and nutrition to the heart muscle and discovered that cholesterol was part of the problem. She studied the effects of sugar and other dietary products on the health of the arteries.

Later she did pioneering work on the effects of cigarette smoke on the functioning of the lungs. She continued this project when the team moved to Albert Einstein College of Medicine, and she also taught courses in biochemistry to medical students. She focused her research on the breakdown of the circulatory system caused either by advanced age or by hypertension. She also led efforts to increase the enrollment of minority students in medical schools and graduate science programs.

As was the case with many women scientists, she had strong encouragement as a child to excel in her studies. Her father had wanted to be a chemist but had had funds for only one semester at Cornell University. Marie felt she was fulfilling her father's goal when she majored in chemistry. Many years later, in 1988, she contributed a gift to Queens College for scholarship aid to black students in the physical sciences and named the scholarship in her father's honor. She was fortunate in selecting the schools she attended. Queens College was a new school and still very small at the time, so she was able to receive individual attention from her instructors. She also was able to work as a student laboratory assistant and tutor to earn money toward tuition for graduate school. While she was attending Columbia University, World War II was at its height, and many men were serving in the military, which meant that women were finding career opportunities in chemistry that previously had been reserved for men. Daly was able to obtain funding from the university to complete her degree program.

She was named a fellow of the American Association for the Advancement of Science, the New York Academy of Sciences, and the American Heart Association. She is a member of the American Chemical Society and the American Society of Biological Chemists. Her research interests are arterial smooth muscle and creatine transport and metabolism. Her photograph is included in *Distinguished African American Scientists of the 20th Century.*

***Bibliography:*** *American Men and Women of Science* 11–19; *Blacks in Science and Medicine; Distinguished African American Scientists of the 20th Century; Notable Twentieth-Century Scientists; Women in Chemistry and Physics.*

# *Darden, Christine Voncile (Mann)*
(1942– )
***aeronautical engineer***

***Education:*** B.S., Hampton Institute, 1962; M.S., Virginia State College, 1967; D.Sc. in engineering, George Washington University, 1983

***Professional Experience:*** High school teacher, 1962–1964; research assistant in physics, Virginia State College, 1965–1966, instructor in mathematics, 1966–1967; data analyst, National Aeronautics and Space Administration (NASA), Langley Research Center, 1967–1973, aerospace engineer, 1973–1989, leader of Sonic Boom Team, 1989–

***Married:*** Walter L. Darden, Jr., 1963

***Children:*** 2

***Christine Darden*** is recognized as an expert on the sonic boom and the creator of a computer software program that is used across the United States for simulating a sonic boom in a wind tunnel. Initially her interest was in mathematics, but when she started working for NASA she realized that engineers use a great deal of mathematics and physics in their work. She took advantage of NASA's program of providing further education for their employees to obtain a graduate degree in mechanical engineering from George Washington University. After completing her doctorate, she attended management classes that are conducted for NASA employees with the goal of promotion to research administrator.

As an undergraduate she majored in education because she thought there would not be jobs available in mathematics for black women. After teaching public school for a few years, she started taking graduate classes while her husband was attending Virginia State College. She secured a research assistantship in the Physics Department at that institution, and her research involved analyzing air quality and determining the presence of specific kinds of pollutants. She was a graduate instructor for one year before the family moved to Hampton, Virginia.

She had three job offers, but she selected the job at NASA because of its salary. Initially she was doing very routine calculations for the engineers, but as the research became more computer oriented she wrote software programs for the engineers and started taking doctorate-level classes in both mathematics and engineering science.

After successfully completing a difficult fluid mechanics course, she enrolled in the engineering program at George Washington University. At the time, there were few black men and very few women of any race in engineering. The subject of her dissertation, the environmental impact of the supersonic transport (SST) aircraft that was then being designed in both the United States and Europe, was directly related to her work at NASA. Aircraft moving at speeds above the speed of sound create a wave of pressure in the air, and when that pressure wave reaches the ground, people in the area hear a loud boom. The sound wave can be powerful enough to shatter windows and damage structures.

Other engineers at NASA were building models of aircraft to test them in wind tunnels, but Darden was asked to develop a computer program that simulated the sound wave. When the managers saw that the wind tunnel tests and the computer program gave the same results—and the latter was much cheaper and faster than the former—they promoted her to be the leader of the Sonic Boom Team. One area of her research was to redesign the airplane to change the shape of the wing and to blunt the nose to minimize the sonic boom. Later the federal government decided not to invest in the SST because of its expense, but the NASA project continued because military aircraft sometimes reach supersonic speeds as they fly across populated areas. U.S. federal regulations specify that the Concorde, built by the French and the British, cannot reach supersonic speeds in populated areas, so those planes do not fly in the United States because of the financial considerations of flying at lower speeds. Darden is also looking at other environmental impacts of supersonic flights, such as the effect on the ozone layer of the atmosphere.

She started attending school at a very young age; her mother, a public school teacher, took her daughter at age three with her because day care was not available. Christine began learning the lessons with the students instead of playing with her toys in the back of the classroom, so she was ready for kindergarten at the age of 4 and was only 15 when she entered undergraduate school. While still in elementary school, she would take apart things, such as her bicycle, to see how they worked—fortunately, she was able to reassemble the bike. Her favorite teacher in high school was the geometry teacher, which influenced her interest in mathematics.

She is a member of the National Technical Association and the American Institute of Aeronautics and Astronautics. She received the Certificate of Outstanding Performance from the Langley Research Center in 1989, 1991, and 1992. She is the author of more than 40 technical papers. Her photograph is included in *Notable Twentieth-Century Scientists, Distinguished African American Scientists of the 20th Century,* and *Blacks in Science, Ancient and Modern.*

**Bibliography:** *Blacks in Science, Ancient and Modern; Blacks in Science and Medicine; Distinguished African American Scientists of the 20th Century; Notable Twentieth-Century Scientists;* Vare, E., *Mothers of Invention.*

# *Davis, Margaret Bryan*
(1931– )
## *paleoecologist, palynologist, ecologist*

***Education:*** B.A., Radcliffe College, 1953; Ph.D. in biology, Harvard University, 1957; honorary degree: M.S., Yale University, 1974

***Professional Experience:*** Fellow, Department of Biology, Harvard University, 1957–1958, and Department of Geoscience, California Institute of Technology, 1959–1960; research fellow, Department of Zoology, Yale University, 1960–1961; research associate, Department of Botany, University of Michigan, 1961–1964, associate research biologist, Great Lakes Research Division, 1964–1970, associate professor, Department of Zoology, 1966–1970, research biologist, Great Lakes Research Division and professor of zoology, 1970–1973; professor of biology, Yale University, 1973–1976; professor of ecology and head, Department of Ecology and Behavioral Biology, University of Minnesota, 1976–1981, professor, 1981–1983, Regents Professor of Ecology, 1983–

***Married:*** Rowland Davis, 1956, divorced ca. 1970

***Margaret Davis*** is a distinguished paleoecologist who is renowned for her analysis of ancient pollen to determine trends in plant growth and migration. Palynology is the study of pollen from ancient plants, and as an undergraduate at Radcliffe, she took a course on paleobotany and became intrigued by the vegetational history of the late Quaternary period, some 10,000 years ago. (The Quaternary period, the present period of earth history, originated about 2 million years ago.) She believed that the best method to understand and interpret the history of ancient plant life is to understand the physiology and ecology of flora (or plants) rather than just the stratigraphic interpretation of pollen records. She received a Fulbright fellowship to study at the University of Copenhagen in 1953–1954, and her research took her to Greenland, where she recorded plant pollen deposited during the interglacial period. Combining her research with her studies at Harvard, she received a doctorate in biology in 1957.

She continued her studies as a National Science Foundation postdoctoral fellow at Harvard and then at the California Institute of Technology, where she concentrated on geology. As a research fellow at Yale, she studied the relationship between pollen in lake sediments and vegetation composition in order to enhance the precision of pollen records for describing past vegetation. She moved to University of Michigan's Department of Botany, and she attracted international attention with a paper, published in 1963 in the *American Journal of Science,* on the theory of pollen analysis. For years, scientists had assumed that fossil pollen produced by trees tens of thousands of years ago could provide a clear picture of plant life during the period. Since some tree species produce more pollen than others, the scientists had suggested that a correction factor ranging from 4:1 to 35:1 be used to equalize the difference. Davis's research on lake-bed sediments showed that these correction factors could range as much as 24,000:1.

Davis also compiled maps for eastern North America depicting the migration of various species of trees during the past 14,000 years. Her maps indicate that the temperate-forest trees moved at different rates and in different directions. Her work cannot be treated as just an esoteric study, as it has implications for the current debate over the various theories of global warming. One topic that elicits vociferous debate among scientists, environmentalists, and citizens is whether the earth is in the process of cooling or warming, and which is the worst scenario. Using data provided by the National Aeronautics and Space Administration (NASA) and the National Oceanographic and Atmospheric Administration (NOAA), she predicted in 1989 that in the next 100 years, sugar maple trees will disappear across the southern edge of their current range in the middle of the country and will shift eastward in Minnesota. Beech trees will disappear from the United States except in northernmost Maine, and scattered blocks of growth will open up in Canada.

She returned to Yale as a professor of biology for three years and then accepted a position at the University of Minnesota where she is now the Regents Professor of Ecology. She was elected to membership in the National Academy of Sciences in 1982. She has also served on numerous committees, such as the International Union of Quaternary Research of the National Academy of Sciences and the National Research Council (1966– ), delegate of the National Academy of Sciences to the International Union of Quaternary Research Congress (1969, 1973, 1977, and 1982), and member of the advisory panel for geological records of global changes of the National Science Foundation (1981– ). She is a fellow of the Geological Society of America and of the American Association for the Advancement of Science. She is a member of the American Quaternary Association (president, 1978–1980), American Society of Limnology and Oceanography, Ecological Society of America (president, 1987–1988), and the International Society for Vegetative Science.

Her research is focused on paleoecology and biogeography of American forest communities, especially late-Quaternary history as recorded by fossil pollen; watershed-lake interactions and ecosystem development over long time intervals; sedimentary processes in lakes; and biotic responses to climatic changes.

***Bibliography:*** *American Men and Women of Science* 11–19; Herzenberg, C., *Women Scientists from Antiquity to the Present; Notable Twentieth-Century Scientists;* Rossiter, M., *Women Scientists in America; Who's Who in America,* 51st ed., 1997; *Who's Who of American Women,* 20th ed., 1997– 1998.

# *Davis, Ruth Margaret*
(1928– )
## *computer scientist, mathematician*

***Education:*** B.A., American University, 1950; M.A., University of Maryland, 1952, Ph.D. in mathematics, 1955; honorary degree: D.Eng., Carnegie-Mellon University, 1979

***Professional Experience:*** Mathematician, U.S. National Bureau of Standards, 1950; research associate, Institute of Fluid Dynamics and Applied Mathematics, University of Maryland, 1952–1955; mathematician, David Taylor Model Basin, 1955–1958, head, Operations Research Division, 1957–1961; staff assistant, Office of the Special Assistant for Intelligence and Reconnaissance, Office of the Director of Defense Research and Engineering, U.S. Department of Defense, 1961–1967; associate director for research and development, National Library of Medicine, 1967–1968; director, Lister Hill National Center for Biomedical Communications, 1968–1970; director, Center for Computer Science and Technology, National Bureau of Standards, 1970–1972; director, Institute for Computer Science and Technology, 1972–1977; deputy to secretary of defense for research and engineering, U.S. Department of Defense, 1977–1979; assistant secretary for energy, U.S. Department of Energy, 1979–1981; president, chief executive officer, and founder, Pymatuning Group, Inc., 1981–

***Concurrent Positions:*** Lecturer, University of Maryland, 1955–1956 and American University, 1957–1958; consultant, Office of Naval Research, 1957–1958; adjunct professor of engineering, University of Pittsburgh, 1981–

***Married:*** 1955

**Ruth Davis** is a pioneer in computer science who is credited with programming three of the first digital computers—SEAC, ORDVAC, and UNIVAC I. She is also responsible for securing worldwide acceptance of a data encryption standard, enabling the United States to become a leader in robotics, and implementing a medical literature retrieval system and a satellite hookup to link the sick in remote Alaska with doctors in the outside world. The posts she had held probably are the most sensitive ever held by a mathematician, a computer expert, or a woman. Her first two jobs involved working for Admiral Hyman Rickover in developing the first computer programs for nuclear reactor design and establishing the U.S. Navy's first command-and-control technical organization. She was the second woman to receive "the man of the year" award from the Data Processing Management Association (1966)—the first was the computer pioneer Grace Murray Hopper (1906–1992). Davis was elected to membership in the National Academy of Engineering in 1976. She has worked successfully in government, academia, and industry.

After receiving her undergraduate degree, she worked for one year as a mathematician for the National Bureau of Standards before returning to school to complete her master's degree. She was a research associate at the University of Maryland until she received her doctorate in mathematics. She was employed as a mathematician for the David Taylor Model Basin, which is a government laboratory, where she became head of the Division of Operations Research in 1957. Operations research is the analysis, usually involving mathematical treatment, of a process, problem, or operation to determine its purpose and effectiveness and to gain maximum efficiency.

She became staff assistant for intelligence and reconnaissance in the Office of the Director of Defense Research and Engineering and then did pioneering research in information technology for the National Library of Medicine between 1967 and 1970. Medical literature today probably is the most accessible of any type of scientific literature, for the National Library of Medicine pioneered computerized indexing of medical literature quickly and accurately. The information is available through computerized databases to the scientist in the laboratory as well as to the practicing physician in the hospital or the office. It is often available to students and citizens in public and academic libraries and on the Internet.

Davis was appointed director of the Institute of Computer Science and Technology at the National Bureau of Standards where she developed standards for data encryption, or coding of data for computing. As deputy to secretary of research and engineering for the Department of Defense, she was involved in early work on robotics between 1977 and 1979. She concluded her government work as assistant secretary of resource applications for the Department of Energy. In 1981, she founded her own company, Pymatuning Group, Inc., of Arlington, Virginia, a consulting firm.

She has been a member of the board of directors of several companies, including Control Data Corporation, United Telecommunications, Inc., and Aerospace Corporation. She has served on advisory groups for the University of Pennsylvania School of Engineering and Science and for the University of California, Berkeley, School of Engineering. She has received the Gold Medal of the Department of Commerce (1972), the Rockefeller Public Service Award for Professional Accomplishment and Leadership (1973), the National Civil Service League Award (1976), and the Ada Augusta Lovelace Award in Computer Science (1984). She is a fellow of the American Association for the Advancement of Science, American Institute of Aeronautics and Astronautics, and Society for Information Display. She is a member of the American Mathematical Society, Mathematical Association of America, Council on Library Resources, and National Academy of Public Administration. Her research interests are automation, electronics, computers, and energy. Her photograph is included in *Infosystems* (May 1980).

**Bibliography:** *American Men and Women of Science* 11–19; Herzenberg, C., *Women Scientists from Antiquity to the Present;* Ireland, N.,

*Index to Women of the World . . . Suppl.; Journal of Computers in Mathematics and Science Teaching* 1982–1983; O'Neill, L., *Women's Book of World Records and Achievements;* Stanley, A., *Mothers and Daughters of Invention; Who's Who in Engineering,* 9th ed., 1995.

# *Deer, Ada E.*

(1935– )

## *sociologist, political and social activist*

***Education:*** B.A. in social work, University of Wisconsin, Madison, 1957; master's degree in social work, Columbia University, 1961; student, University of Wisconsin, Madison, law school, ca. 1970; honorary degrees: doctorate in public service, Northland College, 1974; doctorate, University of Wisconsin, 1974

***Professional Experience:*** Group worker for youth, New York City, 1958–1960; program director, neighborhood home, Minneapolis, 1961–1964; coordinator of Indian Affairs, University of Minnesota, 1964–1967; trainer, Project Peace Pipe, Peace Corps, Arecibo, Puerto Rico, 1968; school social worker, Minneapolis public schools, 1968–1969; director, Upward Bound, University of Wisconsin, Stevens Point, 1969–1970; director, Program Recognizing Individual Determination through Education, 1970–1971; vice president and lobbyist, National Committee to Save Menominee People and Forest, Inc., 1972–1973; chair, Menominee Restoration Committee, 1974–1976; senior lecturer, School of Social Work and American Indian Studies Program, University of Wisconsin, Madison, 1977–; assistant secretary for Indian affairs and head of Bureau of Indian Affairs (BIA), U.S. Department of the Interior, 1993–

***Concurrent Position:*** Legislative liaison, Native American Rights Fund, 1979–1981

A*da Deer,* a member of the Menominee Indian tribe, was the first woman named to head the Bureau of Indian Affairs (BIA), the largest bureau in the Department of the Interior. It provides health, education, and other services to about 2 million Native Americans who are citizens of nearly 500 recognized American Indian and Alaskan native tribal governments; the bureau also oversees the conservation of natural resources on more than 56 million acres of Indian lands.

Deer led the battle to gain restoration of the Menominee's status as a federally recognized tribe. She successfully lobbied Congress to pass the Menominee Restoration Act, which was signed into law in 1973, and the next year she became the first woman to serve as chair of her tribe. The Menominee, whose name means People of the Wild Rice, are located along the Menominee River in Wisconsin and Michigan, and their tribe was one of the few to successfully resist the U.S. government's efforts to move them west of the Mississippi River in the 1850s.

At that time, the Wolf River Treaty gave them what they thought would be eternal sovereignty over a 250,000-acre reservation and federal protection from future claims by white settlers, but in the 1950s, the federal government began to force Native Americans to assimilate into the general population by withdrawing reservation status from several tribes. This policy meant that when the law was signed in 1961, the Menominee Reservation became a separate county in Wisconsin. It also meant that all BIA services to the tribe ceased, leaving its members without money to maintain their hospitals, schools, and other services. It also subjected tribal members to paying income tax. Since the people had no income, the tribal leaders made some unwise decisions to raise money to establish a tax base. The Indians had no experience in business management or in self-government, and by 1972, Menominee County was the poorest county in the state and the poorest in the nation.

Although Deer had enrolled in law school, she left after one semester to help her people. She had spent several years as a social worker, and in 1970, she established a corporation called the National Committee to Save the Menominee People and Forest and served as its chief lobbyist. The Menominee Restoration Act, which officially restored federal recognition to the Menominee, made the tribe's members eligible for federal services again and placed their tribal land assets into a trust. Passage of the act is said to have been the first time a single tribe succeeded in changing federal policy concerning Indians. The tribe's success inspired other tribes to petition and receive restoration of federal recognition.

In 1974, Deer was elected chair of the Menominee Restoration Committee, an interim tribal government, which made her the chief of the tribe. She created the administrative structure for a new tribal government; oversaw financial, legislative, and judicial affairs; and guided the development of a tribal constitution. She left the post in 1976 and in 1977 joined the faculty of the University of Wisconsin, Madison, as a lecturer in both the School of Social Work and the American Indian Studies Program. She also instituted programs to assist low-income students in making the transition from a rural setting to the university by establishing a scholarship for American Indians and by establishing a multicultural center to foster the understanding of all cultures, including that of the Native Americans.

Her primary role model in her social and political activism has been her mother. Constance Deer was a white public health nurse on the Menominee Reservation, which is where she met her future husband, a tribal member. At that time, the BIA program for helping the Indians was centered on destroying their culture. However, Constance Deer loved the culture of the people with whom she worked, and she became a fierce crusader for Indian rights.

When Ada Deer entered the University of Wisconsin, she was one of only two American Indians in a student body of 19,000. She was the first member of her tribe to graduate from the university, and at Columbia University, she was the first Native American to receive a master's degree in social work. She was a trainer in a program operated by the Peace Corps in Arecibo, Puerto Rico, to recruit American Indians for the corps. She is currently serving as director of the Bureau of Indian Affairs while she is on leave from the University of Wisconsin, Stevens Point.

She has served on commissions and committees too numerous to mention, and she has received numerous awards. She has twice been an unsuccessful candidate for election to Congress. She is a member of the American Civil Liberties Union, National Organization for Women, National Women's Political Caucus, National Congress of American Indians, National Association of Social Workers, Common Cause, and the Nature Conservancy. Her photograph is included in *Current Biography* (1994) and *Native North American Almanac.*

***Bibliography:*** *Current Biography* 1994; *Indians of Today; Native North American Almanac; Who's Who of American Women,* 20th ed., 1997–1998.

# Delgado, Jane L.
(1953– )
***psychologist***

***Education:*** B.A., State University of New York at New Paltz, 1973; M.A., New York University, 1975; M.S. in urban policy and sciences, W. Averell Harriman School, 1981; Ph.D. in psychology, State University of New York at Stony Brook, 1981

***Professional Experience:*** Children's talent coordinator, Children's Television Workshop, 1973–1975; research assistant, State University of New York at Stony Brook, 1975–1979; social science analyst, U.S. Department of Health and Human Services, 1979–1983, health policy adviser 1983–1985; president and chief executive officer, COSSMHO, 1985– ; private practice in psychology, 1979–

***Married:*** Herbert Lustig, 1981

***Jane Delgado*** is the president and chief executive officer of the only national organization that focuses on the improvement of health and human services for the nation's Hispanic population. The organization, the National Coalition of Hispanic Health and Human Services Organizations (COSSMHO), was founded in 1985, and one of Delgado's first projects as president was to implement a major outreach program to educate and inform Hispanics about AIDS. Other major projects involve women's health and environmental health. She often is called upon by Congress to provide the latest health statistics on Hispanics.

Delgado's family immigrated from Havana, Cuba, to New York City in 1955, where she was reared by her mother after her father abandoned the family. Although she had little knowledge of English when she entered kindergarten, she learned very quickly and by the third grade had been placed in a "gifted" class. She was disappointed that being "gifted" did not mean she would receive presents. By the time she reached high school, she was unchallenged by school and developed her own plan to speed up graduation. She entered the State University of New York (SUNY) New Paltz at age 16 as a psychology major and graduated when she was 19. She began a master's degree program at New York University in social and personality psychology and financed her studies by working as the children's talent coordinator for the television show *Sesame Street.* This position meant she was in charge of selecting the children who appeared on the show, and she developed a test to determine which children had good television personalities. She also initiated a movement to include handicapped children on the show.

She was rejected the first time she applied for the doctoral program at SUNY Stony Brook because, at age 22, she was considered too young. However, her second application was accepted, and she worked as an instructor at the New York Experimental and Bilingual Institute. Between 1977 and 1979, she was a consultant for the Board of Cooperative Educational Services where she provided psychological and educational services for bilingual children, their parents, teachers, and school officials. At Stony Brook, she directed a three-year study focusing on language development as a predictor of learning disabilities in children. This study covered the United States, Colombia, and Brazil. In 1981, she not only received her doctorate in clinical psychology but had also earned a master of science degree in urban policy and sciences.

Delgado joined the U.S. Department of Health and Human Services in 1979 and worked in the Office of Human Development Services. There she managed the grants and contracts and managed projects concerning Hispanics, black colleges, undocumented workers, etc. She served as liaison with the international office and met foreign dignitaries. When she joined the newly created Office of Community Services, she oversaw $400 million in block grants and served as acting chief of the branch. She then moved to the Office of the Secretary where she dealt with officials at the federal, state, and local levels on policy issues.

She was selected the president of COSSMHO when it was founded by a group of mental health professionals who recognized the need for an organization to represent all Hispanics in the United States. It is a private nonprofit organization that receives federal grants and contracts, foundation support, corporate support, and membership dues. Delgado has received many awards, such as the Surgeon General's Award (1992). Her photograph is included in *Notable Hispanic American Women.*

***Bibliography:*** *Notable Hispanic American Women; Who's Who of American Women,* 20th ed., 1997–1998.

# *Densen-Gerber, Judianne*
(1934– )
## *psychiatrist, physician, lawyer, social activist*

***Education:*** B.A., Bryn Mawr College, 1956; L.L.B., Columbia University, 1959, J.D., 1969; M.D., New York University, 1963

***Professional Experience:*** Lawyer in private practice, 1961– ; psychiatric resident, Bellevue Hospital, New York City, 1964–1965, Metropolitan Hospital, 1965–1967; member of core staff, Addiction Services Agency, 1966–1967; founder, Odyssey House, 1967, clinical director, 1967–1969, executive director, 1967–1974, president of board, 1974–1978; president, founder, and chief executive officer, Odyssey International Inc., 1978– ; attending physician, various hospitals, 1985–

***Married:*** Michael Baden, 1958

***Children:*** 3

***Judianne Densen-Gerber*** is known for her pioneering work in drug rehabilitation. She also is a psychiatrist, lawyer, and activist against child pornography. Although she was able to make some headway in solving some serious social problems by leading fights for legislation, many of the problems still are current today. She received her law degree with the intent of obtaining a medical degree so she could teach medical jurisprudence. However, when her second child died a week after birth, the resulting acute mental stress impelled her to change to psychiatry. She was in her residency at Metropolitan Hospital and pregnant with her third child when she asked the department chair for maternity leave; he responded by giving her an easy assignment in the drug research unit. At the time, it was widely believed that narcotics addicts could not be treated successfully, so it was thought she could complete her residency with little effort on her part. In 1966, however, some of her patients decided they wanted to quit using the experimental heroin substitute. The hospital administrators were appalled because they feared their drug research might be jeopardized, so they removed her from the drug addiction ward and discharged the rebellious patients.

Later, the patients asked her to continue to help them become drug free, and she founded Odyssey House. She theorized that the root cause of drug addiction was the individual's sense of hopelessness and lack of self-confidence. These problems should be treated by group therapy and individual development within a highly structured communal setting so that the addict could be cured and prepared for his or her return to normal life. Although this treatment has now been the standard procedure for a number of years, it was controversial in the 1960s and brought her a great deal of criticism.

As her program became well known, juvenile addicts began asking to join it, but the New York State Department of Social Welfare did not allow Odyssey House to treat anyone under the age of 16. Although authorities claimed there were only 28 cases of heroin-addicted juveniles, she pointed out that 224 teenagers had died from heroin overdoses in New York City alone. After picketing the mayor and the governor, plus appearing on national television, she was able to obtain funding for the juvenile program in 1971. She received so much harassment from city officials over funding that she resigned as head of Odyssey House in 1978 and created Odyssey International, a nonprofit agency that promotes health care for the disadvantaged.

Her work with addicts drew her attention to the needs of sexually abused children, and she helped write the federal legislation that created the National Center on Child Abuse and Neglect in 1973. Another of her causes was child pornography. When she testified before the House Judiciary Subcommittee on Crime, she brought a collection of child pornography books and began to read them aloud in the presence of the television network news cameras. When committee members protested, she reminded them it was their responsibility to clean up the distribution of such material. Some of her other campaigns have been even more controversial than the ones already mentioned. She proposed the legalization of marijuana to enable authorities to concentrate on more serious evils, such as heroin addiction, and she has also proposed that prostitution should be legalized for the greater safety and protection of the women involved.

She has written several books about her reforms, including *Child Abuse and Neglect as Related to Parental Drug Abuse and Other Antisocial Behavior* (1978), *Walk in My Shoes: An Odyssey into Womanlife* (1976), and *We Mainline Dreams: The Odyssey House Story* (1973). She is a member of American Medical Association, Society of Medical Jurisprudence, and American Psychiatric Association. Her photograph is included in *Current Biography* (1983) and *Particular Passions.*

***Bibliography:*** *Contemporary Authors* v. 37–40R; *Current Biography* 1983; *Particular Passions; Who's Who of American Women,* 20th ed., 1997–1998.

# *De Planque, E. Gail*
## (1945– )
## *physicist*

***Education:*** B.A. in mathematics, Immaculata College, 1967; M.S., Newark College of Engineering, 1973; Ph.D. in physics, New York University, 1983

***Professional Experience:*** Physicist, Atomic Energy Commission, 1967–1982, deputy director, Environmental Measurements Laboratory, U.S. Department of Energy, 1982–1987, director, 1987–1991; member, Nuclear Regulatory Commission, 1991–1995; consultant, 1995–

***Concurrent Positions:*** Chair of Health Physics Society's standing working group, American National Standards Institute, 1973–1975, 1980– ; cochair, Committee for International Intercomparison of Environmental Dosimeters, 1974– ; U.S. expert delegate to the international committee for Development of an International Standard on Thermoluminescence Dosimetry, ca. 1977

***Gail De Planque*** is renowned as an expert on radiation physics and radiation dosimetry. She was elected a member of the Nuclear Regulatory Commission for the term 1991–1995 and elected to membership in the National Academy of Engineering in 1995. A renowned woman engineer, in 1997 she was selected to chair the planning committee for a series of conferences to encourage women to become engineers. The project, which was to start late 1997 or early 1998, of the National Academy of Engineering is to be called Celebration of Women in Engineering: Dispelling Myths, Profiling Excellence and will include setting up a Web site. According to academy data, only 2 percent (42) of the academy's 2,000 or so members are women although women engineers compose about 8 percent of the workforce and 20 percent of the undergraduates enrolled in engineering.

After receiving her undergraduate degree, she obtained a position as a research physicist with the Radiation Physics Division of what is now the Department of Energy. She was appointed deputy director in 1982 of the Environmental Measurements Laboratory and director in 1987. The Environmental Measurements Laboratory is a direct descendant of the Manhattan Project and is particularly famous for its long-standing global radiation fallout programs as well as research on radiation dosimetry, radon, and radiation problems associated with nuclear facilities and weapons testing. As director she was responsible for the guidance, direction, and management of the programs, activities, budget, and administrative functions of the laboratory. She currently is a consultant.

Her professional activities have included extensive participation in standards management and development both nationally and internationally. She is a member of the National Council on Radiation Protection and Measurements and was chair of an International Atomic Energy Agency international advisory committee to study the radiological situation on the Mururoa and Fangataufa Atolls, the site of French nuclear weapons testing in the South Pacific. She was the U.S. expert delegate to a standards committee to develop an international standard on thermoluminescence dosimetry and a member of the visiting committee for the Department of Advanced Technology of the Brookhaven National Laboratory. She has served on the editorial board of *Radiation Protection Dosimetry* and on the scientific advisory and editorial committees of the series International Conferences on Solid-State Dosimetry. Her interest in promoting careers in science is seen in her membership on the Engineering Department's advisory committee for the New Jersey Institute of Technology since 1985.

She was elected a fellow of the American Nuclear Society and is a member of the American Physical Society, Association of Women in Science, Health Physics Society, and American Association for the Advancement of Science. Her research has centered on experimental and theoretical investigations involving the application of the basic physics of radiation interactions with matter to problems of radiation protection. Her areas of investigation include solid-state dosimetry, radiation transport and shielding, environmental radiation, nuclear facilities monitoring, and problems of reactor and personnel dosimetry. Her photograph is included in *Science* (July 25, 1997). She is listed as "Gail De Planque" and "E. Gail De Planque" in various sources. Some information was supplied in a letter to the author dated July 5, 1997.

***Bibliography:*** *American Men and Women of Science* 14–19; *Who's Who in America,* 51st ed., 1997; *Who's Who in Science and Engineering,* 3d ed., 1996–1997; *Who's Who in Technology Today* v. 5; *Who's Who of American Women,* 20th ed., 1997–1998.

# DeWitt-Morette, Cecile Andrée Paule
(1922– )
**theoretical physicist**

***Education:*** Student, University of Caen, 1943; diploma, University of Paris, 1944, Ph.D. in theoretical physics, 1947

***Professional Experience:*** Member, Institute for Advanced Studies, Ireland, 1946–1947; member, University Institute for Theoretical Physics, Copenhagen, 1947–1948; member, Institute for Advanced Study, Princeton University, 1948–1950; teacher and researcher, Institut Henri Poincare, France, 1950–1951; research associate and lecturer, University of California, Berkeley, 1952–1955; visiting research professor, University of North Carolina, Chapel Hill, 1956–1967, director, Institute of Field Physics, 1958–1966, lecturer in physics, 1967–1971; professor of astronomy, University of Texas, Austin, 1972–1983, professor of physics, 1983–1993, Jane and Roland Blumberg Centennial Professor of Physics, 1993–

***Concurrent Position:*** Director and founder, Summer School of Theoretical Physics, Les Houches, France, 1951–1972

***Married:*** Bryce S. DeWitt, 1951

***Children:*** 4

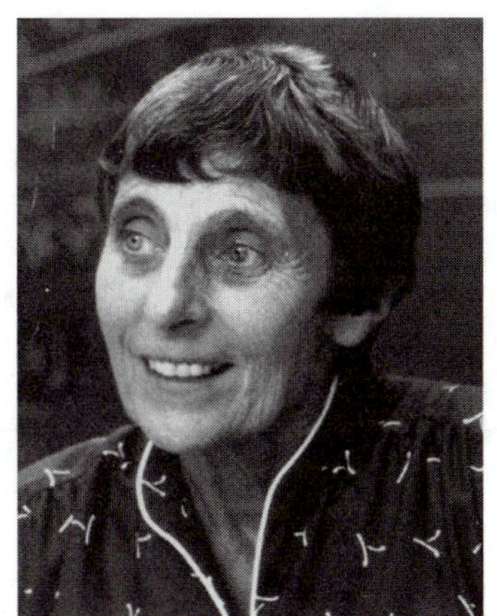

*Cecile DeWitt-Morette* has received international recognition as a pioneer theoretical physicist of modern times. She is credited with bringing stability to teaching physics in France by founding a summer school of theoretical physics with a distinguished and international team of lecturers. This school, L'Ecole de Physique des Houches, has been held every year since 1951. Les Houches, as it is generally called, has been the model for similar programs initiated, with her assistance, in Varenna, Italy, and in the United States as the Battelle Rencontres in Seattle.

She was born in France and was attending college during the World War II German occupation of France. Since her mother felt that medicine would be too physically demanding, Cecile began studying physics, first at the University of Caen and then at the University of Paris. At the University of Paris, she worked in a laboratory directed by Frederic Joliot and Irene Joliot-Curie. Except for a few experimentalists such as the Joliots, French physics, particularly theoretical physics, was outdated. For example, quantum mechanics was not included in the curricula, and few people were working in that area. With the assistance of the Joliots and the Allied military authorities, she went to England in 1946 where she met with the physicist Paul Dirac. She then stayed a year in Ireland at the Institute for Advanced Studies where she gained additional knowledge.

After receiving her doctorate from the University of Paris, she was invited to become a member of the University Institute for Theoretical Physics in Copenhagen for a year, and then J. Robert Oppenheimer invited her to the Institute for Advanced Study at Princeton for two years. In both of these two assignments she was able to meet most of the top theoretical physicists in the world, and they had the opportunity to see her research commitment and creativity. While at Princeton, she became acquainted with Richard P. Feynman and learned the theory of path integration from him. This topic became one of her lifelong research interests.

Also at Princeton she met her future husband, Bryce S. DeWitt, and they were married in 1951. For several years she had been pondering the question of the poor quality of French physics, and she was able to obtain some money from the French Ministry of Education to start the summer school of theoretical physics in the city of Les Houches, which is near Mont Blanc. The first session consisted of 30 students, half of them French and the rest international, who studied basic courses on advanced topics. The quality of the school is indicated by the fact that 13 of the lecturers during the first 15 years of the school later received Nobel Prizes. A year after she started the school at Les Houches, the Italian Physical Society asked her to help start a similar school in Varenna. In 1958, the North Atlantic Treaty Organization (NATO) established a program to support summer study institutes in Western Europe, such as the one in Les Houches. The money was to be used both for direct grants to the institutes and for living and travel expenses of participants from NATO countries.

Meanwhile, in 1951, she had accompanied her husband to the Tata Institute of Fundamental Research in Bombay where he had a Fulbright grant. The next year he joined the nuclear weapons laboratory at Livermore, California, and she obtained a position as a lecturer at the University of California, Berkeley. In 1956, Bryce accepted the directorship of the Institute of Field Physics at the University of North Carolina, and Cecile became codirector; both were given the title of visiting research professor. A few years later, Bryce was named director and chair, but Cecile was demoted in 1967 from research professor to lecturer—in spite of the fact that she had served from 1957 to 1966 as director of the university's Institute of Natural Science and had played a crucial role in attracting money to the university. Although the university cited nepotism rules for this decision, such rules had never been published in the official regulations. She continued operating Les Houches from her home in the United States, and in 1967, she helped initiate the Battelle Rencontres in Seattle and continued to oversee it until 1972. Her research had suffered during the period at North Carolina because she devoted so much time to administrative efforts.

The couple accepted faculty positions at the University of Texas, Austin, where they both were given tenured positions as full professors. However, Cecile was given only a half-time position and assigned to the Astronomy Department owing to fears of nepotism, but the couple was able to collaborate on research with the support of their two departments. In 1983, she was able to move to the Physics Department, and in 1987, she received a full-time appointment. She resigned the directorship of Les Houches in 1972 but remains a member of the board of trustees.

Her professional expertise is in the interplay between physics and mathematics. Several of her papers have broken new ground in areas such as semiclassical expansions, path integrals, and stochastic processes. She has published several books, including *Particles Elementaires* (1951), *Analysis, Manifolds, and Physics* (1977; rev. ed., 1982), *Path Integration in the Non Relativistic Quantum Mechanics* (1978), and *Analysis, Manifolds, and Physics, Part II* (1992). She received from the French government the Chevalier Ordre National Du Merite (1981) for establishing Les Houches, and she has also received the L'Ordre des Palmes Academiques (1991) and the Prix du Rayonnement Français (1992). She was elected a fellow of the American Physical Society, and she is a member of the European Physical Society. Her research includes theory of field elementary particles, mathematical physics, and gravitation.

***Bibliography:*** *American Men and Women of Science* 11–19; *Who's Who in America,* 51st ed., 1997; *Who's Who of American Women,* 20th ed., 1997–1998; *Women in Chemistry and Physics.*

# *Dicciani, Nance Katherine*
(1947– )
## *chemical engineer*

***Education:*** B.S., Villanova University, 1969; M.S., University of Virginia, 1970; Ph.D. in chemical engineering, University of Pennsylvania, 1977, M.B.A., 1986

***Professional Experience:*** Superintendent of water treatment, City of Philadelphia, 1972–1974; research engineer, Air Products and Chemicals, Inc., 1977–1978, research manager, 1978–1981, director of research for the process systems group, 1981–1984, director of research and development for a division, 1984–1986, general manager of the division, 1986–1988, director of commercial development, 1988–1991; vice president and business director, Rohm and Haas Company, 1991–

***Nance Dicciani*** has made significant contributions in the pure sciences, in the application of new technologies in industry, and in managing major industrial corporations. While still in graduate school, she explored new areas of applying chemical engineering to medical imaging; the result was a pioneering effort in developing the ultrasonic scanning devices that now are used routinely to examine women during pregnancy. This type of medical engineering has been in the forefront of research for the past 20 years and continues to be so today.

In common with many women scientists and engineers, Dicciani's parents encouraged her interest in science. As early as the fifth grade she planned a career in the sciences, and she pursued an undergraduate degree in chemical engineering because that allowed her to combine her love for mathematics with a deep interest in the hard sciences, especially physics and chemistry. It also is a practical science and gave her a chance to work in a field where the results of her efforts would make an impact.

After receiving her master's degree in chemical engineering, she worked for four years with the Philadelphia Department of Public Works, including three years as the city's superintendent of water treatment. She returned to graduate school, this time at the University of Pennsylvania. Her thesis topic involved the application of chemical engineering to medical imaging, a joint research project undertaken by the university, the National Science Foundation, and the government of the Soviet Union. Later she returned to the university to receive an M.B.A. from Wharton Business School, one of the five top business schools in the United States.

Her first position in industry was as a process engineer with Air Products and Chemicals, Inc., where she rose rapidly, receiving two promotions within two years. She was then appointed director of research for the process systems group, and her final appointment with Air Products was as general manager of the Chemical Commercial Development and Technology group. She then joined Rohm and Haas Company, one of the world's largest chemical companies, as vice president and business director of the Petroleum Chemicals Division.

In her career, Dicciani has made contributions in the areas of petrochemicals, energy, chemical processes, wastewater treatment, and catalysis of the production of commercially important petrochemicals. She believes that anyone with a love of science—or any field—can succeed with hard work, determination, and self-confidence. She has shrewdly chosen a field where it is possible to achieve recognition for one's contributions, chosen significant projects to work with, and bolstered her expertise by advanced education. As she rose in the corporate structure, she obtained a master's degree in business to make herself a more effective manager.

She is active professionally in supporting engineering education by serving as a member of the chemical engineering advisory boards at both the University of Virginia and the University of Pennsylvania. She is a member of the American Institute of Chemical Engineers and the Society of Women Engineers. Her areas of research include mass transfer, three-phase fluid dynamics, heterogeneous kinetics and catalysis, and separation science. Her photograph is included in *Notable Twentieth-Century Scientists.* Her name is spelled both "Nancy" and "Nance" in the various sources.

***Bibliography:*** *American Men and Women of Science* 16–19; *Notable Twentieth-Century Scientists.*

# *Douglas, Mary (Tew)*
(1921– )
## *anthropologist*

***Education:*** B.A., Oxford University, 1943, M.A., 1947, B.Sc., 1948, Ph.D. in anthropology, 1951
***Professional Experience:*** Civil servant, 1943–1946; anthropological fieldwork in the Belgian Congo (Zaire or Congo), 1949–1950; lecturer in anthropology, Institute of Anthropology, Oxford University, 1951; lecturer and then professor of social anthropology, University of London, 1951–1977; director of the culture program, Russell Sage Foundation, New York City, 1977–1981; Avalon Professor of the Humanities, Northwestern University, 1981–1985; lecturer, Princeton University, ca. 1986–
***Married:*** James A. T. Douglas, 1951
***Children:*** 3

***Mary Douglas*** is a social anthropologist who is known internationally for her studies of religion and symbolism in tribal and contemporary society, pollution, and moral order and for grid and group analysis. As an undergraduate at Oxford, she studied philosophy, politics, and economics. She interrupted her studies in 1943 during World War II to volunteer for national service, working for the Colonial Office. She returned to Oxford to obtain a master's degree in anthropology as well as a B.Sc. She conducted fieldwork in the Belgian Congo (Zaire or Congo) among the Lele tribe as a basis for her dissertation. She married James A. T. Douglas, an economist, in 1951, the same year she received her doctorate and began her long association with the University of London. She retired from that university to serve as the resident scholar and director of the culture program at the Russell Sage Foundation. Later she taught at Northwestern University as the Avalon Professor of the Humanities, a joint appointment in history and the literature of religion. Her last appointment was teaching at Princeton University for several years.

She was one of the first anthropologists to attempt to relate moral philosophy and religion in a systematic manner with social behavior. She examines social accountability throughout her work and devised a formula for classifying social relations by two independent variables—grid and group—to explain changes in rite, symbol, and myth in a systematic way. She explains that "group" is the experience of a bounded social unit and that "grid" refers to rules that relate one person to others. She analyzed cultures and their underlying social organizations by looking at the various combinations of grid and group.

Douglas probably is best known for her studies of pollution, in which she explores how rituals and purity and impurity form part of an accountability system. She sees food as another system of social information and proposes that the choice of animals and plants to be eaten, how they are prepared, and how they are presented is socially structured and organized. In contemporary society, she sees that goods are social markers; consumption of goods is a means for attaining and keeping power. This relationship may be seen in countries that suffer famines; sometimes the foods and supplies that are donated by other countries are confiscated by a rebel group or by the central government so the food never reaches the starving citizens.

Another area she treated was to compare ideas about pollution in both tribal and industrial societies. She feels that beliefs surrounding pollution are culturally determined and have little to do with an object's relationship to dirt or danger. This idea also touches on current society as the environmental protection movement that started in the 1960s is still being debated. She dispels the theory that religion and science cannot coexist and suggests that religion and ritual will continue to play an important role because social relations may change but they do not disappear. In the 1990s, membership in organized religions dropped, but the evangelical and other movements gained followers.

Douglas has written a number of books, including *The Lele of the Kasai* (1963), *Purity and Danger: An Analysis of Concepts of Pollution and Taboo* (1966), and *The World of Goods: An Anthropological Theory of Consumption* (1979). She has received numerous awards, such as the Rivers Memorial Medal (1968) and the Bernal Prize (1994). She is a fellow of the Zoological Society of London and a member of the Royal Anthropological Institute.

***Bibliography:*** *Contemporary Authors* v. 197–100; *Who's Who in America,* 51st ed., 1997; *Women Anthropologists.*

# *Drake, Elisabeth (Mertz)*
## (1936– )
## *chemical engineer*

***Education:*** B.S. in chemical engineering, Massachusetts Institute of Technology, 1958, D.Sc. in chemical engineering, 1966

***Professional Experience:*** Staff consultant in cryogenics, Arthur D. Little, Inc., 1958–1964, senior engineer, 1966–1970, senior engineer of safety and fire technology, 1971–1977, manager of risk assessment group, 1977–1978, department head of safety and fire technology section, 1978–1980, vice president of technological risk management, 1980–1982; Cabot Professor and chair of Chemical Engineering Department, Northeastern University, 1982–1986; vice president of technical risk management, Arthur D. Little, Inc., 1986–1989, consultant, 1990–1994; associate director of new technology, Energy Laboratory, Massachusetts Institute of Technology, 1990– , director 1994–1995

***Concurrent Positions:*** Lecturer, University of California, Berkeley, 1971; visiting professor, Massachusetts Institute of Technology (MIT), 1973–1974; corporate manager, MIT, 1981–1986

***Married:*** Alvin W. Drake, 1957, divorced 1984

***Children:*** 1

***Elisabeth Drake*** is a chemical engineer who is known for her expertise in safety standards and other aspects of environmental safety. Very early in her career, in 1972, she invented a fractionation method and apparatus. Fractionation separates a mixture into ingredients or into portions having different properties, and an apparatus of this type is a valuable contribution to the chemical industry. After receiving her undergraduate degree, she accepted a position at Arthur D. Little, Inc., an international management and technology consulting firm. Her early work was involved in cryogenics, which is the branch of physics that deals with very low temperatures. The term "cryogenics" was coined about 1955 or 1960, which means that she was working on the cutting edge of research and development in this new field.

Drake was promoted to the senior staff after she completed her doctorate. She switched fields to be manager of risk analysis and then vice president of technical risk management. Risk management is the technique of assessing, minimizing, and preventing accidental loss to a business through the use of safety measures, insurance, etc. She accepted a position as chair of the Chemical Engineering Department at Northeastern University in 1982, then returned to work at A. D. Little as vice president of technical risk management. She continued to consult for the company after she left in 1990 to join the Massachusetts Institute of Technology as associate director of new technology in the Energy Laboratory, becoming director between 1994 and 1995.

She has long been active in committees on safety standards. She was a member of the Technical Pipeline Safety Standards Committee of the U.S. Department of Transportation from 1980 to 1985 and a member of the managing board of the Center for Chemical Process Safety from 1988 to 1990. She has been vice chair of the committee that reviews and evaluates the U.S. Army's chemical stockpile disposal program of the National Research Council since 1993.

She was elected to membership in the National Academy of Engineering in 1992. She is a fellow of the American Institute of Chemical Engineers and a member of the American Association for the Advancement of Science and the American Chemical Society. Her research interests include energy technology, risk assessment and control of hazardous material, liquefied natural gas technology and safety, cryogenic engineering, and risk management.

***Bibliography:*** *American Men and Women of Science* 12–19; Vare, E., *Mothers of Invention; Who's Who in America,* 51st ed., 1997; *Who's Who in Science and Engineering,* 3rd ed., 1996–1997; *Who's Who of American Women,* 20th ed., 1997–1998.

## *Dreschhoff, Gisela Auguste-Marie*
(1938– )
### *radiation physicist, geophysicist*

***Education:*** B.S., Technical University of Braunschweig, 1961, M.S., 1965, Ph.D. in physics, 1972

***Professional Experience:*** Staff scientist, radiation protection, Physikalisch Technisch Bundesanstalt, Germany, 1965–1967; research associate, nuclear waste disposal, Kansas Geological Survey, 1971–1972; deputy director, Radiation Physics Laboratory, Space Technology Center, University of Kansas, 1972–1984, codirector, 1984–

***Concurrent Positions:*** Visiting assistant professor of physics, University of Kansas, 1972–1974, adjunct assistant professor, 1974– ; associate professional manager, Division of Polar Programs, National Science Foundation, 1978–

G*isela Dreschhoff* is renowned for her research in Antarctica to survey for radioactive uranium, thorium, and potassium. As background information, until the late 1960s U.S. women scientists were not permitted to conduct research in Antarctica although women from other countries were permitted to do so by their respective governments. This prohibition was made possible because the U.S. base at Antarctica was a naval base and the only transportation was provided by the U.S. Navy. However, there had been a few American women who had financed their own trips (the details of the fight to open research to women is described by Barbara Land in *The New Explorers* [1981]). In 1978, several years after American women were permitted access to Antarctica, Dreschhoff was appointed by the National Science Foundation to coordinate and manage the airborne surveys for the entire geophysics program that the foundation sponsored there. One year she was the only woman living at a remote base during the research season with 15 scientists and an equal number of naval personnel.

Just a few months after receiving her U.S. citizenship papers, the German-born scientist was headed to Antarctica for the first time. After completing her undergraduate training at Braunschweig, she obtained a position as a staff scientist at Physikalisch Technisch Bundesanstalt in Germany where she was involved in safety procedures to be used around nuclear reactors. In 1965, she was measuring the levels of radioactive fission products in German air, soil, water, and plants. In 1967, when she attended a conference sponsored by the International Atomic Energy Agency, she met an American scientist from the University of Kansas who was working on the effects of radiation on solid bodies in space. He had several contracts from the National Aeronautics and Space Administration (NASA) and the U.S. Air Force and offered her a job.

She took a one-year leave from the institute in Germany but, at the end of the year, decided to stay in Kansas. She completed the requirements for her doctorate while working as a research associate and then as a visiting assistant professor in the Department of Physics and Astronomy. In 1972, she was appointed deputy director of the Radiation Physics Laboratory. Four years later, she was en route to Antarctica as a principal investigator. Because she speaks fluent German as well as English and French, she is a valuable participant in international research projects.

Although the popular press interpreted the first year's survey as a search for a potential uranium mine in Antarctica, the project was the start of a general radiometric survey to determine the distribution of uranium, thorium, and radioactive potassium, if any. All nations involved were trying to formulate a policy to govern the future use of resources buried under the polar ice. The survey was planned to last at least five years, and the team experimented with a new system that combined airborne surveys with on-the-ground measurements. Using a helicopter, the scientists would fly over an area while monitoring the readings on a gamma-ray spectrometer. When there were sufficient peaks in the readout over one area, the helicopter would land and the scientists would check their findings with more precise instruments.

Dreschhoff is a member of the American Physical Society, American Geophysical Union, American Polar Society, American Association for the Advancement of Science, Explorers' Club, and the U.S. Naval Institute. Her areas of research are remote sensing, nuclear waste disposal, reactor radiation protection, and geophysics of the polar regions. Photographs are included in Land's *The New Explorers*.

***Bibliography:*** *American Men and Women of Science* 14–19; Ireland, N., *Index to Women of the World . . . Suppl.;* Land, B., *The New Explorers; Who's Who in America,* 51st ed., 1997.

# *Dresselhaus, Mildred (Spiewak)*
## (1930– )
## *solid-state physicist*

***Education:*** B.A., Hunter College, 1951; Fulbright fellowship, Cavendish Laboratory, Cambridge University, 1951–1952; M.A., Radcliffe College, 1953; Ph.D. in physics, University of Chicago, 1958; honorary degrees: about eight

***Professional Experience:*** National Science Foundation fellowship, Cornell University, 1958–1960; staff member, Lincoln Laboratory, Massachusetts Institute of Technology (MIT), 1960–1967, Abby Rockefeller Mauze Visiting Professor, Department of Electrical Engineering and Computer Science, 1967–1968, professor, 1968–1973, associate head of department, 1972–1974, Abby Rockefeller Mauze Professor of Electrical Engineering, 1973–1985, director of Center for Materials Science and Engineering, 1977–1983, professor, Department of Electrical Engineering and Computer Science, 1968– , professor, Department of Physics, 1983– , Institute Professor, MIT, 1985–

***Married:*** Gene Dresselhaus, 1958

***Children:*** 4

*Mildred Dresselhaus* is a renowned solid-state physicist who holds a joint appointment as professor in the Department of Electrical Engineering and Computer Science and professor in the Department of Physics at the Massachusetts Institute of Technology (MIT). In 1985, she was made an Institute Professor, a lifetime honor that has been conferred on no more than 12 active professors in the university. She also has the distinction of having been elected to membership in both the National Academy of Engineering (1974) and the National Academy of Sciences (1985). Only one other woman listed in this volume—Johanna Maria Henrica Levelt Sengers—shares this honor. Dresselhaus has contributed new knowledge about the electronic properties of many materials, particularly semimetals.

She rose from poverty to become an internationally recognized scientist. As a child during the depression, she worked in sweatshops and factories to help support the family, but she managed to continue attending school and taking music lessons at the same time. Her brother was a child prodigy on the violin, and both children were given free lessons, although Mildred was not as talented as her brother. When she applied for admission to Hunter College High School, she passed the entrance exams, receiving a perfect score on the math section. She had difficulty with her lessons at first because of the poor quality of education at the elementary school she had attended, but she was soon in the top group of her classes. She continued to work by tutoring her fellow students.

She entered Hunter College as an elementary education major, but her science instructors, recognizing her talent, persuaded her to major in science. She received a degree in physics and went to the Cavendish Laboratory at Cambridge University on a Fulbright fellowship. Cavendish is the premier physics installation in England, and while there, she was accepted as a woman scientist partially because she was an American and somewhat of a curiosity to the other students. Her musical background gave her an entrée into many cultural and social activities there. After completing her master's degree at Radcliffe College, she received a scholarship to the University of Chicago, which at that time had the most prominent Department of Physics in the United States. Her research centered on the new area of solid-state physics—superconductors in a magnetic field—because she felt it would be a good topic. In fact, she was left to her own devices because none of the faculty members knew much about the topic.

As soon as she had completed her doctorate, she married Gene Dresselhaus, whom she had met as a fellow student in the Physics Department. He had already accepted a position as a junior faculty member at Cornell University, and since Cornell had nepotism rules that kept husband and wife from working in the same department, she accepted a National Science Foundation fellowship. After two years, the couple found joint appointments at Lincoln Laboratory, Massachusetts Institute of Technology.

Solid-state physics, which is defined as dealing with matter in a condensed state, not in gaseous or liquid form, was just becoming a prominent area of research. Russia had launched Sputnik in 1957, and that event spurred the United States to speed up research on new materials. While other scientists were working on semiconductors, Dresselhaus started her research on superconductors, such as lead and tin. In these early years, she was able to combine research and family because she and her husband were collaborating on their research, and they had a full-time baby sitter to take care of their four children. After several years, Lincoln Laboratory became involved in more applied research than she was interested in. She received a one-year appointment to teach physics in the Department of Electrical Engineering and Computer Science at MIT, and after she introduced a graduate-level course in solid-state physics, the department asked her to continue teaching. In 1977 she was named director of the Center for Materials Science and Engineering and continued her teaching. Later she became a full professor in both electrical engineering and physics.

In the course of her teaching, she noticed that there were very few women, about 400 each year, attending MIT and that they were quartered in a very dismal dormitory. She started an informal discussion forum for women students about careers in science, which led to her appointment to the university's undergraduate women's admissions program where she was able to effect a change in the number of women being admitted. She has long been active in her professional associations in recruiting women students to careers in science and engineering.

Her most important work, starting in the 1980s, was done on analyzing carbon. She and her associates found that carbon contained hollow clusters, each containing 60 atoms. These clusters are called Buckminster Fullerenes (named for the scientist Buckminster Fuller), or Buckeyballs, because of their shape. They are important for their potential use as a delivery system for drugs and as an extremely strong form of wire tubing. Today, they are about the hottest thing to hit chemistry since the Bunsen burner.

Dresselhaus states that she has been fortunate in her career in selecting new areas of research that proved to be interesting. She focuses on research rather than on the development of products, preferring to work five years ahead of a practical use. Aside from the problem with nepotism at Cornell, she has not experienced many problems with discrimination. Even in graduate school at Chicago, when there were only one or two women in the program, she was able to fit in because she tutored some of her fellow students. Relations at MIT always have been very good. When she was a young mother, her colleagues criticized her because at times she was an hour late for work while she waited for the baby sitter to arrive; she just ignored their remarks.

She tells young people they can determine if they have an aptitude for science by two essential ingredients: a liking for mathematics and a sense of logic. She says that research is somewhat haphazard; it does not progress in the straight line in which it is presented in a published paper. She encourages women to play around with ideas. As a young scientist, she was working in a backwater of science, and no one took her seriously. However, her accomplishments prove she made correct choices. She tells women scientists to relax, enjoy every moment of life, act and be yourself, exploit every opportunity that comes your way, stick up for yourself, and arrange your personal affairs so you can succeed in your professional activities.

She received the National Medal of Science in 1990 and has also received numerous other awards and committee assignments. She is a fellow of the American Academy of Arts and Sciences, American Physical Society (president, 1984), and Institute of Electrical and Electronics Engineers; she is a member of the Society of Women Engineers. Her research includes electronic, optical, and magneto-optical properties of solids; semimetals; semiconductors; magnetic semiconductors; graphite; and intercalation compounds. An early autobiography was published in Ruth Kundsin's *"Successful Women in the Sciences."* Her photograph is included in *Notable Twentieth-Century Scientists, Journeys of Women in Science and Engineering,* and *Science* (September 26, 1997).

***Bibliography:*** *American Men and Women of Science* 11–19; Herzenberg, C., *Women Scientists from Antiquity to the Present;* Ireland, N., *Index to Women of the World . . . Suppl.; Journeys of Women in Science and Engineering;* Kundsin, R., *"Successful Women in the Sciences"; Notable Twentieth-Century Scientists;* Rossiter, M., *Women Scientists in America; Who's Who in America,* 51st ed., 1997; *Who's Who in Engineering,* 8th ed., 1991; *Who's Who in Science and Engineering,* 3d ed., 1996–1997; *Who's Who of American Women,* 20th ed., 1997–1998.

# *Dunbar, Bonnie J.*
(1949– )
## *biomedical engineer, ceramics engineer, astronaut*

***Education:*** B.S. in ceramic engineering, University of Washington, 1971, M.S. in ceramic engineering, 1975; Ph.D. in biomedical engineering, University of Houston, 1983
***Professional Experience:*** Staff engineer, Boeing Computer Services, 1971–1973; senior research engineer, Space Division, Rockwell International, 1976–1978; staff member, National Aeronautics and Space Administration (NASA), 1978– , astronaut, 1981– , mission specialist STS 61-A (1985) and STS-32 (1990), payload commander, shuttle *Columbia flight* STS-50 (1992) and STS-71 (1995), special assistant to deputy associate administrator, 1993
***Concurrent Positions:*** Visiting scientist, Harwell Laboratories, England, 1975; adjunct assistant professor of mechanical engineering, University of Houston
***Married:*** Ronald M. Sega, 1988

***Bonnie J. Dunbar*** has spent more hours in space than any of the other women astronauts except Shannon Lucid and more hours than many of the men. She applied for the astronaut program in 1978 and worked as a staff member until she was accepted for the one-year training program in 1980. She is one of the eight original women astronauts accepted in 1978 and 1980.

It seems impossible that a woman reared on a farm in a remote area of the state of Washington could have a career in space. She became fascinated with space flight as a child and in high school set her goal of becoming an astronaut. With the encouragement of a teacher, she studied all of the math and science courses that were available in high school. At the University of Washington there were only six women in an engineering class of 2,000 students, and she faced discrimination for the first time. Some faculty members routinely told the women that they were unable to do the class work, but such comments only spurred her to succeed. She originally planned to major in aeronautical engineering but found that Boeing Corporation was reducing employment. The head of the Ceramic Engineering Department, who had received a NASA contract to work on thermal insulation systems for the space shuttle, was recruiting students, and she switched to that program. Ceramic engineering is an element of materials engineering and includes everything that is not a metal and not a plastic.

After receiving her undergraduate degree, she went to the University of Illinois to study bioengineering. However, her brother was killed in Vietnam, and she returned to Washington after a few months to accept a position as a staff engineer for Boeing Computer Services. There she honed her computer skills and, as recreation, learned to scuba dive, a skill she knew she would need in astronaut training. Since she was unable to secure a job in materials engineering at Boeing, she returned to the university for her master's degree. This time she worked on another NASA grant for ionic diffusion material for sodium beta alumina batteries to be used in space.

She accepted a short appointment as a visiting scientist at Harwell Laboratories in England to do materials research on turbine blades. Turbine blades are part of a turbine engine, such as an aircraft engine, and must withstand extremely high temperatures. As recreation she learned parachute jumping, another skill she would need for astronaut training. She joined the Rockwell International Space Division, the prime contractor for the space shuttle, to help develop equipment and processes for the manufacture of the space shuttle's ceramic-tile heat shield. She was the only ceramic engineer on the team and won the Rockwell Engineer of the Year award in 1978. Rockwell encouraged her to apply for the astronaut program and promised her a job if she later left the program.

Dunbar joined NASA as a staff engineer in 1978 and performed key guidance and flight control duties for the Skylab reentry mission in 1979. Her first shuttle flight was aboard STS 61-A *Challenger* in October 1985. On STS-32 in 1990, she had the major responsibility for the Remote Manipulator System (RMS) to retrieve the Long Duration Exposure Facility (LDEF) satellite that had been in orbit since 1984. As payload commander for the 1992 space shuttle *Columbia* flight, she oversaw 31 experiments in materials science, fluid dynamics, combustion science, and biotechnology. Among the most important was the crystal growth furnace, which was designed to process up to six large samples at temperatures above 1,300 degrees Celsius. She flew a fourth mission on STS-71 in 1995. She was a member of the crew that picked up David Wolf when he completed his Mir assignment in 1998.

On a continuing basis she works as chief of the Astronaut Office's science support groups, which advise researchers on the design and operation of hardware for a wide variety of space experiments. She received a doctorate in biomedical engineering in 1983, on a part-time basis and with NASA's permission, in order to enhance her expertise in all types of materials for a wide variety of applications. As research for her degree, she examined the effect of space flight on bone strength and calcium. Her husband, Ronald M. Sega, is also an astronaut, an engineer and physicist who flew on STS-60 (1994) and STS-76 (1996).

Bonnie Dunbar has received several awards, including *Design News*'s Engineer of the Year Award (1993), only the sixth person to receive the award. She also received the National Engineering Award of the American Association of Engineering Societies (1992). She is a member of the American Association for the Advancement of Science, American Ceramic Society, Biomedical Engineering Society, Materials Research Society, National Institute of Ceramic Engineers, Arnold Air Society, and Angel Flight. Her photograph is included in *Design News* (February 22, 1993, and May 3, 1993), *Journeys of Women in Science and Engineering*, Karen O'Connor's *Sally Ride and the New Astronauts*, and A. R. Oberg's *Spacefarers of the '80s and '90s*.

***Bibliography:*** *American Men and Women of Science* 19; Ireland, N., *Index to Women of the World . . . Suppl.; Journeys of Women in Science and Engineering;* Oberg, A. R., *Spacefarers of the '80s and '90s;* O'Conner, K., *Sally Ride and the New Astronauts;* U.S. National Aeronautics and Space Administration, *Astronaut Fact Book; Who's Who in Science and Engineering*, 2d ed., 1994–1995.

# E

## *Earle, Sylvia Alice*

(1935– )

### *marine botanist, oceanographer, environmentalist*

***Education:*** B.S., Florida State University, 1955; M.A., Duke University, 1956, Ph.D in botany, 1966; honorary degrees: numerous

***Professional Experience:*** Fisheries research biologist, U.S. Fish and Wildlife Service, 1957; instructor in biology, St. Petersburg Junior College, 1963–1964; research associate in marine biology, Cape Haze Marine Laboratory, 1964–1965, resident director, 1966–1967, senior research associate in marine biology, 1967– ; instructor, Tulane University, 1968; research fellow, Farlow Herbarium, Harvard University, 1967–1975, researcher, 1975– ; research scholar, Radcliffe Institute for Independent study, 1967–1969; research associate in botany, Natural History Museum of Los Angeles County, 1970–1975; research biologist and curator, California Academy of Sciences, 1976– ; research associate, University of California, Berkeley, 1969–1975; fellow in botany, Natural History Museum, 1989– ; chief scientist, U.S. National Oceanic and Atmospheric Administration (NOAA), 1990–1992, adviser to the administrator, 1992–1993

***Concurrent Positions:*** Founder, president, and CEO, Deep Ocean Technology, Inc., 1981–1990; founder, president, and CEO Deep Ocean Engineering, 1982–1990, board of directors, 1992–

***Married:*** Jack Taylor, 1957, divorced 1966; Giles Mead, 1966, divorced 1975; Graham Hawkes, 1986, divorced ca. 1990

***Children:*** 3

***Sylvia Earle*** is known internationally as a marine botanist and oceanographer. Thirteen years before the first woman astronaut Sally Ride flew on a space mission, Earle and four other women oceanographers spent two weeks living in an underwater habitat called Tektite II as part of a government-funded project. She was the first woman to be selected as chief scientist of the National Oceanic and Atmospheric Administration (NOAA); during her administration, she led the investigations into the pollution of the Persian Gulf that resulted from Iraq's burning of the Kuwait oil refineries and the pollution of Prince William Sound, Alaska, after the supertanker *Exxon Valdez* ran aground in 1989. Her colleagues dub her "Her Deepness" for the records she has set in ocean diving.

She spent part of her childhood on a farm in New Jersey where she studied the aquatic life in a pond on the property. She said she took notes on her observations although no one taught her to do so. Later, when the family moved to Florida, she had the entire Gulf of Mexico as her backyard. She made her first dive in a summer scuba-diving course five miles offshore in the Gulf, and she was fortunate that scuba gear had been developed ten years or so by the time she took up diving. Prior to that development, people had had to depend on heavy helmets and pressurized suits; as a result, few people dived for recreational purposes. The scuba gear changed the entire direction of marine biology. Previously, scientists could only observe specimens caught in drag nets; now, they could observe specimens in their habitats.

Earle graduated from high school at 16 and quickly obtained her undergraduate degree from Florida State at 19 and her master's degree from Duke at 20. She found that her experience in the Duke graduate school made her aware of what she had to achieve as a professional, for the school had a definite standard of excellence. For her doctoral thesis, she chose to study the biology of algae. The research dragged on for several years, being interrupted by marriage to zoologist Jack Taylor, motherhood, and several jobs. In 1964, she was invited to join an expedition to the Indian Ocean sponsored by the National Science Foundation, which led to invitations to join several other expeditions. In one way, she was fortunate that her research on algae spanned several years because she was able to make comparisons on changes in the habitat over time, something many doctoral students do not have the opportunity to do. The year 1966 was a significant one: she received her doctorate, she and her husband divorced, she became resident director of the Cape Haze Marine Laboratory, and she married Giles Mead.

The couple moved to Cambridge, Massachusetts, where she obtained a position as a research fellow at Harvard University. In 1970, the couple moved to Los Angeles where Giles was appointed director of the Natural History Museum of Los Angeles County; Sylvia also received an appointment there. The same year she was appointed team leader of the group of women oceanographers who lived underwater for two weeks in Tektite II. The purpose was not only to observe the marine environment but also to determine the effects of isolation on aquanauts. NASA used the data in planning future space flights when people would orbit for several weeks or months. The reason the crew was composed only of females was that the sponsors could not accept men and women scientists' living together underwater. Although there were 16 tests involving all-male teams, the women's test received the most publicity. As team leader, Earle received invitations to give speeches to various groups, and these provided opportunities to talk about preserving the environment. She also published articles for the general public in *Oceans, Harper's,* and *National Geographic.* At this time, she also participated in local social life as the wife of the museum director, conducted her research, oversaw a household of six children (three her husband's, two hers, and one theirs). The marriage began to fall apart, and the couple divorced in 1975.

Earle started setting diving records in 1979 when she dived to 1,250 feet, a very dangerous depth. She was using a Jim Suit, named for Jim Jarratt who had tested it. This futuristic suit of plastic and metal armor was secured to a manned submarine in the Pacific close to Oahu. When the submarine reached the prescribed depth, the operators released Earle from the sub on a 18-foot tether. She roamed the ocean floor for two and a half hours, taking notes, until the sub pulled her to the surface via the tether. In 1982, she formed a company, Deep Ocean Engineering, with Graham Hawkes, the engineer who had designed the Jim Suit, to design and manufacture easy-to-use submersibles capable of exploring the midwaters of the ocean to a depth of about 6,000 feet. One of their first designs was Deep Rover, a one-person submersible about the size of a Volkswagen "beetle," a very maneuverable, relatively inexpensive vehicle. Deep Rover was completed in 1984, and Earle was one of the first three individuals to test it at the 3,000-foot depth. She and Graham Hawkes married in 1986.

Among her long-term research projects was a study of humpback whales living in Alaskan and Hawaiian coastal waters. Between 1976 and 1980, she worked with Roger and Katherine Payne, who record humpback songs. Sylvia was the one who swam with the whales—but it is still a mystery how the whales sing. She took a leave from Deep Ocean Engineering to serve as chief scientist for NOAA. She is still involved in the operation of the company although she and Hawkes divorced.

In Joyce Tietz's book *What's a Nice Girl Like You . . . ,* Earle is quoted as stating that she does not regard herself as adventurous. She just goes anywhere that is required for her to perform the work she wants to do. The desire to be first is also not a motivation. She is not competitive except that she is always attempting to surpass herself, to excel beyond her own standard of excellence.

She is the author of many scientific papers as well as articles for the general public. She wrote the books *Exploring the Deep Frontier* (1980) and *Sea Change* (1995). She is a corporate member of the Woods Hole Oceanographic Institution and has received all manner of awards, including being the first woman to receive the Lowell Thomas Award of the Explorers' Club (1980). She is a fellow of the American Association for the Advancement of Science and of the Explorers' Club. She is a member of the International Phycological Society, Phycological Society of America, American Society of Ichthyologists and Herpetologists, American Institute of Biological Sciences, and Ecological Society of America. One of the more extensive discussions of her research is in the *New Yorker* (July 3, 1989). There are many photographs in *Current Biography* (1992), *Scientific American* (April 1992), *Notable Twentieth-Century Scientists,* and *Geographical Magazine* (February 1997). A video of her work entitled "Oceanography" aired in the *Discovering Great Minds of Science* series of the Public Broadcasting System in 1996. She is listed as "Sylvia Mead" in some sources.

***Bibliography:*** *American Men and Women of Science* 11–13; *Current Biography* 1992 and 1972; Herzenberg, C., *Women Scientists from Antiquity to the Present;* Ireland, N., *Index to Women of the World . . . Suppl.; Notable Twentieth-Century Scientists;* Rossiter, M., *Women Scientists in America;* Teitz, J., *What's a Nice Girl Like You . . . ; Who's Who in America,* 51st ed., 1997.

# *Edwards, Cecile Hoover*

(1926– )

***nutritionist, biochemist***

***Education:*** B.S., Tuskegee Institute, 1946, M.S., 1947; Ph.D. in nutrition, Iowa State University, 1950; diplomate in human nutrition, American Board of Nutrition, 1963

***Professional Experience:*** Research associate in nutrition, Iowa State University, 1949–1950; assistant professor and research associate in foods and nutrition, Tuskegee Institute, 1950–1956, head of Department of Foods and Nutrition, 1952–1956; professor of nutrition, North Carolina A&T State University, 1956–1971, chair of Department of Home Economics, 1968–1971; chair of Department of Home Economics, Howard University, 1971–1974, dean of School of Human Ecology, 1974–1986, professor of nutrition, 1971–

***Concurrent Positions:*** Dean, School of Continuing Education, Howard University, 1986–1987; collaborator, Bureau of Human Nutrition and Home Economics, Agricultural Research Service, U.S. Department of Agriculture, 1952–1955; adjunct professor, University of North Carolina, Chapel Hill, 1971; project director, National Institute of Child Health and Human Development, 1985–1989

***Married:*** Gerald Alonzo, 1951

***Children:*** 3

C***ecile Edwards*** is a nutrition researcher and educator who has devoted her career to improving the nutrition and well-being of disadvantaged people. She enrolled in Tuskegee Institute at the age of 15 with a major in home economics and minors in nutrition and chemistry. She knew she was not interested in dietetics but in improving nutrition through research. After receiving a master's degree in chemistry from Tuskegee, she received her doctorate in nutrition from Iowa State. Her research project was on methionine, an essential amino acid. She returned to Tuskegee as a faculty member and research associate and was appointed head of the Department of Foods and Nutrition in 1952. She later expanded her research to the amino acid composition of food, the utilization of protein from vegetarian diets, and the planning of well-balanced and nutritious diets, especially for low-income and disadvantaged people both in the United States and abroad.

She accepted a position at Howard University in 1971 as chair of the Department of Home Economics but was assigned the task of designing a new curriculum for the School of Human Ecology. In 1969, Arthur Jensen had advanced the theory in a scientific paper that blacks were inherently inferior and that providing education, nutrition, and other resources could not bring them into equality. Edwards's major goal was to disprove the Jensen hypothesis. The School of Human Ecology conducted research and evaluated work that provided resources for low-income people so they could help themselves and taught parenting, child care, nutrition, budgeting, job skills, and other skills useful in overcoming obstacles. These new curricula reflect a trend in the 1970s in many home economics departments in universities; indeed, many were dropping the words "home economics" and replacing them with terms that better reflected the biochemical nature of their nutrition research and the general scientific basis for their curricula.

Starting in 1985, she directed a five-year project sponsored by the National Institute of Child Health and Human Development to study the nutritional, medical, psychological, socioeconomic, and lifestyle factors that influence pregnancy outcomes for low-income women. She served as editor of the May 1994 issue of *Journal of Nutrition* entitled *African American Women and Their Pregnancies.*

Edwards has served on numerous commissions and committees involving human health and nutrition. She is a member of the American Institute of Nutrition, American Home Economics Association, Society for Nutrition Education, and American Dietetic Association. Her research centers on studies of amino acids. Her photograph is included in *Notable Twentieth-Century Scientists.*

***Bibliography:*** *American Men and Women of Science* 11–19; *Blacks in Science and Medicine;* Herzenberg, C., *Women Scientists from Antiquity to the Present; Notable Twentieth-Century Scientists; World Who's Who in Science.*

# *Edwards, Helen Thom*
(1936– )
## *accelerator physicist*

***Education:*** B.A., Cornell University, 1957, M.A., 1963, Ph.D. in physics, 1966

***Professional Experience:*** Research associate, Laboratory for Nuclear Studies, Cornell University, 1958–1970; research, Fermi National Accelerator Laboratory, 1970–1987, head, Accelerator Division, 1987–1989; head and associate director, Superconducting Division, Superconducting Supercollider Laboratory, 1989–1992; guest scientist, Fermi National Accelerator Laboratory, 1992–

***Concurrent Position:*** MacArthur fellow, 1988

***Helen Edwards*** is known internationally as an accelerator physicist who supervises the design and building of accelerators. She has been responsible for two of the largest in the United States: the Tevatron at Fermi Laboratory and the Superconducting Supercollider in Texas. Unfortunately, the latter project has never been completed because Congress refused to provide further funding in 1992. The significance of her work is that she provides the instrumentation to enable other scientists to gather data on the nature of subatomic particles. She was elected to membership in the National Academy of Engineering in 1988.

In elementary and high school, she liked nature, biology, and the natural sciences; she also enjoyed mechanical tasks so she could see how things were put together and how they worked. When she was ready for college, she applied to the top engineering schools, and her parents steered her to Cor-

nell because it had a few more women students than some of the other schools. She did experience some gender bias at Cornell, though, from instructors who thought it was a waste of time to educate women in the sciences. Most faculty members were very supportive of her work, however.

She decided to stay at Cornell for her graduate degree because the school already had an international reputation for pioneering work in the construction of particle accelerators. She was appointed a research associate in the Laboratory for Nuclear Studies where she was primarily responsible for commissioning (or ensuring that it was in operating order) the 12-GeV electron synchrotron. A synchrotron, which also is called an atom smasher or particle accelerator, is an electrostatic or electromagnetic device that produces high-energy particles and focuses them on a target. The GeV is a unit of measurement for the energy level of accelerated particles equivalent to a billion electron volts. In 1970, Edwards was invited to join the research team at the Fermi Laboratory where she was instrumental in commissioning the 400-GeV main accelerator and commissioning auxiliary equipment. In 1987, she was one of the supervisors assigned to oversee the completion of the world's highest energy superconducting particle accelerator, called the Tevatron. This accelerator can produce an energy level of 1 TeV, the equivalent of 1,000 GeV, as it collides protons and antiprotons moving in opposite directions.

The construction of a particle accelerator is a complicated and complex operation requiring the effort of hundreds of people. Edwards's role was that of group leader, one of the chief designers, and overall project coordinator for the Tevatron. She received the U.S. Department of Energy's Ernest O. Lawrence Award in 1986 for her work on this project, and in 1988, she was awarded a MacArthur fellowship. All of the other recipients of these two awards in those years were men. In 1989, she was a corecipient of the President's National Medal of Technology and was further honored by being selected to be head and associate director of the Superconducting Division of the Superconducting Supercollider (SSC) Laboratory from 1989 to 1992. The SSC was designed to produce collisions at 40 TeV, or 40 trillion electron volts. Currently, she is continuing her research at the Fermi National Accelerator Laboratory.

She is quoted in *Notable Women in the Physical Sciences* as saying that although she has the technical knowledge for these projects, the important part of what she does is getting people to work together and to coordinate their efforts with one another. The power of teamwork cannot be overlooked. When asked if she would choose the same career path, she says she would. However, she thinks it is harder and harder today to conduct new research because so many bureaucratic obstacles and high costs get in the way.

She is a member of the American Physical Society. Her photograph is included in *Notable Twentieth-Century Scientists* and *Notable Women in the Physical Sciences.*

***Bibliography:*** *American Men and Women of Science* 17–19; *Notable Twentieth-Century Scientists; Notable Women in the Physical Sciences.*

# *Ehrlich, Anne (Howland)*
(1933– )
## *environmental scientist, author*

***Education:*** Student, University of Kansas, 1952–1955; honorary degree: LL.D, Bethany College, 1990
***Professional Experience:*** Technician, Department of Entomology, University of Kansas, 1955; research assistant and biological illustrator, Department of Biological Sciences, Stanford University, 1959–1972, research associate, 1972–1975, senior research associate, 1975– ; associate director, Center for Conservation Biology, Stanford University, 1987– ; board of directors, Center for Innovative Diplomacy, Pacific Institute, Rocky Mountain Biological Laboratory
***Married:*** Paul R. Ehrlich, 1954
***Children:*** 1

***Anne Ehrlich*** is known as an author who has had a great impact on the current debates about the future of population and the earth. She has been author, coauthor, or contributor to more than 25 books on topics such as population growth, food resources, extinction of species, and human ecology. She met her husband while she was at the University of Kansas, and after their marriage, the couple moved to Stanford University where Paul completed his doctorate. Anne started working as a research assistant for the Department of Biological Sciences in 1959, was promoted to research associate in 1972, and became a senior research associate in 1975. In 1987, she was appointed the associate director of the Center for Conservation Biology.

Her writings are characterized by extensive research and clear prose. She is especially forceful in presenting the negative aspects of a topic. For example, *The Golden Door: International Migration, Mexico, and the United States* (1979) brings a wealth of detail about the issues related to international migration that we still face today. One reviewer called it an excitingly scary book. Another reviewer called *Extinction: The Causes and Consequences of the Disappearance of Species* (1982) a readable volume that provides a compendium of facts, events, and theories of evolution, biology, environmental history, and ecology. One of the couple's most recent books is *Betrayal of Science & Reason: How Anti-Environmental Rhetoric Threatens Our Future* (1996) in which they argue that although some improvements have been made, most environmental problems have not been solved but are rapidly getting worse. They discuss overpopulation, global warning, and natural resource limits.

The Ehrlichs are not without their critics, whom the couple calls leaders of "the brownlash." One topic on which the Ehrlichs receive much criticism is that of population forecasts. For example, in 1968, when they published *The Population Bomb,* there were 3.5 billion human beings. The Ehrlichs warned that the planet could not support that number of people and predicted that in the 1970s, the world would undergo famines—hundreds of millions of people would starve to death. That did not happen. Instead, food production soared worldwide, prices dropped, and growers experienced a surplus.

As a sequel to the earlier book, they published *The Population Explosion* in 1990. In that book, with the population then at 5.3 billion, they stated that the world has hundreds of billions fewer tons of topsoil and hundreds of trillions fewer gallons of groundwater with which to grow food crops than in 1968. The excess numbers of people have overloaded both the environment and human communities, and the result will be global warming, acid rain, a larger hole in the ozone layer, crime, viral epidemics, and homelessness, to name but a few of the problems that will increase. They forecast a billion or more deaths from starvation and disease and dissolution of society as we now know it. All of these are topics on which it is difficult to find consensus.

Anne Ehrlich has received several awards for her work, including being named to the Global 500 Roll of Honour for Environmental Achievement of the United Nations (1989). She is an honorary fellow of the California Academy of Science and a member of the American Humanist Association.

***Bibliography:*** *American Men and Women of Science* 15–19; *Contemporary Authors* v. 61–64 and CAN-8; *Who's Who in America*, 51st ed., 1997; *Who's Who in Science & Engineering*, 3d ed., 1996–1997.

# *Elders, (Minnie) Joycelyn (Jones)*
(1933– )
## *endocrinologist, pediatrician*

***Education:*** B.A., Philander Smith College, 1952; certified physical therapist, Brooks Army Medical School, 1954; M.D., University of Arkansas, 1960; diplomate, American Board of Pediatrics, 1964; M.S., in biochemistry, University of Arkansas Medical School, 1967; honorary degrees: several
***Professional Experience:*** Intern in pediatrics, University of Minnesota Hospital, 1960–1961; resident, Medical Center, University of Arkansas, 1961–1964, instructor, 1964–1967, assistant professor, 1967–1971, associate professor, 1971–1974, professor of pediatrics, 1976–1987; director of Arkansas Department of Health, 1987–1993; surgeon general, U.S. Public Health Service, 1993–1994; professor of pediatrics, Medical Center, University of Arkansas, 1994–
***Concurrent Positions:*** National Institute of Child Health and Human Development research fellow, 1964–1967, career development award from the National Institute of Child Health and Human Development, 1967
***Married:*** Oliver B. Elders, 1960
***Children:*** 2

***Joycelyn Elders*** was the second woman and the first African American to be appointed to the post of Surgeon General of the United States, succeeding the first woman to hold the post, Antonia Novello. Elders has had a remarkable life. She was a sharecropper's daughter in rural Arkansas who worked with her family in the fields before she worked as a maid to pay her way through undergraduate school. Although she became a physician, she had never seen a doctor until her first year of college—she had planned to become a laboratory technician until that meeting. She enlisted in the U.S. Army as a first lieutenant to receive her certification as a physical therapist and then used the GI Bill to enter medical school, where she was the only woman in her class. Although this was the time of the civil rights movement, she was so busy with her schooling that she did not take part in it. Her medical specialty is endocrinology, which is the branch of biology dealing with the endocrine glands and their secretions; this includes the thyroid, the adrenal, and the pituitary.

After completing her residency, she rose rapidly through the ranks on the pediatrics faculty of the University of Arkansas Medical Center. In 1987, then Arkansas governor Bill Clinton appointed her director of the Arkansas Department of Health. In this position she established school-based health clinics to combat the state's teen pregnancy rate, which was the second highest in the nation. President Clinton appointed her surgeon general in 1993. Her responsibilities were primarily to disseminate information about widespread health problems such as smoking-related illnesses and sexually transmitted diseases. She also managed the commissioned corps, a uniformed service whose members are assigned to medical trouble spots as needed. As surgeon general she held the rank of a three-star admiral, which is the reason she wore a uniform when she appeared in public. She had other responsibilities for the Public Health Service's offices of population affairs, minority health, and women's health and the President's Council on Physical Fitness and Sports.

At the time that she was nominated, there were delays in the confirmation hearings because she advocated controversial measures such as widespread condom distribution, sex education, abortion rights, imposing higher excise taxes on alcohol as well as on tobacco, and the medical use of marijuana. She continued to be outspoken during the 15 months she was in office. After she was fired by President Clinton in 1994, she returned to Arkansas where she again became a professor of pediatrics at the University of Arkansas Medical Center. In a brief autobiography published in the book *Journeys of Women in Science and Engineering,* she says it did not worry her that she was fired as surgeon general because presidents have fired many people over the years.

She is a member of the Society for Pediatric Research, Endocrinology Society, and American Federation for Clinical Research. Her autobiography is *Joycelyn Elders, M.D.: From Sharecropper's Daughter to Surgeon General of the United States of America* (1996). Although she has faced her share of prejudice and discrimination, she does not dwell on them in this book. She focuses instead on the transformation of a poor black girl into a medical scientist. There are also photographs in *Current Biography* (1994), *Scientific American* (November 1993), and *Ebony* (February 1997). Her listing in some sources is "M. Joycelyn Elders" or "Minnie Joycelyn Elders."

***Bibliography:*** *American Men & Women of Science* 12–19; *Current Biography 1994; Journeys of Women in Science and Engineering; Who's Who of American Women,* 19th ed., 1995–1996.

# *Elmegreen, Debra Meloy*
(1952– )
***astronomer***

***Education:*** B.A., Princeton University, 1975; M.A., Harvard University, 1977, Ph.D. in astronomy, 1979

***Professional Experience:*** Research assistant, Thermophysics Division, Goddard Space Flight Center, 1969, Laboratory of Cosmic Ray Physics, Naval Research Laboratory, 1971–1972, Spectros Division, National Bureau of Standards, 1973, Kitt Peak National Observatory, 1974, Arecibo Observatory, 1975; teaching fellow, Harvard University, 1977; Carnegie fellow, Mt. Wilson and Las Campanas Observatory, 1979–1981; visiting astronomer, Royal Greenwich Observatory and Institute of Astronomy, Cambridge University, 1981; visiting scientist, T. J. Watson Research Center, IBM Corporation, 1982–1988; assistant professor of astronomy, Vassar College, 1985–1989, associate professor, 1990– , department chair, 1993–

***Concurrent Positions:*** Chair, Committee on Status of Women in Astronomy, American Astronomical Society; director, New York State Science Talent Search

***Married:*** Bruce Elmegreen, 1976

***Children:*** 2

**Debra Elmegreen** is known for her research on galaxies. After receiving her doctorate from Harvard University, she had a series of short appointments at several observatories and was a visiting scientist at IBM. Such a record of research often is just a reflection of the competition for employment in the field of astronomy as astronomy and related fields receive small amounts of funding compared to the number of qualified people who are searching for positions. She received an appointment as assistant professor of astronomy at Vassar College in 1985, advanced to associate professor in 1990 and department chair in 1993. Vassar College is considered to have a unique position in American astronomy as the first American woman astronomer, Maria Mitchell (1818–1889), served as the first director when the college's observatory was built in the 1860s.

Debra Elmegreen's research on spiral galaxies has resulted in a new method for classifying these galaxies. The primary feature of spiral galaxies is the waves that shape the spiral, waves that arise from the gravitational pulls within the galaxy. The earth is part of a spiral galaxy, and researchers estimate that spiral galaxies represent about one-third of the estimated 100 billion galaxies in the observable universe. Research indicates that spirals show three distinct regions: a central bulge, a nearly spherical halo, and a flattened disk. The central bulge usually spans a few thousand light-years, is basically round, and contains old, reddish, and low-mass stars. The halo of a spiral surrounds the disk and contains old stars similar to those in the bulge. Inside the halo, the disk contains most of the galaxy's stars and gives the galaxy its characteristic spiral bulge.

The earth's galaxy, typical of large spirals, contains about 200 billion stars spread mostly through its disk, which is 100,000 light-years across and about 3,000 light-years thick. A gas, usually hydrogen gas, floats among the stars in the disk. Some of the gas forms clouds, with the largest clouds being concentrated in or near the spiral arms. In conjunction with her husband, she has proposed a classification scheme based on the size of the spiral arms, since all spirals have the same components. Because most galaxies seem to be tilted to our line of sight, the researchers use computer imaging to make the arms seem round and to enhance the contrast against the disk.

Debra Elmegreen is a member of the American Astronomical Society, Royal Astronomical Society, and International Astronomical Union. Her research centers on optical and millimeter observations of external galaxies to study sites of star formation and the origins of spiral structure.

***Bibliography:*** *American Men and Women of Science* 15–19.

# *Estes, Clarissa Pinkola*

(1943– )

***psychologist***

***Education:*** B.A., Loretto Heights College, 1976; Ph.D. in psychology, Union Institute, Cincinnati, Ohio, 1981; diploma in analytical psychology, Inter-Regional Society of Jungian Analysts, Zurich, 1984

***Professional Experience:*** Psychoanalyst in private practice, Denver, 1971– ; developer and teacher of Writing as Liberation of the Spirit program in state and federal prisons in the United States, 1971– ; cocoordinator of Women in Transition Safe House, Denver, 1973–1975; executive director, C. G. Jung Center for Education and Research; cofounder and codirector of Colorado Authors for Gay and Lesbian Equal Rights; founder, Guadeloupe Foundation

***Children:*** 3

**Clarissa Estes** is a certified Jungian analyst who wrote the best-selling book *Women Who Run with Wolves: Myths and Stories of the Wild Woman Archetype* (1992). She received her certification after studying at the Jung Institute in Zurich, Switzerland. Jung's theory is that every person possesses a collective unconscious and archetypes—archetypes are defined as collectively inherited unconscious ideas, patterns of thought, images, etc., that are universally present in individual psyches. Estes explains these archetypes by including in her book the myths she learned from her Mexican and Hungarian relatives.

Her parents were Mexicans of Spanish and Indian descent, but she was adopted as a young child by a couple who had immigrated to the United States from Hungary. She was reared in a community in southern Michigan surrounded by farms, woods, orchards, and the Great Lakes. The community was diverse with people from Eastern Europe, Mexico, and Puerto Rico plus African Americans. In her thirties, she found her original family, but she had no difficulty in bridging the gap between the two families and the two cultures. In fact, she found she could understand herself better after meeting her Mexican family.

While in her twenties, she moved to the Denver area where she received an undergraduate degree in psychotherapeutics. In 1976, she received a doctorate in ethnoclinical psychology, which is a study of both clinical psychology and ethnology, the latter emphasizing the study of the psychology of groups, particularly tribes. She entered private practice in Denver, developed a writing program to be used in state and federal prisons, and served as executive director of the C. G. Jung Center in Denver for a time.

In her private practice, she found there was nothing in formal psychology to help her female patients. She felt that traditional psychology is often silent about deeper issues that are important to women—the intuitive, a woman's way, a woman's knowing, her creative fire. She thought that folklore and fairy tales could address some of these issues and started writing down the myths and tales she had heard from family, friends, and strangers from all types of backgrounds to use in her practice. These myths brought out the information that she wanted to impart to her patients. She recorded the myths on audiocassettes and began to sell them locally. She tried without success to interest the Jung Center in publishing them, but a publisher's representative heard about them and contacted her about handling the book.

Her book hit the market at the right time, as Bill Moyers had just produced his acclaimed television series on myths by Joseph Campbell. Estes views stories as medicine to stimulate the imagination and strengthen various aspects of the psyche. In the book she says the woman who is able to rely on gut feeling to make choices can be compared to a wolf. "Wolves are deeply intuitive, intensely concerned with their young, their mates, and their pack. They are experienced at adapting to constantly changing circumstances, they are fiercely stalwart and very brave" (quotation in *Contemporary Authors*). She says she received letters from men as well as women praising the book; the men say the book helps them understand the women in their lives—mothers, wives, daughters, friends, and lovers.

She has written two additional books of folklore and myths: *The Faithful Gardener: A Wise Tale about That Which Can Never Die* (1995) and *The Gift of Story* (1994). Her books cannot be considered New Age, nor are they accepted by feminists. They seem to be in a category of their own. Her photograph is included in *Notable Hispanic American Women* and *Newsweek* (December 21, 1992).

***Bibliography:*** *Contemporary Authors* v. 143; *Notable Hispanic American Women; Who's Who in America,* 51st ed., 1997.

# *Estrin, Thelma A.*
## (1924– )
### *computer scientist, biomedical engineer, electrical engineer*

***Education:*** B.S., University of Wisconsin, 1948, M.S., 1949, Ph.D. in electrical engineering, 1951

***Professional Experience:*** Researcher, Neurological Institute, Columbia Presbyterian Hospital, New York City, ca. early 1950s; researcher, Weizmann Institute of Science, Israel, 1953–1955; research engineer, Health Science Center, University of California, Los Angeles (UCLA), 1960–1970, director, Data Processing Laboratory, Brain Research Institute, 1970–1980; director, Division of Electronic Computer and Systems Engineering, National Science Foundation, 1982–1984; professor of engineering, Computer Science Department, University of California, Los Angeles, 1980–1991, assistant dean, School of Engineering and Applied Science, 1984–1991, director, Department of Engineering and Science Extension, 1984–1991, emeritus professor of computer science, 1991–

***Concurrent Positions:*** Fulbright fellow, Weizmann Institute of Science, Rehovot, Israel, 1963; principal investigator, U.S. Public Health Service grant, Data Processing Laboratory, Brain Research Institute, University of California, Los Angeles, 1970–1980, adjunct professor of anatomy and computer science, 1978–1980

***Married:*** Gerald Estrin, 1941

***Children:*** 3

***Thelma Estrin*** is renowned for her research in the application of computer technology to neurophysiological research. The ideas she has developed have been applied by medical researchers to create internal brain maps of patients based on external imaging prior to survey and for identifying the epileptic foci in the brain. She was the first woman to be certified as a clinical engineer. She participated in designing and building the first computer in the Middle East at the Weizmann Institute of Science in Israel from 1953 through 1955, and she was one of the team leaders who designed and established the first general-purpose computer for brain research at the University of California, Los Angeles (UCLA), in 1961.

She and her husband were history majors during World War II when they were recruited for the war effort. Her husband enlisted in the army and was sent to the Signal Corps. After an intensive engineering assistant course at the Stevens Institute of Technology, Thelma was placed at a tool and model shop called Radio Receptor Company. After the war, both enrolled at the University of Wisconsin where they obtained their bachelor's, master's, and doctoral degrees in electrical engineering.

Gerald was invited to join computer pioneer John Van Neumann's team at Princeton University to design and build the first digital electronic computing machine, but neither universities nor corporations were interested in hiring women as engineers in the 1950s. One reason was there was a large pool of male engineers who had been released from military service plus newly graduated engineers who had received their education via the GI Bill. Another reason was the general view that women's interest in engineering and science was merely transitory and should not be taken seriously. Through personal contacts, Thelma obtained a research position in the Electroencephalography (EEG) Department of the Neurological Institute at Columbia Presbyterian Hospital in New York, which met her goal of using her training and creativity humanely by choosing to do research on the electrical activity of the brain.

Although she commuted to her job in New York City four hours daily, she was involved to some extent in Von Neumann's work at Princeton. However, through an oversight, she was not credited for her contributions. Her name is listed in the index to Herman Goldstine's book *The Computer from*

*Pascal to Von Neumann* (1972), but she is not mentioned on the page indicated. Gerald Estrin is specifically credited with writing the first engineering type of diagnostic code for the computer.

In 1953, Israeli scientists invited Gerald to build a version of the digital computer for the Weizmann Institute of Science, and Thelma participated in building the first computer in the Middle East. Meanwhile the Princeton project had been completed, so the couple returned to Los Angeles where Gerald had received a professorship in engineering at UCLA. Since nepotism rules excluded Thelma from an appointment in the Engineering School, she became associated with the Medical School. With a collaborator, she designed and established for the Brain Research Institute the first general-purpose computer facility for brain research, called the Data Processing Laboratory, in 1961. It was the first integrated computer laboratory expressly designed and established to develop computer technology for nervous system research. The laboratory was supported by National Institutes of Health grants starting in 1962 and made pioneering contributions in the following areas: analog to digital conversion, data acquisition and processing, signal analysis, interactive graphics, modeling and simulation, distributed processing systems, and laboratory computer systems. In 1970, Thelma was appointed director of the laboratory and principal investigator.

She is also credited with several of the innovations that were developed in the laboratory. In 1961, she introduced digital techniques for recording the impulse firing pattern of neurons, and while on a second Fulbright year in Israel in 1963, she worked on automated pattern recognition techniques to use in identifying EEG patterns preceding brain seizures and in finding ways of using feedback to avert such seizures. Between 1965 and 1970, she designed an on-line analog-to-digital system, and during the 1970s, she studied the novel uses of interactive graphics as a brain research tool.

When nepotism rules were lifted, she joined the Computer Science Department in UCLA's School of Engineering and Applied Science in 1980 as a full professor. One of her graduate students in the 1980s developed an expert system for microcomputers; this is a version of the concept of artificial intelligence (AI). AI is defined as the capacity of a computer to perform operations analogous to learning and decision making in humans, by using an expert system, a program for Computer-Aided Design (CAD) or Computer-Aided Manufacturing (CAM), or a program for the perception and recognition of shapes in computer vision systems.

Also during the 1980s she was appointed assistant dean of the School of Engineering and Applied Science and director of the Department of Engineering Science Extension. She retired as emeritus professor of computer science in 1991, but she remains very active in promoting the role of women in science and engineering. In a brief autobiography in *Journeys of Women in Science and Engineering,* she says that in the 1980s, her focus shifted to women's careers in engineering both at UCLA and on the national level while working with the Institute for Electrical and Electronics Engineers (IEEE). She says women engineers have the skills to be managers but that young women today need a great deal of energy to manage a career. She advises that if a woman decides on an engineering career and wants to marry, she should select a supportive partner who believes in her having a technical career. Two of the Estrin daughters are computer engineers, and the third is a physician.

One of Thelma's papers is included in the fall 1996 issue of *IEEE Annals of the History of Computing* in a section on the role of women in computing; in this paper, "Women's Studies and Computer Science: Their Intersection," she points out that both fields emerged as academic disciplines in the 1960s. However, they evolved along very different paths. She looks at the differences among science, engineering, and the humanities and suggests that feminist epistemology could introduce new ideas for gaining knowledge that will also make computer science more relevant for minority and low-income students.

Among her awards is the 1981 Society of Women Engineers Achievement Award for her work in biomedical engineering. She is a fellow of the Institute of Electrical and Electronics Engineers, the Institute for the Advancement of Engineers, and the American Association for the Advancement of Science. She is a member of Alliance for Engineering in Medicine and Biology, Biomedical Engineering Society, Association for Computing Machinery, and Society of Women Engineers. Her research involves the application of technology and computers to health care delivery, computer methods in the neurosciences, electrical activity of the nervous system, and engineering education. Her photograph is included in *Journeys of Women in Science and Engineering.*

***Bibliography:*** *American Men and Women of Science* 14–19; Herzenberg, C., *Women Scientists from Antiquity to the Present; Journeys of Women in Science and Engineering; Notable Twentieth-Century Scientists;* O'Neill, L., *The Women's Book of World Records and Achievements;* Rossiter, M., *Women Scientists in America;* Stanley, A., *Mothers and Daughters of Invention; Who's Who in Engineering,* 9th ed., 1995; *Who's Who in Technology Today* v. 6.

# *Eyer, Diane Elizabeth*
## (1944– )
## ***psychologist***

***Education:*** B.A., Bucknell University, 1966; Ph.D. in psychology, University of Pennsylvania, 1988

***Professional Experience:*** Poetry therapist, Institute of Pennsylvania Hospital, 1971–1973; counselor, Philadelphia Institute for Gestalt Therapy, 1971–1975; assistant therapist in private practice, ca. 1970s; teaching assistant, University of Pennsylvania, 1983–1985, research assistant, 1984–1987; instructor, Rutgers University, 1985–1989; instructor, Temple University, 1986–1987; lecturer, University of Pennsylvania, 1991–

***Married:*** Jack W. Eyer, 1991

***Diane Eyer*** is a psychologist who examines the reasons that people utilize to explain what they do. Often the reasons are very complicated and sometimes conflict with the "actual" reasons. As she explains in an interview in *Contemporary Authors,* in graduate school she became fascinated with the question of what psychologists thought was normal or healthy, which led her to look at the frequent fads in child-rearing that were based on such psychological concepts. She concentrated on one psychological construct, mother-infant bonding, to see how science interacted with social forces to create this fad. The result was her book *Mother-Infant Bonding: A Scientific Fiction* (1992). Her second book on this theme is *Motherguilt: How Our Culture Blames Mothers for What's Wrong with Society* (1996). In addition, she has contributed to several other books concerning motherhood and has published articles in popular magazines such as *Esquire, Glamour,* and the *Wall Street Journal* and has worked as a reporter and feature writer for the *Bethlehem Globe-Times.* She has produced, narrated, and edited documentary and educational films and has worked as an editorial consultant on many publications.

In her book *Motherguilt,* she discusses the scientific explanations that are given for beliefs about maternal instinct and the ideology of motherhood. She theorizes that the pseudoscientific concept of "maternal bond" is one method of curbing the interest of mothers in such things as employment for wages outside the home and argues that this concept deflects attention from the public support of families. The real need, in her opinion, is to provide substantial tax cuts, paid parental leave, and regulated, subsidized day care instead of blaming women for having unnatural feelings.

After receiving her undergraduate degree, Eyer worked as an assistant therapist in private practice and as a poetry therapist in a hospital. It is a standard treatment to use the arts in therapy, whether music, painting, poetry, fiction, or some other art form. After working as a counselor, she entered the University of Pennsylvania where she received her doctorate in psychology. Meanwhile, she worked as an instructor at Rutgers University and Temple University and held teaching and research assistantships at the University of Pennsylvania.

Her research interests include the history of developmental psychology, child growth studies, women in abusive relationships, and the fallibility of attachment theories. She is a member of the National Women's Studies Association and Society for Research in Child Development.

***Bibliography:*** *Contemporary Authors* v. 143.

# *Faber, Sandra (Moore)*

(1944– )

***astronomer, cosmologist***

***Education:*** B.A., Swarthmore College, 1966; Ph.D. in astronomy, Harvard University, 1972; honorary degree: D.Sc., Swarthmore College, 1986

***Professional Experience:*** Assistant professor/assistant astronomer, Lick Observatory, University of California, Santa Cruz, 1972–1977, associate professor/associate astronomer, 1977–1979, professor/astronomer, 1979–

***Concurrent Positions:*** Alfred P. Sloan Foundation fellow, 1977– ; science advisory committee, National New Technology Telescope, 1983–1984; board of trustees, Carnegie Institution of Washington, 1985– ; chair, Keck Telescope Science Steering Committee, 1987–1990; member, Hubble Space Telescope Strategy Panel, 1990, Users Committee, 1990, Wide Field Camera Team, 1985–

***Married:*** Andrew L. Faber, 1967

***Children:*** 2

***Sandra Faber*** is known internationally for her research on the origin of the universe and of galaxies in particular, a special branch of astronomy called "cosmology." She has discovered correlations between galaxies' features—called scaling laws—that enable astronomers, having measured some features, to predict others. One of the more prominent, called "the Faber-Jackson law," is that larger elliptical galaxies have stars that are orbiting more rapidly than those in smaller ones. Another of her theories is that much of the matter in the universe is in the form of massive, invisible halos surrounding galaxies and that this cold, dark matter has played a determining role in the origin and development of galaxies and clusters of galaxies. Previously, the theory was that the universe was formed by hot, neutrino-based matter.

Faber and six associates formed a collaboration called the Seven Samurai in the 1980s. They found irregularities in the Hubble flow of galaxies and theorized that matter in the universe is clumped into immense concentrations that perturb the smooth expansion of the universe by their gravitational attraction. She says that galaxies can properly be described as the building blocks of the universe. She was involved in the design of the Hubble Space Telescope and in correcting the lens after it was launched into space. She was elected to membership in the National Academy of Sciences in 1985.

She developed an interest in science early in her childhood through looking at specimens in a microscope, observing the stars through a telescope, and reading books. She majored in physics and minored in mathematics and astronomy at Swarthmore College, then entered graduate school in astrophysics at Harvard. She said that when she used the Swarthmore observatory, she was spellbound by the view through the telescope. The director of the observatory at Swarthmore at the time was Sarah Lippencott, who was her mentor. Faber said in an interview in the July 1990 issue of *Omni* that it was unfortunate that physics was at a transition phase in the 1960s when she was studying it, as the subject seemed a maze of unrelated and unsatisfactory theories. Later, after the physicists had sorted out the theories of particle physics, they used the tools that astronomers had developed to prove their theories and produce a new cosmology.

Faber elected to study for her doctorate at Harvard, although it was not the best choice for observational physics, to be near her husband who still was attending Swarthmore. Her first experience using the Harvard observatory was not promising; she fell off the observer's deck of the telescope the very first night. She and her husband moved to Washington, D.C., because of her husband's job at the Naval Research Laboratory, and she was able to use the computers at the Carnegie Institution's Department of Terrestrial Magnetism to compile data for her thesis—on punch cards, no less.

When she completed her doctorate, her husband had decided to study law, which proved to be a wise choice for the couple when they sought to find employment opportunities for both partners. He was accepted by Stanford Law School, and she obtained a position as assistant professor/assistant astronomer at the Lick Observatory at University of California, Santa Cruz. As the first female staff member in the history of the Lick Observatory, she did not feel any discrimination. Having a tenure-track position freed her from the usual problem young astronomers have in finding grants to support their research at various observatories, and the excellent facilities at Lick enabled her and Robert Jackson, a fellow graduate student, to develop the Faber-Jackson scaling law mentioned above. With the implementation of new detector technology, she was able to observe hot stars and interstellar gas in galaxies. She began to publish influential theoretical papers about the physical processes, such as that galaxies are surrounded by massive halos. The presence of this matter is betrayed by its effect on the motion of matter that can be seen. Further, this unseen matter has been responsible for the very formation of galaxies.

Her next major activity was the collaboration of the Seven Samurai and their identification of the Great Attractor, the nearest huge supercluster of galaxies. The gravitational attraction of the Great Attractor accelerates everything in an immense region of space. Other important work by the Seven Samurai was to estimate the distance of every galaxy. They made a map of all of the elliptical galaxies surrounding the Earth in space and discovered that large mass concentrations were causing irregularities in the Hubble flow.

Faber has also been involved in designing, securing funds for, and operating a number of significant astronomical instruments. She was one of the astronomers who started the project to build the 10-meter Keck Telescope at Mauna Kea, Hawaii, currently the largest optical telescope in the world. She was part of the team responsible for the Wide-Field Planetary Camera for the Hubble Space Telescope and helped diagnose the problem with the telescope's mirror and prepare a plan to fix it.

When she was interviewed for the January–February 1992 issue of *Mercury* about women in astronomy, she said that women astronomers are slowly gaining more acceptance. The number of women in graduate school in the field has grown significantly, and the increased presence of women in managerial positions in all fields is making it easier for women to gain administrative positions in astronomy also.

Faber has received numerous prizes, such as the Bart J. Bok Prize of Harvard University (1978) and the Heineman Prize of the American Astronomical Society (1986), and she has also received invitations to give guest lectures throughout the world. She is a member of the International Astronomical Union, American Astronomical Society, and American Academy of Arts and Sciences. Her research involves formation and evolution of normal galaxies, stellar populations in galaxies, galactic structure, stellar spectroscopy, cluster of galaxies, and cosmology. She has participated in several documentaries on Public Television stations, such as "Mysteries of Deep Space" (1997). Her photograph is included in *Mercury* (January–February 1992), *Omni* (July 1990), and *Physics Today* (March 1986).

***Bibliography:*** *American Men and Women of Science* 13–19; Herzenberg, C., *Women Scientists from Antiquity to the Present;* Ireland, N., *Index to Women of the World . . . Suppl.; Notable Twentieth-Century Scientists; Notable Women in the Physical Sciences; Who's Who in America,* 51st ed., 1997; *Who's Who in Science & Engineering,* 3d ed., 1996–1997.

# *Farquhar, Marilyn (Gist)*
(1928– )
## *cell biologist, experimental pathologist*

***Education:*** B.A., University of California, Berkeley, 1949, M.A. in experimental pathology, 1953, Ph.D. in experimental pathology, 1955

***Professional Experience:*** Junior research pathologist, University of California, 1953–1954; research assistant, Department of Anatomy, University of Minnesota Medical School, 1954–1955; assistant research pathologist, University of California, San Francisco, 1956–1958; research associate, Department of Cell Biology, Rockefeller University, 1958–1962; associate research pathologist, University of California, San Francisco, 1962–1964, associate professor of pathology, 1964–1968, professor in residence, 1968–1970; professor of cell biology, Rockefeller University, 1970–1973; professor of cell biology and pathology, Yale University School of Medicine, 1973–1987, Sterling Professor of Cell Biology and Pathology, 1987–1989; professor of pathology, Division of Cellular and Molecular Medicine, University of California, San Diego School of Medicine, 1990–

***Married:*** John Farquhar, 1951, divorced ca. 1968; George Palade, 1970

***Children:*** 2

***Marilyn Farquhar*** is renowned as a pioneer cell biologist who has advanced scientific knowledge of the mechanisms of renal disease and protein trafficking within cells. She was elected to membership in the National Academy of Sciences in 1984. She grew up in the Central Valley of California, which is a farmland area. She developed her interest in nature from her father, who often took her on horseback rides to the mountains. Her parents encouraged both of their daughters to receive a college education, and a family friend, a woman pediatrician, influenced Marilyn's interest in medicine and biology.

She majored in zoology as a premedical student, and she was one of three women in her medical school class at the University of California, San Francisco. After about two years in the program, she became fascinated with the nature of diseases and shifted to a program in experimental pathology instead of obtaining a medical degree. In 1951, she married another medical student and decided that switching to research would allow more flexibility in raising a family. During graduate school, she was fortunate to work with a professor who had the only electron microscope in the entire medical center. This availability allowed her to be involved in the very beginning of applications of electron microscopy in the new field of cell biology.

For her postdoctoral work, she and her husband moved to the University of Minnesota where she was involved in kidney research. In 1958, they went to Rockefeller University where she joined the laboratory of George Palade, the future Nobel Prize winner whose group had the most active and productive team working in cell biology in the country. She was fortunate that the places her husband chose for his career development were also ideal for her. During her graduate and postdoctoral research she was talented enough to make a number of discoveries in basic biomedical research, including the mechanisms of kidney disease, the organization of functions that attach cells to one another, and the mechanisms of secretions—that is, the mechanisms by which cells produce and release their products.

She returned in 1962 to the University at San Francisco as a faculty member, rising to the rank of full professor. She returned to Rockefeller University in 1970 as a professor of cell biology, the only woman professor at the institution. She and her husband had divorced earlier, and she married George Palade in 1970. The couple moved to Yale University School of Medicine in 1973 as full professors to start a new Department of Cell Biology, and they built one of the premier departments of this type in the country. In 1974, George received the Nobel Prize in Physiology and Medicine for his discovery of ribosomes, the cell organ that synthesizes proteins. In 1990, both were actively recruited to move to the University of California, San Diego, where they started and became codirectors of the new Division of Cellular and Molecular Medicine in the Medical School.

Farquhar and her husband both could be classified as workaholics, but they do also enjoy music, opera, and outdoor recreation. Marilyn is proud of the research contributions she has made in her field. As a woman who has achieved success, she is in a position to provide special encouragement as a role model for young women beginning their careers. The overriding driving force that has motivated her career has been the joy of discovery. She says that she has been fortunate to be living and working in a time when the opportunities for discovery and the growth in knowledge of biological sciences has been greater than at any other time in history.

She has received honors and awards, including the E. B. Wilson Medal of the American Society for Cell Biology (1987), the Homer Smith Award of the American Society of Nephrology (1988), the Distinguished Scientist Medal of the Electron Microscopy Society of America (1987), and the National Institutes of Health Merit Award (1988). She is a member of the American Academy of Arts and Sciences, American Society for Cell Biology (president, 1981–1982), American Association of Pathologists, American Association of Anatomists, American Society of Nephrology, Endocrine Society, and Histochemical Society. Her research includes intracellular membrane along the exocytic and endocytic, cellular and molecular bases of glomerular permeability and pathology, structure and function of Golgi complex and lysosomes, and the composition of glomerular basement membrane. Her photograph is included in *Notable Women in the Life Sciences.*

***Bibliography:*** *American Men and Women in Science* 11–19; Herzenberg, C., *Women Scientists from Antiquity to the Present; Notable Twentieth-Century Scientists; Notable Women in the Life Sciences; Who's Who in America,* 51st ed., 1997; *Who's Who of American Women,* 20th ed., 1997–1998; *World Who's Who in Science.*

# *Fausto-Sterling, Anne*
## (1944– )
## *embryologist*

***Education:*** B.A., University of Wisconsin, 1965; Ph.D. in developmental genetics, Brown University, 1970

***Professional Experience:*** Instructor in medical science, Brown University, 1971–1972, assistant professor, 1972–1977, associate professor, 1977–1986, professor of medical sciences in the Division of Biology and Medicine, 1986–

***Concurrent Position:*** Visiting professor, University of Amsterdam 1986

***Married:*** Nelson Fausto, 1966, divorced

***Anne Fausto-Sterling*** is noted for her research on biological theories about women. Embryology is the science dealing with the formation, development, structure, and functional activities of embryos; as a scientist, she has avoided linking gender with sexual determinism, which is the biologically and genetically inherited aptitude of each human being. She criticizes the myths that sex-related hormones control one's destiny as a man or a woman. Some of the cultural assumptions are that men are naturally more intelligent than women, females possess an inherently inferior ability to perceive spatial relations among objects or to understand the intricacies of mathematics than do their male counterparts, and hormonally induced mood fluctuations affect a woman's ability to function in society. Fausto-Sterling argues that the political goal

to relegate women to traditionally subordinate positions within society has influenced much of the study done in both biology and genetics. Much has been published to justify cultural biases that discriminate against women, which has been seen as a backlash against the feminist movement, feminism being defined as the doctrine advocating social, political, and all other rights of women equal to those of men.

In 1985, she published a summary of her research in the book *Myths of Gender: Biological Theories about Women and Men,* in which she raises doubts about how valid the scientific studies are that support the traditional view of the subordinate woman when the studies are based on social biases. She discusses each of the myths in turn, pointing out the underlying social biases. In each case, the conclusions do not meet basic scientific procedures as the myths are based on inadequate evidence, many alternative explanations, and circular reasoning. A second edition of the book was published in 1992 and includes some new material on brain research and on homosexuality.

The book has been criticized because it has a feminist bias. Fausto-Sterling is a feminist, and she, in turn, criticizes her critics for their poor scholarship. An example is her article "Attacking Feminism Is Not a Substitute for Good Scholarship" in the August 1995 issue of *Politics and the Life Sciences.* Her primary argument there is that the critics have read selectively instead of examining all of the material that is available on the topic.

She received her undergraduate degree from the University of Wisconsin in 1965, was married in 1966, and received her doctorate from Brown University in 1970. She immediately began teaching at Brown as an instructor and rose through the ranks to full professor. She was granted tenure at Brown for her work on *Drosophila,* the fruit fly. She found that research in molecular biology had become crowded and very competitive and switched to more basic research on the evolution and regeneration of freshwater flatworms called *Planaria.* These flatworms have five different modes of reproduction: three asexual and two sexual. In a brief autobiography in *Journeys of Women in Science and Engineering,* she encourages young people to look around and find the field and lifestyle that they find compatible: "Young people should see science as an enormously diverse set of worlds in which it's possible to find a comfortable place if one works hard enough and doesn't believe everything grown-ups say."

In addition to her scientific papers, Fausto-Sterling is editing a book series—Race, Gender, and Science—for Indiana University Press. She has received many honors, including a National Science Foundation grant (1971); Wellesley Center for Research on Women, Mellon fellowship (1980–1981) and travel fellowship (1984–1985); appointment as fellow, Pembroke Center for Research and Teaching on Women (1982); and a grant from Wayland Collegium (1983). She is a fellow of the American Association for the Advancement of Science and is a member of the Society for Developmental Biology and of the International Society for Developmental Biology. Her research interests are developmental biology; biological theories about women; and gender, race, and science. She is listed in editions 12 to 14 of *American Men and Women of Science* under "Sterling" but under "Fausto-Sterling" in later editions. Her photograph is in *Scientific American* (November 1993) and *Journeys of Women in Science and Engineering.*

***Bibliography:*** *American Men and Women of Science* 12–19; *Contemporary Authors* v. 137; *Journeys of Women in Science and Engineering.*

# Fedoroff, Nina Vsevolod
(1942– )
## molecular biologist

***Education:*** B.S., Syracuse University, 1966; Ph.D. in molecular biology, Rockefeller University, 1972

***Professional Experience:*** Assistant professor of biology, University of California, Los Angeles, 1972–1974, Damon Runyan-Walter Winchell Cancer Research Fund Fellow in molecular biology, School of Medicine, 1974–1975; National Institutes of Health fellow, Carnegie Institution of Washington, 1975–1977, research associate, 1977–1978, staff scientist, 1978–1994; director, Biotechnical Institute, Pennsylvania State University, 1995– ; Willamon Professor of Life Sciences, 1995–

***Concurrent Position:*** Professor, Department of Biology, Johns Hopkins University, 1979–1994

***Married:*** Joseph Hacker, 1959, divorced 1962; Patrick Gaganidze, 1966, divorced 1978; Michael Broyles, 1990

***Children:*** 2

*Nina Fedoroff* is renowned for her success in duplicating and analyzing genetically the transposable elements in maize (corn), first identified by the American geneticist Barbara McClintock (1902–1992). After meeting McClintock at a conference, Fedoroff became so intrigued with the idea of transposable elements that she changed the direction of her scientific research and began her study in earnest when she was appointed to a position at the Carnegie Institution in Washington, D.C. Fedoroff not only replicated McClintock's work, but she also discovered that the transposable elements were mobile in plants other than maize. Other molecular biologists quickly picked up the system of cloning from her work and used the maize transposable elements to mark and clone genes in other plants. She is the author of the book *Dynamic Genome: Barbara McClintock's Ideas in the Century of Genetics* (1992) and was elected to membership in the National Academy of Sciences in 1990.

Fedoroff's academic interests were apparent at an early age. While still in high school, she took some college courses in history and taught music. She first married in 1959, and although she had a child, entered Syracuse University on a scholarship. After she and her first husband were divorced, she earned tuition and living expenses by working as a freelance flutist, music teacher, and a Russian-English translator. Since her parents were Russian immigrants, she was fluent in the language, and at one time, she was assistant manager of the Translation Bureau of *Biological Abstracts.* She married Patrick Gaganidze after receiving her undergraduate degree. At one point she considered becoming a professional musician and was hired as a flutist by the Syracuse Symphony Orchestra. However, at a chamber music concert she met James D. Watson, who had won the 1962 Nobel Prize with Francis Crick for their work on DNA, and she was so intrigued she returned to school to study medicine.

With a National Science Foundation undergraduate summer grant, she spent three months at the Woods Hole Marine Biological Laboratory where she was exposed to so many new techniques and concepts that she wanted to devote her life to research. She received a National Science Foundation grant for her graduate work at Rockefeller University, receiving her degree in 1972, the same year her second child was born.

She received a temporary appointment at the University of California, Los Angeles, as an acting assistant professor. There she taught classes and conducted research on ribonucleic acid (RNA). She then received a postdoctoral fellowship from the Damon Runyon–Walter Winchell Cancer Research Fund and another fellowship from the National Institutes of Health. With the latter, she joined the Department of Embryology at the Carnegie Institution in Washington, D.C., in 1975. She received a permanent position there as a staff scientist in 1978, the same year that she was divorced a second time. At Carnegie, her early work was studying replications of viruses that destroy bacteria, and her studies shed light upon ribosomes, the principal sites of protein synthesis. She then turned to cloning and molecular genetic analysis of maize transposable elements. These elements, known as "jumping genes," were of interest because of their ability to move to new positions on the chromosome. Her work has contributed substantially to the development of the entire field of plant molecular biology.

She has been very active in training students in plant biology, traveling to universities to give lectures, meet with classes, and hold informal meetings with students. She also has been very active in recombinant DNA and genetic engineering controversies. She has been communicating her ideas on the subject by lecturing, writing popular and technical articles, and appearing on television documentaries and radio talk shows. She has personal concerns about introducing genetically engineered organisms into the environment.

She has been a member of a number of commissions, including the Science Advisory Panel on Applications of Genetics, Office of Technological Assessment, U.S. Congress (1979–1980); member of NIH Recombinant DNA Advisory Committee (1980–1985); and member of the Council on Life Science and Board of Basic Biology (1985–1990). She is a member of the American Academy of Arts and Sciences and the American Association for the Advancement of Science. Her research interest is transposable elements in maize.

***Bibliography:*** *American Men and Women of Science* 14–19; *Notable Twentieth-Century Scientists; Who's Who in America,* 51st ed., 1997; *Who's Who of American Women,* 20th ed., 1997–1998.

# *Ferguson, Angela Dorothea*

(1925– )

***pediatrician***

***Education:*** B.S., Howard University, 1945, M.D., 1949

***Professional Experience:*** Instructor in pediatrics, Howard University School of Medicine, 1953–1959, assistant professor, 1959–1963, professor, 1963–1990, associate pediatrician, Freedmen's Hospital, 1953–1970, head, University Office of Health Affairs, 1970–1979, associate vice president for health affairs, 1979–1990; retired 1990

***Concurrent Positions:*** Staff member, District of Columbia General Hospital, 1963–1990

***Married:*** Charles M. Cabanis, 1951

***Children:*** 2

***Angela Ferguson*** has been recognized for her research on the symptoms and treatment of sickle-cell anemia, a hereditary disease among people of African descent. She was born in Washington, D.C., and although her father was a public school teacher, the family lived on the edge of poverty. In elementary school she worked in the cafeteria in exchange for her school meals. In high school she first focused on business courses because she felt she would be unable to attend college, but by her second year of high school, she had discovered that she liked science courses and that she was intelligent enough to do well in them. She enrolled in Howard University so she could live at home while attending school. Her parents paid her tuition the first year, but she received scholarships after that. By the second year of college her interests had shifted from chemistry and mathematics to biology, and she began considering medical school. She wanted to become both a researcher and a physician. In medical school she majored in pediatrics, which involves the treatment of infants and young children.

After completing her residency, she started a private pediatrics practice, but she found that she was unable to answer parents' questions about their children because all research on developmental physiology had been conducted on children with a European background, not on African-American children. She obtained a research position at Howard University's School of Medicine and its teaching hospital, Freedmen's Hospital, to gather data on the physiology of children from the well-baby clinics around the United States. The data on height and weight from these records could be used to estimate the expected size at each age level. In examining the records, she found that a large number of black children suffered from sickle-cell anemia, a hereditary disease that causes red blood cells to function improperly. Healthy red blood cells are doughnut shaped, but diseased red blood cells are folded into a sickle shape, which affects the easy flow of blood in veins and arteries.

In attempting to develop a method for detecting the disease in young children, Ferguson found that the early symptoms closely resemble many other medical conditions. In infants, the symptoms resemble those of arthritis; between the ages of 2 and 6, the symptoms look like a shortage of certain vitamins in the diet; between 6 and 12 years, most children show no symptoms or only very mild ones; and after 12 years of age, the disease can return with the most common symptom being skin ulcers. She started giving each newborn infant a blood test to detect the condition at the earliest possible time. If a patient required surgery, he or she could be given oxygen after coming out of the anesthesia. For 5-year-olds, the severe symptoms could be reduced by drinking extra water every day, especially if a small amount of baking soda were dissolved in it.

In the 1960s, she decided to shift her focus to administrative work. She was instrumental in developing plans to build a new teaching hospital, one that included a children's wing, to replace the outdated Freedmen's Hospital. In 1970, she was appointed to be in charge of the University Office of Health Affairs, which included responsibility for facility development, student health services, research, and advanced instruction for all degree programs at the Howard University Medical School. The new Freedmen's Hospital opened in 1975, and in 1979, she was named the associate vice president for health affairs. She retired in 1990.

Among her awards is the Certificate of Merit of the American Medical Association. She is a member of the Society for Pediatric Research, Society of Nuclear Medicine, National Medical Association, and the New York Academy of Sciences. Her photograph is included in issues of *Ebony* (May 1964, January 1954, August 1960, and September 1963).

***Bibliography:*** *American Men and Women of Science* 11; *Blacks in Science and Medicine; Distinguished African American Scientists of the 20th Century.*

# Fischer, Irene (Kaminka)

(1907– )

## *geodesist, mathematician*

***Education:*** M.A. in mathematics, University of Vienna; M.A. in descriptive geometry, Vienna Institute of Technology, 1931; postgraduate study, University of Virginia and Georgetown University, 1950–1957; honorary degree: Dr.Eng., University of Karlsruhe, 1975

***Professional Experience:*** Teacher of mathematics, description geometry, and engineering drawing in Vienna, Austria, secondary schools, 1931–1938; researcher, Massachusetts Institute of Technology, 1942–1944; mathematician, Geodesy Branch, Defense Mapping Agency Topographic Center, 1952–1958, geodesist, 1958–1962, supervisory geodesist, 1962–1965, supervisory research geodesist, 1965–1977, branch chief, 1962–1977; retired 1977

***Concurrent Positions:*** Teacher in secondary schools and colleges in the United States, 1941–1945

***Married:*** Eric Fischer, 1930

***Children:*** 2

***Irene Fischer*** is known as a geodesist and mathematician. Her specialty is geodesy, which is the branch of applied mathematics that deals with the measurement of the shape and area of large tracts of country, the exact positions of geographical points, and the curvature, shape, and dimensions of the earth. After her schooling, she taught in secondary schools in Austria before coming to the United States during World War II. After teaching and working as a researcher, she obtained a position at the Defense Mapping Agency Topographic Center, U.S. Department of the Army, where she held research and supervisory positions. She was elected to membership in the National Academy of Engineering in 1979.

Geodesy is a special branch of mathematics and one in which few women are employed. In her work she contributed data that were used for the Mercury, Gemini, and Apollo projects, which were among the first experimental flights conducted by the National Aeronautics and Space Administration (NASA). NASA required precise topographical data on both the earth and the seas in order to plan and execute these experimental flights. The primary responsibility of the mapping agency, of course, is data for military use, even in peacetime. Fischer wrote two books, *Geometry* (1965) and *Basic Geodesy: The Geoid—What's That?* (1973), in addition to hundreds of articles in professional journals. The geoid is an imaginary surface that coincides with mean sea level in the ocean and its extension through the continents.

In the 1950s and 1960s, she published a series of papers in the *Journal of Geophysical Research* on work conducted at the Defense Mapping Agency on the geoid. In the 1970s, she published papers on work on bathymetry, which is the measurement of the depth of oceans, seas, etc., and the compilation of the topographical data. During her years of employment at the agency, she was involved in using all of the new technology, from the introduction of computers to satellite observations. In 1969, she was a member of the committee that compiled South American data for the Pan-American Institute of Geography and History. She was also a member of the special study group on the history of geodesy for the International Association of Geodesy.

Among the awards she received were the Meritorious Civilian Service Award, Department of the Army (1957), the Bronze Leaf Cluster (1966), the Research and Development Achievement Award (1966), and a Decoration for Exceptional Civilian Service (1967); Distinguished Civilian Service Award, Department of Defense (1967); Outstanding Career Woman, Defense Mapping Agency (1975), Meritorious Service Medal (1977); National Civil Service League Career Award (1976); and the designation of Federal Retiree of the Year (1978). She is a fellow of the American Geophysical Union and a member of the International Association of

Geodesy. Her areas of research include the figure of the earth, shape of the geoid, parallax and distance of the moon, Fischer ellipsoid, deflections at sea, mean sea level slopes, and history of geodesy.

***Bibliography:*** *American Men and Women of Science* 11–19; Rossiter, M., *Women Scientists in America; Who's Who in Engineering,* 9th ed., 1995; *Who's Who of American Women,* 20th ed., 1997–1998.

# *Fisher, Anna L.*
## (1949– )
## *physician, astronaut*

***Education:*** B.S. in chemistry, University of California, Los Angeles, 1971, M.D., 1976, M.S. in chemistry, 1987

***Professional Experience:*** Emergency room physician, Los Angeles area hospitals, 1977–1978; mission specialist, National Aeronautics and Space Administration (NASA), 1978–1979, astronaut, 1980–1990, flight STS 51-A of orbiter *Discovery,* 1984, Space Station Support Office, 1990–

***Married:*** William F. Fisher, 1978

*Anna Fisher* has the distinction of being the first mother to fly in space. She was one of the six women astronauts selected in 1978 from more than 1,250 women applicants. She and her husband William F. Fisher were the first married couple in the astronaut program; he was selected in 1980 and later returned to civilian employment. She decided at age 13 that she would like to be an astronaut, but she felt it was such an impossible dream that she did not talk about it for fear people would laugh. Later she decided on a career in medicine because it would be the best qualification to have if she ever had the chance to be an astronaut.

She earned her medical degree and was working as an emergency room specialist when NASA announced that a new group of astronauts with revised requirements would be selected. She and her then-fiancé both applied for admission to the program; a week after they married, she was chosen, probably because of her background in the physical sciences as well as the medical sciences. The couple moved to Houston where Anna started her training and Bill worked as an emergency room physician. After he, too, was accepted, they planned to fly on the same mission but abandoned the idea after she became pregnant. She and her husband continued to work as emergency room physicians one weekend per month while they were in the astronaut program in order to maintain their skills.

Anna Fisher's assignments as an astronaut included developing and testing the Remote Manipulator System, verifying flight software, and providing medical backup in rescue helicopters. She and Bill served as emergency physicians for a number of the launchings and landings, and she was on-orbit capsule communicator for the STS-9 mission. Her first space flight was on November 8, 1984, on the second flight of the orbiter *Discovery.* The crew accomplished the first space salvage in history, retrieving the Palapa B-2 and Westar VI satellites. In her later work in the Space Station Support Office, she became the crew representative for space station development training, operations concepts, and health maintenance.

One early problem was that the spacesuits needed to be redesigned to fit the women, who usually were not as tall or as heavy as the men. One of the changes the women asked for was a two-piece suit for a better fit. At NASA, Fisher helped Hamilton-Standard, the manufacturer of the suit, develop one that was more comfortable for the women whose upper-body strength was not as great as the men's. She also tested a shuttle-tile repair kit in which epoxy was sprayed into the place of a lost or broken thermal tile—which proved to be unnecessary after the first and second flights of *Columbia.* She helped Martin-Marietta test and develop the manned maneuvering unit (MMU), the rocket-powered backpack that allows an astronaut to propel himself or herself around while wearing a space suit.

In talking about her career, she said the three qualifications for either a woman or a man in the astronaut program, in addition to a basic background in the sciences, are the capacity to understand orbital mechanics, a certain amount of physical coordination and endurance, and a need to believe in what you are doing. She explains that one factor that delayed the introduction of women into the astronaut program is that few women were test pilots, which would have given them the experience to work with new spacecraft. Originally there was a great deal of opposition from the male astronauts as well as many of the men employed by NASA to select women for the program. Fisher says she has encountered opposition in her career, but she has always thought that only reflected the men's own insecurity. The slights from colleagues may have hurt her feelings, but she did not worry about them.

There are numerous articles and several books, primarily written in the 1980s, about the first eight women astronauts. In 1996, the women were included in a special issue of *Working Woman* honoring 350 women who changed the world from 1976 to 1996. Her photograph is included in A. R. Oberg's *Spacefarers of the '80s and '90s,* Karen O'Connor's *Sally Ride and the New Astronauts,* Phyllis Read and Bernard Witlieb's *The Book of Women's Firsts* (1992), *Working Woman* (May 1980 and November–December 1996), *MS Magazine* (June 1986), and *U.S. News & World Report* (February 23, 1981).

***Bibliography:*** Herzenberg, C., *Women Scientists from Antiquity to the Present;* Ireland, N., *Index to Women of the World . . . Suppl.;* Oberg, A. R., *Spacefarers of the '80s and '90s;* O'Connor, K., *Sally Ride and the New Astronauts;* Read, P., *The Book of Women's Firsts;* U.S. National Aeronautics and Space Administration, *Astronaut Fact Book.*

# *Fitzroy, Nancy (Deloye)*
## (1927– )
## *engineer*

***Education:*** B.ChE., Rensselaer Polytechnic Institute, 1949; honorary degrees: D.Sc., New Jersey Institute of Technology, 1987; D.Eng., Rensselaer Polytechnic Institute, 1990

***Professional Experience:*** Assistant engineer, Knolls Atomic Power Laboratory, 1950–1952; development engineer, Hermes Missile Project, General Electric Company, 1952–1953, development engineer, 1953–1963, heat transfer engineer, Advanced Technology Laboratories, 1963–1965, consultant in heat transfer, Research and Development Center, 1965–1971, manager of heat transfer consulting, 1971–1974, strategy planner, 1974–1976, advanced concepts planner and proposal manager, 1976–1979, program development manager, Gas Turbine Division, 1979–1982, manager of energy and environment programs, Turbine Market and Projects Division, 1982–1987; consultant in fields of gas turbines, nuclear energy, and space vehicles, 1987–

***Married:*** Roland V. Fitzroy, Jr., 1951

***Nancy Fitzroy*** is known for her research in the properties of materials, heat transfer, and fluid flow that she conducted at General Electric Company. She was first assigned to a team to solve a thorny heat transfer problem: how to keep the high temperatures produced by an atomic reaction from escaping the nuclear reactor of an atomic generator or a nuclear submarine. Later she worked on keeping the delicate electronic equipment in space satellites at room temperature while the skin of the satellite was being alternately superheated and supercooled. She has also designed more-standard products such as toasters and microwave ovens. She says that toasters can present more problems than missiles and satellites because outer space is basically uniform but no two pieces of bread are alike.

When she was a senior in high school, she still had not applied to any colleges because she did not want to major in English, which is what most of her friends planned to do. When one of her teachers facetiously suggested engineering as a career, she thought at first he was joking, but after she considered the possibility, she applied to two engineering schools and was accepted by both. She was the first woman chemical engineering student at Rensselaer, but she was accepted by her fellow students. However, there was not a women's restroom in the building in which many of her classes were held; for her sophomore year, the faculty decided to appropriate one of the men's rooms for her use.

She was appointed to a position at General Electric Company (GE) where she stayed in various capacities for the next 30 some years; her husband also worked for GE. During that period she was one of the first to study heat transfer surfaces in nuclear-reactor cores, and she holds a patent in the area of cooling integrated circuits, having invented a thermal chip that is used to measure temperatures in such circuits. She also developed a thermal protection system for hardened radar antennae that was utilized in the U.S. early warning system. Her work reflects the interdisciplinary nature of engineering, as she can be considered both a chemical and a mechanical engineer. In the 1970s, she took on more administrative responsibilities. As a strategy planner she planned long-range goals in the corporate research and development programs before she retired in 1987 to be an independent consultant. She shared her expertise with fellow employees by teaching in the GE Advanced Engineering Course between 1962 and 1967. She is the author of the *GE Heat Transfer and Fluid Flow Data Books* (1955–1974), which were used throughout industry and academe. She is considered the most accomplished woman helicopter pilot in the country.

Although she feels the outlook for women engineers is positive, she says women still need encouragement to enter what is considered a masculine profession. She encourages women engineers to participate in the high school and college career-day programs. Not all societal pressures are directed at women. For example, she said that when she continued working after marriage, men would ask her husband if he could not afford to support a wife.

She was elected to membership in the National Academy of Engineering in 1995. She received the Achievement Award of the Society of Women Engineers (1972), the Federation of Professional Women Award (1984), the Demers Medal of Rensselaer Polytechnic Institute (1975), and the Centennial Medallion of the American Society of Mechanical Engineers (1980). She is a fellow of the American Society of Mechanical Engineers (president, 1986–1987) and a member of the American Institute of Chemical Engineers, National Society of Professional Engineers, and Society of Women Engineers. Her photograph is included in *Cosmopolitan* (April 1976) and *Design News* (December 1, 1986).

***Bibliography:*** *American Men and Women of Science* 12–19; Herzenberg, C., *Women Scientists from Antiquity to the Present;* Ireland, N., *Index to Women of the World . . . Suppl.; Notable Twentieth-Century Scientists; Who's Who in America,* 51st ed., 1997; *Who's Who in Engineering,* 9th ed., 1995; *Who's Who in Science and Engineering,* 3d ed., 1996–1997.

# *Flanigen, Edith Marie*
(1929– )
***inorganic chemist***

***Education:*** B.A., D'Youville College, 1950; M.S., Syracuse University, 1952; honorary degree: D.Sc., D'Youville College, 1983

***Professional Experience:*** Research chemist, Union Carbide Corporation, 1952–1960, senior research chemist, 1960–1962, research associate, 1962–1967, senior research associate, 1967–1969, senior research scientist, 1969–1973, corporate research fellow, 1973–1982, corporate senior research fellow, 1982–1988; senior research fellow, UOP, Inc., 1988–

***Edith Flanigen*** is renowned for her research on synthetic molecular sieves and synthetic zeolites, which are used in industry as catalysts. Molecular sieves are compounds with molecule-size pores, such as sodium aluminum silicate; zeolites are hydrated silicates of aluminum with alkali metals. She was elected to membership in the National Academy of Engineering in 1991 and has received two of the primary awards in chemistry: the Perkin Medal of the Society of Chemical Industry (1992) and the Garvan-Olin Medal of the American Chemical Society (1993). In the 1960s, she developed a synthetic emerald for industrial use.

After receiving her master's degree, she joined the Linde Division of Union Carbide Corporation as a research chemist. She advanced through the research side of the corporation, and in 1982, she was named a corporate senior research fellow, the first woman to achieve that distinction. In the early 1970s, the laboratories in which she worked were relocated to White Plains, New York. In 1988, Union Carbide assigned Linde Division's molecular sieve and catalyst business to the UOP, Inc. subsidiary of AlliedSignal Corporation as a part of making UOP a joint venture of Union Carbide and AlliedSignal.

Flanigen was the first woman to be awarded the Perkin Medal in its 86-year history. The medal especially recognizes her synthesis of molecular sieves as new classes of materials—the synthesis of aluminophosphate and silicoaluminophosphate. These substances are cousins of synthetic zeolites, which are widely used as catalysts and sorbents. Her earliest contributions to the field of chemistry were new methods to make synthetic zeolites. These are metal aluminosilicates. Although zeolites are found in nature, scientists, including Flanigen, have found ways to make naturally and nonnaturally occurring structures by heating aqueous alumina-silica gels at 100 degrees Celsius to 450 degrees Celsius. When a fellow Linde Division researcher made small amounts of a new type of zeolite called "zeolite Y" that showed promise as a fluid-cracking catalyst in oil refining, Flanigen succeeded in making large amounts of the zeolite.

In the early 1960s, Lincoln Laboratory contracted with the Linde Division to make synthetic emeralds for masers, which were microwave forerunners of lasers. Flanigen devised a process to make emeralds by using temperature and pressure to control the different solubilities of aluminum, silicon, beryllium, and chromium oxides in aqueous gels. Linde later marketed these as synthetic gemstones that are used in jewelry.

When she received the notice in 1991 that she would be awarded the Perkin Medal, she was not surprised that the invitation stated she should wear white tie and tails. After all, she was the first woman to receive the medal, and her hosts forgot to revise the invitation. She states that it is an unbelievably emotional thing to find a new material, and her team has developed nearly 200 such compounds. After brainstorming with her fellow researchers, she groups the various ideas into a range of options on which the team votes. Usually the group decides on just a few goals. She feels the vote is a critical strategy to get the total commitment of everyone.

She is a member of the Mineralogical Society of America, American Chemical Society, and American Association for the Advancement of Science. Her research includes inorganic and physical chemistry research in crystalline molecular sieves, zeolites, adsorbents, and catalysts; hydrothermal synthesis of mineral phases, particularly silicates; and crystal growth. Her photograph is included in *Business Week* (January 18, 1993) and *Chemical & Engineering News* (March 9, 1992).

***Bibliography:*** *American Men and Women of Science* 11–13, 15, 18–19; *Who's Who in Science and Engineering,* 3d ed., 1996–1997; *Who's Who of American Women,* 20th ed., 1997–1998.

# *Fossey, Dian*
## (1932–1985)
## *primatologist, zoologist, anthropologist*

***Education:*** B.A., San Jose State College (now San Jose State University), 1954; Ph.D., Cambridge University, 1976 (or 1974)

***Professional Experience:*** Occupational therapist, Kosair Crippled Children's Hospital, Louisville, Kentucky, 1955–1966; scientific director, Karisoke Research Centre, Ruhengeri, Rwanda, 1967–1980 and 1983–1985, project coordinator, 1980–1983

***Concurrent Position:*** Visiting associate professor of anthropology, Cornell University, 1980–1982

***Dian Fossey*** was the international authority on the mountain gorilla at the time of her death in 1985. One of the unsolved mysteries in science is who murdered her at her research station in Rwanda. Although several people or groups were suspected, there was only a cursory investigation by the undermanned Rwanda police. One of her associates and several native employees were accused of the crime, but the consensus is that poachers who were angry with her broke into her cabin during the night and killed her. She was buried on the mountain in the graveyard that she had established for her gorillas.

Numerous people could be said to be suspects as Fossey was a controversial person who attracted strong likes and dislikes. A portion of her problems could be attributed to the fact that she was a workaholic and she expected everyone to have the same devotion and tenacity to her work that she did. Another strong factor was that she conducted research, often alone, in a primitive area with limited funds. The political situation in African countries often is precarious, and Rwanda even today experiences political upheavals. Years of these types of stresses would wear down anyone, and at times she experienced what we now call burnout.

During her lifetime she was known as one of "Leakey's ape ladies." The famous anthropologist Louis S. B. Leakey had the goal of conducting extensive research on the three major primate groups—chimpanzees, gorillas, and orangutans—and comparing the results to his lifelong study of early humans. He was a mentor for the three women who conducted these studies—Jane Goodall, Dian Fossey, and Birute Galdikas—and felt that women were more thorough investigators than men. Leakey preferred women with little scientific background because they would concentrate on the task they were assigned and not be sidetracked by other theories and interests. The three women fulfilled this requirement, but they changed the way primatologists conduct research by studying animals as individuals with life histories, as humans are studied. The three women met as a group only three times: in 1970, at Jane Goodall's home in London; in 1974, at the Wenner-Gren Conference on Great Apes in Austria; and in 1981, at the Second Conference on Great Apes in Los Angeles.

Fossey had a lifelong interest in animals. She enrolled in the preveterinary medicine program at the University of California, Davis, but transferred to San Jose after two years and earned a degree in occupational therapy. While in college, she became an accomplished equestrian, which drew her to a job in Louisville, Kentucky, the heart of the horse country, where she was an occupational therapist at a crippled children's hospital. She realized her dream to see the gorillas that the primatologist George Schaller had described in his book *The Mountain Gorilla: Ecology and Behavior* (1963) when she took out a three-year bank loan in 1963 for $8,000 to finance a seven-week safari. Rather than follow the usual tourist route, she hired a "white hunter" to lead her to specific places. Her first stop was the Olduvai Gorge in Tanzania to visit Mary and Louis Leakey. She also stopped in the Congo (or Zaire) to see the mountain gorillas and visited friends in Rhodesia (or Zimbabwe) where she met Alexie Forrester, to whom she later became engaged. She returned to the United States to continue her work, pay off the loan, and keep up contacts with Leakey.

Leakey was interested in not only sponsoring research on gorillas but also protecting them from further encroachments. After he had secured funds, he offered Fossey this two-pronged project in 1966; she immediately accepted. After a two-week orientation with Jane Goodall, Fossey set up camp, with the assistance of wildlife photographer Alan Root, in Zaire's Parc National des Virungas. Soon there was a civil war, and the rebels expelled all white people. Fossey was held prisoner for several weeks until she escaped across the border into Uganda when her guards became drunk one day. Leakey reestablished her with supplies and native staff, this time in Rwanda's Parc National des Volcans. Her fiancé tried to persuade her to return to America, but she decided to stay in Africa and broke their engagement.

Her research station is located in a remote area in a high rain forest. The mountains are 9,000 feet high, and the station can be reached only by a three-to-five-hour climb up muddy and steep animal paths. No vehicles can penetrate the dense forest. The weather is foggy, damp, and chilly most of the year. Fossey developed a unique research methodology. Instead of observing the animals from a distance, she gradually habituated them to her presence by imitating their sounds and behavior. The gorillas were shy and peaceful; they charged at humans and other animals only when threatened or approached without warning.

Her research was funded by the Leakey Foundation, the Wilkie Foundation, and the National Geographic Society. When she realized that she would need a doctorate if her work were to be accepted by the scientific community, Leakey arranged for her to attend Cambridge University to take the necessary course work to prepare a thesis. By this time, her work was attracting international attention, and many visitors and tourists were flocking to see her gorillas. She accepted graduate students starting in 1970, but her relationship with them was often stormy. She expected the students to perform prodigious amounts of work under extremely harsh working conditions; some departed after only a day or two when they saw the camp. Even after she received her doctorate, some of the students denigrated her work because she had started her research as an amateur; some journals would not accept her papers because of her unconventional background. One task the students did accomplish was to prepare a census of the gorilla population in 1981; it indicated the number had declined 50 percent since Schaller wrote his book.

In the late 1970s, Fossey became increasingly obsessed with protecting the gorillas. The population was declining, and one of her favorites, Digit, was murdered. She used his death to start a campaign to save the species, and money started pouring in for the Digit Fund to hire antipoaching patrols and equipment. Rwanda is one of the most densely populated countries in Africa, and it was only natural that people would attempt to graze their cattle or clear land for farming in the park where the gorillas lived. Fossey became obsessive about catching the poachers and farmers to the extent of destroying crops and traps, killing cattle, and harassing people.

Several scientists and government officials suggested that one solution would be to establish a gorilla family in a reasonably accessible area of the mountains where tourists could be brought to observe the group. This solution solved the problem of visitors' disturbing the scientific work, provided employment for the local people as tour guides and taxi drivers, promoted the Rwandan tourist industry, and brought needed money to the country. The plan was set up in 1980, in spite of Fossey's opposition, as the Mountain Gorilla Project under Alexander (Sandy) Harcourt and Bill Weber, who had been her associates.

At the time, Fossey was experiencing health problems because of poor diet. She also suffered from emphysema but would not stop smoking. In 1980, she accepted a visiting associate professorship at Cornell University where she wrote her book *Gorillas in the Mist* (1983). The book was a compilation of much of the information reported in her previous publications, but the details are given more in an anecdotal style than as a technical treatise. When she returned to the research station, she continued her war against the poachers and farmers until she was murdered in 1985.

Dian Fossey was an impressively attractive woman. She was more than six feet tall, had dark hair, and dressed fashionably when "in civilization." In the camp, she dressed in jeans and boots. She was extremely loyal to her friends, and she maintained contacts with her California and Kentucky friends for many years. In 1974, she again contemplated marriage, this time with a local French physician, Dr. Pierre Weiss. However, they did not marry, and he returned to France. Birute Galdikas mentions in her book *Reflections of Eden* (1995) that Fossey had a wild sense of humor, which many people did not understand, that consisted of put-downs and double entendres.

Fossey received the Franklin Burt Award from the National Geographic Society (1973) for outstanding research and the Joseph Wood Krutch Medal from the Humane Society of the United States (1984) for outstanding conservation work. Since the recent civil war in Rwanda there has been little information about the situation of the research station, but according to an advertisement in the November 1997 issue of *National Geographic,* Fossey's project managers are seeking funds as the Dian Fossey Gorilla Fund International with an address in Atlanta, Georgia. Her book, *Gorillas in the Mist,* was made into a popular movie of the same title and released in 1988. There are numerous books about her, including Sy Montgomery's *Walking with the Great Apes* (1991), F. Mowat's *Woman in the Mists: The Story of Dian Fossey and the Mountain Gorillas of Africa* (1987), Bettyann Kevles's *Watching the Wild Apes: The Primate Studies of Goodall, Fossey, and Galdikas* (1976), and Harold T. P. Hayes's *The Dark Romance of Dian Fossey* (1990). There are numerous photographs in these books and in *National Geographic* articles.

**Bibliography:** *Contemporary Authors* v. 113, 118, and CANR-34; *Current Biography* 1985 and 1986; Herzenberg, C., *Women Scientists from Antiquity to the Present;* Ireland, N., *Index to Women of the World . . . Suppl.; Notable Twentieth-Century Scientists;* Read, P., *Book of Women's Firsts.*

# Fox, Marye Anne
(1947– )
## organic chemist, physical chemist

***Education:*** B.S., Notre Dame College, 1969; M.S., Cleveland State University, 1970; Ph.D. in organic chemistry, Dartmouth College, 1974

***Professional Experience:*** Instructor in physical science, Cuyahoga Community College, 1970–1971; fellow and research associate in chemistry, University of Maryland, 1974–1976; assistant professor of chemistry, University of Texas, Austin, 1976–1980, associate professor, 1981–1985, professor of chemistry, 1985–1987, Rowland Pettit Centennial Professor, 1987–1992, M. June and J. Virgil Waggoner Regents Chair, 1992–

***Married:*** 1969, divorced; James K. Whitesell, 1990

***Children:*** 5

*Marye Fox* is renowned for her research to solve major problems in organic photochemistry and electrochemistry. She and her team members have pioneered the interdisciplinary field of organic photoelectrochemistry; electrochemistry is the branch of chemistry that deals with chemical changes produced by electricity and the production of electricity by chemical changes. There is an unusual breadth in her research. She is cited for having a mastery of problems found in physical, inorganic, and analytical chemistry and applying them when tackling the problems of organic chemistry. She was one of the first researchers to apply the research techniques of physical organic chemistry to reactions occurring on surfaces and to recognize semiconductor particles as ideal microenvironments for initiating controlled redox chemistry (redox means oxidation reduction).

Fox says she had no qualms about deciding on science as a career while in high school because, at the time, almost everyone who was reasonably bright was interested in science. She chose chemistry because that field enabled her to steer clear of the messy aspects of biology as well as the extreme emphasis on math that is found in physics. She married a medical student after receiving her undergraduate degree, and since he was in Ohio, she entered the master's program at Cleveland State so she could complete her degree in one year even while supporting her husband. She accomplished this feat by teaching at the local community college. She was then able to successfully pursue her own professional development while she followed her husband around the country. When her husband received a residency at Hanover, New Hampshire, she entered the doctoral program at Dartmouth. She was pregnant her second year at Dartmouth and had to decide whether to continue her studies or put a hold on a scientific career. Instead of leaving the program, she completed her doctorate in three years.

When her husband was drafted and sent to Washington, D.C., she obtained a postdoctoral appointment at the University of Maryland. When he set up a practice in Austin, Texas, she secured a faculty research appointment at the University of Texas there, where she advanced quickly in professorial rank. Somewhere along the way she and her husband divorced, and she remarried in 1990. She had three sons with her first husband and two with her second.

She was elected to membership in the National Academy of Sciences in 1994. In addition to numerous other awards, she received the Garvan Medal of the American Chemical Society in 1988 and was the Arthur C. Cope Scholar in 1989. She was a member of the National Science Board, the group that advises the National Science Foundation, from 1991 to 1996. She has authored or coauthored more than 100 scientific articles and is a coauthor of the book *Organic Chemistry* (1994), a textbook that has received complimentary reviews. One feature of the book is that the authors establish connections between organic chemistry and the students' professional interests, which are usually in biological or health-related areas.

She is a member of the editorial advisory boards of the *Journal of Organic Chemistry*, the ACS Symposium Series, and Advances in Chemistry. She has been an associate editor of the *Journal of the American Chemical Society* since 1986. She is a fellow of the American Association for the Advancement of Science and a member of the American Chemical Society, Electrochemical Society, and American Society for Photobiology. Her research interests include organic photochemistry, electrochemistry, and physical organic mechanisms. Her photograph is included in *Chemical & Engineering News* (December 5, 1988, and March 15, 1993) and in *Science* (May 24, 1991).

***Bibliography:*** *American Men and Women of Science* 14–19; *Who's Who in America*, 51st ed., 1997; *Who's Who of American Women*, 20th ed., 1997–1998.

# *Free, Helen (Murray)*
(1923– )
***clinical chemist***

***Education:*** B.A., College of Wooster, 1944; M.A. in laboratory management and health care administration, Central Michigan University, 1978; honorary degrees: D.Sc., College of Wooster, 1992; D.Sc., Central Michigan University, 1993

***Professional Experience:*** Control chemist, Miles Laboratories Corporation, 1944–1946, research chemist, Biochemical Section, 1946–1959, associate research biochemist and group leader, Ames Research Laboratories, 1959–1964, Ames Product Development Laboratory, 1964–1966, Ames Technical Service, 1966–1969, new product manager for clinical test systems, Ames Growth and Development, 1969–1974, senior new product manager for microbiological test systems, 1974–1976, director of special test systems, Ames Division, 1976–1978, director of clinical laboratory and reagents, Research Division, 1978–1982, professional relations for Diagnostic Division, Miles, Inc., 1982–

***Concurrent Positions:*** Adjunct professor of biochemistry, Goshen College; adjunct professor of management, Indiana University, South Bend

***Married:*** Alfred H. Free, 1947

***Children:*** 6

***Helen Free*** is recognized as a pioneer in the field of diagnostic chemistry. Starting in the 1940s, she has been involved in the development of convenient test systems involving chemical reagents and the instrumentation to accompany those tests. Her research led to the development of the convenient tablet tests for urinalysis and to the introduction and development of easy dip-and-read tests for various urinary conditions. Clinical laboratory diagnostic methods and devices were comparatively primitive in the 1940s and 1950s, and her pioneer research contributed greatly to remedying that situation. Today, the test procedures that she has developed are used in clinical laboratories throughout the world.

She is the only woman scientist to reach the executive level in the Miles Laboratories Corporation of Elkhart, Indiana. The company's famous product is Alka-Seltzer, but Free worked on the development of chemical reagents, microbiology reagents, and sophisticated instrumentation for clinical diagnosis. The tests that she developed include blood chemistry, histology, and cytology as well as urinalysis.

In common with many women scientists, Free's parents encouraged her to make good grades in school, and her father encouraged her to become a physician. At the College of Wooster, she initially majored in Latin but later changed to chemistry. When she completed her undergraduate degree, she started working for Miles Laboratories as a chemist and advanced up the corporate ladder to director of clinical laboratory reagents. During her time with the company, it acquired Ames Laboratories, which became the research arm while Miles remained the manufacturing arm of Miles Laboratories Corporation. When she retired in 1982, she continued as a consultant for the corporation by handling professional relations for the Diagnostic Division, Miles, Inc.

She is the author or coauthor of more than 200 papers, many of them written with her husband, who also worked for Miles. She also holds seven patents. She sharpened her administrative skills by obtaining a master's degree in laboratory management and health care administration from Central Michigan University in 1978 through a program offered off-site in many states. She and her husband coauthored the book *Urinalysis in Clinical Laboratory Practice* (1976; 2d ed., 1980), which is still considered the standard text on the subject. She also edited *Modern Urine Chemistry* (1986), which was published by Miles.

Helen Free has been very active in professional organizations, serving as president of the American Association for Clinical Chemistry in 1990 and president of the American Chemical Society in 1993. She was awarded the Garvan Medal of the American Chemical Society (ACS) in 1980, an award for distinguished service to chemistry by women chemists. The citation included recognition of her leadership in the development of clinical test systems that streamlined work in medical laboratories around the world, and she also was cited for her service to the ACS and for being an inspiration to women chemists. In 1980, she also received the Distinguished Alumni award of the College of Wooster. While she was president of ACS, she urged members to participate in outreach to students and citizens to bring chemistry into their everyday lives. In 1995, she was the first recipient of the Helen M. Free Public Outreach Award.

She is a fellow of the American Institute of Chemists and American Association for the Advancement of Science. She is a member of the American Chemical Society (president, 1993), American Association for Clinical Chemistry (president, 1990), Association of Clinical Scientists, and Royal Society of Chemistry. Her photograph is included in several issues of *Chemical & Engineering News* (September 24, 1990; November 25, 1991; January 4, 1993; and September 25, 1995).

***Bibliography:*** *American Men and Women of Science* 14–19; *Notable Women in the Physical Sciences; Who's Who in Science and Engineering,* 3d ed., 1996–1997; *Who's Who in Technology Today* v. 6; *Who's Who of American Women,* 20th ed., 1997–1998; *Women in Chemistry and Physics.*

# *Friedl, Ernestine*

(1920– )

## *cultural anthropologist, ethnologist*

***Education:*** B.A., Hunter College, 1941; Ph.D. in anthropology, Columbia University, 1950

***Professional Experience:*** Lecturer in anthropology, Brooklyn College, 1942–1944; instructor in sociology, Wellesley College, 1944–1946; lecturer in sociology and anthropology, Brooklyn College, 1946–1947; lecturer, Queens College, 1947–1951, instructor, 1951–1956, assistant professor, 1956–1960, associate professor, 1960–1973, professor, 1973, chair, Department of Anthropology and Sociology, 1965–1968, chair, Department of Anthropology, 1968–1969, executive officer of Ph.D. program in anthropology, 1969–1970; professor of anthropology and department chair, Duke University, 1973–1978, professor of anthropology, 1978–1986, professor emeritus, 1986– ; adjunct professor, Princeton University, 1987–1991

***Married:*** Harry L. Levy, 1942, died 1981

*Ernestine Friedl* is a cultural anthropologist who is known for her studies of Greek village life, peasant society, urban migration studies, and the social and cultural variables of sex role variation. As department chair at two universities and as president of two associations, she has had a major role in the development of the field of anthropology. She was born in Hungary and immigrated to New York with her parents at the age of two. Graduating from high school during the depression, she was encouraged by her parents to develop a career in order to earn her own living.

When she entered Hunter College, both tuition and books were free, but it took her nine years to complete her doctorate because she had to teach full-time. As an undergraduate, she first thought of majoring in psychology, but one course was sufficient to change her mind. After meeting an anthropology faculty member socially, she started taking courses in that field with the idea of teaching. Her husband, who already had received his doctorate, explained to her that teaching at the university level required a doctorate, but she started teaching at Brooklyn College when she had completed only a year and a half of course work. When her husband entered the army during World War II, she accepted a position outside New York City at Wellesley College. After the war, she returned to New York and in 1947 began teaching at Queens College, where she remained for the next 27 years. Her husband was a faculty member in classics at Hunter College and Fordham University and later vice chancellor of the City University of New York. Ernestine moved to Duke University in 1973 as professor and chair of the Anthropology Department, retiring in 1986. She then was an adjunct professor at Princeton University for several years.

She did a brief study of the Chippewa Indians of Wisconsin during the summers of 1941 through 1943; this experience formed a foundation for a historical dissertation on leadership styles and their relation to political organization. She focused on the relations of the Chippewa with Europeans from the first arrival of the Jesuits in the seventeenth century to 1948 and also used the resources of the Bureau of Indian Affairs for the study.

After she received tenure at Queens in 1954, she applied for fieldwork funds to study post–World War II changes in rural communities. She chose Greece because no Americans had worked there since the war, and her husband, a classicist, could do comparative research on ancient and modern Greek languages and cultures. On the advice of Margaret Mead and others, Friedl chose a small rural community of about 200 people, a workable number if she wanted to meet each person. She stressed those aspects of village life that the inhabitants considered important: family, economic advancement of the family through dowry, education, and the acquisition of urban housing and jobs. Her husband accompanied her when she interviewed the men because, given the culture of the time, she would not have been able to do so alone. The study was published as the book *Vasilika: A Village in Modern Greece* (1962). In 1964–1965, she did fieldwork among the community's members who had migrated from Vasilika to Athens.

One factor that impressed her about the Greek village was how powerful the women were, for they had more power and influence than the appearance of deference and spatial segregation would suggest. This fact led her to investigate what anthropologists knew about the comparative position of women and resulted in her book *Women and Men: An Anthropologist's View* (1975). In this study of the gender role definition of hunting and gathering societies and of horticultural societies, she looked for necessary conditions that might influence the degrees of dominance men held over women, ranging from severe oppression to close-to-equal status.

Before she became a member of the Committee on the Status of Women in Anthropology (of the American Anthropological Association), she thought women anthropologists did not have any problems even though she was a student at Columbia during the time that faculty member Ruth Benedict (1887–1948) was not named head of the Anthropology Department although everyone expected it. Benedict was a world-renowned anthropologist, but she was not promoted to full professor at Columbia until shortly before she died. The students at the time were not aware of the political factors involved in such appointments. Friedl's committee found that although most women anthropologists received their doctorates from 14 highly ranked universities, the women were not hired by those universities. Unlike their male classmates, who were hired by the universities from which they were graduated, the women were hired by small liberal arts colleges and state universities that had fewer research opportunities. Friedl herself had encountered few problems in her own career.

Since the mid 1970s, anthropological and feminist theories have questioned the attitude that women and men are viewed by their basic biological differences. This attitude leads to such myths that men are more intelligent than women and that women are unable to understand geometry and higher levels of mathematics. This situation led Friedl to challenge anthropologists to question basic assumptions about biologically and genetically based distinctions. In the *Annual Review of Anthropology* (1995) she states: "Qualities of character, personality, and intelligence . . . are being imputed to so-called cultural differences among diverse populations, and too often they are construed as genetic differences."

She is a fellow of the American Academy of Arts and Sciences, the American Association for the Advancement of Science, and the American Anthropological Association (president, 1975). She is a member of American Ethnological Society (president, 1967). Her autobiography, "The Life of an Academic: A Personal Record of a Teacher, Administrator, and Anthropologist," appeared in the *Annual Review of Anthropology* (1995). The article includes a photograph.

***Bibliography:*** *American Men and Women of Science* 11–13; *Contemporary Authors* v. 37–40R; Rossiter, M., *Women Scientists in America; Women Anthropologists.*

# *Friend, Charlotte*
## (1921–1987)
## *medical microbiologist*

***Education:*** B.A., Hunter College, 1944; Ph.D. in bacteriology, Yale University, 1950; honorary degrees: D.Sc., Medical College of Ohio, 1983; Ph.D., Brandeis University, 1986

***Professional Experience:*** Associate member, Sloan-Kettering Institute, 1949–1966; professor and director, Center for Experimental Cell Biology, Mt. Sinai School of Medicine, 1966–1987

***Concurrent Positions:*** Associate professor of microbiology, Sloan-Kettering Division, Medical College of Cornell University, 1952–1966

***Charlotte Friend*** pioneered the approach that a virus causes cancer and a vaccine could be developed against it. Her major research effort involved leukemia of childhood, but she paved the way for a large number of other avenues of research. She was the first to show that animals could be immunized with retrovirus preparations and protected against developing the disease. Her experiments indicating that such protection is possible are frequently cited by researchers who are trying to develop a vaccine against the human immunodeficiency virus (HIV). Her system was the forerunner for other cell culture models to study other types of cancer. However, her first paper on leukemia was scorned at a meeting in 1956 of the American Association for Cancer Research, for her audience was unable to discuss rationally such an unorthodox idea given by a woman just a few years out of graduate school. It was not until an internationally known scientist replicated her work and assisted her in publishing the paper that researchers would even consider her ideas.

Friend might have been motivated to work in the field of microbiology by the death of her father from bacterial endocarditis when she was three years old; when she was ten, she wrote a paper for a school assignment on why she wanted to be a bacteriologist. She attended the Hunter College High School in New York, a school for girls who were planning to attend college. There was no tuition, just as Hunter College itself was free. However, to help with family expenses while attending Hunter, she worked in a physician's office during the day and took classes at night. After graduation in 1944 she joined the WAVES, the women's division of the U.S. Navy at the time, as an ensign and was promoted to lieutenant junior grade after basic training. She was assigned to be second in command at the hematology laboratory at the naval hospital in Shoemaker, California. Upon her discharge, she used the GI Bill to obtain a doctorate from Yale. Her first two years at Yale she chose to take classes with the medical students to gain a good foundation on anatomy, pathology, and other subjects that would be important to research.

She received an appointment at the Sloan-Kettering Institute for Cancer Research where she began her outstanding career in research. Although the director of Sloan-Kettering did not agree with her theory of the virus, he supported her completely in her research. The theory was that, contrary to the prevailing medical opinion, leukemia is caused by a virus. She was soon successful in vaccinating mice against leukemia by injecting a weakened form of the virus, now called "the Friend virus," into healthy mice so they could develop antibodies to fight off the normal virus. She presented the paper on this new discovery at the 1957 meeting of the American Association for Cancer Research to a much more receptive audience. She received the Alfred P. Sloan Award for Cancer Research and another award from the American Cancer Society in 1962. She was elected to membership in the National Academy of Sciences in 1963.

In 1966, she moved to the newly formed Mt. Sinai School of Medicine as professor and director of the Center for Experimental Cell Biology. Her one request was that she should not teach; she wished to devote her time to research. However, she had to seek her own grants to support her research, a task that involves a great deal of time. She continued her work on leukemia, and in 1972 announced the discovery of a method to alter a leukemia mouse cell in a test tube so that it would no longer multiply. Through chemical treatment, the malignant red blood cell could be made to produce hemoglobin, as do normal cells. Friend was diagnosed with lymphoma in 1981, but very few people knew of the diagnosis as she did not want reviewers of grants or manuscripts that she submitted to be influenced by her illness. She continued to conduct research in the lab while undergoing therapy, carrying on business as usual. One of her last public appearances was in 1986 when she received an honorary degree from Brandeis University.

Charlotte Friend had a strong personality and would defend her theories vigorously. She was also very generous with her time in working in the professional associations of which she was a member. She was the first woman president of the New York Academy of Sciences, and she was president of the American Association for Cancer Research 20 years after her first paper was scorned. In her last years she was very much concerned that her success in developing vaccines for some types of cancers might result in more funds being targeted for patient care than for research. Naturally her discoveries were widely discussed in newspapers and popular magazines and created a great deal of public interest, and to the end of her life she was worried about the future funding for cancer research.

She received many awards during her career, including the Presidential Medal Centennial Award of Hunter College (1970), the Virus-Cancer Program Award of the National Institutes of Health (1974), and the Jocobi Medallion of Mt. Sinai Medical Center (1984). She was a member of the American Association for Cancer Research (president, 1976), New York Academy of Sciences (president, 1978), American Association of Immunologists, American Society of Hematology, and Tissue Culture Association. There are photographs in Iris Noble's *Contemporary Women Scientists of America* and in *Biographical Memoirs* of the National Academy of Sciences (1994).

***Bibliography:*** *American Men and Women of Science* 11–17; Herzenberg, C., *Women Scientists from Antiquity to the Present;* Ireland, N., *Index to Women of the World . . . Suppl.;* Noble, I., *Contemporary Women Scientists of America; Notable Twentieth-Century Scientists; Notable Women in the Life Sciences;* Rossiter, M., *Women Scientists in America;* Stanley, A., *Mothers and Daughters of Invention.*

# *Fromkin, Victoria Alexandria (Landish)*
(1923– )
## ***linguist, neurolinguist***

***Education:*** B.A., University of California, Berkeley, 1944; M.A., University of California, Los Angeles, 1963, Ph.D. in linguistics, 1965
***Professional Experience:*** Research linguist, University of California, Los Angeles, 1965–1966, assistant professor of linguistics, 1966–1968, associate professor, 1968–1972, professor of linguistics, 1972– , chair of department, 1972–1976, dean of graduate division, 1979–1989, vice chancellor of graduate programs, 1980–1989
***Concurrent Positions:*** Member of executive board, Center for Applied Linguistics; chair of Council of Graduate Deans, University of California, 1985–1986
***Married:*** Jack Fromkin, 1948
***Children:*** 1

***Victoria Fromkin*** is known as a linguist who has conducted research in neurological problems. Linguistics is the science of language that encompasses phonetics, phonology, morphology, syntax, semantics, pragmatics, and the history of linguistics. She has served on many distinguished committees and has been a prolific writer in the field. She was elected to membership in the National Academy of Sciences in 1996.

After receiving her doctorate, she accepted a position at the University of California, Los Angeles, in the Linguistics Department. She advanced quickly through the ranks to professor of linguistics and department chair in 1972. Later she served other administrative responsibilities as dean of the graduate division and vice chancellor for academic programs.

She has been an active scholar, serving as a member of the editorial boards of *Brain and Language, Studies in African Linguistics,* and *Journal of Applied Psycholinguistics.* She has investigated many aspects of the subject in her books *Introduction to Language* (1974; 2d ed., 1978), *Language, Speech, and Mind* (1988), *Speech Errors as Linguistic Evidence* (1974), and *Errors in Linguistic Performance: Slips of the Tongue, Ear, Pen, and Hand* (1980). She also edited *Tone: A Linguistic Survey* (1978) and has discussed her research on dyslexia in some of her more recent papers.

Fromkin has served on distinguished committees, being a member of the linguistics panel of the National Science Foundation (1976–1978); linguistics delegate to the National Academy of Science of China (1974); member of National Institutes of Health Sensory Disorder and Language Section (1982–1984); member of the National Research Council Committee on Basic Research Behavior and Social Sciences (1982–1988); president of the Association of Graduate Schools of the Association of American Universities (1988); and U.S. delegate and member of the executive board of the International Permanent Committee on Linguistics. In addition to her responsibilities for women faculty members and students in her capacity as department chair, dean, and later, vice chancellor, she has been active in promoting the role of women scientists, including being a member of the National Science Foundation Advisory Panel on Faculty Awards for Women in Science and Engineering from 1990 to 1991.

In correspondence with the author in June and July 1997, Fromkin said she was totally surprised when she was notified that she had been elected to membership in the National Academy of Sciences but that the election has not changed her life. She encourages young women to pursue a career in her field of linguistics.

The range of her interests is indicated by the professional associations in which she is active. She is a fellow of the Acoustical Society of America, the American Psychological Society, and the New York Academy of Sciences. She is a member of the Linguistics Society of America (president, 1985) and the American Association of Phonetic Sciences. Her research includes brain mechanisms underlying language and cognition, using data from normal spontaneous speech errors, aphasia patients, and normal experimental speech production and perception studies. Some information was supplied in a telephone conversation and correspondence with the author in June and July 1997.

***Bibliography:*** *American Men and Women of Science* 11, 16–19; *Contemporary Authors* v. 89–92.

# *Fuchs, Elaine V.*

(1950– )

## ***cell biologist, molecular biologist, biochemist, geneticist***

***Education:*** B.S. in chemistry, University of Illinois, 1972; Ph.D. in biochemistry, Princeton University, 1977

***Professional Experience:*** Research fellow in biochemistry, Massachusetts Institute of Technology, 1977–1980; assistant professor of biochemistry, University of Chicago, 1980–1985, associate professor of molecular and cell biology and biochemistry, 1985–1988, investigator and professor of molecular genetics, molecular and cell biology, and biochemistry, Howard Hughes Medical Institute, University of Chicago, 1988–

***Married:*** David T. Hansen, 1988

***Elaine Fuchs*** is renowned for her research in molecular genetics. She was identified early in her career as an outstanding scientist, and she was named a Presidential Scholar in 1982. She also received the President's Young Investigator Award of the National Science Foundation for 1985–1990. After completing her postdoctoral research at the Massachusetts Institute of Technology, she received an appointment as an assistant professor at the University of Chicago. In the short span of eight years she was promoted to professor and investigator for the prestigious Howard Hughes Medical Institute at that university. She was elected to membership in the National Academy of Sciences in 1996.

In her research on human skin genes, she is seeking cures for cancer and other diseases of the skin, esophagus, and bronchial tubes. She has focused on understanding the biochemical mechanisms that regulate genes during the growth and differentiation of the inner or basal epidermis cells. During differentiation, the basal cells stop multiplying, migrate to the skin's surface, and then undergo morphological and biochemical changes, the most pronounced being the production of keratin proteins. A malfunction of this process characterizes many skin diseases. In basal-cell carcinomas, for example, the cells do not differentiate at all ("differentiate" in biological terminology means that cells or tissues change from relatively generalized to specialized kinds during development).

Fuchs's current research involves the molecular biology of gene expression in differentiating human epidermal cells and in transgenic mouse epidermis, biochemical changes in the cytoskeletal architecture during differentiation, and effect of Vitamin A and growth factors on gene expression in normal and cancerous epithelial cells. She has published numerous research papers and has served as associate editor of the *Journal for Cell Biology* since 1993.

She has received many other awards, such as the Andrew Mellon fellowship, University of Chicago (1980), R. R. Bensely Award of the American Association of Anatomists (1988), the Searle Scholar Award of Searle Corporation (1981), the career development award of the National Institutes of Health (1982), the William Montagna Award of the Society of Investigative Dermatology (1995), and the Keith Porter award of the American Association of Cell Biology (1996). She is a fellow of the American Academy of Arts and Sciences. She is a member of the Institute of Medicine of the National Academy of Sciences, American Society for Cell Biology, American Society of Biological Chemists, and Society for Investigative Dermatology. Her photograph is included in *Science Digest* (December 1984) as one of America's top 100 young scientists.

***Bibliography:*** *American Men and Women of Science* 15–19; Ireland, N., *Index to Women of the World . . . Suppl; Who's Who in America,* 51st ed., 1997; *Who's Who of American Women,* 20th ed., 1997–1998.

# *Futter, Ellen Victoria*
(1949– )
## *naturalist, museum director*

***Education:*** Student, University of Wisconsin, 1967–1969; B.A., Barnard College, 1971; J.D., Columbia University, 1974; honorary degrees: LL.D, Columbia University, Hamilton College, and New York Law School; DHL, Amherst College and Hofstra University
***Professional Experience:*** Associate in law firm, 1974–1980; acting president, Barnard College, 1980–1981, president, 1981–1993; president, American Museum of Natural History, 1993–
***Married:*** John A. Shutkin, 1974
***Children:*** 2

***Ellen Futter*** was appointed president of the American Museum of Natural History in New York City in 1993 and is a lawyer and a former college president. Although she is not a scientist, she considers herself a naturalist with a genuine interest in many areas that are represented in the museum's collections. As a child she collected shells, rocks, and butterflies and still has a personal collection of shells. She was hired by the museum board of directors for her administrative ability. Although the board had started a program of modernization several years earlier, they needed fresh ideas on selecting exhibits, marketing, promotions, and technology.

While Futter was president of Barnard College, she increased fund-raising, built a new dormitory with some of the funds, and negotiated an agreement with Columbia University to permit women to enroll in that university's undergraduate programs—up to that time, Barnard had been a women's college, and the Columbia undergraduate curriculum had been restricted to men. In an interview in the March 13, 1995, issue of the *New Yorker,* she said that her experience at Barnard gave her "a keen appreciation for process, a real understanding of the importance of the culture of the institution, of community. . . . It's more than a sense of being careful; it's being true to the institutional values."

The American Museum of Natural History has a long tradition of exhibits, education, and research. When it opened in 1869, the directors originally accepted material that seemed to be of popular interest. During the late 1800s, libraries, museums, and trade schools were established to educate the working-class population, many of whom were immigrants. Later, after touring some of the European museums, the directors added the element of research, and the American Museum became, and still is, one of the leading resources in anthropology and paleontology. In the late 1800s and early 1900s, anthropologists, some of them women, collected vast amounts of data and artifacts about the Native American tribes, some of which were wiped out during the westward migration of whites. The museum has one of the largest collections of animal fossils of the American continent. More than 60 percent of the artifacts are not on display but are used for research.

The curators today still spend a high percentage of their field research on topics that may not relate to any of the exhibits. Their salaries are competitive with the top university researchers, and they also have the security of tenure. One of Ellen Futter's concerns is to provide more opportunities in science for women and minorities.

As a young woman without a scientific background heading the museum, she has been successful in working with the staff and researchers. Her forte is what is known in the business world as "positioning"; she is consciously positioning her institution for a return to a long-forgotten prominence. She has overseen sprucing up the exhibits, but she has not made major changes in the concepts. She asks the curators to think strategically about exhibitions that can reach a wider audience and about taking the museum to classrooms and the general public. She used the museum's 125th birthday anniversary in 1993 to launch a barrage of events.

Her goal is to cultivate a new image of the museum as an involved, vital place. In 1994, the *New York Times* reported on the front page on a Friday that a museum paleontologist had discovered the first fossil embryo of a carnivorous dinosaur. By the time the museum opened on Saturday morning, the embryo, as well as an enlarged illustration and a video, was on display in the rotunda.

Futter is also active in the business and social arenas. She is a member of the Council on Economic Development. She has received several awards, including an award from Albert Einstein College of Medicine/Yeshiva University, the Abram L. Sachar award of Brandeis University, medal of distinction from Barnard College, and Excellence Medal from Columbia University. She is a member of the American Academy of Arts and Sciences, the National Institute of Social Sciences, and bar associations. Her photograph is included in *People Weekly* (September 8, 1980), *Natural History* (January 1994), *Scientific American* (July 1994), and the *New Yorker* (March 13, 1995).

***Bibliography:*** *Who's Who of American Women*, 20th ed., 1997.

# G

## *Gailliard, Mary Katharine*

(1939– )

***theoretical physicist***

***Education:*** B.A., Hollins College, 1960; M.A., Columbia University, 1961; D.Sci. in theoretical physics, University of Paris-Sud, Orsay, 1964 and 1968
***Professional Experience:*** Research assistant, Centre National de Recherche Scientifique, Paris, 1964–1968, research associate, 1968–1973, head of research, 1973–1979, director of research, 1980–1981; professor of physics, University of California, Berkeley, 1981–
***Concurrent Positions:*** Visiting scientist, European Organization for Nuclear Research, Geneva, 1964–1981; National Accelerator Laboratory, Batavia, Illinois, 1973–1974, 1983; Institute for Theory of Physics, University of California, Santa Barbara (1985); principal investigator, National Science Foundation grant, 1982– ; faculty senior scientist, Lawrence Berkeley Laboratory, 1981–
***Children:*** 3

**Mary Gaillard** is known internationally for her research in theoretical physics, specifically on gauge theories and supergravity. She has held distinguished appointments with the Centre National de Recherche Scientifique in Paris and several of the laboratories in the United States, such as Fermilab and Lawrence Berkeley Laboratory. Although she was born in New Brunswick, New Jersey, and educated at two American universities, she received her doctorate in France and was employed primarily in Europe for a time. She was elected to membership in the National Academy of Sciences in 1991.

She has received numerous awards and distinguished lectureships, such as the Prix Thibaud (1977), Loeb Lecture in Physics of Harvard University (1980), Warner-Lambert Lecture, University of Michigan (1984), E. O. Lawrence Memorial Award (1988), chancellor's distinguished lectureship, University of California, Berkeley (1981), and appointment as science director, Les Houches summer school (1981). She has served on a number of distinguished committees, such as the Technical Assessment Committee on University Programs, U.S. Department of Education, 1982; member, Subpanel on New Facility High-Energy Physics Advisory Panel, U.S. Department of Energy, 1983; visiting committee for Fermilab, 1983–1985, Astrophysics Advisory Committee, 1985–1988, Physics Advisory Committee, 1986–1990; advisory committee, Theoretical Advanced Study Institute of Elementary Particle Physics, 1983–1988; advisory board, Institute for Advanced Studies, University of California, Santa Barbara, 1985–1988; Subcommittee on Oversight Review, National Science Foundation Theoretical Physics Program, 1988; and review committee, Argonne National Laboratory High Energy Physics Division, 1988–1990.

She has written many scientific publications, has edited two books—*Weak Interactions* (1977) and *Gauge Theories in High Energy Physics* (1983)—and has been an editor for a series published by Springer Verlag since 1988. She has been active in professional associations and chaired the Committee on the Status of Women in Physics of the American Physical Society in 1985. She is a fellow of the American Academy of Arts and Sciences and the American Physical Society and a member of the American Association for the Advancement of Science. Her research interests include elementary particle theory, phenomenology of gauge theories, physics of the early universe, unification of fundamental interactions, supercollider physics, and effective theories of particle physics based on superstring theories.

***Bibliography:*** *American Men and Women of Science* 17–19; *Who's Who in America,* 51st ed., 1997; *Who's Who in Science and Engineering,* 3d ed., 1996–1997; *Who's Who of American Women,* 20th ed., 1997–1998.

# *Galdikas, Birute Marija Filomend*

(1946– )

## *primatologist, anthropologist*

***Education:*** B.S. in psychology, University of California, Los Angeles, 1966, M.S. in archaeology, 1969, Ph.D. in anthropology, 1978
***Professional Experience:*** Head, orangutan research station, Tanjung Puting Nature Reserve, Borneo, 1971– ; visiting professor of anthropology, Simon Frasier University, 1981–
***Married:*** Rod Brindamour, 1969, divorced 1979; Pak Bohap bin Jalan, 1981
***Children:*** 3

***Birute Galdikas*** is the international authority on the orangutan. In 1971, armed with a master's degree, some field experience, and a small grant from the Leakey Foundation, she set out for Borneo to study orangutans. The scientists who had previously searched for orangutans often had been unable to find even one to study, but within a week of arriving in the rain forest in Borneo, Galdikas had spotted a female with her baby.

Even Galdikas says it seems incongruous that the world renowned anthropologist Louis S. B. Leakey would entrust a study to a young woman who had limited scientific experience. For a number of years, Leakey had the goal of studying the three major primate groups—the gorilla, the chimpanzee, and the orangutan—in order to compare the results with his own research on early humans. He preferred to select inexperienced people to conduct his studies, and he preferred to select women because they were more thorough in their work and tended to be more diligent without being distracted by outside activities and alternate theories. The three women he found to conduct the studies—Jane Goodall, Dian Fossey, and Birute Galdikas—often were referred to as "Leakey's ladies" or "the ape ladies"; but in their work, they changed the methods by which primatologists conduct research by studying animals as individuals with life histories, as human studies are conducted. The three women met as a group only three times: in 1970, in Jane Goodall's home in London; in 1974, at the Wenner-Gren Conference on Great Apes in Austria; and in 1981, at the Second Great Ape Conference in Los Angeles.

Galdikas was born in Wiesbaden, Germany, her parents having fled Lithuania when the Soviets took over that country after World War II. In 1948, the family emigrated to Toronto, Canada. She began her studies at the University of British Columbia, but when her family moved to southern California to join other family members, she transferred to the University of California, Los Angeles (UCLA). She had been fascinated with orangutans since childhood and had studied most of the material available on the subject. In California, she observed the orangutans in the Los Angeles zoo.

Galdikas met Leakey when he talked to one of her graduate anthropology classes at UCLA about his project on orangutans, and she volunteered for the project. Leakey approved of her husband, Rod Brindamour, because having spent his teenage years working in Canadian logging camps, he could administer the research site and deal with the Indonesian authorities for her. She had a much stronger scientific background than either Goodall or Fossey, having spent a semester at the University of Arizona

Field School at Ft. Apache, Arizona, at the Grasshopper archaeology site and two summers in Yugoslavia working on an international field project on Neanderthals.

While en route to Borneo, the couple visited Goodall in London and Africa and Mary Leakey in Africa. They did not go to Fossey's research site because she was not in residence at the time. When they arrived in Borneo, government officials escorted them on a long trek up the river to a swamp in the rain forest that was their research site. The housing consisted of one straw hut on stilts in which Birute, Rod, the cook, the assistants, and visitors all lived together. Several years later, the government built them a sturdy wooden house in which they lived alone, the staff having other quarters.

Orangutans are difficult to study because the males travel alone and the females travel with their children and perhaps another mother in the dense swampy forest of Borneo and Sumatra. The forest canopy is 20 or more feet above the ground, and the Borneo swamp is no Garden of Eden. Although there are fruit trees and edible plants, most are far above the ground and often are too sparse for researchers to attempt to use as food. Birute and Rod subsisted on rice, canned sardines, powdered milk, and tea. The animals are difficult to observe because they spend little time on the ground—the word "orangutan" means "people of the forest." It may seem strange that a bright orange object such as an orangutan could not be seen, but the forest canopy is very dense and the underbrush is so thick that the animals disappear into the foliage. One of the first tasks was for Rod to cut trails through the forest so the researchers could follow the orangutans as they moved from tree to tree.

Research on orangutans is a lifetime effort, for the animals have a life span of 50 to 60 years. The females mature about age 8 but do not have their first offspring until about age 12. Although the females in captivity breed about every five years, those in the wild breed about every eight years, so a female may have only two or three offspring during her lifetime. The animals are solitary by necessity. Food is plentiful in the rain forest, but the animals feed about 60 percent of the time, and an individual one can strip a tree of its fruit in a day. They establish separate territories and usually feed only within that territory. They seem to operate in slow motion, feeding and resting throughout the day. In an interview in the July 1987 issue of *Omni,* Galdikas says she considers the orangutans to be very intelligent. Although they do not use tools in the way that chimpanzees work a stick to get termites, "they have incredible cognitive abilities that they use in locomoting and in processing food, abilities that are equivalent to those required for tool use. . . . They aren't so excitable as chimps. There is a reserve, a detachment about them. They don't allow you too close to them. That serenity has always appealed to me."

As part of the negotiations with the Borneo government to use the forest preserve for her research, Galdikas agreed to rehabilitate captive orangutans. The laws prohibiting keeping them as pets are frequently flouted, and as the captive animals mature, they become very destructive. Galdikas comments in her autobiography that rehabilitating the captives actually gave her insight into how orangutan mothers rear their young. Since the young are dependent on their mothers even at age three or four, the rehabs adopted Galdikas as their mother, clinging to her 24 hours a day. After she had suffered through the first batch of infants, she transferred the next batch to the ones already rehabilitated. She keeps the rehabs separate from the wild population to avoid transferring disease from one group to another and to protect the food supply of the wild troop. An added benefit is that there is a constant batch of rehabs around the research station that visitors can see. Rod worked with the authorities to remove the poachers and farmers from the forest preserve.

After Birute began to report her preliminary findings at international meetings there was scientific interest in her work, and visitors started arriving. She also has students from the University of Jakarta on a regular rotating basis. She and Rod returned to Los Angeles for short periods in order to prepare her thesis, and after she received her doctorate, the two divorced. Rod stayed in North America to pursue his own career in computer science and to rear their son in civilization with his new wife. However, Birute had committed herself to spending her life in Borneo with the orangutans. Rod returned to Canada with their son, whom Birute sees regularly when she is in British Columbia to teach and lecture at Simon Frasier University. Later she married a Dayak tribesman, Pak Bohap bin Jalan, and they have two children. She has established the Orangutan Foundation, which is located in Los Angeles.

Her autobiography is *Reflections of Eden: My Years with the Orangutans of Borneo* (1995). There is information about her in Sy Montgomery's *Walking With the Great Apes* (1991) and Bettyann Kevles's *Watching the Wild Apes: The Primate Studies of Goodall, Fossey, and Galdikas* (1976). There are photographs of her in *Omni* (July 1987), *Discover* (December 1994), *International Wildlife* (March–April 1990), and *National Geographic* (October 1975 and December 1980). The Discovery Channel has broadcast a one-hour program on her work; the tape was prepared in the late 1980s and is available in the *Wild Discovery* series.

***Bibliography:*** *Current Biography 1995*; Yount, L., *Twentieth-Century Women Scientists.*

# *Gantt, Elisabeth*
(1934– )
***botanist***

***Education:*** B.A., Blackburn College, 1958; M.Sc., Northwestern University, 1960, Ph.D. in biology, 1963
***Professional Experience:*** National Institutes of Health (NIH) research associate in microbiology, Dartmouth College Medical School, 1963–1966; NIH research associate in microbiology, Radiation Biology Laboratory, Smithsonian Institution, 1966–1988; professor of botany, University of Maryland, 1988–
***Married:*** R. Raymond, 1958
***Children:*** 1

***Elisabeth Gantt*** is noted for her work on plant physiology and biological structure. After receiving her doctorate from Northwestern University, she was a National Institutes of Health research associate in microbiology, first at Dartmouth College Medical School and then at the Radiation Biology Laboratory of the Smithsonian Institution. She then joined the University of Maryland as a professor in the Botany Department. She was elected to membership in the National Academy of Sciences in 1996.

Born in Yugoslavia, Gantt immigrated to the United States and received degrees from Blackburn College and Northwestern University. For many years her research has focused on examining the process of photosynthesis, which, especially in plants, is defined as the synthesis of complex organic materials, especially carbohydrates, from carbon dioxide, water, and inorganic salts using sunlight as the source of energy and with the aid of chlorophyll and associated pigments.

She has received numerous awards and honors such as the Darbaker Prize of the Botany Society of America (1958) and the G. M. Smith Medal of the National Academy of Sciences (1994). She was a member of the board of fellows and associates of the National Research Council from 1973 to 1976. She has been active in professional organizations, serving as president of the American Society of Plant Physiologists in 1989 and the Phycological Society of America in 1978.

She is a fellow of the American Association for the Advancement of Science. In addition to the associations listed above, she is a member of the American Institute of Biological Sciences, American Society for Photobiology, and Japan Society of Plant Physiologists. Her research centers on structures of photosynthetic apparatus, localization and characterization of phycobiliproteins, and membrane structure.

***Bibliography:*** *American Men and Women of Science* 11–19; Herzenberg, C., *Women Scientists from Antiquity to the Present;* Ireland, N., *Index to Women of the World . . . Suppl.; Who's Who in America,* 51st ed., 1997; *Who's Who in Science and Engineering,* 3d ed., 1996–1997.

# *Garmire, Elsa (Meints)*

(1939– )

## *physicist, electrical engineer*

***Education:*** B.A., Radcliffe College, 1961; Ph.D. in physics, Massachusetts Institute of Technology, 1965

***Professional Experience:*** Research fellow, Massachusetts Institute of Technology, 1965–1966; scientist, Electronics Research Center, National Aeronautics and Space Administration (NASA), 1966; research fellow in electrical engineering, California Institute of Technology, 1966–1973; senior research scientist, Center for Laser Studies, University of Southern California, 1974–1978, professor of electrical engineering and physics, 1981–1992, associate director of center, 1978–1983, director of center, 1984–1995, William Hogue Professor of Engineering, 1992–1995; dean of Thayer School of Engineering, Dartmouth College, 1995–1997; professor of engineering sciences, Dartmouth College, 1997–

***Concurrent Positions:*** President, Laser Images, Inc.; member of technical staff, Aerospace Corporation, 1975–1992

***Married:*** Gordon P. Garmire, 1961, divorced 1975; Robert H. Russell, 1979

***Children:*** 2

***Elsa Garmire*** has had a distinguished career in laser research since receiving her doctorate in nonlinear optics under Charles H. Townes, who received the Nobel Prize in Physics. The term "laser" is an acronym for light amplification by stimulated emission of radiation; the term was coined about 1960. The author remembers when there was much discussion about how to pronounce the word—as "layser" or as "lazer." Elsa Garmire married after completing her undergraduate degree and continued working in the division of sponsored research while she was in graduate school. The couple moved to California where her husband had a fellowship and later a professorship at the California Institute of Technology.

She had an appointment as a research fellow in electrical engineering at the California Institute of Technology between 1966 and 1973, but between 1969 and 1973, she was working only a limited schedule as a part-time research fellow or part-time senior research fellow. Throughout her career, she has been conducting major research in the front ranks of laser studies in America. In 1974, she was appointed a senior research scientist at the Center for Laser Studies at the University of Southern California and was promoted to professor of electrical engineering and physics, associate director of the Center for Laser Studies, and then director of the center. She was the first woman to be appointed to the engineering faculty at the University of Southern California and became the William Hogue Professor of Engineering there in 1992. She was elected to membership in the National Academy of Engineering in 1989 and to the American Academy of Arts and Sciences in 1996. In 1995 she became the dean of the Thayer School of Engineering at Dartmouth College, the first woman dean of engineering in an Ivy League school.

Garmire's expertise is reflected in the number of consultations in which she has been involved. She has consulted for Standard Telecommunication Labs in England (1974), Northrop Corporation (1975–1977), TRW Corporation (1988–1989), and McDonnell Douglas of St. Louis (1990–1994). She also was president of Laser Images, Inc. She has published more than 200 papers in scientific journals and has been awarded ten patents. She has been associate editor of both *Optics Letters* and *Fiber and Integrated Optics.*

She is a fellow of the Institute of Electrical and Electronics Engineers, the American Physical Society (APS), the Optical Society of America (OSA) and the Society of Women Engineers. She has been on the boards of APS, OSA, and the IEEE Lasers & Electro-Optics Society and received an achievement award from the Society of Women Engineers in 1994. Her research is focused on lasers, integrated optics, nonlinear optics, spectroscopy, and quantum electronics.

***Bibliography:*** *American Men and Women of Science* 11–19; *Who's Who in America,* 51st ed., 1997; *Who's Who in Engineering,* 9th ed., 1995; *Who's Who in Science and Engineering,* 2d ed., 1994–1995; *Who's Who of American Women,* 20th ed., 1997–1998.

# *Gayle, Helene Doris*

(1955– )

## *pediatrician, epidemiologist*

***Education:*** B.A. in psychology, Barnard College, 1976; M.D., University of Pennsylvania, 1981; M.S. in public health, Johns Hopkins University, 1981

***Professional Experience:*** Residency in pediatrics, Children's Hospital Medical Center, Washington, D.C., 1981–1984; epidemiology training program, Centers for Disease Control and Prevention (CDC), 1984–1987, coordinator of acquired immune deficiency syndrome (AIDS) and human immunodeficiency virus (HIV) in children and teenagers, 1987– ; coordinator of CDC with the U.S. Agency for International Development, ca. 1990

***Helene Gayle*** is renowned worldwide for her work on acquired immune deficiency syndrome (AIDS) and human immunodeficiency virus (HIV) prevention and control. Growing up during the time of the civil rights movement, she was conscious of the importance of making a contribution to society. She majored in psychology as an undergraduate before attending medical school; after hearing a noted researcher speak about smallpox eradication, she added a master's degree in public health. She was a resident and intern in pediatrics before joining the epidemiology training program at the Centers for Disease Control and Prevention (CDC) in Atlanta, Georgia. Epidemiology is the branch of medicine that deals with the incidence and prevalence of disease in large populations and with the detection and cause of epidemics of infectious diseases. By the mid 1980s, when Gayle was in the first years of her work, AIDS was reaching epidemic proportions.

In her various assignments at CDC, she has concentrated on the effect of AIDS on children, adolescents, and their families, both in the United States and worldwide, and she found that the U.S. black community, especially black women, is at high risk with respect to contracting the AIDS virus. For example, in the late 1980s, black women constituted 52 percent of the female AIDS population nationwide although they represented only 11 percent of the population, and black children constituted 53 percent of the children in the nation who had AIDS. She has focused her attention on educating the populations of both the United States and Africa on ways to prevent HIV infection, the virus that causes AIDS, because currently there is not a vaccine available. By studying the virus's effect on people in various societies and age groups, researchers hope to find better ways to prevent, diagnose, and treat the deadly infection. One approach is to encourage female-specific prevention, such as female condoms or vaginal virucides, especially in those countries where women are more often infected but have less control over sexual interaction.

The problem with controlling AIDS is that transmission is the result of personal behaviors that are culturally influenced. In a news release published in many newspapers in September 1997, Gayle said recent successes in treating AIDS have resulted in a general feeling that HIV is no longer the threat it used to be. However, cases of gonorrhea among homosexual men have more than doubled at some U.S. clinics, which suggests that safe sex is not being taken seriously. The author of one article in the May–June 1995 issue of *Public Administration Review* praises Gayle for her accomplishments in AIDS prevention efforts and public policy. She has been instrumental in getting disparate groups—including minority, gay, and church communities—involved so they have a better understanding of what the government does about AIDS. She has also used her interpersonal-relations skills to successfully build bridges and foster communication between the federal government and various communities. Another area in which she has made a significant contribution, according to the article, is in the development of preventive tools and technologies for women to use. The present prevention tools, such as the use of condoms, are all linked to male-controlled behavior.

Gayle has received numerous awards, such as the U.S. Public Health Service achievement medal. She is a member of the editorial board of *Annual Review of Public Health.* Her photograph is included in *Black Enterprise* (October 1988) and *Ebony* (November 1991).

***Bibliography:*** *Blacks in Science and Medicine; Notable Twentieth-Century Scientists.*

# *Geller, Margaret Joan*
(1947– )
## *astrophysicist, cosmologist, astronomer*

***Education:*** B.A., University of California, Berkeley, 1970; M.A., Princeton University, 1972, Ph.D in physics, 1975; honorary degree: D.Sc., Connecticut College (1995)

***Professional Experience:*** Fellow in theoretical astrophysics, Center for Astrophysics, 1974–1976; research associate, Harvard University, 1976–1980, assistant professor, 1980–1983; astrophysicist, Smithsonian Astrophysical Observatory, 1983– ; professor of astronomy, Harvard University, 1988–

***Concurrent Position:*** Senior visiting fellow, Institute of Astronomy, Cambridge University, 1979–1980

***Margaret Geller*** is one of the foremost cosmologists of the twentieth century. Cosmology is the branch of astronomy that deals with the general structure and evolution of the universe, and since the 1980s, she has worked on surveys of the distribution of galaxies in the universe. She and her team constructed three-dimensional maps that revealed, for the first time, that galaxies such as the earth's own Milky Way are arranged in very large patterns resembling soapsuds. In the nearby universe, thin walls marked by thousands of galaxies surround vast dark regions in which there are very few galaxies. In 1989, Geller and her collaborator, John Huchra of Harvard, discovered "the Great Wall," a huge arc of galaxies spanning the area the scientists surveyed. The wall is a chain of galaxies on the order of 500 million by 200 million by 15 million light-years in extent; this is the largest coherent structure yet seen in the universe.

Those are among the most significant discoveries about galaxies in more than 60 years. The galaxies were first described by Edwin Hubble in the 1930s when he verified that other galaxies exist and that those galaxies are flying away from earth's as the universe expands. The light waves emitted by the receding galaxies are stretched and thereby nudged toward the red end of the spectrum; the faster the recession, the greater the redshift. Therefore, the distance to a far-off galaxy can be gauged from its redshift, and it was theoretically possible to map the three-dimensional distribution of galaxies instead of just their position in the sky. Hubble and his associates did not prepare the maps because he theorized that the universe was smooth and featureless. It is also tedious work to determine the redshift of even one galaxy.

In the 1970s, observatories started replacing photographic plates with more-efficient electronic detectors, and using these instruments, observers could take a redshift in half an hour rather than an entire night. The detectors also could be used with an ordinary telescope rather than one of the giant ones, such as the telescope at Mt. Palomar. Geller and Huchra began a systematic redshift survey in 1985 to find out how many galaxies there are in a given volume of space; they, too, expected the galaxy distribution to be smooth. They took a representative slice across the sky and assigned a graduate student to construct a map of the survey's redshifts. The map revealed the "soapsuds," the blank spaces, and the Great Wall. Since 1985, team members have prepared additional "slices" of redshifts and are continuing the project. Other observatories that have newer electronic detectors are mapping other areas of the universe.

In common with many other women scientists, Geller was encouraged by her parents to pursue her interests in mathematics and science as a child. When she found school boring, her parents coached her in algebra at home and encouraged her to read widely. She was born while her father was a graduate student at Cornell University, and when he later worked as an x-ray crystallographer at Bell Labs, he would take her to his laboratory to show her how to measure x-ray diffraction photographs. At that time, Bell Labs was on the leading edge of research on the maser, the laser, and the transistor, and Geller's father conveyed his enthusiasm for his work to his children. Margaret majored in physics at the University of California, Berkeley, and received a National Science Foundation predoctoral fellowship in the Physics Department at Princeton. One of the physics faculty members advised her to enter a field that would be coming of age by the time she finished her doctorate; he advised either astrophysics or biophysics as particularly promising areas. She chose astrophysics and was only the second woman to earn a doctorate in physics from Princeton.

Although at first she found her work as a research associate at Harvard rather boring, she challenged herself to work on questions that interested her. While visiting the Institute of Astronomy at Cambridge University, she decided to examine the large-scale structure of the universe, of which little was known. She joined forces with Huchra, who specializes in using telescopes to gather the necessary data for these explorations, to complement her theoretical, analytical view. When she became a professor, she was only the second woman astronomer to receive tenure at Harvard; the first was Cecelia Payne-Gaposchkin (1900–1979).

In addition to Geller's scientific publications, she has prepared two films for the general public. The video *Where the Galaxies Are* (1991), which premiered at the National Air and Space Museum, is a general description of her work; the film *So Many Galaxies . . . So Little Time* (1992) provides insights into the lives and work of scientists and their students. She is concerned about subtle cultural factors that could steer women away from careers in science. In her own experience, one elementary school teacher tried to discourage her interest in math and science, and the Physics Department at Princeton did not welcome her with open arms, but many of the faculty members were very supportive of her work and career. She feels that women are more concerned about security than men are and are not as willing to take risks. In order to be a successful scientist or successful at any creative endeavor, one has to take risks.

She was elected to membership in the National Academy of Sciences in 1992. She has received one of the MacArthur awards (1990), the Newcomb-Cleveland Prize of the American Academy of Arts and Sciences (1990), and the Helen Sawyer Hogg Prize of the Royal Astronomical Society of Canada (1993), the last named for the woman (1905– ) who cataloged variable stars in globular clusters. Geller has been on the editorial review board for *Science* since 1991. She is a fellow of the American Physical Society and the American Association for the Advancement of Science and a member of the American Academy of Arts and Sciences, International Astronomical Union, and American Astronomical Society. Her research includes nature and history of the galaxy distribution, the origin and evolution of galaxies, and x-ray astronomy. She was interviewed for the television program "Mysteries of Deep Space" in the *NOVA* series on public television in 1997. Her photograph is included in *Current Biography* (1997), *Science* (May 24, 1991), *Physics Today* (November 1990), *Time* (January 20, 1986), *Omni* (August 1991), and *Scientific American* (November 1993).

***Bibliography:*** *American Men and Women of Science* 13–19; *Current Biography 1997; Notable Twentieth-Century Scientists; Who's Who in Science and Engineering,* 3d ed., 1996–1997.

# *Giblett, Eloise Rosalie*
## (1921– )
## ***hematologist, geneticist***

***Education:*** Student, Mills College, 1939–1940; B.S., University of Washington, 1942, M.S. in microbiology, 1947, M.D., 1951

***Professional Experience:*** Intern and resident, University of Washington, 1951–1952, postdoctoral fellow, 1953–1955, clinical associate, School of Medicine, 1955–1957, clinical instructor, 1957–1958, clinical assistant professor, 1958–1961, clinical associate professor, 1961–1967, research professor of medicine, 1967–1987; associate director, Puget Sound Blood Center, 1967–1979, executive director, 1979–1987, emeritus professor and emeritus executive director, 1987–

***Concurrent Positions:*** Postdoctoral fellow, Medical School, University of London, 1953–1955

***Eloise Giblett*** is known for her discovery that an inadequate supply of two specific enzymes causes inherited deficiencies in the body's immune system. She also discovered a wide range of new inherited characteristics, called genetic markers, including blood groups and serum proteins. She was interested in music as a career until she became intrigued with science while attending Mills College. After completing her undergraduate degree at the University of Washington, she joined the WAVES, the women's branch of the U.S. Navy at the time, as a medical technician. She then used funds from the GI Bill to attend medical school, receiving an M.S. in microbiology and then an M.D. degree. She fulfilled her internship and residency at the University of Washington in 1951–1952 and continued as a postdoctoral fellow at the same institution, as well as in medical school at the University of London from 1953 to 1955, specializing in hematology and human genetics.

She accepted a joint appointment as full professor at the University of Washington and associate director of the Puget Sound Blood Center in 1967. In the mid 1970s, she discovered that deficiencies of the enzymes adenosine deaminase and nucleoside phosphorylase caused inherited immunodeficiencies because both are vital in the purine cycle (purines are fundamental constituents of nucleic acids). She also led the research on gene therapy to treat these deficiencies. Another important discovery was the new genetic markers, especially her findings regarding polymorphisms in blood cell enzymes (polymorphism in genetics refers to genes in the human blood groups O, A, B, and AB). She also did important research in blood group antibodies.

Giblett has published more than 200 papers and textbook chapters on various aspects of inherited characteristics, particularly those in human blood. These include iron kinetics, red cell destruction owing to isoantibodies, detection of variants in blood group antigen, serum protein, red cell enzyme genetic systems, and changes in red cell antigen associated with marrow stress. She is the author of the book *Genetic Markers in Human Blood* (1969). She has participated on many significant committees and commissions as a member of the National Institutes of Health Genetics Study Section; the National Heart, Lung, and Blood Research Review Committee; the National Blood Resources Committee; and the Food and Drug Administration Toxicology Advisory Committee. In the 1960s, she was associate editor of the journals *Transfusion* and *American Journal of Human Genetics.*

She was elected to membership in the National Academy of Sciences in 1980 and has received the Emily Cooley Award (1975), the Karl Landsteiner Award (1976), and the Philip Levine Award (1978). She is a member of the American Society of Hematology, American Society of Human Genetics (president, 1973), American Association of Immunologists, and Association of American Physicians.

***Bibliography:*** *American Men and Women of Science* 11–19; Herzenberg, C., *Women Scientists from Antiquity to the Present; Notable Twentieth-Century Scientists; Who's Who in America,* 51st ed., 1997; *World Who's Who in Science.*

# *Glusker, Jenny (Pickworth)*
(1931– )
## *crystallographer, cancer researcher*

***Education:*** B.A., Somerville College, Oxford University, 1953, M.A. and D.Phil. in chemistry, 1957; honorary degree: D.Sc., College of Wooster, 1985

***Professional Experience:*** Research fellow in x-ray crystallography, California Institute of Technology, 1955–1956; research associate, Institute for Cancer Research, Philadelphia, 1956–1967, director, 1966– , assistant member, 1967, member, 1967–1979, senior member, 1979–

***Concurrent Positions:*** Research associate professor, University of Pennsylvania, 1969–1979, adjunct professor, 1980–

***Married:*** Donald L. Glusker, 1955

***Children:*** 3

***Jenny Glusker*** is renowned for her work in x-ray crystallography. She is a leading authority on chemical carcinogenesis based on the structure determinations of various carcinogens. She has performed calculations on simple aromatic hydrocarbons that act as models for polycyclic aromatic hydrocarbons, and she has studied many antitumor agents that inhibit chemical carcinogenesis. X-ray crystallographic data are powerful tools, for they provide a three-dimensional structure, the absolute configuration, and the preferred conformations of a sample.

In her youth, both of her parents encouraged their children's interest in science. Both parents were physicians and wished Jenny to pursue medicine as a career. Her mother was a member of the first class of women students in the medical school at Glasgow University during World War I, and she encouraged both of her daughters to combine marriage with a career. When Jenny was reading for her degree at Somerville College, her tutor was Dorothy Hodgkin, who later received a Nobel Prize. She worked with Hodgkin again while pursuing her doctorate, contributing to research on the structure of vitamin $B_{12}$. She met her future husband when he was a Rhodes Scholar in England. The two went to the United States in 1955, where they were married, and each had a postdoctoral appointment at the California Institute of Technology, Jenny being a member of Linus Pauling's research team. The couple then faced the problem of finding jobs at the same location. She found a position at the Institute for Cancer Research, and Donald found one at Rohm and Haas, a chemical company, both in Philadelphia.

Fortunately, the director of the institute encouraged married women to work and permitted them to work part-time schedules when their children were small. He also arranged that the researchers could teach at the University of Pennsylvania and supervise graduate students for the university. When their youngest child was two years old, in 1966, the director of the institute died after a brief illness, and Jenny was offered the position. She accepted the position and continued with her important research. She followed the general strategy of using the results of x-ray crystallographic studies on small molecules having biological activity to try to discover the mechanisms of action in biological systems that involve the interactions between small molecules and macromolecules. She has helped to determine the mechanisms of a number of important biochemical processes and has contributed to understanding the mode of action of certain carcinogens.

Glusker has published more than 100 scientific articles, written two books, and edited six others. Her books are *Crystal Structure Analysis: A Primer* (1972; 2d ed., 1985) and *Crystal Structure Analysis for Chemists and Biologists* (1994). She is the editor of *Acta Crystallographica* and serves on the editorial boards of several other journals. Several sources have commented on her careful and precise work and her ability to pull together large masses of structural and biochemical information into a consistent, plausible general mechanism. She has been very active in promoting the careers of many young researchers either through her teaching at the university or while supervising their graduate work at the institute. Among the awards she has received are the Garvan Medal of the American Chemical Society (1979) and the Fankuchen Award of the American Crystallographic Association (1995).

She is active in several professional associations, such as the American Association for the Advancement of Science, American Crystallographic Association (president, 1979), American Chemical Society, American Society of Biological Chemists, and Biophysical Society. Her research includes infrared spectroscopy; molecular structures in general; mechanisms of enzyme reactions from x-ray crystallographic studies of enzymes and their substrates and inhibitors; and studies of polycyclic mutagens and carcinogens, and the metabolic products of carcinogens. A partial list of her publications is included in *Women in Chemistry and Physics*, and her photograph is in *Chemical & Engineering News* (September 11, 1978).

***Bibliography:*** *American Men and Women of Science* 11–19; *Notable Women in the Physical Sciences;* Rossiter, M., *Women Scientists in America; Who's Who in Science and Engineering*, 3d ed., 1996–1997; *Women in Chemistry and Physics.*

# Goldberg, Adele
(1945– )
## computer scientist, information technologist

*Education:* B.A., mathematics, University of Michigan; M.S., and Ph.D in information science, University of Chicago, 1973

*Professional Experience:* Researcher in educational technology, Stanford University; research scientist, Xerox Corporation, Palo Alto Research Center (PARC), 1973–1988; founder, president, and chief executive officer, ParcPlace Systems, 1988–1992, chair of board of directors, 1992–1996, independent researcher on computer science courses, 1996–

*Children:* 2

*Adele Goldberg* is one of the few women whose contributions to the development of the personal computer in the 1970s is generally acknowledged. She worked at Xerox Corporation's prestigious think tank at Palo Alto, California, familiarly referred to as PARC. One author refers to the development of the personal computer as information technology's Manhattan Project—the Manhattan Project was the name of the massive effort to develop the atomic bomb during World War II.

With advanced degrees in information technology, she was teaching at Stanford University when Alan Kay, a computer whiz at Xerox, contacted her about developing programs for a computer that he called Smalltalk, which was the name of both the computer and the program. The purpose of Smalltalk was to improve productivity among computer programmers by developing a very simple programming language, and with her experience in instructional technology, Goldberg wrote demonstrations that were simple enough for children to use. Xerox at that time was notorious for allowing promising projects to languish in the labs—it already had a computer called Star that used icons, windows, and the mouse, but it did not bring the item into production, and competitors stole the market. However, Smalltalk had many of the same features; this type of computer is called an "object-oriented" computer.

Adele Goldberg's specific contributions are that she was instrumental in testing the computer and its software and that she persuaded Xerox to allow her and three partners to form a subsidiary to market Smalltalk. With her contacts in the education community, she went into public schools to have children play with the equipment and develop class projects. She was able to pull off this miracle by her understanding of computer systems and the way people work with them. She succeeded by sheer diligence. At one point the Xerox management dragged its feet about approving this testing, so she and Kay loaded the computers in a van, took them to a school, worked with the teachers and students, and left the equipment for their use for a year.

She managed the project starting in 1979, and she also headed projects to design other programming languages and environments, interface technology, and user applications. By 1987, she and Kay knew they had a viable product in Smalltalk, and they tried, without success, to persuade Xerox to market it. Adele hammered out an agreement with the corporation allowing her to spin off the product so that she and her partners could form a subsidiary, ParcPlace Systems, to further develop and market the computer. Adele and three other Xerox researchers were the stockholders; she was founder, president, and CEO.

At the time, the primary programming languages for mainframes were COBOL and C++, and it was the consensus of programmers that C++ was a beast to learn. Smalltalk was designed to be used for both mainframes and personal computers, and the applications were limitless: business processes, games, educational interactions, document publishing, manufacturing control. ParcPlace Systems ran a test on the relative ease of learning C++ and Smalltalk, and the result was that programmers could require up to 18 months to become proficient in C++ while ordinary COBOL programmers could become productive on Smalltalk in a matter of weeks and proficient in six months or less.

Goldberg was president and CEO until 1992 when she became the company's chief strategist and chair of the board of directors. The company went public in 1994. In 1995 or 1996, the company became ParcPlace-Digital, and she resigned as chair of the board. She now helps create new computer science courses at community colleges in the United States and at universities abroad and is also involved as a board member of Cognito Learning Media, a new company formed to provide multimedia software for science education.

She has published a number of articles in computing journals and several books: *Smalltalk–80: The Interactive Programming Environment* (1984), *Smalltalk–80: The Language and Its Implementation* (1983; rev. ed., 1984), and *Succeeding with Objects: Decision Frameworks for Project Management* (1995). In the last, she summarizes her experiences in creating and managing object technology at the Xerox Palo Alto Research Center and at ParcPlace Systems. She has received several awards such as the Association of Computer Machinery's Software Systems Award (1987). She is a member of the Association for Computing Machinery (president, 1984–1986) and the American Federation of Information Processing Societies. Her photograph is included in *Notable Twentieth-Century Scientists* and *Forbes* (October 7, 1996).

***Bibliography:*** *Notable Twentieth-Century Scientists;* Stanley, A., *Mothers and Daughters of Invention.*

# *Good, Mary (Lowe)*
## (1931– )
## ***inorganic chemist, radiation chemist***

***Education:*** B.S., Arkansas State Teachers College (now University of Central Arkansas), 1950; M.S., University of Arkansas, 1953, Ph.D. in inorganic chemistry and radiation chemistry, 1955; honorary degrees: at least 14

***Professional Experience:*** Instructor in chemistry, Louisiana State University, Baton Rouge, 1954–1956, assistant professor, 1956–1958; associate professor, Louisiana State University, New Orleans, 1958–1963, professor of chemistry, 1963–1974, Boyd Professor, 1974–1980; vice president and director of research, UOP, Inc., 1980–1985, director of research, Signal Research Center/AlliedSignal, Inc., 1985–1986, president of Engineering Materials Research, 1986–1988, senior vice president of technology, AlliedSignal Research and Technology Laboratory, 1988–1993; under secretary for technology, U.S. Department of Commerce, 1993–

***Married:*** Bill J. Good, 1952

***Children:*** 2

Mary L. Good is a renowned chemist who has achieved prominence for her research and teaching in academia and her administrative capabilities in industry and the federal government. Her early work in solvent extraction of metal complexes was focused on describing the chemical and physical properties of chemical species in an organic solvent, and she was one of the first researchers to apply Mossbauer spectroscopy to basic chemical research, namely, the solution of solid-state chemistry problems. Her significant work in this area was demonstrating that detailed chemical and structural information could be obtained for systems containing ruthenium. Her third major effort was in chemical evaluation of antifouling coatings, which are used to remove barnacles from ships in the U.S. Navy and the maritime industry. She was elected to membership in the National Academy of Engineering in 1987.

She was encouraged by her parents, both college graduates, to pursue a college education. When she entered college she at first majored in home economics with the idea of teaching in a public school, but in her first semester, her chemistry professor so inspired her with his enthusiasm for science that she switched her major to chemistry. She received her degree at age 19 with a major in chemistry and minors in mathematics and physics. Both her master's and doctoral degrees are in inorganic chemistry and radiochemistry. She met Bill Good in a chemistry class at Arkansas State, and they married in 1952.

Before she received her doctorate, she was appointed as an instructor of chemistry and the director of the radiochemistry laboratory at Louisiana State University (LSU) at Baton Rouge. In 1958, she and her husband were invited to join the faculty at the newly founded branch of LSU in New Orleans, she in the Chemistry Department and he in the Physics Department. She was promoted to professor in 1967 and in 1974 was named the Boyd Professor of Chemistry. The Boyd professorship is a university-wide distinguished professorship and a lifetime appointment. When she returned to the Baton Rouge campus in 1978, she was named the Boyd Professor of Materials Science in the Division of Engineering Research.

Even with her teaching, research, and family responsibilities, she has been very active in the American Chemical Society (ACS). She was chair of the board of directors in 1978 and 1980 and president in 1987. She received the Garvan Medal of the Society in 1973; this award is given annually to an American woman chemist. Those two recognitions for her work brought her national attention, and in 1980, she was appointed to the National Science Board, the oversight committee for the National Science Foundation; she served a second term from 1988 to 1992.

Also in 1980, she was offered the position of vice president and director of research for Universal Oil Products (UOP), Inc., an opportunity she has described as a challenge she could not refuse. The company had a highly regarded research center doing very interesting research. This was a time of mergers and acquisitions in industry, and although there were changes in name during the next few years, she essentially continued working for the same company, whether it was called UOP or AlliedSignal. She mentions that when she was interviewed by corporate executives about her ability to manage a large budget, she said her experience on the board of directors for the American Chemical Society qualified her for the position as that society not only oversees conferences but also publishes books and journals, operates an information service through *Chemical Abstracts*, and specifies standards for undergraduate and graduate chemical education.

When she accepted the position with UOP, her husband took advantage of the opportunity to retire from teaching and research to start a new career as an artist. Mary's next career change was in 1993 when she was appointed undersecretary for technology for the U.S. Department of Commerce. Her first assignment in that position was to oversee the clean car initiative between the Big Three auto manufacturers and the government to develop a car that is capable of operating at 82 miles per gallon.

An article in the June 11, 1990, issue of *Chemical & Engineering News* includes the statement that if you want to get something done in chemistry or in science in general, one of the better ways to succeed is to appoint Mary Good to the oversight committee, preferably as chair. She has served on numerous prestigious committees, one being the President's Council of Advisors on Science and Technology on which she served in 1991; this group guides and shapes U.S. scientific policy. In addition to participating in many research associations, she has been active in supporting the role of women. She has been president of the Zonta International Foundation, a philanthropic arm of Zonta International, a multinational organization dedicated to improving the status of women and encouraging high ethical standards in business. The foundation awards the Amelia Earhart fellowship to women in graduate studies in aerospace science.

Good has received the Parsons Award of the American Chemical Society (1991), the first woman to receive this recognition for outstanding public service by an ACS member, and she was named scientist of the year by *Industrial Research & Development* in 1982. In addition to publishing more than 100 scientific papers, she is the author of the books *Integrated Laboratory Sequence* (1970) and *Biotechnology and Materials Science: Chemistry for the Future* (1988). She is a fellow of the American Association for the Advancement of Science and a member of the American Chemical Society (president, 1987) and International Union of Pure and Applied Chemistry. There are photographs in *Notable Twentieth-Century Scientists, Notable Women in the Physical Sciences,* and *Chemical & Engineering News* (June 11, 1990, and October 15, 1995).

***Bibliography:*** *American Men and Women of Science* 11–19; Herzenberg, C., *Women Scientists from Antiquity to the Present;* Ireland, N., *Index to Women of the World . . . Suppl.; Notable Twentieth-Century Scientists; Notable Women in the Physical Sciences; Who's Who in America,* 51st ed., 1997; *Who's Who of American Women,* 20th ed., 1997–1998; *Women in Chemistry and Physics.*

## *Graham, Frances (Keesler)*
(1918– )
***psychophysiologist***

***Education:*** B.A., Pennsylvania State University, 1938; Ph.D. in psychology, Yale University, 1942; honorary degree: D.Sc., University of Wisconsin, 1996

***Professional Experience:*** Assistant and instructor in medical psychology, Washington University, St. Louis, 1941–1948, instructor and research associate, 1953–1957; instructor in psychology, Barnard College, 1948–1951; independent researcher, 1951–1957; research associate, University of Wisconsin, Madison, 1957–1964, associate professor of pediatrics, 1964–1968, professor, 1968–1980, professor of psychology, 1969–1980, Hilldale Research Professor, 1980–1986; research professor of psychology, University of Delaware, 1986–

***Concurrent Positions:*** Psychologist and acting director, St. Louis Psychiatric Clinic, 1942–1944

***Married:*** David Graham, 1941

***Children:*** 3

***Frances Graham*** is known for her research on the psychology of attention and the use of physiological measurement in the study of cognition and perception. A leading developmental psychologist, she has advanced psychological knowledge of the first months of life and been instrumental in developing measures and analyses for this field. As an undergraduate at Pennsylvania State University, she was a mathematics major until a required course in psychology steered her in another direction. In her graduate program at Yale, she first explored child clinical work.

After her marriage in 1941, she moved to St. Louis where she held positions in a city clinic and at Washington University. She negotiated half a day per week for research and developed a memory-for-designs test for brain damage that still is used. While her husband was at Cornell Medical College from 1948 to 1951, Graham taught at Barnard College. When they returned to the St. Louis area, she decided to be a self-supporting research investigator. She obtained grants to study the consequences of low blood oxygenation during the first postnatal hour, which eventually played a pivotal role in prenatal risk research.

In 1957, the Grahams moved to the University of Wisconsin, Madison, where she received an appointment as a research associate in pediatrics. In 1964, when she received a National Institute of Mental Health Research Scientist Award, she also became a tenured associate professor. She was promoted to professor of pediatrics in 1968 and received a joint appointment in psychology in 1969. Since the research scientist award paid her salary, she was able to teach and at the same time explore the electronics equipment available for research. She discovered that an unexpected stimulus change results in a slower cardiac rate, and other research efforts centered on the blink reflex of the human eye. In 1986, the Grahams moved to the University of Delaware where Frances received a full-time appointment in psychology. Her research there has centered on cardiac orienting and reflex modulation.

She has received awards, including the Distinguished Scientific Contribution of the Society for Psychophysiological Research (1981) and the Distinguished Alumna Award from Pennsylvania State University (1983). She was the Hilldale Research Professor at the University of Wisconsin and was named a William James fellow of the American Psychological Society in 1990. She was a consultant to both the National Institute of Neurological Disease and Blindness from 1958 to 1970 and the President's Commission on Ethics in Medicine and Biomedical and Behavioral Research from 1979 to 1981. She received the Wilbur L. Cross Medal of Yale University in 1992 and the Gold Medal of the American Psychological Foundation in 1995.

She was elected to membership in the National Academy of Sciences in 1988 and is a fellow of the American Association for the Advancement of Science. She is a member of the Society for Psychophysiological Research (president, 1974), Society for Research in Child Development (president, 1975–1977), American Psychological Association, Federation of Behavior Psychological and Cognitive Sciences, Acoustical Society of America, International Society for Developmental Psychobiology, and Society of Experimental Psychologists. A photograph and selected bibliography are included in the April 1991 issue of *American Psychologist.*

***Bibliography:*** *American Men and Women of Science* edition 11–19; *Who's Who in America,* 51st ed., 1997; *Who's Who of American Women,* 20th ed., 1997–1998.

# *Graham, Susan Lois*
(1942– )
***computer scientist***

***Education:*** B.A. in mathematics, Harvard University, 1964; M.S., Stanford University, 1966, Ph.D. in computer science, 1971

***Professional Experience:*** Associate research scientist and adjunct assistant professor of computer science, Courant Institute of Mathematical Science, New York University, 1969–1971; assistant professor of computer science, University of California, Berkeley, 1971–1976, associate professor, 1976–1981, professor, 1981–

***Concurrent Position:*** Lecturer, IBM Canada Laboratory, 1988–1992; visiting professor, Computer Science Department, Stanford University, 1981, Forsythe lecturer, 1993

***Married:*** 1971

***Susan Graham*** is known for her expertise in programming language design and implementation. While working toward a doctorate from Stanford University, she was a research scientist at the prestigious Courant Institute of Mathematical Science, an appointment that also carried teaching responsibilities. She then obtained a position in the Computer Science Department of the University of California, Berkeley, where she advanced from assistant professor to full professor in only ten years—the rate of advancement is indicative of the quality of her research and teaching. She was elected to membership in the National Academy of Engineering in 1993.

Her area of research is the study of programming languages for very large systems and networks. This work involves compiler transformations for high-performance computing, developing languages and interactive software, detecting faults in software, orchestrating interactions among parallel computations, and the design and implementation of practical data breakpoints. Often one reads about glitches in large computer programs that disrupt service and/or anger customers—an example is the breakdown in service of the Internet service America Online in 1997. Some of these glitches can cost thousands of dollars to repair and retest the system. Some academic computer experts regularly consult for companies that need assistance in setting up or repairing their computer networks or to train their programmers, and Susan Graham was a lecturer at the IBM Canada Laboratory for IBM programmers from 1988 to 1992.

One of the more coveted scientific committee appointments is to the U.S. President's Committee on the National Medal of Science, which recommends the persons to receive the medal; Graham was a member of that committee between 1994 and 1996. Her expertise has also been sought by government agencies. She was a member of the advisory committee, Division of Computer and Computation Research, of the National Science Foundation from 1987 to 1992 and of that foundation's program for science and technology centers from 1987 to 1991 as well as being a member of the committee on physical science, mathematics, and applications of the National Research Council from 1992 to 1995. Several universities have sought her expertise in evaluating their science curricula, and she became a member of the visiting committee for applied sciences at Harvard University in 1995 and of the visiting committee for engineering and applied science at the California Institute of Technology in 1994.

Her very active research has been funded by the National Science Foundation since 1974. She has been editor of *Communications of the Association for Computing Machinery* (1975–1979) and editor in chief of *Transactions on Programming Languages and Systems* (1978–1992). She was appointed the Forsythe Lecturer of the Computer Science Department at Stanford University in 1993 and was a visiting professor for the same department in 1981.

She is a fellow of the American Association for the Advancement of Science, the Association for Computing Machinery, and the American Academy of Arts and Sciences. She is a member of the Institute of Electrical and Electronics Engineers. Her research includes programming language design and implementation, syntax error recovery, parsing, and code generation and optimization.

***Bibliography:*** *American Men and Women of Science* 13–19; *Who's Who in Science and Engineering,* 3d ed., 1996–1997.

# *Grandin, Temple*
(1947– )
***animal scientist***

***Education:*** B.A. in psychology, Franklin Pierce College, 1970; M.S. in animal science, Arizona State University, 1975; Ph.D. in animal science, University of Illinois, Urbana, 1989
***Professional Experience:*** Livestock editor, *Arizona Farmer Ranchman,* 1973–1978; equipment designer, Corral Industries, Phoenix, Arizona, 1974–1975; independent consultant, Grandin Livestock Systems, Urbana, Illinois, 1975–1990, Fort Collins, Colorado, 1990– ; lecturer, then assistant professor, Animal Science Department, Colorado State University, 1990–
***Concurrent Position:*** Chair, handling committee, Livestock Conservation Institute, Madison, Wisconsin, 1976–

***Temple Grandin*** is known for her pioneer work as an animal scientist who specializes in designing equipment for handling livestock on farms, in feedlots, and in slaughtering facilities. She is a remarkable person who has controlled autism to lead a productive life. In fact, she coached the actor Dustin Hoffman for his role as a savant autistic person in the movie *The Rain Man* (1988). Her autism is thought to be a mild type called "Asperger's syndrome," a category used for a less-incapacitating form of autistic disorder. It is thought that many people who are dyslectic or hyperactive may be slightly autistic but learn as children to control themselves to lead normal lives.

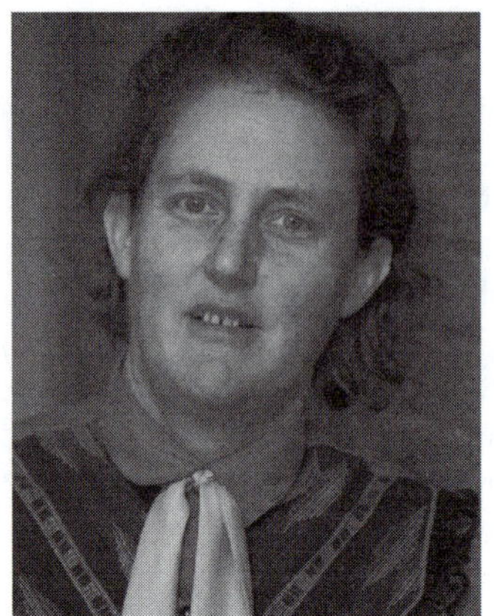

As a child Grandin was uncontrollable, but her mother refused to place her in an institution as she was advised to do. Grandin did not speak until she was three years old, and her mother and aunt worked heroically with her to control her involuntary actions. Her mother finally found a special preschool where Grandin could be given individual attention, and she was later able to attend high school and continue on to college. Grandin also is grateful to a high school science teacher who sparked her interest in science and introduced her to the scientific literature that real scientists use, such as *Psychological Abstracts* and *Index Medicus.*

One time while she was in high school, she was visiting her aunt's farm and noticed that the workers were using a "squeeze chute" to hold cattle while inoculating them. She also noticed that the cattle seemed to be very calm in this chute. Grandin persuaded her aunt to let her try the chute, and she herself felt very relaxed afterward. At home she built a chute from cardboard and plywood and used it regularly. One problem autistic persons have is they cannot endure close contact with others, or to be hugged or embraced, or even to shake hands. However, Grandin felt the chute to be a substitute for the hugs she had been unable to allow her mother and others to give her. In college, one of the psychologists told her that the chute was worthless, but she persuaded 40 students to try the chute, and 25 found it relaxing.

The experience with the squeeze chute led to her career in designing equipment and facilities to handle livestock. Although she still is appalled when going to slaughterhouses, she designs safe and calming methods for handling livestock. Instead of having cattle walk down a straight chute, she has designed chutes that curve slightly because cattle tend to walk in circles. The sides of the chutes are six feet high and walls are solid so the cattle will not be disturbed by seeing workers or equipment. She also instructs workers on farms, at feedlots, and in slaughterhouses on how to work humanely with livestock to keep them calm and easy to manage.

When Grandin was in graduate school, she had a part-time job in a feedlot and then began to sell the chutes that she had developed. She says the reason she understands livestock is that animals think in pictures just as she does. Autistic persons have difficulty understanding emotions or reading body language in others, and many autistic people compare themselves to Data, the android in the television show *Star Trek,* for he, too, is always puzzled about emotions. Grandin forms mental pictures of a person who is angry, and when she sees someone who acts like that picture, she knows the person is angry. It is as if she stores videos in her mind. People are amazed that she can write books, reports, and scientific papers and draw plans, but she plans these projects in her mind before she puts them on paper.

In an interview for *Journeys of Women in Science and Engineering,* she says that most people she has worked with did not know until recently that she is autistic. She says she has never felt she was discriminated against because she is autistic although she has been discriminated against because she is a woman. Especially when she was starting her consulting business, she found that many men would not allow her to visit feedlots or slaughterhouses because she was a woman. However, as she gained recognition for her work, she was able to overcome many of these barriers.

She is coauthor of her biography *Emergence: Labeled Autistic* (1986), and she wrote *Thinking in Pictures: And Other Reports from My Life with Autism* (1993). There also is information about her in Oliver Sacks's book *An Anthropologist on Mars: Seven Paradoxical Tales* (1995)—the title is a term she used to describe herself to Sacks. She has also written *Recommended Animal Handling Guidelines for Meat Packers* (1991) and *Livestock Handling and Transport* (1993) as well as papers describing how to conform to the strictures for handling meat to be used by various religious groups, such as Jews and Muslims.

She has received the Distinguished Alumni Award from Franklin Pierce College (1989) and the Industry Innovator Award from the *Meat Marketing and Technology Magazine* (1994) and was named one of the processing stars of 1990 by the magazine *National Provisioner.* She is a member of the Autism Society of America, American Society of Animal Science, American Society of Agricultural Engineers, and American Meat Institute. Her photograph is included in *Current Biography* (1994), *New Yorker* (December 27, 1993–January 3, 1994), and *Journeys of Women in Science and Engineering.*

***Bibliography:*** *Current Biography 1994; Journeys of Women in Science and Engineering; Who's Who of American Women,* 20th ed., 1997–1998.

# *Granville, Evelyn (Boyd)*
(1924– )
## *mathematician, computer scientist*

***Education:*** B.A., Smith College, 1945; M.A. in mathematics and physics, Yale University, 1946, Ph.D. in mathematics, 1949; honorary degree: honorary doctorate, Smith College, 1989

***Professional Experience:*** Research assistant, New York University Institute of Mathematics and Mechanics, 1949–1950; associate professor of mathematics, Fisk University, 1950–1952; mathematician, U.S. National Bureau of Standards, 1952–1953; applied mathematician, Diamond Ordnance Fuze Laboratory, U.S. Army, 1953–1956; mathematician, International Business Machines Corporation (IBM), 1956–1960; researcher, Space Technology Laboratories, 1960–1963; research specialist, North American Aviation Space and Information Systems Division, 1963–1967; associate professor, later professor, of mathematics, California State University, Los Angeles, 1967–1984; professor of mathematics, Texas College, Tyler (later University of Texas, Tyler), 1985–1988, Sam A. Lindsey Chair and visiting professor, 1990–

***Married:*** Gamaliel M. Collins, 1960, divorced 1967; Edward V. Granville, 1970

***Evelyn Granville*** is known for her contributions to the Vanguard and Mercury space programs in analyzing orbits and computing rocket trajectories. She also has been an outstanding professor of mathematics at three universities. She was one of the first two black women in the United States to receive doctorates in mathematics, and she was also the first black female mathematician in the United States to receive an honorary degree when Smith College awarded her one in 1989. When asked to summarize her major accomplishments, she replied that the first was showing that women can do mathematics and second was letting people know that African-American women have brains, too.

She grew up in segregated Washington, D.C., in a family that was supported by a single mother after her parents separated. Her high school had a number of well-qualified teachers who encouraged her in her studies, and her mother and aunt also supported her interest in higher education. She planned to teach high school mathematics and science. She won a partial scholarship to Smith College, and her family provided financial support the first year. After that year, she lived in a cooperative where the students waited tables and helped with the cooking for their room and board. In the summers, she worked as a mathematician for the National Bureau of Standards (during World War II, there were many job opportunities for women because so many men were engaged in military service). She thought of majoring in astronomy but did not favor the isolation of working in a great observatory—she regretted that decision when she became involved in the space industry. She financed her graduate school education by awards, a fellowship from Smith College, a Julius Rosenwald fellowship for promising black students, and a postdoctoral fellowship from the Atomic Energy Commission. She received her doctorate in 1949.

After spending a postdoctoral year at New York University, she sought a university post. Although she had a degree from a recognized university, she was unable to obtain a position at a university that had a doctoral program, possibly because she was a woman and an African American. She finally secured an appointment as associate professor at Fisk University, then moved to the National Bureau of Standards as a mathematician. A year later, the projects she was working on were transferred to the Diamond Ordnance Fuze Laboratories of the U.S. Army. There she consulted for the ordnance engineers and scientists on analyzing the mathematical problems that arose in the development of missile fuzes.

In 1956, Granville moved to IBM as a mathematician and staff assistant and worked on the formulation of orbit computations and computer procedures for the Vanguard and Mercury space probes. She also was a consultant in numerical analysis and a programmer for the IBM 650 and 704 computers. In 1960, she moved to the Computation and Data Reduction Center of U.S. Space Technology Laboratories to participate in research studies on the methods of orbit computation; she became a research specialist for the Apollo Engineering Department in celestial mechanics, trajectory and orbit computation, numerical analysis, and digital computer techniques at North American Aviation's Space and Information Systems Division.

She married the Reverend G. M. Collins in 1960 and became heavily involved in his ministry and in the care of his three children from a previous marriage while pursuing her own career. They divorced in 1967, the same year she joined the faculty of California State University, Los Angeles, as an associate professor of mathematics. She did not confine her work to the college classroom, for she also taught a supplementary half-time mathematics program in an elementary school and directed an after-school program in mathematics enrichment for students in kindergarten through fifth grade. She married again in 1970 to Edward V. Granville. In 1984, they both retired from their jobs and moved to his home state of Texas. Evelyn was appointed a professor of mathematics at University of Texas, Tyler, and taught mathematics and computer science there full time for three years. She was named to the Sam A. Lindsey Chair and has been a visiting professor since 1990.

She wrote a textbook, *Theory and Application of Mathematics for Teachers* (1975; rev. ed., 1978), that has had extensive use. She has been active in educational commissions in California and on the national level and is a member of the American Mathematical Society and the Mathematical Association of America. There are photographs in *Notable Twentieth-Century Scientists* and *Black Women in America.* She is listed in some sources as "Evelyn Collins" or as "Evelyn Boyd."

***Bibliography:*** *American Men and Women of Science* 10; *Black Women in America; Blacks in Science and Medicine; Distinguished African American Scientists of the 20th Century; Notable Twentieth-Century Scientists; Women of Mathematics.*

# *Grasselli, Jeanette (Gecsy)*

(1928– )

## *analytical chemist, spectroscopist*

***Education:*** B.S., Ohio University, 1950; M.S. in chemistry, Case Western Reserve University, 1958; honorary degrees: D.Sc., Ohio University and Clarkson University, 1986, Wilson College, 1994, Case Western Reserve University and Notre Dame College, 1995; D.Eng., Michigan Technological University, 1989

***Professional Experience:*** Chemist and infrared spectroscopist, Research and Development, BP America, Inc. (formerly Standard Oil of Ohio, or Sohio), 1950–1956, project leader, absorption spectroscopy group, 1956–1970, supervisor of molecular spectroscopy, 1970–1981, director of analytical science laboratory, 1981–1983, director of technical support department, 1983–1985, director of corporate research and environmental and analytical science, 1985–1989; retired 1989; director of research enhancement and distinguished visiting professor, Ohio University, 1990–

***Married:*** Robert Grasselli, 1957, divorced 1985; Glen R. Brown, 1987

***Jeanette Grasselli*** has made major contributions to the advancement of science and to the advancement of women in science. She has developed new problem-solving techniques in analytical chemistry that solve real-life problems such as identification of contaminants in gasoline, analyzing the structure of new plastics, and analyzing pollution problems in the environment. She has served on several committees involving careers of women in science and engineering on both the state and the national levels. She has held the highest administrative position of any woman at BP America, Inc.

When she was a child, her parents emphasized to both her and her younger brother that they should have a college education. While she was in high school, she was captivated by science in her first course in chemistry, and she dropped her career goal of majoring in English. She received a four-year scholarship to Ohio University where she majored in chemistry. She joined BP of America (formerly Standard Oil of Ohio) after receiving her undergraduate degree and worked through the ranks to become the first woman director of corporate research and environmental and analytical science.

During her career, she was responsible for developing many innovative applications for molecular spectroscopy; these applications are now at the forefront of industrial practice. She has made major advances in in-situ analyses, computerized spectroscopy, and systematized data retrieval and storage. She is noted for her expertise in problem solving and says problem solvers must be able to work on teams, learn to communicate well, and utilize and cross-apply techniques from other disciplines when necessary.

Although spectrometry had been used since the late nineteenth century, it was not until World War II that electronics were developed to make the instrumentation that was necessary to solve complex problems. Spectroscopy is an analytical technique to measure the interaction of electromagnetic radiation with matter. The methods are nondestructive and require only small amounts of sample, thus providing data at the atomic and molecular levels. The instruments are used in solving problems in academia, government, industry, and the environment.

When Grasselli was hired as part of the problem-solving team, she was put in charge of a new instrument called an infrared spectrometer and told to see what she could do with it. Her first project was to analyze World War II German airplane fuel formulations to see how the Germans were able to obtain such long flight ranges for their planes. She became one of the foremost contributors to infrared and Raman spectrometry of the century and also utilized nuclear magnetic resonance spectroscopy to a lesser extent. She even consulted with the coroner's office in Cleveland, Ohio, to help with the work of that office. Now it is common practice to analyze unknown samples at crime scenes, and the forensic analytical methods are the same as the analytical methods used in industrial laboratories.

She found she needed to know more about physical and organic chemistry for her work and enrolled as a part-time student at Case Western Reserve University to earn a master's degree. While attending classes, she met Robert Grasselli, also a Standard Oil chemist, who was studying there. They married in 1957, and she adopted his name professionally. He continued in school to obtain his doctorate, but she stopped at the master's level to devote time to her career. She advanced rapidly through the corporate ranks; as her husband became uncomfortable with her success, the couple divorced in 1985. She married Glen Brown, dean of colleges at Case Western Reserve, in 1987. She retired in 1989 and was appointed a distinguished visiting professor at Ohio University in 1990. She still is sought after as a speaker and consultant on spectroscopy, science education, and careers for women scientists and engineers.

Grasselli is the author of *The Analytical Approach* (1983) and coeditor of *Atlas of Spectral Data and Physical Constants of Organic Compounds* (2d ed., 1975) and *Practical Spectroscopy Series,* vols. 1–3, *Infrared and Raman* (1977). In 1986, she received the Garvan Medal of the American Chemical Society, an award that is given annually to an American woman chemist. She has also received the Distinguished Service Award of the Society for Applied Spectroscopy (1985) and the Fisher Award in Analytical Chemistry of the American Chemical Society (1993). She was named to Ohio Women's Hall of Fame in 1989 and the Ohio Sciences and Technology Hall of Fame in 1991. She has served on distinguished committees, such as the National Science Foundation Advisory Committee for Analytical Chemistry (1982–1984), Energy Research Advisory Board of the U.S. Department of Energy (1987–1989), the visiting committee of the National Institute of Standards and Technology (1988–1991), the Smithsonian Institution's exhibition advisory board (1990–1994), and the U.S. National Committee of the International Union of Pure and Applied Chemistry (chair, 1992–1995).

She has been active in promoting careers for women as a member of the International Women's Forum and National Research Council's Committee on Women in Science and Engineering (1995). She is a member of the American Chemical Society, Society for Applied Spectroscopy (president, 1970), Coblentz Society, Federation of Analytical Chemistry and Spectroscopy Societies, and American Association for the Advancement of Science. Her photograph is included in *Chemical & Engineering News* (October 14, 1985) and *Notable Women in the Physical Sciences.* A list of her publications is included in *Women in Chemistry and Physics.*

***Bibliography:*** *American Men and Women of Science* 11–19; *Notable Women in the Physical Sciences; Who's Who of American Women,* 19th ed., 1995–1996; *Women in Chemistry and Physics.*

# *Greer, Sandra Charlene*
(1945– )
## *physical chemist*

***Education:*** B.S., Furman University, 1966; M.S., University of Chicago, 1968, Ph.D. in chemistry, 1969
***Professional Experience:*** Research chemist, National Bureau of Standards, 1969–1978; associate professor of chemistry, University of Maryland, 1978–1983, professor of chemistry, 1983– , department chair, 1990–1993
***Married:*** 1968
***Children:*** 2

***Sandra Greer*** is a physical chemist known for her research in thermodynamics in both government and academia. Thermodynamics is the science concerned with the relations between heat and mechanical energy or work and the conversion of one into the other. Contrary to popular views of chemists, she does not work with test tubes and glassware. She has an electronics laboratory that constitutes a blend between physics and chemistry. Her major interest is critical phenomena, which is a phase change in which two forms of matter that are very different gradually grow more alike because of temperature and pressure variation.

Her interest in chemistry began early, and her parents purchased chemistry sets and a microscope for her to encourage her interest in science. She received her undergraduate degree in chemistry with a minor in mathematics from Furman University, a small liberal arts school with an excellent Chemistry Department. Her college adviser suggested that she attend the University of Chicago. She had no trouble being accepted there, and she found that although the competition was strong, she had no trouble in keeping up. She married another chemistry graduate student during college, and they both secured positions at the National Bureau of Standards after graduation.

She worked in the Heat Division of the Institute of Basic Standards at the bureau and remarked that it was there that she first saw other women actually doing scientific work, aside from women students in college. It was important for her to see women functioning as both professional scientists and as people. The administrators in her division were very supportive of women employees, and when her twins were born, she was on leave for several months and then worked part time for several years without any hassles. Although she did not feel any discrimination, she observed that women scientists with the same credentials as men were classified one whole government position grade below the men.

In 1978, Greer joined the faculty of the University of Maryland as an associate professor in the Department of Chemistry. She was promoted to professor in 1983 and served as department chair from 1990 to 1993. She said she enjoys the combination of teaching and research, although she teaches only one course per semester. One factor that contributes to her satisfaction is that as a tenured faculty member, she can control her own grant money, meaning she can select her own equipment and hire her own graduate and postdoctoral students. When she worked for the government, the project managers controlled the grant money. The university also provides greater opportunity to do research that does not have to be goal oriented.

Although she has not experienced much overt discrimination in her career, she found that when she first started working, people were too helpful; she had to fight to get people to let her handle the laboratory equipment. She believes that in handling the equipment and learning all of its capabilities, one can expand or contract one's project. She also feels that it was important to her career to have a husband who would carry his share of the load. When their children were small, she would leave for work early in the morning and return by the time school was over in the afternoon. Her husband would leave for work later to await the arrival of the sitter or take the children to nursery school. Her advice to people considering a career in science is, if you love it, do it.

Greer is a fellow of the American Physical Society and a member of the American Chemical Society, American Association for the Advancement of Science, and Association of Women in Science. Her research interests include experimental thermodynamics of phase transitions and critical phenomena and of fluid mixtures. Her photograph is included in Alice Fins's *Women in Science.*

**Bibliography:** *American Men and Women of Science* 12–19; Fins, A., *Women in Science;* Herzenberg, C., *Women Scientists from Antiquity to the Present.*

# *Greibach, Sheila Adele*
(1939– )
## *computer scientist, mathematician*

***Education:*** B.A., Radcliffe College, 1960, M.A., 1962; Ph.D. in applied mathematics, Harvard University, 1963

***Professional Experience:*** Lecturer in applied mathematics, Harvard University, 1963–1965, assistant professor, 1965–1969; associate professor, University of California, Los Angeles, 1969–1972, professor, 1972– , vice chair of computer science, 1985–

***Married:*** Jack W. Carlyle, 1970

***Children:*** 1

*Sheila Greibach* is known for her research in several areas of theoretical computer science, especially automata theory and formal languages. While at Harvard she worked on a project in mathematical linguistics and automatic translation. Automata in the elementary sense are things that are capable of acting automatically without outside interference. Greibach is working at a very basic level of computer science, and the impact of her work is not obvious to the average programmer. Her theoretical research benefits individuals involved in developing fundamental concepts and philosophies that must precede the evolution of subsequent techniques. She works in areas that benefit those people who are involved in transform analysis, transform-centered design, transaction analysis, and various exploratory problem-solving methodologies that are used by designers of systems. The effects of automata theory and formal-language research are normally not felt by programmers until the results finally influence such matters as efficiency of compilation, the relationship of structured design to structured programming techniques, and the use of incrementation.

Her interest in science is a natural one because her father, the inventor Emil Greibach, held more than 20 patents. After receiving her undergraduate and master's degrees from Radcliffe College, she attended graduate school at Harvard University. She was both a lecturer and an assistant professor at Harvard before joining the faculty at the University of California, Los Angeles (UCLA), where she advanced through the ranks to professor and vice chair of computer science. She served as a consultant to the Rand Corporation and System Development Corporation between 1964 and 1970.

Her standing as a pioneer in computer science is apparent by her inclusion in the article "Brief Notes on Six Women in Computer Development" in the winter 1982–spring 1983 issue of *Journal of Computers in Mathematics and Science Teaching*. She has published more than 50 technical papers and the book *Theory of Program Structures: Schemes, Semantics, Verification* (1975). She is a member of the American Mathematical Society, Association for Computing Machinery, Institute of Electrical and Electronics Engineers, and Society for Industrial and Applied Mathematics. Her research includes theoretical computer science in general with emphasis on formal languages, algorithms, and computational complexity.

***Bibliography:*** *American Men and Women of Science* 11–19; Stanley, A., *Mothers and Daughters of Invention.*

# *Gross, Carol A. (Polinsky)*

(1941– )

***bacteriologist***

***Education:*** B.S., Cornell University, 1962; M.S., Brooklyn College, 1965; Ph.D. in bacteriology, University of Oregon, 1968

***Professional Experience:*** Postdoctoral fellowship, University of Oregon, 1969–1973; project associate, University of Wisconsin, 1973–1976, assistant scientist, McArdle Laboratory for Cancer Research, University of Wisconsin, 1976–1979, associate scientist, 1979–1981, assistant professor of bacteriology, 1981–1988, professor, 1988–1992; professor, Department of Stomatology and Microbiology, University of California, San Francisco, 1993–

***Concurrent Position:*** Visiting professor, Department of Chemistry, Nanjing, 1985

***Children:*** 2

**Carol Gross** is a noted bacteriologist who specializes in studying the production of cell proteins in response to heat. She also has conducted research on the ribonucleic acid (RNA) polymerase enzyme that regulates various functions in both DNA and RNA. She received her undergraduate degree from Cornell University in 1962 and her master's degree from Brooklyn College in 1965. While she was attending Brooklyn College, she met and married her husband. They have two children, one born in 1965 after she completed her master's degree and the other born in 1969 after she completed her doctorate from the University of Oregon.

She immediately began a postdoctoral fellowship at Oregon and in 1973 became a project associate at the University of Wisconsin studying RNA, which is any of a class of single-stranded molecules transcribed from DNA in the cell nucleus or in the mitochondrion or chloroplast. She developed an interest in cancer research and moved to the McArdle Laboratory for Cancer Research at the University of Wisconsin as an assistant scientist and advanced to associate scientist. She moved to a faculty position in 1981 when she became an assistant professor in the university's Department of Bacteriology and became a full professor in 1988. In 1993, she joined the University of California, San Francisco, as a professor in the Department of Stomatology (diseases of the mouth) and Microbiology.

One of her major interests is how cell proteins respond to intense heat. When cells are subjected to high temperatures, nearly all begin to produce large quantities of certain proteins, and these are characterized by their ability to grow and thrive at what is ordinarily a lethal temperature. She is looking at the function that these proteins serve and the precise nature of how they operate. Another project is the structure and function of RNA polymerase, an enzyme that binds compounds in and transcribes DNA, thus regulating how DNA interacts with the cell. Her doctoral thesis was on the subject of E. coli bacteria, and she continues to publish papers on this topic. *Escherichia coli* is a species of rod-shaped anaerobic bacteria in the large intestine of humans and other animals; it is sometimes pathogenic.

She was elected to membership in the National Academy of Sciences in 1992 and has received numerous honors. In 1985, she became a member of the scientific advisory committee of the Damon Runyon–Walter Winchell Cancer Research Fund, a prestigious funder of research. She was named editor of the *Journal of Bacteriology* in 1990 and became a member of the editorial board of *Genes and Development* the same year. She is a member of the American Academy of Arts and Sciences.

***Bibliography:*** *Notable Twentieth-Century Scientists.*

# *Gross, Elizabeth Louise*

(1940– )

***biochemist***

***Education:*** B.A., University of California, Los Angeles, 1961; Ph.D. in biophysics, University of California, Berkeley, 1967

***Professional Experience:*** Research associate in biochemistry, C. F. Kettering Research Laboratory, 1967–1968; assistant professor, Ohio State University, 1968–1973, associate professor, 1973–1979, professor of biochemistry, 1979–

**Elizabeth Gross** is credited with inventing photovoltaic cells that use living organisms—"living batteries," as they are popularly called. The photovoltaic effect is a phenomenon identified about 1960 in which the incidence of light or other electromagnetic radiation upon the junction of two materials induces the generation of electromotive force. In simple terms, a photovoltaic cell converts sunlight directly into electricity. In about 1982, Gross was credited with producing 2,000 microvolts of power at 4–5 percent efficiencies. She devised a way to use a cheap carbon electrode instead of platinum in the chloroplast solar battery. A chloroplast is a plastid containing chlorophyll, and a plastid is a small, double-membrane organelle of plant cells and certain protists occurring in several forms as the chloroplast and containing ribosome, prokayotic DNA, and often pigment. In other words, she is seeking a way to harness the plant world's use of photosynthesis as a "green solar battery."

Although the 2,000-microwatt output that she reported is about half the output of a standard flashlight battery, it does have potential. In a silicon cell the energy produced must be used immediately or stored in another battery; Gross's cell is a battery. One potential use is as a rooftop solar-collector battery. In the 1980s, there was great interest in photovoltaic cells by major companies, and in addition to using them in space vehicles and satellites, there was scientific and popular interest in preserving the fossil fuel resources through substituting solar-powered cars, solar heat, etc. In 1997, manufacturers still were talking about solar energy as a way of reducing air pollution in the environment and preserving fossil fuel reserves, and Gross was still improving her chloroplast solar battery.

After receiving her undergraduate degree from the University of California, Los Angeles, she received a doctorate in biophysics from the University of California, Berkeley. She worked as a research associate in biochemistry before joining the faculty of Ohio State University, where she currently is a professor of biochemistry. She is a member of the Biophysical Society, American Society of Biological Chemists, American Society of Plant Physiologists, American Chemical Society, and International Solar Energy Society. Her research includes biophysical and biochemical studies of chloroplast membrane proteins including plastocyanin and the pigment-protein complexes, biological solar energy, and chloroplast solar batteries.

***Bibliography:*** *American Men and Women of Science* 15–19; Stanley, A., *Mothers and Daughters of Invention.*

# *Guttman, Helene Augusta (Nathan)*
(1930– )
## *microbiologist, biochemist*

***Education:*** B.A., Brooklyn College, 1951; M.A., Harvard University, 1955 and Columbia University, 1958; Ph.D. in bacteriology, Rutgers University, 1960

***Professional Experience:*** Research technician in immunology, Public Health Research Institute, New York City, 1951–1952; assistant microbiologist, Haskins Labs, 1952–1956, research associate, 1956–1959, staff member, 1959–1964; research associate, Goucher College, 1960–1962; assistant professor of biochemistry and cell physiology, University College and Graduate School of Arts and Sciences, New York University, 1962–1965, associate professor, 1965–1967; from associate professor to professor of biological sciences, University of Illinois, Chicago Circle, 1967–1975, professor of microbiology, College of Medicine, 1969–1975, faculty associate in urban systems laboratory, College of Engineering, 1974–1975, associate director of research, 1975; expert, Office of the Director, Heart, Lung, and Blood Institute, 1975–1977, research resources coordinator, Office of Program Planning and Evaluation, 1977–1979; deputy director of science advisory board, U.S. Environmental Protection Agency, 1979–1980; program coordinator, Science Education Coordinating Office, Science and Education Directorate, U.S. Department of Agriculture, 1980–1983, associate director, Beltsville Human Nutrition Research Center, 1983–1989, animal care coordinator, National Program Staff, Agricultural Research Service, 1989–

***Married:*** Newman Guttman, 1962

***Helene Guttman*** is known for her work in nutritional biochemistry and microbiology. After receiving her undergraduate degree from Brooklyn College, she worked for the Public Health Research Institute, and Haskins Labs before receiving one master's degree from Harvard and a second from Columbia. She received her doctorate from Rutgers in 1960 and was a research associate at Goucher College for two years before joining the faculty of New York University. She moved to the University of Illinois, Chicago Circle, as an associate professor, was promoted to professor, and obtained a joint professorship in the College of Medicine.

She left academia in 1975 to work in the Office of the Director of the Heart, Lung, and Blood Institute of the National Institutes of Health and then moved first to the Office of Planning and Evaluation and second to the U.S. Environmental Protection Agency. She joined the U.S. Department of Agriculture in the Science and Education Directorate, was appointed associate director of the Beltsville Human Nutrition Research Center, and then moved to the position of animal care coordinator of the Agricultural Research Service. She has brought a vast amount of knowledge and experience to each of those positions. Currently her office is issuing a series of bulletins and papers about animal care, a high-profile topic for the government owing to the activities of the friends of animals groups that are attempting to ban animal experimentation in research, proposing to turn livestock loose to fend for itself, and encouraging all citizens to become vegetarians. Some of the animal rights groups are aggressive to the point of invading laboratories and destroying equipment, and in some communities, such groups have picketed stores that sell fur coats or sell meat.

Guttman has been involved in activities concerning women and women scientists such as chairing the Professional Opportunities for Women Commission of the American Institute of Chemists (1974–1978) and serving on the advisory board of *Creative Women* (starting in 1970). She has also served as a member of the Status of Women Microbiologists Commission (1980–1985) and was a member of the education committee of the Illinois Commission on the Status of Women (1974–1975).

She is the author of *Experiments in Cellular Biodynamics* (1972) and editor of *Science and Animals: Addressing Contemporary Issues* (1989). She is a fellow of the American Institute of Chemists, American Academy of Microbiology, New York Academy of Sciences, and American Association for the Advancement of Science. She is a member of the American Society for Microbiology, American Society of Biological Chemists, American Society for Cell Biology, and American Society of Clinical Nutrition. Her research interests include behavioral biochemistry; control of inducible syntheses, especially small peptides, enzymes, and antibodies; isolation and purification of bioactive natural products; nutrition biochemistry; and drug mode of action at the cellular level.

***Bibliography:*** *American Men and Women of Science* 11–19; Herzenberg, C., *Women Scientists from Antiquity to the Present; Who's Who in America,* 51st ed., 1997; *Who's Who of American Women,* 20th ed., 1997–1998; *World Who's Who in Science.*

# H

## *Haas, Mary Rosamond*
(1910– )
***linguist, anthropologist***

***Education:*** B.A., Earlham College, 1930; Ph.D. in linguistics, Yale University, 1935; honorary degrees: D.Lit., Northwestern University, 1975; LHD, University of Chicago, 1976, Earlham College and Ohio State University 1980

***Professional Experience:*** Research worker, Yale University, 1936–1938; committee on research on American native language, American Council of Learned Societies, 1938–1941, research fellow, committee on research on modern Oriental languages, 1941–1946; lecturer in Siamese, University of California, Berkeley, 1943–1947, assistant professor of Siamese and linguistics, 1947–1952, associate professor Siamese and linguistics, 1952–1957, professor of linguistics, 1957–1977, acting department head, 1956–1957, department head, 1958–1964, emeritus professor of linguistics, 1977–

***Married:*** Morris Swadesh, divorced; Heng R. Subhanka, divorced

***Mary Haas*** is renowned as a leader in anthropological linguistics not only because of her work on American Indian languages but also because of her pioneering research on the relationship of ethnology and sociology to language. The latter includes men's and women's speech, word taboos, word games, kinship vocabulary, and language contact. In the 1940s, during World War II, she responded to the national need for expertise on languages of the Far East and published several grammars and dictionaries of Thai and Burmese (previously called Siamese). After her appointment to the faculty of the University of California, Berkeley, in 1947, she returned to her interests in American Indian linguistics and was instrumental in founding the Survey of California Indian Languages at Berkeley in 1953. She was department chair at Berkeley in 1958 and president of the Linguistics Society of America in 1963 at a time when it was very unusual for a woman to achieve these honors. She was elected to membership in the National Academy of Sciences in 1978.

Her first fieldwork in her graduate studies was with the Nitinat tribe of British Columbia. For her doctoral research, she went to Louisiana to work with the lone surviving speaker of Tunica. She later published a grammar, a dictionary, and a text collection of the Tunica language. Her research launched her career as the principal authority on the languages of the native southeastern United States, including Natchez and Muskogean families, and she later studied many other North American linguistic families. Her work provided solid corroboration of studies conducted by anthropologists, archaeologists, and ethnologists.

Her awards include the Berkeley Citation of the University of California, Berkeley, in 1977 and the Wilbur Cross Medal of the Yale Graduate Association the same year. In 1986, she was honored at the Haas Festival Conference on Native American Linguistics held at the University of California, Santa Cruz. *In Honor of Mary Haas* (1988) is a collection of papers presented by colleagues and former students at the conference. Several reviewers complained that the book does not reflect the esteem and unanimous affection for her that was apparent at the conference and that it obscures Mary Haas as the memorable character all know her to be.

One reviewer summarized her contributions in the fall 1992 issue of *American Indian Quarterly.* "Many of Mary Haas' students came to the study of Native American languages from a society that assumed that not only the cultures but the languages embodying the concepts of those cultures were primitive, if not downright barbaric. Haas made us aware from the beginning of the complexity and subtlety and beauty of these languages, and in turn, her intellectual children and grandchildren have helped teach the world this lesson. She insisted on the highest standards of work any scholar could demand, and never let her students forget the importance and urgency of what they were doing, nor that the work that cried out to be done was nearly endless (and still is)."

In addition to her books on the Thai language, she published *The Prehistory of Languages* (1969) and *Language, Culture, and History* (1978) and was still publishing scientific papers in the 1990s. She is a member of the Linguistics Society of America (president, 1963), American Anthropological Association, American Oriental Society, and American Academy of Arts and Sciences.

***Bibliography:*** *American Men and Women of Science* 11; *Contemporary Authors* v. 9–12R; Ireland, N., *Index to Women of the World . . . Suppl.;* Rossiter, M., *Women Scientists in America.*

# *Hamilton, Margaret*
(1936– )
### *computer scientist, systems engineer*

***Education:*** Student, University of Michigan, 1955; B.A., Earlham College, 1958
***Professional Experience:*** Public school teacher, 1959; programmer, Massachusetts Institute of Technology, 1960, Philco-Ford Sage Project and Air Force Cambridge Research Laboratory, 1961–1963, programmer, Massachusetts Institute of Technology, 1963–1965; programmer for Apollo project, Massachusetts Institute of Technology Draper Laboratory, supervisor, assistant director, 1965–1977 or 1978; cofounder and codirector of Higher Order, Inc., 1978–
***Married:*** Hamilton, 1958, divorced 1967; Dan Lickly, 1969
***Children:*** 1

***Margaret Hamilton*** is known as one of the chief systems analysts on the Apollo spacecraft project. She was assistant director of the Draper Laboratory of the Massachusetts Institute of Technology (MIT) when the on-board computers and guidance instruments for all the manned moon missions were designed. She said that as one of the first programmers hired, she became acquainted with all phases of the project and had a general knowledge of everything that happened in Apollo. Often when other personnel had problems with a program, they would come to her for assistance. Her overall knowledge of the project enabled her to solve the problems and win promotions. Eventually she was promoted to assistant director. At the peak of the Apollo project, she supervised about 100 engineers, mathematicians, programmers, and technical writers. She oversaw two separate subgroups—one for the on-board computer in the command module, the other for the computer in the lunar excursion module (LEM).

The programs her group devised were very complex. Before each Apollo mission (all of them took place between 1968 and 1972), she had to try to anticipate all possible eventualities and program the two computers to be ready for them. The computers had to process a great many simultaneous inputs and give commands instantly. Not all commands were given from the on-board computers, because Mission Control, spacecraft instruments such as radar, and the astronauts were all issuing commands. In fact, one program established the order in which the computer must do the various jobs it was asked to do at once. For example, during the Apollo landing, astronaut Neil Armstrong reported a 1201–1202 alarm. The television commentators reported that it indicated a computer malfunction, but instead, the alarm merely alerted Armstrong, Mission Control, and Draper Lab that the computer was overloaded. The problem was a radar switch in the wrong position.

In the early days of the Apollo project there was room for invention on the programmers' part, but after the National Aeronautics and Space Administration (NASA) accepted the program, MIT could not revise an item without going through red tape at NASA. The feeling was that since the Apollo flight to the moon was a success the first time, there was no need to change even one instruction. After the first moon landing, the MIT part of the project was greatly reduced, and one of Hamilton's major responsibilities then was to obtain contracts for further work and to give the group new direction. Later projects that she oversaw were a biomedical bedside computer, a new computer language and compiler, security systems, control systems for aircraft, a data management system for the Department of Transportation, air traffic control instrumentation, the space shuttle, the unmanned Mars landing, and Skylab.

She has an unusual family background in that both sets of grandparents and both parents had college degrees. After receiving her undergraduate degree in mathematics, she married and taught math and French to grades 7 through 12 in a public school for a year while her husband completed his undergraduate degree. They moved to Boston so he could attend Brandeis University and later Harvard Law School. She planned to work on her master's degree at Brandeis, but after having a baby, she obtained a job at MIT as a programmer for a professor doing meteorological prediction and statistical long-range weather forecasting. She then worked for Philco-Ford's Sage Project, a radar defense system that tracked unknown aircraft. At the same time, she did general programming for satellite tracking at the Air Force Cambridge Research Laboratory. She returned to MIT in 1963 to do programming for another meteorology professor and joined the Apollo program in 1965. About 1977 or 1978 she founded a computer company to develop industrial systems, Higher Order, Inc., with a former colleague. The software they developed was designed to catch mistakes, such as a missing step in a manufacturing process, before they happen.

Before she first went to work, she had a stereotypical image of a career woman as one who is aggressive and thinks only her career is important. She wanted to work, but she wanted to be happily married, too, and she has been able to combine her professional life and her family life successfully. She received her share of comments from people who wondered at her working after she had a child; she merely said her husband was in graduate school and they needed the money. She believes it is the men who lack self-confidence who need to discredit the work of women, and in her private life, she avoids men who are unkind to women or regard them as toys. She freed herself of personal exploitation by refusing to allow men to exploit her. Her photograph is included in *Fortune* (June 25, 1984) and Joyce Teitz's *What's a Nice Girl Like You. . . .*

***Bibliography:*** Ireland, N., *Index to Women of the World . . . Suppl.;* Teitz, J., *What's a Nice Girl Like You. . . .*

# Hammel, Heidi
(1960– )
**astronomer**

***Education:*** B.S., Massachusetts Institute of Technology, 1982; Ph.D. in physics and astronomy, University of Hawaii, 1988
***Professional Experience:*** Team member, NASA Voyager Imaging Science Team, Neptune Encounter, 1989; principal research scientist, Massachusetts Institute of Technology, 1990–
***Concurrent Positions:*** Team leader, NASA Hubble Space Visible/New-UV Imaging Team, Comet Shoemaker–Levy 9 Collision with Jupiter, 1994

**Heidi Hammel** rose to prominence very early in her career because she had a solid background in her field. She wrote her dissertation on Neptune and was thus a logical choice for the team that oversaw the Voyager encounter with Neptune in 1989. That work, in turn, resulted in the assignment to be the team leader for the Comet Shoemaker–Levy 9 Collision with Jupiter in 1994. During the television coverage of the Shoemaker–Levy 9 event, her ability to explain the phenomena in language the general public could understand, and in an enthusiastic manner, endeared her to numerous viewers. Although some astronomers criticize her excitement, they agree that she does a very good job of explaining complex concepts in simple terms.

As a child she was told by her parents that she could be anything she wanted to be. They read to their children, and they also stressed the joy of reading everything. They purchased a toy telescope for her to use in her first experiences of sky watching, and although she was not particularly intent on a career in astronomy, she often visited the planetarium in Harrisburg, Pennsylvania, where the family lived. Instead, she was a math wizard. Her math instructor encouraged her to apply to the Massachusetts Institute of Technology (MIT), but when she asked her chemistry instructor to write a letter of recommendation, he refused, saying that she would never be accepted. When she was accepted, he said the only reason was that she was a woman and the school needed to fill a quota. In her sophomore year, she started her astronomy courses but felt out of place. However, the instructor convinced her that she could do the work. She received her undergraduate degree in earth and planetary science and enrolled in graduate school at the University of Hawaii, Manoa, in Honolulu because that school had the largest and best telescopes for the subject she was studying. Her dissertation was on the clouds and structure of Neptune.

Her first job was at the Jet Propulsion Laboratory of the National Aeronautics and Space Administration (NASA) in Pasadena, California. She was a member of the imaging team for Voyager 2's encounter with Neptune in 1989, and she has said that that assignment gave her experience with spacecraft and with performing in a high-pressure situation. In 1990, she was appointed a principal research scientist at MIT, and in 1994, she was selected to be the team leader for the Comet Shoemaker–Levy 9 Collision with Jupiter, with headquarters at the Johns Hopkins University Space Telescope Science Institute. Her experience with explaining science to the public started in graduate school when she was assigned to give lectures on the visit of Halley's comet to earth in 1986. She says that she prefers to talk very simply and plainly, and even at a science conference, people who are not familiar with her work but want to learn something have no difficulty with her presentations.

She has published more than 30 scientific papers and has received several awards: NASA Group Achievement Award for Voyager Science Investigation (1990), the Vladimir Karapetoff Award from MIT in recognition of her contributions to science and education (1994), and the Klumpke-Roberts Award of the Astronomical Society of the Pacific (1995). The last award is named for Dorothea Klumpke-Roberts (1861–1942), an American woman who worked for the Paris Observatory between 1887 and 1901 and was renowned for her work in charting and cataloging stars. There are photographs of Hammel in the *Chronicle of Higher Education* (July 27, 1994) and *Notable Women in the Physical Sciences.* In 1997, she appeared on a television documentary on the Discovery Channel, "Hubble Space Telescope." A video of the show is available.

***Bibliography:*** *Notable Women in the Physical Sciences.*

# *Harris, Jean Louise*

(1931– )

## *specialist in internal medicine, allergist*

***Education:*** B.S., Virginia Union University, 1951; M.D., Medical College of Virginia, 1955; honorary degree: D.Sc., University of Richmond, 1981

***Professional Experience:*** Intern, Medical College of Virginia, 1955–1956, resident in internal medicine, 1956–1957, fellow, 1957–1958; fellow, Strong Memorial Hospital, School of Medicine, University of Rochester, 1958–1960; instructor in medicine, College of Medicine, Howard University, 1960–1968, assistant professor of community health practice, 1969–1972; professor, Virginia Commonwealth University, 1973–1979, clinical professor of family practice, 1978; secretary of human resources, Commonwealth of Virginia, 1978–1982; president and chief executive officer, Ramsey Foundation, 1988–1992; senior associate director, medical affairs, University of Minnesota Hospital and Clinic, 1992–

***Concurrent Positions:*** Research associate, Walter Reed Army Institute of Research, 1960–1963; private practice in internal medicine and allergies, 1964–1971; chief, Bureau of Resources Development, District of Columbia Department of Health, 1967–1969; director, Center for Community Health Consultants, Department of Health, Education, and Welfare, 1969–1977; assistant clinical professor of community medicine, Charles R. Drew Postgraduate Medical School, Los Angeles, 1970–1972; executive director, National Medical Association Foundation, 1970–1973; vice president of state marketing programs, Control Data Corporation, 1982–1984, vice president of state government affairs, 1984–1986, vice president of business development, 1986–1988

***Married:*** Leslie J. Ellis, Jr., 1955

***Children:*** 3

***Jean L. Harris*** is known as a specialist in internal medicine and an allergist who has held high-level positions in academia, state government, federal government, private industry, and professional associations. She was one of the youngest persons and the first black woman to graduate from a segregated medical school in Virginia, and she was also the first woman and first black person to be named to the cabinet of a Virginia governor when she was named secretary of human resources in 1978.

In academia, she has been a clinical professor of family practice at Virginia Commonwealth University, a fellow at the Medical College of Virginia, a senior associate director at the University of Minnesota Hospital and Clinic, a fellow at the School of Medicine of the University of Rochester, and an instructor in medicine at Howard University's

College of Medicine. In state government, she has been a member of the cabinet in Virginia and chief of the Bureau of Resources Development of the District of Columbia Department of Health. She has had numerous appointments in the federal government, such as research associate at the Walter Reed Army Institute of Research and director of the Center for Community Health Consultants of the Department of Health, Education and Welfare. On the association level, she was executive director of the National Medical Association Foundation, and she worked for Control Data Corporation in various capacities. She was also engaged in private practice of internal medicine and allergies. Although many of these appointments overlapped, she handled them all.

She has also had high-level appointments to committees, such as being a member of the recombinant DNA advisory committee of the National Institutes of Health (1979–1982), vice chairman of the National Commission on Alcoholism and Alcohol Related Diseases (1980–1981), member of the President's Private Sector Initiative Task Force (1981–1982), member of the Defense Advisory Commission on Women in the Service (1985–1988), and member of the Advisory Council on Sickle Cell of the National Heart, Lung, and Blood Institute (1975–1979).

She is a fellow of the Royal Society of Health and a member of the Institute of Medicine of the National Academy of Sciences, the American Academy of Medical Administrators, and the American Public Health Association. In an interview for the November 1981 issue of *Ebony* she said that earlier in her career the Medical College of Virginia was so conservative the administrators would not give her an appointment to the faculty but that later she was able to return to the school as an administrator, and she thought that the South now offered great opportunities for blacks. Her photograph is included in *Ebony* (July 1955 and November 1981).

***Bibliography:*** *American Men and Women of Science* 14–19; *Blacks in Science and Medicine; Who's Who of American Women*, 20th ed., 1997–1998.

# *Harris, Mary (Styles)*
(1949– )
### *geneticist, epidemiologist*

***Education:*** B.A., Lincoln University, 1971; Ph.D. in genetics, Cornell University, 1975

***Professional Experience:*** National Cancer Institute fellowship, New Jersey University of Medicine and Dentistry, 1975–1977; instructor in genetics, School of Medicine, Morehouse College, 1978–1986; president, Harris & Associates Ltd., 1986–1987; chief executive officer, BioTechnical Publications, 1987–

***Concurrent Positions:*** Research associate in tumor virology, Rutgers Medical School, 1975–1977; director of administration, Sickle Cell Foundation of Georgia, Inc., 1977–1986; National Science Foundation Residency, 1979–1980; scientist in residence, television station WGTV, University of Georgia, 1979, adjunct public service assistant, 1979–1980; assistant director of science and public policy, Atlanta University, 1981–1982; instructor in human genetics, Emory University, 1982; director of genetic service, Georgia Department of Human Resources, 1982–1985

***Married:*** Sidney Harris, 1972

***Children:*** 1

M***ary Harris*** is known for her work on genetics testing of children in her capacity as executive director of the Sickle Cell Foundation of Georgia and state director of genetics service in Georgia. In 1979, she employed an unusual technique for educating the public: she used a National Science Foundation grant to work with broadcasters to produce a series of television documentary programs on the relationship between science and medicine. Sickle-cell anemia, which occurs primarily among Africans or persons of African descent, is a chronic hereditary blood disease in which the red blood cells become sickle-shaped and nonfunctional. If the condition is identified at birth, it can be controlled; thus, the importance of genetic testing. If the disease is not identified, the children may die at an early age.

Harris was encouraged to enter the medical field because her father was a physician with a practice in the African-American section of Miami, Florida. Her parents encouraged her to read at an early age, and through her reading, she developed an interest in science. After her father died when she was nine years old, the family struggled financially. The schools were just beginning to desegregate in 1963 when she entered high school, and she was among the first blacks to attend an integrated school. Outside of school, in the evenings and on weekends, she served as a volunteer at a local black-owned medical laboratory. In return for her volunteering, the staff showed her how to use the equipment and how to do routine biological tests.

She was one of the first women to enter Lincoln University in Pennsylvania, and since she spent a great deal of time with the premed students, people assumed she was headed to medical school. Colleagues of her father arranged, through a minority recruitment program, to reserve a place for her at the University of Miami Medical School, but she preferred to concentrate on research and declined the appointment. Instead, she was awarded a Ford Foundation fellowship to study molecular genetics. She married after graduating from Lincoln, and she and her husband, who was a graduate student in engineering, entered Cornell, which had an excellent program in molecular genetics.

Harris received a postdoctoral fellowship from the National Cancer Institute for research on the chemical composition of viruses. She chose the New Jersey University of Medicine and Dentistry for her postdoctoral research, and her husband obtained a position at nearby Bell Laboratories. Mary took over an ongoing project to discover materials that would retard the growth of viruses, and in order to acquaint herself with the project, she tried to replicate some of the experiments that her predecessor had completed. However, she was unable to reproduce the same positive conclusions, and it was finally determined that the previous researcher had used contaminated materials in all of the experiments. Harris next worked on a new project dealing with the chemical structure of viruses and genetically important molecules, and this project was successful.

Not wanting to continue a career in grant-supported basic research, she accepted a position as director of administration of the Sickle Cell Foundation of Georgia, and her husband joined the faculty of Georgia State University. After her successful series of television documentaries had received a positive response, she was invited to become state director of genetics service for Georgia, a newly created position.

When her husband was offered a position at Claremont College in California, the couple decided he should accept it, and in California, Mary founded her own consulting firm, Harris & Associates, to assist companies that were engaged in genetic engineering. Many new companies that develop products based on genetic engineering need help in explaining their activities to the general public, to prospective customers, and to various government officials, and Harris's experiences provided a good background for helping these companies build their reputations. She received a grant from the National Cancer Institute to produce a new series of television programs on the particular health problems of African Americans, and the company, BioTechnical Publications, also produces audiovisual educational materials on a broad range of health care issues encountered by women and minorities. Harris also does a series of radio features on a number of public health topics.

She is a member of the American Public Health Association and the American Society of Human Genetics. Her photograph is included in *Jet* (February 21, 1980).

***Bibliography:*** *American Men and Women of Science* 14–19; *Blacks in Science and Medicine; Distinguished African American Scientists of the 20th Century.*

# *Harrison, Faye Venetia*
(1951– )
***anthropologist***

***Education:*** B.A., Brown University, 1974; M.A., Stanford University, 1977, Ph.D. in anthropology, 1982
***Professional Experience:*** Assistant professor of anthropology, University of Louisville, 1983–1989; associate professor of anthropology, University of Tennessee, Knoxville, 1989–
***Married:*** William L. Conwill, 1980
***Children:*** 3

***Faye Harrison*** is an anthropologist who has concentrated her research on how people of African descent both shape and are shaped by their cultural environments. She has studied people from the Cape Verde Islands off the coast of Africa who have immigrated to the United States, natives of the West Indies who immigrated to London, West Indian families who live in the West Indies, and the oral histories of her own ancestors who lived in North Carolina and Virginia.

She became interested in different cultures as a child when her family moved into a house that contained a closet full of old *National Geographic* magazines. She started comparing the racial views she had experienced in Norfolk and Tidewater Virginia with those in other countries, as revealed by those magazines. She was a serious child who excelled in her studies and received encouragement from her teachers. Even in high school she focused her attention on the cultures of Latin America, which she thought would be an interesting area to investigate, and studied Spanish, Portuguese, and French. She was so skilled in her Spanish studies that a local sorority provided scholarship money for her to travel to Puerto Rico with a group of other language students.

She received a full university scholarship to Brown University where she realized that anthropology was the course of study that she needed. In her senior year, she had the opportunity to undertake an independent research project and looked at the attitudes and opinions of a special group of high school students whose ancestors had come to the United States from the Cape Verde Islands. She selected this group to study because the Cape Verdeans had retained their original language of Portuguese. Upon graduation from Brown, she received a fellowship to spend a year in London. There she studied the lives of a group of West Indians from the Caribbean who had immigrated to England and compared the differing beliefs and behaviors of the Caribbean people with those of the English.

She received a one-year full university fellowship for graduate work at Stanford University, and for her doctoral program, she chose to follow up her London investigation and study West Indian families living in the West Indies; her work was funded by a Fulbright-Hayes program. She studied people in the slum areas of Kingston, Jamaica, and although these slum people were thought to be unemployed, she found they earned a living within an informal economic system. They bought and sold material goods among themselves and also provided goods and services to the larger community on an informal or casual basis. Many actually ran their own businesses. She returned to Kingston each summer for a number of years after receiving her doctorate to detect trends in the everyday life of the slums. She found that the informal trade of the 1970s gradually shifted to illegal drug dealing in the late 1980s and early 1990s and that the group activities that had been centered on sports became gang-related activities involving the smuggling drugs and guns.

Harrison was first a faculty member at the University of Louisville and then was appointed an associate professor at the University of Tennessee, Knoxville. In addition to her scientific papers, she has edited *Black*

*Folks in Cities Here and There* (1988) and *Decolonizing Anthropology: Moving Further Toward an Anthropology for Liberation* (1991). She has also been an associate editor of *Urban Anthropology* since 1992 and a consulting editor for *Women and Aging* since 1990. She is active in civil rights efforts, such as organizing the Kentucky Rainbow Coalition and being a member of Black Women Organized for Power, Louisville, and of Alliance Against Women's Oppression, Louisville. She is also a member of the Association of Black Anthropologists (president, 1989–1991) and the International Union of Anthropological and Ethnological Sciences. Her photograph is included in *Distinguished African American Scientists of the 20th Century.*

***Bibliography:*** *Distinguished African American Scientists of the 20th Century; Who's Who in America,* 51st ed., 1997; *Who's Who of American Women,* 19th ed., 1995–1996.

# *Harrison-Ross, Phyllis Ann*
(1936– )
***pediatrician, psychiatrist***

***Education:*** B.S., Albion College, 1956; M.D., Wayne State University College of Medicine, 1959

***Professional Experience:*** Instructor of pediatrics, Cornell Medical School, 1961–1962; instructor in pediatrics and psychology, Albert Einstein College of Medicine, 1966–1968, assistant professor, 1968–1972; professor of clinical psychiatry, New York Medical College, 1972–

***Concurrent Positions:*** Fellowship in adult psychiatry, Albert Einstein College of Medicine, 1964–1966; Medical Review Board, New York State Commission of Corrections, 1970

***Married:*** Edward Ross, 1970

***Phyllis Harrison-Ross*** has pioneered the rehabilitation of children who are considered hopelessly retarded, emotionally disturbed, or physically disabled. Between 1966 and 1972, she helped to develop beginning programs in physical and mental therapy for the young. Previously, there had not been any school programs for the disturbed children; they had just stayed at home. She helped to design special programs and developed models that were duplicated in the public schools so that such children could have a learning environment.

She practices psychiatry in Spanish Harlem, and she states that poverty is probably one of the major causes of disorders in children. Living in poverty and seeing the things that poverty produces in a community is probably the number-one cause of mental problems, whether they show up as mental illness, learning disabilities, mental retardation, alcoholism, or problems of child abuse. She says she switched from pediatrics to psychiatry because she enjoys talking with her patients; she is an outgoing person who requires conversation and contacts. In her practice, children up to five years of age are brought to be treated for phobias that range from an inability to speak or a refusal to eat to the dread of walking downstairs, or just a plain fear of living. One form of therapy to help children gradually overcome a speaking block is to have five or ten parents and children seated in a circle having a group sing. Other forms of therapy, including water play, painting, and the manipulation of puppets, are part of the curriculum. Harrison-Ross says that one of the chief problems for black and Hispanic mothers is to find reliable child care, and she endorses the government program for child care in Sweden.

At one time, she was involved with patients as a forensic psychiatrist for the Medical Review Board of New York State. She was responsible for investigating all deaths that occurred in jails, the development of medical hygiene services for underserved members of the population, and investigating alcoholism and drug abuse problems. She has also written psychological textbooks for junior and senior high school students.

Her parents, each of whom had college degrees, gave her a great deal of attention when she was a child, and they pushed her toward the professions of law or medicine. However, they cautioned her about the problems a black woman would encounter in trying to succeed in a profession. She received her undergraduate degree at age 20 and her M.D. at age 23. She said she was not discriminated against in college as a black but that there was sexual discrimination. The fraternities were segregated and all male, so there was no possibility of her joining one of them.

She has received several awards, including Distinguished Alumnus of Albion College (1976), the Leadership in Medicine Award of the Susan Smith McKinney Stewart Medical Society (1978), and the Award of Merit of the Public Health Association of New York City (1980). She was president of the Black Psychiatrists of America in 1976–1978. Her photograph is included in W. Rayner's *Wise Women.*

***Bibliography:*** *Blacks in Science and Medicine;* Herzenberg C., *Women Scientists from Antiquity to the Present;* Rayner, W., *Wise Women.*

# *Haschemeyer, Audrey Elizabeth Veazie*

(1936– )

## ***biochemist, environmental physiologist***

***Education:*** B.S., University of Illinois, 1957; Ph.D. in physical chemistry, University of California, Berkeley, 1961

***Professional Experience:*** Research associate in biology, Massachusetts Institute of Technology, 1961–1964; assistant biologist, Massachusetts General Hospital, 1965–1969; associate professor of biological science, Hunter College, 1969–1974, professor of biology and biochemistry, 1974– , chair of department of biological science, 1980–

***Concurrent Positions:*** Associate, Harvard Medical School, 1967–1969; member of graduate faculty, City University of New York, 1969– ; chief scientist, research vessel *Alpha Helix,* Caribbean-Pacific, 1978; project director, U.S. Antarctic Research Program, 1978– ; chief scientist, U.S. Coast Guard Cutter *Polar Star,* Ross Sea, 1981; member of corporation, Marine Biological Laboratory, Woods Hole, Massachusetts, 1969–

***Children:*** 2

***Audrey Haschemeyer*** is known for the research she conducted for a number of years on fish in Antarctica. Her goal was to learn from the fish how temperature changes can affect some of the complex life processes in humans. Her research capabilities have been recognized by the awarding of a National Science Foundation grant for the project. In the 1970s, she was studying how fish make specific protein molecules, and she was measuring how long the fish required to produce the protein molecules at various temperatures. Unfortunately, North American fish go into a hibernation state about 10 degrees Celsius, but she learned that fish in McMurdo Sound do not seem affected by low temperatures. While lining up funding for a trip to Antarctica, she took a job in 1978 as the chief scientist aboard the *Alpha Helix,* a research ship operated by the Scripps Institution of Oceanography, and studied tropical fish in the Galapagos Islands.

She received a three-year grant from the National Science Foundation for her Antarctic research project, and her team members were able to make very precise measurements of the production of protein molecules by the fish. The team would go out by helicopter to hunt cracks in the ice to use as natural openings for fishing—it was not usually necessary to drill through the ice—set traps, and return the next morning to collect the fish. At times team members camped on the ice, but usually they stayed at night in the plain, serviceable quarters assigned to the scientists. They were able to identify the antifreeze protein in the fish and learned that about half of all the protein in the blood of Antarctic fish is this special protein. The fish have a triggering mechanism that turns off the antifreeze protein in warm weather and turns it on in cold weather.

Although American women scientists were not allowed to conduct research in Antarctica until the 1969–1970 season, there seem to be few restrictions on their work now, and they fill a variety of jobs in both winter and summer. The reason women were previously restricted is that the only travel and living accommodations for Americans were under the control of the U.S. Navy, and it was only after women scientists from other countries were on site that the navy lifted their restrictions against women. Haschemeyer said that she and her women assistants felt no negative discrimination during all of their seasons on site. They were respected as scientists and received very warm treatment.

She is a fellow of the American Association for the Advancement of Science and a member of the American Physiological Society, American Society of Biological Chemists, and Biophysics Society. Her research interests are regulation of protein synthesis in higher organisms, cold adaptation of fish, mechanism of action of the thyroid hormone, and biological reaction rates in living organisms. Her photograph is included in Barbara Land's *The New Explorers.*

***Bibliography:*** *American Men and Women of Science* 12–19; Ireland, N., *Index to Women of the World . . . Suppl.;* Land, B., *The New Explorers.*

# *Hatfield, Elaine Catherine*
(1937– )
***psychologist***

***Education:*** B.A., University of Michigan, 1959; Ph.D. in psychology, Stanford University, 1963

***Professional Experience:*** Assistant professor, University of Minnesota, 1963–1964, associate professor of sociology and psychology, 1964–1966; associate professor of psychology, University of Rochester, 1966–1968; associate professor, University of Wisconsin, Madison, 1968–1969, professor of sociology and psychology, 1969–1981; professor of psychology, University of Hawaii, Manoa, 1981– , chair of department, 1981–1983

***Concurrent Positions:*** Research associate, Wisconsin Family Studies Institute, 1980–1981; family therapist, King Kalakua Center, 1982–

***Married:*** G. W. Walster, 1962, divorced; Richard L. Rapson, 1982

***Elaine Hatfield*** is known for her research and publications on love, sex, and family life. Her work is marked by solid research instead of the extravagant claims that have characterized the writings of some psychologists of her generation. She has examined a wide range of topics, including some cross-cultural studies of the preferences of men and women in marital partners in the United States, Russia, and Japan and college students' dating patterns in the three countries. Within the family structure she has looked at marital fairness over the life span of the couple and problems faced by families of developmentally disabled children.

She is the coauthor of several general psychology texts, such as *Interpersonal Attraction* (1969; 2d ed., 1978), *Human Sexual Behavior* (1974), and *Introduction to Psychology* (1979). However, her book *A New Look at Love* (1978) brought her popular attention, and the American Psychological Association named her the recipient of their National Media Award in 1979 for this publication. *Mirror, Mirror: The Importance of Looks in Everyday Life* (1987) struck a chord with many people who were concerned about contemporary society's emphasis on good looks over integrity and performance. Hatfield begins with defining good looks from culture to culture and ends with discussing the pros and cons of look-improvement campaigns. In Western culture, the experiences of the good-looking and the homely differ greatly; looks affect sex, marriage, self-image, personality, and social skills.

That book was followed by *Psychology of Emotion* (1992), *Love, Sex, and Intimacy: Their Psychology, Biology, and History* (1993), *Emotional Contagion* (1994), and *Love and Sex* (1996). *Love, Sex, and Intimacy* is an update of the earlier book *A New Look at Love,* and in it, the authors approach the study of relationships from multiple perspectives. They discuss not only heterosexual dating and marital relationships but other types of close relationships such as homosexual ones.

After receiving her doctorate, Hatfield was appointed assistant professor at the University of Minnesota and advanced to associate professor in two years. She moved to the University of Rochester as associate professor and then to the University of Wisconsin, Madison, where she was soon promoted to professor of sociology and psychology. She received an appointment at the University of Hawaii at Manoa as professor in 1981.

She has received the distinguished scientist award of the Society for Scientific Study of Sex (1994) and the award of the Society of Experimental Social Psychology (1993). She is a fellow of the American Psychological Association, the Society for the Psychological Study of Social Issues, and the American Sociological Association. She is a member of the Society of Experimental Social Psychology and of the American Association of Sex Educators and Counselors. She is listed under several names in various sources: "Elaine C. Hatfield," "Elaine Walster," and "Elaine Hatfield Walster."

***Bibliography:*** *American Men and Women of Science* 11–13; *Contemporary Authors* v. 25–28R, CANR-10, CANR-17, and CANR-38; *Who's Who in America,* 51st ed., 1997.

# *Hay, Elizabeth Dexter*

(1927– )

### *embryologist, cell biologist, anatomist*

***Education:*** B.A., Smith College, 1948; M.D., Johns Hopkins University, 1952; honorary degrees: M.A., Harvard University, 1964; D.Sc., Smith College, 1973, Trinity College, 1989, and Johns Hopkins University, 1990

***Professional Experience:*** Intern, University Hospital, Johns Hopkins University, 1952–1953, instructor in anatomy, School of Medicine, 1953–1956, assistant professor, 1956–1957; assistant professor, Medical College of Cornell University, 1957–1960; assistant professor, Harvard Medical School, 1960–1964, Louise Foote Pfeiffer Associate Professor of Embryology, 1964–1969, chair, Department of Anatomy, 1975–1993, Louise Foote Pfeiffer Professor of Embryology, 1969– , professor of cell biology, 1993–

***Elizabeth Hay's*** work as a cell biologist, embryologist, and anatomist is significant because her research on cellular mechanisms aids the understanding of the metastasis of cancer cells, birth defects, and childhood diseases. During her undergraduate years at Smith College, she spent her summers working at the Marine Biological Laboratory at Woods Hole, Massachusetts, on limb regeneration; that work was one of her first projects when she joined the Anatomy Department at Johns Hopkins Medical School as an instructor. She concentrated on salamanders and their ability to grow new limbs, and at Hopkins, she had use of an electron microscope and was one of the first researchers to use it in the study of biological structure. In 1957, she moved to Cornell Medical College to conduct research with Don Fawcett, one of the foremost electron microscopists.

When Fawcett received an appointment as chair of the Department of Anatomy at Harvard Medical School, Hay became an assistant professor in the same department and, while there, published several important studies on limb regeneration. She was among the first successfully to apply autoradiography to the electron microscope, autoradiography being the technique of recording on photographic emulsion the radiations emitted by radioactive material in the object being studied.

Hay and Jean-Paul Revel published a series of papers using the technique to localize metabolic activities in cells. In 1961, they demonstrated DNA synthesis in the nucleolus long before the widespread acceptance of the idea that the nucleolus contains DNA (the nucleolus is a dense spherical accumulation of fibers and granules found in the nucleus of most eukaryotic cells). Their studies of organelle function indicated that the epidermis secreted collagen, a very debatable theory at that time. In 1969, they published a monograph on the fine structure of the developing avian cornea that has become a classic in the field, and since that time, Hay has concentrated on studies of eye tissues and the functions of collagen and other extracellular matrix molecules. Her research has had a profound impact on cell and developmental biology, and she was elected a member of the National Academy of Sciences in 1984.

Hay's father was a physician who had hoped that Elizabeth's twin brother, Jack, would follow a medical career. However, Jack died in 1942, and when Elizabeth's mentor at Smith College advised her to pursue an M.D. degree instead of a Ph.D., she was delighted to tell her father that she would become a physician. The reason for the advice was that at the time, women with doctorates in biology could find jobs only in the smaller women's colleges, like Smith, and there was far more mobility with an M.D. She was the first woman to chair an academic department at Harvard Medical School; her appointment is significant because, during her tenure at the school, there usually have been only two other women members of the department. She accepted the job because otherwise the school would have hired someone from outside the department as chair.

Hay is the author of the books *Regeneration* (1966) and *Fine Structure of the Developing Avian Cornea* (1969) and editor of *Macromolecules Regulating Growth and Development* (1974) and *Cell Biology of Extracellular Matrix* (1981; 2d ed., 1991). She has received the Distinguished Achievement Award of the New York Hospital–Cornell Medical Center Alumni Council (1985), the Alcon Award for Vision Research (1988), the E. B. Wilson Award of the American Society for Cell Biology (1989), the Excellence in Science Award of the Federation of American Societies for Experimental Biology (1990), and the Salute to Contemporary Women Scientists Award of the New York Academy of Sciences (1991).

She is a member of the Society for Developmental Biology (president, 1973–1974), the American Association of Anatomists (president, 1981–1982), American Society of Zoologists (president, 1976–1977), the American Academy of Arts and Sciences, and International Society of Developmental Biology. Her research includes origin of cells in amphibian limb regeneration; fine structure of developing muscle, cartilage, skin, and eye; collagen synthesis by epithelium; tissue interaction in the developing cornea; and the immunohistochemistry of collagen. Her photograph is included in *Notable Women in the Life Sciences.*

**Bibliography:** *American Men and Women of Science* 11–19; Herzenberg, C., *Women Scientists from Antiquity to the Present; Notable Twentieth-Century Scientists; Notable Women in the Life Sciences; Who's Who in America,* 51st ed., 1997; *Who's Who in Science and Engineering,* 3d ed., 1996–1997.

# Healy, Bernadine Patricia
(1944– )
## cardiologist, health administrator

***Education:*** B.A., Vassar College, 1965; M.D., Harvard Medical School, 1970; diplomate, American Board of Medical Examiners, American Board of Cardiology, American Board of Internal Medicine

***Professional Experience:*** Intern in medicine, Johns Hopkins Hospital, 1970–1971, assistant resident, 1971–1972; staff fellow, section of pathology, National Heart, Blood, and Lung Institute, 1972–1974; fellow, Cardiovascular Division, Johns Hopkins University School of Medicine, 1974–1976, fellow, Department of Pathology, 1975–1976, assistant professor of medicine and pathology, 1976–1981, associate professor of medicine, 1977–1982, assistant dean for postdoctoral programs and faculty development, 1979–1984, associate professor of pathology, 1981–1984, professor of medicine, 1982–1984; active staff, medicine and pathology, Johns Hopkins Hospital, 1976– ; deputy director, Office of Science and Technology Policy, Executive Office of the President, 1984–1985; chair of Research Institute, Cleveland Clinic Foundation, 1985–1991, senior health and science policy adviser, 1994– ; director of National Institutes of Health (NIH), 1991–1993; vice chair of President's Council of Advisors on Science and Technology, 1990–1991; member of Special Medical Advisory Group, Department of Veterans Affairs, 1990–1991, chair of advisory panel for Basic Research for 1990s, Office of Technical Assessment, 1990–1991

***Concurrent Positions:*** Member, visiting committee, Board of Overseers, Harvard Medical School and School of Dental Medicine, 1985–1991; member, national advisory board, Johns Hopkins Center for Hospital Finance and Management, 1987–1991; member, Board of Overseers, Harvard College, 1989– ; trustee, Edison BioTech Center, Cleveland, 1990–

***Married:*** George Bulkley, divorced 1981; Floyd D. Loop, 1985

***Children:*** 2

*Bernadine Healy* is a cardiologist and health administrator known for her research in and advocacy of women's health issues. She was the first woman to head the National Institutes of Health (NIH), from 1991 to 1993, and when she was president of the American Heart Association, she initiated pioneering research into women's heart disease. At the time, heart disease was considered a man's disease, but she demonstrated that more women than men die from that disease.

As head of NIH she initiated a large-scale study of the effects of vitamin supplementation, hormone replacement therapy, and dietary modification on women between the ages of 45 and 79. Probably one of the most significant problems she attacked was that most of the clinical tests of medications were being conducted on adult males, even medications that were designed for women and children. She established the policy that NIH would fund only those clinical trials that included both women and men when the condition being studied affected both genders. In addition to heart disease, she also fought to increase funding for other conditions that affect women, such as breast cancer, depression, osteoporosis, and AIDS. She pointed out that although most research has been conducted primarily on men, women make up the fastest-growing group of people with AIDS, especially women of color, who account for most of the women with AIDS.

Healy had a great deal of experience in health administration, particularly at Johns Hopkins University and at the Cleveland

Clinic, before she was appointed NIH director. In addition, she had served as the president's deputy director of the White House Office of Science and Technology Policy in 1984–1985 and 1990–1991. She joked that NIH was in such poor shape that no man would accept the appointment. The agency had been without a permanent director for 20 months, and scientists were leaving in droves to accept better salaries elsewhere.

A serious problem, and one that still exists today, is that scientific questions were embroiled in politics, such as the congressional ban on fetal-tissue research. Before Healy was appointed, Congress was investigating alleged cases of scientific misconduct, and the agency had been accused of sexism and racism in hiring and promotion. Another controversy arose when she approved patent applications for 347 genes, believing that patenting genes would promote, not hinder, the ability to access information about them and also contribute to much-needed international debate on the subject. She exerted strong leadership in handling these problems, some successfully, others not successfully.

She has attributed her ambitious nature to her father's conviction that women should have every opportunity in life that men have. As a child, she envisioned being either a nun or a physician until her father pointed out that she was too independent to take orders from a priest in a convent. Her father actually defied the Catholic Church when he removed Bernadine from the parochial school and sent her to Hunter College High School, a public school that prepared girls for college. At that time, it was thought that girls should not be overeducated because their role was to be good Catholic mothers.

She attended Vassar College on a scholarship, majoring in chemistry with a minor in philosophy, and when she graduated from Harvard University Medical School, she was one of only ten women in a class of 120 students. Since she had previously attended all-female schools, she experienced sexism for the first time at Harvard; her fellow students criticized her for depriving a man of the opportunity to attend that prestigious school. She had a long, successful career at Johns Hopkins, but she still was faced with problems of sexism that she encountered there. However, at NIH she was able to point out and undermine the subtle but pervasive bias in medical research against treating women's diseases separately from men's.

She has served on numerous committees and commissions related to medicine and health and has managed to continue her medical practice and treat patients. She published a book for the general public, *Staying Strong and Healthy from 9 to 99* (1995), in which she encourages women to take charge of their health. She received an award from the American Heart Association (1983–1984), and she is a member of the Institute of Medicine of the National Academy of Sciences, the American Federation for Clinical Research (president, 1983–1984), American Heart Association (president, 1988–1989), American Medical Women's Association, and Association of Women in Science. Her research includes cardiovascular research and medicine, neurobiology, immunology, cancer, artificial organs, atherosclerosis, musculoskeletal disorders, and molecular biology. Her photograph is included in *Current Biography* (1992), *Notable Twentieth-Century Scientists,* and *Working Woman* (September 1992).

***Bibliography:*** *American Men and Women of Science* 17–19; *Current Biography 1992; Notable Twentieth-Century Scientists; Who's Who in America,* 51st ed., 1997; *Who's Who in Science and Engineering,* 3d ed., 1996–1997.

# *Helm, June*
(1924– )
## *anthropologist, ethnologist*

***Education:*** Student, University of Kansas City, 1941; Ph.D., University of Chicago, 1944, M.A., 1949, Ph.D. in anthropology, 1958
***Professional Experience:*** Sessional lecturer in anthropology, Carleton University, 1949–1959; field officer, Northern Coordination and Research Center, Department of Northern Affairs and Natural Resources, Canada, 1959–1960; assistant professor of anthropology, University of Iowa, 1960–1963, associate professor, 1963–1966, professor, 1966–
***Concurrent Positions:*** Adviser to Indian Brotherhood for Northwest Territories, Canada, 1974; consultant for Mackenzie Valley Pipeline Inquiry, Canada, 1975–1976
***Married:*** Richard MacNeish, 1945, divorced 1958; Pierce E. King, 1967

***June Helm*** is a sociocultural anthropologist known for her ethnographic accounts of the Déné Indians, the hunting and gathering people of Canada's Northwest Territories. Her research contradicts that of other anthropologists in the areas of territorial groups, ethnohistory, political leadership, and sociocultural change; her work offers a continuous and detailed picture of a particular region; and she has consistently made use of historical documents since the beginning of her research.

Helm married archaeologist Richard MacNeish in 1945 so she could accompany him to Mexico for his dissertation fieldwork—it was common at the time for researchers who planned to conduct joint fieldwork to marry. After completing her master's dissertation, she suffered a writer's block and did not continue with her doctorate. The couple moved to Canada in 1949 where her husband worked for the National Museum of Canada. Accompanying him on a fieldtrip to the Northwest Territories in 1950, Helm accepted a position to teach English to children of the Slave Indians, a division of the Déné/Athabaskan people, which gave her an entrée to the community as an ethnologist and opened up a career-long study for her. She has focused on the Déné Indians of Canada's Northwest Territories for most of her professional life.

When the couple returned to Ottawa, she read all she could find about the Déné and noticed that the family terminology she had recorded differed from that reported in other studies and that the socioterritorial organization of this small bush community did not match what had been attributed to it. She also raised questions about northern Athabaskan leadership styles. After three additional trips to Déné communities, she used the information she had gathered as the basis for her doctoral dissertation. She received her doctorate in 1958, the same year the couple divorced, and accepted a position at the University of Iowa.

She continued her studies of the peoples in the northwestern subarctic and their relations with other Déné and whites during the past 200 years. One characteristic of her work is that she uses historical documents. For example, some studies indicated that epidemic diseases led to an estimated 80 percent reduction in the population, but she found that from 1829 to the mid-twentieth century, the population remained static. She concluded that the elimination of female infanticide after 1860, perhaps because of the influence of missionaries and traders, served as a counterbalance to deaths from epidemic diseases.

Helm's mother was very influential in her decision to seek a career, and as a result of her mother's drive and attention, she did not feel any limits because she was a woman. The family had little money for education, and she was awarded a scholarship for college. She spent her first year at the University of Kansas City and, owing to an increase in the family's finances during World War II, then entered first a two-year program at the University of Chicago and later the master's program.

She has published several books, including *Lynx Point People: The Dynamics of a Northern Athapaskan Band* (1961) and *Indians of the Subarctic* (1976), and edited the *Handbook of North American Indians*, volume 6, *Subarctic* (1976) and *Social Contexts of American Ethnology, 1840–1984* (1985). She is a fellow of the American Association for the Advancement of Science and the American Anthropological Association (president, 1985–1987). She is a member of the Ethnological Society of America.

***Bibliography:*** *American Men and Women of Science* 11–13; *Who's Who in America*, 51st ed., 1997; *Who's Who of American Women*, 20th ed., 1997–1998; *Women Anthropologists.*

# *Herzenberg, Caroline Stuart (Littlejohn)*
(1932– )
***physicist***

***Education:*** B.S., Massachusetts Institute of Technology, 1953; M.S., University of Chicago, 1955, Ph.D. in physics, 1958; honorary degree: D.Sc, State University of New York, 1991
***Professional Experience:*** Research associate in nuclear physics, University of Chicago, 1958–1959, and Argonne National Laboratory, 1959–1961; assistant professor of physics, Illinois Institute of Technology (IIT), 1961–1967, Research Corporation grant, 1963–1964; research physicist, IIT Research Institute, 1967–1970, senior physicist, 1970–1971; consultant, 1971–1972; visiting associate professor of physics, University of Illinois Medical Center, 1972–1974; consultant, 1974–1975; lecturer in physics, California State University, Fresno, 1975–1976; physicist, Argonne National Laboratory, 1977–
***Married:*** Leonardo Herzenberg, 1961
***Children:*** 2

***Caroline Herzenberg*** is a physicist who is known for her pioneering research on the Mossbauer effect, for studying the first lunar samples returned to earth from the Apollo missions, and for developing analytic instruments for fossil fuel studies. In addition, she has publicized the accomplishments of women scientists and worked to further the science careers of young women.

After completing her doctorate, she continued as a postdoctoral fellow at the University of Chicago where she participated in measuring the products of nuclear reactions between lithium isotopes and those of lithium, beryllium, and boron. These studies pioneered some of the earliest heavy-ion work. As a postdoctoral fellow at the Argonne National Laboratory, her research focus shifted to Mossbauer spectroscopy. She and several colleagues verified the existence of and went on to do pioneering work on the Mossbauer effect, which is the phenomenon whereby the atom in a crystal undergoes no recoil when emitting a gamma ray, giving all the emitted energy to the gamma ray and resulting in a sharply defined wavelength. The phenomenon was named between 1955 and 1960 in honor of Rudolph Mossbauer.

Herzenberg was appointed assistant professor of physics at the Illinois Institute of Technology (IIT) in 1961 where she continued work on the Mossbauer effect while studying experimental low-energy nuclear physics using a small Van de Graaff accelerator. She set up a Mossbauer-effect research facility and began to explore geological applications of the effect. She published the spectra of different rock types, noting the potential for using the Mossbauer spectrometry technique to analyze rocks and minerals from lunar and planetary surfaces. She submitted a proposal to the National Aeronautics and Space Administration (NASA) and was appointed a principal investigator for analyzing the lunar samples from the Apollo missions. Since the Mossbauer technique requires minute samples for nondestructive testing, it was an ideal analytical technique. Her group clearly identified the presence of free metallic iron and ilmenite and verified the presence of other iron-containing minerals in the lunar samples.

Unfortunately, at the same time she was notified of the grant, she was denied tenure at IIT. She managed to obtain appointments, first as a research physicist and then as a senior physicist, at IIT Research Institute so she would have laboratory space for the analyses. Naturally, the university administrators made a concerted effort to keep a lucrative NASA grant on their campus, and it is shocking that she spent the next five or so years as an independent consultant and on temporary assignments while she hunted for a full-time position.

In 1977, she was appointed as a physicist at the Argonne National Laboratory, where she still works. There she joined a fossil-energy instrumentation program that focused on developing instrumentation for process control of a new generation of coal conversion and combustion plants. She developed nuclear techniques for noninvasive measuring of the composition and flow rate of coal slurries and pulverized coal in pneumatic transport pipes. During the 1980s, she studied fossil energy utilization, radioactive waste disposal, technology for arms control verification, and radiological emergency preparedness.

Her childhood was similar to that of many women scientists in that, although they were not particularly interested in science, her parents fostered her interest in the natural sciences. Not following the sex stereotyping of the time, her mother did not want her to play with dolls but provided teddy bears, toy soldiers, and toy guns. Caroline had an inauspicious start in school by flunking kindergarten because she could not skip properly, name all the colors, or socialize adequately with other children. While she was in high school, she won the Westinghouse Talent Search, which enabled her to attend the Massachusetts Institute of Technology as an undergraduate.

In 1989, she was the first scientist to be inducted into the Chicago Women's Hall of Fame. In addition to her scientific publications, she has written *Women Scientists from Antiquity to the Present* (1986), a compendium of sources for information about women scientists, and also has published several papers on the historic role of women in science.

She is a fellow of the American Association for the Advancement of Science and the American Physical Society. She is a member of the Association of Women in Science (president, 1988–1990) and the Federation of American Scientists. Her research interests include low-energy experimental nuclear physics, Mossbauer-effect studies, lunar sample analysis, nuclear analysis methods, instrumentation development, fossil energy utilization technology, radioactive isotope applications, nuclear radiation physics, history of science, and technological emergency preparedness.

***Bibliography:*** *American Men and Women of Science* 11–19; Herzenberg, C., *Women Scientists from Antiquity to the Present; Notable Twentieth-Century Scientists; Who's Who in Engineering,* 9th ed., 1995; *Who's Who of American Women,* 20th ed., 1997–1998; *Women in Chemistry and Physics.*

# *Hewlett, Sylvia Ann*
(1946– )
***economist***

***Education:*** B.A., Cambridge University, 1967, M.A, 1971; Ph.D. in economics, London School of Economics and Political Science, 1973
***Professional Experience:*** Research fellow, Cambridge University, 1972–1974; assistant professor of economics, Barnard College, 1979–1981; vice president for economic studies, United Nations, 1981–1986; author, 1986–
***Married:*** Richard Weinert
***Children:*** 4

***Sylvia Hewlett*** is an economist who has provided sharp criticism of the situation for women in the United States since the feminist movement of the 1970s. It is her contention that American women, and the American family, are in worse condition than at any other time in the nation's history. Her chief argument is that in the drive for equality in the workplace, the feminists ignored the fact that many women want to be mothers and therefore did not demand paid medical and maternity leaves, tax exemptions for children, or government-funded child care, guarantees that are prevalent in many European countries.

She herself supported the feminist movement for a number of years, and while she was teaching at Barnard College, she was amazed to find she was allowed only a few weeks' paid leave when she and her husband had their first child. When she attempted to establish maternity leaves and child care facilities, both her female and male colleagues told her she was asking too much. When she had a miscarriage, people were even less sympathetic when she explained she needed extra time to recover. She found it was impossible for her to complete the requirements for tenure at Barnard because of her family responsibilities and accepted a position with the United Nations as vice president for economic studies.

As a graduate student at Cambridge, she had been involved in economic studies in South America, and she published several books during her career based on her economics research, including *The Cruel Dilemma of Development: Twentieth-Century Brazil* (1980), *Brazil and Mexico: Patterns in Late Development* (1982), and *The Global Repercussions of U.S. Monetary and Fiscal Policy* (1984). However, she is best known for her studies of the effects of the American feminist movement.

She was born in Wales in a working-class environment that made her conscious of social injustice at an early age. However, her father, a teacher, encouraged her to study and do well in school, and when she was 13, he took her on a trip to Cambridge University and told her she could go to a place like that if she worked hard. When she entered Cambridge she found herself at a disadvantage because she did not speak standard British English, and she had difficulty overcoming the rigid social-class barriers. However, she persevered with her studies and earned degrees at Cambridge and a doctorate at the London School of Economics and Political Science.

She set off a storm of criticism when she published her book *A Lesser Life: The Myth of Women's Liberation in America* (1986) in which she argued that the focus of the U.S. feminist movement to attain equality through the passage of the Equal Rights Amendment was misguided and irrelevant to most American women. Believing the feminists had ignored the needs of working mothers, she said they confused equal rights with equal treatment and ignored the realities of family life. They did not attempt to enact legislation to provide support services, such as paid medical and maternity leaves, increased tax exemptions for families, paid child care subsidies, and adequate child care facilities. The situation is further complicated by the facts that family income has been reduced year after year and the divorce rate quadrupled in 20 years. Divorced mothers with children find that their standard of living drops 73 percent the first year after a divorce while that of their ex-husbands rises 42 percent. Hewlett cites the programs for government support of families in the Scandinavian countries as the programs to copy.

Her second book on this topic, *When the Bow Breaks: The Cost of Neglecting Our Children* (1991), again stirred controversy. In that book, she provides additional data on the gap in wages between women and men, the low income of divorced women with children, the lack of adequate child care facilities, and the need for family subsidies. She mentions the need for prenatal care and the need for better-educated children. However, the most provocative statistics are those that compare the amount of federal money available for the elderly and for children. She argues that Americans are spending too much money providing bypass surgery for 70-year-old citizens and just pennies for prenatal care. In her most recent book, *The War against Parents: What We Can Do for America's Beleaguered Moms and Dads* (1998), she argues that business, government, and even our culture make raising children impossible. Her photograph is included in *Time* (August 26, 1991) and *People Weekly* (May 4, 1998).

***Bibliography:*** *Contemporary Authors* v. 118 and 123.

# *Hite, Shere*

(1942– )

***cultural historian, author***

***Education:*** B.A., University of Florida, 1964, M.A. in history, 1968; student, Columbia University, 1968

***Professional Experience:*** Director of Feminist Sexuality Project, National Organization for Women (NOW), 1972–1978; director, Hite Research International, 1978– ; instructor in female sexuality, New York University, 1977– ; lecturer; author

***Married:*** Friedrich Hoericke, 1985

***Shere Hite's*** research on human sexuality has been considered in some circles as pioneering as that of the late Alfred Kinsey and the team of William Masters and Virginia Johnson. Using the approach of asking people about their sex lives and views of sex, her investigation started in 1971 when, while working at the National Organization for Women (NOW) office in New York City, she saw a pamphlet entitled "The Myth of Female Orgasms" and decided to prepare a questionnaire on the issue under NOW's sponsorship. Using NOW's mailing lists and advertisements in various popular publications, she asked that women send in their views. This was the beginning of four major surveys that she has conducted.

Her first book was *The Hite Report: A Nationwide Study of Female Sexuality* (1976), which was based on a four-year study of about 3,000 women who responded to her questionnaire. The responses she received did not resemble the information she saw in the pamphlet, and her general conclusion was that the current notions on sexuality must be revised if women are to receive sexual fulfillment. She said that women's sexual difficulties were the fault of a male-oriented pattern of sexual expression. The book was an instant best-seller and continues to be in print. Some critics regarded the work on a par with the Kinsey and Masters/Johnson books; others criticized it as being unscientific because only 3,000 women responded to the 100,000 questionnaires distributed. They theorized that only women who were unhappy responded to the survey while Kinsey and Masters/Johnson were authority figures who had used interviews and laboratory research in gathering their data. However, a recent biography of Kinsey indicates, what had long been speculated, that he fabricated some of his data. Masters/Johnson also have experienced reduced credibility after their publication on AIDS in 1988.

Equally controversial, *The Hite Report on Male Sexuality* (1981) presents primarily verbatim responses to a questionnaire by more than 7,000 males between the ages of 13 and 97. Just as the women had indicated, many men said they also felt trapped by sexual stereotypes, craved emotional intimacy, and found themselves unable to talk openly about their sexual angers, anxieties, and desires. Many critics again pointed out that Hite was using responses from a self-selected group instead of a statistically valid sampling. The severest critics called the book representative of the hard-line feminist interpretation that sexual differences and problems are the result of the patriarchal culture and the age-old male suppression of women.

Hite's third book, *Women and Love: A Cultural Revolution in Progress* (1987), again was based on a questionnaire, this time one distributed through women's clubs and organizations across the country. About 4,500 women responded to the inquiry, out of the 100,000 copies distributed, and the result was that women of all ages experience increasing emotional frustration and gradual disillusionment in their personal relationships with men. This book was also criticized because the survey method probably attracted unhappy women rather than a cross-sampling of both happy and unhappy women. Some critics complained about the male bashing, the bloated generalizations, and the rambling prose in this book.

The last book in the "Hite report" series is *The Hite Report on Family: Growing up under Patriarchy* (1994). This work, too, is based on a questionnaire distributed through popular magazines and various organizations. About half of the 3,000 responses were received from the United States, and the rest came primarily from Western Europe. Hite's interpretation of the responses is that we need to break away from the traditional family headed by a patriarch and give children the freedom to choose other lifestyles. She says that the recent changes in the family, especially the increased divorce rates, do not signal a crisis; instead, they are evidence that the family is finally becoming democratized. The book was published in England, but although the American publisher Dutton purchased the U.S. rights, publication of the book in the United States was canceled.

The blasts of criticism for the first two books angered Hite, but she has still published several additional books. "The Hite reports" have often been criticized for an unorthodox methodology, anti-male bias, and occasionally sloppy prose style, but for many social scientists, they represent a mother lode of information about a period in American culture when there was an unprecedented confrontation of the traditional ideas of home and family.

She was born Shirley Diana Gregory and adopted by her stepfather, Raymond Hite. At some point she started calling herself "Shere," pronounced "Share." She lived with her grandparents for a time, then went to Florida to live with other relatives. She was gifted in music, and for a time she wanted to be a classical composer. However, she majored in history at the University of Florida and then moved to New York City where she attended graduate school at Columbia University briefly but dropped out of school. Not satisfied with the curriculum, she worked as model for the Wilhelmina Agency and then obtained the position at NOW headquarters where she started her surveys. She has lectured at many universities. The negative criticism of her book *Women and Love* prompted her to leave the United States for Europe in 1987, and according to a newspaper item in March 1996, she has adopted the German citizenship of her husband, composer and concert pianist Friedrich Hoericke. There are photographs in *Current Biography* (1988) and *MS* magazine (September–October 1994).

***Bibliography:*** *Contemporary Authors* v. 81–84 and CANR-31; *Current Biography 1988; Good Housekeeping Woman's Almanac;* Ireland, N., *Index to Women of the World . . . Suppl.; Who's Who in America,* 51st ed., 1997; *Who's Who of American Women,* 20th ed., 1997–1998.

# *Hoffman, Darleane (Christian)*
(1926– )
***nuclear chemist***

***Education:*** B.S., Iowa State University, 1948, Ph.D. in physical chemistry, 1951
***Professional Experience:*** Assistant, Ames Laboratory, U.S. Atomic Energy Commission, 1947–1951; chemist, Oak Ridge National Laboratory, 1951–1952; chemist, Los Alamos National Laboratory, 1952–1971, associate group leader, 1971–1978, division leader, Chemistry–Nuclear Chemistry Division, 1979–1981, leader, Isotope Nuclear Chemistry Division, 1981–1984; professor of chemistry, Nuclear Science Division, Lawrence Berkeley Laboratory, University of California, 1984– ; director, Glenn T. Seaborg Institute of Transactinium Science, Lawrence Livermore National Laboratory, 1991–
***Married:*** Marvin Hoffman, 1951
***Children:*** 2

*Darleane Hoffman* is a major international figure in nuclear chemistry. In her early research on the separations processes of the heavy elements, she developed techniques that still are in use today, and her original interest in chemical separations has made her a leading figure in the studies of the heaviest elements. For more than two decades she has conducted her research at the major national laboratories, and she is director of the Seaborg Institute of Transactinium Science at the Lawrence Livermore National Laboratory. It was at Los Alamos that she discovered plutonium-244 in nature. In 1987, her group performed the first aqueous chemistry on hahnium (element 105) using the longest known isotope, which has a half-life of only 35 seconds. Between 1987 and 1990, in collaboration with German and Swiss scientists, her group produced and studied isotopes of element 103 (Lr) and element 105 as Ha-262 and Ha-263. She was awarded the National Medal of Science in 1997.

Her father was a schoolteacher, and mathematics was his favorite subject. Darleane, too, was very interested in mathematics but also spent much time on musical activities and learned to play several instruments. She was undecided whether to select math or art in college, but she entered as an applied art major. In a required chemistry course her freshman year she found that she liked chemistry best of anything she was studying, primarily because of an excellent teacher. As a junior, she secured a research assistantship at Iowa State University's Institute of Atomic Research and became fascinated with the study of radioactivity. She continued at Iowa State as a graduate student and met her future husband there; they married shortly after she received her doctorate in 1951. When she accepted a position at Oak Ridge National Laboratory, her husband remained at Ames to complete his degree in physics; they both moved to Los Alamos after he completed his degree. Darleane was appointed professor of chemistry at the University of California in 1984 and became director of the Glenn T. Seaborg Institute in 1991.

Hoffman's team has focused on the chemical and nuclear properties of the transplutonium elements. The team members represent one of only two or three groups in the world that has access to the required accelerators and heavy element targets as well as expertise in the radiochemical and nuclear techniques and data acquisition systems required for these studies. She published a paper "The Heaviest Elements" on elements heavier than fermium in the May 2, 1994, issue of *Chemical & Engineering News.* She considers one of the most-important applied programs she has been associated with to be when she was a project leader of the radionuclide migration project at the Nevada test site in 1975. The project was to determine the potential for radionuclide migration away from the site of underground nuclear tests, and it later led to the Nevada Nuclear Waste Storage Investigation Program to find a suitable site for an underground nuclear repository at the Nevada test site.

She was the first woman to receive the Award for Nuclear Chemistry of the American Chemical Society (1983), and in 1989 she received the Garvan Medal of the American Chemical Society, which is awarded each year to an American woman chemist. Among her committee appointments, she has been a member of the Cold Fusion Panel of the Department of Energy to examine claims to the discovery of cold fusion (1989–1990). She has published more than 150 scientific papers; a partial list is included in *Women in Chemistry and Physics.* She is a fellow of the American Institute of Chemists and the American Physical Society and a member of the American Chemical Society and the American Association for the Advancement of Science. Her research interests are low-energy and spontaneous fusion, radionuclide migration in the environment, nuclear waste management, production mechanisms for heavy element isotopes, and chemical and nuclear properties of the heaviest elements. Her photograph is included in *Chemical & Engineering News* (May 2, 1994, and September 25, 1989).

***Bibliography:*** *American Men and Women of Science* 11–19; Rossiter, M., *Women Scientists in America; Who's Who in America,* 51st ed., 1997; *Who's Who in Science and Engineering,* 3d ed., 1996–1997; *Who's Who of American Women,* 20th ed., 1997–1998; *Women in Chemistry and Physics.*

# *Hollinshead, Ariel Cahill*
## (1929– )
## *pharmacologist, cancer researcher*

***Education:*** B.A., Ohio University, 1951; M.A., George Washington University, 1955, Ph.D. in pharmacology, 1957; honorary degree: D.Sc., Ohio University, 1977

***Professional Experience:*** Research fellow in virology, Baylor University Medical Center, 1958–1959; assistant professor of pharmacology, George Washington University, 1959–1961, associate professor of pharmacology, 1961–1973, head and director, Laboratory for Virus and Cancer Research, 1964–1989, professor of medicine, George Washington Medical Center, 1974–1991; professor of medicine emeritus, 1991–

***Married:*** Montgomery Hyun, 1958

***Children:*** 2

***Ariel Hollinshead*** is renowned as being the first person to identify animal and human antigens in cancerous tumors, and she is also the first to purify, develop, and test cancer-gene products that induce long-lasting cell-mediated immunity. In her research, she devised a new technique for isolating the antigens intact from the membranes by using low-frequency sound, which gently separates out the antigens without damaging them. In the 1970s, she started her research by investigating vaccines for human lung cancer; in the 1980s, she moved into the field of ovarian cancer; and recently she has been developing new forms of HIV and AIDS therapy.

Like many women scientists, as a child Ariel Hollinshead was encouraged by her parents to succeed. Both parents were college graduates, and they brought her up to feel equal to her older brother. She was inspired to pursue an investigative career in the sciences when at age 15 she read Paul De Kruif's *The Microbe Hunters* (1926). She received her undergraduate degree from Ohio University and her graduate degrees in pharmacology from George Washington University. After her marriage in 1958, she had a postdoctoral fellowship in virology at Baylor Medical School for two years but returned to Washington, D.C., to rejoin George Washington University as an assistant professor. She was promoted through the ranks to become professor of medicine in 1974. Between 1964 and 1989, she headed the Laboratory for Virus and Cancer Research.

Her comments about being a female engaged in medical research were that you get knocked down a great deal but you just get up and fight. She was an early advocate of mentoring and networking for women in the sciences and has established prizes for papers on this topic. When discussing combining a career with family, she mentioned fulfilling her expected role of ironing seven shirts each week, planning meals, purchasing groceries, and preparing meals. She said she made a little chart to convert teaspoons and pounds into milliliters and grams because she had never cooked but had had many chemistry courses.

She was the first woman appointed to chair the Review Board of Oncology for the Veterans Administration in 1977. Among her awards are Medical Woman of the Year Award of the Board of American Medical Colleges (1975–1976), and Star of Europe (1980). She is a fellow of the American Academy of Microbiology and American Association for the Advancement of Science. She is a member of the New York Academy of Sciences, International Society for Preventive Oncology, Society for Experimental Biology and Medicine, American Society for Microbiology, American Association of Cancer Research, American Association of Immunologists, and American Medical Writers Association. Her research interests include chemotherapy of animal virus diseases and cancer; nucleoprotein chemistry of viruses; cancer immunogenetics; environmental carcinogens; and first isolation, purification, and identification of animal and human tumor-associated antigens. Her photograph is included in *Science News* (June 12, 1980).

***Bibliography:*** *American Men and Women of Science* 12–19; Herzenberg, C., *Women Scientists from Antiquity to the Present;* Ireland, N., *Index to Women of the World . . . Suppl.; Notable Women in the Life Sciences;* Stanley, A., *Mothers and Daughters of Invention; Who's Who in America,* 51st ed., 1997; *Who's Who of American Women,* 20th ed., 1997–1998.

## *Horner, Matina (Souretis)*
(1939– )
***psychologist***

***Education:*** B.A., Bryn Mawr College, 1961; M.S., University of Michigan, 1963, Ph.D., in psychology, 1968; honorary degrees: about 20

***Professional Experience:*** Lecturer, University of Michigan, 1968–1969; lecturer, Department of Social Relations, Harvard University, 1969–1970, assistant professor of clinical psychology, 1970–1972, consultant, University Health Services, 1971–1989; associate professor of psychology, 1972–1989 and president, Radcliffe College, 1972–1989; president emeritus, 1989– ; executive vice-president, TIAA-CREF, 1989–

***Married:*** Joseph L. Horner, 1961

***Children:*** 3

***Matina Horner*** is known for her research on the analysis of achievement motivation among women. Her theory is that many highly intelligent women fear that academic or business success will undermine their femininity and that they will be criticized for their ambition rather than encouraged in it. Such women develop strong anxieties and unconsciously underachieve. Horner started her study of achievement motivation while still an undergraduate in the late 1950s; while conducting research for her doctorate in the

1960s, she found that although male students were confident of success in work, life, family, etc., after graduation, female students were inconsistent in their replies. She explained this difference by the fact that by the women's junior year in college, their parents were encouraging them to look for success through a secure marriage and family rather than to risk failure seeking personal achievement in a career. This mixed message was causing the fear-of-success syndrome.

When she was teaching at Harvard and then president of Radcliffe, she found that although Radcliffe women were highly intelligent, they were not finding outstanding, responsible jobs in high-profile careers as graduates of other women's colleges were. She did a series of studies of both Harvard and Radcliffe students and found that the Harvard students, all male, had the stereotype of Radcliffe women as dull, uninteresting, and unattractive. She concluded that the universities should eliminate this stereotype of successful women, which had become ingrained in the minds of both males and females. Women must be guided into feeling confident about themselves and comfortable with their success while men must learn to be more comfortable in working and socializing with successful women. Although the situation has improved since the 1960s and men and women are successfully working together, there is still much to be done. As president of Radcliffe, Horner continued her efforts to integrate the two schools. She retired in 1989 to become executive vice president of TIAA-CREF, a private retirement insurance agency for educators.

A gifted child, she was encouraged academically by her professor father. After receiving her undergraduate degree, she married Joseph Horner, an engineering student, and they entered graduate school at the University of Michigan where both received doctorates. Matina was appointed as a lecturer and then assistant professor at Harvard before she was named the president of Radcliffe at age 32, the youngest president in the college's history. She is a member of the American Psychological Association and the American Association for the Advancement of Science. Her photograph is included in *Current Biography* (1973), *The 100 Greatest American Women,* and *U.S. News & World Report* (November 23, 1981).

***Bibliography:*** *American Men and Women of Science* 13; *Current Biography 1973;* Herzenberg, C., *Women Scientists from Antiquity to the Present;* Ireland, N., *Index to Women of the World . . . Suppl.; The 100 Greatest American Women; Who's Who in America,* 51st ed., 1997; *Who's Who of American Women,* 20th ed., 1997–1998.

# *Horning, Marjorie G.*
(1917– )
***pharmacologist, biochemist***

***Education:*** B.A., Goucher College, 1938; M.S., University of Michigan, 1940, Ph.D. in biological chemistry, 1943; honorary degree: D.Sc., Goucher College, 1977
***Professional Experience:*** Research associate in pediatrics, University of Michigan Hospital, 1944–1945; research chemist, University of Pennsylvania, 1945–1950; biochemist, National Heart Institute, 1951–1961; associate professor of biochemistry, College of Medicine, Baylor University, 1961–1969, professor of biochemistry, Institute for Lipid Research, 1969– ; adjunct professor of biochemical and biophysical sciences, University of Houston
***Married:*** Evan Horning, 1942, died ca. 1993

***Marjorie Horning*** is renowned for her pioneering research on techniques for studying how drugs are broken down and used by the human body. She is particularly known for her study in the 1960s and 1970s of the transfer of drugs from a pregnant woman to her child. As late as 1968, the placenta was considered a barrier that kept the fetus from harm, but Horning showed that virtually every drug taken by a pregnant woman reaches her unborn child, as taken or in the form of breakdown products. This research underlies all recent work in preventing drug-induced birth defects. She also found that drugs taken by a nursing mother will reach her child through breast milk.

Horning's research had significant implications during the 1980s and 1990s when the number of babies who were born with drug or alcohol addiction increased, a result of the prevalence of drug addiction during the period. In her early research, however, she found that many mothers did not consider nonprescription medications "drugs" and did not realize that aspirin or remedies for other physical conditions were passed on to their children. Nor did they realize that the medicine, drugs, and alcohol could cause birth defects or later behavioral or learning problems in their offspring. What is important is that physicians have the data they need to warn parents about the effects of alcohol and other drugs. Currently, physicians are advising prospective mothers and fathers to quit alcohol, drugs, and cigarettes as much as six months prior to conceiving a child.

In the scientific community, Horning is probably best known for her research techniques. She and her husband, Evan, were at the forefront of applying gas chromatology to the solution of biological problems in the 1950s, and their use of trace analysis by gas chromotography was a major breakthrough for the field of analytical biochemistry in the early 1960s. Later, Marjorie used mass spectrometry to identify the metabolic switching of drug pathways, and recently, she has worked with the atmospheric pressure ionization mass spectrometer, which allows detection at minute levels. The Hornings received the Outstanding Achievement in Mass Spectrometry Award from the American Chemical Society in 1989.

When Marjorie began her research, she faced all the barriers that women scientists had to face in the 1940s. She worked as an unpaid aide in a University of Pennsylvania lab because women simply were not hired for laboratory work. She worked at the National Heart Institute for 11 years before moving to Baylor University as an associate professor, later professor. In 1977, she received the Garvan Medal of the American Chemical Society, which is awarded annually to an American woman chemist, and she and her husband shared the Warner-Lambert Award of the American Association of Clinical Chemists in 1976. She is a member of the American Association for the Advancement of Science, American Society of Pharmacology and Experimental Therapeutics, American Chemical Society, and New York Academy of Sciences. Her research includes analytical biochemistry, drug metabolism, gas chromatography and mass spectrometry, and toxicology. Her photograph is included in *Chemical & Engineering News* (September 25, 1989).

***Bibliography:*** *American Men and Women of Science* 11–19; Ireland, N., *Index to Women of the World . . . Suppl.;* Levin, B., *Women and Medicine;* Stanley, A., *Mothers and Daughters of Invention.*

# Hoy, Marjorie Ann (Wolf)
(1941– )
***entomologist, geneticist***

***Education:*** B.A., University of Kansas, 1963; M.S., University of California, 1966, Ph.D. in entomology, 1972
***Professional Experience:*** Research geneticist, University of California, Berkeley, 1964–1966; lecturer in biology, Fresno State College, 1967–1968, 1973; laboratory technician, Division of Biological Control, University of California, Berkeley, 1968–1970; research entomologist, Connecticut Agricultural Experiment Station, 1973–1975; research entomologist, Northeast Forest Experiment Station, U.S. Forest Service, 1975–1976; assistant professor, University of California, Berkeley, 1976–1981, associate professor, 1981–1982, professor of entomological science, 1982–1992, emeritus professor of entomological science, 1992– ; Fischer Davies and Eckes Professor of Biological Control, Department of Entomology and Nematology, University of Florida, Gainesville, 1992–
***Married:*** James B. Hoy, 1961
***Children:*** 1

*Marjorie Hoy* is renowned for her pioneering work in developing an integrated management program (IMP) of pest control for spider mites in crop plants. The traditional methods for artificial pest control have been developing pesticide chemicals, breeding pest-resistant plants, and using natural predators to control the pests. Each method has its drawbacks, but integrated pest management incorporates all three approaches and seeks control rather than eradication. IMP pest-control plans emphasize biological controls over chemical controls and use genetics to improve both the pest resistance of the crop plants and the predatory efficiency or survival rate of the pest's predators.

Her research involved the spider mites that infest California's almond orchards, and her team devised techniques for mass producing the resistant spider mites, effectively dispersing them, and establishing them in the orchards. Team members also monitored the mite population relative to its prey as well as its levels of pesticide resistance so that chemicals can be cautiously applied to aid it, or new releases can augment its numbers. Resistant species of mites lasted through the winter and retained their pesticide resistance for as long as three or four years. The control program has also been used for apples, peaches, and grapes, and today, it is standard procedure for many other crop plants. One benefit is that the program reduces the amount of pesticides that are spread in fields and eventually percolate into the groundwater. It also reduces the cost of producing a number of crops.

Hoy is one of the few women listed in this volume who is associated with agricultural research. After receiving her doctorate in entomology from Berkeley, she was first a lecturer in biology at Fresno State College and then a laboratory technician in the Division of Biological Control at Berkeley. She and her husband moved to the East Coast where she obtained a position as a research entomologist first at the Connecticut Agricultural Experiment Station and then at the Northeast Forest Experiment Station of the U.S. Forest Service. The couple later returned to Berkeley where Marjorie began as an assistant professor of entomological science, advanced through the ranks to professor, and retired in 1992. She and her husband then moved to Florida where she is currently an eminent scholar at the University of Florida, Gainesville, in the Department of Entomology and Nematology.

She has received the Bussart Memorial Award (1986) and the Founder's Memorial Award of the Entomological Society of America (1992). She is the editor or coeditor of several books: *Genetics in Relation to Insect Management* (1979), *Recent Advances in*

*Knowledge of the Phytoseiida* (1982), *Biological Control of Pests by Mites* (1983), *Biological Control of Agricultural IPM Systems* (1985), and *Insect Molecular Genetics* (1994). She is a fellow of the American Association for the Advancement of Science and a member of the Entomological Society of America and International Organization for Biological Control of Noxious Animals and Plants. Her research includes genetics and biological control of insect and mite pests, genetic selection of pesticide-resistant predators and parasites for integrated pest management programs, and risk assessment for releases of transgenic arthropod natural enemies.

***Bibliography:*** *American Men and Women of Science* 13–19; Stanley, A., *Mothers and Daughters of Invention; Who's Who in America,* 51st ed., 1997; *Who's Who in Science and Engineering,* 3d ed., 1996–1997; *Who's Who of American Women,* 20th ed., 1997–1998.

# *Hrdy, Sarah C. (Blaffer)*

(1946– )

## *evolutionary biologist, primatologist*

***Education:*** B.A., Radcliffe College, 1969; Ph.D. in behavioral biology, Harvard University, 1975

***Professional Experience:*** Instructor in anthropology, University of Massachusetts, 1973; lecturer in biological anthropology, Harvard University, 1975–1976, fellow in biology, 1977–1978; associate, Peabody Museum, 1979– ; professor, University of California, Davis, 1984–

***Concurrent Position:*** Visiting associate professor of anthropology, Rice University, 1981–1982

***Married:*** Daniel B. Hrdy, 1972

***Children:*** 3

***Sarah Blaffer Hrdy*** is renowned for her research on evolutionary biology. As a graduate student at Harvard in 1974, she proposed the controversial theory that infanticide is an adaptive evolutionary strategy among a primate, the langurs in India. After she heard Paul Ehrlich lecture about the dangers of overpopulation, she decided to study the monkeys called Hanuman langurs, of which there are dense populations in parts of India. Her original theory was that overpopulation prompted the langur males to kill a rival's offspring, but she found that whenever a male became dominant in a group, he would kill his predecessor's offspring so he could breed with the mothers. The next dominant male followed the same pattern, and although few males were actually seen to kill, the babies just disappeared. Before the 1970s, most researchers viewed animal societies as smoothly running systems in which each member fulfilled his or her role in the group, and it was thought that primate societies in particular were utopias that humans would do well to emulate.

Although there was a great uproar of protest when she proposed this theory, especially from other researchers who studied langurs, by the 1980s the view was that infanticide was normal behavior in primates as well as humans and other creatures. For example, lions are known to kill the offspring of their rivals, and when bird eggs hatch over a period of days, the late arrivals often are pecked to death by their older siblings. Infanticide has also been reported among mice, ground squirrels, bears, deer, prairie dogs, foxes, fish, wasps, and bees. The practice of preferring male offspring to female among some cultures and primitive human tribes has been known for many years, and some researchers now are examining child abuse as a possible indicator of potential infanticide in society.

She moved on to examine the role of women in evolutionary biology, and in her book *The Woman That Never Evolved* (1981), she contradicts the theory that women are evolutionarily selected to be weaker than men. She agrees that there is a size differential between men and women but argues that the theories that meek women must be looked after are merely designed to rationalize the tyranny of what other researchers have called "patriarchy." Another theory, reported in *Science* (April 25, 1997), is based on the fact that women in primitive societies often live 40 or more years past menopause. She presented the argument that the older women gathered food for the family while the mothers in the family nurtured the children, which contradicts the view that the human family evolved because males were needed to provision mothers.

Following the completion of her doctorate, she was a lecturer and fellow at Harvard before being appointed an associate at the Peabody Museum in 1979; she was also appointed a professor at the University of California, Davis, in 1984. She has published several other books, namely, *Black Man of Zinacantan: A Central American Legend* (1972), *Langurs of Abu: Female and Male Strategies of Reproduction* (1980), *Human Ethology* (1989), and *The Evolution of Sex* (1990).

She was elected to membership in the National Academy of Sciences in 1990 and is a fellow of the Animal Behavior Society and of the American Academy of Arts and Sciences. She is a member of the American Society of Naturalists, American Society of Primatologists, American Anthropological Association, and International Primatological Society. Her research is centered on the evolution of primate social behavior. Her books are listed under "Sarah Blaffer," and she is listed in references as either "Sarah Blaffer" or "Sarah Hrdy."

***Bibliography:*** *American Men and Women of Science* 15–19; *Contemporary Authors* v. 107.

# *Huang, Alice Shih-Hou*

(1939– )

***microbiologist***

***Education:*** Student, Wellesley College, 1957–1959; B.A., Johns Hopkins University, 1961, M.A., 1963, Ph.D. in microbiology, 1966; honorary degrees: M.A., Harvard University, 1980; D.Sc., Wheaton College, 1982, Mt. Holyoke College, 1987, and Medical College of Pennsylvania, 1991

***Professional Experience:*** Assistant professor of zoology, National Taiwan University, 1966; postdoctoral fellow, Salk Institute of Biological Science, 1967; postdoctoral fellow in biology, Massachusetts Institute of Technology, 1968–1969; assistant professor, Harvard Medical School, 1971–1973, associate professor, 1973–1979, professor of microbiology and molecular genetics, 1979–1991; dean of science, New York University, 1991–

***Concurrent Position:*** Director, Laboratory of Infectious Diseases, Children's Hospital Medical Center, Boston, 1979–1981

***Married:*** David Baltimore, 1968

***Children:*** 1

***Alice Huang*** is known for a discovery that led to a major breakthrough in understanding how viruses function. The discovery was reverse transcriptase, an enzyme that allows viruses to convert their genetic material into deoxyribonucleic acid (DNA). In searching for clues on how to prevent viruses from replicating, she isolated a rabies type of virus that produced mutant strains that interfered with viral growth.

In her work with David Baltimore at the Massachusetts Institute of Technology, one of the viruses she studied made ribonucleic acid (RNA) from RNA instead of from DNA. This work led to Baltimore's research on tumor viruses and the discovery of the enzyme called reverse transcriptase, which converted RNA to DNA instead of the reverse. While at Harvard Medical School, Huang studied a rabies-like virus that produced mutant strains that interfered with further growth of the viral infection. She was seeking to understand where the mutants came from and how they affected the viral population. For this research, she was awarded the Eli Lilly Award in Microbiology and Immunology (1977).

She was born in China, where her father was a bishop in the Anglican Episcopal Ministry, but when China was taken over by the communists in 1949, her parents sent their four children to the United States so they would have better opportunities than in China. Alice was ten years old when she arrived in the United States, and she became a citizen her senior year in high school. She was influenced to choose medicine as a career by the number of people with illnesses she had seen in China, and while in school at Johns Hopkins University, she decided to pursue medical research rather than to become a physician. She was appointed an assistant professor at Harvard Medical School in 1971 and advanced through the ranks to become professor of microbiology and molecular genetics in 1979. She was elected president of the American Society for Microbiology in 1978, the first Asian American to head a national scientific society in the United States. In 1991, she was appointed dean of science at New York University.

Although her first love continues to be basic research, she views her role in administration at New York University as important and necessary. She mentions the exhilaration that she receives from research, because at the point of discovery, she is the only person who has the information and knowledge of the discovery. She would attempt to transmit this joy to a student by telling him or her they were the only two people in the world to have knowledge of a new discovery. Although she has experienced rapid advancement in her career, she says there is a glass ceiling for Asian Americans and she has experienced it. In an interview for a top-level position, she suspected that the selection committee had no intention of offering the job to an Asian American, and at the close of the interview, the committee members agreed that they did not.

She is a fellow of the Infectious Diseases Society of America and a member of the American Association for the Advancement of Science, American Society for Biochemistry and Molecular Biology, American Society for Microbiology (president, 1988–1989), and New York Academy of Sciences. There is a photograph in *Science* (November 13, 1992) and *Scientific American* (November 1993).

***Bibliography:*** *American Men and Women of Science* 11–19; *Notable Twentieth-Century Scientists; Who's Who in Science and Engineering,* 3d ed., 1996–1997; *Who's Who of American Women,* 19th ed., 1995–1996.

# *Hubbard, Ruth (Hoffman)*
(1924– )
***biologist, biochemist***

***Education:*** B.A., Radcliffe College, 1944, Ph.D. in biology, 1950; honorary degrees: D.Sc., Macalester College and University of Toronto, 1991; LHD, Southern Illinois University, 1991

***Professional Experience:*** Research fellow in biology, Harvard University, 1950–1958, research associate, 1959–1974, lecturer, 1968–1973, professor, 1973–1990, emeritus professor of biology, 1990–

***Concurrent Position:*** Member of corporation, Marine Biological Laboratory, Woods Hole, Massachusetts, 1971–

***Married:*** Frank Hubbard, 1942, divorced 1951; George Wald, 1958

***Children:*** 2

R*uth Hubbard's* career has been a series of careers. She is known for her research on the biochemistry and photochemistry of vision in vertebrates and invertebrates, which she published in many articles and reviews between 1940 and 1970. In the 1970s, she started looking at women's health and at the position of women in academia and research. Later, she began examining the ethics of gene therapy and genetic testing.

After receiving her doctorate, she worked in George Wald's laboratory at Harvard investigating vision. She specifically studied the architecture of visual pigments such as rhodopsin, a molecule that responds to light. The team discovered that light changes the shape of visual pigments that, in turn, initiate all the changes that lead to electrical charges and ultimately to neurotransmission. Wald received the Nobel Prize in Medicine in 1967 for his laboratory's work on vision. During the Vietnam War, Hubbard encountered a mental block when she questioned whether the data she gathered on vision were worth killing a squid in order to study it for that data.

About the same time, she was asked to give a talk on women scientists to the American Association for the Advancement of Science. After she interviewed other women, she realized how similar their experiences had been. She found that none of them had real jobs but had been relegated to the position of associate, lecturer, or assistant. She joined a group at Harvard that petitioned the university to examine the status of women, and as a result, in 1973 she became the first woman to receive tenure in the sciences at Harvard. After that, she added courses on health and women's issues to her continuing courses on photochemistry. After receiving tenure, she was asked by a reporter if she thought she had received tenure because she was a woman. She replied that the reason she had not received tenure previously was that she was a woman.

She comments that a career is always talked of in terms of a woman's problem rather than in terms of a problem for society. The issue is always phrased as how are women going to be able to structure work and family as if the same were not an issue for men. Having a career was a given in her family. She grew up in Austria, and both of her parents were physicians. In their social class, it was expected that women would be professionals and hire people to care for their children, and she had always assumed she would be a physician and have a family. She has written and edited a number of books that reflect her interest in women and their health, including *Genes and Gender II: Pitfalls in Research on Sex and Gender* (1979), *Biological Woman: The Convenient Myth* (1982), *Woman's Nature: Rationalizations of Inequality* (1983), *The Shape of Red: Insider/Outsider Reflections* (1988), *Women Look at Biology Looking at Women* (1989), *The Politics of Women's Biology* (1990), and *Profitable Promises: Essays on Women, Science, and Health* (1994).

She is currently preoccupied with genetics and molecular biology because society is oversimplifying science and assigning every trait, including behaviors, to genetics. She argues that searching to identify all genes, including those for diseases, will necessitate ethical choices that society will have to confront. She mentions potential abuse by insurers who may deny coverage because of genetic conditions and says that finding a gene for breast cancer, for example, may obscure other potential causes of cancers, such as environment. Her views on this topic are included in the book *Exploding the Gene Myth* (1993).

She is a member of the American Association for the Advancement of Science, American Society of Biological Chemists, Biophysical Society, and Society of General Physiologists. Her research includes chemistry of vision, synthesis of visual pigments, health education of nonprofessionals, women's biology and health, sociology of science, and predictive genetic testing. Her photograph is included in *Scientific American* (November 1993 and June 1995).

***Bibliography:*** *American Men and Women of Science* 11–19; *Contemporary Authors* v. 116 and CANR-41; Herzenberg, C., *Women Scientists from Antiquity to the Present;* Ireland, N., *Index to Women of the World . . . Suppl.; Notable Women in the Life Sciences;* Rossiter, M., *Women Scientists in America; Who's Who in America,* 51st ed., 1997.

# *Hubbell, Sue (Gilbert)*
## (1935– )
## ***nature writer***

***Education:*** Student, Swarthmore College, 1952–1954, University of Michigan, 1954–1955; B.A., University of Southern California, 1956; M.S. in library science, Drexel University, 1963

***Professional Experience:*** Acquisitions librarian, Trenton State College, 1963–1967; elementary school librarian, Rhode Island, 1967–1968; serials librarian, Brown University, 1968–1972; commercial beekeeper in Missouri, 1973– ; writer, 1985–

***Married:*** Paul Hubbell, 1955, divorced 1983; Arne Sieverts, 1988

***Children:*** 1

***Sue Hubbell,*** a nature writer, is regarded as one of the primary naturalists writing on insects today, and her articles have been published in journals such as *Natural History* and *Smithsonian Magazine.* After working as a university librarian for several years, she moved to the Ozark Mountains in southern Missouri and became a commercial beekeeper. Her first book of essays, *A Country Year: Living the Questions* (1986), describes her reflections on life and her experiences with nature during the course of one year. Reviewers praised her clear prose and accuracy of descriptions of the scenes and events of nature that she told about. She lived alone on her farm for more than 12 years, earning a living from her 18 million honeybees. After her second marriage in 1988, she and her husband have divided their time between Missouri and Washington D.C., where he is employed.

Her second book, *A Book of Bees . . . and How to Keep Them* (1988), can be read as a how-to manual for bee-keeping, and it established her reputation as one of the best living writers about the insect world. Even if a reader has no interest in engaging in bee-keeping, he or she can appreciate her account of her experiences that reinforce her mutually dependent relationship with the bees. In a strict sense, one does not "keep" bees; one comes to terms with their wild nature. In a related article, "Trouble With Honeybees," published in the May 1997 issue of *Natural History,* she tells of the role of honeybees in American agriculture since colonial days. This article was especially pertinent because the previous year, parasitic mites and harsh winter weather had eliminated 80 percent of the honeybee colonies in some parts of the country.

In her book *Broadsides from the Other Orders: A Book of Bugs* (1993), Hubbell accomplishes the impossible task of describing 13 insect orders without putting her readers to sleep. She takes her readers to California to learn about the multimillion-dollar ladybug business, recounts the mating activities of camel crickets she observed in her home terrarium, tells about her participation in an annual butterfly count in Wyoming, and expounds on the 100-year history of humankind's attempts to eradicate the destructive gypsy moth. She ranges from the stance of an amateur naturalist to that of a bemused observer of efforts to control the insect world.

When she moved to Missouri in the 1970s, she was prompted by a back-to-the-land idealism and political disenchantment to live cheaply and grow her own vegetables. Over the years she wrote a series of essays for the *St. Louis Post-Dispatch,* and she has reprinted these in her book *On This Hilltop* (1991). She describes her lot as a novice bee-keeping farmer in the Ozarks and her neighbors, who consist of longtime farmers and hippies who garden by moonlight. She has unforgettable stories about her pickup truck, which she named Press on Regardless, plus the usual chicken and dog stories. In ironic fashion, she treats her country material with a healthy dose of cynicism.

Hubbell describes her experiences commuting between Washington, D.C., and the Missouri Ozarks in *Far Flung Hubbell: Essays from the American Road* (1995). Often she herself trucks products from her farm to markets as far away as the northeastern part of the country, and this book is another collection of essays on diverse subjects such as truck stops, bug art, the anatomy of an Elvis sighting, and a magician's convention. Many of these essays originally appeared in the *New Yorker.*

***Bibliography:*** *Contemporary Authors* v. 120 and CANR-47.

# *Hunt, Eva (Verbitsky)*
(1934–1980)
## *cultural anthropologist*

***Education:*** B.S., Universidad Femina, Mexico City, 1953; student, Escuela Nacional de Anthropologia, 1953–1957; M.A., University of Chicago, 1959, Ph.D. in anthropology, 1962
***Professional Experience:*** Research associate, Northwestern University, 1961–1962; instructor, University of Chicago, 1965–1969; associate professor of anthropology, Boston University, 1969–1978, professor, 1978–1980
***Married:*** Robert Hunt, 1960
***Children:*** 1

***Eva Hunt*** was a cultural anthropologist who was an expert on Mesoamerican culture. She and her husband, Robert Hunt, took the lead among anthropologists working in Mexico by conducting regional research. In an entire district in the state of Oaxaca, not just one small village, they studied the ways institutions such as the courts, the schools, and the markets have served different groups and created structures whereby individuals of varying cultures and classes can meet to resolve problems and exchange information and goods. They were also concerned with how irrigation systems affected social and political choices.

Hunt's primary area of interest was the study of kinship systems, and she published a number of significant articles on the topic. She said that anthropologists working in

Mesoamerica had missed the importance of kinship ties because they were looking for segmented social groups, which did not exist. The kinship system is very much tied to the land, and kinship groups tend to split up over conflicts for control of the land. She also felt that the role played by other institutions, such as the national government, had been overlooked in these kinship splits. The best-known work of her very short career is *The Transformation of the Hummingbird: Cultural Roots of a Zinacantecan Mythical Poem* (1977), in which she explains the importance of the hummingbird to Mesoamerican cultural history because it is one of the manifestations of the Aztec god Huitzilopochtli.

She was born in Argentina, but her family moved to Mexico City in the early 1950s. The women in her family led active professional lives—her grandmother was a physician, and her mother was a specialist in childhood education—and Eva was expected to prepare for a career. She was a talented painter, and she continued to paint throughout her life. She enrolled in both undergraduate school and graduate school in anthropology in Mexico City. Through the influence of several American anthropologists, she decided to continue her studies at the University of Chicago, which was noted for its focus on Mexican anthropology. Although she spoke little English and read it poorly, she was able to arrange with faculty members to do her exams and papers in Spanish until she gained sufficient knowledge of English. She married fellow anthropologist Robert Hunt in 1960.

She was a research associate at Northwestern University for one year, and it was there that she started on her study of kinship in her teaching and research. She obtained an appointment as an instructor teaching undergraduate anthropology at the University of Chicago—at the time, no women were teaching in the graduate school at Chicago. It was unfortunate that she was unable to supervise graduate students, but they were able to tap her expertise in Mexican culture in seminars. The couple moved to the Boston area where Eva obtained a position as an associate professor at Boston University and later was promoted to full professor. She died of brain cancer in 1980 after fighting the disease for five years.

Although she enjoyed the recognition she received for her contributions to anthropology, she believed that women of her generation still had more trouble than men in establishing themselves as anthropologists, and she criticized those women who glossed over the problem. For example, she was disappointed that Margaret Mead in her autobiography did not describe the difficulties that she had had in gaining acceptance by colleagues in the field. However, Eva Hunt did not join the feminist movement that swept across the university campuses in the 1970s. She preferred to work to improve the status of women on an individual basis by encouraging promising female students and offering herself as a positive role model.

Her photograph is included with her obituary in *American Anthropologist* (December 1981). A partial list of her publications is given in *Women Anthropologists.*

***Bibliography:*** *Women Anthropologists.*

# *Hutchins, Sandra Elaine*
(1946– )
## *computer scientist, communications engineer*

***Education:*** B.A., University of California, San Diego, 1967, Ph.D. in information and computer science, 1970

***Professional Experience:*** Assistant professor of electrical engineering, Purdue University, 1970–1972; senior staff engineer in communications, TRW Defense & Space Systems, 1972–1977; senior scientist, communications, and engineering manager, Linkabit Corporation, 1977–1979; technical director, voice processing, ITT Defense Communications Division, 1981–1982; technical director and principal, Emerson & Stern Associates, 1983–

***Concurrent Positions:*** Instructor, Loyola Marymount University, 1973–1974, and University of California, Davis, Extension, 1978–

S*andra Hutchins* is known for her expertise in voice processing in computer software and hardware. She has an undergraduate degree in physics with a minor in linguistics. After teaching for two years in the Electrical Engineering Department of Purdue University, she worked in computer software and hardware design for a number of corporations. She has specialized in design and management of real-time software and hardware for communications, specifically voice processing, message switching, secure computing, modems, and personal computers. She was a senior staff engineer in communications for five years with TRW Defense & Space Systems and technical director of voice processing at ITT Defense Communications Division. She served as engineering manager for two different corporations—Linkabit Corporation and ITT. She holds at least two patents, one for digital compression of speech and one for computer recognition of speech in severe noise environments.

As technical director of Emerson & Stern Associates, a software and systems design consulting firm, she oversees a line of educational programs, games, puzzles, and software for home management. These can be run by total novices on unsophisticated computers. Several were chosen for a 1985 Smithsonian Institution exhibit on American games, and the company advertises its ability to create user-oriented programs for any computer in any language.

However, Hutchins's focus is on programs that enable computers to respond to human speech and to natural English. In computer terminology, she is creating a lexical analyzer, which is the next step in computers—to enable users to bypass the keyboard. Although the obvious use is to speed up work, in taking inventories, for example, probably the largest block of time could be saved in the health care industry, which is an area where there is a great emphasis on reducing cost. One area of savings would be for the physician to dictate to the computer the patient diagnosis, indicate the prescriptions or tests needed, and forward the file to the billing department. Currently, in many clinics the physician's instructions have to be transcribed by a clerical employee from a tape to the computer.

Hutchins is a member of the Institute of Electrical and Electronics Engineers and of the Association for Computing Machinery. Her research includes communications, information theory, and signal processing.

***Bibliography:*** *American Men and Women of Science* 12–15; Stanley, A., *Mothers and Daughters of Invention.*

# *Intriligator, Devrie (Shapiro)*

(1941– )

***space physicist, astrophysicist***

***Education:*** B.S., in physics, Massachusetts Institute of Technology, 1962, M.S., 1964; Ph.D. in planetary and space physics, University of California, Los Angeles, 1967

***Professional Experience:*** Assistant research geophysicist, Institute of Geophysics and Planetary Physics, University of California, Los Angeles, 1967; research associate, Space Science Division, Ames Research Center, National Aeronautics and Space Administration (NASA), 1967–1969; research fellow in physics, California Institute of Technology, 1969–1972, assistant professor, 1972–1980, member, Space Science Center, 1978–1983; staff member, Stauffer Hall of Science, University of Southern California, 1974–1977, assistant professor of physics, 1977–1979; senior research physicist, Carmel Research Center, 1979– , director of Space Plasma Laboratory, 1980–

***Married:*** Michael Intriligator, 1963

***Children:*** 4

***Devrie Intriligator*** is renowned for her research in space physics and astrophysics and for her expertise in designing measurement instruments for interplanetary spacecraft. Among the projects in which she has participated are the Pioneer 10 and 11 missions to the outer planets, the Pioneer-Venus Orbiter, and the Pioneer 6, 7, 8, and 9 heliocentric missions.

She explains her unusual name (Devrie) by saying her parents composed it, but she has sometimes found it to be handy because people think she is a man when they see her name on a proposal or a staff list. She began doing physics experiments as a high school sophomore—she would just set them up from the information that she had read—and she won a national prize in a Future Scientist of America contest in her senior year. She received financial aid to enroll in college, but the dean of women at the first school she attended would not permit her to enroll in physics, and she had to give up the financial aid when she transferred to the Massachusetts Institute of Technology (MIT) the following year. The person in charge of scholarships and loans at MIT refused to give her money because, he said, women do not continue to work and they merely take up space in a class.

She held a number of jobs in college to support herself. She was a research assistant in the cosmic ray group at MIT in 1960, and prior to her senior year, she was a consulting physicist for the Institute of Physics, University of Milan, where she consulted on cosmic-ray balloon experiments. She continued as a graduate student at MIT and worked as a physicist in the cosmic-ray branch of the Air Force's Cambridge Research Laboratory from 1962 to 1963. When her husband received an appointment to teach at University of California, Los Angeles (UCLA), she transferred to that school to complete her doctorate.

Since UCLA would not accept her credits from MIT, she had to repeat a number of courses, but in the course of the three years she spent studying at UCLA, she became interested in solar wind plasma physics and decided to add it as a specialty. The solar wind plasma is a stream of particles—electrons, protons, and other ions—that continually flow from the sun and is responsible for many features of the solar system and the earth's environment. After graduation she won a prestigious National Academy of Sciences Resident Research Associateship for use at NASA's Ames Research Center where she was the principal investigator of the positive-ion probe on the UCLA Small Scientific Satellite. She also was a coinvestigator of the Ames solar wind plasma probes on several Pioneer spacecraft in orbit around the sun.

At the California Institute of Technology, where she began working in 1969, she analyzed data sent back from instruments aboard the Pioneer spacecraft in orbit around the sun. She was coinvestigator of the Ames solar wind plasma probe for the Pioneer 10 and 11 missions to Jupiter, and she was also a member of the plasma measurement team for the outer planet missions to Jupiter, Saturn, Uranus, Neptune, and Pluto. In her current position as director of the Space Plasma Laboratory, she is continuing her research on cosmic rays and solar winds.

Although many women scientists have dismayed their employers by continuing to work close to the birth of a child, Intriligator even had to obtain a note from her physician to give to officials at the California Institute of Technology certifying it was safe for her to continue working. After the birth of a child, she said, she began working at home after about three days, started back to work for an hour or two within a week, and returned to her full schedule within three or four weeks. As is true for many couples, she and her husband sometimes go grocery shopping at two o'clock in the morning. She does most of the cooking but hires help for the cleaning and has always had live-in help for the children. She emphasizes that it is important for a woman scientist to have a husband who is committed to seeing her succeed in her career. A man must be sure of himself and not regard his wife's having a career as a threat.

She is a coeditor of the book *Exploration of the Outer Solar System* (1976) and has written numerous scientific papers. She has received three achievement awards from NASA and is a member of the American Geophysical Union, American Physical Society, and American Association for the Advancement of Science. Her research includes high-energy nuclear physics, plasma physics, and astrophysics. Her photograph is included in Joyce Teitz's *What's a Nice Girl Like You. . . .*

***Bibliography:*** *American Men and Women of Science* 12–19; Teitz, J., *What's a Nice Girl Like You . . . ; Who's Who in America,* 51st ed., 1997; *Who's Who in Science and Engineering,* 3d ed., 1996–1997; *Who's Who of American Women,* 20th ed., 1997–1998.

# Jackson, Jacquelyne Mary (Johnson)
(1932– )
***sociologist***

***Education:*** B.S., University of Wisconsin, Madison, 1953, M.S., 1955; Ph.D. in sociology, Ohio State University, 1960
***Professional Experience:*** Assistant professor to associate professor, Southern University, 1959–1962; professor of sociology and department chair, Jackson State College, 1962–1964; assistant professor, Howard University, 1964–1966; assistant professor of medical sociology, Duke University Medical Center, 1968–1971, associate professor, 1971–
***Concurrent Position:*** Visiting professor of sociology, St. Augustine's College, 1969–
***Married:*** Frederick A. S. Clarke, 1955, divorced 1959; Murphy Jackson, 1962
***Children:*** 2

***Jacquelyne Jackson*** is known for her research on minority aging and for her participation in the civil rights movement. She has had a number of firsts in her career. She was the first black woman to receive a doctorate in sociology from Ohio State University, she was the first full-time black faculty member to be hired at the Duke University Medical Center, and she was the first black person on the medical school faculty to be tenured.

She and her fraternal twin, Jeanne, had a solid middle-class background that emphasized the importance of education. They did not experience any negatives associated with being female. Both of their parents were college graduates, and their father was director of the School of Business at Tuskegee Institute. At the institute, there were leaders in many areas who served as role models for Jacquelyne. After receiving her doctorate, she was a faculty member at Southern University, a professor of sociology at Jackson State College, and an assistant professor at Howard University before joining the faculty of the Duke University Medical Center as an assistant professor of medical sociology.

Her work has always been connected to real people and real issues. Her interest in minority aging grew out of the experience of elderly friends who had to sell their houses to pay for medical care. Later, one friend was in a racially segregated ward in New Orleans's Charity Hospital, and Jackson organized her students to donate "black" blood for the woman because blood was segregated at the time.

She became involved in the civil rights movement while teaching at Jackson State College. When a group of civil rights advocates was forbidden to hold a meeting at Jackson State for fear of creating racial unrest, she secured the support of Charles Evers, brother of Medgar Evers, to schedule the meeting at another site in the city. She took part in the 1963 march in Washington, D.C., and in 1962, she published *These Rights They Seek,* a study of the Tuskegee Civic Association, the Montgomery Improvement Association, and the Alabama Christian Movement for Human Rights. She has also published articles in *Black Scholar, Essence,* and *Ebony* as well as scientific journals.

She helped to found the *Journal of Minority Aging,* and in 1980 she published *Mi-*

*norities in Aging*, which has become a classic in the field. She advocates using responsible research to influence federal legislation and national, state, and local programs and policies. One problem she sees is that of romanticizing the black family and the problems it faces. As an example, she cites the critics of Alice Walker's *The Color Purple* who deny that the character "Mister" ever existed. Jackson is a fellow of the Gerontological Society of America and a member of the Association of Social and Behavioral Scientists, National Council on Family Relations, American Sociological Association, and Caucus of Black Sociologists.

***Bibliography:*** *American Men and Women of Science* 11–13; *Contemporary Authors* v. 37–40R; Ireland, N., *Index to Women of the World . . . Suppl.*; *Notable Black American Women.*

# *Jackson, Shirley Ann*

(1946– )

## ***elementary particle physicist***

***Education:*** B.S., Massachusetts Institute of Technology, 1968, Ph.D. in physics, 1973; honorary degrees: Bloomfield College, Fairleigh Dickinson University, Cheyney University, Villanova University, and St. Peter's College

***Professional Experience:*** Research associate in theoretical physics, Fermi National Accelerator Laboratory, 1973–1974, 1975–1976; visiting science associate, European Organization for Nuclear Research, Geneva, 1974–1975; research associate, Stanford Linear Accelerator Center and Aspen Center for Physics, 1976–1977; technical staff in theoretical physics, AT&T Bell Laboratories, 1976–1991; professor of physics, Rutgers University, 1991– ; chair of Nuclear Regulatory Commission (NRC), 1995– ; chair of International Nuclear Regulators Association (INRA), 1997–

***Married:*** Morris A. Washington, ca. 1979

***Children:*** 1

***Shirley Ann Jackson*** is renowned as a theoretical physicist who has researched and taught in the area of particle physics and condensed matter physics. This is the branch of physics that uses theories and mathematics to predict the existence of subatomic particles and the forces that bind them together. Her research includes Landau theories of charge density waves in one and two dimensions, transport properties of random systems, and correlation effects in electron-hole plasmas. In 1995, she was appointed the chair of the Nuclear Regulatory Commission (NRC), the federal agency that regulates the uses of nuclear materials and technology throughout the United States to ensure the protection of public health, safety, and the environment. Jackson has had several firsts in her career. She was the first African American woman to receive a doctorate in any field from the Massachusetts Institute of Technology (1973), and she is the first woman and first African American to serve as chair of the NRC.

Her area of interest in physics is the study of subatomic particles found within atoms. Subatomic particles, which are usually very unstable and short-lived, can be studied in several ways. One method uses a particle accelerator, a device in which nuclei are accelerated to high speeds and then forced to collide with a target to separate them into subatomic particles. Another method detects their movements using certain types of nonconducting solids. Jackson has conducted research using both methods at a number of prestigious physics laboratories in both the United States and Europe. At the Fermi National Accelerator Laboratory she studied hadrons, and at the European Organization for Nuclear Research in Switzerland she explored theories of strongly interacting elementary particles. She has also lectured in physics and conducted research at the Stanford Linear Accelerator Center.

When Jackson joined AT&T Bell Laboratories, she explored theories of phases transitions in solids and the physics of two-dimensional systems. She performed seminal work in such areas as charged density waves in layered compounds, polaronic aspects of electrons on the surface of liquid helium films, and optical and electronic properties of semiconductor strained-layer superlattices. She joined Rutgers University as professor of physics in 1991, and there her research has focused on electronic and optical properties of low-dimensional systems, primarily two-dimensional or quasi-two-dimensional systems, looking at other kinds of excitations and how they affect the properties of electrons. She has looked particularly at spin fluctuations and how they affect the electrical and optical properties of electrons in two-dimensional semiconductors. She continued to consult for Bell after joining Rutgers; in fact, she still had an office there for a time.

In her present position as chair of the NRC, she talks of several areas that require attention: ensuring an efficient and technologically sound process for renewing the licenses of existing nuclear power plants; ensuring safety in an economically competitive environment as electric utilities are deregulated; incorporating risk perspectives and risk assessment methodologies into nuclear energy regulation; and ensuring safety in the disposal of spent reactor fuel. The NRC has about 3,000 employees and an annual budget of about half a billion dollars. With the May 1997 formation of the International Nuclear Regulators Association, Jackson was elected as the group's first chair. The association consists of the most senior nuclear regulatory officials from Canada, France, Germany, Japan, Spain, Sweden, the United Kingdom, and the United States.

As a child growing up in Washington, D.C., Jackson and her siblings were encouraged by their parents to study hard and to excel. She was a strong student, and she built soapbox go-carts with her sister. She benefited from the U.S. response to Sputnik by being able to participate in one of the many accelerated educational programs in the country to nurture scientific talent. She was a member of the honors program in the seventh grade, finished the high school curriculum early, and took college-level courses in her senior year. One of her teachers noted her mathematical ability and encouraged her to apply to the Massachusetts Institute of Technology (MIT), from which she received her doctorate. She received several scholarships while she was at MIT. However, to provide additional money to help pay her tuition and living expenses, she worked as a technician in the nutrition and food science laboratory at the university. She credits her parents as her ultimate role models because of the way they lived their lives and imparted solid values to their children. She says she has been able to manage both family and career because she has a very supportive husband, who is also a physicist.

She has been active in professional groups to encourage more women and minorities to pursue scientific and technological occupations. She has also been active in civic affairs, such as when she was appointed by the governor of New Jersey to the Commission on Science and Technology. She received the Thomas Alva Edison Science Award (ca. 1990) for her contributions to physics and for her promotion of science and the New Jersey Governor's Award in Science (1993). She is a member of the American Physical Society, American Academy of Arts and Sciences, American Association for the Advancement of Science, New York Academy of Sciences, and National Society of Black Physicists (president, 1980–1982). Her photograph is included in *Journeys of Women in Science and Engineering* and *Ebony* (July 1996), and she was inducted into the National Women's Hall of Fame in 1998.

***Bibliography:*** *American Men and Women of Science* 13–19; *Blacks in Science and Medicine; Distinguished African American Scientists of the 20th Century;* Herzenberg, C., *Women Scientists from Antiquity to the Present;* Ireland, N., *Index to Women of the World . . . Suppl; Journeys of Women in Science and Engineering; Notable Black American Women; Notable Twentieth-Century Scientists; Who's Who in America,* 51st ed., 1997; *Who's Who of American Women,* 20th ed., 1997–1998.

# *Jemison, Mae Carol*
(1956– )
## *physician, astronaut*

***Education:*** B.S., chemical engineering, B.A., African and Afro-American Studies, Stanford University, 1977; M.D., Cornell University Medical School, 1981

***Professional Experience:*** Intern, University of Southern California Medical Center, 1981–1982; general practitioner, INA–Ross Loos Medical Group, Los Angeles, 1982; medical officer in Sierra Leone and Liberia, Peace Corps, 1983–1985; physician, Cigna Health Plan of California, 1985–1987; astronaut, 1987–1993, mission specialist, STS-47 on *Endeavour,* 1992; teaching fellow, Dartmouth College, 1993– ; founder and director of Jemison Group, Houston TX, 1993–

***Mae Jemison*** is a physician who has focused her life not only on science but also on contributing to her world. She graduated from Stanford University with a double major in chemical engineering and African and Afro-American Studies. She was involved in many extracurricular activities such as dance and theater groups, and while she was in medical school, she volunteered for a summer school experience in a Thai refugee camp and also engaged in health studies in Kenya in 1979 on a grant from the International Travelers Institute.

While in the Peace Corps as a medical officer in Sierra Leone and Liberia, she was manager of health care for Peace Corps volunteers; in addition to her administrative duties, she developed curricula and taught volunteer personnel and implemented guidelines on public health and safety issues for volunteers. She developed and participated in research projects on hepatitis B vaccine, schistosomiasis, and rabies in conjunction with the National Institutes of Health and the Centers for Disease Control. After she entered the astronaut program she became the first woman of color in the world to travel in space (the first black astronaut, male or female, was Guion Bluford, who flew four missions between 1983 and 1992). Jemison left the astronaut program in 1993 to found the Jemison Group, a company that seeks to research, develop, and market advanced technologies.

At the time that she received her undergraduate degrees, the National Aeronautics and Space Administration (NASA) announced that it was seeking candidates for the space shuttle program, and although one of her long-term goals was to be an astronaut, she decided to complete her biomedical training first. When NASA reopened the program in 1986 after the *Challenger* accident, she applied and was one of 15 chosen from a field of some 2,000 applicants in 1987. After completing the training program, she worked for the usual five years before making her first space flight. She was assigned to the space shuttle *Endeavour* on mission STS-47 (September 12–20, 1992) and conducted experiments concerning weightlessness, tissue growth, and the development of semiconductor materials. One of the experiments was to test whether or not motion sickness in space could be alleviated by the use of biofeedback techniques; it was successful. She investigated the loss of calcium in human bones in space and the effects of weightlessness on the fertilization and embryologic development of frogs.

In interviews following the flight, she said she hoped her historic flight would enhance American society's appreciation of the abilities of both women and members of minority groups. She is passionate about women's rights, saying that women must take full responsibility for their lives and that more women should demand to be involved in the space program. That is an area where women can get in on the ground floor and possibly help direct where space exploration will go in the future. Her credo is, don't be limited by others' limited imaginations. She encourages children, not to look to her for inspiration, but to follow their own dreams, not hers or anyone else's.

Growing up in Chicago, one of her favorite pastimes was going to the Museum of Science and Industry. She credits her success to her parents, who nurtured their children, and her teachers, who allowed her to explore ideas on her own. She had a childhood dream of flying into space and went through a phase in high school when she read stacks of astronomy books—not science fiction, but actual texts. She hopes her success will inspire people everywhere, especially African American children, to strive to realize their goals, however unrealistic they might seem. She explains her participation in extracurricular activities by stressing that a person has to be well rounded.

After spending five years in the astronaut program, Jemison left in 1993 to become a teaching fellow at Dartmouth College and to found her own company. One of her company's projects is to establish a space-based telecommunication system to facilitate health care delivery in countries of the developing world. One of the honors she has received was having a public school in Michigan named for her. In 1996, she hosted a television program, "World of Wonder," on the Discovery Channel in which she introduced the research of several women scientists. There are photographs in most of the sources listed below plus *Ebony* (February 1997).

***Bibliography:*** *Black Women in America; Blacks in Science and Medicine; Current Biography 1993; Distinguished African American Scientists of the 20th Century; Notable Black American Women; Notable Twentieth-Century Sciences;* Schneider, D., *ABC-CLIO Companion to Women in the Workplace;* U.S. National Aeronautics and Space Administration, *Astronaut Fact Book.*

# *Johnson, Barbara Crawford*

(1925– )

## *aerospace engineer*

***Education:*** B.S. in general engineering, University of Illinois, 1946

***Professional Experience:*** Engineer, Rockwell International Space Division, 1950s, project leader for Hound Dog air-to-ground weapon used by B-52 bombers as well as Navaho missiles, supervisor of Entry Performance Analysis, 1961–1968, system engineer, manager for Apollo program, 1968–1972, manager, Mission Requirements and Integration for Rockwell Space Systems Group, 1973–1983, retired 1984

***Married:*** Robert Johnson

***Children:*** 1

***Barbara Johnson*** is known for her work at Rockwell International Space Division on the manned space flight program for the National Aeronautics and Space Administration (NASA). She is one of the many woman scientists and engineers who have played significant roles in the space program as employees of NASA or of NASA contractors. She reports that as a child, she loved looking at the stars and planets and she still thinks there is life out there in other galaxies.

After graduating from the University of Illinois, the first women to receive an undergraduate degree in engineering from that school, she started working for Rockwell in the 1950s. Her major in college had been general engineering with an emphasis on aeronautical engineering. Rockwell was one of the primary contractors for NASA, and one of her major contributions was to create the Entry Monitor System (EMS), the backup entry guidance system designed for the Apollo space missions. The EMS is a graphic display for the astronauts to use in the case of a primary guidance failure, and similar graphic displays are now a part of the instrument panels of virtually all spacecraft and aircraft and are even currently available in many automobiles.

One of her first assignments on joining the corporation was to be the project leader for developing the Hound Dog air-to-ground missile used by the B-52 bomber. She supervised the project from concept to design to configuration, performance, and stability analysis of the weapon. She also was involved in the development of the Navaho missile, and in the 1960s, she was supervisor of the Entry Performance Analysis team, which determined the trajectories that enabled the Apollo aircraft to reenter the earth's atmosphere safely; if it entered on too shallow a trajectory, there was a danger of overheating; if too deeply, the astronauts would experience unbearable gravitational forces. Before the 1960s, a spacecraft had never re-entered the earth's atmosphere from hypervelocity, which is a speed greater than that of the earth's rotation. It was during the 1960s also that she developed the Entry Monitor System (EMS).

She was appointed system engineering manager for the Apollo program in 1968 and in that capacity, she supervised system analysis in support of a lunar landing and exploration, the Apollo-Soyuz test program, and numerous auxiliary projects and studies. During the Apollo-Soyuz test program, she supervised a staff of over 200 people. In 1973, she was named manager of Mission Requirements and Integration for Rockwell, which meant she directed the mission, flight performance, and trajectory design analysis of the space shuttle and orbiter projects. She retired in 1984.

Johnson received a medallion from NASA for her role in the first Apollo landing on the moon, and she has also received the Achievement Award of the Society of Women Engineers (1974), the Distinguished Alumni Merit Award from the University of Illinois (1975), and the Outstanding Engineer Merit Award of the Institute for the Advancement of Engineers (1976). She is a member of the American Institute of Aeronautics and Astronautics and a fellow of the Institute for the Advancement of Engineers. Her photograph is included in *Notable Twentieth-Century Scientists.*

***Bibliography:*** Herzenberg, C., *Women Scientists from Antiquity to the Present;* Ireland, N., *Index to Women of the World . . . Suppl.; Notable Twentieth-Century Scientists;* O'Neill, L., *Women's Book of World Records and Achievements;* Vare, E., *Mothers of Invention; Who's Who in Engineering*, 9th ed., 1995.

# Johnson, Virginia (Eshelman)
(1925– )
## psychologist, sex therapist

**Education:** Student, Drury College, 1940–1942, University of Missouri, 1944–1947; student, Washington University, St. Louis (no degree)
**Professional Experience:** Research staff, Washington University, St. Louis, School of Medicine, Division of Reproductive Biology, 1957–1960, research assistant 1960–1962, research instructor, 1962–1964; research associate, Reproductive Biology Research Foundation, St. Louis, 1964–1969, assistant director, 1969–1973, codirector, 1971–1973; codirector, Masters and Johnson Institute, 1973–1994; director, Virginia Johnson Masters Learning Center, St. Louis, 1994–
**Married:** George Johnson, 1950, divorced 1956; William H. Masters, 1971, divorced 1992
**Children:** 2

*Virginia Johnson* is renowned for her pioneer studies, with William H. Masters, of human sexuality under laboratory conditions. Part of her work at the Reproductive Biology Research Foundation in St. Louis and later at the Masters and Johnson Institute involved counseling many clients and teaching sex therapy to many practitioners. Masters as a young medical student had thought of doing research on the physiology of sex, and one of his mentors had suggested that he establish himself as a scientist and gain some maturity before undertaking such a sensitive subject. By the late 1950s, he had become a respected professor of obstetrics and gynecology at the Washington University School of Medicine when he started his project in the Division of Reproductive Biology. He hired Virginia Johnson, an outgoing, mature, intelligent woman, to interview volunteers for his research project.

Gathering scientific data by electroencephalography (EEG), electrocardiography, and the use of color monitors, the two measured and analyzed 694 volunteers. In addition to a description of the four stages of sexual arousal, they gained other valuable data, including evidence of the failure of some contraceptives, the discovery of a vaginal secretion in some women that prevents conception, and the observation that sexual enjoyment need not decrease with age. They created the nonprofit Reproductive Biology Research Foundation in 1964, began training couples to combat their sexual problems, and wrote a scientific text, *Human Sexual Response* (1966), describing their research. Although the book was advertised only in scientific journals, within a few months it had become a best-seller. More than 300,000 copies had been sold by 1970 in spite of the dull, scientific prose in which it was written.

The two researchers went on the lecture circuit to discuss their findings. In their second book, *Human Sexual Inadequacy* (1970), they discussed the possibility that sex problems are more cultural than physiological or psychological. The two married in 1971, and their next book, *The Pleasure Bond: A New Look at Sexuality and Commitment* (1975), was written for the average reader and advised total commitment and fidelity to the partner as the basis for an enduring sexual bond. They expanded their counseling to dual-sex therapy teams and conducted workshops for marriage counselors and other professionals. In 1973, they founded the Masters and Johnson Institute, with Johnson supervising the everyday business and Masters concentrating on the scientific work.

In *Homosexuality in Perspective* (1981), the couple gave an account of their research on homosexual sexual practices and problems. One of their controversial conclusions was that homosexuality is a "learned" behavior and that homosexuals can be "converted." Dr. Robert Kolodny coauthored the next book, *Crisis: Heterosexual Behavior in the Age of AIDS* (1988), which included the prediction of a large-scale outbreak of the virus in the heterosexual community and some wildly exaggerated comments on how AIDS can be transmitted. Several prominent medical authorities questioned this study, and the adverse publicity hurt the team. Masters and Johnson quietly dissolved the institute; the couple divorced in 1992. Later Virginia founded the Virginia Johnson Masters Learning Center in St. Louis, which produces instructional material for couples with sexual problems.

Although Virginia Johnson has no medical credentials, she has been regarded as a professional sex therapist by the medical community. She had been considering returning to college to obtain a degree in sociology at Washington University when she obtained a job with Masters. She continued to take courses for several years but dropped out as a doctoral candidate in 1964 because of the pressure of work at the institute. She had attended two other colleges but at those had been primarily interested in music.

She had had two brief marriages before marrying George Johnson, a musician, and had worked for a legal newspaper and in the advertising department of a local television station. She sang with Johnson's band until the couple divorced. She was an ideal person to conduct the initial interviews for Masters, for she was pleasant, intelligent, mature, soft-spoken, and a mother. Soon she was promoted to research assistant, research instructor, and eventually codirector of the institute. She and Masters made a unique contribution to our knowledge of human sexuality. In 1997, the couple was profiled in the *Biography* series on the Arts & Entertainment Channel; a video of the program is available. She is a member of the American Association for the Advancement of Science and the Society for the Study of Reproduction. Her photograph is included in *Current Biography* (1976), William Rayner's *Wise Women, The 100 Greatest American Women,* and *Time* (March 21, 1988).

***Bibliography:*** *Contemporary Authors* v. 21–24R; *Current Biography 1976;* Herzenberg, C., *Women Scientists from Antiquity to the Present;* Ireland, N., *Index to Women of the World . . . Suppl.; Notable Twentieth-Century Scientists; The 100 Greatest American Women;* Rayner, W., *Wise Women;* Sochen, J., *Movers and Shakers.*

# *Johnston, Mary Helen*
## (1945– )
## *metallurgical engineer*

***Education:*** B.S., Florida State University, 1966, M.S., 1969; Ph.D. in metallurgical engineering, University of Florida, 1973

***Professional Experience:*** Member of metallurgical staff, University of Alabama, Huntsville, 1969– ; materials engineer, George Marshall Space Flight Center, National Aeronautics and Space Administration (NASA), 1969–

***Concurrent Positions:*** Principal investigator, Marshall Space Flight Center, NASA, 1976– ; president, Metallurgical Engineering Technology of Alabama, Inc., 1982–

***Mary Johnston*** is known for her expertise in failure analysis while working at the George Marshall Space Flight Center of the National Aeronautics and Space Administration (NASA). As a metallurgist, she was concerned with the stability of the metal and materials parts that the spacecraft was composed of. There always is a possibility that a part might malfunction or break when exposed to the extremes of soaring heat or frigid cold in space, and the failure could occur in any part of a spacecraft, including bolts and screws.

Although she worked for NASA for a number of years, she was never part of the astronaut program. In the 1970s, she started planning for the time when women would be accepted into the space program, and she was among the women employees who taught themselves how to function in a weightless environment. She started working at the Huntsville installation as a student in the cooperative education program, which meant she would spend a part of each year in school and a part in Huntsville to earn the money for her tuition. She had wanted to be in the space program since Alan Shepard's flight on Mercury–3 in 1961. One of her chemistry professors was John Llewellyn, who had withdrawn from the astronaut program after he had been selected; this made her realize that one could be a scientist and fly (the original astronauts were all military test pilots, and some of them did not have college degrees).

Johnston was the first woman to graduate from Florida State University in engineering, and when she started graduate school at the University of Florida, some of the faculty members were appalled. Several women had enrolled previously in engineering there but had left when they married a fellow student, taking their husbands with them. However, she remained in the program and received her doctoral degree. She was a co-op student at Marshall for six years before becoming a full-time employee.

When she chose her major of metallurgical engineering, materials processing in space did not exist as a specialty. However, in 1974, she participated in an all-woman crew of experimenters in a five-day simulation of a Spacelab mission set up by NASA at Marshall because NASA needed to know how difficult it would be to handle materials processing experiments in space. These experiments require a lot of power and put out a lot of heat, and Johnston predicted that nuclear radiation detector material would be a good material for a Spacelab experiment. One advantage of metallurgical research in space is that the zero gravity environment in space allows for more control; whereas on earth, it is more difficult to study the processes involved in metals when the metals are cooled. Later she was assigned to be the backup payload specialist on Spacelab–3, but she did not go into space.

Johnston advises people interested in space to choose an area that looks as if it will have a large number of space flights, such as the biomedical or pharmaceutical areas, and become involved in them. She says one must subconsciously aim oneself in the direction one wants to go. She did this, and it was fortuitous that she happened to be at Marshall when the opportunity to be a member of the five-day simulation of a Spacelab mission arose. She predicts that some day special technical companies may be a source of space employment. In the future, companies may put together research teams in materials processing or medical experiments, and these teams will work on contract for NASA rather than NASA's preparing its own teams. Her photograph is included in A. R. Oberg's *Spacefarers of the '80s and '90s.* She is a member of American Society for Metals and National Society of Professional Engineers.

***Bibliography:*** *American Men and Women of Science* 15–18; Ireland, N., *Index to Women of the World . . . Suppl.;* Oberg, A. R., *Spacefarers of the '80s and '90s.*

# *Jones, Anita Katherine*
(1942– )
***computer scientist***

***Education:*** B.A. in mathematics, Rice University, 1964; M.A. in English, University of Texas, Austin, 1966; Ph.D. in computer science, Carnegie Mellon University, 1973

***Professional Experience:*** Programmer, International Business Machines Corporation (IBM), 1966–1968; assistant professor of computer science, Carnegie Mellon University, 1973–1978, associate professor, 1978–1981; vice president and founder, Tartan Laboratories, Pittsburgh, 1981–1987; freelance consultant, 1987–1988; professor and department chair, Computer Science Department, University of Virginia, 1988–1993; director, Defense Research and Engineering, U.S. Department of Defense, 1993–1997; professor, computer science, University of Virginia, 1997–

***Married:*** William A. Wulf, 1977

***Children:*** 2

***Anita Jones*** is renowned for her research in the area of computer software and systems. When she was director of Defense Research and Engineering for the U.S. Department of Defense (DOD), she was the department's senior official for research and technology matters. Her responsibilities included management of DOD science and technology programs; all in-house laboratories and research, development, and engineering centers; university research initiatives; and the Advanced Research Projects Agency. The last-mentioned agency was responsible for designing ARPAnet, the predecessor of the Internet. In one interview, she said that DOD is pursuing dual-use technology to develop technology that will serve as a basis for both commercial and military products. The agency is also exploring technology to reduce the cost of buying and operating military systems; one technology that is of highest priority is information technology in the broadest sense, which includes modeling and simulation, high-performance computing, and the application of information technology to manufacturing. Other areas of priority are sensor technology and the two new areas of microelectromechanical systems and nanotechnology.

Jones was interviewed for the June 23, 1997, issue of *Business Week,* and in that interview she said the fundamental problem in information technology is that programming is difficult and there is no current breakthrough that makes programming easy. "It takes a long time to build new systems when you just have general purpose programming languages." She predicted that in 15 years, virtual reality (VR) simulations will be used extensively in education and job training, pointing out that the military invented high-fidelity simulations for flight training and it still bankrolls the most cutting-edge applications. "Exercises of this sort require staggering processing power—beyond the reach of academic labs. But with price reductions pushed by games, high-end simulations will soon be widely available."

In the private sector, she was a member of the faculty of Carnegie Mellon University in computer science for several years and then professor and department chair in the same field at the University of Virginia. She returned to Virginia after leaving DOD in 1997. She has edited two books—*Foundations of Secure Computation* (1971) and *Perspectives in Computer Science* (1977)—in addition to writing numerous scientific papers. Prior to being appointed director of DOD, she was a consultant for the National Science Foundation, Defense Advanced Research Projects Agency, and National Research Council. She was a trustee of Mitre Corporation and a director of Science Applications International Corporation. She has been a member of the Defense Science Board (1985–1993) and the U.S. Air Force Science Advisory Board (1980–1985). She received the Air Force Meritorious Civilian Service Award in 1985.

She was elected to membership in the National Academy of Engineering in 1994. She is a fellow of the Association for Computing Machinery and a member of the Institute of Electrical and Electronics Engineers. Her research includes design and implementation of programmed systems on computers, including enforcement of security policies on computers, operating systems, and scientific data bases. Her photograph is available in *Business Week* (June 23, 1997) and *Aerospace America* (July 1994).

***Bibliography:*** *American Men and Women of Science* 13–19; *Who's Who in America,* 51st ed., 1997; *Who's Who in Science and Engineering,* 3d ed., 1996–1997; *Who's Who of American Women,* 20th ed., 1997–1998.

# Kanter, Rosabeth (Moss)

(1943– )

## *sociologist, management consultant*

***Education:*** Student, University of Chicago, 1962–1963; B.A., Bryn Mawr College, 1964; M.A., University of Michigan, 1965, Ph.D. in sociology, 1967; postdoctoral studies, Harvard University, 1975–1976; honorary degrees: 17

***Professional Experience:*** Instructor in sociology, University of Michigan, 1967; assistant professor of sociology, Brandeis University, 1967–1973; associate professor of administration, Harvard University, 1973–1974; associate professor of sociology, Brandeis, 1974–1977; associate professor of sociology, Yale University, 1977–1978, professor, 1978–1985, department chair, 1982; partner, Goodmeasure, Inc., 1977–1980, chair of the board, 1980– ; professor of business administration, Harvard, 1986–

***Concurrent Position:*** Editor, *Harvard Business Review,* 1989–1992

***Married:*** Stuart A. Kanter, 1963, died 1969; Barry A. Stein, 1972

***Children:*** 1

***Rosabeth Moss Kanter*** is renowned as the person who has revolutionized management by introducing humanism into the workplace. Magazine articles refer to her as "the guru" of management (a guru is an intellectual or spiritual guide or leader or a mentor). She has brought a fresh, multidisciplinary perspective to the study of organizations. In her landmark book *Men and Women of the Corporation* (1977), she debunked the notion that the right personality is the key ingredient for success. Her research indicated that the structure of a company and a person's position within it determines her or his behavior and promotability. Her statements that people can be products of their jobs, not the reverse, was particularly important for women, who usually are told they do not have the personality to be a manager when they have never been able to develop leadership skills in powerless jobs.

After Kanter developed some of these ideas in a slide presentation, she and her second husband, Barry Stein, wrote *A Tale of "O"* (1980). In a whimsical manner she described how x's and o's are treated differently and revealed the insidious effect of discrimination in organizations. In her next book, *The Change Masters: Innovation for Productivity in the American Corporation* (1983), she shifted her perspective from that of an outsider to that of a high-profile adviser to management. She advised companies on how to stimulate entrepreneurial efforts in an organization. This was the groundbreaking work of intrapreneurship—that is, entrepreneurship within a company—and established that management technique in the business arena. She revealed how innovation affected profits when she compared the financial performance of the most progressive companies to that of the least progressive. In 1977, she and her husband established a management consulting firm, Goodmeasure, Inc., in which she was the managing partner for several years before reducing her profile to chair of the board in 1980.

In *World Class: Thriving Locally in the Global Economy* (1995), Kanter describes how corporate leaders have managed to adapt to changing circumstances, a very hot topic. She emphasizes the alternatives to job insecurity and economic chaos that have been brought on by the increasing globalization of industry. A later book, *Rosabeth Moss Kanter on the Frontiers of Management* (1997), is a compilation of articles previously published in the *Harvard Business Review* on subjects such as strategy, innovation, and leadership. She continues to write for that journal although, having been the first female editor in the history of the *Review,* she left that post in 1992. In 1997, she also published *Innovation: Breakthrough Thinking at Du Pont, GE, Pfizer, and Rubbermaid.*

Her expertise in management and administration seems an odd contrast to her earlier research. While she was teaching sociology at Brandeis, she visited numerous communes and participated in several social experiments. Those experiences plus the results of a questionnaire that was distributed among the members of 20 communes resulted in the book *Commitment and Community: Communes and Utopias in Sociological Perspective* (1977), and she published a second book on the topic, *Communes: Creating and Managing the Collective Life* (1973). Her first attempts to apply the techniques of sociological research to corporations met with criticism, but her book *Men and Women of the Corporation* established her as a serious analyzer of the sociology of corporations.

She also has had some influence on the political scene. She was an adviser to Senator Gary Hart in 1986 for his second presidential campaign, and she was closely associated with Governor Michael Dukakis of Massachusetts in his campaign for the presidency in 1988. She and Dukakis wrote *Creating the Future: The Massachusetts Comeback and Its Promise for America,* which was published in 1988 to coincide with his campaign. In 1994, Massachusetts governor William Weld appointed her to his Council on Economic Growth and Technology and named her cochair of his International Trade Task Force.

Kanter is a member of the board of overseers of the Malcolm Baldrige National Quality Award sponsored by the U.S. Department of Commerce, and she is also a member of the American Sociological Association, American Association for Higher Education, and Society for the Study of Social Problems. Her photograph is included in *Current Biography* (1996) and *Working Woman* (September 1986).

***Bibliography:*** *Contemporary Authors* v. 77–80 and CANR-14; *Current Biography 1996;* Herzenberg, C., *Women Scientists from Antiquity to the Present;* Ireland, N., *Index to Women of the World . . . Suppl.;* Liechtenstein, G., *Machisma; Who's Who in America,* 51st ed., 1997; *Who's Who of American Women,* 20th ed., 1997–1998.

# *Karp, Carol Ruth (Vander Velde)*
(1926–1972)
***mathematician***

***Education:*** B.A., Manchester College, 1948; M.A., Michigan State University, 1950; Ph.D. in mathematics, University of Southern California, 1959

***Professional Experience:*** Instructor in mathematics, New Mexico Agricultural and Mechanical College (now New Mexico State University), 1953–1954; instructor in mathematics, University of Maryland, 1958–1960, assistant professor, 1960–1963, associate professor, 1963–1966, professor, 1966–1972

***Married:*** Arthur L. Karp, 1952

**Carol Karp** was renowned for her research on logic, particularly infinitary logic in mathematical logic. Logic is defined as the science that investigates the principles governing correct or reliable inference, and her book *Languages with Expressions of Infinite Length* (1964), based on her doctoral thesis, was the first systematic explanation of the theory of infinitary logic. While still a graduate student she had participated in a seminar in 1956 on infinitary logic at Berkeley, and after receiving her graduate degree, she continued working on her ideas while she was at the University of Maryland. The book has a different focus from the thesis and includes the results of other people's work. Infinitary logic is a modification of calculus, and the formulas are formed from symbols representing variables, constants, functions, and relations; in addition, she introduced four new symbols representing conjunction of infinite sets.

During the time she was completing her doctorate at the University of Southern California, she was hired as an instructor at the University of Maryland. However, after receiving her degree she advanced rapidly to the rank of full professor owing to international recognition of her work. She was able to recruit other logicians to join her on the Maryland faculty, and the group had a steady stream of graduate students. She was instrumental in bringing several important participants to the colloquia that she sponsored, and she and her husband even had a home with an extra apartment in which visiting logicians were frequently housed.

Her intellectual standards were extremely high. Although she was considerate toward her students and younger faculty members, she was unfailingly honest in appraising their mathematical contributions and promise. She advised working toward a doctorate only if one expected to make research the most important part of one's professional career. She refused to allow her students to graduate until their results met her own high standards for publishability.

Her parents encouraged their children to pursue a college education. The family was very conservative and belonged to the Dutch Reformed Church. The children as teenagers were not allowed to dance or to attend movies, but Carol did learn to play the viola, and after completing her master's degree, she traveled around the country as a violist in an all-woman orchestra for a time. While her husband was in the U.S. Navy, they lived in Japan from 1957 to 1958. She developed breast cancer in 1969, but she continued her schedule of teaching and research until 1971 when she was too ill to work. She died in 1972.

At the time of her death she was working on a second book, but the manuscript was very incomplete. Colleagues and friends prepared a memorial volume, volume 492 in the series Lecture Notes in Mathematics, *Infinitary Logic: In Memoriam Carol Karp* (1975), which incorporates many of her ideas and notes. A list of her publications is included in *Women of Mathematics.* She was a member of American Mathematical Society, Mathematical Association of America, and Association for Symbolic Logic.

***Bibliography:*** *American Men and Women of Science* 11–13; Herzenberg, C., *Women Scientists from Antiquity to the Present; Women of Mathematics.*

# Kaufman, Joyce (Jacobson)
(1929– )
## quantum chemist, pharmacologist

***Education:*** B.S., Johns Hopkins University, 1949, M.A., 1959, Ph.D. in chemistry and chemical physics, 1960; DES in theoretical physics, Sorbonne, 1963
***Professional Experience:*** Research chemist, U.S. Army Chemical Center, Maryland, 1949–1952; research assistant, Johns Hopkins University, 1952–1960; staff scientist, Martin Company Research Institute for Advanced Studies, 1960–1962, head, quantum chemistry group, 1962–1969; associate professor of anesthesiology, School of Medicine, and principal research scientist in chemistry, Johns Hopkins, 1969–1977, associate professor, Department of Surgery, 1977–
***Married:*** Stanley Kaufman, 1948
***Children:*** 1

*Joyce Kaufman* has gained a distinguished national and international reputation in a wide variety of fields—chemistry, physics, biomedicine, and supercomputers—on both the experimental and the theoretical levels. Her specialties include theoretical quantum chemistry, experimental physical chemistry, and chemical physics of energetic compounds; the last includes explosives, rocket fuels, oxidizers, and energetic polymers.

She also has examined the application of those techniques and experimental animal studies to biomedical research, including pharmacology (mechanism of the action of drugs and anesthetics); drug design; molecular modeling; and toxicology, including prediction toxicity and toxicology. She is also knowledgeable in nuclear chemistry and radiochemistry and has been successful in using quantum chemical and other theoretical techniques as well as experimental chemical physics techniques in determining the guidelines for effective drug action in a number of different areas. These include major tranquilizers, narcotics and narcotic antagonists, and carcinogens. She has effectively used the computer—especially the San Diego Supercomputer Center, at the invitation of the National Science Foundation—for quantum chemical and theoretical prediction of toxicity and toxicology.

She published a landmark paper in 1980 in which she introduced a new theoretical method for coding and retrieving certain carcinogenic polycyclic aromatic hydrocarbons. Since that time, at least 30 papers have been written by other researchers using and expanding the concept. In her position in the Department of Surgery at Johns Hopkins School of Medicine, she works with interns and residents in the area of theoretical quantum chemical and experimental physiochemical studies of central nervous system drugs. These include narcotics and narcotic antagonists, major tranquilizers, psychotropic drugs, general anesthetics, and spinal anesthetics. She also has several postdoctoral fellows plus visiting scientists working with her in the Department of Chemistry.

She always has been excellent in mathematics and interested in science, and she says she knew she wanted to be a chemist after she read a biography of Marie Curie at the age of eight. She had learned to read before she was two years old, and by the time she was six, she had read all of the children's books in the local public library. A librarian then suggested that she read biographies of famous people, especially scientists. She was chosen to attend a high school for exceptional students who were allowed to complete the three-year curriculum in two years. She married while she still was in undergraduate school, and after receiving her undergraduate degree, she worked as a technical librarian at the Army Chemical Center where she set up a scientific indexing system for their technical reports. During the 1950s, it was common practice for companies and agencies to hire women scientists, even those with doctorates, as librarians specializing in scientific literature rather than to employ them in the laboratories. However, Kaufman was able to transfer to a position as a research chemist after one year.

Her chemistry professor at Johns Hopkins invited her to return to the university to work with him on a research contract, and he later convinced her to obtain a doctorate. She worked with him on kinetics of isotopic exchange reactions of the boron hydrides and the chemical physics studies of those and related compounds. She was then invited to join Martin Company's Research Institute for Advanced Studies to do theoretical research on the application of quantum mechanics to problems in chemistry. She returned to Johns Hopkins in 1969 where she has an appointment in the Department of Surgery.

She has received a number of awards: the Garvan Medal of the American Chemical Society (1974) for her research on quantum calculations of drug actions; the Gold Medal of the Martin Company each year for three years (1964–1966); and the Dame Chevalier of the Centre National de la Recherche Scientifique, France (1969). She is a fellow of the American Physical Society and the American Institute of Chemists and a member of the American Chemical Society. Her research includes physiochemistry and theory of drugs that affect the central nervous system, computer systems, experimental chemical physics, chemical effects of nuclear transformation, isotopic exchange reactions of boron hydrides, and quantum chemistry. A partial list of her publications is included in *Women in Chemistry and Physics,* and her photograph is included in *Notable Women in the Physical Sciences.*

***Bibliography:*** *American Men and Women of Science* 11–19; Herzenberg, C., *Women Scientists from Antiquity to the Present;* Ireland, N., *Index to Women of the World . . . Suppl.; Notable Women in the Physical Sciences; Women in Chemistry and Physics.*

# *Keller, Evelyn (Fox)*

(1936– )

## *physicist, mathematical biologist, molecular biologist*

***Education:*** Student, Queens College, 1953; B.A., Brandeis University, 1957; M.A., Radcliffe College, 1959; Ph.D. in physics, Harvard University, 1963

***Professional Experience:*** Instructor, New York University, 1962–1963, assistant research scientist, 1963–1966; assistant professor, Graduate School of Medical Science, Cornell University, 1966–1969; associate professor of molecular biology, New York University, 1970–1972; associate professor, Division of Natural Science, State University of New York (SUNY) at Purchase, 1972–1982; visiting fellow, Massachusetts Institute of Technology, 1979–1980, visiting scholar, 1980–1984, visiting professor, 1985–1986; professor of humanities and mathematics, Northeastern University, 1982; senior fellow, Cornell University, 1986–1987; professor of rhetoric, Women's Studies and History of Science, University of California, Berkeley, 1989–1993; professor, history and philosophy of science, Massachusetts Institute of Technology, 1993–

***Married:*** Joseph B. Keller, 1964, divorced 1974

***Children:*** 2

***Evelyn Keller*** is known for her work in the fields of theoretical physics, molecular biology, and mathematical biology. However, she taught a course in women's studies in 1974 while working at the State University of New York (SUNY) at Purchase, and since that time, she has examined the psychological basis for scientific beliefs and given science a feminist critique.

She was not interested in science as a child even though both her older brother and sister tried to entice her into the field. While a freshman at Queens College, she was receiving low grades in freshman composition until she started writing about George Gamow and quantum mechanics. Her brother persuaded her to transfer to Brandeis University where she decided to major in physics to gain admittance to medical school. After she wrote her senior thesis on Richard Feynman, she became hooked on science. She won a National Science Foundation fellowship and decided to attend Harvard.

However, as she describes in *Working It Out* (1977) and other sources, she learned to hate Harvard. Although she was a superior student, the faculty and fellow students told her she could not possibly understand physics; that she lacked any fear of physics was proof of her ignorance. At the time, physics was viewed as a skill of calculation, but she saw it as a means for deep inquiry into nature. She was ready to quit school after two years, but her brother took her to the Cold Spring Harbor Laboratory for the summer and she found that the biologists there treated her much better than the physicists did. She wrote her thesis on molecular biology and received her doctorate in physics.

She held several successive and concurrent positions, married, and had two children—and faced another crisis when the roles of wife, mother, teacher, and scientist conflicted. Through the teachings of the women's movement and therapy, she began to see that the difficulties she had experienced in graduate school were not her fault. Someone suggested she write about the geneticist Barbara McClintock (1902–1992), and what she planned as just a brief article turned out as a book, *A Feeling for the Organism: The Life of Barbara McClintock* (1983). McClintock had worked for years in relative obscurity at Cold Spring Harbor on the genetics of maize (corn). She had discovered that genes can move from one area on the chromosomes to another, a finding known as "jumping genes" that now helps molecular biologists identify, locate, and study genes. It was not until scientists started observing similar phenomena in their own work that McClintock received any credit. She received the Nobel Prize for this discovery more than 32 years after publishing her first findings; Keller's biography of her conveys the frustration of a scientist who endured the incomprehension of her colleagues concerning her great insights.

Keller continued to question the way science is carried out and published *Reflections on Gender and Science* (1985), which generated much controversy, for in the work she emphasizes the importance of intuition in science and speculates what science might be like if it were gender free. After teaching in the Women's Studies and History of Science Department at the University of California, Berkeley, she accepted a position as professor of history and philosophy of science at the Massachusetts Institute of Technology in 1993.

She is a member of the American Association for the Advancement of Science, and her research includes mathematical models of chemotaxis and pattern formation and the psychological basis of scientific beliefs. Her photograph is included in *Working It Out*.

***Bibliography:*** *American Men and Women of Science* 11–19; *Contemporary Authors* v. 125 and CANR-51; Herzenberg, C., *Women Scientists from Antiquity to the Present;* Ireland, N., *Index to Women of the World . . . Suppl.; Notable Women in the Life Sciences; Working It Out.*

# *Kempf, Martine*
(1958– )
***computer scientist***

***Education:*** Student in astronomy, Friedrich Wilhelm University, Bonn, 1981–1983
***Professional Experience:*** Owner and manager, Kempf, Sunnyvale, California, 1985–

*Martine Kempf* is known for her research on voice commands for computer programs. She invented a breakthrough voice recognition microcomputer dubbed Katalavox, a name derived from the modern Greek word *katal,* which means "to understand," and *vox,* which is Latin for "voice." While she was a student in Bonn, she saw many German teenagers who had been born without arms because their mothers had taken thalidomide during pregnancy and reasoned that a voice recognition system would enable them to drive cars. Learning to program on an Apple computer, she succeeded in directly transforming the human voice's analog signals into the computer's digital signals. Further refinements enable Katalavox to respond to a spoken command in 0.008 of a second, compared with one or two seconds for competing systems.

When she tried to start her own company in France to market the device, the French government backed out of a promise of a $100,000 loan. She immediately went to the United States where she found financing in Sunnyvale, California, to start her company. The device weighs only five pounds, and to program it, the user merely repeats a command such as "right" or "left" three times. The computer stores the information in its erasable-programmable memory, which saves the information even after the system is turned off.

In addition to being of use for people with physical difficulties, such as the German teenagers or quadriplegics, the device has applications in microsurgery, for surgeons can use voice commands to focus the magnifying devices instead of focusing them manually. People who have lost their voice because of cerebral palsy, strokes, or other damage can also use it, and it has other potential uses in issuing commands to robots on automobile assembly lines or controlling cameras mounted on the external robotic arm of a space shuttle. Another potential use is in a mobile phone to control a car by spoken commands. Kempf also invented the Comeldir Multiplex Handicapped Driving Systems for people who must operate cars with their feet rather than their hands.

Kempf has two incentives to work in this area. One is that her father, a polio victim, designed a car he could drive with his hands and is currently customizing cars for others with disabilities. The other incentive is that in the 1970s, she nearly died from eating unwashed strawberries that had been sprayed with fertilizer containing arsenic. She then vowed to help other people. She dismisses the stereotype that women do not have mechanical or electrical expertise. She not only designed the software for her device but designed and built the hardware, designing the board and soldering the circuits herself. A voice-controlled wheelchair has been featured in a mystery novel: in *Dismissed with Prejudice* by J. A. Jance (1989), one of the products a computer entrepreneur designs is a voice-operated wheelchair.

There are photographs of Martine Kempf in E. Vare's *Mothers of Invention* and *People Magazine* (May 26, 1986).

***Bibliography:*** Stanley, A., *Mothers and Daughters of Invention;* Vare, E., *Mothers of Invention; Who's Who of American Women,* 20th ed., 1997–1998.

# *Kidwell, Margaret Gale*
(1933– )
***evolutionary geneticist***

***Education:*** B.Sc., Nottingham University, 1953; M.S., Iowa State University, 1962; Ph.D. in genetics, Brown University, 1973
***Professional Experience:*** Officer, Ministry of Agriculture, London, 1955–1960; associate in research, Brown University, 1966–1970, research fellow, 1973–1974, research associate, 1974–1975, investigator, 1975–1977, assistant professor, 1977–1980, associate professor, 1980–1985, professor, 1985; professor of ecology and evolutionary biology, University of Arizona, 1985– , head, ecology and evolutionary biology, 1992–
***Married:*** widowed
***Children:*** 2

*Margaret Kidwell* is renowned for her research on *Drosophila,* the common fruit fly. In the 1990s, her team discovered that sometime around 1950, genes of one fruit fly jumped to another species. Since that time, "the jumping genes" have spread like wildfire, so that today, essentially all fruit fly populations, except those maintained in isolation in laboratories, carry the same elements. The theory is that a tiny parasitic mite lives in association with both species. Although there have been reports of other possible gene transfers between species, principally by viruses, this discovery was the first indication that a mite or anything like it can transfer genetic material.

The transfer of genetic material between species could have a major impact on evolution. The elements are called "transposons," which are DNA sequences that can move around in the genome and cause mutations if they happen to land in a gene. However, if lateral transfers of genetic material between species occur frequently, that could complicate the work of researchers who are attempting to study the evolutionary relationships among species. Kidwell, a pioneer in this research, was the one who zeroed in on the mite. Since the two species of fruit flies cannot breed, the team recognized that the material had to have been transferred by some agent.

After receiving her doctorate from Brown University, she accepted a position with the university as a research scientist, then transferred to the professorial ranks as an assistant professor in 1977 and rose rapidly to the positions of associate professor and then professor. She moved to the University of Arizona in 1985 as professor of ecology and evolutionary biology, being named head of both in 1992.

She was elected to membership in the National Academy of Sciences in 1996. She is a fellow of the American Association for the Advancement of Science and of the American Academy of Arts and Letters and a member of the American Genetics Association (president, 1991), American Society of Naturalists, Genetics Society of America, and Society for the Study of Evolution. Her research interests include *Drosophila* genetics and evolution, recombination transposable elements, and speciation.

***Bibliography:*** *American Men and Women of Science* 14–19.

# *Kieffer, Susan Werner*
(1942– )
## *geologist, volcanologist, mineral physicist*

***Education:*** B.S. in physics and mathematics, Allegheny College, 1964; M.Sc. in geological sciences, California Institute of Technology, 1967, Ph.D. in planetary science, 1971; honorary degree: D.Sc., Allegheny College, 1987
***Professional Experience:*** Research geophysicist, University of California, Los Angeles, 1971–1973, assistant professor, 1973–1978, associate professor, 1978–1979; geologist, U.S. Geological Survey, 1978–1990; professor, Arizona State University, 1989–1993, regents professor, 1991–1993; professor and head, Department of Geological Science, University of British Columbia, 1993–1995; cofounder and head, Kieffer & Woo, Inc., Palgrave, Ontario, 1996–
***Married:*** 1966
***Children:*** 1

S*usan Kieffer* is renowned as an expert on volcanoes both on earth and on Io, Venus, Mars, and other planets. Her expertise on the hydraulics of lava flow also transfers to her studies of the hydraulics, sediment transfer, rapids, and waves in rivers. She also participated in the studies of asteroid impact on earth at the Chicxulub crater in Mexico. She was elected to membership in the National Academy of Sciences in 1986.

She has worked for government agencies as well as for several universities. Her most recent appointment was professor and head of the Department of Geological Sciences at the University of British Columbia in Canada. After receiving her doctorate, she secured a position as a research geophysicist at the University of California, Los Angeles, and then transferred to professorial rank as an assistant professor and then associate professor. She moved to the U.S. Geological Survey for 12 years, and then returned to academe as a professor at Arizona State University before moving to the University of British Columbia in 1993. In 1996 she cofounded Kieffer & Woo, a consulting firm.

Her expertise in volcanoes ranges from earth to planetary sites. She has studied geysers, volcanoes, and the volcanic environment on earth as well as on other planets and has found that simulated volcanic eruptions on earth, Venus, and Mars produce plumes with different fluid dynamic regimes. A major portion of the differences are caused by differing atmospheric pressures and ratios of volcanic vent pressure to atmospheric pressure. She did extensive studies of the hydraulics of lava flow and erosion furrows after the eruption of Mount St. Helens in Washington State in 1980, and she has also studied the hydraulics of river flow in areas such as the Colorado River. In her study of geysers, she explored Old Faithful in Yellowstone National Park by lowering a robot down its vent.

Although it is commonplace for asteroids to strike other planets, it is a comparatively rare occurrence when they strike earth. Kieffer collaborated with Walter Alvarez in his study of the crater left by an asteroid striking the earth at Chicxulub in Mexico, a study that supported Alvarez's theory that the dust cloud from this impact blotted out the sun while circling the earth, thus killing the vegetation that was the food supply for the dinosaurs. Kieffer and Alvarez coauthored a paper about the study, and the research is also discussed in Alavarez's book *T-Rex and the Crater of Doom* (1997).

Kieffer received a MacArthur fellowship in 1995, a prestigious award consisting of a five-year grant to support her research in a field of her choosing. She has also received the Mineralogical Society of America Award (1980), Meritorious Service Award of the Department of Interior (1987), Spendiarov Prize of the Soviet Academy of Sciences (1990), and the Day Medal of the Geological Society of America (1992). She is the coeditor of *Microscopic to Macroscopic Atomic Environments to Mineral Thermodynamics* (1985). She is a fellow of the American Geophysical Union and a member of the Meteoritical Society, Geological Society of America, and American Academy of Arts and Sciences ("meteoritical" refers to meteors). Her research includes geological physics, high-pressure geophysics and impact processes, shock metamorphism of natural materials, thermodynamic properties of minerals, mechanisms of geyser and volcano eruptions, and river hydraulics.

***Bibliography:*** *American Men and Women of Science* 13–19; *Who's Who in America,* 51st ed., 1997; *Who's Who in Science and Engineering,* 3d ed., 1996–1997; *Who's Who in Technology Today* v. 4; *Who's Who of American Women,* 19th ed., 1995–1996.

# *Kimble, Judith*

(1949– )

***geneticist***

***Education:*** B.A., University of California, Berkeley, 1971; Ph.D. in biology, University of Colorado, Boulder, 1978

***Professional Experience:*** Postdoctoral fellow, Laboratory of Molecular Biology, Cambridge, England, 1978–1982; assistant professor, Laboratory of Molecular Biology and Department of Biochemistry, University of Wisconsin, Madison, 1983–1988, associate professor, 1988–1992, professor, 1992– , professor, Department of Medical Genetics, 1993– , investigator, Howard Hughes Medical Institute, 1994–

***Judith Kimble*** is renowned for her research on elegans, a type of nematode—nematodes are unsegmented worms of the phylum Nematoda and have an elongated, cylindrical body. After completing her undergraduate degree at the University of California, Berkeley, Kimble spent two years at the University of Copenhagen Medical School as an assistant before she received a National Science Foundation predoctoral fellowship at the University of Colorado, Boulder. After receiving her doctorate, she was a postdoctoral fellow at the Laboratory of Molecular Biology in Cambridge, England, from 1978 to 1982. For two of those years (1978–1980), she received the Jane Coffin Childs postdoctoral fellowship, and for the remaining two years (1980–1982), she had a National Institutes of Health postdoctoral fellowship.

After joining the Department of Biochemistry at the University of Wisconsin, Madison, as an assistant professor, she received the National Institutes of Health Research Career Development Award for 1984–1989. She was promoted to associate professor in 1988 and professor in 1992 and received the Pound Award for Excellence in Research from the university in 1988 and the Romnes faculty fellowship in 1990. In 1993, she also became a professor in the Department of Medical Genetics at Wisconsin. She has published about 40 scientific articles in primary journals such as *Developmental Biology; Genetics; Cell; Developmental Genetics;* and *Proceedings of the National Academy of Sciences.*

Kimble was elected to membership in the National Academy of Sciences in 1995. She has served on several prestigious committees, such as the Damon Runyon–Walter Winchell Cancer Research Fund Scientific Advisory Board (1992–1996) and the Searle Scientific Advisory Board (1997– ) and has been active in several professional associations, such as the Society of Developmental Biology (secretary, 1987–1990) and the American Society for Cell Biology (council member, 1994– ). She is also a member of the American Academy of Arts and Sciences. This information was supplied to the author in correspondence in June 1997.

***Bibliography:*** National Academy of Sciences. *Organization and Members,* June 30, 1995.

# King, Mary-Claire
(1946– )
## *geneticist, epidemiologist*

***Education:*** B.A. in mathematics, Carleton College, 1966; Ph.D. in genetics, University of California, Berkeley, 1973

***Professional Experience:*** Visiting professor, University of Chile, Santiago, 1973; assistant professor of epidemiology, School of Public Health, University of California, Berkeley, 1974–1980, associate professor of epidemiology, 1980–1984, professor of epidemiology, 1984–1996, professor of genetics, Department of Genetics and Molecular Biology, 1989–1996, American Cancer Society Professor of genetics and epidemiology, 1994–1996; professor of genetics, Division of Medical Genetics, University of Washington, 1996–

***Married:*** Robert Colwell, 1973, divorced 1980

***Children:*** 1

**M*ary-Claire King*** is renowned for her research on breast cancer. In 1990, she predicted the existence of the gene BRCA1 that, if damaged, can predispose women to breast and ovarian cancer. The next year, she and other researchers discovered the chromosomal location of a gene that causes a form of inherited deafness, and another of her discoveries consists of the genetic clues to the reason why some men infected with HIV-1 develop AIDS faster than others. She has used her expertise in DNA sequencing for other humanitarian efforts, for example, assisting Argentine human rights groups to identify hundreds of children who had been kidnapped between 1978 and 1983 and reuniting them with their families.

When she enrolled in graduate school at the University of California, Berkeley, King began working toward a doctorate in biostatistics in order to combine her talent in mathematics with problems in medicine. However, taking a course in genetics prompted her to change her course of study. She had chosen Berkeley for its reputation for political activism as well as its academic superiority, but when then-governor Ronald Reagan called in the California National Guard after a series of Vietnam War protests on campus in 1969, she took leave from school to work for the consumer advocate Ralph Nader as a research fellow at his Center for the Study of Responsive Law. There she worked on projects such as determining the effects of pesticides on farmworkers.

One of her Berkeley professors invited her to obtain her doctorate in evolution. His theory was that humans and apes had evolved from lineages that diverged at least 5 million years ago, but when she examined the genetic differences between humans and chimpanzees, she found that the genomes differed by less than 1 percent. Their paper caused quite a stir when it was published in *Science* (April 11, 1975). She had already gone to Chile to teach at the University of Chile on an exchange program funded by the Ford Foundation by the time the paper was published. She did postdoctoral research on epidemiology back at Berkeley, was appointed an assistant professor of epidemiology, and rose through the ranks to be named professor in 1984. She had concurrent appointments as professor of epidemiology and professor of genetics until 1996 when she moved to the University of Washington.

Although she started her research on breast cancer in the 1970s, she made very little headway until the early 1980s when breakthroughs in molecular biology led to the mapping of more genetic markers. Her team was very close to finding the gene BRCA1 when it was located by a team at the University of Utah Medical Center in 1994. Although very much disappointed, she continues her work because the gene is unusually prone to mutation; researchers had found at least 30 distinct mutations by the end of 1994. However, researchers are saying that there may be another gene, which they have named BRCA2. She approaches the genetic analysis of breast and ovarian cancer not only as a researcher but as a person who has a family history of breast cancer, for as she explains, breast cancer is genetic.

King has used her skills in genetic searching to help the U.S. government identify the remains of soldiers who had been listed as missing in action in the Vietnam War, and she has aided the government of El Salvador in identifying the remains of villagers killed in a massacre. She is using sequencing of mitochondrial DNA in her work with the Human Genome Diversity Project, work that will enable scientists to examine how humans migrated out of Africa or how some people, after the same exposure to viruses or bacteria, become ill while others do not. The latter research has been applied to her study of why some homosexual men who have been exposed to HIV develop AIDS while others do not. Since mutations of the gene BRCA1 often result in breast or ovarian cancer, she says in a special issue of *Business Week* on biotechnology (March 10, 1997) that she wants to start a clinical test on whether the gene can be used to develop a therapy. Tests on mice indicate that those with ovarian cancer live much longer when given a normal version of the gene.

She has served on various committees of the National Cancer Institute, National Institute of Medicine, and National Institutes of Health (NIH) and on the advisory board of NIH's Office of Research on Women's Health. She was considered for the directorship of the National Institutes of Health in 1991, but she declined because she is not interested in that level of administrative responsibility. She is a member of the American Society of Human Genetics and Society for Epidemiologic Research. Her research includes the genetics and epidemiology of breast cancer and other common chronic diseases, pedigree analysis, and human and primate molecular evolution. One of several books that describes her contributions is *Breakthrough: The Race to Find the Breast Cancer Gene* (1996) by Kevin Davies and Michael White. Her photograph is included in *Current Biography* (1995), *Discover* (October 1990), and *Parade* (April 21, 1996).

***Bibliography:*** *American Men and Women of Science* 13–19; *Current Biography 1995; Who's Who in America,* 51st ed., 1997; *Who's Who in Science and Engineering,* 2d ed., 1994–1995; *Who's Who of American Women,* 20th ed., 1997–1998.

# *Klinman, Judith (Pollock)*

(1941– )

## *biochemist, physical organic chemist*

***Education:*** B.A., University of Pennsylvania, 1962, Ph.D. in organic chemistry, 1966

***Professional Experience:*** Postdoctoral fellow, Isotope Department, Weizmann Institute of Science, Israel, 1966–1967, Department of Chemistry, University College, London, 1967–1968; postdoctoral associate, Institute for Cancer Research, Philadelphia, 1968–1970, research associate in biochemistry, 1970–1972, assistant member, 1972–1977, associate member, 1977–1978; associate professor of chemistry, University of California, Berkeley, 1978–1982, professor of chemistry, 1982– , professor of molecular and cell biology, 1993– , chancellor's professor, 1996–1999

***Concurrent Positions:*** Assistant professor, medical biophysics, University of Pennsylvania, 1974–1978

***Married:*** Norman R. Klinman, 1963, divorced 1978

***Children:*** 2

***Judith Klinman*** is renowned for bringing the principles and tools of physical organic chemistry to bear on biological processes. Her research has led to two recent breakthroughs: the discovery of a new redox cofactor in eukaryotes and the demonstration of hydrogen tunneling in enzymatic reactions. She also has been a leading figure in the use of isotope effects to probe enzymatic-reaction mechanisms and transition states. In 1994, she was awarded the Repligen Award of the Division of Biological Chemistry of the American Chemical Society and elected a member of the National Academy of Sciences in the same year.

After she received her doctorate, she was a postdoctoral fellow at the Weizmann Institute of Science in Israel and then was affiliated with the Department of Chemistry at the University College, London. First a postdoctoral associate at the Institute for Cancer Research in Philadelphia, she was promoted to research associate and later became an associate member there. Concurrently, she was assistant professor of biophysics at the University of Pennsylvania, for the administrators of the institute had arranged that the members could have joint appointments at the University of Pennsylvania so they could teach there and supervise graduate students. She joined the University of California, Berkeley, in 1978 as an associate professor and became professor of chemistry in 1982. She has had a joint appointment as professor of molecular and cell biology since 1993, and she was appointed to be a chancellor's professor of the university from 1996 to 1999.

In a telephone conversation with the author on July 3, 1997, Klinman said that the high point of her career was developing a new class of proteins and cofactors involving polypeptide chains. Another was finding evidence for the importance of quantum mechanics, which may have fundamental applications to how proteins function. She said she was happy she received the honor of being elected to the National Academy of Sciences at the height of her career because the honor will further benefit her career. She talked of the need for people to be selected at a young age because election to that body will help them obtain grants and secure appointments; election at a later time—for example, at retirement—cannot benefit them as much. She said she would encourage women to follow a career in biochemistry if they have a predilection for it. It is an extremely difficult discipline with many subfields, but it presents opportunities for creative outlets. It also involves an enormous amount of effort, for one must establish a research group, find funding, teach, write, oversee graduate students, travel, give seminars, etc., while maintaining a family life. She loves her work and has no regrets about choosing it as a career.

She has received awards, such as the Merit Award of the National Institutes of Health (1992) and being named a fellow of the Japanese Ministry of Science (1996). She is a member of the American Academy of Arts and Sciences, American Society for Biochemistry and Molecular Biology, and American Chemical Society. Her research centers on the mechanism and regulation of enzyme action. Her photograph is included in *Chemical & Engineering News* (February 21, 1994).

***Bibliography:*** *American Men and Women of Science* 11–19; *Who's Who in America,* 51st ed., 1997; *Who's Who in Science and Engineering,* 3d ed., 1996–1997; *Who's Who of American Women,* 20th ed., 1997–1998.

# *Kreps, Juanita (Morris)*
(1921– )
***economist***

***Education:*** B.A., Berea College, 1942; M.A., Duke University, 1944, Ph.D. in economics, 1948
***Professional Experience:*** Instructor in economics, Denison University, 1945–1946, assistant professor, 1947–1950; lecturer, Hofstra College, 1952–1954, and Queens College, 1954–1955; visiting assistant professor of economics, Duke University, 1955–1958, assistant professor, 1958–1961, associate professor, 1962–1967, professor, 1967–1972, James B. Duke Professor of Economics, 1972–1977, vice president of university, 1973–1977, vice president emeritus 1979– ; secretary of commerce, U.S. Department of Commerce, 1977–1979
***Concurrent Positions:*** Director of undergraduate economics studies, dean of Women's College, 1969–1972
***Married:*** Clifton H. Kreps, 1944
***Children:*** 3

*Juanita Kreps* is an economist who focused her research on women's employment, and she was the first woman secretary of commerce of the U.S. Department of Commerce. She was also the first professional economist to hold that cabinet post. Prior to that time, the secretaries had supported the interests of business, but she stated she would support the interests of the public, including consumers, as well as those of business. The late 1970s was a period of high unemployment owing to the restructuring of industries, and corporations were experiencing increased competition from abroad in industries such as steel and automobiles, traditionally the strong sectors of U.S. industry. While she was working to revitalize industry, she was also working to increase social consciousness among businesspeople.

Kreps was born in Harlan County, Kentucky, where coal mining was the primary industry. For many years the area has experienced high unemployment, especially during the depression when Juanita was a child. She worked her way through college on a work-study program at Berea College, a small college that pioneered work-study programs for a student body drawn from the impoverished areas of the southern Appalachian Mountains. She decided to major in economics after her first class in the subject because it seemed especially relevant to her situation.

She attended graduate school at Duke University, again working to support herself. She taught part-time and served as a junior economist with the National War Labor Board in the summers of 1943 and 1944; she even interrupted her graduate studies to teach economics at Denison University as an instructor and assistant professor. After receiving her doctorate, she lectured at Hofstra College and Queens College before returning to Duke as a visiting assistant professor in 1955 and then joining the full-time faculty in 1958. She advanced through the ranks to become professor of economics and then received the prestigious appointment as the James B. Duke Professor of Economics in 1972.

Meanwhile, she served as dean of the Women's College for three years. During the early 1900s, many universities had solved the problem of admitting women as students by establishing separate women's colleges, especially at the undergraduate level. Usually women faculty members were appointed as deans, which at least allowed some women to gain administrative experience. Kreps was later appointed to be a vice president of the university. After she completed her term as secretary of the Department of Commerce, she continued to write and lecture, and she served on many committees and commissions prior to 1990.

She specialized in labor demographics with particular emphasis on the employment of women and older workers. One book for which she is still known is *Sex in the Marketplace: American Women at Work* (1971), which identified gaps in the information about women workers. She explored such fundamental questions as why women enter the same occupations year after year, why their proportion of advanced degrees remains so low, and why so many exchange the monotony of housework for equally dull and low-paying office and factory jobs. Another book, *Sex, Age, and Work: The Changing Composition of the Labor Force* (1975), explores the effect of changing patterns of sex, age, and marriage on future manpower policies. In 1975, she organized a conference called "Women and the American Economy" that produced a policy document endorsing the Equal Rights Amendment, recommending stronger affirmative action programs at universities, and urging public education for preschool children.

As a highly respected economist, Kreps attracted attention from leading corporations that were under pressure in the early 1970s to add women to their boards of directors. She was named to the board of the New York Stock Exchange plus the boards of several companies such as Western Electric and Eastman Kodak. She was the first woman director for most of them; although she realized these were token appointments, she accepted in order to pave the way for other women to receive similar appointments. She resigned from the directorships when she was appointed secretary of commerce.

She is a fellow of the Gerontological Society of America and of the American Academy of Arts and Sciences; she is a member of the American Economic Association. Her photograph is included in *Current Biography* (1977) and Peggy Lamson's *In the Vanguard.*

***Bibliography:*** *American Men and Women of Science* 11–13; *Contemporary Authors* v. 130; *Current Biography 1977;* Ireland, N., *Index to Women of the World . . . Suppl.;* Lamson, P., *In the Vanguard;* Read, P., *Book of Women's Firsts;* Schneider, D., *ABC-CLIO Companion to Women in the Workplace; Who's Who in America,* 51st ed., 1997; *Who's Who in Science and Engineering,* 3d ed., 1996–1997; *Who's Who of American Women,* 20th ed., 1997–1998.

# *Krim, Mathilde (Galland)*
(1926– )
## *geneticist, virologist*

***Education:*** B.S., genetics, University of Geneva, Switzerland, 1948, Ph.D. in cytogenetics, 1953

***Professional Experience:*** Junior scientist and research associate, Weizmann Institute, Israel, 1953–1959; research associate in virology, Division of Virus Research, Cornell University Medical College, 1959–1962; associate, Sloan Kettering Institute of Cancer Research, 1962–1975, associate and member, 1975–1986; associate research scientist, St. Luke's Roosevelt Hospital Center and College of Physicians and Surgeons, New York City, 1986–

***Married:*** Arthur B. Krim, 1958

***Children:*** 1

***Mathilde Krim*** is a distinguished geneticist and virologist who left the laboratory in 1986 in order to devote her time to raising funds for AIDS research. She established an AIDS research laboratory at St. Luke's Roosevelt Hospital in New York City, which she is funding. While working at the Sloan Kettering Institute for Cancer Research in cancer viruses, she became intrigued with the possibility that the protein interferon, which is produced naturally by almost all animal species and even some plants, might inhibit tumors and modify some properties of the immune system in animals. She felt this would be a significant area of research, particularly in 1974 when a Swedish physician announced some success with interferon's stopping the recurrence of highly malignant bone cancer in a number of patients.

She began to press Sloan Kettering to establish an interferon laboratory and also sought funding from the National Institutes of Health and the National Cancer Institute. When the results of the Swedish tests were discredited, there was great controversy over the efficacy of interferon, which was very expensive as a natural substance. After a researcher cloned the interferon gene, it was possible to produce interferon in large quantities, and Krim was then appointed as head of Sloan Kettering's interferon evaluation program, which she had established in 1975. During her tenure, Sloan Kettering won Food and Drug Administration (FDA) approval to use interferon to treat certain types of leukemia.

Krim initially became involved in AIDS research through studies of the effectiveness of interferon in treating Karposi's sarcoma, a cancer that afflicts many AIDS patients. She became incensed that the public funding for research aimed at preventing the disease was inadequate, and in 1983 she founded the AIDS Medical Foundation, which awarded grants for promising AIDS research. In 1985, she merged her group with another to form the American Foundation for AIDS Research, which she cochairs.

She has proven to be a formidable fundraiser. Her husband, chair of United Artists and later founder of Orion Pictures, has many influential friends in both politics and the entertainment industry, and her social position plus her reputation as a prominent scientist has enabled her to secure unprecedented amounts of funding for AIDS research. The actress Elizabeth Taylor became the foundation's honorary chairperson and often appears at fund-raising activities, thus guaranteeing good press coverage. In recent years, the drug azidothymidine (AZT) has been approved by the FDA for use in the treatment of AIDS. Although Krim no longer does laboratory research, she keeps abreast of current scientific problems. She also began alerting people to another health threat, the multidrug-resistant tuberculosis (MDRTB), which is a serious problem among people who are HIV positive as well as the homeless, people in prison, and the poor.

As a child, her interest in science was encouraged by her grandfather, who was a teacher. Her father was a zoologist, and she had decided by age seven that she wanted a career in biology. The family moved to Switzerland from Italy in 1932 to escape depressed economic conditions, and she received her degrees from the University of Geneva. During World War II, Switzerland remained a neutral country, and she was little affected by the war. However, after she saw newsreels of the Jewish people who were released from concentration camps, she became involved in Jewish activities at the university. She married a Jewish medical student, whose name is unknown, and moved to Israel where she had a daughter. She worked for the Weizmann Institute after her divorce, remarried, and moved to New York City. At the Weizmann Institute, she was involved in research to determine the sex of an unborn child through amniocentesis, a procedure that involves analyzing the fetal chromosomes found in the amniotic fluid surrounding a fetus.

Among her activities, she has been a member of the Committee of 100 for National Health Insurance (1969– ); trustee of the Rockefeller Foundation (1971– ); and president of the Commission to Study Ethical Problems in Medical, Biomedical, and Behavioral Research (1980– ). She is a member of the American Association for the Advancement of Science, American Cancer Society, and American Association of Mental Deficiency. Her research includes structure of chromosomes, prenatal determination of sex, aberrations in human sexual development, cell biology and mechanisms of oncogenic transformation, and interferon research. Her photograph is included in *Current Biography* (1987), *Notable Twentieth-Century Scientists, MS Magazine* (January 1986), *Time* (fall 1990), and *Advocate* (November 16, 1993).

***Bibliography:*** *American Men and Women of Science* 11–19; *Current Biography 1987; Notable Twentieth-Century Scientists; Who's Who in America,* 51st ed., 1997; *Who's Who in Science and Engineering,* 3d ed., 1996–1997; *Who's Who of American Women,* 20th ed., 1997–1998.

# *Krueger, Anne (Osborn)*
(1934– )
***economist***

***Education:*** B.A., Oberlin College, 1953; M.S., University of Wisconsin, 1956, Ph.D. in economics, 1958; honorary degree: Ph.D., Honoris Causis, Hacettepe University, Ankara, Turkey, 1990

***Professional Experience:*** Instructor in economics; University of Wisconsin, Madison, 1958–1959; assistant professor of economics, University of Minnesota, 1959–1963, associate professor, 1963–1966, professor, 1966–1982; vice president of economics and research, World Bank, Washington, D.C., 1982–1986; arts and sciences professor of economics, Duke University, 1986–

***Concurrent Positions:*** Research associate, Upper Midwest Economic Study, 1962–1964; international economist, Bankers' Trust Company, 1961–1962; research associate, National Bureau of Economic Research, 1969–1976, member of senior research staff, 1977– ; consultant, World Bank, 1986–

***Married:*** William R. Krueger, 1953, divorced 1957; James M. Henderson, 1981

***Children:*** 1

A***nne Krueger*** is an economist who is known for her expertise on international trade and economic development. She holds a joint appointment as professor of economics at Duke University and as a consultant for the World Bank, Washington D.C. She also has a position as a member of the senior research staff of the National Bureau of Economic Research and has been a consultant for many organizations. She has authored, coauthored, or edited more than 15 books on trade, development, economic change, developing countries, exchange rates, and economic aid.

Her father was a physician and might have played a role in her selection of a career. She married the same year she received her undergraduate degree and divorced the year prior to receiving her doctorate. She received an appointment as an instructor in economics at the University of Wisconsin, Madison, and one year later was appointed an assistant professor at the University of Minnesota. She advanced through the ranks to become a professor in 1966. Meanwhile, she started on a series of consultancies as a research associate of the Upper Midwest Economic Study (1962–1964). She received an appointment as a vice president of economics and research for the World Bank for the period 1982–1986 and continues as a consultant to the present time.

Among other consultancies, she has been an international economist for the Bankers' Trust Company and has held the position at the National Bureau of Economic Research mentioned above. She has also been a consultant for the U.S. Agency for International Development (1965–1972), the National Science Foundation, (1971– ), and the Brookings Institution (1988– ). Among the honors she has received are the Robertson Award of the National Academy of Sciences (1984) and the Bernhard-Harms Prize of the Kiel Institute of World Economics (1990).

One of her more comprehensive publications was sponsored by the National Bureau of Economic Research and was published by the University of Chicago Press, the three-volume *Trade and Employment in Developing Countries* (1983; 2d ed., 1988) of which she is the sole author of two of the three volumes. Later books are *Political Economy of Policy Reform in Developing Countries* (1994) and *American Trade Policy: A Tragedy in the Making* (1995). She continues to publish numerous papers in the economics journals.

She was elected to membership in the National Academy of Sciences in 1995. She is a fellow of the American Academy of Arts and Sciences and the Econometric Society; she is a member of the American Economic Association and the Royal Economic Society.

***Bibliography:*** *American Men and Women of Science* 11–13; *Contemporary Authors* v. 37–40R, CANR-15, and CANR-32.

# *Kubler-Ross, Elisabeth*

(1926– )

***psychiatrist***

***Education:*** M.D., University of Zurich, 1957; honorary degrees: 16
***Professional Experience:*** Intern, Community Hospital, Glen Cove, New York, 1958–1959; research fellow, Manhattan State Hospital, 1959–1962; fellow in psychiatry, Psychopathic Hospital, University of Colorado Medical School, 1962–1963, instructor in psychiatry, Colorado General Hospital, 1962–1965; assistant professor of psychiatry, Billings Hospital, University of Chicago, 1965–1970; medical director, Family Service and Mental Health Center, Chicago, 1970–1973; president, Ross Medical Associates, 1973–1977; president and chair of the board, Shanti Nilaya Growth and Health Center, Escondido, California, 1977–
***Concurrent Positions:*** Resident, Montefiora Hospital, 1961–1962; member of staff, LaRabida Children's Hospital and Research Center, 1965–1970, chief consultant and research liaison section, 1969–1970
***Married:*** Emmanuel R. Ross, 1957
***Children:*** 2

***Elisabeth Kubler-Ross*** is a psychiatrist and a pioneer in a new field of health care. She challenged the taboo surrounding death. The scientific name for her work is "thanatology," which is the study of the effects of death and dying, especially the investigation of ways to lessen the suffering and address the needs of the terminally ill and their survivors. This research is currently a topic for debate as one group of people support assisted suicide for terminally ill patients while another group supports the hospice concept. A hospice is a health care facility for the terminally ill that emphasizes pain control and emotional support for the patient and family, typically refraining from taking extraordinary measures to prolong life.

It was while teaching psychiatry that she began to address the issue of death in the case studies of her dying patients. While she was teaching at Billings Hospital in Chicago in 1965, she instituted an interdisciplinary seminar on death in which she proposed having a series of conversations with the terminally ill that would make it possible for them to express their feelings during the crisis. She points out that treatment of the dying had changed from taking place at home in the comforting presence of family and friends to occurring in impersonal institutional settings where death is seen as a failure of the technological expertise of physicians, who wish to prolong life. She identifies the five stages that dying patients experience—denial, anger, bargaining, depression, and acceptance—and her work has paved the way for more-humane treatment of the terminally ill by medical personnel. Hospice care has been established as an alternative to dying in hospitals, and there is more emphasis on counseling for families of dying patients. Her book *On Death and Dying* (1969) was instrumental in bringing about this change.

Her seminars on death at Billings were popular with the students, and she continued to give them for several years. However, the school and faculty criticized them because the lectures were not scientific enough. After *Life* magazine published an article about her work, she started receiving invitations to speak at seminars throughout the United States and Canada, but she also continued to see patients and their families in her regular practice. Later she prepared another book, *AIDS: The Ultimate Challenge* (1987), specifically for people who suffer from that affliction. In it, she focuses on the medical, moral, and social implications of the disease and the need for compassion in dealing with the thousands of men, women, children, and babies who are its victims.

Kubler-Ross was the firstborn of a set of identical triplet girls. She weighed only two pounds at birth, but her mother refused to allow the babies to be taken to a hospital, believing that it was essential to have the personal loving care of family members. The girls were so identical that even the parents could not tell them apart, and Kubler-Ross relates that one of their teachers gave all three C's in class because he could not tell which one was not doing her own work.

Living in Switzerland, the family was not affected by World War II, but in an effort to break away to form her own distinctive identity, she volunteered in a hospital where refugees from other European countries were being treated; seeing so many people who had suffered from the war left a deep impression on her. After she received her medical degree, she married a fellow student, an American, and the two went to the United States to complete their training.

She decided to specialize in pediatrics because she felt children were the most helpless of patients. She was accepted as a resident at New York's Columbia Presbyterian Medical Center, but pregnancy kept her from taking that position. Her only option at this point was a residency at a public mental institution, so she went to Manhattan State Hospital. Her work there with persons deemed "hopeless" led her to become a psychiatrist. While she was teaching at Colorado General Hospital and treating chronic schizophrenics, she achieved some success using a technique that she later used in her work with the dying, namely, she began asking the patients what they thought would be most helpful to them. She has been operating her own clinic since 1977.

She is a member of the American Association for the Advancement of Science, American Holistic Medical Association, American Medical Women's Association, American Psychiatric Association, and American Psychosomatic Society. She has written at least nine books in addition to the ones mentioned above. Her autobiography is *The Wheel of Life: A Memoir of Living and Dying* (1997), and in that work she says she has undergone out-of-body experiences, had meetings with spirit guides, and has had visions of fairies. One reviewer had a negative opinion of that book. Earlier, Derek Gill published a biography of her, *Quest: The Life of Elisabeth Kubler-Ross* (1980). Her name is spelled "Kuebler-Ross" in some sources. Her photograph is included in Lynn Gilbert and G. Moore, eds., *Particular Passions: Talks with Women Who Have Shaped Our Times*, Deborah Felder's *The 100 Most Influential Women of All Time*, and *Mother Earth News* (May–June 1983).

***Bibliography:*** *American Men and Women of Science* 19; *Contemporary Authors* v. 25–28R; *Current Biography 1980;* Felder, D., *The 100 Most Influential Women of All Time;* Gilbert, L., and Moore, G., *Particular Passions: Talks with Women Who Have Shaped Our Times;* Ireland, N., *Index to Women of the World . . . Suppl.; Who's Who in America,* 51st ed., 1997; *Who's Who in Science and Engineering,* 3d ed., 1996–1997; *Who's Who of American Women,* 20th ed., 1997–1998.

# *Kuhlmann-Wilsdorf, Doris*
(1922– )
## *physicist, metallurgist*

***Education:*** B.S., University of Göttingen, 1944, M.S., 1946, Ph.D. in materials science, 1947; honorary degree: D.Sc., University of Witwatersrand, Johannesburg, 1954
***Professional Experience:*** Fellow in materials science, University of Göttingen, 1947–1948; fellow in physics, Bristol University, England, 1949–1950; lecturer in physics, University of Witwatersrand, Johannesburg, 1950–1956; associate professor of metallurgy, University of Pennsylvania, 1957–1961, professor, 1962–1963; professor of engineering physics, University of Virginia, 1963–1966, professor of applied science in Physics and Metallurgical Science Department, 1966–
***Concurrent Position:*** Visiting professor of physics, Pretoria University, 1982–1983
***Married:*** Heinz G. F. Wilsdorf, 1950
***Children:*** 2

*Doris Kuhlmann-Wilsdorf* is renowned for her research as a metallurgist and materials scientist. Her most significant work may be her design for electrical metal-fiber brushes to be used as sliding electrical contacts. If the U.S. Navy were to modify ship drives, the brushes could lead to a widespread use of electrical motors on naval vessels, which would result in ships that are lighter, more maneuverable, and more efficient. Currently navy ships use diesel-fueled engines.

Her area of expertise is called tribology, which is the study of the effects of friction on moving machine parts and of methods of lubrication. Another of her contributions is the development of a model for surface deformation, which takes into account erosion as well as friction and wear. She has also investigated the behavior and properties of various metals, such as studying why rolled aluminum sheets crinkle under pressure while other sheet metals break.

Prior to entering college in Germany, she served as an apprentice metallographer and materials tester for two years. After receiving her doctorate from Göttingen, she continued her research with several postdoctoral appointments at both that university and the University of Bristol. At the latter, she studied under Nobel laureate Nevill F. Mott. She and her husband then were lecturers at the University of Witwatersrand in Johannesburg. The couple then went to the United States, where she was appointed associate professor at the University of Pennsylvania while her husband became director of laboratories at the Franklin Institute, which is also located in Philadelphia. After her promotion to professor, the couple moved to the University of Virginia where both received appointments as professors in the Physics and Materials Science Department.

She stresses that it is essential to include women in scientific fields. Women represent 50 percent of the population, and people are throwing away 50 percent of the talent when they say women cannot do this or that. Based on her teaching experience, she feels that women have a particular innate dedication to hard work and reliability.

She was elected to membership in the National Academy of Engineering in 1994. She has served as consultant to corporations such as General Motors Technical Center, Chemstrand Research Laboratories, and General Dynamics Corporation as well as for the National Institute for Standards and Technology. She has published over 250 scientific papers and has received numerous honors and awards, including the Society of Women Engineers Achievement Award (1989), the Ragnar Helm Scientific Achievement Award of the Institute of Electrical and Electronics Engineers (1991), the Medal for Excellence in Research of the American Society of Engineering Education (1965 and 1966), and the Heyn Medal of the German Society of Materials Science (1988). She is a fellow of the American Society for Metals and the American Physical Society and a member of the American Society of Mechanical Engineers and Society of Women Engineers. She is listed in some sources under "Wilsdorf" and in some others under "Kuhlmann," but she seems to have been using "Kuhlmann-Wilsdorf" in recent years.

***Bibliography:*** *American Men and Women of Science* 11–19; Herzenberg, C., *Women Scientists from Antiquity to the Present; Notable Twentieth-Century Scientists; Who's Who in America,* 51st ed., 1997; *Who's Who in Science and Engineering,* 3d ed., 1996–1997; *World Who's Who in Science.*

# *Kurtzig, Sandra L. (Brody)*
## (1946– )
## *computer scientist, aeronautical engineer*

***Education:*** B.S. in chemistry and mathematics, University of California, Los Angeles, 1968; M.S. in aerospace engineering, Stanford University, 1968

***Professional Experience:*** Mathematical analyst, TRW Systems, 1967–1968; marketing representative, General Electric Corporation, 1969–1972; chair of the board, chief executive officer (CEO), and president, ASK Computer Systems, Mountain View, California, 1972–1985, chair of the board, 1986–1989, chair, president, and CEO, 1989–1993, founder and chair, the ASK Group, Inc., 1972–1993, retired, 1993–

***Married:*** Arie Kurtzig, divorced

***Children:*** 2

***Sandra Kurtzig*** is a true computer pioneer who founded her own company, ASK Computer Systems, in 1972, stepped down from running the company in 1985, and returned to take over the company again in 1989 to save it from failure. ASK is the largest public company founded by a woman and probably will be recognized in the history books as one of the success stories of the 1970s minicomputer boom. The company's integrated software products for manufacturers, primarily its MANMAN Information System, are industry standards and are available as turnkey solutions for minicomputers, particularly those manufactured by Digital Equipment and Hewlett-Packard. When Kurtzig returned to the company in 1989, she expanded the product line by developing portable applications software to run on multiple computer platforms in addition to those at Digital and Hewlett-Packard. She also started adapting the software to specific niche markets such as the automotive market.

She was a 25-year-old homemaker looking for a way to create a part-time job for herself while rearing her two sons when she started the company with only a $2,000 investment in one of the bedrooms of the apartment where the family lived. The name of the company is derived from her and her husband's initials—Arie and Sandra Kurtzig, ASK. She started developing innovative programs for businesses, such as one for a newspaper company to monitor its carriers, and later created minicomputer programs and information systems to help manufacturers optimize inventory, improve product quality, reduce operating expenses, and improve customer service. The ASK systems route information flowing from the various parts of a company to the department that needs it. She had the foresight to design software to run on minicomputers when they were just starting to become popular, and in the late 1970s, she started selling computer hardware along with ASK software to provide customers with turnkey systems. By 1983, the company had 200 employees and a reputation for success. Because Kurtzig financed all of the company's growth from earned income rather than borrowing venture capital, she has received huge returns on her investment. Every ASK Computer Systems employee also owns stock.

By the mid 1980s, the company had become very successful, and she decided to step down as CEO and replace herself with someone she personally selected. She then spent several years giving lectures, traveling, building a vacation house in Hawaii, and enjoying herself. Unfortunately, her successor was not as creative as she, and company sales began to slump and the product line needed overhauling. The board of directors asked Kurtzig to return. In order to save the company, she returned as CEO, launched new products for the current market, and increased the research budget from 20 percent to 50 percent of sales. Her employees were delighted with her return because she has a warm personal style.

She believes in personal contact. She has a style of walking around and stroking people and tries to compliment them in front of their peers. She feels that a woman can show a warmth that a man often cannot. When the company stages its annual users' conference, she holds the meetings close to headquarters so all research and development engineers can attend, and ASK engineers take turns staffing a separate area designed to solicit customers' questions and suggestions. For example, to get its portable software line off the ground, ASK put together a special customer council. ASK executives show their latest product designs and solicit each member's suggestions, and the company also sends its engineers to council members' manufacturing plants to work out problems.

Kurtzig's keen business instincts probably are derived from her parents' influence. Her father was a residential real estate developer, and her mother helped in the business; both always discussed business at the dinner table. Sandra was a diligent student in high school and completed both high school and college in three and a half years each. Some colleagues attribute her three-year vacation from her business as a reaction to burnout. She spent part of the time writing her autobiography, *CEO: Building a $400 Million Company from the Ground Up* (1991), in which she describes starting her own successful business in a male-dominated field. She thinks being a woman in a primarily men's profession is a nonissue for her. She was one of only a few women studying math and aeronautical engineering in college, and she has rarely encountered other women in manufacturing companies or in upper management. Although she has observed instances of sex discrimination, she has not encountered it herself as the boss. There are photographs in *Infosystems* (May 1980), *Business Week* (November 12, 1990), *Working Woman* (July 1990), *Business Marketing* (April 1990), *Time* (fall 1990), and *Computerworld* (March 21, 1994).

***Bibliography:*** Stanley, A., *Mothers and Daughters of Invention; Who's Who in Science and Engineering*, 3d ed., 1996–1997.

# *Kwolek, Stephanie Louise*
(1923– )
## *polymer chemist*

***Education:*** B.S., Carnegie Institute of Technology, 1946; honorary degree: D.Sc., Worcester Polytechnic Institute, 1981

***Professional Experience:*** Chemist, Fibers Department, Experimental Station, E. I. Du Pont de Nemours and Company, 1946–1959, research chemist, 1959–1967, senior research chemist, 1967–1974, research associate, 1974–1986, retired 1986

***Concurrent Position:*** Consultant in polymer chemistry, 1986–

***Stephanie Kwolek*** is renowned as the inventor of the polymer that is manufactured by Du Pont under the trade name Kevlar. She spent her entire career at Du Pont, primarily working at the experimental station in Wilmington, Delaware, and she has continued to consult for the company since her retirement in 1986. In 1996, she was one of the Du Pont employees featured in print ads and in television commercials describing the company's research. She received the 1997 Perkin Medal of the Society of Chemical Industry for her inventions of liquid-crystal aromatic polyamides, especially the product known as Kevlar. She is only the second woman to receive the prize in its 91-year history; it is awarded annually to an outstanding chemist. In a White House ceremony in 1996, she received the nation's highest technology honor, the National Medal of Technology. She is also a member of the National Inventors' Hall of Fame.

She joined Du Pont after graduating from college because she wanted to earn money to attend medical school; the job with the company was just a temporary measure. However, the work turned out to be so interesting, she stayed. In the 1940s, women at Du Pont were able to work in the laboratory for a few years, then they would be pushed into so-called women's jobs. She was able to retain her research position because she was involved at the very beginning of the research that led to the discovery of low-temperature polymerization; she was already making discoveries. By the 1960s, Du Pont had rather liberal labor practices for hiring women as professionals, even those who were wives of employees.

In 1959, Kwolek won the first of her many prizes, a publication award from the American Chemical Society (ACS), and she is one of only a few women to win anything but the Garvan Medal from that society. She first gained national attention in 1960 for her work creating long molecule chains at low temperatures; these are synthetic, petroleum-derived fibers that have incredible stiffness and strength. Her discovery of the method to spin these fibers led to her winning the ACS Award for Creative Invention in 1980, and the invention led to the commercial production of aramid fibers, a multimillion-dollar industry. Many of her patents and scientific honors were awarded to "S. L. Kwolek," to disguise her gender.

She reminisces that in 1964 she was asked to scout for the next generation of fibers; the goal was high-performance fibers from intractable polymers. She persevered in the hot and humid Delaware summer and developed a liquid crystalline solution that eventually enabled the scientists to spin the polymer. The compound had such high tensile strength that she ran the tests again and again to make sure she had not made an error before reporting her discovery to the laboratory director. This polymer resembles nylon, except the hydrocarbon in nylon is replaced by aromatic rings. The ring structure prevents the polymer from bending, which gives the material its rigidity. The resulting product, Kevlar, is used in radial tire cords, composites, rope, thermal insulating clothing, and bulletproof vests.

It is for the use of Kevlar in bulletproof vests that she receives the most accolades, and she hears from police all over the country whose lives have been saved by the vests. In the first 20 years of use, about 2,000 police officers wearing Kevlar vests took a bullet and survived. These officers have formed the Survivors Club, a joint venture between Du Pont and the International Chiefs of Police Association. One man even brought his vest to Kwolek for an autograph.

Since her retirement, in addition to consulting, she has been giving lectures in schools about science and careers in science. She receives telephone calls from all over the country from students seeking help with homework, and children in her neighborhood come to interview her for their term papers.

She is a member of the American Chemical Society and American Institute of Chemists. Her research includes condensation polymers, high-temperature polymers, low-temperature interfacial and solution polymerizations, high-tenacity and high-modulus fibers and films, liquid crystalline polymers, and solutions and melts. Her photograph is included in *Scientific American* (March 1997) and *Chemical & Engineering News* (March 3, 1997).

***Bibliography:*** *American Men and Women of Science* 11–19; Rossiter, M., *Women Scientists in America*; Vare, E., *Mothers of Invention; Who's Who in Science and Engineering*, 3d ed., 1996–1997; *Who's Who in Technology Today* v. 3.

# LaBastille, Anne
(1938– )
***ecologist***

***Education:*** Student, University of Miami, Coral Gables, 1951–1953; B.S., Cornell University, 1955; M.S., Colorado State University, 1958; Ph.D. in biology, Cornell University, 1969
***Professional Experience:*** Wildlife tour leader, National Audubon Society, Palm Beach, Florida, 1955–1956; organizer and coleader, wildlife tours, Miami, Florida, 1955–1963; owner, comanager, and naturalist, Covewood Lodge, Big Moose, New York, 1956–1964; ranger, naturalist, Everglades National Park, Florida, 1964; assistant professor, Department of Natural Resources, Cornell University, 1969–1971, research associate, Laboratory of Ornithology, 1971–1973; freelance wildlife ecologist, consultant, writer, and photographer, 1971–
***Married:*** divorced

***Anne LaBastille*** is known as an ecologist who has done extensive work on preserving the wildlife habitat of several species of birds. One of her extensive projects was her work with a flightless bird known as the giant pied-billed grebe that was found at only one large lake in Guatemala. There was little known about this waterbird until she began the first systematic study of its characteristics, and no photographs or drawings of it had ever been made. She established a sanctuary for the birds and monitored the population, obtaining grants from the World Wildlife Fund and the Smithsonian Institution to support her work. She persuaded the Guatemalan government to designate the grebe's habitat as the country's first wildlife refuge, but even so, the population dwindled, at first because of an earthquake that drastically lowered the water level of the lake and then because of pollution from sewage discharging from the weekend houses and condominiums that surrounded the lake. The local people called her "Mama Poc," based on the name for the grebe used by the local Indians, and she records her experiences in her book *Mama Poc: Story of the Extinction of a Species* (1990).

After receiving her undergraduate degree from Cornell University, LaBastille spent her summers conducting wildlife tours in Florida and winters operating a lodge in upstate New York while working on her master's degree at Colorado State University. She returned to Cornell to obtain her doctorate and worked as a research associate in the internationally known Laboratory of Ornithology at Cornell while she started working freelance as a wildlife ecologist, consultant, and writer. She wrote two books under the name Anne LaBastille Bowes: *Birds of the Mayas* (1964), which comprises folktales and a guide to the birds of Yucatan and Guatemala, and *Bird Kingdom of the Mayas* (1967), which presents the folklore of birds.

After she was divorced, she built a log cabin on 22 acres of lakefront forestland in upstate New York where she lived alone with her dog for a time and still continues to reside. She describes her experiences living in the Adirondacks and the plants and animals she has met in the woods in the book *Woodswoman* (1976). Continuing this theme, she wrote of other women naturalists in *Women and Wilderness* (1980), in which she examines the historical role of women in wilderness living and activity. She profiles 15 women whose lives and professions have centered on the outdoors, including Eugenie Clark, Jane Goodall, Elizabeth Agassiz, and Delia Akeley. Some of the 15 are field scientists or are employed in technical jobs such as park rangers, marine and wildlife biologists, or professional environmentalists. Others merely enjoy hunting, fishing, or just being in the backwoods. In *Beyond Black Bear Lake* (1987), she reflects on her further experiences in upstate New York; this book might be considered "Woodswoman II."

The success of the first book and her environmental activities brought unwelcome interruptions to her wilderness life. Fans started arriving unannounced at her boat dock for a visit, and she received numerous requests for publications, interviews, and speeches. With the assistance of friends, she moved deeper into the Adirondacks woods to build another cabin, one that is a 45-minute walk and canoe ride from the first cabin. She reflects on her life there as well as her work as a consultant and conservationist. She has published an additional book, *The Wilderness World of Anne LaBastille* (1993), which consists of selections from never-before-published poems and short stories as well as color photographs. It includes her experiences as an Adirondack guide leading diverse groups in the wilderness. One reviewer describes the book as a congenial trip through poems, photographs, and stories about places and people one would like to visit.

LaBastille continues to lecture at universities, conduct research sponsored by the World Wildlife Fund and other organizations, and write for journals—one article being "How the King of Birds Was Chosen and Other Mayan Folk Tales" in the March–April 1997 issue of *International Wildlife.* She is a fellow of the Explorers' Club and a member of the American Ornithologists' Union and the National Audubon Society.

***Bibliography:*** *Contemporary Authors* v. 57–60 and CANR-8.

# *Lancaster, Cleo*
(1948– )
***physiologist***

***Education:*** B.S., Elizabeth City State University, 1971; M.S. in biomedical science, Western Michigan University, 1979

***Professional Experience:*** Research assistant, Brookhaven National Laboratory, 1971; research associate in ulcer research, Upjohn Company, 1971–1989, senior research associate in Safety Pharmacology, 1989–

***Cleo Lancaster*** is renowned as a pioneer in research leading to new ulcer therapies. She is an expert in the field of prostaglandin cytoprotection, which is the cellular protection of the gastric lining by the use of hormone-like fatty acids. At Upjohn Company, she has been developing experimental models of such gastrointestinal diseases as ulcers, diarrhea, pancreatitis, and colitis in order to discover natural or synthetic chemicals to treat such conditions. In the early 1970s, she studied the ulcer-causing effects of nicotine and linked smoking to duodenal ulcers in humans. She has compared the effects of ibuprofen versus aspirin as an irritant to the gastrointestinal tract, and she has also examined a steroid used in organ transplant patients that causes ulcers. Another irritant she has studied is the combination of alcohol and aspirin that causes ulcers.

Her major work, which spanned 1971–1991, revealed that prostaglandins can be used to inhibit gastric acid secretion. Prostaglandins are fatty acids produced in many parts of the body although initially it was thought they were produced only in the prostate gland. They stimulate muscle contraction and function with the autonomic and central nervous systems. Her research showed that prostaglandins stimulate mucus/bicarbonate production and increase the cell resistance of the stomach lining, thus preventing ulcers. She has two patents: one for a treatment of pancreatitis and the second for treating ulcers with oxolate derivatives, an asthma preparation. She also contributed to developing surgical techniques for the research of gastric secretion.

She has said that growing up on a farm influenced her appreciation for living things; that she learned comparative anatomy from their farm animals, which prevented her from being repulsed in anatomy or physiology classes. She was influenced to study biology by one of her high school teachers. Originally she planned to be a biology teacher, but in her third year of college she decided on a career in research because she wanted the challenge of discovery. She worked as a research assistant in radiation genetics at the Brookhaven National Laboratory the summer after she received her undergraduate degree, and she joined the Upjohn Company in the fall as a research associate in gastrointestinal, or ulcer, research. She received her master's degree in biomedical science while working for Upjohn. Since 1989 she has been a research associate in the Safety Pharmacology group, where she is responsible for the evaluation of new drugs and their effects on the gastrointestinal tract.

She received the Laboratory Special Recognition Award of the Upjohn Company. She is a member of the American Association for the Advancement of Science and the New York Academy of Sciences. Her research interests include experimental gastroenterology and the development of experimental models of ulcers, gastric lesions, pancreatitis, and surgical methods to study gastric secretion.

***Bibliography:*** *American Men and Women of Science* 17–19; *Notable Twentieth-Century Scientists.*

## *Leacock, Eleanor (Burke)*
(1922–1987)
***cultural anthropologist***

***Education:*** Student, Radcliffe College, 1939–1942; B.A., Barnard College, 1944; M.A., Columbia University, 1946, Ph.D. in anthropology, 1952

***Professional Experience:*** Research assistant, Department of Psychiatry, Cornell University Medical College, 1952–1955; lecturer, Department of Anthropology and Sociology, Queens College, 1955–1956; special consultant, U.S. Department of Health, Education and Welfare, 1957–1958; codirector of research, suburban interracial housing, Teaneck, New Jersey, 1958–1960; senior research associate, schools and mental health project, Bank Street College of Education, 1958–1965; lecturer, Department of History and Economics, Polytechnic Institute of Brooklyn, 1962–1963, associate professor, 1963–1967, professor of anthropology, 1967–1972; professor of anthropology, City College of New York, 1972–1987, chair, 1972–1975, 1978–1984

***Concurrent Positions:*** Part-time lecturer, City College of New York, 1956–1960, 1966–1967, and Washington Square College, 1960–1961

***Married:*** Richard Leacock, 1941, divorced 1962; James Haughton, 1966

***Children:*** 4

***Eleanor Leacock*** was a prominent cultural anthropologist known for her studies of the changing social and gender relations among the natives of Labrador, her reevaluations of the work of the Marxist Friedrich Engels, her contributions to feminist theory, and her analyses of racism in American education. However, along with other women who were married, had children, and were considered radicals, she was unable to secure a full-time job teaching anthropology for 11 years after receiving her doctorate. She was exposed to radical theories early in life, for her father was a literary critic and social philosopher and the family's social circle included artists, political radicals, and writers who lived in Greenwich Village. At Radcliffe and Barnard she was active in student radical groups. In 1944, when she applied for a position in Washington, D.C., to assist in the war effort, the Federal Bureau of Investigation denied her clearance.

When she accompanied her husband, a filmmaker, to Europe in 1948–1949, she began archival research in Paris on changes in the social organization of an Indian people in Labrador, the Montagnais-Naskapi (Innu), following the introduction of the fur trade. The next year she started her field research in Labrador, and her research changed the prevailing interpretation of private property in hunter-gatherer societies. She found that although the rights to trap in given places were privatized, the rights to gather, fish, hunt for food, and so on were still communal. It had been thought that these societies were patriarchal, but she found that there was flexibility in the relations between women and men. She recorded stories that the residents told her, typed them, and presented them to the tribes. Previously only Bible texts had been transcribed into their native language, Innu, for them.

Her first full-time position teaching anthropology began in 1963 when she was appointed associate professor of anthropology at the Polytechnic Institute of Brooklyn. This job security allowed her to devote increased effort to her writing and research, and she achieved recognition for her work on anthropology and education, on class and culture in urban schools, and on reevaluating the work of early Marxists. She was invited to be the chair of the Anthropology Department at City College in 1972 to rebuild the program there. She was extremely supportive of junior colleagues owing to her own struggles to be taken seriously as an anthropologist. She died unexpectedly in Honolulu in 1987 after suffering a stroke in Western Samoa where she was conducting fieldwork.

She published more than 70 papers and books; a partial list of her publications is included in *Women Anthropologists.* She was a fellow of the American Anthropological Association and the Society for Applied Anthropology and a member of the American Ethnological Society. An obituary with her photograph is included in the March 1990 issue of *American Anthropologist.*

***Bibliography:*** *American Men and Women of Science* 11–13; *Contemporary Authors* v. 122, 37–40R, and CANR 15; *Women Anthropologists.*

# Ledley, Tamara (Shapiro)
(1954– )
## climatologist

*Education:* B.S., University of Maryland, 1976; Ph.D. in meteorology, Massachusetts Institute of Technology, 1983
*Professional Experience:* Research associate, Rice University, 1983–1985, assistant research scientist, 1985–1990, senior faculty fellow in climatology/earth system science, 1990– ; associate research scientist, Texas A&M University, 1990–
*Concurrent Position:* Assistant director, Solar Institute, 1993; lecturer in space physics and astronomy, Rice University, 1990–1991, visiting lecturer in geology and geophysics, 1993
*Married:* Fred D. Ledley, 1976
*Children:* 2

*Tamara Ledley* is known for her research on the role of the polar regions in shaping climate on a wide range of time scales by examining how the interaction of atmosphere and sea with ice and oceans influences climate change. Her research has involved studies conducted in both Alaska and Antarctica, and she has also been active in presenting information on climatology to elementary school children as well as to university students. There is sometimes confusion about the difference between meteorology and climatology. Meteorology is the science dealing with the atmosphere and its phenomena, including weather and climatology. Climatology is the science that deals with the phenomenon of climate or climatic conditions.

Ledley was a member of the working team at the Alaska facility for the National Aeronautics and Space Administration (NASA) in 1988 and a member of the McMurdo Sound working team in 1990. She also was a participant in the workshop on the Arctic initiative of the Office of Naval Research in 1988 and a participant in the U.S. Global Change Research program's climate modeling forum in 1988. She was a fellow in scientific computing at the National Center for Atmospheric Research in Boulder, Colorado, in 1978 and served as a conservator for the Houston Museum of Natural Science from 1989 to 1990. She has worked at Rice University since 1983, and since Rice is located in Houston and NASA has a major science facility there, she has had access to people and projects on the cutting edge of events in climatology.

In her work of bringing science to the schools, she has participated in many outreach programs. She was the director of the weather project for a teacher training program at the George Observatory, Rice University, from 1990 to 1992; codirector of the Rice–Houston Museum of Natural Science Summer Solar Institute in 1993; and consultant for the elementary science curriculum project of the Houston Museum of Natural Science from 1989 to 1990. On the university level, she was a lecturer in space physics and astronomy at Rice from 1990 to 1991 and a visiting lecturer in geology and geophysics in 1993.

On the national level, she was appointed associate editor of the *Journal of Geophysical Research—Atmosphere* in 1993, one of the primary journals in her field. She became a member of the committee on global and environmental change of the American Geophysical Union in 1993, and she is a member of the American Association for the Advancement of Science, American Meteor Society, American Geophysical Union, and Ocean Society. Her research includes the role of the polar regions in shaping climate.

***Bibliography:*** *American Men and Women of Science* 18–19; *Who's Who in Science and Engineering*, 3d ed., 1996–1977; *Who's Who of American Women*, 20th ed., 1997–1998.

# *Leeman, Susan (Epstein)*
(1930– )
## *endocrinologist, physiologist*

***Education:*** B.A., Goucher College, 1951; M.A., Radcliffe College, 1954, Ph.D. in physiology, 1958; honorary degrees: D.Sc., State University of New York at Utica/Rome, 1992
***Professional Experience:*** Instructor in physiology, Harvard Medical School, 1958–1959; fellow in neurochemistry, Brandeis University, 1959–1962, senior research associate in biochemistry, 1962–1966, adjunct assistant professor, 1966–1968, assistant research professor, 1968–1971; assistant professor of physiology, Laboratory of Human Reproduction and Reproductive Biology, Harvard Medical School, 1972–1973, associate professor, 1973–1980; professor of physiology, Medical School, University of Massachusetts, 1980–1992, director, Interdepartmental Neuroscience Program, 1984–1992; professor of pharmacology, Boston University Medical School, 1992–
***Married:*** Cavin Leeman, 1957, divorced
***Children:*** 3

***Susan Leeman*** is considered one of the founders of the field of neuroendocrinology based on her research on peptides. She is renowned for her work with substance P and neurotensin, peptides that help govern the functioning of the nervous, endocrine, and immune systems. Neuroendocrinology is the study of the anatomical and physiological interactions between the nervous and endocrine systems. During the 1960s, when she was conducting research at Brandeis, she made a chance finding of a chemical that turned out to be substance P, which had been discovered in the 1930s but had never been isolated. She and her colleagues isolated and characterized the peptide. She was elected to membership in the National Academy of Sciences in 1991.

Substance P is a transmitter that is distributed throughout both the central and the peripheral nervous systems and the spinal cord. One of its functions is to stimulate the secretion of saliva, and it is important in neuroimmune interactions and seems to play a role in inflammatory responses. During her work with this peptide, Leeman also discovered another one, neurotensin, which is involved in the relaxation and contraction of the blood vessels. This peptide is found in both the central nervous system and the gastrointestinal tract. It may be involved in psychiatric disorders and, perhaps, regulation of the menstrual cycle.

After she received her undergraduate degree in physiology, she worked for a time in New York City before continuing her study of science. She explains that in the 1950s, women were not supposed to do anything. Both of her parents were college graduates, and her father was a prominent metallurgist. She became interested in neuroendocrinology in graduate school and continued her research throughout her career. Also while in graduate school she started her work on corticotropin, a hormone used in the treatment of rheumatoid arthritis and rheumatic fever. It was while she was trying to purify corticotropin at Brandeis that she made the chance finding of substance P.

She has received numerous awards, including the Excellence in Science Award of Eli Lilly and Company (1993), the Burroughs-Wellcome Visiting Professorship Award (1992), and the Fred Conrad Koch Award of the National Academy of Sciences (1994). She is a member of the Endocrine Society, Society for Neuroscience, American Association for the Advancement of Science, and American Physiological Society. Her research centers on neuroendocrinology. Her photograph is included in *Notable Twentieth-Century Scientists.*

***Bibliography:*** *American Men and Women of Science* 11–19; *Notable Twentieth-Century Scientists; Who's Who in Science and Engineering,* 2d ed., 1994–1995; *Who's Who of American Women,* 19th ed., 1995–1996.

# *Leopold, Estella Bergere*

(1927– )

## *paleoecologist*

***Education:*** Ph.B., University of Wisconsin, 1948; M.S., University of California, Berkeley, 1950; Ph.D. in botany, Yale University, 1955

***Professional Experience:*** Research botanist, Paleontology and Stratigraphic Branch, U.S. Geological Survey, Denver, 1955–1976; professor of botany and forest products and director of Quaternary Research Center, University of Washington, Seattle, 1976–1982, professor, Department of Botany and College of Forest Resources, 1982–1989, professor of environmental studies, 1989–1994, professor of botany, 1989–

***Concurrent Position:*** Adjunct professor, Department of Biology, University of Colorado, 1967–1976

***Estella Leopold*** is known as one of the leading authorities on paleoecology, which is the study of prehistoric organisms and their environments. She describes her work as comparing the pollen and spores that exist today with those found in rocks for a particular time period. In this way researchers try to determine the landscape and climate represented by fossils, which are probably the most-important evidence of environments of the past. She was elected to membership in the National Academy of Sciences in 1974.

She developed her interest in ecology in her childhood under the tutelage of her father, the conservationist and writer Aldo Leopold. Although they lived in Madison, Wisconsin, the family spent weekends on their farm 50 miles north of their home. The farm was not the usual type featuring corn and soybeans; instead, the family planted tree seedlings and restored an old cornfield back to the tall-grass prairie it was meant to be. All five Leopold children followed careers in science, and Estella and her two brothers, Starker and Luna, are all members of the National Academy of Sciences.

In reading about the Leopold family, it is somewhat confusing that Estella has the same name as her mother, Estella Bergere Leopold. The younger Estella received an undergraduate degree in botany from the University of Wisconsin, Madison, where her father taught wildlife management. After receiving her master's degree from the University of California, Berkeley, she hesitated to pursue a doctorate at the University of California, Los Angeles, because she heard that the professors there were hard on women students. On the advice of friends, she chose Yale University instead. Although she was the only woman graduate student in science there, she felt very comfortable in her situation.

Instead of pursuing a teaching position, she chose a career as a research paleoecologist with the U.S. Geological Survey in Denver. In her research in the Rocky Mountains, she found that extinction and evolution are highest in the middle of the continent because of the variable seasonal changes, while the coastal areas, which have more moderate climates, are able to sustain older species, such as the giant redwood. She was one of the leaders in the successful campaign to save Colorado's Florissant fossil beds, and in 1962, the National Park Service decided to designate the fossil beds as a national monument, but did not enact legislation. Meanwhile, developers started building recreational subdivisions in the park. In 1969, the Defenders of Florissant, Inc., persuaded the U.S. Congress to enact legislation to designate 6,000 acres for the national monument.

She retired from the Geological Survey in 1976 to direct the Quaternary Research Center at the University of Washington, Seattle (the Quaternary period, the present period of the earth's history, originated about 2 million years ago). She left the center in 1982 but remained with the university as professor of botany. She has served on many distinguished scientific committees on conservation and ecology and is a fellow of the American Association for the Advancement of Science (president, 1995) and of the Geological Society of America. She is a member of the American Quaternary Association (president, 1982–1984), Botanical Society of America, Ecological Society of America, and American Academy of Arts and Sciences. Her research includes late Cenozoic paleobotany, palynology, paleoecology, and paleoclimate; pollen and spore floras of the late Cenozoic age; and the history of western grasslands. Her photograph is included in *Science* (March 7, 1980).

**Bibliography:** *American Men and Women of Science* 11–19; Herzenberg, C., *Women Scientists from Antiquity to the Present;* Ireland, N., *Index to Women of the World . . . Suppl.; Notable Twentieth-Century Scientists;* O'Neill, L., *Women's Book of World Records and Achievements.*

# Lesh-Laurie, Georgia Elizabeth

(1938– )

## *developmental biology*

***Education:*** B.S., Marietta College, 1960; M.S., University of Wisconsin, 1961; Ph.D. in biology, Case Western Reserve University, 1966

***Professional Experience:*** Instructor in biology, Case Western Reserve University, 1965–1966; assistant professor of biological science, State University of New York at Albany, 1966–1968; assistant professor, Case Western Reserve University, 1969–1973, associate professor, 1974–1977, assistant dean, 1973–1976; professor of biology, Cleveland State University, 1977–1990, chair, Department of Biology, 1977–1981, dean, College of Graduate Studies, 1981–1986, dean, College of Arts and Sciences, 1986–1990, interim provost, 1989–1990; vice chancellor of academic affairs, University of Colorado, 1990–

***Married:*** 1969

**Georgia Lesh-Laurie** is renowned for her research on a drug that can be used in place of digitalis for the treatment of congestive heart failure. Digitalis, made from the purple foxglove plant, increases the heart's pumping power without increasing oxygen demand, but patients with kidney problems are unable to use it. Lesh-Laurie's stimulant is a protein found in the toxin of the hydra, a small freshwater cousin of the jellyfish, and the protein was discovered after people stung by jellyfish noticed a sudden neurological and cardiovascular response. Sponsored by the American Heart Association, she continued work in the 1980s on developing a drug incorporating the protein.

The hydra belongs to the phylum Cnidarian, which is characterized by a specialized stinging structure in the tentacles surrounding the mouth. The phylum includes hydra, jellyfish, sea anemones, and corals, and these invertebrates have a nematocyst, which is an organ consisting of a minute capsule containing an ejectable thread that causes a sting.

Early in her career Georgia Lesh-Laurie assumed administrative responsibilities in addition to her teaching and research. She served as assistant dean for three years at

Case Western Reserve, and at Cleveland State University, she was department chair, dean of the College of Graduate Studies, dean of the College of Arts and Sciences, and interim provost for a year. She moved to the University of Colorado as vice chancellor of academic affairs in 1990.

She is a member of the American Association for the Advancement of Science, American Society of Zoologists, Society for Developmental Biology, New York Academy of Sciences, and American Society for Cell Biology. Her research consists of the study of the neural control of developmental events in Cnidarian systems and the role of nematocyst products on the mammalian cardiovascular system.

***Bibliography:*** *American Men and Women of Science* 12–19; Stanley, A., *Mothers and Daughters of Invention.*

# *Levelt-Sengers, Johanna Maria Henrica*

(1929– )

***physicist***

***Education:*** B.Sc., University of Amsterdam, 1950, Drs, 1954, Ph.D. in physics, 1958; honorary degree: D.Sc., Technical University of Delft, 1992

***Professional Experience:*** Assistant, Van der Waals Laboratory, University of Amsterdam, 1954–1958, 1959–1963; research associate, instructor in theoretical chemistry, University of Wisconsin, 1958–1959; physicist, Heat Division, Institute of Basic Standards, U.S. National Bureau of Standards, 1963–1978, physicist and supervisor, Thermophysical Division, National Engineering Laboratory, 1978–1987, senior fellow, Thermophysical Division, National Institute of Standards and Technology, 1983–1995, emeritus 1995–

***Concurrent Positions:*** Visiting professor, University of Louvain, Belgium, 1971; visiting scientist, University of Amsterdam, 1974–1975

***Married:*** Jan V. Sengers, 1963

***Children:*** 4

***Johanna Levelt-Sengers*** is renowned for her research on critical phenomena and fluid mixtures. She is one of the two women in this volume who is a member of both the National Academy of Sciences and the National Academy of Engineering; she was elected to membership in the former in 1996 and the latter in 1992. The other person who has dual memberships is Mildred Dresselhaus.

In a letter to the author dated September 25, 1997, Levelt-Sengers said: "The honorary doctorates presented to my husband and me in 1992 at the Technical University of Delft, Netherlands, in the presence of the Queen of the Netherlands, formed the highest point in my career. This ceremony gave me recognition in my country of birth for my achievements in the U.S.A. Our joint election for these honors recognized the importance of our marriage to our professional success. Finally, receiving an honorary degree at the Technical University meant that my training as a physicist did not prevent me from having an impact on engineering."

She said that each time she was notified of her election, first to the National Academy of Engineering and second to the National Academy of Sciences, the initial reaction was disbelief; the second was a feeling of great pleasure and gratitude to the colleagues and supervisors who had prepared and carried through the nominations on her behalf. She said that both academies are acutely aware of the low number of women members but that they are making a special effort to encourage nominations of women.

She says the climate for women scientists at the National Bureau of Standards, now called the National Institute of Standards and Technology, is quite favorable. Even when she joined the National Bureau of Standards in 1963 there were highly respected women scientists there, some in leadership positions. She said that "young women should not fear to enter fields that have traditionally been male domains. If they are well prepared, willing to work hard, and enjoying their work, they can build satisfying careers in the fields of science and engineering, but probably in quite different areas than those I worked in. There is very little a woman cannot do once she sets her mind to it." The career picture in science is in a state of flux, and there are many new areas that women can consider.

She has received numerous awards, such as the Edward Uhler Condon Award of the National Bureau of Standards (1975), the Silver Medal Award (1972) and the Gold Medal Award (1978) of the Department of Commerce, and the Alexander von Humboldt Award (1991). Her research includes thermodynamic properties of fluids and fluid mixtures; critical phenomena in fluids; equation of state, theoretical and experimental; and supercritical aqueous systems. She is a fellow of the American Physical Society and a member of the American Society of Mechanical Engineers, American Institute of Chemical Engineers, American Chemical Society, and International Association for the Properties of Water and Steam (president, 1991–1991). She is listed as "Sengers" and "Levelt Sengers" in various sources. Some information was also supplied in a second letter to the author dated July 8, 1997.

***Bibliography:*** *American Men and Women of Science* 12–19; Herzenberg, C., *Women Scientists from Antiquity to the Present; Who's Who in America,* 51st ed., 1997; *Who's Who of American Women,* 20th ed., 1997–1998.

# *Linares, Olga Frances*

(1936– )

## *anthropologist*

***Education:*** B.A., Vassar College, 1958; Ph.D. in anthropology, Harvard University, 1964
***Professional Experience:*** Instructor in anthropology, Harvard University, 1965; lecturer in anthropology, University of Pennsylvania, 1966–1971; research scientist then senior scientist, Smithsonian Tropical Research Institute, 1973– ; research curator, Center for American Archaeology, Peabody Museum, Harvard University, 1974–
***Married:*** Martin H. Moynihan

*Olga Linares* is recognized for her research on the rural populations of western Africa and Central America. She is working in the area of economic anthropology among primarily agrarian populations and looks not only at the types of crops that are grown and marketed but also at the sexual division of labor. She examines the social, spatial, and temporal relations in archaeological perspective. She was elected to membership in the National Academy of Sciences in 1992.

The strength of her research can be seen in the book *Power, Prayer, and Production: The Jola of Casamance, Senegal* (1992). The central thesis is that ideology and production are part of the same system and any consideration of the division of labor—whether by gender, age, status, or ethnic identity—must take into account the influence of ideology. She compares three communities that are engaged in intensive wet-rice cultivation but structure their agriculture very differently. One is a non-Muslim community in which both men and women commune with spirit shrines, and relations between the generations and the sexes tend to be reciprocal and cooperative. Another community has adopted Islam and has divided production along territorial, generational, gender, and kinship lines. The third community also is Islamic and there is a strong Islamic community nearby; this group has more extreme inequality and social separation between the sexes and the generations. In each case, Linares examined the same set of factors: marriage and residence patterns, cropping and land tenure arrangements, the role of ritual and religious powers and duties, the organization of labor, the effects of introduced technologies, and the dynamics of social power and conflict.

After an appointment as a lecturer in anthropology at the University of Pennsylvania, she secured joint appointments with the Smithsonian Tropical Research Institute, first as a research scientist and then as a senior scientist, and with the Center for American Archaeology at the Peabody Museum of Harvard University as a research curator. She is a fellow of the American Association for the Advancement of Science and a member of the American Anthropological Association, African Studies Association, Royal Anthropological Association, and Latin American Studies Association. Her research centers on agrarian practices and political economy of western African and Central American rural populations and on human adaptations to the tropical forest, past and present.

***Bibliography:*** *American Men and Women of Science* 18–19.

# *Lippincott, Sarah Lee*
(1920– )
## *astronomer*

***Education:*** Student, Swarthmore College, 1938–1939; B.A., University of Pennsylvania, 1942; M.A. in astronomy, Swarthmore College, 1950; honorary degree: D.Sc., Villanova University, 1973

***Professional Experience:*** Research assistant in astronomy, Swarthmore College, 1942–1951, research associate, 1952–1972, lecturer, 1961–1976, director of Sproul Observatory, 1972–1981, professor, 1977–1981, emeritus professor of astronomy and emeritus director, Sproul Observatory, 1981–

***Concurrent Positions:*** Visiting associate astronomer, Lick Observatory, 1949, and California Institute of Technology, 1978

***Married:*** Dave Garroway, 1980, died

S***arah Lippincott*** is known for her research in astrometry, which is the branch of astronomy that deals with the measurement of the positions and motions of celestial bodies. One of her projects has been to look for extrasolar planets or planet-like companions to nearby stars. The Sproul Observatory has had a long-term program of tracing the motions of stars within five parsecs of the Earth to look for such perturbations. The data, going back an average of 50 years, are on photographic plates containing images of those stars; these are in the archives of the observatory. Lippincott found three stars that were candidates for having unseen companions.

In addition to her work at Swarthmore, she was a visiting associate astronomer at the Lick Observatory (1949) and at the California Institute of Technology (1978). She was a Fulbright fellow in France from 1953 to 1954 and a member of the French solar eclipse expedition to Oland, Sweden, in 1954. One of her students who has become famous is the cosmologist Sandra Faber. Lippincott spent her entire professional career at Swarthmore College, beginning as a research assistant and being promoted to research associate and then lecturer before becoming director of the Sproul Observatory. She was appointed to the faculty as professor of astronomy in 1977 and retired in 1981.

She has published numerous papers in scientific journals and is coauthor of the book *Point to the Stars,* of which three editions were published between 1963 and 1976. She is a member of the American Astronomical Society and International Astronomical Union (president, 1973–1976). Her research includes parallaxes of nearby stars; double stars, search for planetary companions to nearby stars, stellar masses, and chromosphere studies.

***Bibliography:*** *American Men and Women of Science* 11–19; *Contemporary Authors* v. 17–20R; *Who's Who in Technology Today* v. 5, *Who's Who in America,* 51st ed., 1997.

# *Liskov, Barbara Huberman*
(1939– )
## *computer scientist*

***Education:*** B.A. in mathematics, University of California, Berkeley, 1961; M.S. in computer science, Stanford University, 1965, Ph.D. in philosophy, 1968

***Professional Experience:*** Programmer, Mitre Corporation, 1961–1962; programmer, Harvard University, 1962–1963; research assistant, Stanford University, 1963–1968; member of technical staff, Mitre Corporation, 1968–1972; professor of computer science and engineering, Massachusetts Institute of Technology, 1972– , NEC professor of software science and engineering, 1984–

***Concurrent Positions:*** Consultant, Digital Equipment Company, Hewlett-Packard, NCR, Prime Computers, and BBN Corporation.

***Married:*** 1970

***Children:*** 1

*Barbara Liskov* is recognized as an expert on computer software, and her research is at the forefront of the field of computer software science and engineering for computer operating systems. In the 1990s, her papers covered such esoteric topics as dynamic programs for updating systems, providing high availability using lazy replication, disconnected operation in object-oriented database systems, controlling cyclic distributed garbage by controlled migration, fault-tolerant distributed garbage collection in a client-server object-oriented database, behavioral notion of subtyping, remote mobile objects in user interfaces and data storage, language-independent interface of a persistent object system, and the use of a modified object buffer to improve the write performance of an object-oriented database. She was elected to membership in the National Academy of Engineering in 1988.

The software with which she works obviously is not designed for personal computers. One problem with computer technology today is that while the computers being designed are increasingly faster and more diversified, the software available sometimes does not permit programmers to take advantage of the increased sophistication. This difficulty sometimes can cause interruptions in service, loss of data, or a total breakdown. For example, in 1997 when the America Online system overloaded because of a huge surge in customer use, the system crashed for several days. The managers in the company who were attempting to increase membership apparently did not anticipate the huge number of new members and had not arranged to increase the system's capacity. There were also problems in integrating new software into existing programs that were used for the system.

Liskov has a strong background in computer science. In addition to her formal education, she worked for Mitre Corporation for several years and has consulted for major computer hardware companies such as Digital Equipment and Hewlett-Packard. She holds a distinguished professorship at the Massachusetts Institute of Technology. In addition to publishing numerous papers in scientific journals, she is coauthor of two books: *CLU Reference Manual* (1981) and *Abstraction and Specification in Program Development* (1986). She is a member of the Institute of Electrical and Electronics Engineers and Association for Computing Machinery; she is a fellow of the American Academy of Arts and Sciences. Her research includes programming methodology, distributed computing, programming languages, and operating systems.

*Bibliography:* *American Men and Women of Science* 17–19; *Who's Who in Science and Engineering,* 2d ed., 1994–1995; *Who's Who of American Women,* 19th ed., 1995–1996.

# Long, Irene (Duhart)

(1951– )

### *aerospace physician*

*Education:* B.A. in biology, Northwestern University, 1973; M.D., St. Louis School of Medicine; M.S. in aerospace medicine, Wright State University School of Medicine, 1981

*Professional Experience:* Resident in general surgery, Cleveland Clinic, Mt. Sinai Hospital, Cleveland, and later Ames Research Center of National Aeronautics and Space Administration (NASA); chief, Occupational Medicine and Environmental Health Office, NASA Kennedy Space Center, 1982–

*Irene Long* is one of the highest-ranking professional women at the National Aeronautics and Space Administration (NASA). She is the first black female chief of the Occupational Medicine and Environmental Health Office, which means she is responsible for overseeing not only the health of the astronauts but also the health of some 18,000 workers, civil servants, and contractors at the Kennedy Space Center. Her office even administers physicals to employees. She works with a team of physicians to provide medical services to the astronauts in emergency cases, such as an aborted mission, and she oversees inspecting workspaces at the Kennedy Space Center to protect employees from exposure to various possible hazards—toxic chemicals, fire, decompression—when a spacecraft is launched. She coordinates the efforts of the Department of Defense, environmental health agencies, and the astronaut office when they work together to stage successful launches, as well as to prepare for emergency situations.

Long's staff also participates in the research projects that are performed by the astronauts by supplying technical expertise and providing equipment and laboratory facilities to the principal investigators who design the life sciences experiments that are placed aboard the shuttle. In her own research, Long has shown that people with the sickle-cell trait, which is different from the sickle-cell disease, should not be banned from flying. She found that the lower oxygen level does not cause the red blood cells of people with the trait to sickle, which can cause an extremely painful ailment because the sickle cells impede the flow of blood. Another area of research is her work with the Johnson Space Center's collection of medical data on the condition of astronauts, including the effects of space on the individuals' physiology and the consequences of weightlessness.

Her goal since childhood has been to be a medical officer on a space shuttle flight. At the age of nine, after seeing the reports of the space program on television, she told her parents she was going to have a career in aerospace medicine; she then spent Sunday afternoons with her father watching airplanes taking off and landing at Cleveland's airport. After she received her M.D. degree, she enrolled in the Wright State University School of Medicine to earn a master's degree in aerospace medicine, Wright State being one of the few schools that offer this degree. She says she has realized her dream of blending her love for medicine and aviation.

Long is proud of one of the programs she has helped create to encourage women and minorities to have careers in science and engineering, the Space Life Sciences Training Program. The goal is to encourage minorities and female college students to take part in space life sciences. Participants in the program spend six weeks at the Kennedy Space Center studying space physiology in plants, animals, and humans; learning how to develop experiments; and becoming acquainted with the basic concepts of teamwork. Her photograph is included in *Notable Twentieth-Century Scientists* and *Ebony* (September 1984).

***Bibliography:*** *Notable Twentieth-Century Scientists.*

# *Long, Sharon (Rugel)*

(1951– )

## ***developmental biologist, molecular biologist***

***Education:*** B.S., California Institute of Technology, 1973; Ph.D. in biology, Yale University, 1979

***Professional Experience:*** Research fellow, Department of Biology, Harvard University, 1978–1981; assistant professor, Department of Biological Science, Stanford University, 1982–1987, associate professor, 1987–1992, professor, 1992– ; investigator, Howard Hughes Medical Institute, 1994–

***Married:*** Harold J. McGee, 1979

***Children:*** 2

***Sharon Long*** is renowned for her studies in plant genetics. She identified and cloned the genes that allow bacteria to locate and enter certain plants; she has worked with the rhizobium bacterium that invades the roots of such legumes as alfalfa, soybeans, and peas and lives symbiotically with the plant, receiving moisture and protection from it and producing nitrogen for the plant's growth. Her specific contribution is genetically to alter the bacterium to make better invaders. Her research involves allowing the bacterium to invade other major food crops, which will enable farmers to reduce the amounts of nitrogen fertilizer that are spread on food crops and eventually are washed off by rain into streams and rivers. She was elected to membership in the National Academy of Sciences in 1993 as one of its younger members.

She has had a distinguished career in research. She received a Presidential Young Investigators Award of the National Science Foundation for 1984–1989 and a MacArthur fellowship for 1992–1997. She was cited as one of America's top 100 young scientists in *Science Digest* (December 1984). Business journals such as *Business Week* and *Fortune* are also interested in science news, and she was cited by *Fortune* (October 8, 1990) as one of America's hot young scientists.

Long rose quickly through the academic ranks. After an appointment as a research fellow at Harvard University, she was appointed an assistant professor at Stanford University in 1982, promoted to associate professor in 1987, and became a professor in 1992. She is currently also an investigator with the prestigious Howard Hughes Medical Institute. She is a fellow of the American Association for the Advancement of Science, American Academy of Arts and Sciences, and American Academy of Microbiology and a member of the Genetics Society of America, American Society of Plant Physiologists, American Society for Microbiology, and Society for Developmental Biology. Her research includes genetics and developmental biology of symbiotic nitrogen fixation in legumes, the role of plasmids in symbiosis, plant cell biology, and plant molecular biology. Her photograph is included in *Science Digest* (December 1984) and *Fortune* (October 8, 1990).

***Bibliography:*** *American Men and Women of Science* 15–19; Ireland, N., *Index to Women of the World . . . Suppl.;* Stanley, A., *Mothers and Daughters of Invention; Who's Who in America,* 51st ed., 1997; *Who's Who in Science and Engineering,* 3d ed., 1996–1977.

# Low, Barbara Wharton
(1920– )
**biochemist**

***Education:*** B.A., Oxford University, 1942, M.A., 1946, D.Phil. in chemistry, 1948
***Professional Experience:*** Research fellow, California Institute of Technology, 1946–1947; research associate, Harvard Medical School, 1948, associate in physical chemistry, 1948–1950, assistant professor, Harvard University, 1950–1956; associate professor of biochemistry, College of Physicians and Surgeons, Columbia University, 1956–1966, professor, 1966–1985, professor of biochemistry and molecular biophysics, 1985–1990, emeritus professor and special lecturer, 1990–
***Concurrent Position:*** Associate member, Laboratory of Physical Chemistry, Harvard University, 1950–1954
***Married:*** Metchie J. E. Budka, 1950, died 1995

*Barbara Low* is known both for her early research in penicillin and for her later work with proteins. In *Who's Who in America* she mentions her achievements, which include determination of the three-dimensional structure of penicillin and the structure determination of the protein implicated in neurological block. She is credited with discovery of the pi helix, and she was codeveloper of the use of heavy atoms in protein crystal structure determination. She introduced low-temperature studies for protein data collection, interdicted Polaroid photography of protein x-ray diffraction patterns, and established the probable binding site of snake venom neurotoxins to the acetylcholine receptor. More recent research includes studying curare-like toxins that interact with acetylcholine receptors. Curare is a resin-like substance that is derived from tropical plants of the genus *Strychnos.* Curare is used by Indians in South America for poison arrows, but in physiological experiments and medicine it is employed for arresting the action of the motor nerves.

Born and educated in England, Low moved to the United States in 1946 and became first a research associate at Harvard Medical School and then a faculty member at Harvard University. She received an appointment at the College of Physicians and Surgeons at Columbia University where she rose through the ranks to professor of biochemistry and molecular biophysics and was named emeritus professor in 1990. She has received many distinguished appointments such as senior research fellow of the National Institutes of Health (1959–1963), where she received a career development award (1963–1968); consultant for the U.S. Public Health Service; visiting professor at the University of Strasbourg and Tohoku University; and invited lecturer at the Chinese Academy of Science (1981) and at the Academy of Science, USSR (1988). She has published articles in chemical, biochemical, biophysical, and crystallographic journals.

She is a fellow of the American Academy of Arts and Sciences and a member of the American Association for the Advancement of Science, American Institute of Physics, American Society of Biological Chemists, American Crystallographic Association, Biophysical Society, and International Society on Toxinology. Her research includes x-ray crystal structure of nonenzyme proteins and peptides, particularly snake venom postsynaptic neurotoxins, cytotoxins, and membrane proteins; protein-protein interactions; prediction of protein conformation; curaremimetic toxins and their interaction with acetylcholine receptors; and choleic acids.

***Bibliography:*** *American Men and Women of Science* 11–19; *Who's Who in America,* 51st ed., 1997; *Who's Who of American Women,* 20th ed., 1997–1998; *World Who's Who in Science.*

# Lubchenco, Jane

(1947– )

## marine ecologist, conservation biologist

*Education:* B.A., Colorado College, 1969; M.S., University of Washington, 1971; Ph.D. in ecology, Harvard University, 1975; honorary degrees: D.Sc., Drexel University, 1992; D.Sc., Colorado College, 1993; D.Sc., Bates College, 1997

*Professional Experience:* Assistant professor of ecology, Harvard University, 1975–1977; assistant professor of zoology, Oregon State University, 1977–1982, associate professor, 1982–1988, professor, 1988, department chair, 1989–1992, distinguished professor, 1993–

*Concurrent Positions:* Principal investigator, National Science Foundation, 1976– ; research associate, Smithsonian Institution, 1978– ; science adviser, Ocean Trust Fund, 1978–1984

*Married:* Bruce A. Menge, 1971

*Children:* 2

*Jane Lubchenco* is an ecologist who is making an impact on research in marine environments. Her work has focused on marine plant–herbivore interactions, chemical ecology, predator-prey interactions, algal ecology, and life histories. She is also interested in biodiversity and sustainable ecological systems. She was elected to membership in the National Academy of Sciences in 1996.

It is remarkable that she has been able to accomplish so much when for 10 years, she was a half-time assistant professor at Oregon State University handling a full schedule of field research in Panama plus teaching, engaging in research, and participating in professional associations. It is even more remarkable that she was promoted to associate professor with tenure during this period.

After she and her husband had been married for several years, they sought employment at a research university where they could split a tenure-track faculty position, each working half-time, in order to combine family and career. They found such a position at Oregon State University. Many of the land grant universities, such as Oregon State, have such an arrangement for their agricultural extension people; as the Lubchencos explain in the April 1993 issue of *BioScience,* Oregon State split one tenure-track position into two separate, independent, and half-time tenure-track positions. After their children were in school, they increased their assignments to three-quarters of a faculty position for two years and then increased it again to full-time status.

Grant funds for research in their field decreased during that ten-year period, which meant enforcing strict economy. The university has since offered the same arrangement to three other couples, but the Lubchencos recommend that participants should ask for a one-and-a-half faculty position split into two three-quarter positions to allow time for all of their faculty and professional responsibilities. Jane and her husband endorse this arrangement as a method to attract more women into science and also to enhance overall faculty well-being and performance. There was a precedent for Jane to work part-time, as her mother was a pediatrician who practiced part time when her children were young, returning to a full-time career when the children were older.

Jane conducted field research in Panama from 1977 to 1983. She has received the Mercer Award of the Ecological Society of America for the best paper on ecology (1979) and has been president of the Ecological Society of America (1992–1993) and the American Association for the Advancement of Science (1997). She received a MacArthur Foundation fellowship in 1993.

Lubchenco has been active in national and international efforts in ecology. She helped draft the Sustainable Biosphere Initiative of the Ecological Society of America in 1991 and coauthored an article published in the July 25, 1997, issue of *Science* entitled "Human Domination of Earth's Ecosystems." In that article, the authors describe how human alteration of the earth is substantial and growing.

She is a fellow of the American Association for the Advancement of Science (president, 1996) and of the American Academy of Arts and Sciences. She is a member of the Ecological Society of America (president, 1992–1993), Phycological Society of America, American Society of Naturalists, and American Institute of Biological Sciences. Some of her papers in the years 1971–1977 were published under the name "Jane Menge." Her research includes evolutionary population and community ecology, biodiversity, conservation biology, ecological causes and consequences of global change; marine ecology; algal ecology; algal life histories, biogeography, chemical ecology, and sustainable ecological systems. Some information was supplied in a letter to the author dated August 8, 1997.

***Bibliography:*** *American Men and Women of Science* 14–19; *Notable Women in the Life Sciences; Who's Who in Science and Engineering,* 2d ed., 1994–1995; *Who's Who in Technology Today* v. 6.

# *Lubic, Ruth (Watson)*

(1927– )

***anthropologist, nurse-midwife***

***Education:*** Diploma, School of Nursing Hospital, University of Pennsylvania, 1955; B.S., Teachers College, Columbia University, 1959, M.A., 1961, Ed.D. in applied anthropology, 1979; certificate in nurse-midwifery, State University of New York at Brooklyn, 1962; honorary degrees: 3

***Professional Experience:*** Faculty member, School of Nursing, New York Medical College, and Maternity Center Association, State University of New York School of Nurse-Midwifery, Downstate Medical Center, 1955–1958; nurse, Memorial Hospital for Cancer and Allied Diseases, New York, 1955–1958; clinical associate, Graduate School of Nursing, New York Medical College, 1962–1963; general director, Maternity Center Association, 1970–1995, director, clinical projects, 1995–

***Concurrent Positions:*** Consultant in midwifery, nursing, and maternal and child health, Office of Public Health and Science, U.S. Department of Health and Human Services, 1995–

***Married:*** William J. Lubic, 1955

***Children:*** 1

***Ruth Lubic*** is known for her contributions to the public health field, particularly those related to childbearing women and their relatives, as she has been a driving force behind the expansion of the midwifery profession in the United States. In the early part of the twentieth century, most babies were born at home, often with the assistance of a lay midwife rather than a physician. By the middle of the century, almost all babies were delivered in hospitals by obstetricians. During World War II, army health insurance covered only hospital births, and for many years thereafter, few hospitals permitted midwives to deliver babies. However, the Maternity Center Association of New York was founded in 1918 as a nonprofit health agency dedicated to the advancement of education about childbearing and improving the care given to women during pregnancy and birth and after delivery. The center established a school of nurse-midwifery in 1931 that continues today.

During her nursing training, Lubic observed that maternity patients often were treated with condescension and insensitivity by the doctors and that often they did not receive the prenatal and postnatal information they needed. These observations contrasted with her own experience in 1959 when her obstetrician allowed her husband to be present in the delivery room and to remain there with her and their newborn child for an hour after birth. She received her certificate in nurse-midwifery from State University of New York at Brooklyn in 1962, but while working for the center, she realized that her limited knowledge of different cultures was barring her from responding adequately to the needs of some of her clients. Therefore, she entered the graduate program in applied anthropology at Columbia University's Teachers College and earned an Ed.D. degree in 1979. She had become director of the Maternity Center Association in 1970.

The childbearing centers that are operated by nurse-midwives attempt to humanize obstetric care and accommodate a demand for family-centered maternity care. They typically set up birthing rooms that feature fewer technical devices, such as monitors; encourage breast-feeding and keeping the mother and newborn in the same hospital room; and allow the father and other family members to be present during the delivery. Since such centers routinely accept only low-risk mothers and obstetricians are on hand for all deliveries to handle any unforeseen complications, the number of successful deliveries is high. The centers emphasize prenatal instruction for the family as well as for the mothers and offer normal postnatal counseling and assistance with recovery and infant care. A public health nurse visits the family the day after the mother leaves the hospital and at other times if necessary. Although nurse-midwife programs still receive criticism from some medical personnel and medical associations, they are gaining increased acceptance. In fact, many the traditional hospitals have adopted a number of the innovations such as birthing rooms and family participation as part of the general trend of humanizing medical care.

Lubic's father was a pharmacist, and during the Great Depression, many people sought medical advice from him rather than going to a physician. Ruth was encouraged to enter the nursing field by friends and relatives; after her father's death, she worked in the pharmacy, which her mother now operated, and entered nursing school at the age of 25 after saving enough money for tuition and expenses. After receiving her diploma, she worked in a hospital while taking night courses at Teachers College to earn her undergraduate degree in 1959.

She has received the Rockefeller Public Service Award from Princeton University (1981) and the Lillian D. Wald Spirit of Nursing Award from the Visiting Nurse Service of New York (1994). She is the first nurse ever to be honored with a MacArthur Foundation grant. She is coauthor of the book *Childbearing: A Book of Choices* (1987). She is a member of the Institute of Medicine of the National Academy of Sciences, the American Public Health Association, American College of Nurse-Midwives, and National Association of Childbearing Centers (president, 1983–1992). Her photograph is included in *Current Biography* (1996).

***Bibliography:*** *American Men and Women of Science* 15–16; *Current Biography 1996; Who's Who in America,* 51st ed., 1997; *Who's Who of American Women,* 20th ed., 1997–1998.

# Lubkin, Gloria (Becker)
(1933– )
***physicist***

***Education:*** B.A., Temple University, 1953; M.A. in physics, Boston University, 1957
***Professional Experience:*** Mathematician, Aircraft Division, Fairchild Stratos Corporation, 1954, and Letterkenny Ordnance Depot, U.S. Department of Defense, 1955–1956; physicist, technical research group, Control Data Corporation, 1956–1958; acting chair, Department of Physics, Sarah Lawrence College, 1961–1962; vice president Lubkin Associates, 1962–1963; associate editor, *Physics Today*, 1963–1969, senior editor, 1970–1984, editor, 1985–
***Married:*** Yale J. Lubkin, 1953, divorced 1968
***Children:*** 2

G***loria Lubkin*** is known for her professional manner of presenting the news of the physics profession for more than 25 years in *Physics Today*, the publication of the American Institute of Physics. She is an expert on science policy and has conducted several roundtables on issues in science that have been published in the journal, including problems such as "Science under Stress" published in the February 1992 issue. At that roundtable, the panel considered the problem that physicists spend more time looking for funding than doing the actual research. Another roundtable was "New Challenges for the National Labs" (February 1991), which consisted of a discussion about the future of America's government laboratories. "Physics Research in Industry" was the topic in February 1988; "Whither Now Our Research Universities?" in March 1995. In the last, panel members scrutinized the nation's research universities, which are having to redefine their objectives because of financial and social problems. These are substantial articles, each consisting of 14–18 pages.

Lubkin came to the journal with a solid background of experience. While working on her master's degree, she had worked as a mathematician for Fairchild Stratos Corporation and the U.S. Department of Defense, and she was a physicist with Control Data Corporation before serving as acting chair of the Physics Department at Sarah Lawrence College. She joined the staff of *Physics Today* as an associate editor and rose through the ranks to the position of editor. As such, she maintains a significant position in the male-dominated profession of physics.

She has received appointments to significant committees and commissions. She was a member of the Nieman Advisory Committee of Harvard University (1978–1982) after being a recipient of a Nieman fellowship (1974–1975). In the American Physical Society, she has been a member of the executive commission of the Forum of Physics and Society (1977–1978) and a member of the executive committee of the History of Physics Division (1983– ). She has been cochair of the advisory commission for the Theoretical Physics Institute of the University of Minnesota (1987–1988) and of the oversight committee (1989– ). She was also a consultant for the Center for the History and Philosophy of Physics of the American Institute of Physics (1966–1967).

In 1990, the University of Minnesota established the Gloria B. Lubkin Professorship of Theoretical Physics. She is a fellow of the American Physical Society and the American Association for the Advancement of Science and a member of the New York Academy of Science and the National Association of Science Writers. She is coauthor of the book *Reactor Handbook*, volume 3, part 8 (1962). Her research includes nuclear physics; science policy; and physics reporting, writing, and editing.

***Bibliography:*** *American Men and Women of Science* 11–19; Ireland, N., *Index to Women of the World . . . Suppl.*; *Who's Who in America*, 51st ed., 1997; *Who's Who in Technology Today* v. 5; *Who's Who of American Women*, 20th ed., 1997–1998.

# *Lucid, Shannon (Wells)*
(1943– )
***biochemist, astronaut***

***Education:*** B.S., University of Oklahoma, 1963, M.S., 1970, Ph.D. in biochemistry, 1971
***Professional Experience:*** Senior laboratory technician, Oklahoma Medical Research Foundation, 1964–1966, research associate, 1974– ; chemist, Kerr McGee, 1966–1968; astronaut, National Aeronautics and Space Administration (NASA), 1978– , missions STS 51-G, STS-34, STS-43, STS-58, STS-76/*Mir*
***Married:*** Michael F. Lucid
***Children:*** 3

***Shannon Lucid*** is known internationally for her world records: first, in 1996 she set the record for the most hours for a woman in space, and second, in 1996 she set a U.S. record for any astronaut by spending six months in space. She is the first woman to fly on the space shuttle three times and the first to be awarded the Congressional Space Medal of Honor (1996). She was a member of the first group of women to be selected for the space program in 1978, and she is one of 21 women who were inducted into the National Women's Hall of Fame in Seneca Falls, New York, in 1998. It is significant that she received this last honor because she believes that the opportunity for women to join the space program came from the women's movement, which actually began around the turn of the century at a meeting in Seneca Falls. The push for equal opportunity in all kinds of jobs in the 1970s paved the way for more organizations to hire women to fill responsible jobs.

Although she was not the first mother to fly in space, she probably had the oldest children when she did so. She says she became interested in space flight even before the United States had a manned space program and that she decided she wanted to be an astronaut when she was in the fifth or sixth grade. In common with many of the female astronauts, she planned her education carefully, earning degrees in chemistry and biochemistry before obtaining a position at the Oklahoma Medical Research Foundation. She knew what she wanted to do, prepared herself for it, and was ready to step in when the opportunity came along. Although she was slightly older than the other women astronauts, she did not hesitate to apply for the program.

Lucid's family has supported her at every step. She always has worked outside the home, and her children are accustomed to their mother's having a job. Her husband left his job and secured another as a mining engineer for a petroleum company in Houston when the family moved there. She had an unusual upbringing. Born in China, she was incarcerated in a prisoner-of-war camp with her missionary parents when she was only six weeks old, and the family returned to the United States as part of a prisoner exchange when she was a year old.

Although there were negative reactions among the NASA male personnel and the male astronauts when women were chosen for the program, many agreed later that the women do excellent work. Shannon said the women just want to be treated like the men in the program. They view themselves as ordinary people who happen to have very interesting jobs. Once she commented that although the women do the same work as the men, nobody asks the men about how their children feel about their work. Even in her *Mir* assignment, which was mainly to gauge the effects of long-term space flight on humans, she could not escape snide remarks from the Russian scientists. When she received the assignment to *Mir*, an executive officer of the Russian space agency said they would be happy to have a woman aboard the space station because women love to clean. Her Russian fellow cosmonauts said they liked to have her there because she made tea for them when they returned from their space walks.

During the 1980s, there was much publicity about the women astronauts, and there are numerous photographs of Lucid in many of the weekly news magazines. There was extensive coverage of her 1996 *Mir* mission, and many photographs of her appeared in the weekly news magazines as well as in the sources cited below. She is listed in the November–December 1996 issue of *Working Woman* as one of the "350 Women Who Changed the World 1976–1996."

***Bibliography:*** *American Men and Women of Science* 19; Herzenberg, C., *Women Scientists from Antiquity to the Present;* Oberg, A. R., *Spacefarers of the '80s and '90s;* O'Connor, K., *Sally Ride and the New Astronauts;* Read, P., *Book of Women's Firsts;* U.S. National Aeronautics and Space Administration, *Astronaut Fact Book; Who's Who in Science and Engineering,* 3d ed., 1996–1977; *Who's Who of American Women,* 20th ed., 1997–1998.

# *Lurie, Nancy (Oestreich)*
(1924– )
***anthropologist***

***Education:*** B.A., University of Wisconsin, Madison, 1945; M.A., University of Chicago, 1947; Ph.D. in anthropology, Northwestern University, 1952; honorary degree: LL.D, Northland College, 1976

***Professional Experience:*** Instructor in anthropology and sociology, University of Wisconsin, Milwaukee, 1947–1949, 1951–1952; substitute instructor in anthropology, University of Colorado, 1950; research associate, Peabody Museum, Harvard University, 1954–1956; lecturer in anthropology, Rackham School, University of Michigan, 1957–1959, lecturer, School of Public Health, 1959–1961, assistant professor, 1961–1963; associate professor of anthropology, University of Wisconsin, Milwaukee, 1963–1967, professor, 1967–1972, department chair, 1967–1972; cultural anthropologist, Milwaukee Public Museum, 1972–

***Concurrent Positions:*** American Association for the Advancement of Science grant, National Archives, 1953–1954; adjunct faculty member, University of Wisconsin, Milwaukee, 1972–

***Married:*** Edward Lurie, 1951, divorced 1963

***Nancy Lurie*** is a cultural anthropologist known for her studies of North American Indians and her work in applied and action anthropology (action anthropology is defined as anthropological research that is combined with helping to identify and solve community problems). Her work centers on the Winnebago, and she was adopted by a member of that tribe, Mitchell Redcloud, Sr., whom she interviewed during the course of her graduate research. Her adoption gave her an entrée to Redcloud's family when she later conducted extensive research into the role of Native American women, whom she felt were ignored in most histories of Native Americans. One of her books—*Mountain Wolf Woman, Sister of Crashing Thunder* (1961)—consists of an autobiography of one of Redcloud's family members. As part of her action anthropology, Lurie consults with and acts as an expert witness for law firms that represent Indian clients before the U.S. Indian Claims Commission.

She developed an early interest in anthropology after her father took her at the age of eight to meet the anthropologists at the Milwaukee Public Museum to learn about American Indians. As soon as she was old enough to ride the public transportation alone, she spent many hours at the museum and worked in the Anthropology Department as a volunteer. In the summer between her junior and senior years of college she conducted her first fieldwork among the Wisconsin Winnebago; there was very little information about this group available at the time. She continued her research on the Winnebago in graduate school on the topics of child care and training. Her first employment was in a newly created position, instructor in anthropology at the University of Wisconsin, Milwaukee, while she continued her studies toward her doctorate. Her graduate thesis compared cultural change in the Nebraska and Wisconsin enclaves of the Winnebago. Her work as an expert witness before the U.S. Indian Claims Commission has usually involved land questions, for such hearings require ethnohistorical research and testimony concerning tribal identities, boundaries, land use, and occupancy.

She met and married her husband while she was attending graduate school. She first obtained a position as lecturer in anthropology at the University of Michigan. Because of nepotism rules (her husband held a position in the History Department at Michigan), she was unable to secure a faculty position; after her husband left the university, she was able to secure a regular appointment. During the late 1950s and early 1960s, she collaborated on research with June Helm on the northern Athabaskan Indians, studying the Dogrib settlements in the Canadian Northwest. Among her action anthropology projects, several involved the Winnebago and Menominee tribes. In 1972 she changed direction in her career and left the university for a full-time position as curator and head of the anthropology section of the Milwaukee Public Museum, the first woman to head one of the museum's scientific sections.

Her work has done much to dispel stereotypical notions about American Indians. She is conscious of the political nature of anthropological work and its consequences. She reveals much about the desires of the people to live within their value systems and at the same time respects the desire of individuals who wish to assimilate into the larger society. She views herself as a consultant to the Native Americans and respects their control over information concerning them. She has received numerous honors and awards. She is a fellow of the American Anthropological Association (president, 1983–1985) and a member of the American Association for the Advancement of Science, American Ethnological Society, and Society for Applied Anthropology. Her research includes North American Indians, especially ethnology and ethnohistory; action anthropology; ethnohistory; and museology. A partial list of her publications is included in *Women Anthropologists.*

***Bibliography:*** *American Men and Women of Science* 11–13; *Contemporary Authors* v. CANR-16 and 1–4R; *Women Anthropologists.*

# McCammon, Helen Mary (Choman)

(1933– )

## *geologist, marine biologist*

***Education:*** B.Sc., University of Manitoba, 1955; M.S., University of Michigan, 1956; Ph.D. in geology, Indiana University, 1959

***Professional Experience:*** Research technician in stratigraphy, Manitoba Department of Mines and Natural Resources, 1952–1959; lecturer in geography, University of North Dakota, 1961; assistant professor of geology, Department of Earth Science, University of Pittsburgh, 1963–1968, associate professor, 1968; visiting associate professor of geology, Department of Geology, University of Illinois at Chicago, 1968–1970; research associate in geology, Field Museum of Natural History, Chicago, 1969–1972; director of environmental science, Environmental Protection Agency, Boston, 1973–1976; senior oceanography and marine scientist, Environmental Research Division, U.S. Department of Energy, 1977–1979, director, 1979–1991, deputy director of Environmental Science Division, 1991–

***Married:*** Richard B. McCammon, 1956

***Children:*** 2

***Helen McCammon*** is a geologist who is also known for her work in marine physiology and ecology. Like many scientists, her research requires broad interdisciplinary knowledge. Currently she is deputy director of the Environmental Science Division of the U.S. Department of Energy, and her responsibilities include overseeing ecological research and overseeing the division's budget. Prior to that she was the senior oceanography and marine scientist in the same agency. Her background includes considerable experience in research and teaching geology in several universities plus a stint as a geologist at the Field Museum of Natural History in Chicago. However, her research included studies of living animals as well as terrestrial and marine environments, the usual subjects of geologists.

After she completed her dissertation on paleontology for her doctorate in geology, she decided to study how marine organisms live today before trying to interpret how they lived in the past and started to research living invertebrates, especially brachiopods. They were common 300 million years ago and can still be found in New Zealand, the Antarctic, and other cold-water regions. Her fieldwork took her to many of these places, but because geology is a male-dominated field, she had problems in obtaining funding and having her papers published. For example, the standard description of the food pyramid is that lesser animals are eaten by more-advanced animals in the food chain. McCammon's experiments indicated that this was not the case with brachiopods, but her paper on the topic was not given the award for the best paper of the year because receiving the award would be more valuable to a man's career than to a woman's.

She also faced discrimination at the University of Illinois, Chicago when the department head decided to discontinue her salary in order to hire a man and asked her to continue teaching as an unsalaried faculty member. Her husband was a faculty member at the university at the time, but her position had been only that of a visiting associate professor. She refused to accept the arrangement and accepted a position at the Field Museum of Natural History instead. However, throughout her career she did receive strong research support from many male colleagues in her department and other departments in the universities in which she worked.

She reports that her husband's support was a valuable asset during the times of professional stress, and he also shared the responsibility of raising their two children. The couple worked at the same location throughout most of their marriage. Helen always hired a full-time housekeeper when the children were small, and whenever she received a raise in salary, she would increase the housekeeper's wages because she wanted to give other women the breaks she wanted for herself. Although her relatives criticized her career, her husband supported her work. She said that one result of her working was that the children learned to be self-reliant and helped with the chores when they were growing up. Both she and her husband involved the children in their research, and whenever they went to biological stations, the children helped by collecting animals to study and assisted in the laboratory.

For several years the family spent considerable time commuting. Helen commuted from Boston to Chicago and Washington, D.C., where her husband was working for three years. During that time, her husband and children went to New Zealand for a year, and she visited them there. She advises women to go after the best jobs, not the ones with the least resistance where one will be paid peanuts. Many women build fences around their opportunities, citing family or other responsibilities; in her own career, when she was moving from the university and research to government and management, she sought professional job counseling. She felt the advice was so valuable that she has conducted job-hunting and resume-writing seminars for women in geology. She has also given workshops for women geologists on how to interview for positions, training them how to answer embarrassing questions although, supposedly, such questions no longer can be asked.

McCammon is a fellow of the American Association for the Advancement of Science and a member of the American Geological Institute, American Society of Zoologists, Oceanic Society, and American Society of Limnology and Oceanography. Her research includes the impact of energy activities in coastal oceans and terrestrial environments ranging from arctic tundra to temperate forest and desert regions as well as marine physiology and ecology. Her photograph is included in A. Fins's *Women in Science.*

***Bibliography:*** *American Men and Women of Science* 11–13, 18–19; Fins, A., *Women in Science; Who's Who of American Women,* 19th ed., 1995–1996.

# McClellan, Catharine
(1921– )
*anthropologist*

*Education:* B.A., Bryn Mawr, 1942; Ph.D. in anthropology, University of California, Berkeley, 1950

*Professional Experience:* Ethnographer, National Museum of Canada, 1950–1951; visiting assistant professor of anthropology, University of Missouri, 1952; assistant professor, University of Washington, Seattle, 1952–1956; assistant professor and department chair, Barnard College, Columbia University, 1956–1961; associate professor, University of Wisconsin, Madison, 1961–1965, professor, 1965–1973, Bascom Professor of Anthropology, 1973–

*Married:* John Hitchcock, 1974

*Catharine McClellan* is a cultural anthropologist who is known as an expert on the cultural history of the peoples of Alaska and the Yukon Territory. She gathered the oral literature and life histories of Arctic and subarctic peoples for more than 35 years. Her research on Native Americans began when she was still an undergraduate, when she began studying under anthropologist Frederica de Laguna at Bryn Mawr and worked with her for a number of years. While in graduate school, she made an ethnographic survey of the natives of the Yukon Territory for the National Museum of Canada, which involved being the first U.S. researcher to use the Hudson Bay Company's newly opened archives in London. After receiving her graduate degree, she spent the summer as de Laguna's assistant conducting archaeological and ethnological investigations of the Tlingit Indians in Angoon, Alaska. The following year she did ethnographic work in the Yukon Territory of Canada.

While on the faculty of the University of Washington, Seattle, she and de Laguna studied the Yakutat Tlingit and the Atna Athabaskans of Copper River, Alaska, and made an archaeological survey of the Taku River in British Columbia. Prior to joining Barnard College, McClellan spent six months with the Alaskan Inuit for the U.S. Public Health Service. While at the University of Wisconsin, she gathered the oral traditions and cultural history of northern Athabaskans.

Her research is characterized by time-intensive fieldwork, exhaustive data collection, and an avoidance of using theoretical models too exclusively. She is described as having the ability to see Indian culture in Indian terms. Her criteria for good fieldwork requires multiple visits, corroborative evidence, meticulous detail, and repeated participant observation of cultural events. She impresses her students with their ethical responsibilities toward the groups they study. For example, she has written very little on witchcraft because that is a taboo subject among her informants. She examined the first encounters of the Athabaskans with whites and found that the natives' stories about the first encounters provide an additional context for how the Yukon Indians perceive their world. She has also looked at why access to major sources of power among the southern Yukon Indians differ for women and men.

Unlike many women anthropologists of her generation, McClellan does not believe that being a woman restricted her career options or limited the nature of her anthropological work. Although she served on various committees in the 1970s that addressed women's rights, she was not involved in the organized feminist movement. She did not experience any restrictions in her fieldwork; in fact, she found that being a woman was an advantage. During the 1940s and 1950s, white males in the Yukon were viewed as game wardens or agents of the government, but white women usually were viewed as missionaries or schoolteachers. She sometimes found herself in the role of the model white woman serving tea to visiting dignitaries in exchange for the freedom she was given to conduct her research.

Her parents provided a private school education for their four children. They encouraged Catharine's interest in botany and the natural world and sent her to Bryn Mawr, which her mother and older sister also had attended. Prior to World War II, Catharine and several other students and faculty received training from the U.S. Navy, and during the war, she worked for the navy in communications intelligence and ended her service with the rank of lieutenant in the naval reserve. She received her doctorate under the GI Bill.

She is a fellow of the American Association for the Advancement of Science and the American Anthropological Association. She is a member of the American Ethnological Society (president, 1965) and Society for American Archaeology. Her research has focused on the cultural history of northwestern North America; a partial list of her publications is included in *Women Anthropologists.*

***Bibliography:*** *American Men and Women of Science* 11–13; *Women Anthropologists.*

# *Maccoby, Eleanor (Emmons)*
(1917– )
***psychologist***

***Education:*** Student, Reed College, 1934, 1936; B.S., University of Washington, Seattle, 1939; M.A., University of Michigan, 1949, Ph.D. in psychology, 1950; honorary degrees: D.Sc., University of Cincinnati, 1975, and Russell Sage College, 1977

***Professional Experience:*** Study director, Division of Program Surveys, U.S. Department of Agriculture, 1943–1946; study director, Survey Research Center, University of Michigan, 1946–1948; lecturer, then researcher, Laboratory of Human Development, Department of Social Relations, Harvard University, 1950–1958; associate professor of psychology, Stanford University, 1958–1966, professor, 1966–1987, department chair, 1973–1976, Barbara Kimball Browning Professor, 1979–1987, professor emeritus 1987–

***Married:*** Nathan Maccoby, 1938, died 1992

***Children:*** 3

***Eleanor Maccoby*** is recognized as one of the prominent and influential psychologists in developmental and social psychology. Her landmark studies of the socialization of young children and the critical dimensions of their social behavior influence research today, and her reviews of the research and theories of gender differences have significantly influenced the direction of later research. She was elected to membership in the National Academy of Sciences in 1993.

In 1966, she edited a book, *The Development of Sex Differences,* on the differences in the development of male and female children, and the chapter she wrote explored the reasons boys and girls perform differently on intellectual tests. A sequel to this book was her landmark study, *The Psychology of Sex Differences* (1974), in which she and her coauthor attempted to bring objectivity to the research on gender-related studies. They examined about 1,600 studies and developed the theory that gender-typed behavior is a joint product of biological predispositions, social shaping, and cognitive self-socialization processes. They said there was no evidence that girls are more social than boys, that girls are more suggestible than boys, or that girls lack the motivation to achieve. In assessing the validity of the most widely held beliefs about sex differences, they concluded four were fairly well established: girls have greater verbal ability than boys, boys excel in visual-spatial ability, boys excel in mathematical ability, and males are more aggressive. This book was immediately controversial, but it was recognized as the first step toward a scientific investigation of sex differences.

Maccoby continued her interests in children's socialization and development differences with a study of children from birth to age six. In her book *Social Development* (1980), she reported that family socialization processes influence, and are influenced by, the sequences of the children's development changes and that children's development is limited by the nature and effect of parent-child interactions. She emphasized the importance that the partners in a relationship, including parent-child relations, be willing to be influenced by the other. In the late 1980s, she conducted another study of the family by examining a large group of divorcing families. The results of this study were published as *Dividing the Child: Social and Legal Dilemmas of Custody* (1992). Her most recent book on the topic is *The Two Sexes: Growing Up Apart, Coming Together* (1998), in which she explores how individuals express their sexual identity at successive periods of their lives and in different social contexts.

She did not have the average upbringing for girls of her age. Her parents permitted her to be a tomboy, climbing trees and playing marbles, and when she caddied for her father at the local golf course, she pretended she was a boy. Her parents were members of the Theosophical Society, which advocated a vegetarian diet and interests in spiritualism and extrasensory perception (ESP). However, the discovery in a high school experiment with a set of ESP cards used for mind reading that the cards contained subtle markings steered her toward a no-nonsense approach to life.

She received a one-year scholarship to Reed College but did not have funds to continue, and she worked as a secretary for a year before returning to Reed where she took her first course in psychology. She was so impressed with the subject that she transferred to the University of Washington, Seattle, for further study. In the fall of her senior year she married a fellow student, Nathan Maccoby, and the couple moved to Oregon State College where her husband taught for one year. In 1940, they moved to Washington, D.C., where Nathan worked for the U.S. Civil Service Commission, and Eleanor obtained a position with the noted Rensis Likert in the Division of Program Surveys of the Department of Agriculture. There she gained experience in applied psychology by conducting public opinion surveys of wartime programs such as fuel oil rationing and the sale of war bonds. Likert moved his organization to the University of Michigan as the Institute for Social Research while Eleanor completed the work in Washington for the group. She later joined the Survey Research Center at Michigan while working on her doctorate.

After her husband had obtained his doctorate at Michigan, the couple moved to Boston University where Nathan had received an appointment. Eleanor conducted research for her thesis at B. F. Skinner's laboratory in the Psychology Department at Harvard University. When she received her doctorate, she was a lecturer in the Department of Social Relations at Harvard and then joined the Laboratory of Human Development there to conduct interviews of mothers for a socialization study on child-rearing practices. When the major investigator left the department, she was assigned to teach his courses in child psychology. She and her husband adopted a second child and, later, a third, so she worked half-time for a number of years. The couple moved to Stanford University for a one-year project, but both were offered faculty appointments there, she in the Psychology Department and he in communications (because of nepotism rules, the couple could not work in the same department). It was at Stanford that Eleanor began her work on gender studies.

She has received numerous prizes, such as the distinguished scientific contributions award of the American Psychological Association (1988), the Kurt Lewin Memorial Award (1991), and the Gold Medal Award for Life Achievement in Psychological Science of the American Psychological Association (1996). She has published more than 100 papers, books, and reports. She is a fellow of the Society for Research in Child Development (president, 1981–1983) and the American Psychological Association. She is a member of the Social Science Research Council and American Academy of Arts and Sciences. Her photograph is included in *Psychology Today* (November 1987), *Journal of*

*Social Issues* (summer 1992), and *American Psychologist* (April 1989 and August 1996).

***Bibliography:*** *American Men and Women of Science* 11–13; *Contemporary Authors* v. 113; Ireland, N., *Index to Women of the World . . . Suppl.; Who's Who in America,* 51st ed., 1997; *Who's Who of American Women,* 20th ed., 1997–1998; *Women in Psychology.*

# *McFadden, Lucy-Ann Adams*

(1952– )

### *astronomer, geophysicist*

***Education:*** B.A., Hampshire College, 1974; M.S., Massachusetts Institute of Technology, 1977; Ph.D. in geology and geophysics, University of Hawaii, 1983

***Professional Experience:*** Research associate, Institute of Astronomy, University of Hawaii, 1977–1978; research assistant, Planetary Geoscience Division, Hawaii Institute of Geophysics, 1978–1983; research associate, Department of Geology, University of Maryland and Goddard Space Flight Center, National Aeronautics and Space Administration (NASA), 1983–1984, research associate, astronomy program, University of Maryland, 1984–1986, assistant research scientist, astronomy program, 1984–1986 and 1986–1987, planetary astronomy program, 1985; assistant research scientist, California Space Institute, University of California, San Diego, 1987–

***Concurrent Positions:*** Principal investigator, planetary geology program, NASA, 1984– ; National Science Foundation visiting professor, University of Maryland, 1992–1994

***Married:*** Gregory S. McFadden, 1982

***Children:*** 2

***Lucy-Ann McFadden*** is recognized as a planetary scientist and a specialist in remote sensing. In recent years she has specialized in searching for earth-approaching asteroids and dead comets that are formed elsewhere in the solar system. Books and movies that provide fictional accounts of unknown objects from outer space striking the earth have been quite popular with the general public, and some authors even suggest using laser beams to destroy such objects that seem to imperil the earth.

Her research involves determining the surface composition of planet-crossing asteroids to understand their nature, source, and evolution. She studies the relationship between asteroids and comets based on the composition of solid components, and she also studies the reflectance properties of meteorites as a means of developing interpretive techniques of remotely measured spectra of asteroids and comets. She uses ultraviolet spectroscopy to determine the composition of comets and examines the applications of automation techniques for space science.

McFadden was a member of a scientific program that scans the skies for near-earth objects. As she explains in an article in the August 1992 issue of *Astronomy,* between 1,500 and 2,000 asteroids and dead comets roam space near the earth. Most of them pass earth at high speed millions of miles away, but those that come closer give astronomers a method for understanding the solar system's past. The small bodies in the inner solar system contain primarily rock and metal while those in the outer solar system contain ices and dark, carbon-based compounds.

Dead comets and asteroids are difficult to see because they do not give off the long, glowing tails that new comets do, but astronomers are interested in tracking all objects—there is a theory that a meteor or an asteroid struck the earth and caused the demise of the dinosaurs and many other species 65 million years ago—and scanning the skies takes place every month for two weeks during the dark of the moon using the Schmidt telescope atop Mt. Palomar in California. Two teams take turns observing to search systematically for faint, fast-moving objects. Gene and Carolyn Shoemaker, members of one team, first identified the Shoemaker-Levy comet that impacted Jupiter during their routine observations.

The study of near-earth asteroids is important because their composition tells about the material the solar system was formed from. The difference in composition among various types indicates how material was spread through the solar system while it was forming, and by bouncing radar beams off their surfaces, astronomers can determine the sizes, shapes, and compositions of the objects. McFadden has published numerous papers on the characteristics of the objects that she has studied and also participated in the observations of the Shoemaker-Levy comet. She has been the principal investigator of NASA's planetary geology program since 1984, which has included observations of Mars, the moon, and other planets. Having previously worked at the University of Maryland and the Goddard Space Flight Center, one of the principal space-observation centers, she now works at another principal observation center, this one at the California Space Institute at the University of California, San Diego.

She is a member of the American Association for the Advancement of Science, American Astronomical Society, American Geophysical Union, and Meteoritical Society ("meteoritical" refers to meteors).

***Bibliography:*** *American Men and Women of Science* 16–19; *Who's Who of American Women*, 19th ed., 1995–1996.

# *McNutt, Marcia Kemper*
(1952– )
***geophysicist***

***Education:*** B.A., Colorado College, 1973; Ph.D. in earth science, Scripps Institution of Oceanography, 1978
***Professional Experience:*** Visiting associate professor, University of Minnesota, 1978–1979; geophysicist, U.S. Geological Survey, 1979–1982; assistant professor, Department of Earth Science, Massachusetts Institute of Technology, 1982–1986, associate professor, 1986–1988, professor, 1989– , Griswold Professor, 1991–
***Married:*** 1978
***Children:*** 3

*Marcia McNutt* is renowned for her research on plate tectonics using a variety of techniques including the Geosat global-positioning satellite. She is particularly known for her work on mapping the ocean floor and measuring the depth of the ocean. Plate tectonics, a science that developed about 1965–1970, is the theory of global tectonics in which the lithosphere is divided into a number of crustal plates, each of which moves on the plastic asthenosphere more or less independently to collide with, slide under, or move past adjacent plates. The lithosphere is the solid portion of the earth, as distinguished from the atmosphere; the asthenosphere is the region below the lithosphere and is variously estimated to be from 50 to several hundred miles thick; the rock is less rigid than that above and below but rigid enough to transmit transverse seismic waves.

The study of plate tectonics seeks to explain how the continents were formed and to predict how the plates will move into new patterns. Although geologists have mapped much of the land portion of the earth, data on the oceans are still being revealed. One problem has been that data have been classified as secret in the United States owing to the military requirements of the U.S. Navy. The data that have been released can indicate new locations for fishing or for oil drilling as well predicting the future activity of underwater volcanoes.

McNutt has worked particularly on mapping areas of the southern oceans, which had remained uncharted because they are far from shipping lanes and not of strategic importance from the military standpoint. The standard method has been to use echo sounders by deploying entire arrays of acoustic transceivers on the hulls of ships to measure the ocean depth in a swath several kilometers wide. The data are useful because they can indicate what offshore areas of Africa were contiguous to known oil-rich basins off Brazil when the continents separated 160 million years ago. McNutt has improved this research by using highly sensitive radar altimeters in earth orbit to sense minute changes in sea level caused by the gravitational attraction of topography on the seafloor; the radar altimeters measure the water density by hitting the water/rock interface on the ocean floor. The measurements obtained by the echo sounders and by the radar altimeters provide similar readings, but the orbiting altimeters provide a much higher resolution than the echo sounders.

A few years ago, the Department of Defense finally released the previously classified Geosat altimetry data. Researchers from the Scripps Institution of Oceanography and the National Oceanic and Atmospheric Administration (NOAA) converted the raw data into usable form and placed the results in the public domain via the Internet; they also provided the software package to access the data on the same source. However, for several years now, the European ERS-1 satellite has returned publicly available data on the oceans, of comparable resolution and accuracy to that obtained by Geosat.

McNutt received the James B. MacElwane Medal of the American Geophysical Union in 1988, an award that recognizes significant contributions to geophysics by a young scientist. She is or has been a member of the National Aeronautical and Space Administration (NASA) Science Steering Group Geopotential Research Mission (1978– ), the Committee on Geodesy of the National Research Council (1982–1984), the Geodynamics Committee, (1984–1987), and the committee on earth science, (1987– ). She is also a member of the American Geophysical Union. Her research includes studies of long-term rheology of the earth's crust and upper mantle using gravity and topography data, isotasy, paleomagnetism of seamounts, and thermal modeling of the lithosphere. Her photograph is included in *U.S. News & World Report* (December 30, 1991), and she was featured on the Public Broadcasting System's television series *Discovering Women* in April 1995.

***Bibliography:*** *American Men and Women of Science* 15–19; *Who's Who in America,* 51st ed., 1997; *Who's Who of American Women,* 20th ed., 1997–1998.

# *McSherry, Diana Hartridge*

(c. 1945– )

### *medical physicist, computer scientist*

***Education:*** B.A., Harvard University, 1965; M.A., Rice University, 1967, Ph.D. in nuclear physics, 1969

***Professional Experience:*** Fellow, nuclear physics, Rice University, 1969; research physicist in ultrasonics, Digicon, Inc., 1969–1974, executive vice president of medical ultrasound, 1974–1977; president, cardiology analysis systems, Digisonics, Inc., 1977–1982; vice president, Digicon, Inc., 1980–1987; chief operating officer, Cogniseis Development, Inc., 1987–

***Concurrent Positions:*** Chair of the board, Information Products Systems, Houston, 1982–1986

***Married:*** 1977

***Children:*** 1

*Diana McSherry* is a research biophysicist known for her development of computer-based cardiology analysis systems and has worked in the specific areas of echocardiology, ventriculography, and hemodynamics. Echocardiology uses reflected ultrasonic waves to examine the structure and functioning of the heart; ventriculography involves examining the ventricles of the heart, which are the lower chambers on each side of the heart that receive blood from the atria and in turn force it into the arteries; and hemodynamics is the branch of physiology dealing with the forces involved in the circulation of the blood.

The system she developed uses ultrasonic waves and computer processing to produce images of the heart and circulation system, and it was a major breakthrough in the 1970s when scientists were just beginning to develop the software for medical applications. Her product permits physicians to view the inside of a patient's body without making an incision; the ultrasound is reflected from the heart, producing an image that is refined after being fed into a computer.

After receiving her doctorate from Rice University, she was a fellow in nuclear physics there for one year and then spent the rest of her career working in corporations. She started as a research physicist in ultrasonics at Digicon, Inc., before being promoted to executive vice president of medical ultrasound and then president of cardiology analytical systems of Digisonics, Inc. She was promoted to vice president of Digicon, Inc., and then became chief operating officer (COO) of Cogniseis Development, Inc. All three companies may be the same company with variations in name; it is difficult to trace some of the early private software companies through various mergers and name changes. She also served on the board of directors as chair for Information Products Systems, Houston. It was not unusual for women to hold management positions in companies in the early computer industry; there are numerous examples elsewhere in this volume. Several women have pointed out that they had successful careers because they were involved in an infant industry at an early stage before computers became a male-dominated area.

She is a member of the Institute of Electrical and Electronics Engineers, American Institute of Ultrasound in Medicine, American Physical Society, and American Heart Association. Her research centers on computer-based cardiology systems.

***Bibliography:*** *American Men and Women of Science* 14–19; Herzenberg, C., *Women Scientists from Antiquity to the Present.*

## *McWhinney, Madeline (Houston)*
(1922– )
***economist***

***Education:*** B.A., Smith College, 1943; M.B.A., New York University, 1947
***Professional Experience:*** Economist, Federal Reserve Bank, New York City, 1943–1973, chief financial and trade statistician, 1955–1959, assistant vice president, 1965–1973; president and chief executive officer, First Women's Bank, New York City, 1974–1976; senior consultant, Dale, Elliott & Company, New York, 1977–
***Concurrent Position:*** Member of board of governors, American Stock Exchange, 1977–1981
***Married:*** John D. Dale, 1961
***Children:*** 1

***Madeline McWhinney*** is known as the first female officer of the Federal Reserve Bank of New York City and the highest-ranking women in the Federal Reserve System for many years. She also has the distinction of being the first president and chief executive officer of the First Women's Bank, New York City. It is unusual to have two firsts in a conservative area such as banking. She wrote an undergraduate thesis on the devaluation of gold, and when she joined the Federal Reserve Bank she was assigned to a task involving the money market as it related to daily demands for currency and for gold. She succeeded in this task, thus earning more and more challenging assignments that resulted in promotions. She went to night school in the early years to earn an M.B.A. from New York University to aid her in her job. She also took several courses toward a doctorate in economics but did not complete those studies.

She left the Federal Reserve Bank to become the president of the First Women's Bank because she believed women needed such an institution to guarantee them equal credit opportunities. This was the first full-service commercial bank in the United States to be predominantly owned and operated by women. After the bank made some ridiculous loans, she realized that the organizers had wanted her to set up the bank legally but that the board of directors would operate it. The board consisted of feminists such as Betty Friedan who tended to overlook the fact the bank was living beyond its means with ill-advised loans and spending money on expensive space and furnishings; within six months, it had a $400,000 operating deficit. McWhinney left the bank after two years to join her husband's management consulting firm.

She credits her interest in banking to her father, who was a vice president of a bank in Denver. When she was a child, he would discuss banking with her, and she soon developed an intense interest in the subject; she worked for his bank during her summer vacations in high school. After graduating from Smith College, she moved to New York City to look for work in a bank trust department, but she selected the Federal Reserve System because of its higher salaries and liberal opportunities for advancement.

She became the first woman officer of the Federal Reserve Bank in 1960 when she was appointed chief of the newly established Market Statistics Department, which monitors the government securities market. In 1965, she became the first woman assistant vice president, and in that capacity, she developed a program to computerize statistical processing and economic analyses for the research and statistics function of the bank. As president of the First Women's Bank, she was able to stabilize the bank's finances after the first year so it could continue operations. Although many shareholders and depositors were women, about 40 percent of the customers were men, and many large corporations such as CBS, Delta Airlines, and Mobil Oil Corporation opened business and commercial accounts. She was a member of the board of governors of the American Stock Exchange during this period and also served on the boards of several companies.

She is a member of the American Finance Association. Her photograph is included in *Current Biography* (1976), W. Rayner's *Wise Women,* and *The 100 Greatest American Women.*

***Bibliography:*** *Current Biography 1976; The 100 Greatest American Women;* Rayner, W., *Wise Women; Who's Who in America,* 51st ed., 1997.

# *Margulis, Lynn (Alexander)*
(1938– )
## *cell biologist, microbiologist*

***Education:*** B.A., University of Chicago, 1957; M.S., University of Wisconsin, 1960; Ph.D. in genetics, University of California, Berkeley, 1965; honorary degrees: D.Sc., Southeastern Massachusetts University, 1989, Westfield State College, 1989, and Plymouth State College, 1990

***Professional Experience:*** Postdoctoral researcher, Brandeis University, 1963–1965; assistant professor of biology, Boston University, 1966–1971, associate professor, 1971–1977, professor, 1977–1988, Distinguished University Professor of Biology, 1986–1988; Distinguished University Professor of Botany, University of Massachusetts, 1988–

***Married:*** Carl Sagan 1957, divorced 1963; Thomas N. Margulis, 1967, divorced 1980

***Children:*** 4

*Lynn Margulis* has been called the most gifted theoretical biologist of her generation, and she is one of the few living scientists who has shifted a paradigm. Starting when she was a student at the University of Chicago, she has questioned accepted truths about evolution, heredity, and cell biology. Her research on evolutionary links between cells containing nuclei and cells without nuclei led her to formulate a symbiotic theory of evolution in the 1970s that finally is becoming more widely accepted in the scientific community. Prior to her work, scientists held that evolution was based on natural selection.

One of her current theories that has not been accepted is that the earth as a whole is alive. This idea is popularly known as "the Gaia hypothesis," named for the Greek goddess of the earth and proposed by the chemist James Lovelock. Margulis is providing some evidence for this theory in her research on protozoa, algae, seaweeds, molds, and microbes that prompted *Omni* magazine to dub her "the wizard of ooze" in 1985. However, one theory of Lovelock and Margulis's that has proved to be true is that Mars has no evidence of living organisms, which was supported by the data from the *Viking* space probe launched by the National Aeronautics and Space Administration (NASA) in 1976. When Margulis was elected to membership in the National Academy of Sciences in 1983, she said she was totally shocked, and she viewed the honor as an indication that her theories were being accepted by the scientific community.

Her theory of symbiosis proposes that eukaryotes (cells with nuclei) evolved when different kinds of prokaryotes (cells without nuclei) formed symbiotic systems to enhance their chances for survival. The first such symbiotic fusion would have taken place between fermenting bacteria and oxygen-using bacteria. All cells with nuclei, she theorizes, are derived from bacteria that formed symbiotic relationships with other primordial bacteria some 2 billion years ago. It is now widely accepted that mitochondria—those components of eukaryotic cells that process oxygen—are remnants of oxygen-using bacteria. She argues that the primary mechanism driving biological change is symbiosis and that competition plays a secondary role.

The manuscript in which she first presented her symbiotic theory was rejected or lost by 15 journals before it was published in the *Journal of Theoretical Biology* in 1966 under the name Lynn Sagan. Her comprehensive exposition of the theory is presented in the book *The Origin of Eukaryotic Cells* (1970) and the revised version published as *Symbiosis in Cell Evolution* (1981). By the time the second book was published, the scientific establishment had finally accepted the idea that mitochondria and chloroplasts evolved symbiotically. The first cells with mitochondria, the organelles that produce energy for the cell, appeared about 1.4 billion years ago when large quantities of oxygen first entered the earth's atmosphere. The first cells with chloroplasts, the organelles that convert sunlight into energy, probably evolved later. Margulis's last and by far most-controversial symbiotic theory is that the nucleated cells' ability to move within organisms is due to a merger with spirochetes, which are tiny, spiral-shaped, and highly mobile bacteria. However, to date there is no reasonable body of evidence to support this theory.

Margulis was a superior student in school, and at age 15 she was accepted into an early entrant program at the University of Chicago. At the time, Chicago had an innovative teaching program in which students' reading assignments were, not textbooks, but the original works of the world's great scientists. A course in natural science prompted her to ask questions throughout her life, such as what is heredity. She met Carl Sagan, a graduate student in physics, and they married when she received her undergraduate degree at age 19.

The couple moved to the University of Wisconsin where Lynn received her master's degree in zoology and genetics. They moved again to the University of California, Berkeley, where she received her doctorate. The couple then divorced, and she moved to Brandeis University with their two sons for postdoctoral research. She received an appointment as an adjunct assistant of biology at Boston University and progressed through the ranks to become full professor and then Distinguished Professor of Biology. She married crystallographer Thomas Margulis in 1967, but they divorced in 1980. She received an appointment as Distinguished University Professor of Botany at the University of Massachusetts in 1988.

She has received many awards and committee appointments and published more than 130 scientific papers and books, several of the latter with her son Dorion Sagan. She is a fellow of the American Association for the Advancement of Science and a member of the International Society for the Study of the Origin of Life and International Society for Evolutionary Protistology ("protistology" refers to the taxonomic kingdom of protists such as protozoans, eukaryotic algae, and slime molds). Her research includes origin and evolution of cells, cytoplasmic genetics, microtubules and kinetosomes, evolution of biochemical pathways, morphogenesis in protists, and spirochetes of termites. Her photograph is included in *Current Biography* (1992), *Science* (April 19, 1991), and *Smithsonian* (August 1989).

***Bibliography:*** *American Men and Women of Science* 11–19; *Contemporary Authors* v. CAN-4 and 53–56; *Current Biography 1992;* Herzenberg, C., *Women Scientists from Antiquity to the Present; Notable Twentieth-Century Scientists; Who's Who of American Women,* 20th ed., 1997–1998.

# *Marrack, Philippa Charlotte*
(1945– )
## *immunologist*

***Education:*** B.A., Cambridge University, 1967, Ph.D. in biological sciences, 1970
***Professional Experience:*** Fellow in immunology, University of California, San Diego, 1971–1973; fellow in immunology, University of Rochester, 1971–1974, associate, 1974–1975, assistant professor of immunology, 1975–1979; associate professor, Department of Biophysics, Biochemistry, and Genetics, University of Colorado Health Science Center, 1980–1985, professor, 1985, professor, Department of Microbiology and Immunology, 1988–
***Concurrent Position:*** member, Department of Medicine, National Jewish Hospital and Research Center, 1979– ; Head, Division of Basic Immunology, National Jewish Center of Immunology and Respiratory Medicine, 1988–1990
***Married:*** John Kappler, 1974
***Children:*** 2

***Philippa Marrack*** is renowned for her research on the body's immune system and the intricate web of defenses it raises against viruses, bacteria, and other trespassers. Her particular interest is how the body accepts or rejects its own tissues, which is the study of the T lymphocytes that control the immune system. She and her husband, John Kappler, are among the leading scientists conducting this research.

The T cells are formed in the thymus gland, which is located behind the breastbone. There, any T cells that show a tendency to attack the self are quickly culled before they can do any harm, and the perfect T cells develop in the thymus until they are ready to emerge as mature immune cells. The team feels this is one of their most important discoveries. However, at times, the system breaks down, for the researchers have found that superantigens play a role in at least two different kinds of diseases. One group is made of up of autoimmune conditions—arthritis, juvenile diabetes, multiple sclerosis, and Graves' disease (a thyroid condition)—in which the immune system turns on its own tissue. The other group involves conditions in which the immune system apparently becomes wildly overstimulated and releases a flood of poisons, such as toxic shock syndrome or even common food poisoning. Marrack was elected to membership in the National Academy of Sciences in 1989.

Very little was known about the T cells in the immune system until the late 1960s. Researchers at that time concentrated on another group of white blood cells, the B lymphocytes, which secrete antibodies that attach themselves to foreign invaders and brand them for destruction. However, Marrack's research indicated that the T cells help the B cells do their job. Although there are billions of types of T cells in the body, usually only one type will react to any given antigen. Therefore, the T cell identifies the specific antigen and triggers the B cell to start reproducing antibodies.

She started her research on T cells while a graduate student at Cambridge because her thesis adviser was working in this area, and she decided to go to the University of California, San Diego, for her graduate work because she and some friends decided San Diego had much better weather than Cambridge. As a fellow in immunology there, she joined the laboratory of R. W. Dutton, who had recently learned to grow cultures of T lymphocytes, and there she met John Kappler, who also was working in the laboratory. They married in 1974 and moved to the University of Rochester where she was a postdoctoral fellow in immunology.

After she won an American Heart Association investigatorship to do basic research, she was recognized as an equal partner with Kappler, and they are now considered as a single entity, "Kappler-and-Marrack." They have slightly different interests and work styles, but over the years they have studiously minimized professional conflicts. For research publications, the person who performed the principal experiments is always the first listed author; the one who primarily wrote the paper is the last author named. Their careers are intertwined, and there have not been problems in combining careers and family life. Marrack's parents moved to the United States and lived close by to care for the children when they were young.

She has received the Feodor Lynen Medal (1990) and the William B. Coley Award of the Cancer Research Institute (1991). She is a member of the American Association of Immunologists and the American Heart Association. Her research includes study of functional and maturational heterogeneity of mouse T cells, mode of antigen recognition, and action of helper T cells. Her photograph is included in *Discover* (December 1991) and *Scientific American* (August 1992).

***Bibliography:*** *American Men and Women of Science* 14–19; *Who's Who in Science and Engineering*, 3d ed., 1996–1977.

# *Matola, Sharon Rose*
## (1954– )
## *conservationist*

***Education:*** Student, University of Iowa, 1976–1978; B.A. in biology, University of South Florida, Sarasota, 1981

***Professional Experience:*** Founder and director, Belize Zoo and Tropical Education Center, 1983–

**S*haron Matola*** is a conservationist who founded and directs the Belize Zoo and Tropical Education Center in the small Central American nation of the same name, the first zoo to be established in Belize, formerly British Honduras. The facility is intended to introduce the Belizeans to their native wildlife in natural settings, and she has done more than any other individual or group to arouse the consciousness of the government and people of Belize to help ensure the protection of the country's wildlife and wilderness areas.

After receiving an undergraduate degree in biology, Matola was working toward a master's degree in mycology at the University of South Florida when she saw an advertisement for dancers for a circus that was traveling to Mexico and thought she would use the opportunity to collect fungi in Mexico for her research. Later she added lion taming to her portfolio of skills with the circus. When she was transferred to a larger circus that traveled only to cities, she was not able to collect research samples, so she accepted a position as an assistant to a wildlife photographer to handle the animals that he was filming in Belize. Within a few months the photographer departed for another assignment, leaving her with the animals. Some of the animals had been born in captivity and could not be released in the wild, and she did not have funds to feed them.

On a dirt road that is the major east-west highway in Belize, she put signs on the cages describing the animals and opened a zoo in January 1983. Soon she had a steady stream of visitors who paid a small admission fee, and she traveled to many schools to talk about wildlife and the animals in the zoo. She received the approval of the Ministry of Education to establish a special school program whereby a visit to the zoo is part of the yearly agenda for every child in the small nation. Although the species represented are native to Belize, most adults and children have never seen the animals.

Matola's goal was a modern zoological facility. An architect donated a comprehensive plan for a new facility, and she obtained financial contributions from the World Wildlife Fund, Inter-American Foundation, Conservation International, other similar organizations, business organizations, and individuals. The new zoo opened in 1991 on 1,000 acres. The visitor's center is named for the British conservationist Gerald Durrell whose foundation, the Wildlife Preservation Trust International, was a major contributor. The facility includes a library, a plant for generating solar power, a plot for food crops, and facilities for the zoo's captive breeding and release program. In 1992, the government gave an adjoining 1,700-acre tract for a field research station.

Matola acts as an unpaid official adviser to the government on natural resources and the environment, and she has made progress in protecting forested areas and other regions from development. At her suggestion, British troops and members of the Belize Defense Force receive natural history instruction along with their wilderness training. She has led a program to preserve the world's four tapir species, all of which are endangered (the tapir is the national animal of Belize). Her lifelong commitment to preserving nature leads many people to place her in the category of Dian Fossey or Birute Galdikas.

As a child, Matola was an outdoors person, keeping worms as pets and bringing home a jarful of butterflies. After high school she enlisted in the U.S. Air Force where she performed routine inspections of aviation survival equipment. She was one of the few women who attended the air force's jungle survival training school in Panama, but she left the service after two and a half years because it was too much of an old boys' club. Her photograph is included in *Current Biography* (1993) and *International Wildlife* (November–December 1992).

***Bibliography:*** *Current Biography 1993.*

# *Matson, Pamela Anne*
## (1953– )
## ***soil scientist, environmental scientist***

***Education:*** B.S. in biology, University of Wisconsin, Eau Claire, 1975; M.S. in environmental science, Indiana University, 1980; Ph.D. in forest ecology, Oregon State University, 1983

***Professional Experience:*** Fellow, Department of Entomology, North Carolina State University, 1983; research scientist, Ames Research Center, National Aeronautics and Space Administration (NASA), 1983–1993; professor, Department of Environmental Science Policy and Management, University of California, Berkeley, 1993–

***Pamela Matson*** is renowned for her pioneering research into the role of land-use changes on global warming. She is analyzing the effects of greenhouse gas emissions resulting from tropical deforestation and investigating the effects of intensive agriculture on the atmosphere, especially the effects of tropical agriculture and cattle ranching. She is finding ways in which agricultural productivity can be expanded without increasing the level of greenhouse gases. In an article in the July 25, 1997, issue of *Science,* she states that intensification of agriculture by the use of high-yielding crop varieties "has contributed substantially to the tremendous increases in food production over the past 50 years. Land conversion and intensification, however, also alter the biotic interactions and patterns of resource availability in ecosystems and can have serious local, regional, and global environmental consequences. The use of ecologically based management strategies can increase the sustainability of agricultural production while reducing off-site consequences."

She was elected to membership in the National Academy of Sciences in 1994, and she was selected to be a MacArthur fellow for 1995–2000. After receiving her doctorate, her research first focused on forest ecology and then broadened to include many other areas in the global environment. She has been a part of numerous significant commissions in ecology, including being a member of the National Academy of Science Board on Global Change, National Science Foundation long-term Ecological Research Program, NASA's Boreal Ecosystem-Atmosphere Exchange Study Advisory Committee, and NASA's Mission to Planet Earth Advisory Committee. She was also chair of the Sustainable Biosphere Initiative Steering Committee of the Ecological Society of America. She has published more than 90 papers and book chapters and is coeditor of the book *Biogenic Trace Gases: Measuring Emission from Soil and Water* (1995).

In a telephone conversation on June 26, 1997, she said she was totally surprised when she was elected to the National Academy of Sciences because she felt she was just beginning her best work. One result of her election is that she has been more in demand to present papers and serve on committees—and her level of recognition has increased. She said she has had to learn how to say "no" to requests. She also said the high point of her career is her current research collaboration with social scientists, agronomists, and environmental scientists, for they are really breaking new ground. Other high points have been her election to the National Academy of Sciences and receiving the MacArthur fellowship.

She has found no problem, as a woman, receiving recognition for her work. She finds that women work better on interdisciplinary teams than men do, for women are much better at recognizing other approaches and looking at the different perspectives of other members. She encourages women to enter her field of ecology and environmental science, saying that the twenty-first century will be the century of the environment.

Among the other awards she has received are the NASA Exceptional Service Award (1994) and the University of Wisconsin, Eau Claire, Distinguished Alumni Award (1996). She is a member of the American Academy of Arts and Sciences, Ecological Society of America, American Association for the Advancement of Science, American Geophysical Union, and American Institute of Biological Sciences.

***Bibliography:*** *American Men and Women of Science* 19; *Who's Who in America,* 51st ed., 1997; *Who's Who in Science and Engineering,* 3d ed., 1996–1977.

# *Matthews, Alva T.*

(c. 1930– )

***engineer***

***Education:*** Student, Middlebury College, Barnard College; B.S., Columbia University, 1955, M.S., 1957, Ph.D. in engineering science, 1965

***Professional Experience:*** Design engineer, Weidlinger Associates, 1957– ; senior research engineer, Rochester Applied Science Associates; consultant, 1977–

***Concurrent Positions:*** Instructor in civil engineering, Columbia University School of Engineering; adjunct associate professor, Department of Mechanical and Aerospace Sciences, University of Rochester, c. 1975

***Married:*** A. R. Solomon

***Children:*** 1

***Alva Matthews*** is a research engineer who is recognized for her work in the field of structural analysis and wave propagation in solids. In her structural analysis work, she has designed helicopter blades and satellite-tracking antennae and analyzed auto accidents in order to learn how to build safer cars. As a wave propagation specialist, she has studied earthquakes to see how shock waves are transmitted through soil and rocks and how buildings can be designed to withstand earth tremors.

After receiving her master's degree, she joined Weidlinger Associates, a construction engineering firm, as a design engineer, and when she completed her doctorate, she was named senior research engineer. Her work involved the mechanical behavior of materials under great pressures, such as how nuclear weapons blasts might affect buildings. Later, when she was a senior research engineer with Rochester Applied Science Associates in Rochester, New York, she conducted research on the dynamics of helicopter blades and worked on the reconstruction and analysis of automobile accidents. She developed software for the design and development of the Telstar Tracking antennae, which have been used in transmitting television pictures and telephone messages. At the same time, she was an instructor of civil engineering at Columbia and lectured in the evenings at the University of Rochester.

She decided to become an engineer at age 15. Her parents encouraged her to achieve without limitations, and she saw the possibilities of an engineering career when she accompanied her father, an industrial builder, to construction sites. When she enrolled in the engineering program at Middlebury College, an adviser told her engineering was too difficult for a girl and she would never find a job. She ignored this advice. When she was a student worker in a contractor's field office, she was prohibited from entering the tunnels because of the superstition that women cause tunnel collapses (there is a similar superstition that women cause mines to collapse). At Columbia University, she was the first woman to attend the Engineering School's surveying camp, and since there were no facilities for women, she had to stay at a guest house away from the camp. One day while using a surveying transit, or telescopic instrument used for measuring horizontal and sometimes vertical angles, Alva saw her future husband through the lens instead of the angles upon which she should have been concentrating!

Matthews has found that a career in engineering has provided flexibility for her. She said that if a woman is going to have a husband and family, she needs a career that can be either expanded or contracted during different periods. She was able to reduce her workload for several years after the couple had a child, continuing to work as a consultant for Xerox Corporation and other firms on a part-time basis.

Several of her publications are recognized as pioneering studies, particularly in the areas of pressure-wave propagation and vibrations in elastic media. She has received the Society of Women Engineers Achievement Award for her work in shock analysis, elasticity, and structural design (1971) and the Engineering Award of the Federation of Engineering and Scientific Societies of Drexel University (1976). She is a member of the American Society of Mechanical Engineers. Her photograph is included in *Cosmopolitan* (April 1976).

***Bibliography:*** Ireland, N., *Index to Women of the World . . . Suppl.; Notable Twentieth-Century Scientists;* O'Neill, L., *The Women's Book of World Records and Achievements;* Stanley, A., *Mothers and Daughters of Invention.*

# *Medicine, Beatrice A.*
(1924– )
***anthropologist***

***Education:*** B.Sc., South Dakota State University; M.A., Michigan State University; Ph.D. in anthropology, University of Wisconsin, 1983
***Professional Experience:*** Faculty member in anthropology at University of Washington, University of British Columbia, University of Calgary, Michigan State University, University of South Dakota, Dartmouth College, and Stanford University; assistant professor of anthropology and acting director of Native American Studies, San Francisco State University; associate professor of anthropology, California State University, Northridge; associate professor emeritus
***Married:*** James Garner, divorced
***Children:*** 1

*Beatrice Medicine* is recognized as an expert on the study of tribal traditions among the Dakota Indians. She is one of the few Native American women to earn an advanced degree in anthropology, and she has worked to dispel anthropological myths that have tended to oversimplify and homogenize Native American cultures. In her writing and teaching, she has established a more realistic picture of the plurality and diversity of Native American life from the real and complex Native American perspectives. She has been especially interested in the changing American Indian family and in women's roles, real and perceived, past and present. She has directed Native American studies programs at several universities, including the Native American Studies Program at San Francisco State University and the Native Centre at the University of Calgary, Alberta.

Although she has spent much of her life in an academic atmosphere, she has always maintained strong ties to her reservation home. She was born and raised on the Standing Rock Sioux Reservation in northern South Dakota, and her family stressed maintaining tribal traditional cultural identity and encouraged her to pursue her interest in researching Native American culture. Much of her work has focused on the study of tribal traditions among the Dakota Indians. Several of the women anthropologists listed in this volume have researched Native American society and culture to dispel the myths that surround the history of the American Indians, but Beatrice Medicine is one of the very few Native American women to pursue this research at the university level. Much erroneous information exists because the first narratives and histories were written by white men who were the product of a patriarchal society and they largely ignored or incorrectly reported the role of women in Native American society.

In addition to her research on her own people, Medicine has been involved in work with the aboriginal peoples of New Zealand, Australia, and Canada. She has been extensively involved in the field of mental health, focusing on issues such as alcohol and drug abuse among Native Americans. The title of her doctoral thesis was "An Ethnography of Drinking and Sobriety among the Lakota Sioux." She has been an advocate for Indian leadership and has worked to establish a network of Indian social service centers in urban areas.

She has published more than 60 articles and chapters in books. She is a member of the American Anthropological Association and Society for Applied Anthropology. Some sources report that she received her doctorate from Michigan State University while others, including the *Dissertation Abstracts* database, list the University of Wisconsin. Her photograph is included in *Indians of Today.*

***Bibliography:*** Bataille, G. M., *Native American Women; Indians of Today; Native North American Almanac; Notable Native Americans.*

# Menken, Jane Ava (Golubitsky)
(1939– )
## *demographer*

***Education:*** B.A., University of Pennsylvania, 1960; M.S., Harvard University, 1962; Ph.D. in sociology and demography, Princeton University, 1975
***Professional Experience:*** Assistant in biostatistics, Harvard University School of Public Health, 1962–1964; mathematical statistician, National Institute of Mental Health, 1964–1966; research associate, Department of Biostatistics, Columbia University, 1966–1969; member of research staff, Office of Population Research, Princeton University, 1969–1971, 1975–1987, assistant director, 1978–1986, associate director, 1986–1987, professor of sociology, 1980–1982, professor of sociology and public affairs, 1982–1987; professor of sociology and demography, University of Pennsylvania, 1987– , UPS Foundation Professor of social sciences, 1987– , director, Population Studies Center, 1989–1995
***Married:*** Matthew Menken, 1960, divorced 1985; Richard Jessor, 1992
***Children:*** 2

*Jane Menken* is recognized as one of the expert demographers in the United States, and for a number of years she was director of the Population Studies Center of the University of Pennsylvania, one of the primary centers in the country. Demography is the science of vital and social statistics, such as birth, death, diseases, and marriage. It differs from statistics, which is the science that deals with numerical facts or data, in that demography is centered on the populations—the people—and the interpretation of trends and forecasting future trends.

Not all population studies involve dry, dull data. Many involve controversial social issues, such as an example of Menken's work that was described in *People Weekly* of July 21, 1980, while she was employed at Princeton University's Office of Population Research. The Supreme Court had just ruled that the federal government had the right to refuse to pay for abortions with Medicaid funds, and the reporter asked Menken what the impact of this decision had been. She replied that there had been about 300,000 federally funded abortions in the United States prior to August 1977 when the Hyde Amendment took effect; in 1978, there had been only 2,000. However, many women had still been able to obtain free abortions through state services, but now, since the states receive Medicaid funds from the federal government, the Supreme Court ruling prohibited the states from continuing to provide free abortions with federal funds.

A current topic in population studies is the aging of Americans. The projection for the United States as a whole is that, as a result of advances in health and medicine, people are living longer than in previous generations. On the other hand, people in some age groups are healthier than the people in later generations. Both aspects are creating profound problems for the future of Social Security and health insurance, for example.

In her career, Menken worked for the federal government for a short time as a statistician for the National Institute of Mental Health but has primarily been employed by major universities with distinguished reputations in demography, such as Princeton University and the University of Pennsylvania. She has served on numerous panels and commissions including serving as a member of the population advisory committee for the Rockefeller Foundation (1981–1993), member of the committee on AIDS research of the National Academy of Sciences

(1987–1994), cochair of a panel on data and research priorities for arresting AIDS in sub-Saharan Africa (1994– ), and member of the Commission on Behavioral and Social Sciences and Education (1991– ). She was a Center for Advanced Study in Behavioral Sciences fellow in 1995–1996.

Menken was elected to membership in the National Academy of Sciences in 1989. She is a coauthor of the book *Mathematical Models of Conception and Birth* (1973) and editor of *Natural Fertility* (1979), *Teenage Sexuality, Pregnancy, and Childbearing* (1981), and *World Population and U.S. Policy: The Choices Ahead* (1986). She is a fellow of the American Association for the Advancement of Science and a member of the American Academy of Arts and Sciences, Population Association of America (president, 1985), American Public Health Association, American Sociological Association, Society for the Study of Social Biology, and International Union for the Scientific Study of Population.

***Bibliography:*** *Who's Who in America*, 51st ed., 1997; *Who's Who of American Women*, 20th ed., 1997–1998.

# *Mertz, Barbara (Gross)*
(1927– )
***archaeologist, writer***

***Education:*** Ph.B., University of Chicago, 1947, M.A., 1950, Ph.D. in Egyptology, 1952
***Married:*** Richard R. Mertz, 1950, divorced 1968
***Children:*** 2

***Barbara Mertz*** is an Egyptologist who has turned her research skills and knowledge of various countries into writing popular novels that have been hugely successful. One recognition of her research on Egypt was her television appearance in a segment on Ramses II in the *Ancient Mysteries* series first broadcast on the Arts & Entertainment Channel in 1996. She began college as an education major, which was a tradition in her family, but finding herself bored with her classes, she transferred to the Oriental Institute of the University of Chicago, which she had started visiting as a child, and she obtained her doctorate there. The Oriental Institute is the premier center in the United States for the subject of Egypt. In common with many young women in the 1950s, Mertz stayed at home after her marriage to rear her children. Although she wanted to be an archaeologist, one thing she could do while at home was write.

She began with several nonfiction books for the general public in the 1960s, the first being *Temples, Tombs, and Hieroglyphs: The Story of Egyptology* (1963). The reviewers commented on how well she captured the life of the ancient Egyptians and described some of the colorful archaeologists who had explored the country. They praised her lively treatment of the subject. The next book was *Red Land, Black Land: The World of the Ancient Egyptians* (1966), which reviewers called a witty and informative tour of the world of the ancient Egyptians. She took the mummies out of the tombs and turned them into living, thinking, feeling human beings. Her third book was *Two Thousand Years in Rome* (1968), written with her husband, a historian. In this book, they compared the prehistoric, medieval, Renaissance, and baroque Rome with the modern metropolis by surveying the surviving monuments.

After trying without success to publish fiction, Mertz hit on the formula of writing suspense novels. The first, written under the pseudonym Barbara Michaels, was *The Master of Blacktower* (1966), and she has been publishing about one novel per year in this genre ever since. She adopted the pseudonym of Elizabeth Peters for her mystery novels.

Mertz has three primary heroines, each of whom has avid readers breathlessly waiting for a new book. The first is Jacqueline Kirby, a librarian who turns to writing romance novels. Mertz then drew on her expertise in

Egyptology for her Amelia Peabody novels. Amelia is a late-nineteenth-century archaeologist who has a number of adventures in Egypt with her archaeologist husband and son. One has the feeling that the descriptions are historically correct and that the characteristics attributed to known, and named, archaeologists of the period are accurate also. One reviewer says that Mertz uses almost every cliché character and plot twist of Victorian fiction in these books. The third set of novels features Vicky Bliss, an American curator working for a German museum, which gives the author the opportunity to place Vicky's adventures in Germany, Italy, and Switzerland. Although most of Mertz's plots and characters reveal meticulous research, most of the Barbara Michaels books differ from an Elizabeth Peters in tone, for the former are more serious and contain more supernatural elements.

Amelia Peabody is an outspoken, forthright woman who will not admit she has limitations. In an interview for *Contemporary Authors,* Mertz says that since she has started writing about Amelia, she has taken on many of her characteristics. "In a way she gave me the courage to speak my mind . . . I was Miss Mealymouth for the first forty years of my life. Now people laugh raucously when I say that, which I take as a great compliment." She is especially careful with her research for the Amelia novels because they involve a specific chronology. She has to assure that she does not commit any errors, such as talking about the tomb of Tutankhamen when it was not discovered until 20 year later or mention using flashlights when archaeologists still were using candles in the tombs.

In her personal life, Mertz is a champion of women's rights. She was one of the founders of the organization Sisters of Crime, which champions fair treatment of women authors. One area the organization is pursuing is to see that women's books are reviewed in the press, a primary source for information about new publications. She mentions that it is essential for all women to have access to child care, health care, and protection. She envisions women will receive pay for staying home if that is what they want to do. In the *Contemporary Authors* interview, she states, "I think women are going to have to be on their toes forever, and in as nice a way as possible, but as firmly as possible, insist on their rights."

She advises young writers that they should not be obsessed with the best-seller list. Very few people make that list, and a writer can still make a very comfortable living and have a very good time situated at the top of the midlist. She also questions the advisability of traveling around on publicity tours if doing so interferes with writing.

***Bibliography:*** *Contemporary Authors* v. CANR-11, 21–24R, and CANR-36.

# *Michel, Helen (Vaughn)*
(1932– )
## *nuclear chemist*

***Education:*** B.S. in chemistry, University of California, Berkeley, 1955; Student, Indiana University, 1955–1956

***Professional Experience:*** Chemist, University of California, Berkeley, Radiation Laboratory (later called Lawrence Radiation Laboratory), 1956–1990; retired 1990

***Married:*** Maynard Michel, 1957

*Helen Michel* has achieved great success and worldwide recognition for her expertise in operating the complex electronic instruments in the Lawrence Radiation Laboratory in Berkeley, California. Her analyses have led to many important scientific discoveries, and she has achieved startling success in the fields of nuclear science, archaeometry, geochemistry, and plant biology (archaeometry refers to dating archaeological specimens through specific techniques such as radiocarbon dating).

One study she conducted brought a vast amount of publicity to the laboratory. The group was asked in 1975 to assist in determining the authenticity of an artifact called the Plate of Brass. Historical evidence indicated it had been left by Sir Walter Drake, the English explorer, in the sixteenth century when his ship the *Golden Hind* landed on the coast of what is now California. The plate had been discovered in 1936 in San Francisco, and it was being kept in the Bancroft Library at Berkeley. Its authenticity had been confirmed by historians and scientists, but there still were questions about its origin. After examining samples of the metal as well as the plate itself by X-ray fluorescence, atomic absorption, and emission spectroscopy, Michel determined that the Plate of Brass was not authentic and that it had probably been made in the last half of the nineteenth century or the early part of the twentieth. Similar studies conducted at Oxford University verified her conclusions.

In the 1960s, the laboratory team began to undertake studies into the provenance of ancient pottery, that is, determining the place where the clay fabric of the pots originated. This work utilized neutron activation analysis, in which nuclear techniques are used to measure the chemical abundance of many elements in pots of unknown origin to compare with the known chemical abundance patterns of ancient pottery from different parts of the world.

In another instance, her expertise in soil analysis was crucial in a long-term project to determine the source of iridium at the time of the Cretaceous-Tertiary (KT) boundary in many parts of the world (the Cretaceous-Tertiary boundary occurred 65 billion years ago at the time of the extinction of the dinosaurs). The physicist Luis Alvarez and his geologist son Walter proposed the theory that a giant asteroid impacted the earth at the time of the KT boundary. The resulting dust cloud circled the earth, blotted out the sun, and killed the vegetation on which the dinosaurs and other large mammals fed. This event led to the demise of these creatures plus many species of vegetation. Michel was instrumental in verifying this theory by her meticulous analysis of samples over a period of more than ten years.

The search was further complicated when the scientist Richard Muller published a theory that a star circles the sun and every 26 million years an asteroid breaks off, impacts the earth, and causes mass extinction. He called this "the Nemesis star" or "the death star." However, eventually the impact crater of the asteroid proposed by the Alvarezes was discovered in 1991 in Chicxulub, Mexico—the crater had remained unrecognized for so long because it was underwater. Because the impact had occurred at the water's edge, the tsunami, an unusually large sea wave, that had resulted from the impact was responsible for other results that had not previously been explained. Michel's contributions are described in Luis Alvarez's book *Adventures of a Physicist* (1987), Walter Alvarez's *T-Rex and the Crater of Doom* (1997), and books written about the Nemesis star.

Michel decided on a career in chemistry when she was in the sixth grade. Her parents gave her a chemistry set, and she was intrigued by the odors that she could manufacture. When one of her teachers offered a science class after school, she decided to attend, but it was the day the experiment blew up that was the turning point in directing her toward chemistry. It was difficult in the 1950s for women to obtain any job, so having obtained a part-time job at the Radiation Laboratory in Berkeley in the Division of Nuclear Chemistry while she was still an undergraduate, she postponed further education upon graduation and accepted a full-time position as a chemist there. (She did spend a year in graduate work at Indiana University before returning to Berkeley.) She married Maynard Michel, a fellow scientist at Berkely, in 1957. She was treated as an equal by her colleagues; her name was always included as a coauthor on all of the papers describing research in which she participated.

In the 1960s, she and her husband took up the hobby of breeding orchids. They kept expanding their hobby into a business, the Orchid Ranch, in Livermore, California, and when the couple retired from Lawrence Laboratory, she took over much of the daily supervision of the business. A list of her publications is included in *Women in Chemistry and Physics*. Her photograph is included in both of the Alvarez books.

***Bibliography:*** *Women in Chemistry and Physics.*

# *Micheli-Tzanakou, Evangelia*
(1942– )
## ***neurophysicist, biomedical engineer, biophysicist***

***Education:*** B.S., University of Athens, 1968; M.S., Syracuse University, 1974, Ph.D. in physics, 1977

***Professional Experience:*** Fellow in biophysics, Physics Department, Syracuse University, 1977–1980; assistant professor of biomedical engineering, Department of Electrical Engineering, Rutgers University, 1981–1985, associate professor, 1985–1990, professor and department chair, 1990– , codirector of graduate program in biomedical engineering, 1992– , faculty member, computer science and electrical engineering departments

***Concurrent Positions:*** Consultant for Eye Defect and Engineering Research Foundation, 1978–1980, consultant in biophysics, Syracuse University, 1980–1981

***Evangelia Micheli-Tzanakou*** is a physicist who does extensive research on brain function. She is renowned for her research in using optimization techniques to bring understanding to problems of brain functions and dysfunctions, and she has pursued a multiphase quest in order to gain this understanding. Some of the methods she developed are used in cardiology to predict the prognosis of heart attack patients, and she has compared people who age normally with patients who have Alzheimer's and Parkinson's diseases. She has developed a set of algorithms for modeling the visual system and applied this technique to other functions of the nervous system and to research other brain functions, such as pattern recognition. In 1994, her research indicated that people with advanced educational and occupational attainment are able to cope longer before the onset of Alzheimer's, a finding that has proved controversial.

Biomedical engineering, or bioengineering, is a relatively new discipline that developed about 1960–1965. It involves the application of engineering principles and techniques to problems of medicine and biology, and in many schools and departments, it is an interdisciplinary effort on the part of physicians, biophysicists, electrical engineers, and computer scientists. Some researchers have expertise in several or all of these disciplines. An example of Micheli-Tzanakou's work was presented in a paper in 1996 in which she and her coauthor described designing a neuromime circuit to be used for modeling nerve networks from living organisms by using very large-scale integration (VLSI) technology.

She was born in Greece, and after receiving her undergraduate degree in physics from Athens University, she taught in a high school in Athens before journeying to the United States to resume her education. She joined the staff at Syracuse University where she completed her graduate work, and she continues her research there. In her work, information processing by the visual system is examined by computer-controlled techniques; recordings are done both in animals and in humans with a response feedback method by which the information flow is reversed and a feature extractor becomes a feature generator.

She advises young people to pursue the field that inspires their passion. One should go for whatever education pleases one the most, she says, because that is where success will be found. She is surprised by the lack of ethics among some scientists and encourages young women to seek role models from among scientists of integrity whether they are men or women. Many women think they need a woman as a role model, but gender does not matter.

She is a founding fellow of the American Institute for Medical and Biological Engineering. She is also a fellow of the Institute of Electrical and Electronics Engineers and a member of the Society for Neuroscience, Association for Research in Ophthalmology, and Biophysical Society. Her research includes pattern recognition; digital signal processing of biological signals; neural networks, data compression, and image reconstruction; hearing aids and neural network modeling of the brain. Her photograph is included in *Notable Twentieth-Century Scientists.* She is listed under "Evangelia Tzanakou" in editions 15–18 of *American Men and Women of Science.*

***Bibliography:*** *American Men and Women of Science* 15–19; *Notable Twentieth-Century Scientists.*

# *Mielczarek, Eugenie Vorburger*

(1931– )

## *solid-state physicist, biophysicist*

***Education:*** B.S., Queens College, 1953; M.S., Catholic University, 1957, Ph.D. in physics, 1963
***Professional Experience:*** Physicist, U.S. National Bureau of Standards, 1953–1957; research assistant, Catholic University, 1957–1959, research associate, 1959–1962, assistant research professor, 1962–1965; professor of physics, George Mason University, 1965–
***Concurrent Position:*** Visiting scientist, National Institutes of Health, 1965–
***Married:*** 1954
***Children:*** 2

*Eugenie Mielczarek* is known for her work in biophysics, which is the conjunction between biology and physics. Working with Mossbauer spectroscopy, she is applying the techniques of nuclear physics to biological materials in order to probe the molecular environment around iron atoms. She explains that our bodies contain iron. Persons who have sickle-cell anemia or Cooley's anemia suffer from damaged kidneys and spleens. The red blood cells break down faster in these persons than in healthy individuals, and this breakdown dumps iron into those major organs. Iron chelators, or iron-grabbing compounds, are needed to clean up the excess iron, and we need to understand the atomic environment of iron in iron-chelating compounds in order to prevent the damage caused by the iron buildup.

Her early research was in solid-state metals physics, but she has moved into an area in which the metal is in a biological environment. Solid-state physicists increasingly are studying more-complex biological systems, looking at hemoglobin, cell membranes, and brain waves, all very exciting work because it has application to living systems.

Mielczarek feels she gravitated to science because no physical science was taught in the elementary school she attended. Often elementary teachers in schools that do offer science are insecure in teaching it, and their lack of confidence and information sometimes projects an image to young women that science is too difficult for them. However, her physical science teacher in high school was excellent and encouraged her to pursue physics, and she liked the intellectual challenge. Her father offered to send her to secretarial school, but she insisted on attending Queens College, a public, free university in New York City.

When she had completed her undergraduate degree in physics, she received several job inquiries because employers quickly looked at her name and thought she was male. At the job interview, then, they would offer feeble excuses for not hiring her, such as their company facilities had no restroom for women. She obtained a position at the U.S. National Bureau of Standards, where she met her future husband, and while working at the bureau, she attended Catholic University for her master's degree. After receiving that, she remained at the same university for her doctorate and worked there during that period of time. She enjoyed her work while she was an assistant research professor at the university, but the position did not provide job security or the research support she needed.

Although she has met discrimination in her life, she prefers not to dwell on it. Still, she feels that even though there is now protection under the law, women must work harder and be better than the average men in the field. She says she has been able to continue her career because of her enormously supportive husband and advises young women to choose their husbands carefully or not to marry. She never stopped working (she and her husband always hired people to take care of the children) because women who want to have careers as physicists must maintain their capability. It is all right to work part time, but one must continue to work or else the field will pass them by. She points out the field of physics is changing to encompass computer science, geophysics, biophysics, and engineering, which means there are many areas for women to choose from.

She is a member of the American Physical Society, Biophysical Society, American Association of Physics Teachers, and Association of Women in Science. Her research includes solid-state low-temperature physics, semiconductors, Mossbauer spectroscopy of metal and biological compounds, biophysics, and Fermi surfaces of metals. Her photograph is included in A. Fins's *Women in Science.*

**Bibliography:** *American Men and Women of Science* 11–19; Fins, A., *Women in Science;* Herzenberg, C., *Women Scientists from Antiquity to the Present.*

# *Mitchell, Mildred Bessie*
(1903– )
## *clinical psychologist*

***Education:*** B.A., Rockford College, 1924; M.A., Radcliffe College, 1927; Ph.D. in psychology, Yale University, 1931

***Professional Experience:*** Professor of education and mathematics, Lees College, 1927–1928; psychologist, George School, 1931–1933; chief psychologist, New Hampshire State Hospital, 1933–1936; vocational director, U.S. Employment Service in New Hampshire, 1936; psychologist, Bellevue Hospital, New York City, 1937; chief psychologist, Psychopathic Hospital, Iowa State University, 1938–1939; psychologist, Mt. Pleasant and Independence Street Hospitals, 1939–1941; clinical psychologist, State Bureau of Psychological Services, Minnesota, 1941–1942; member of WAVES, 1942–1945; vocational appraiser, Veterans Guidance Center, City College New York, 1945–1946; psychologist, Domestic Relations Court, New York City, 1946–1947; chief psychologist, Veterans Administration Mental Hygiene Clinic, Ft. Snelling, Minnesota, 1947–1951, Veterans Administration Center, Dayton, Ohio, 1951–1958; clinical psychologist, Aerospace Medical Laboratory, Wright-Patterson Air Force Base, 1958–1960, research psychologist, Bionics Section, Aeronautical Systems Division, 1960–1963; associate professor of psychology, University of Tampa, 1965–1967; lecturer in behavioral science, University of South Florida, 1967–1970; retired 1970

***Married:*** Ira Spear, 1947

*Mildred Mitchell* has had a distinguished career as a clinical psychologist, but she is best known for her early contributions to the development of the science of bionics. Although the term *bionics* conjures up visions of robots in science fiction movies, it is a scientific discipline that is increasingly important today. Bionics means utilizing electronic devices and mechanical parts to assist humans in performing difficult, dangerous, or intricate tasks by supplementing or duplicating parts of the body. Tasks can range from the design of glove boxes to handle radioactive material in clean rooms to the design of artificial limbs to replace those lost to accident or disease. Bionics was a new science in the 1960s, and psychologists, biologists, physicians, chemists, physicists, mathematicians, and engineers teamed up to duplicate electronically the functions of people, animals, and plants.

She became involved in bionics in the late 1950s when she was asked by the U.S. Air Force to assist in the psychological evaluation of the 31 men who were being evaluated for the seven openings for astronaut training in the Mercury program. Initially, she was asked only to test the applicants' reaction to isolation, but later she was appointed to the selection team. Since no one had yet traveled in space, the selection committee did not have any criteria on which to base their selections and decided to choose experienced pilots who had flown planes at very high altitudes. The committee members devised tests that simulated the pressures of high altitude and the resultant stresses on the body. They studied men who had flown higher and faster than other men in testing new aircraft, and although Mitchell supported the idea of selecting women for the astronaut program, her recommendation was not implemented for almost 20 years.

The scientists knew that even experienced pilots had difficulty performing some actions such as manipulating the controls during takeoffs and landings because of high gravity (G) forces. When Mitchell was head of the bionics section, Aeronautical Systems Division, Aerospace Medical Laboratory, she designed an artificial muscle that could take over such operations and could also assist if an astronaut who had experienced long periods of weightlessness found his muscles had become weak or impaired. The artificial muscle is very light in weight. It is composed of 130,000 separate inelastic fibers imbedded in a tube of material, and when molded together, the fibers look like a thin stalk of celery. However, the device can lift even heavy equipment. She also designed what she called a "nail bender" that can bend an iron nail with a puff of air. Her group designed a man-made "biological clock," which duplicates through machinery the natural mechanism that tells animals whether it is day or night, even if their environment has been artificially altered.

Today, the bionic equipment that is being designed is often vastly different from what was built more than 30 years ago. There have been advances in materials, in computer simulation of muscle action, and in the need for specific bionic equipment. The numerous space flights during this period also have contributed to our knowledge of human activity, such as the weakening of bones and muscles as a result of weightlessness. However, Mitchell and her teams made significant contributions to this new science.

After working with the air force, she accepted positions teaching at several academic institutions, and during her career, she was involved in improving the status of women psychologists. In 1951, she published a landmark report in the journal *American Psychologist* on the status of women psychologists who were members of the American Psychological Association. The data indicated that women had not been elected as fellows or officers, nor had they been appointed to committees in proportion to their numbers and qualifications. Naturally this report caused an uproar in the association and resulted in some reforms. She mentions that the reason she changed jobs frequently is that most did not offer opportunities for advancement. Often, a man less qualified than she was hired as her supervisor.

After retiring, she traveled and frequently gave speeches and lectures about bionics and her experiences in the astronaut program. Among the honors she has received is the distinguished technical achievement award of the U.S. Air Force (1962 and 1964). She is a fellow of the American Association for the Advancement of Science, the American Psychological Association, and the International Council of Women Psychologists. There is a photograph in Mary Hoyt's *American Women of the Space Age.*

***Bibliography:*** Hoyt, M., *American Women of the Space Age;* Rossiter, M., *Women Scientists in America;* Stanley, A., *Mothers and Daughters of Invention;* Vare, E., *Mothers of Invention.*

# *Morawetz, Cathleen (Synge)*
(1923– )
## *applied mathematician*

***Education:*** B.S., University of Toronto, 1944; M.S., Massachusetts Institute of Technology, 1946; Ph.D. in mathematics, New York University, 1951; honorary degrees: 8
***Professional Experience:*** Research associate, Massachusetts Institute of Technology, 1951–1952; research associate, Courant Institute, New York University, 1952–1957, assistant professor of mathematics, 1957–1960, associate professor, 1960–1966, professor of mathematics, 1966– , associate director, Courant Institute of Mathematical Science, 1978–1984, director, 1984–1988, chair, Department of Mathematics, 1981–1984, Samuel F. B. Morse Chair of Arts and Sciences
***Married:*** Herbert Morawetz, 1945
***Children:*** 4

C*athleen Morawetz* is renowned for her research in applied mathematics. She is the first woman in the United States to head a mathematical institution, the Courant Institute of Mathematical Science, and there are only one or two other women mathematicians of her generation who have achieved distinction in their careers. Her work has been in applications of partial differential equations. Her doctoral thesis and her early work involved the mathematical analysis of transonic flow, which has practical applications in the design of aircraft as it involves the study of flow past an airfoil, such as the wing of an airplane. At very fast speeds, shock waves will develop and will increase the drag on an aircraft, which has important implications for the design of supersonic aircraft. In the 1960s, her research indicated that the equations of transonic flow show that a shock wave must occur if a plane goes fast enough, no matter how the wings are designed; engineers now settle for designing airfoils with small shocks.

Later she concentrated on the mathematics associated with the scattering of waves in the inverse mode. When a wave—electromagnetic, sound, or elastic—hits a barrier, it interacts with that barrier, and the wave can be reflected, absorbed, or transmitted depending on such factors as the wave frequency and the properties of the barrier. The problem in scattering theory is to analyze how the interaction takes place and what can be observed from a distance. One class of problems in scattering theory is inverse scattering. After the wave is sent in, there are some data on how it was scattered, but the problem is to find what the wave hit to cause the disturbance. Some applications of this theory have solved problems in x-ray diffraction, and mathematical analyses of high-frequency waves are the basis of techniques used in medicine to visualize internal organs as well as techniques used in geology to search for oil fields.

Her father was the mathematician John Synge, who was known for his work in tensor analysis. He did not push his daughter toward a career in mathematics because, although he felt she had talent, he did not think she was willing to work hard enough. She wanted to go to California Institute of Technology to study engineering, but the school did not accept women at that time. At the University of Toronto, therefore, she concentrated on applied mathematics because she found it esthetically appealing to use mathematics to describe natural phenomena. She took off a year during her third year of college to work for an inspection board in Quebec during World War II.

After obtaining her master's degree, she moved to New York City where her husband had a job. When she inquired about working at AT&T Bell Laboratories, she was told her name would be placed in a pool of women applicants who had bachelor's degrees. She obtained a temporary job at New York University in the Mathematics Department to edit mathematician Richard Courant's book *Supersonic Flow and Shock Waves* (1948). She says that she did not formally apply to the graduate school but just started taking classes and eventually wrote a thesis on imploding shock waves. She spent several years working part time for the department supported by navy contracts. She joined the faculty as an assistant professor in 1957 and moved rapidly through the ranks, being selected associate director of the Courant Institute in 1978 and director in 1984.

She is known for her seemingly endless array of new ideas for solving mathematical problems, but she herself admits she is not ranked with the greatest talents of the century. Almost never has a woman been one of the superstars of mathematics. Some psychologists theorize that women are inherently less capable of mathematical reasoning than men, but she does not think there is a difference between men and women in this respect. Her own experience leads her to believe that social conditions discourage most talented women from becoming mathematicians.

It was rare at the time for a man to encourage his wife to work outside the home, but her husband encouraged her to succeed and urged her to hire housekeepers to cook, clean, and help care for their four children. The Mathematics Department at New York University also was very supportive by giving her maternity leaves as well as promotions in rank. However, she did experience social pressures to stay at home. When her husband was offered a job at General Electric Corporation, she applied for one also; she was told that "GE wives do not work."

She was elected to membership in the National Academy of Sciences in 1990. She is a fellow of the American Association for the Advancement of Science and the American Academy of Arts and Sciences. She is a member of the American Mathematical Society,

Society for Industrial and Applied Mathematics, and Mathematical Association of America. Her research includes applications of partial differential equations to wave propagation, transonic flow, etc. There are photographs in *New York Magazine* (December 21, 1992) and *More Mathematical People.*

***Bibliography:*** *American Men and Women of Science* 11–19; *More Mathematical People; Notable Twentieth-Century Scientists; Who's Who in America,* 51st ed., 1997; *Who's Who in Science and Engineering,* 3d ed., 1996–1977; *Who's Who of American Women,* 20th ed., 1997–1998; *Women of Mathematics.*

# *Moss, Cynthia Jane*
(1940– )
## *wildlife biologist*

***Education:*** B.A. in philosophy, Smith College, 1962
***Professional Experience:*** Reporter and researcher for *Newsweek,* 1964–1968; assistant to veterinarian researcher in Nairobi, 1969; research assistant, Athi Plains and Tvavo National Park, 1970; freelance journalist, 1970–1971; editor, *Wildlife News,* 1971–1985; codirector of Amboseli Elephant Research Project, 1972–
***Concurrent Position:*** Senior associate, African Wildlife Foundation, 1985–

***Cynthia Moss*** is one of the foremost experts on the African elephant in the world, and for many years, she and her associate Joyce Poole led the fight to stop the world trade in ivory. In many parts of Africa, public officials and park employees were participating in the illegal killing of elephants for their ivory tusks; since it is the older male and female elephants that have the largest tusks, they were the targets of the poachers. Elephants are highly social animals who live in families led by a female, and the entire social structure of the animals was being threatened. The killing was also threatening the gene pool whereby the strongest males sire most of the young animals. Elephants have a long gestation period, an even longer maturation, and often live more than 50 years. Young males do not leave their families until they are teenagers, and females remain with the family group for life. If the older adults are killed, the families lose the wisdom of the elders on the foods to eat, the locations of water and shelter, and the best migration routes.

During the 1980s, Moss and Poole temporarily set aside their research projects to work with Richard Leakey to protect the elephants in Kenya and to stop the worldwide ivory trade. It was about this time that Leakey lost his legs in an airplane accident and was no longer able to participate in his family's long-term archaeological work. The three worked together to have the African elephant designated an endangered species by the Convention on International Trade in Endangered Species in 1989.

Moss's unique research on animals has been compared to the work of Jane Goodall and Birute Galdikas. One of Moss's contributions is her scheme of identifying elephants by their ears. The size, shape, and condition of the ears are unique to each elephant; she set up a file of photographs of the front, both sides, and back of individual elephants plus sketching the shape and condition of the ears and the tusks. The ears often had tears in them, and the tusks had scratches, broken points, etc. She also used Jane Goodall's scheme of naming the elephants according to their families, but because there are more families than letters in the alphabet, she used combinations, such as AA, AB, AC, etc., and BA, BB, BC, etc. All members of a family have names starting with the same letter. For example, she named one female in the "J" group for Joyce Poole; the matriarch for that particular family was Jezebel. Moss also studied the elephants' family structure and social patterns and became an authority on the subject.

She is famous for her research that shows the male African elephants experience musth, a condition of increased aggression and increased sexual activity that had previously been attributed only to male Indian elephants. However, the daily observations of Moss and Poole revealed that African elephants experience it also. The two women have also conducted pioneer studies of elephant vocalizations and have identified many calls and behaviors that signal what the elephants will do—either charge or move away. Using sophisticated equipment that was designed to study the vocalization of whales, Poole also found that elephants communicate at sound levels below the comprehension of the human ear. Another insight Moss discovered is that in times of drought, the elephants do not breed and therefore reduce the number of babies that will require food.

In common with many people, Moss fell in love with Africa on a brief visit to the country, and after working as a journalist for a number of years, she moved to Africa permanently in 1968 and worked with several established researchers before assuming the codirectorship of the Amboseli Elephant Research Project in 1972. She is also a senior associate of the African Wildlife Foundation, a conservation organization that is based in Washington, D.C., but she remains in Africa. She wrote the book *Portraits in the Wild: Behaviour Studies of East African Mammals* (1975), an overview of the country, and *Elephant Memories: Thirteen Years in the Life of an Elephant Family* (1988), which describes her work in Amboseli National Park. *Echo of the Elephants* (1992) is a portrait of one of the elephants who is named Echo, and *Little Big Ears* (1996) is a book for juveniles.

One method that Moss and Poole employed to gather worldwide support for the banning of the ivory trade was to invite photographers and newspaper people from all over the world to visit Amboseli to photograph the elephants and tell their story. For this reason, most of the footage on elephants that one sees on television programs and in the movies was photographed at Amboseli in the mid and late 1980s; one of the films features Echo the elephant. There are numerous photographs available, such as in *Current Biography* (1993), *Scientific American* (December 1994), Moss's own books, and Joyce Poole's autobiography, *Coming of Age with Elephants* (1996).

***Bibliography:*** *Contemporary Authors* v. 65–68; *Current Biography 1993; Who's Who of American Women,* 20th ed., 1997–1998.

# *Murray, Sandra Ann*

(1947– )

## ***molecular biologist, cell biologist***

***Education:*** B.S., University of Illinois at Chicago, 1970; M.S. in biology, Texas Southern University, 1973; Ph.D. in anatomy, University of Iowa, 1980

***Professional Experience:*** Instructor in biology, Texas Southern University, 1972–1973; National Institutes of Health research fellow, University of California, Riverside, 1980–1982; assistant professor of anatomy, University of Pittsburgh Medical School, 1982–1989, associate professor of cell biology and physiology, 1989–

***Concurrent Positions:*** Researcher, Marine Biological Laboratory, Woods Hole, 1986–1990; visiting scientist, Scripps Research Institute of Molecular Biology, 1991–1992; associate professor, Health Officers Institute, Office of Defense, Addis Ababa, Ethiopia, 1996–

***Sandra Murray*** is known for her research in molecular and cell biology. She uses molecular biological, biochemical, and morphological methods to study how cells function, what brings about normal functions in a cell population, what controls the rate of cell population growth if a normal population has been injured, and how that compares with the daily process of aging and replenishing that population. She looks at what is different in cancer cell populations and examines the capacity of cells to send signals from one cell to an adjacent cell via structures called "connexons" that are associated with controlling the function of cells and the rate of cell population growth. She also studies signal transduction; that is, when one cell gives off a peptide hormone that brings about a response in another cell by interacting with molecules on the external side of the cell membrane.

She rarely uses animals in her work. She studies cells in culture and sometimes human tissue taken from donors, which gives her control over the environment in which the cell lives and the ability to limit the number of variables in a way that is not possible with organisms. One long-term goal of her work is being able to replace cells in the body. However, in order to do so, you must be able to control the immune systems of the person to whom you are giving the cells. For example, in treating tumor cells, the goal is to stop the cells from growing and not affect the rest of the cells in the body.

She became interested in science at a very early age. Her arm was paralyzed for a time because of a broken clavicle, and in response to her questions about why her arm had stopped working, the hospital staff gave her old medical books to read. She also participated in science fairs, but she usually selected projects that were too ambitious, such as a cure for cancer. Her family was very supportive of her interests in science; if she had homework, she did not have to do chores. She always felt there was no limitation to being a woman and going into any field that she wanted to go into. Her mother set a good example for her by working in the family business as well as operating her own business.

Murray did not know there were fields women did not go into until she went to college. Although a high school counselor told her that "colored girls don't become research scientists," Murray did not believe her. In high school she worked as a laboratory aide at the University of Illinois Medical School and was participating in special science classes at the University of Chicago. She supported herself at Texas Southern University by working as a teaching assistant in genetics, but her major professor at the University of Iowa told her she could not expect to keep up with the class in genetics because, he theorized, as a black person, her family for generations had had an inadequate diet. When she made good grades, he told her that her lighter skin probably indicated she had non-African blood that allowed her to do well. She decided that her only recourse to such statements was to transfer to a different department with a different adviser. She went on to succeed in her class work and to receive her doctorate. At the University of Pittsburgh Medical School, she is one of the few women and persons of color in that institution.

Although she finds her peers very supportive, she feels that a white man's career is nurtured in ways that may not be made available to a woman or to a minority person. It may be neglect rather than hostility, but people forget to tell a minority or female faculty member information that they need to know. However, she warns women that they should learn to say no to many committee appointments: accept the invitation to serve on the finance committee but reject the one that plans to redecorate the conference room. In order to encourage minority students to seek careers in science and technology, she schedules visits to institutions with high minority enrollments to make contact with the students.

She is a member of the American Society of Cell Biology, American Society of Biological Chemists, American Association of Anatomists, Tissue Culture Association, and Endocrine Society. Her photograph is included in *Distinguished African American Scientists of the 20th Century* and *Journeys of Women in Science and Engineering*.

***Bibliography:*** *Distinguished African American Scientists of the 20th Century; Journeys of Women in Science and Engineering; Who's Who in America,* 51st ed., 1997; *Who's Who of American Women,* 20th ed., 1997–1998.

# Nader, Laura
(1930– )
***cultural anthropologist***

***Education:*** B.A., Wells College, 1952; Ph.D. in anthropology, Radcliffe College, 1961
***Professional Experience:*** Assistant professor of anthropology, University of California, Berkeley, 1960–1965, associate professor, 1965–
***Concurrent Positions:*** Fellow, Center for Advanced Study in Behavioral Sciences, 1963–1964; fellow, Woodrow Wilson Center for International Scholars, 1979–1980
***Married:*** Norman Milleron, 1962
***Children:*** 3

**Laura Nader** is renowned for her studies in cultural anthropology that encompass law, anthropology, sociology, and scientific interests. One popular study she conducted in the 1980s indicated that one out of every six purchases in the United States leads to legitimate grounds for complaint. However, consumers either do not complain or rarely get satisfaction when they do because consumers have less power than the manufacturers, stores, or professionals they must deal with. Therefore, consumers can be ignored or fought successfully in court. She also compared the way complaints are handled in advanced and simple societies. In one village in southern Mexico, complaints are heard by a designated referee and usually are resolved the same day. In contrast, a woman in Pennsylvania tried for weeks to convince dealers, manufacturers, and federal agencies that her new stove was a hazard. Before her complaint was resolved, the stove turned itself on and burned down her house.

Nader has published several books on the theme of resolving conflict, particularly in South American societies. She is considered one of the deans of Mexican legal anthropology, and her brother is the consumer advocate Ralph Nader. Among her books on the topic of resolving conflict are *Law in Culture and Society* (1969), *The Disputing Process: Laws in Ten Societies* (1978), and *No Access to Law: Alternatives to the American Judicial System* (1980). In *Harmony Ideology: Justice and Control in a Zapotec Mountain Village* (1990), she explains that the people in the village handle disputes by focusing on reconciliation and compromise, preferring to use the village courts instead of appealing to the district courts where an adversarial form of litigation predominates. She theorized that the "harmony ideology" concept was introduced by the Christian missionaries because the Spaniards favored indirect rule of Indian communities.

*Naked Science: Anthropological Inquiry into Boundaries, Power and Knowledge* (1996) consists of a collection of essays that examine the power of Western science over the other sciences around the globe, such as navigation in Micronesia, herbal medicine in Mexico, nuclear weapons testing, DNA sequence databases, and Japanese primatology. An earlier book on this theme *is Cultural Illness and Health: Essays in Human Adaptation* (1973). Another of her interdisciplinary studies concerns views of motherhood in the United States and Mexico, and it appeared in the journal *Urban Anthropology and Studies of Cultural Systems and World Economic Development* in 1986. "This paper contrasts Latin American women's emphasis on motherhood as a political strategy with the anti-motherhood position of many U.S. feminists to show how both positions reflect different sociocultural conditions and patterns of male domination. The ideal of motherhood in the U.S. has isolated women and weakened their position in the family and society. In Mexico, motherhood is the basis of successful female political action."

Nader is a member of the American Anthropological Association. In addition to her books, she has contributed articles and book reviews to law reviews and to anthropological, sociological, and scientific journals.

***Bibliography:*** *American Men and Women of Science* 11–13; *Contemporary Authors* v. CANR-7 and 17–20R.

# *Napadensky, Hyla Sarane (Siegel)*
(1929– )
## *combustion engineer*

***Education:*** B.S. and M.S. in mathematics, University of Chicago, c. 1950
***Professional Experience:*** Design analysis engineer, International Harvester Company, 1952–1957; instructor, Mechanics Department, Illinois Institute of Technology (IIT), 1964–1966; director of research, IIT Research Institute, Chicago, 1957–1988; vice president, Napadensky Energetics, Inc., 1988–1994; engineering consultant, 1994–
***Married:*** Arnoldo I. Napadensky, 1956
***Children:*** 2

***Hyla Napadensky*** has had a fascinating career as an expert in explosives and propellant safety. Although other women listed in this volume have expertise in handling hazardous chemicals, nuclear materials, and environmental hazards, combustion engineering seems to be an unusual occupation. Somehow explosives sound dangerous, but perhaps working with them is not as dangerous as studying the flow of lava from volcanoes as some women geophysicists do.

She lists her research as the study of accidental fires and explosions during the manufacture, transport, and storage of explosives, propellants, and pyrotechnics. She also studies explosive and initiation mechanisms, facility siting, and systems safety and risk analysis.

After working for five years for the International Harvester Company, she began a career as director of research at the IIT Research Institute, which is involved with research on a contract basis, some of it with federal agencies. Probably many of the studies she conducted for the government are classified as secret and therefore are not included in the standard databases.

Napadensky has conducted research on a wide variety of materials using explosive charges of varying degrees of intensity. One report, published in an engineering journal, discussed the behavior of porous material when rapidly compressed by an explosive. She also did a study on the stress wave propagation in snow and ice for the U.S. Army by comparing Greenland snow to Michigan snow using a low-density explosive charge. She has written about the risks of handling explosives on ships and in harbors.

She prepared a 220-page book for the U.S. Army, *Development of Hazards Classification Data on Propellants and Explosives* (1978), and a similar book for the same agency, *Recommended Hazard Classification Procedures for In-Process Propellant and Explosive Material* (1980). As an internal publication, she prepared data on the TNT equivalency of black powder.

She was elected to membership in the National Academy of Engineering in 1984, and she is a member of the Combustion Institute. Like many of the women profiled in this volume, she later worked for a company, Napadensky Energetics, Inc., and then turned to consulting.

***Bibliography:*** *American Men and Women of Science* 16–19; Herzenberg, C., *Women Scientists from Antiquity to the Present; Who's Who in America,* 51st ed., 1997.

# *Navrotsky, Alexandra A. S.*
(1943– )
## *geochemist, geophysicist*

***Education:*** B.S., University of Chicago, 1963, M.S., 1964, Ph.D. in chemistry, 1967
***Professional Experience:*** Research associate in theoretical metallurgy, Clausthal Technical University, Germany, 1967–1968; research associate in geochemistry, Pennsylvania State University, 1968–1969; assistant professor, Arizona State University, 1969–1974, associate professor, 1974–1977, professor of chemistry and geology, 1978–1985, director, Center for Solid State Science, 1984–1985; professor, Department of Geology and Geophysical Science, Princeton University, 1985– , department chair, 1988–1991, Albert G. Blanke Jr. Professor of Geology and Geophysical Science, 1992–
***Concurrent Positions:*** Program director in chemical thermodynamics, National Science Foundation, 1976–1977

A***lexandra Navrotsky*** is recognized as one of the leaders in combining mineralogical and materials research. As new technological materials become increasingly complex in structure and bonding, they are beginning to resemble the materials that make up our planet; materials science is the study of the characteristics and uses of various materials such as glass, plastics, and metals. The technology was developed about 1960–1965; the science of mineralogy developed about 1680–1690. A mineral is any of a class of substances that occur in nature; usually comprising inorganic substances of definite chemical composition and usually definite crystal structure, such as quartz or feldspar, it may sometimes include rocks formed by these substances as well as certain natural products of organic origin, such as asphalt or coal.

One of the areas she has investigated is the composition of the earth, and she points out that although humans have explored the moon, a journey to the center of the earth remains fictional and technologically unattainable. However, mineral physics can provide some information via laboratory and computational simulations of matter under high pressure and temperature. The earth is composed of, in descending order, the crust, the upper mantle, the transition zone, the lower mantle, the outer core, and the inner core. An interdisciplinary study is examining questions about the earth using mineral physics, seismology, and geodynamics; one of Navrotzky's papers on mantle thermochemistry was published in the July 9, 1993, issue of *Science.*

Her expertise has been recognized by invitations to serve on visiting committees for several prestigious universities, including the Division of Geological Science, California Institute of Technology (1991), Department of Earth and Planetary Science, Harvard University, (1991– ), and Geological Science, Columbia University, 1992– ). She was also a member of the Committee on Mineral Physics of the American Geophysical Union (1983–1993) and a member of the Committee on High Temperature Chemistry of the National Academy of Sciences (1981–1985).

Navrotsky was elected to membership in the National Academy of Sciences in 1993. She has more than 100 publications and is the author of *Physics and Chemistry of Earth Materials* (1994), a textbook designed for a one-semester course for advanced undergraduates and first-year graduate students. She is a fellow of the Mineralogical Society of America (president, 1992–1993), and the American Geophysical Union. She is a member of the American Ceramic Society and Materials Research Society. Her research includes thermodynamics, phase equilibrium and high temperature calorimetry, oxides and oxide solid solutions order-disorder, geochemistry, and geothermal fluids.

***Bibliography:*** *American Men and Women of Science* 12–19; *Who's Who in Science and Engineering,* 2d ed., 1994–1995.

# *Nelkin, Dorothy (Wolfers)*
(1933– )
***sociologist***

***Education:*** B.A. in sociology, Cornell University, 1954
***Professional Experience:*** Research associate, Cornell University, 1963–1969, senior research associate, 1970–1972, associate professor, 1972–1976, professor, science, technology and society policy program, Department of Sociology, 1976–1990, professor of sociology, 1977–1990; university professor and professor of sociology, affiliate professor of law, New York University, 1990– , Clare Booth Luce visiting professor, 1988–1990
***Married:*** Mark Nelkin, 1952
***Children:*** 2

***Dorothy Nelkin*** is a sociologist who has published a long list of books and papers covering the spectrum of social problems. Over a 20-year period, primarily while she was a member of the science, technology, and society policy program at Cornell University, she wrote and coauthored books and papers about migrant labor, nuclear power, housing innovation, university and military research, methadone maintenance, science, technological decisions, the atom, the creation controversy, unsafe work conditions, and medical diagnosis. She later wrote about animal rights and DNA, and an article in the January 16, 1998, issue of *Science* quotes her reaction to physicist Richard Seed's announcement that he was planning to clone humans. She said that Seed should have been ignored. "It's a shame," Nelkin adds, "that the episode hasn't seeded a more worthwhile discussion about the risks and benefits of cloning."

In her book *Workers at Risk: Voices from the Workplace* (1984), she reviews the unsafe conditions that workers of all types encounter. Her research team interviewed workers in museums, beauty shops, research laboratories, and computer assembly plants as well as steel mills, auto assembly plants, and other obvious places for dangerous working conditions. The surveyors found there was no direct link between the actual hazards and people's perceptions of risk. For example, artists and research scientists often feel that the rewards of their job outweigh the risks of handling extremely toxic chemicals. However, many workers complained they lacked information about the chemicals they worked with; it is to be hoped that that situation has improved since the survey was conducted.

*Dangerous Diagnostics: The Social Power of Biological Information* (1994) is a revised edition of a book by the same title published in 1989. In it, the authors review the myriad tests that pronounce people healthy or ill or likely or not likely to suffer any of hundreds of ailments. However, the authors focus on the social implications of the information that these tests provide and question the common belief that information attained through scientific testing is always credible. However, their primary concern is the power and control that accrue to the people who administer the tests and make judgments about how the results are to be applied.

A more recent book is *The DNA Mystique: The Gene as a Cultural Icon* (1994). Although many areas of science today are so esoteric that even scientists in other disciplines cannot comprehend them, the subject of genetics, especially human genetics, has attracted a great deal of public interest. In addition, various political ideologists adopt contrasting views on the questions at stake. The isolation surrounding scientific work has broken down, and politicians, moralists, and campaigners are not content to allow scientists to decide whether and in what sense intelligence, homosexuality, or a propensity to commit crime can be said to be genetically determined. The authors conclude that the DNA mystique implies that the problems of American society cannot be solved through changing the social structure or nurturing patterns but only through biological controls.

Nelkin has been a consultant to the Organization of Economic Cooperation and Development (OECD, 1975–1976) and the Institute of Environment, Berlin (1978–1979) and a member of the National Advisory Council to the Human Genome Project of the National Institutes of Health (1991–1995). She is a fellow of the American Association for the Advancement of Science and a member of the Society for Social Studies of Science (president, 1978–1979). Her research includes sociology; studies between science and the public, science and the media; and the institutional use of scientific information.

***Bibliography:*** *American Men and Women of Science* 19; *Contemporary Authors* v. CANR-31; Herzenberg, C., *Women Scientists from Antiquity to the Present; Who's Who in America,* 51st ed., 1997; *Who's Who in Science and Engineering,* 3d ed., 1996–1977.

# *Neufeld, Elizabeth (Fondal)*
(1928– )
## ***biochemist, enzymologist***

***Education:*** B.S., Queens College, 1948; student, University of Rochester, 1949–1950; Ph.D. in biochemistry, University of California, Berkeley, 1956; honorary degrees: Dr., Universite René Descartes, Paris, 1978, Hahnemann University, 1984; D.Sc., Russell Sage College, 1980
***Professional Experience:*** Research biochemist, National Institute of Arthritis, Metabolism and Digestive Diseases, National Institutes of Health, 1963–1973, chief, Section on Human Biochemical Genetics, 1973–1979, chief, Genetics and Biochemistry Branch, National Institute of Arthritis, Diabetes, and Digestive and Kidney Diseases, 1979–1984, deputy director, Division of Extramural Research, 1981–1983; professor of biological chemistry and department chair, School of Medicine, University of California, Los Angeles, 1984–
***Concurrent Positions:*** U.S. Public Health Service fellow, University of California, Berkeley, 1956–1957, assistant research biochemist, 1957–1963
***Married:*** Benjamin Neufeld, 1951
***Children:*** 2

***Elizabeth Neufeld*** is a leading international authority on human genetic diseases. Her research has provided new insights on the absence of certain enzymes that prevent the body from properly storing certain substances and has led to prenatal diagnosis of such life-threatening fetal disorders as Hurler syndrome. She was awarded the Lasker Award in 1982, the Wolf Prize in Medicine in 1988, and in 1995, she was awarded the National Medal of Science of the National Science Foundation; this award was presented in the White House by President Clinton. She was elected to membership in the National Academy of Sciences in 1977.

Her research focuses on inherited disorders of the connective tissues. These are lysosomal storage diseases in which cells lack certain enzymes needed to process complex sugars. The accumulation of sugars causes the cells to grow and put internal pressure on nerve tissues, which can die from too much pressure. Patients suffer from severe mental and motor deterioration, have vision and hearing problems, and die prematurely, usually before puberty. The diseases are known as the Hurler and Sanfilippo syndromes and are in a group called mucopolysaccharidoses (MPS). Also related to MPS are Tay-Sachs and I-cell diseases. After years of research, her team found that the problem was a defective gene that was causing the sugars to break down at an abnormally slow rate, and further study indicated that a series of enzymes were lacking in the patients. Her work has led to successful prenatal diagnosis and has contributed to the availability of genetic counseling for parents. Future treatments being considered are gene replacement therapy and bone marrow transplant.

Neufeld's parents were Russian refugees living in Paris after the Russian revolution when she was born; the family moved to New York City before the Germans occupied France in 1940. Her parents stressed the importance of education because education cannot be taken away from you, and she became interested in science while in high school through the influence of her biology instructor. After receiving her undergraduate degree, she worked briefly as a research assistant at the Jackson Memorial Laboratory, then studied physiology at the University of Rochester. She moved to the McCollum-Pratt Institute at Johns Hopkins University as a research assistant, then studied for her doctorate at University of California, Berkeley.

She started her scientific studies at a time when few women were choosing science as a career and there were few positions open for women—partly because of the historical bias against women in science and partly because of the influx of men returning from World War II. Few women could be found on the science faculties of colleges and universities, but she persevered in her career because she enjoyed what she was doing. One of her rewards was receiving two of the most prestigious awards in the United States. The first was the Lasker Award for medical research in 1982, the highest honor in the United States for medical research; recipients of that award often later receive the Nobel prize in medicine. The second was the National Medal of Science in 1995, whose recipients are chosen from all scientific disciplines in the United States each year.

She is a fellow of the American Association for the Advancement of Science and a member of the American Society of Human Genetics, American Chemical Society, American Society of Biological Chemists, American Society of Cell Biology, American Society of Biochemistry and Molecular Biology (president, 1992–1993), and American Academy of Arts and Sciences. Her research includes human biochemical genetics, mucopolysaccharidoses; Tay-Sachs disease; synthesis and transport of lysosomal enzymes; and inherited disorders of lysosomal functions. Her photograph is included in *Notable Twentieth-Century Scientists* and *Chemical & Engineering News* (September 12, 1994).

***Bibliography:*** *American Men and Women of Science* 11–19; Herzenberg, C., *Women Scientists from Antiquity to the Present; Notable Twentieth-Century Scientists; Notable Women in the Life Sciences;* Stanley, A., *Mothers and Daughters of Invention; Who's Who in America,* 51st ed., 1997; *Who's Who in Science and Engineering,* 3d ed., 1996–1977; *Who's Who of American Women,* 20th ed., 1997–1998

# New, Maria Iandolo
(1928– )
*pediatrician*

***Education:*** B.A., Cornell University, 1950; M.D., University of Pennsylvania, 1954; diplomate, American Board of Pediatrics, 1960
***Professional Experience:*** Intern in medicine, Bellevue Hospital, 1954–1955; assistant resident in pediatrics, New York Hospital–Cornell Medical Center, 1955–1957, assistant pediatrician, Clinical Research Center, 1957–1959, pediatrician, Outpatient Department, 1959–1963, research investigator, diabetic study group, Comprehensive Care and Teaching Program, 1958–1961, instructor in pediatrics, 1958–1963, associate professor and associate attending pediatrician, 1968–1971, professor of pediatrics and attending pediatrician, 1971– , Harold and Percy Uris professor of pediatric endocrinology, 1978– ; director, Pediatric Metabolism and Endocrine Clinic and division head, Pediatric Endocrinology, 1964– , associate director of pediatrics, Clinical Research Center, 1966–
***Concurrent Positions:*** Adjunct professor, Rockefeller University, 1981– ; attending pediatrician, Pediatrics Department, Memorial Sloan-Kettering Cancer Center, 1979– ; consultant, Albert Einstein College of Medicine, 1974– , and United Hospital, Port Chester, New York, 1977–
***Married:*** Bertrand L. New, 1949, died 1990
***Children:*** 3

*Maria New* has had a long career as a pediatrician specializing in endocrinology at New York Hospital–Cornell Medical Center, and since 1955, she has also maintained a private practice specializing in pediatrics in New York City. She advanced through the ranks to become the pediatrician in chief at the New York Hospital and then moved to a faculty position at Cornell University Medical College, rising to the rank of professor in 1971. She was appointed the Harold and Percy Uris Professor of pediatric endocrinology in 1978 and has also served as an adjunct professor at Rockefeller University since 1981. She was a career scientist on the New York City Health Research Council from 1966 to 1974 and has been attending pediatrician in the Pediatrics Department of the Memorial Sloan-Kettering Cancer Center since 1979.

In addition to her numerous publications, she has served as editor in chief of the *Journal of Clinical Endocrinology and Metabolism* since 1994. She has received multiple honors and awards, including the Robert H. Williams Distinguished Leadership Award (1988), medal of the New York Academy of Medicine (1991), Maurice R. Greenberg Distinguished Service Award (1994), and Humanitarian Award of the Juvenile Diabetes Foundation (1994).

Maria New is one of the editors of a book written for the general public, the two-volume *Disney Encyclopedia of Baby and Child Care* (1995) compiled by four pediatricians. Volume 1, *Infant and Child Development—Birth to Age Six,* outlines the progression of those years and suggests milestones and signs of trouble for various ages. Volume 2, *A to Z Encyclopedia of Child Health & Illnesses,* lists 160 medical and behavioral concerns in alphabetical order. One reviewer recommended that the encyclopedia is most useful to parents as an initial reference, a starting point to further reading.

New was elected to membership in the National Academy of Sciences in 1996. She is a member of numerous associations, such as the American Association for the Advancement of Science, New York Academy of Sciences, American Society of Human Genetics, American Academy of Pediatrics, Society for Pediatric Research, Endocrine Society (president, 1991–1992), American Fertility Society, and American Academy of Arts and Sciences. Her research includes pediatric endocrinology and renal diseases, juvenile hypertension, pediatric pharmacology, and growth and development from the biochemical viewpoint.

***Bibliography:*** *American Men and Women of Science* 11–19; *Who's Who in America,* 51st ed., 1997.

# *Nichols, Roberta J.*
(1931– )
## ***environmental engineer***

***Education:*** B.S. in physics, University of California, Los Angeles, 1968; M.S. in environmental engineering, University of Southern California, 1975, Ph.D. in engineering, 1979
***Professional Experience:*** Mathematician, Missile Department, Douglas Aircraft Company, 1957; mathematician, propulsion department, TRW Space Technology Laboratory, 1958–1960; research associate, Aerospace Corporation, Aerodynamics and Propulsion Laboratory, 1960–1967, Chemical Kinetics Department, 1969–1978, where she established the Air Pollution Laboratory; established Synthetic Fuels Office, State of California, 1978–1979; developer of synthetic fuels, Ford Motor Company, 1979–1989, manager of alternate fuels program, 1989–
***Married:*** Lynn Yakal
***Children:*** 2

***Roberta Nichols*** is renowned as the person who led the U.S. automobile manufacturers in developing alternate fuels and the cars to use those fuels. California and many other states are now requiring manufacturers to build ultra-low-emission vehicles—by 1999, in some cases—and the Environmental Protection Agency has also issued mandates. Roberta has been researching alternative fuels since the late 1970s, becoming interested in such fuels—what she calls "funny fuels"—when she was drag racing boats in California in the 1960s. In 1968, she bought a 1954 methanol-powered Mercedes that she still races occasionally at a race course in Michigan; her personal best speed, 190 miles per hour, was in a 1929 Model A Ford at the Bonneville Salt Flats in Utah. She says her racing experience taught her about engines.

However, it was her father, an aerospace engineer, who introduced her to racing. As a child she went fishing with him and helped him work on cars. When people tell her she is a woman pioneer in engineering, she says she was just a typical tomboy; she didn't know she was not supposed to like that stuff. She has worked for several aerospace companies, and while she was working for Aerospace Corporation, she established the Air Pollution Laboratory. After her first husband died in the mid 1960s, however, leaving her with two children to rear, she decided to return to school part time to obtain degrees in engineering in order to enhance her career opportunities. Her experiences in boat and car racing led her to choose engineering. She has published one paper on methanol-gasoline blends and another comparing hydrogen-powered versus battery-powered automobiles. She has also consulted for the state of California on synthetic fuels.

She joined the Ford Motor Company in 1979 and single-handedly dragged Ford and then the rest of the Detroit automobile manufacturers into the alternative fuels age. She was one of the few people who had the foresight that future clean air laws would alter the use of fuels used to power cars and trucks. She has earned three patents for technologies used in engines that burn fuels of different octane, volatility, and volumetric energy content. She developed ethanol-fueled engines for Ford of Brazil; designed and developed 630 methanol-fueled Escorts, which were used primarily for California government fleets; designed and developed the power train for an alternate fuel vehicle exhibited in 1982; and oversaw the building of 27 natural gas trucks. She is still working on sodium-sulfur technology for batteries and on electric vehicles.

Nichols is the first woman to be elected a fellow of the Society of Automotive Engineers, and she has received the Outstanding Engineer Merit Award of the Institute for the Advancement of Engineering, the Aerospace Corporation's Woman of the Year Award, and the Society of Women Engineers Achievement Award (1988). A photograph of her in her fireproof racing uniform is included in *Business Week* (July 16, 1990) and in *Automotive News* (April 4, 1993).

***Bibliography:*** *Notable Twentieth-Century Scientists.*

# *Novello, Antonia (Coello)*
(1944– )
***pediatrician***

***Education:*** B.S., University of Puerto Rico, 1965, M.D., 1970; M.S. in public health, Johns Hopkins University School of Hygiene, 1982; diplomate, American Board of Pediatrics; honorary degrees: 14

***Professional Experience:*** Intern in pediatrics, University of Michigan Medical Center, 1970–1971, resident in pediatrics, 1971–1973, pediatric nephrology fellow, 1973–1974; pediatric nephrology fellow, Georgetown University Hospital, 1974–1975; private practice, 1976–1978; project officer, National Institute of Arthritis, Metabolism and Digestive Diseases, National Institutes of Health (NIH), 1978–1979, staff physician, 1979–1980, executive secretary, general medicine study section, Division of Research Grants, 1981–1986, deputy director, National Institute of Child Health and Human Development, 1986–1990; surgeon general, U.S. Department of Health and Human Services, 1990–1993; special representative for health and nutrition, UNICEF, 1993–

***Concurrent Positions:*** Clinical professor of pediatrics, Georgetown University Hospital, 1986, 1989; adjunct professor of pediatrics and communicable diseases, University of Michigan Medical School, 1993; adjunct professor of international health, Johns Hopkins University School of Hygiene and Public Health

***Married:*** Joseph R. Novello, 1970

***Antonia Novello*** was the first woman to be selected Surgeon General of the United States, being sworn in by Sandra Day O'Connor, the first woman member of the U.S. Supreme Court, in 1990. Novello was also the first Hispanic and the first Puerto Rican person to hold the position of surgeon general. As a child, she decided to become a physician to ease the sufferings of others—she herself was a victim of a debilitating malady that afflicted her until she reached her early twenties, and for many years she required annual hospitalization. She was inspired by the care her pediatrician gave her to become a pediatrician herself. Her mother pushed her to continue her education to meet her goals.

After receiving her M.D. degree in Puerto Rico, she and her husband moved to the University of Michigan to continue their education. She then had additional training at Georgetown University before she joined the National Institutes of Health (NIH). While with NIH, she received a master's degree in public health from Johns Hopkins University and rose rapidly through the ranks, serving as deputy director of one agency before being appointed surgeon general. Since her predecessor as surgeon general, C. Everett Koop, had been an outspoken person who attracted media attention, Novello also used the position to attract national media attention to health-related issues, but in a more diplomatic manner. She concentrated on the health care of minorities, women, and children; injury prevention; and the problems of domestic violence, alcohol abuse among the nation's youth, and smoking among women and young people. Although she opposes abortion, she seldom discussed the issue while surgeon general, feeling that women should not view abortion as the only issue to tackle.

The surgeon general is considered to be the nation's chief adviser on matters of public health and a spokesperson for the president in such areas. Another responsibility is to oversee the 6,400 active-duty commissioned corps of the U.S. Public Health Service, whose members hold ranks equivalent to those in the U.S. Navy. Consequently, Novello wore a vice admiral's uniform when she appeared in public during her term in office. Public health service members staff health centers on Native American reservations, serve in areas of the country where there is a shortage of medical personnel, conduct quarantine inspection in U.S. ports, engage in basic research, and help out during national medical emergencies.

Novello made headlines in 1992 when she and the executive vice president of the American Medical Association held a news conference to urge R. J. Reynolds Tobacco Company to withdraw its ads featuring the cartoon character Joe Camel because of its appeal to young people. She also attacked alcohol advertising because, in using sports heroes and other people who are physically appealing, it targets young people and encourages underage drinking. Other issues that she targeted were domestic violence, particularly against women; the number of children who are not vaccinated against common infectious diseases; and the widespread lack of proper prenatal care. Because of her interest in children, her office suite was decorated with toys and photographs of children. One person described it as looking like a pediatrician's waiting room rather than a bureaucrat's office, but it was designed to make her visitors feel at ease and to reflect her warm, open manner.

After she left the surgeon general's office, she accepted a position with UNICEF. She has received many awards, such as the Public Health Service Outstanding Medal (1988), Surgeon General Medallion Award (1990), alumni award of the University of Michigan Medical School (1991), Distinguished Public Service Award (1993), and the Elizabeth Blackwell Award (1991)—Elizabeth Blackwell (1821–1910) is considered to have been the first woman physician in modern times. Novello was inducted into the National Women's Hall of Fame at Seneca Falls, New York, in 1994. She is a member of the American Medical Association, International Society of Nephrology, and American Society of Nephrology. Her photograph is included in *Current Biography* (1992) and *Notable Hispanic American Women.*

***Bibliography:*** *American Men and Women of Science* 17–19; *Current Biography 1992; Notable Hispanic American Women; Who's Who in Science and Engineering,* 3d ed., 1996–1977; *Who's Who of American Women,* 20th ed., 1997–1998.

# Ocampo, Adriana C.
(1955– )
***planetary geologist***

***Education:*** Student in aerospace engineering, Pasadena City College, c. 1972–1975; B.S. in geology, California State University, 1983

***Professional Experience:*** Planetary geologist, Jet Propulsion Laboratory, National Aeronautics and Space Administration (NASA), 1983– , science coordinator for *Galileo* mission to Jupiter, 1989–

***Married:*** Kevin O. Pope, 1989

***Adriana Ocampo*** is known as a planetary geologist who has expertise in remote sensing. She is primarily involved in applying traditional geological principles to other celestial bodies, such as stars, moons, comets, and asteroids. However, planetary geologists also study objects on earth that are of extraterrestrial origin, such as meteorite remnants, and she has had experience with that aspect of her field as well. At the Jet Propulsion Laboratory, she has been involved in the *Viking* space mission to explore Mars and the outer planets and in the *Hermes* mission to explore Mercury; as a science coordinator for the *Galileo* mission to Jupiter, she was responsible for one of the spacecraft's four remote sensing instruments. In the early 1990s, she participated in exploring areas of Yucatan in an effort to locate the crater made by an asteroid when it impacted the earth at the time of the Cretaceous-Tertiary (KT) boundary (65 billion years ago). The sulfurous cloud that rose from that impact circled the earth, blocked the sun, and killed the vegetation on which the dinosaurs and large mammals fed, causing the extinction of both.

Ocampo was born in Colombia and lived in Argentina until her family moved to California when she was a teenager. Although she was interested in science, she had difficulty persuading the school adviser in high school that she preferred taking physics and mathematics instead of business courses. She was not allowed to take auto mechanics in high school, but she finally took that course in junior college. While still in high school, she obtained a summer job at the Jet Propulsion Laboratory and continued to work there during her last two years of high school and while she was in college. When she joined the lab as a full-time employee in 1983, she had already worked there ten years. It was through her work there that she decided on a career in planetary geology.

For the *Viking* mission to Mars, she was assigned to produce a photo atlas of one of the moons of Mars. This volume, published in 1984, is the only available atlas of the moon Phobus. For the *Mars Observer* mission, she was responsible for the thermal emission spectrometer, an instrument that was supposed to measure the heat produced by the planet, thus enabling cartographers to create accurate maps. Unfortunately, the mission failed in 1993 when the spacecraft fell silent and spun out of control owing to a malfunction; the instrument remained untested. She was then assigned to oversee the operation of the Near-Infrared Mapping Spectrometer (NIMS), which was mounted on the *Galileo* spacecraft. As one of four remote sensing instruments, NIMS was to measure reflected sunlight and heat from Jupiter's atmosphere and helps scientists determine the planet's composition, cloud structure, and temperature, information that will enable scientists to learn more about the surface chemistry and mineralogy of Jupiter's four moons. *Galileo* was launched in 1989 and was still on track in 1998.

Ocampo and her husband were part of the team searching for the asteroid crater in Yucatan (his company does remote-sensing geological and ecological research). The background of this project is that for a number of years, geologists had found a layer of iridium on the Cretaceous-Tertiary (KT) boundary in various parts of the world. Since iridium is not found on earth but is found on other planets, the physicist Luis Alvarez and his geologist son, Walter Alvarez, developed the theory that a giant asteroid had impacted the earth 65 million years ago, spreading the iridium in the dust cloud that had then circled the earth. Ocampo and her husband participated in verifying this theory, and their contributions are mentioned in Walter Alvarez's book, *T-Rex and the Crater of Doom* (1997).

Her photograph is included in *Hispanic* (September 1996) and *Hispanic Engineer* (fall 1987).

***Bibliography:*** *Notable Hispanic American Women; Notable Twentieth-Century Scientists.*

# *Ochoa, Ellen*
## (1958– )
## *electrical engineer, astronaut*

***Education:*** B.S., San Diego State University, 1980; M.S., Stanford University, 1981, Ph.D. in electrical engineering, 1985

***Professional Experience:*** Researcher, Imaging Technology Division, Sandia National Laboratory, 1985–1988; group leader then chief, Intelligent Systems Branch, Ames Research Center, National Aeronautics and Space Administration (NASA), 1988–1990; astronaut, 1990– , mission STS-56 (1993) and STS-66 (1994)

***Married:*** Coe F. Miles, 1990

***Ellen Ochoa*** is known as an electrical engineer and an astronaut who is a specialist in optics and optical recognition in robotics. While working at Sandia National Laboratory, she developed a process that implements optics for image processing that is normally done by computer. For example, one method she devised removes noise from an image through an optical system rather than using a standard digital computer to do the work. On her first space flight in 1993, she was one of only two scientists on board the shuttle. She played a key role by deploying instruments in space to enable scientists to look at the sun's corona, and she operated the deployment arm under stressful conditions owing to the limited time allotted for the procedure on the short mission.

While still a graduate student, she developed and patented a real-time optical inspection technique for defect detection, and she considers it her most important scientific achievement to date. She joined the technical staff in the Imaging Technology Division of Sandia after receiving her doctorate, and there her research centered on developing optical filters for noise removal and optical methods for distortion-invariant object recognition. She was coauthor of two additional patents, one for an optical system for the nonlinear median filtering of images and another for a distortion invariant optical pattern recognition system.

She had not considered a career as an astronaut until many of her friends in graduate school had applied, but she was the only one of the group to be accepted. She first applied for the program in 1985, and in 1987 she was named one of the top 100 finalists. In 1988 she joined the National Aeronautics and Space Administration (NASA) as a group leader in the Photonic Processing Group of the Intelligent Systems Branch located at the Ames Research Center in California. Photonics is the study and technology of the use of light for the transmission of information, and she was a group leader for a team researching optical image and data-processing techniques for space-based robotics. Six months later, she was promoted to chief of the Intelligent Systems Technology Branch. She was chosen for the astronaut program in 1990 and completed her training in 1991.

Her first flight was in 1993 on the orbiter *Discovery* mission STS-56 that carried the Atmospheric Laboratory for Applications and Science, known as Atlas-2. She was specifically responsible for the primary payload, the Spartan 201 satellite, and she operated the robotic arm to deploy and retrieve it. Her second flight was in 1994 on mission STS-66, the Atmospheric Laboratory for Applications and Science-3 (Atlas-3). This mission continued the Spacelab flight series to study the sun's energy during an 11-year solar cycle in order to learn how changes in the irradiance of the sun affect the earth's environment and climate. On that mission, she was the payload commander.

However, science was not her first choice as a career when she entered college. While she was an undergraduate, she changed her major four times, from music to business to journalism to computer science before finally settling on physics. Her parents had stressed the value of an education to their children, encouraging them to do whatever they wanted to do but placing a high premium on going to college. Following her own advice, their mother took college courses for 23 years, finishing with a triple major in business, biology, and journalism. Ochoa worked incredibly hard both in college and in her positions at Sandia and NASA, even obtaining a pilot's license for small-engine planes because she thought she should learn more about aviation if she wanted to be an astronaut.

As the first female Hispanic astronaut, Ochoa has become a role model for young girls and Hispanics and frequently speaks before school groups. She emphasizes if one studies hard and reaches far enough, the possibilities are endless. She has received several awards, including the NASA Group Achievement Award for Photonics Technology (1991), NASA Space Flight Medal (1993), Women in Science and Engineering (WISE) Engineering Achievement Award (1994), National Hispanic Quincentennial Commission Pride Award (1990), *Hispanic* magazine's Hispanic Achievement Science Award (1991), and the Congressional Hispanic Caucus Medallion of Excellence Role Model Award (1993). She is a member of the Optical Society of America and the American Institute of Aeronautics and Astronautics. Her photograph is included in the first two sources that follow.

***Bibliography:*** *Notable Hispanic American Women; Notable Twentieth-Century Scientists;* U.S. National Aeronautics and Space Administration, *Astronaut Fact Book.*

# *Osborn, Mary Jane (Merten)*
(1927– )
## *molecular biologist, biochemist*

***Education:*** B.A. in physiology, University of California, Berkeley, 1948; Ph.D. in biochemistry, University of Washington, 1958

***Professional Experience:*** Instructor, New York University School of Medicine, 1961–1962, assistant professor, 1962–1963; assistant professor, Department of Molecular Biology, Albert Einstein College of Medicine, 1963–1966, associate professor, 1966–1968; professor of microbiology, University of Connecticut Health Center, 1968– , department head, 1980–

***Married:*** Ralph K. Osborn, 1950

***Mary Osborn*** is renowned for being the first person to demonstrate the mode of action of a major cancer chemotherapeutic agent called methotrexate, an agent that also opposes the physiological effects of folic acid. She is best known for her research into the biosynthesis of a complex polysaccharide known as lipopolysaccharide, which is a molecule that is essential to bacterial cells. She thus helped to identify a potential target for the development of new antibiotics and chemotherapeutic agents. She was elected to membership in the National Academy of Sciences in 1978.

She entered college as a premed student, but by her senior year she had realized that she did not want to treat patients. When she pursued biochemistry courses, she found that she liked bench research and could do it well. Her thesis research examined the functions of the vitamins and enzymes whose action depended on folic acid. However, as a graduate student in 1957, she reported the mode of action of methotrexate, which later became a major cancer chemotherapeutic agent, especially for leukemia.

As a postdoctoral student she moved into the biosynthesis, or the study of the structure building blocks, of a molecule complex polysaccharide named lipopolysaccharide, which is unique to a certain class of bacteria that includes pathogens such as salmonella, shigella, and the cholera bacillus. Lipopolysaccharide is responsible for major immunological reactions and for the bacteria's characteristic toxicity, and her work led to a new understanding of a previously unknown mechanism of polysaccharide formation.

Osborn's parents were high achievers, and their ambitions for Mary were considerable. When as a ten-year-old she talked of becoming a nurse, her parents asked her why she did not want to become a doctor. They supported her interest in science throughout her education. However, she said it was amazing that she sustained an interest in biology after primary and secondary schools because the quality of the science classes in the schools she attended was so poor.

She has served on many important committees and commissions of the National Institutes of Health, the American Heart Association, and the National Academy of Sciences, and from 1980 to 1986, she was a member of the prestigious National Science Board, the board that advises the National Science Foundation. She is a fellow of the American Academy of Arts and Sciences and a member of the American Association for the Advancement of Science, American Society of Biological Chemists (president, 1981–1982), American Chemical Society, Federation of American Societies for Experimental Biology (president, 1982–1983), and American Society for Microbiology. Her research includes the biosynthesis of bacterial lipopolysaccharides and the biogenesis of membranes.

***Bibliography:*** *American Men and Women of Science* 13–19; Herzenberg, C., *Women Scientists from Antiquity to the Present; Notable Twentieth-Century Scientists; Who's Who in America,* 51st ed., 1997; *Who's Who of American Women,* 20th ed., 1997–1998.

# *Owens, Joan Murrell*
(1933– )
***marine biology***

***Education:*** B.A., Fisk University, 1954; M.S., University of Michigan, 1956; B.S., George Washington University, 1973, M.A., 1976, Ph.D. in geology, 1984
***Professional Experience:*** Instructor, English Department, Howard University, 1957–1964; instructor, Education Services, Inc., 1964–1970; instructor then associate professor, Department of Geology and Geography, Howard University, 1984–
***Married:*** Frank Owens

***Joan Owens*** has had a unique experience in that after 20 years of a successful career in one field she returned to college to obtain degrees in an entirely different field, becoming the first African-American woman in the United States to earn a doctorate in geology according to one source. She became fascinated with water animals as a child. Since the family lived in Miami, she had opportunities to see unusual species, such as manatees, alligators, and otters, and in high school she dreamed of a career in marine science. However, when she entered Fisk University, she found that neither women nor African Americans were welcome in that field. Finding her career path blocked, she settled on majoring in fine arts with a double minor in psychology and mathematics, plus taking education courses.

She was admitted to the graduate commercial art program in the School of Architecture at the University of Michigan, but she did not enjoy the program. A fellow graduate student suggested she transfer to the Bureau of Psychological Services, which is part of the School of Education, and she enjoyed her work there because she turned out to have a special talent for working with brain-damaged and emotionally disturbed children. She was invited to join the English Department at Howard University where she taught remedial reading to incoming students. When her husband's job took them to Massachusetts, she obtained a position with Education Services, Inc., where she developed new procedures and programs for teaching English to educationally disadvantaged high school students. She then began designing college remedial programs for the institute, which later transferred her back to its office in Washington, D.C.

Owens was still dreaming of becoming a marine biologist, but none of the colleges in the Washington, D.C., area had an undergraduate program in marine science. A friend suggested that a major in geology and a minor in zoology would be the equal of a formal program in marine science, so with the approval of the chair of the Geology Department, she enrolled at George Washington University. For her research thesis, she was fortunate that the Smithsonian Institution had a project that needed attention. The Smithsonian had a collection of button deep-sea corals, which live at depths well below the layers penetrated by sunlight, and she was able to use the collection of skeletons as the basis for her research. After completing her doctorate, she accepted a position at Howard University in the Department of Geology and Geography. When she started presenting papers at meetings of marine scientists, she perceived an attitude change in geologists and marine scientists toward accepting minorities and women into their fields. She is continuing her research on the classification of button corals with support from major oil companies.

She particularly enjoys teaching beginning science courses because she is able to show students that science can be interesting and relatively easy. In addition, she participates in giving presentations at junior high schools to interest girls in careers in science. She advises her students to keep their own dreams alive.

***Bibliography:*** *Distinguished African American Scientists of the 20th Century.*

# Pardue, Mary Lou
(1933– )
## *cell biologist, developmental biologist*

***Education:*** B.S., College of William and Mary, 1955; M.S., University of Tennessee, 1959; Ph.D. in biology, Yale University, 1970; honorary degree: D.Sc., Bard College, 1985
***Professional Experience:*** Fellow, Edinburgh University, 1970–1972; associate professor of biology, Massachusetts Institute of Technology, 1972–1980, professor, 1980– , Boris Magasnik Professor of Biology, 1995–
***Concurrent Position:*** Instructor in molecular cytogenetics, Cold Spring Harbor Laboratory, 1971–

***Mary Lou Pardue*** is a cell biologist who is known for her work in insect genetics. Her area of specialization is the structure and function of chromosomes in eukaryotic organisms (organisms whose DNA, or deoxyribonucleic acid, which provides the information for reproduction, is contained in their cell's nuclei, or centers). Her work excludes lower organisms such as bacteria and viruses, which are prokaryotic organisms (these have their genetic material located in the cell area surrounding the nucleus, the cytoplasm). Her studies have primarily centered on the breed of fruit fly known as *Drosophila melanogaster.* Because fruit flies have very short lifetimes, the rapid succession of fruit fly generations facilitates a time-saving study of genetic developments. An added benefit is that the flies' gene activity is similar, and therefore applicable, to that of higher organisms. She was elected to membership in the National Academy of Sciences in 1983.

In the late 1960s, while a graduate student at Yale, she and her major professor developed a technique called "in situ hybridization" for localizing, with intact chromosomes, specific nucleotic sequences, which determine traits imparted during reproduction. These experiments were carried out using the chromosomes for the *Drosophila*'s salivary glands. The technique, which was designed to locate genes on the chromosomes, is used to identify the chromosomal regions of DNA that are complementary to specific nucleic acid molecules, or RNAs.

During the mid 1970s, as a faculty member at the Massachusetts Institute of Technology, Pardue concentrated on heat-shock response, which refers to the effects of temperature on genetic activity. Studies of the fruit fly indicated that increases in its environmental temperature that exceed 10 degrees result in the suspension of some genetic activity. Her studies attempted to determine what genes are affected by the heat increase.

In a related area, that of the biology of stress response in an insect muscle cell, she found that stress also resulted in suspending some genetic activity and the associated synthesis of proteins. This research is significant for its potential application in cancer treatment, for an understanding of how to turn genetic activity on and off carries potential benefits in establishing new forms of cancer therapy as well as other scientific/medical treatments.

Pardue has received numerous awards, including the Esther Langer Award for Cancer Research (1977) and the Lucius Wilbur Cross Medal of Yale Graduate School (1989). She was a member of the Science Advisory Council of Abbott Laboratories from 1987 to 1990, the American Cancer Society Advisory Committee on Nucleic Acids and Protein Synthesis from 1990 to 1993, and the Howard Hughes Medical Institute Science Review Board from 1993 to 1994 and has been a member of the National Research Council Board of Biology since 1989. She is a fellow of the American Association for the Advancement of Science and a member of the American Society for Cell Biology (president, 1985–1986), Genetics Society of America (president, 1982–1983), and American Academy of Arts and Sciences. Her research includes structure and function of eukaryotic chromosomes; cell biology of stress responses; and studies of nucleocytoplasmic interactions, RNA metabolism, and transposable elements.

***Bibliography:*** *American Men and Women of Science* 13–19; Herzenberg, C., *Women Scientists from Antiquity to the Present; Notable Twentieth-Century Scientists; Who's Who in America,* 51st ed., 1997; *Who's Who of American Women,* 20th ed., 1997–1998.

# *Partee, Barbara (Hall)*

(1940– )

## *anthropologist, linguist*

***Education:*** B.A. in mathematics, Swarthmore College, 1961; Ph.D. in linguistics, Massachusetts Institute of Technology, 1965; honorary degrees: D.Sc., Swarthmore College, 1989, and Charles University, Prague, 1992

***Professional Experience:*** Assistant professor, University of California, Los Angeles, 1965–1969, associate professor, 1969–1973; associate professor of linguistics and philosophy, University of Massachusetts, 1972–1973, professor, 1973–1990, Distinguished University Professor, 1990– , head, department of linguistics, 1987–1993

***Concurrent Positions:*** Fellow, Center for Advanced Study in Behavior Sciences, 1976–1977; member, board of managers, Swarthmore College, 1990–

***Married:*** Morris H. Partee, 1966, divorced 1971; Emmon W. Bach, 1973

***Children:*** 3

***Barbara Partee*** is a linguist known for her expertise in mathematical methods in linguistics. Linguistics, the science of language, includes phonetics, phonology, syntax, semantics, pragmatics, and historical linguistics. She was elected to membership in the National Academy of Sciences in 1989.

She published *Fundamentals of Mathematics for Linguistics* in 1978, which has been out of print since the 1980s, but many ideas in theoretical linguistics, such as phonology and syntax, have emerged since that time. She is the coauthor of *Mathematical Methods in Linguistics* (1990), which includes many of the new theories. The volume is divided into five parts. Part A, "Set Theory," covers sets, relations, functions, and infinity. Part B, "Logic and Formal Systems," introduces the prepositional and predicate calculi, including natural deduction, Beth tableaux, and axiomatization. Part C, "Algebra," presents abstract algebraic systems including maps, morphisms, groups, semigroups, monoids, lattices, and Boolean and Heyting algebras. Part D, "English as Formal Language," deals with topics in post-1970 model-theoretic semantics, from compositionality through lambda calculus to generalized quantifiers and intensionality. Part E, "Languages, Grammars, and Automata," introduces mathematical linguistics, including formal languages and grammars, trees, the Chomsky hierarchy, and the theory of automata and computability.

Partee also coedited *Properties, Types and Meaning* (1989), a two-volume set of essays originally presented at a 1986 meeting at the University of Massachusetts. Volume 1 is *Foundational Issues* and volume 2, *Semantic Issues.* A later book, *Quantification in Natural Languages* (1995), which she coedited with her husband, Emmon Bach, and others, consists of 20 papers on the subject of semantics, which is the study of meaning, or the study of linguistics developed by classifying and examining change in meaning and form.

She is a member of the Linguistics Society of America (president, 1986), American Philosophical Association, Association for Computational Linguistics, and American Academy of Arts and Sciences.

***Bibliography:*** *Who's Who in America*, 51st ed., 1997; *Who's Who of American Women*, 20th ed., 1997–1998.

# *Paté-Cornell, (Marie) Elisabeth Lucienne*

(1948– )

***industrial engineer***

***Education:*** B.S. in mathematics and physics, University of Marseilles, 1968; M.S. in computer science and applied mathematics, University of Grenoble, 1970; engineer degree in computer science and numerical analysis, Polytechnic Institute of Grenoble, 1971; M.S. in operations research, Stanford University, 1972, Ph.D. in engineering-economic systems, 1978
***Professional Experience:*** Assistant professor, civil engineering, Massachusetts Institute of Technology, 1978–1981; assistant professor, industrial engineering and engineering management, Stanford University, 1981–1984, associate professor, 1984–1989, professor, 1991–
***Married:*** C. Allin Cornell, 1981
***Children:*** 2

*Elisabeth Paté-Cornell* is known for her research in engineering systems analysis that is combined with economic analysis to find realistic solutions to actual problems. In pulling together what had been thought to be separate disciplines to offer a unique approach to problems, she has drawn on her studies in mathematics and physics, computer engineering with an electrical engineering component, economics, and operations research. Operations research (OR), which was developed in 1940–1945, during World War II, for military operations, is the analysis, usually involving mathematical treatment, of a process, problem, or operation to determine its purpose and effectiveness and to gain maximum efficiency. She was elected to membership in the National Academy of Engineering in 1995 as one of the academy's youngest members, and she was the first woman faculty member from Stanford to be elected.

She has employed her expertise in analyzing risk management for the tiles of the space shuttle, and she found that 15 percent of the tiles account for about 85 percent of the risk and that some of the most-critical tiles are not in the hottest areas of the orbiter's surface. She analyzed different maintenance policies for the control of production systems that are subject to deterioration over time—the two policies considered were scheduled preventive maintenance and maintenance on demand. The result indicated, by monitoring the production system, that the preventive maintenance policy can achieve significant savings.

For her doctoral dissertation, she studied seismic risk from a public policy viewpoint, looking at the costs and benefits of reducing earthquake risks in two different ways: the reinforcement of buildings and a long-term investment in earthquake prediction. One solution was engineering oriented—reduce property damage and human casualties caused by earthquakes with different levels of reinforcement for different kinds of buildings. The other involved the reliability of warnings and their use by human beings to reduce risks.

When she left high school she was torn between the sciences and the humanities although she was very much influenced by her engineer father. She chose science because she could enjoy literature and music without being a professional, but the reverse was not true. After completing her master's degree in operations research, she still wanted to work in technical and mathematical analysis as well as the social sciences, so she entered the interdisciplinary department of Engineering-Economic Systems at Stanford to give her the background she needed.

In a telephone conversation with the author on May 28, 1997, Paté-Cornell said the situation for women scientists and engineers had improved over the past 20 years, especially with respect to salary, improvement in working conditions, and being listened to. She said one result of her election to the National Academy of Engineering is that she is listened to more than before.

In 1998, she was a member of the Marine Board of the National Research Council (NRC); chair of an NRC committee on risk assessment and management of marine systems, such as offshore platforms; and a member of the Army Science Board and of the NASA Advisory Council. She finds that working on committees puts her in touch with large organizations that face many operations research problems, and it gives her the opportunity to study uncertainties in real-life decisions.

She feels she has been successful in combining her career with a balanced family life and says that her husband is extremely supportive of her career. She is a member of the Society for Risk Analysis and the Operations Research Society of America. Her research interests are operations research and risk analysis. Her photograph is included in *Journeys of Women in Science and Engineering.*

***Bibliography:*** *Journeys of Women in Science and Engineering; Who's Who in America,* 51st ed., 1997; *Who's Who in Engineering,* 9th ed., 1995; *Who's Who in Science and Engineering,* 3d ed., 1996–1977.

# *Patrick-Yeboah, Jennie R.*

(1949– )

***chemical engineer***

***Education:*** Student, Tuskegee Institute, 1969–1970; B.S., University of California, Berkeley, 1973; Ph.D. in chemical engineering, Massachusetts Institute of Technology, 1979

***Professional Experience:*** Assistant engineer, Dow Chemical Company, 1972, and Stauffer Chemical Company, 1973; research associate, Massachusetts Institute of Technology, 1973–1979; engineer, Chevron Research, 1974, and Arthur D. Little, 1975; research engineer, General Electric Research and Development Center, 1979–1983, and Phillip Morris Company, 1983–1985; manager of fundamental chemical engineering research, Rohm and Haas Company, 1985–1990; assistant to executive vice president, Southern Company Services, 1990–1993; 3M Eminent Scholar and Professor of Chemical Engineering, Tuskegee Institute, 1993–

***Concurrent Positions:*** Adjunct professor, Rensselaer Polytechnic Institute, 1982–1985, and Georgia Institute of Technology, 1985–1987

***Jennie Patrick-Yeboah*** is known as a successful chemical engineer, manager, and educator who has applied her research perceptiveness on behalf of a number of companies and universities. She is the first African American woman to earn a doctorate in chemical engineering, which she received at the Massachusetts Institute of Technology (MIT) in 1979.

Her parents were a working-class couple who emphasized to their five children that knowledge is an escape from poverty. Jennie spent many hours in the local library reading all types of materials, but she particularly enjoyed reading encyclopedias because they enabled her in her imagination to go from her very limited world to one that had everything. She attended segregated elementary and middle schools, but in high school she was one of the first participants in an integrated school in her hometown in Georgia. Racial integration in the schools was a controversial question in the middle to late 1960s, but in spite of heated debate in her community, she decided to attend the integrated school because it had all the scientific equipment she needed for her studies while the school for blacks had none. She attributes her ambition to be successful to seeing how hard her parents' lives were; she wanted to use the gift of her intelligence to be a more independent person. Another influence consisted of her black elementary school teachers who challenged her to look for knowledge and made her feel she had the ability to do whatever she wanted to do.

She was accepted by several outstanding universities but chose to attend Tuskegee Institute as a chemistry major. In her freshman year she decided to switch to chemical engineering because she thought it might be more challenging for her. The school started a program the next year, but it was dropped. However, years later, she returned to Tuskegee as a faculty member in a solid chemical engineering program. After a short time at Tuskegee, she transferred to University of California, Berkeley, to complete her undergraduate degree, working for two chemical companies, Dow and Stauffer, to support herself while she was in school. She then went to MIT where she worked as a research associate while obtaining her doctorate. Her research at MIT involved the concept of superheating, in which a liquid is raised above its boiling temperature but does not become a vapor. She investigated the temperature to which pure liquids and mixtures of two liquids could be superheated. In addition to financial support from fellowships, she worked for Chevron and Arthur D. Little during this period.

She first joined the General Electric Research and Development Center where her work involved research on energy-efficient processes for chemical separation and purification, particularly the use of supercritical extraction. In supercritical processes, the temperature and pressure are varied so that a substance is not a liquid or a gas but a fluid; she received patents for some of this work. She then joined Phillip Morris Company as a project manager in charge of the development of a new business venture on supercritical fluid technology.

She moved to Rohm and Haas Company as a research section manager for the newly formed Fundamental Engineering Research Group. Here she was responsible not only for providing new engineering technology but for improving existing engineering technology within the corporation. In this position she interacted with all aspects of the chemical business, from engineering to marketing to manufacturing, and her group helped to develop improved products, improved processes, and more-cost-efficient processes. Her next move was to Southern Company Services as assistant to the executive vice president. This position emphasized her management skills in both the business and the technical aspects of the company.

Earlier she had held adjunct professorships at two universities, and she now decided to make teaching a larger part of her life. She returned to Tuskegee University as the 3M Eminent Scholar and Professor of Chemical Engineering, and she has stayed there to teach and develop research projects in materials sciences. She is committed to helping minority students find success, particularly in the fields of science and engineering. Her experiences in her integrated high school formed her commitment to aiding students; while she was there, the counselors had attempted to discourage the black students from enrolling in college preparation courses and had emphasized that the black students should set much lower standards or goals than the white students.

Patrick-Yeboah received the Outstanding Women in Science and Engineering Award in 1980 and is a member of the American Institute of Chemical Engineers. Her photograph is included in *Notable Twentieth-Century Scientists* and *U.S. Black Engineer* (fall 1988).

***Bibliography:*** *Blacks in Science and Medicine; Notable Twentieth-Century Scientists.*

# *Payton, Carolyn (Robertson)*
(1925– )
***psychologist***

***Education:*** B.S. in home economics, Bennett College, 1945; M.S. in psychology, University of Wisconsin, Madison, 1948; Ed.D. in counseling, Teachers College, Columbia University, 1962; honorary degree: DHL, Lake Erie College for Women

***Professional Experience:*** Instructor in psychology, Livingston College, 1948–1953; dean of women, Elizabeth City State Teachers College, 1953–1956; associate professor of psychology, Virginia State College, 1956–1959; assistant professor of psychology, Howard University, 1959–1964; chief field selection officer, Peace Corps, 1964–1966, deputy director, Eastern Caribbean section, 1966–1971; assistant professor, Howard University, 1971–1977; director of Peace Corps, 1977–1978; dean of counseling and career development, Howard University, 1979–

***Married:*** Raymond R. Payton, date unknown, divorced 1951

***Carolyn Payton*** is known for her work in counseling and career development, and from 1977 to 1978, she was the first black and the first female director of the Peace Corps. When the Peace Corps was formed in 1961, it was charged with sharing technical skills with requesting countries. Trained volunteers spent two years in host countries working primarily in the areas of agriculture, rural development, health, and education. At first, the corps sent volunteers to Latin America, Africa, and the Middle East, but after 1990 and the end of the Cold War, eastern-bloc countries also began requesting volunteers. Payton joined the Peace Corps in 1964 as a field selection officer and progressed in rank until she was deputy director of the Eastern Caribbean Section in 1966. She returned to Howard University to teach until 1977 when she was named director of the Peace Corps.

In the meantime, the focus of the corps had shifted. In the first phase, new college graduates with liberal arts backgrounds were chosen to work with selected communities on projects. In 1977, the recruits were experienced, highly skilled persons who could fill the specialized needs of developing countries; however, they tended to "teach down" to the people they were sent to help. Most of the volunteers were white and male. Payton planned a paraprofessional training program to train the volunteers to be better teachers and planned to recruit more blacks and women for the program. The Peace Corps no longer was an autonomous organization, however, and it was being administered by the American Council to Improve Our Neighborhoods (ACTION), whose head did not agree with her plans. Payton was forced to resign. However, her resignation had a positive impact in that President Carter realized the corps operated better as an independent organization, and in 1981, the agency once again became independent.

Payton has worked to promote world understanding through cross-cultural interactions in both public and private forums. To quote the citation for her Distinguished Professional Contributions Award from the American Psychological Association in 1982, she believed "that equality and social justice for black Americans would never be achieved so long as the world tolerated rampant poverty, hunger, and illiteracy in the 'less developed' countries. It also became clear that something more than rhetoric was called for to bring about change. To further these beliefs, Payton has worked within colleges and universities to bring about change and has taken opportunities that have arisen from time to time to leave academia and tilt at windmills in the real world."

After receiving her undergraduate degree in home economics, she received a master's degree in psychology and taught at several small colleges before starting work on her doctorate. She continued working at

Howard University after completing that degree, and between her two terms with the Peace Corps, she returned to teach at Howard. She was then appointed dean of counseling and career development at Howard after leaving the corps the second time. She is a fellow of the American Psychological Association, and her photograph is included in *American Psychologist* (January 1983).

***Bibliography:*** *Notable Black American Women.*

# *Peden, Irene (Carswell)*
## (1925– )
## *electrical engineer, radio scientist*

***Education:*** B.S., University of Colorado, 1947; M.S., Stanford University, 1958, Ph.D. in electrical engineering, 1962

***Professional Experience:*** Junior engineer, Delaware Power and Light Company, 1947–1949; junior engineer, Aircraft Radio Systems Laboratory, Stanford Research Institute, 1949–1950, research engineer, 1950–1952, antenna research group, 1954–1957; research engineer, Midwest Research Institute, 1953–1954; research assistant, Hansen Laboratory, Stanford University, 1958–1961, acting instructor in electrical engineering, 1959–1961; assistant professor, University of Washington, Seattle, 1961–1964, associate professor, 1964–1971, professor, 1971– , associate dean of engineering, 1973–1977, associate chair, Electrical Engineering Department, 1983–1986

***Married:*** Leo J. Peden, 1962

***Children:*** 2

***Irene Peden*** is known as a specialist in radio science and electromagnetic wave propagation scattering. She enhanced her reputation as a scientist by conducting geophysical studies of radio wave propagation in Antarctica, where she was the first American woman engineer/scientist to live and work in the interior of that continent. She also accumulated several other firsts. She was the first woman to receive a Ph.D. in electrical engineering from Stanford University—some sources say it was the first in any engineering discipline at Stanford. In the late 1960s, she was the only woman faculty member in the University of Washington, Seattle, Engineering Department, and she was the first woman member of the board of directors of the Institute of Electrical and Electronics Engineers, the primary association in her field. She was elected to membership in the National Academy of Engineering in 1993.

She received recognition for her outstanding research of radio wave propagation through the Antarctic ice pack. At the Byrd Antarctic Research Station in the 1970s, she developed new methods to characterize the deep glacial ice by studying the effect it has on radio waves directed through it, and she has continued this line of research by studying certain properties in the lower ionosphere over Antarctica. In order to conduct her research, she had to develop the methodology for her experiments and also invent the mathematical models to study and interpret the data the team collected. She and her students were the first researchers to measure many of the electrical properties of Antarctic ice and to describe important aspects of very low frequency (VLF) propagation over long paths in the polar region. Later she turned her attention to subsurface exploration technologies, using very high frequency (VHF) radio waves to detect and locate subsurface structures and other targets. Again, she found she had to design the methodology and models to collect and interpret her data.

It is significant for scientific research that although women scientists from other countries had been conducting research at their country's research stations in Antarctica for a number of years, American women were excluded from the U.S. station before Peden was allowed to go in 1970. The U.S. Navy was in charge of the research station and was responsible for transportation to and from the area plus any travel within Antarctica; the navy kept saying the weather was too harsh, there were not adequate living quarters for women, etc. When Peden received a grant from the National Science Foundation (NSF) for research on Antarctic ice, her male graduate students could visit the site, but she was not permitted to. However, the NSF requires that the primary investigator visit a research site at least once during a study; in 1970, NSF representatives finally received approval from the navy for her to make the trip, with a last-minute requirement that she have a female assistant to accompany her. The NSF contacted a woman member of the New Zealand Alpine Club whose scientist husband had been to Antarctica and was eager to go. The two women and four men spent several months on site, and Peden describes her experiences in Barbara Land's *The New Explorers.*

Peden's interest in science was kindled in high school when she enrolled in a required chemistry course. Later her interests shifted to electrical engineering, in which she received her undergraduate degree. She worked for the Stanford Research Institute for a time and received her master's degree from Stanford. She moved to the Hansen Laboratory and taught part time while working on her doctorate. Her research topic was measurement techniques for microwave circuits. She accepted an appointment at the University of Washington, Seattle, as an assistant professor in 1961, advancing in rank to that of professor in 1971.

She has received appointments to numerous committees and commissions and has received awards for her research, including the Society of Women Engineers Achievement Award (1973), U.S. Army's Outstanding Civilian Service Medal (1987), Centennial Medals from the Institute of Electrical and Electronics Engineers (1984) and the University of Colorado (1988), and being named to the 100-member Hall of Fame of the American Society for Engineering Education. She is a fellow of the Institute of Electrical and Electronics Engineers, the American Association for the Advancement of Science, and the Explorers' Club and is a member of American Geophysical Union, New York Academy of Science, and Society of Women Engineers. Her photograph is included in Barbara Land's *The New Explorers* and *Notable Twentieth-Century Scientists.*

***Bibliography:*** *American Men and Women of Science* 11–19; Herzenberg, C., *Women Scientists from Antiquity to the Present;* Ireland, N., *Index to Women of the World . . . Suppl.;* Land, B., *The New Explorers; Notable Twentieth-Century Scientists;* O'Neill, L., *The Women's Book of World Records and Achievements;* Stanley, A., *Mothers and Daughters of Invention; Who's Who in Engineering,* 9th ed., 1995.

# *Pert, Candace Dorinda (Bebe)*

(1946– )

***neurophysiologist***

***Education:*** Student, Hofstra University, 1966; B.A., Bryn Mawr, 1970; Ph.D. in pharmacology, School of Medicine, Johns Hopkins University, 1974

***Professional Experience:*** National Institutes of Health fellow, Johns Hopkins University, 1974–1975; staff fellow, National Institute of Mental Health, 1975–1977, senior staff fellow, 1977–1978, research pharmacologist, 1978–1982, chief, Section on Brain Chemistry, 1982–1988, guest researcher, 1988– ; scientific director, Peptide Design, 1987–1990; adjunct professor of physiology, Georgetown University, 1990–

***Married:*** Agu Pert, 1966

***Children:*** 3

***Candace Pert*** is one of the world's foremost researchers on the chemistry of the brain. She is known as a leading researcher in the field of chemical receptors, which are the places in the body where molecules of a drug or natural chemical can be inserted, thus stimulating or inhibiting various physiological or emotional effects. As a graduate student she was the codiscoverer, with her major professor, of the brain's opiate receptors, the areas in which painkilling substances such as morphine can be inserted. Her work led to the discovery of endorphins, the naturally occurring substances manufactured in the brain that relieve pain and produce sensations of pleasure. After her research turned to other areas, two Scottish scientists eventually discovered endorphins, which may be the most important discovery in brain chemistry in the 1970s, and they were awarded the Lasker Award in Medicine in 1978. Pert's major professor, Solomon Snyder, also shared the Lasker Award, but her name was omitted from the award although she had received her doctorate in 1974. This oversight created a controversy in the scientific world because the Lasker Award has proved to be an early step for eventual recipients of the Nobel Prize.

Her research at the time of the discovery was on neurotransmitters, chemicals that stimulate or inhibit other neurons throughout the body, which in turn regulate the heart and other organs. Receptors evolve from a chain of amino-acid molecules, molecules that are shaped by electrical forces into a three-dimensional shape with an electrically active indentation that recognizes correspondingly shaped molecules. These indentations are the point at which a receptor binds with a chemical substance or neurotransmitter. Pert used radioactive drugs to identify receptor molecules that bonded with morphine and other opiate drugs in animal brain cells and speculated that there might be an unknown neurotransmitter, naturally produced in the body, that explained why opiate receptors existed. However, after initial investigations proved inconclusive, she turned to other research, and it was John Hughes and Hans Kosterlitz who found the transmitters, which they called endorphins. They are naturally occurring substances, manufactured in the brain, that relieve pain, produce sensations of pleasure, and are extremely addictive. Other researchers have found more than a score of other varieties of receptors and corresponding chemicals in the brain.

Her research on peptides and their receptors has led to a new area, the use of a chemical called peptide-T as a potential treatment for AIDS. She has evidence the purified peptide-T prevents viruses from getting into cells by blocking the receptor sites on the cells, and there is also evidence that peptide-T reverses the symptoms of the disease. The first work was done in 1985, and the clinical trials started in the early 1990s. However, the project later was dropped when she was unable to find further funding.

Pert planned to major in English in college although an aptitude test in high school indicated she would make a great mechanical engineer. She left Wheaton College after a few months and entered Hofstra University, which was close to her home on Long Island. She was fairly content at Hofstra until she received a grade lower than she expected on an English paper and she realized there were no "objective standards" in the English Department. She married Agu Pert, a graduate student in psychology, and the couple moved to Bryn Mawr where he obtained a doctorate. She entered Bryn Mawr as a biology major and continued her studies in pharmacology at Johns Hopkins.

She continued her work on neurotransmitters at the National Institute of Mental Health for a number of years. She examined Valium receptors in the brain and the receptors where the street drug PCP, or "angel dust," takes hold, and she also led the team that discovered peptide-T. She left the government laboratory to form her own company, Peptide Design, to encourage research on peptides and worked there from 1987 to 1990. She has since become an adjunct professor in the Department of Physiology at Georgetown University in Washington, D.C., where she has been investigating immune systems and the nature of HIV (human immunodeficiency virus), which causes AIDS.

She talks, in several sources, of her own experiences as a woman scientist who has combined career and family. Although she declines to talk about the controversy concerning the Lasker Award, she has experienced other forms of discrimination. An interview for graduate school consisted mainly of questions about her family and insinuations about her ability to commit herself to a scientific career. She has also found the competitive element in science to be a destructive force at times; for instance, she feels that competition from other teams did not allow her team sufficient research on peptide-T. Competition can be motivating, but it can be carried to extremes. She encourages women to consider careers in science because women have curiosity, observational powers, and good communication skills. They also have analytical minds and can consider many different ideas at once and from many angles.

There is a fairly extensive interview with Candace Pert in *The Omni Interviews;* she is the only woman among the 20 scientists who were interviewed for the book. There is also an interesting one in the September 1992 issue of *American Biological Teacher* in which she discusses her research. In her autobiography, *Molecules of Emotion: Why You Feel the Way You Feel* (1997), she describes her research and her career; an abridged version is available on audiocassette. She won the Arthur S. Fleming Award in 1979 for her research. She is a member of the American Society of Pharmacology and Experimental Therapeutics, American Society of Biological Chemists, and Society for Neuroscience. Her research is on brain peptides and their receptors: chemical characteristics, brain distribution, and function. Her photograph is included in *The Omni Interviews* and *American Biology Teacher.*

***Bibliography:*** *American Men and Women of Science* 15–19; Mount, E., *Milestones in Science and Technology; Notable Twentieth- Century Scientists; The Omni Interviews;* Stanley, A., *Mothers and Daughters of Invention.*

# *Pfeiffer, Jane (Cahill)*
(1932– )
***computer scientist***

***Education:*** B.A., University of Maryland, 1954; postgraduate study, Catholic University of America, 1956–1957; honorary degrees: LHD Pace College, 1978, University of Maryland, 1979, Manhattanville College, 1979, Amherst College, 1980, Babson College, 1981, and University of Notre Dame, 1991

***Professional Experience:*** Systems-engineer trainee, International Business Machines (IBM) Corporation, 1955–1959, site manager, missile tracking station for Mercury space program, 1960–1966; White House fellow at Department of Housing and Urban Development, 1966; executive assistant to Chairman Thomas J. Watson, IBM, secretary of management review committee, 1970, director of communications, 1971, vice president in charge of corporate communications and government relations, 1972–1975; management consultant, 1975–1978; chair of NBC, 1978–1980; business consultant, 1980–

***Married:*** Ralph A. Pfeiffer, 1975

***Jane Pfeiffer*** was known as a knowledgeable business consultant when RCA Corporation asked her to improve the management of NBC, a wholly owned subsidiary of RCA. The television division had lost a large segment of its adult audience when, in 1974, in an attempt to compete with ABC and CBS, it had redirected its programming toward a more youthful market. The company also was losing affiliate stations to other networks. Several years previously, as a vice president of IBM Corporation, she had led the company into sponsoring high-quality television entertainment and public affairs programs. IBM first sponsored the CBS weekly news program *Face the Nation* because, she reasoned, the company would profit from the sales of computers to the businesspeople in the audience. IBM also sponsored several operas and musical programs. In this capacity, she had worked with Fred Silverman, who now was president and chief executive officer of NBC. He first hired Jane Pfeiffer as a consultant in 1978 and then selected her as chair of NBC. She was also elected to the board of directors.

After making several significant changes in the management of the network, she revamped the news department with an increased budget and additional personnel. A very delicate situation arose, for it appeared that some unit managers were involved in embezzling more than a million dollars in company funds. She immediately called in lawyers and accountants from outside to investigate the allegations and contacted the FBI. About ten people were brought up on criminal charges, and she replaced many of the managers and one vice president. Naturally the situation affected morale in the company, and she was criticized for her swift action in handling the problem, because many corporations just fire people who embezzle funds without bringing criminal charges against them. She and Silverman also revamped the 1979 broadcast schedule to include more mature programs, including more news and information. A year later the network still lagged behind its two rivals, and in that same year, the United States boycotted the summer Olympic Games in Moscow, which NBC had contracted to broadcast, which meant a loss of about $10 million in advertising revenues.

Even so, the industry was shocked when Silverman fired Pfeiffer in 1980. There were the usual charges that she had mishandled the embezzlement problem, had fired key managers in many departments, and was not in tune with current trends in entertainment. There were also many derogatory remarks made in the press, such as referring to her as "St. Jane," "the Ayatollah," and "Attila the Nun," the last stemming from her brief interest in becoming a nun while she was in college.

When her father died leaving her mother a widow with two children, her mother started a career in nutrition in order to support the family. Jane's mother, Helen Cahill, eventually became the highest-paid woman in the federal civil service as the chief nutritionist of the Veterans Administration. Jane majored in speech and drama and minored in mathematics as an undergraduate, then enrolled in graduate courses in philosophy at Georgetown University. She spent about six months as a Catholic novitiate but left the convent.

She secured a job as a systems-engineering trainee at IBM, learning and then teaching computer programming. In the 1950s and 1960s, the computer science field was still open to people without science or engineering degrees because college courses in computer science were still in their infancy. She was involved in the government's Mercury space program as the site manager of an IBM missile tracking station in Bermuda. She came to the attention of the top executives when the staff's paychecks did not arrive and she negotiated a loan at a local bank in order to pay the workers. She asked that headquarters rush the reimbursement to her because she had only a short-term loan.

She became the first female White House fellow in 1966 when she worked with the Department of Housing and Urban Development on revamping the old Housing and Home Finance Agency, which gave her opportunities to meet leading government officials. When she returned to IBM, Chairman Thomas J. Watson appointed her his executive assistant. She was named secretary of the management review committee in 1970, director of communications in 1971, and vice president in charge of corporate communications and government relations in 1972. The last appointment meant she was the first woman to be named a vice president at IBM since World War II.

After leaving NBC, Pfeiffer served as a business consultant. She served on the boards of directors of companies such as Ashland Oil, International Paper, and J. C. Penny, and she was a trustee of the National Industrial Conference Board in 1991 and trustee of the Rockefeller Foundation. She has received the Distinguished Alumna Award of the University of Maryland (1975), Humanitarian Award of the National Organization for Women (1980), and the Centennial Alumna Medallion of the University of Maryland (1988).

***Bibliography:*** *Current Biography 1980;* Ireland, N., *Index to Women of the World . . . Suppl.;* Lichtenstein, G., *Machisma; Who's Who in America,* 51st ed., 1997; *Who's Who of American Women,* 20th ed., 1997–1998.

# *Pickett, Mary S.*
(1946– )
## *computer scientist*

***Education:*** B.S. in mathematics, Iowa State University; M.S. in computer science, Purdue University

***Professional Experience:*** Staff research scientist, Computer Science Department, General Motors Corporation, 1971–

*Mary Pickett* has been one of the leaders at General Motors Corporation in using robots to automate manufacturing facilities by designing powerful computer programs to manipulate the robots. Although robots had been used in manufacturing for a number of years, primarily in hazardous locations such as radioactive environments, the automobile industry did not make extensive use of them until the 1980s when it sought additional efficiencies in the workplace to meet the competition for vehicle sales. In 1984, she and a colleague invented the first computer system to integrate robotics, solid (or 3-D) modeling, and simulation. Their design received one of the Year's Top One Hundred Innovations awards given by *Science Digest* in its December 1985 issue.

In any manufacturing facility, there are several dozen kinds of robots, each with different capabilities. Originally managers had to use a manual process to choose the right robot for a given set of tasks, a show-and-teach process that involved great expenditures of time and money. To counteract that problem, Mary Pickett and her coinventor designed RoboTeach. Although the early software specified the desired robot motion, they had no way of describing the robot's environment, and they could not take into account physical obstacles or anticipate collisions. Graphics programs for robots used stick figures, which were too crude for collision detection. Using solid modeling, or 3-D modeling, provides geometrically complete representations of environmental components and their spatial relations. However, the two alone are not adequate for the task. Only by using computer simulation of both the robot and its environment can the sequence of discrete steps in a robot task be converted into the continuous motion of a process, and simulation allows for an accurate representation of the robotic process as it unfolds in its environment.

Although the above all sounds today like ancient computer history, in view of the status of robotics at the time they were real problems that had to be solved; Pickett's work can be compared favorably with the research of other women computer scientists in this volume—for example, those who developed the first personal computers.

Using the system that Pickett developed, manufacturers can verify that the proposed motions will actually do the work desired, and various sequences of motions can be tried out. When the best one is found, it is programmed into the robot's computer. One of the chief benefits is that the robots can be programmed or reprogrammed off-line. The conventional method had been to show and teach a robot each new task, but that method became prohibitive as more and more robots were added to the production line. Therefore, the invention represents savings in time and money.

The introduction of robots into manufacturing not only changed the methods used but also affected the number of people employed in such industries. Formerly, many workers were needed to assemble products on the assembly lines; currently, the companies need fewer employees, but those employees need knowledge of computers and other areas of technology to work effectively. Pickett's photograph is included in *Technology Review* (August–September 1984).

***Bibliography:*** Stanley, A., *Mothers and Daughters of Invention.*

# *Poole, Joyce*
(1956– )
## *wildlife biologist*

***Education:*** B.A., Smith College, 1979; Ph.D. in animal behavior, Cambridge University, 1984
***Professional Experience:*** Researcher, Amboseli Elephant Research Project, 1974–1990; coordinator of elephant conservation and management, Kenya Wildlife Service, 1990–1993; independent researcher, 1993–

***Joyce Poole*** is one of the world's authorities on the African elephant; the other woman authority is her colleague Cynthia Moss. Poole has made several significant contributions to our knowledge of elephants. The first is that male African elephants experience musth—she and Moss were the first to recognize this condition in African elephants—and the second is that she has conducted research on vocalization among elephants, being concerned specifically with vocalization in sound ranges that are below what the human ear is able to detect.

Poole has lived in Africa most of her life. Her family first moved there in 1962 when her father was appointed director of the Peace Corps program in Malawi when she was six years old. She became fascinated with the animals at that time and was greatly disappointed when the family moved to Washington, D.C., when her father was made head of the Peace Corps Africa Program. When it turned out her father did not care for the bureaucracy involved in his job, the family moved in 1965 to Kenya for four years. She chose biology as a career at age 11 after hearing Jane Goodall speak at the National Museum of Kenya about her research. Joyce returned to the United States in 1965 for several years to complete her schooling.

She entered Smith College in 1975, but when her father accepted another job in Africa, this time in Nairobi with the African Wildlife Leadership Foundation, she was allowed to leave school for a year to accompany the family. Her boyfriend at the time, Paul Klingenstein, left Harvard for a year also for research in Kenya. This was about the time that Cynthia Moss was starting her program at Amboseli. With her parents' permission, Poole obtained an unpaid position with Moss.

Poole's primary task was to help compile the vast records on all of the elephants in the preserve. Moss was identifying each elephant by taking three photographs of the head—full face and each side—plus making detailed sketches of the ears and tusks. In its lifetime, each elephant develops distinctive markings in the ears—there are holes, torn edges, missing pieces, etc.—and the tusks are shaped slightly different and also contain cracks or cuts or have pieces or entire tusks missing. Moss also used Jane Goodall's method of naming the elephants by families, and since there are more than 26 families, the alphabet had to be expanded by using AA, AB, AC, etc., BA, BB, BC, etc. Moss further named each family member with a distinctive name. For example, she named one animal "Joyce" in honor of Joyce Poole; the matriarch of that family was Jezebel in the JA family.

Moss assigned Poole to concentrate on identifying the males because Moss already had a great deal of data on the females. The task actually was an arduous one because the males leave the family groups as teenagers and spend their time in small groups scattered throughout the park, unlike the females, who stay with their family groups all of their lives. Many of the family groups stayed close to Moss's camp, even spending the nights sleeping next to the tents, which helped keep other wild animals away from the camp. Poole expanded the photograph file by pasting the photos on punch cards and indexing the physical characteristics via the punched holes.

Poole returned to Smith the following year but spent each summer and some of the Christmas holidays at Amboseli. Since she was concentrating on the male elephants, she noticed from time to time that some of the males had a green discharge from the penis and exhibited aggressive behavior toward others while mating. This seemed to be a condition similar to musth, which was thought to occur only in Asian elephants. Poole used some of the early data for an undergraduate thesis at Smith and later expanded the data for her doctoral work at Cambridge University.

After completing her undergraduate degree, she moved permanently to Amboseli although her mother had returned to the United States after Poole's father had been killed in an accident. She decided to seek a graduate degree and spent a portion of the time over the next few years working up her data in residence at Cambridge University. After she received her doctorate in animal behavior in 1984, she obtained a Guggenheim Foundation postdoctoral position at Princeton University.

Poole and Moss also began a study of the vocalization of elephants. Moss concentrated on the audible vocalization that often is accompanied by physical movements such as head shaking, ear flapping, or foot shuffling; these movements indicate whether the animal is in a good mood or is intending to charge. Poole concentrated on the vocalization at sound ranges that were below what can be detected by the human ear. The two researchers knew there were inaudible vocalizations, for there are times, for example, when an entire family will turn and move in unison without an audible signal from the matriarch. At Princeton, Poole was able to make contacts with people to obtain sound equipment that is used to study whale vocalization; it is called infrasound vocalization, that is, very low frequency vocalization.

In the mid 1980s, there was a huge international market in ivory, which was being supplied by poachers who were killing elephants for their tusks, and the situation was reaching a crisis in the number of elephants that were being slaughtered in Africa. Often the poachers were park rangers who were protected by corrupt government officials. Moss and Poole encouraged film crews to expose the plight of the elephants by allowing the crews to film at Amboseli. Probably the majority of the filming in the world in the late 1980s and early 1990s was done there, and most of the footage shown in nature films and on television programs today probably comes from this one source. Poole and Moss went to the United States in 1987 to try to convince the African Wildlife Fund and the World Wildlife Fund to place elephants on the endangered species list. In 1988, they put aside their research to help with aerial elephant counts throughout Kenya, for owing to their years of study, they could determine the sex and age of an animal on sight.

When Richard Leakey took up the cause of the elephants, the Kenyan government finally started arresting the poachers. Since Leakey had been injured in a plane accident, he was no longer physically able to conduct archaeological field studies, and he turned to supporting the preservation of the elephants. Poole presented a paper showing that killing the older males and females, who had the largest tusks, doomed the young elephants, for elephants have to learn what to eat, where to find water, and where the best paths are between grazing areas. Young are led by the matriarch of their families; young males usually roam in groups with older males. The World Wildlife Fund estimated that elephants would be commercially extinct by 1995 and on the African continent entirely extinct by 2015. The fund finally succeeded in protecting the elephants worldwide and in stopping the ivory trade.

About 1988 Poole realized she had to find a permanent job if she wanted to stay in Africa. Since she had a doctorate, she wanted to establish herself as a researcher instead of just Moss's assistant. Although Moss was unhappy about this decision, it was necessary for Poole's career, and by this time, the two had trained a group of Kenyan elephant specialists who could help Moss continue her work. Poole accepted Richard Leakey's offer to become elephant coordinator of the Kenya Wildlife Service and built a house in Nairobi, but she resigned from the service in protest when Leakey was fired. Since 1993, she has been involved in independent studies in Africa.

About the only source of information about her is her autobiography, *Coming of Age with Elephants* (1996). Her photograph is included in *National Geographic* (April 1996) and *Smithsonian* (July 1996).

# *Pour-El, Marian Boykan*
(1928– )
## *computer scientist, mathematician*

***Education:*** B.A., Hunter College, 1949; M.A., Harvard University, 1951, Ph.D. in mathematics, 1958

***Professional Experience:*** Assistant professor of mathematics, Pennsylvania State University, 1958–1962, associate professor, 1962–1964; associate professor of mathematics, University of Minnesota, 1964–1968, professor, 1968–

***Concurrent Positions:*** Member, Institute for Advanced Study, Princeton, New Jersey, 1962–1964

***Married:*** Akiva Pour-El, 1955

***Children:*** 1

***Marian Pour-El*** is a mathematician who pioneered investigations on the interface between mathematical logic, mathematical analysis, computer science, and physics. Among the topics she studies in her research are the computability/noncomputability of the propagation of waves, the diffusion of heat, eigenvalues, and eigenvectors.

In the 1950s, when Marian Pour-El was a graduate student at Harvard University, it was unusual for a woman to prepare for a career as a mathematician or scientist. A woman's status in society was a reflection of her husband's success. This was not Pour-El's desire for herself. She recalls her first day in class at Harvard. She was surrounded by empty chairs. None of the other students, all men, would sit within two or three places of her. The reason was simple; they were puzzled to find a woman in their midst, and did not know how to react socially. When they discovered that she was as serious about her career as they were about theirs, she was accepted by them as a fellow student. After receiving her Ph.D. from Harvard, Pour-El joined the faculty of Pennsylvania State University as an assistant professor of mathematics. By that time she was married and had a baby daughter. Research, teaching, and childcare kept her very busy.

In 1962, Pour-El took a leave of absence. She accepted a fellowship from the Institute for Advanced Study in Princeton, New Jersey. She and her daughter moved to Princeton, where she spent the next two years on research. Her husband remained in Pennsylvania. In 1964, Pour-El accepted a faculty position as associate professor at the University of Minnesota. Some time later, her husband took a position in industry in Illinois. (At that time the University of Minnesota had a strong nepotism rule so that it was not possible for both husband and wife to hold faculty positions there.) Thus the couple entered upon a lifestyle in which husband and wife lived apart for many years in order to practice their careers. Pour-El described the dynamics of the marriage in an article entitled "Spatial Separation in Family Life: A Mathematician's Choice," which appeared in *Mathematics Tomorrow* (1981). An earlier article entitled "Mathematician" appeared in Ruth Kundsin's 1974 "Successful Women in the Sciences," the report of a symposium sponsored by the New York Academy of Sciences concerning careers of women scientists. In *Who's Who in America* Pour-El said: "In order to practice our careers our family has evolved a pattern of life at variance with the norm. For more than twenty years we have lived apart most of the time. Our strong emotional and personal ties were intensified by the absence of continuous physical nearness. It is my belief that one can succeed personally, socially, and professionally without having to accept the constraints of an existing social order."

Pour-El has lectured by invitation at colloquia, conferences, seminars, and symposia throughout Europe and the United States and in Japan and China. She has also coauthored, with Ian Richards, *Computability in Analysis and Physics* (1989). She is a fellow of the American Association for the Advancement of Science and a member of the American Mathematical Society, the Mathematical Association of America, and the Association for Symbolic Logic. She remains committed to helping women achieve satisfying careers in mathematics and science.

***Bibliography:*** *American Men and Women of Science* 11–19; Herzenberg, C., *Women Scientists from Antiquity to the Present;* Kundsin, R., "Successful Women in the Sciences"; Rossiter, M., *Women Scientists in America; Who's Who in America,* 51st ed., 1997; *Who's Who in Technology Today* v. 5; *Who's Who of American Women,* 20th ed., 1997–1998.

# *Pressman, Ada Irene*

(1927– )

***control systems engineer***

***Education:*** B.S. in mechanical engineering, Ohio State University, 1950; M.B.A., Golden Gate University, 1974

***Professional Experience:*** Project engineer, Bailey Meter Company, 1950–1955; project engineer, Bechtel Power Corporation, 1955–1974, chief control engineer, 1974–1979, engineering manager, 1979–1987; retired 1987

***Married:*** 1969

A***da Pressman*** is acknowledged as an authority in power plant controls and process instrumentation, and she is an expert in both fossil fuel (coal, oil, and diesel) and nuclear power plants. She is especially known for the measures she devised to safeguard people working on the sites of nuclear power plants from the danger of radiation and to protect people living in the vicinity of the plant. She specialized in the area of shutdown systems for these plants and worked to find ways to ensure that a nuclear power plant's turbine, steam engine, and reactor work together properly and safely to generate electrical power. She contributed to the technology of emergency systems, including developing a secondary cooling system that operates from a diesel generator in the event of a primary power source loss.

After working for Bailey Meter Company for a few years, she accepted a position as a project engineer with Bechtel Corporation in Los Angeles, a company that manages nuclear power plants throughout the world. She advanced in responsibilities to the position of engineering manager in 1979. Before she retired in 1987, she managed 18 design teams for more than 20 power generating plants scattered around the world.

She was noted for her involvement in the profession and in women's organizations.

In the 1970s, she successfully campaigned to have the profession of control systems engineering classified as a separate field with the state engineering board of California, and she was the first person to be registered in the new discipline, in addition to being a registered mechanical engineer in California and Arizona. Many state and federal agencies require that a contractor's key personnel on a project be registered engineers, and her work enhanced the professional status of control systems engineers. She was active in promoting careers for women in science and engineering, serving as president of the Society of Women Engineers in 1979–1980.

She has said that her career in engineering was a challenge and an opportunity to do a good job. Since she was one of the few women in a leadership role in the field at the time, she was impelled to develop resourcefulness. She often found that she was given assignments no one else wanted, but these often proved to be opportunities in disguise because they gave her the chance to do things that otherwise she would not have had the chance to do.

She received several awards in her career, including the E. G. Bailey Award of the Instrument Society of America in 1985, the Society of Women Engineers Annual Achievement Award in 1976, and the Distinguished Alumni Award of Ohio State University in 1974. She is a member of the American Nuclear Society, Instrument Society of America, and Society of Women Engineers (president, 1979–1980).

***Bibliography:*** *American Men and Women of Science* 15–19; *Notable Twentieth-Century Scientists; Who's Who in Engineering,* 9th ed., 1995.

# *Prichard, Diana (Garcia)*
(1949– )
## *chemical physicist*

***Education:*** LVN (nursing) degree, College of San Mateo, 1969; B.S. in chemistry and physics, California State University, Hayward, 1983; M.S., University of Rochester, 1985, Ph.D. in chemical physics, 1988
***Professional Experience:*** Research scientist, Photo Science Research Division, Eastman Kodak Company, 1983–
***Married:*** Mark S. Prichard
***Children:*** 2

***Diana Prichard*** is a research scientist who conducts research on fundamental photographic materials for Eastman Kodak Company. She received praise for her graduate work on the behavior of gas phases at the University of Rochester, and the inventiveness of her project brought unusual attention and recognition by the scientific community. Her graduate work involved the high-resolution infrared absorption spectrum, which basically tells how much or what type of atoms or molecules are present, and she was able to construct the first instrument ever to be able to measure van der Waals clusters.

The van der Waals equation accounts for the nonideal behavior of gases at the molecular level. An ideal, or perfect, gas is one that always obeys the known gas laws, and the van der Waals equation allows scientists to predict the behavior of gases that do not strictly follow these laws by factoring in specific corrections. Van der Waals clusters are weakly bound complexes that exist in a natural state but are low in number, and Prichard's work allows scientists to produce these rare clusters by experimental methods in order to study them. Her graduate publications on the subject, such as the one in the *Journal of Chemical Physics* (August 1, 1988), have been cited in more than 100 subsequent publications.

In her position at Eastman Kodak, Prichard conducts basic studies in silver halide materials for photographic systems, and such work is in stark contrast to her early education. Although her parents had themselves received little education, they knew the value of education and supported her interest in learning. She received a degree in nursing and spent several years working and raising her children, but she had always been intrigued by the creativity required to do scientific research. She enrolled in California State University, Hayward, for her undergraduate degree and then moved to the University of Rochester for her master's and doctoral degrees.

She is active in encouraging students to undertake science and engineering careers and founded a program in Rochester called Partnership in Education that provides Hispanic role models in the classroom to teach science and mathematics to students with only limited English proficiency. She also cofounded the Hispanic Organization for Leadership and Advancement (HOLA) at Eastman Kodak, and she is an active member of the Society of Hispanic Professional Engineers.

***Bibliography:*** *Notable Twentieth-Century Scientists.*

# *Prinz, Dianne Kasnic*

(1938– )

***solar-terrestrial physicist***

***Education:*** B.S., University of Pittsburgh, 1960; Ph.D. in physics, Johns Hopkins University, 1967

***Professional Experience:*** E. O. Hulbert fellow in physics and astronomy, University of Maryland, 1968–1971; research scientist, Space Science Division, U.S. Naval Research Laboratory, 1967–1968, 1971–

***Concurrent Position:*** Payload specialist, National Aeronautics and Space Administration (NASA), c. 1980s

***Married:*** 1960

***Dianne Prinz*** is known for her expertise in solar-terrestrial physics, and she is a specialist in designing optical instrumentation. She has conducted research at the U.S. Naval Research Laboratory since 1967, except in the 1980s when she was on special assignment with the National Aeronautics and Space Administration (NASA) as a payload specialist on Spacelab-2.

The *Astronaut Fact Book* of NASA defines payload specialists as "career scientists or engineers selected by their employer or country for their expertise in conducting a specific experiment or commercial venture on a space shuttle mission." However, Dianne Prinz was assigned to be a backup payload specialist and did not have the opportunity to work in space. She said that she acted as a liaison between the experimenters and NASA, defining page displays as they evolved, developing the mission time line, and working up detailed ground command paths. As a specialist in optical instrumentation, she designed the optics and the flight software for instruments aboard Spacelab-2.

In order to fulfill the assignment, she and the other applicants for the position had to pass a fairly strict physical examination. No one explained the purpose of some of these tests—for example, the physicians measured every angle of each joint on the body. The applicants also were tested for claustrophobia in the rescue sphere, which looked like the world's smallest gym. It had been in use so often that "the gym" had a bad odor.

In the late 1970s, NASA was under a great deal of pressure to select women as astronauts. They finally selected the first six in 1978, but in addition, there were large numbers of men and women who were selected as payload specialists but not selected to undergo the astronaut training. On the other hand, those people who did pass their one-year astronaut training program were also designated payload specialists until they finally made a trip in space. In more recent years, many people have waited as long as five years before making their first flight. This situation becomes very confusing to an outsider who is attempting to explain who people are and what they do at NASA, and several reference books provide inaccurate information for that reason.

Prinz is a member of the American Geophysical Union. Her research includes infrared spectroscopy of atmospheric gases and ultraviolet spectroscopy of solar and atmospheric gases. Her photograph is included in A. R. Oberg's *Spacefarers of the '80s and '90s.*

***Bibliography:*** *American Men and Women of Science* 11–19; Ireland, N., *Index to Women of the World . . . Suppl.;* Oberg, A. R., *Spacefarers of the '80s and '90s;* U.S. National Aeronautics and Space Administration, *Astronaut Fact Book.*

# *Profet, Margie*
## (1958– )
## ***biomedical researcher, evolutionary biologist***

***Education:*** B.A. in political philosophy, Harvard University, 1980; B.S. in physics, University of California, Berkeley, 1985

***Professional Experience:*** Computer programmer, National Semiconductor Company in Germany, 1980–1981; MacArthur Foundation fellowship, 1993–1998; independent researcher and author, 1996–

***Margie Profet*** is a creative individual who is presenting new theories relating to how humans adapt to their environment. She has challenged accepted theories on allergies, pregnancy sickness, and menstruation. After receiving two undergraduate degrees, she felt stifled by the constraints of the classroom and the need to meet deadlines, so she decided not to continue further academic training but to pursue her real interest in evolutionary physiology. She supports herself with part-time jobs in order to spend her time asking questions and searching for the answers.

Since she is allergic to various foods and chemicals, she spent time looking for evidence to explain her allergies. In an article published in the March 1991 issue of *Quarterly Review of Biology* entitled "The Function of Allergy: Immunological Defense Against Toxins," she proposed that humans develop allergic reactions as a means of protecting the body from harmful toxins. When the body is exposed to a toxin or when a toxin is ingested, it sends a warning signal through an allergic reaction, which means the allergy serves as one of the last defense mechanisms the body can mount against toxins. She even noted that people with allergies are less likely to develop cancer than individuals without allergies and believes that allergies are an internal warning device for the body.

She next looked at the question of what causes morning sickness during pregnancy. She theorizes that the brain's ability to discern what is toxic becomes recalibrated during pregnancy so that almost any food or odor can cause an aversion to almost anything. Although the condition is commonly called "morning sickness," the aversion can occur any time of the day or night depending on what is eaten. Her hypothesis is that all plants contain toxins that cause birth defects and that pregnancy sickness is a natural defense mechanism which reduces the amount of plant toxins one eats during the first trimester, the period when the embryo is particularly vulnerable to toxins that could cause birth defects. Therefore, morning sickness is the body's defense against birth defects. She presents a detailed explanation of this theory in her book *Protecting Your Baby-to-Be: Preventing Birth Defects in the First Trimester* (1995), which also contains information of interest to lay readers; for instance, there is a chapter on nutrition that discusses the importance of plant-derived nutrients in preventing birth defects.

The third question she has investigated is the reason for menstruation, and she presents the theory that sperm carry pathogens into the uterus and that the menstrual flow allows the uterus to rid itself of bacteria and infection. Menstruation is commonly viewed as merely a monthly waste of blood and energy. However, myriad bacteria that are found in and around the genitals of men and women hitch rides on sperm, thus gaining access to the uterus and fallopian tubes, and menstruation washes away the contaminants that could cause infection or infertility. She published her theory in the September 1993 issue of *Quarterly Review of Biology* as "Menstruation as a Defense against Pathogens Transported by Sperm."

Profet was a bright, inquisitive child who quickly became bored with routine but was a good student—and always asked questions. She studied political philosophy as an undergraduate, which encouraged her to challenge conventional wisdom and search for meaning in life. After graduation from Harvard, she went to Germany where she worked as a computer programmer for National Semiconductor Company. Still seeking answers to questions, she obtained another bachelor's degree, this time in physics, and she then embarked on her program of independent research and writing. She received a MacArthur Foundation fellowship for the five-year period 1993–1998, but the biographical sources do not indicate what new theories she is exploring. There are articles and photographs in *Scientific American* (April 1996), *Omni* (May 1994), *Time* (October 4, 1993), *People Weekly* (October 11, 1993), and *Newsweek* (October 4, 1993).

***Bibliography:*** *Notable Women in the Life Sciences; Who's Who in Science and Engineering,* 3d ed., 1996–1977; *Who's Who of American Women,* 20th ed., 1997–1998.

# R

## *Ramaley, Judith (Aitken)*

(1941– )

### *endocrinologist, reproductive biologist*

***Education:*** B.A., Swarthmore College, 1963; Ph.D. in anatomy, University of California, Los Angeles, 1966

***Professional Experience:*** Assistant professor, anatomy and physiology, Indiana University, 1969–1972; assistant professor, physiology and biophysics, University of Nebraska Medical Center, 1972–1974, associate professor, 1974–1978, professor, 1978–1982, assistant vice president for academic affairs, 1981–1982; vice president of academic affairs, State University of New York at Albany, 1982–1984, acting president, 1984–1985, executive vice president of academic affairs, 1985–1987; executive vice chancellor, University of Kansas, 1987–1990; president, Portland State University, Oregon, 1990–

***Married:*** Robert F. Ramaley, 1966, divorced 1976

***Children:*** 2

**Judith Ramaley** is known as an endocrinologist who is an expert in the physiology of puberty and the control of male and female fertility. In 1981, she started on a new career path when she was appointed assistant vice president for academic affairs at the University of Nebraska Medical Center. She then had a series of administrative appointments at the State University of New York at Albany and the University of Kansas until she was selected as president of Portland State University in Oregon in 1990. Since that time she has pursued her scientific interests on a reduced schedule.

In addition to numerous scientific publications, she is the author of two books, *Progesterone Function: Molecular and Biochemical Aspects* (1972) and *Essentials of Histology* (1974, revised edition, 1978), and the editor of *Covert Discrimination of Women in the Sciences* (1978). The last is a compilation of papers that were presented at an annual national meeting of the American Association for the Advancement of Science and published under its auspices. The symposium was sponsored by the Association of Women in Science, and the theme was that women are not represented as fully as they should be in the scientific professions.

In the Introduction to *Covert Discrimination,* Ramaley states that since World War II, women have not benefited to the same extent as men from the surge in educational opportunities—as can be seen by the few women who are admitted to graduate schools in spite of their high academic achievement. The proportion of women enrolled in and graduating from scientific disciplines has not even returned to the levels of the 1920s when women earned 16 percent of all doctorates. Nor do the statistics support the assumption that women now have an advantage over their male colleagues both in acquiring jobs and in preferred advancement when hired. On the contrary, the unemployment rate in the sciences for women is four times higher than the rate for men with comparable training.

Ramaley has been an active participant in the communities in which she has lived, involving herself in the urban league, planned parenthood, metro family services, the academic women's resource center, the local sports committee, the community progress board, and similar activities. She also became a member of the American Association of Colleges and Universities (AACU) board of directors in 1995. She is the author of an article in the spring 1996 issue of *Journal of Urban Affairs* in which she outlines how Portland State is revising its activities to meet the research and educational needs of the metropolitan region it serves.

She is a fellow of the American Association for the Advancement of Science and a member of the American Association of Anatomists, Endocrine Society, Society for the Study of Reproduction, Society for Neuroscience, and American Physiological Society. Her research includes the physiology of puberty and control of male and female fertility.

***Bibliography:*** *American Men and Women of Science* 11–19; Herzenberg, C., *Women Scientists from Antiquity to the Present; Who's Who in America,* 51st ed., 1997; *Who's Who of American Women,* 20th ed., 1997–1998.

# *Ranney, Helen Margaret*
(1920– )
## *hematologist*

***Education:*** B.A., Barnard College, 1941; M.D., Columbia University, 1947; honorary degree: D.Sc., University of Southern California, 1979

***Professional Experience:*** Assistant professor of clinical medicine, Columbia University, 1958–1960; associate professor of medicine, Albert Einstein College of Medicine, 1960–1965, professor, 1965–1970; professor, State University of New York at Buffalo, 1970–1973; chair, Department of Medicine, University of California, San Diego, 1973–1986, professor of medicine, 1973–1990; distinguished physician, Veterans Administration Medical Center, San Diego, 1986–1991; member of staff, Alliance Pharmaceutical Corporation, San Diego, 1991–

***Helen Ranney*** is known for her research in abnormal hemoglobins and the many facets of research that evolved from what began as relatively simple exercises in physiology, chemistry, and clinical hematology. For many years she has been a major force in medical education, clinical hematology, and blood-related research and training, and for more than 40 years, her work has extended into disciplines and directions as diverse as biochemistry, physical chemistry, immunology, metabolism, genetics, rheology, and analytical technologies. She was elected to membership in the National Academy of Sciences in 1973.

She has had a distinguished career at the Albert Einstein College of Medicine, the State University of New York at Buffalo, and the University of California, San Diego. In 1986 she was honored at the Helen Ranney Symposium held in Tarrytown, New York, the papers of which were published as *Pathophysiological Aspects of Sickle Cell Vaso-Occlusion* (1987), volume 240 in the series Progress in Clinical and Biological Research. One participant described her qualities thus: "Repeatedly, Helen's spirit of inquiry, her ability to get to the core of the problem, her intellectual curiosity, and her creative approaches to getting answers to the questions merged with her sense of fairness and her concern for both the subject and her professional colleagues."

Ranney's awards include the J. M. Smith Prize of Columbia University (1955), Gold Medal of the College of Physicians and Surgeons (1978), and May H. Soley Research Award of the Western Society of Clinical Investigation (1987). She was a member of the board of directors of Squibb Corporation from 1975 to 1989, and she is the author of *Genetics in Hematology* (1990), volume 27 in the series Seminars in Hematology.

She is a fellow of the American Association for the Advancement of Science and a member of the Association of American

Physicians, American Academy of Arts and Sciences, American College of Physicians, American Society of Clinical Investigation, American Society of Hematology, and American Physiological Society. Her research includes the relationship of hemoglobin and red cell membrane in sickle-cell disease and red cell survival. Her photograph is included in *Progress in Clinical and Biological Research,* vol. 240 (1987), edited by R. L. Nagel.

***Bibliography:*** *American Men and Women of Science* 11–19; O'Neill, L., *The Women's Book of World Records and Achievements; Who's Who in America,* 51st ed., 1997; *Who's Who of American Women,* 20th ed., 1997–1998.

# *Reichmanis, Elsa*

(1953– )

## *computer scientist, organic chemist*

***Education:*** B.S., Syracuse University, 1972; Ph.D. in organic chemistry, 1975
***Professional Experience:*** Intern in organic chemistry, Syracuse University, 1975–1976, Chaim Weizmann fellow of scientific research, 1976–1978; member of technical staff in organic chemistry, AT&T Bell Laboratories, 1978–1984, supervisor, Radiation Sensitive Material and Applications Group, 1984–
***Married:*** Francis J. Purcell, 1979
***Children:*** 4

***Elsa Reichmanis*** is known for her contributions to the science of manufacturing integrated circuits, or computer chips. Specifically, her research centers on developing sophisticated chemical processes and materials for computer chips. She holds 11 patents, some of which are for the design and development of organic polymers, called resists, which are used in microlithography (the principal process by which circuits, or electrical pathways, are imprinted upon the tiny silicon chips used in computers). During the multistage process of chip manufacture, layers of resist material are applied to a silicon base and exposed to patterns of ultraviolet light. As portions of the resists harden, they become templates for the application of subsequent layers of positively and negatively charged semiconductors that serve as the channel through which electric current travels. As computer products have become smaller and smaller, it has become more and more of a challenge to develop materials and processes to manufacture them. She was elected to membership in the National Academy of Engineering in 1995.

She received her doctorate in organic chemistry at the age of 22, and after completing a postdoctoral fellowship at Syracuse University, she joined AT&T Bell Laboratories in 1978, where she continues to conduct research. She has received several awards, including the 1993 Society of Women Engineers Annual Achievement Award for her contributions in the field of integrated circuitry and the *Research and Development Magazine* R&D 100 Award for one of the 100 significant inventions of 1992. She was a member of the Committee to Survey Materials Research Opportunities and Needs for the Electronics Industry of the National Research Council in 1987.

In addition to publishing more than 100 scientific papers, she has edited four volumes in the ACS Symposium Series of the American Chemical Society: *The Effects of Radiation on High-Technology Polymers* (1989), *Polymers in Microlithography: Materials and Processes* (1989), *Irradiation of Polymeric Materials: Processes, Mechanisms, and Applications* (1993), and *Microelectronics Technology: Polymers for Advanced Imaging and Packaging* (1995). She also edited a volume of the proceedings of an International Society for Optical Engineering symposium, *Advances in Resist Technology and Processing VI* (1989).

Reichmanis encourages women to embrace both a career and a family. She advises that if you are interested in something and you like doing it, then go for it. As the mother of four children, she says that if you ask yourself how you can manage a career and children, you will never do it; if you try it, everything will fall into place. She is a fellow of the Society of Women Engineers and a member of the American Chemical Society, American Association for the Advancement of Science, and Society of Photo-Optical Instrumentation. Her research includes properties and application of radiation sensitive materials, electronic materials, microlithography, photochemistry, synthesis, and polymers for electronic applications. Her photograph is included in *Notable Twentieth-Century Scientists.*

***Bibliography:*** *American Men and Women of Science* 14–19; *Notable Twentieth-Century Scientists; Who's Who in America,* 51st ed., 1997; *Who's Who in Science and Engineering,* 3d ed., 1996–1997; *Who's Who in Technology Today* v. 3.

# *Reinisch, June Machover*
(1943– )
***psychologist***

***Education:*** B.S., New York University, 1966, M.A., Columbia University Teacher's College, 1970, Ph.D. in psychology, Columbia University, 1976

***Professional Experience:*** Staff research associate in psychiatry, University of California, Los Angeles, School of Medicine, 1973–1974; instructor in psychology, Teachers College, Columbia University, 1974–1975; assistant professor of psychology, Rutgers University, 1975–1980, associate professor, 1980–1982; professor of psychiatry, 1983– , director and professor of The Kinsey Institute for Research in Sex, Gender, and Reproduction, 1982–1993, professor of clinical psychology, Indiana University School of Medicine, 1983–1993, director and professor emeritus, senior research fellow, and trustee, The Kinsey Institute, 1993– ; senior science consultatnt, Strategic Surveys International, Inc., New York, 1997–

***Concurrent Positions:*** Adjunct assistant professor in psychiatry, College of Medicine and Dentistry of New Jersey, Rutgers, 1976–1981; consulting faculty, Sexual Counseling Service, 1977–1980, adjunct associate professor in psychiatry, 1981–1982; professor of psychology, Indiana University, 1982–1993; professor of psychiatry 1983–1993; director and principal investigator, Prenatal Development Projects, 1978– ; president, $R^2$ Science Communications, Inc., 1985– ; visiting senior researcher, Institute of Preventive Medicine, Copenhagen, Denmark, 1994–

***Married:*** Leonard Rosenblum, 1988

***Children:*** 1

***June Reinisch*** is known as the director emeritus of what is probably one of the most controversial social science institutes in the United States, The Kinsey Institute for Research in Sex, Gender, and Reproduction at Indiana University in Bloomington, Indiana. For a number of years after Alfred Kinsey's death in 1956, the institute had seemingly retreated into the background of research in spite of changing public attitudes toward sex and gender during the 1960s and 1970s, although Kinsey's books *Sexual Behavior in the Human Male* (1948) and *Sexual Behavior in the Human Female* (1953), had helped demystify sex and make public discussion acceptable.

June Reinisch was hired by the institute's board of trustees in collaboration with the university administration to build and expand its academic and public missions of research, archiving, and education in order to bring it to national and international prominence again. The institute has a unique affiliation with Indiana University.

In 1947, prior to the publication of Kinsey's first book, the university's president, foreseeing problems with the controversial subject matter, suggested that Kinsey turn his Institute for Research in Sex into a private corporation. That way, the university could escape criticism by pointing to the institute's independence, and the researchers could shield the files of the sex histories from the prying eyes of outraged state officials and the conservative state legislators.

Reinisch was successful in bringing the institute back into the forefront in both the scientific and public arenas. During her 11-year tenure, federal and private research grant funding increased tenfold, the library, archives, art collections, and research and administrative spaces were expanded, modernized, and renovated, the institute's research became multidisciplinary in focus, publications increased, and a public education program was instituted. A series of international multidisciplinary conferences led to the publication of four scholarly volumes by Oxford University Press addressing sex differences, adolescence and puberty, sexual orientation, and AIDS and sexuality. As part of the public education program a thrice weekly column, "The Kinsey Report," answering the public's questions with current research infomration, was syndicated for nine years in newspapers around the world, and a reader-friendly encyclopedia was published addressing questions about sex, gender, and reproduction. Despite its status as a private nonprofit corporation, the institute receives a substantial part of its funding from Indiana University. The remainder is derived from private and public grants, private donations, and income from its publications. Increased public awareness brought increased criticism. Reinisch defended the institute from attacks by conservative political and religious forces. However, the expanded multidisciplinary interests and public education program were criticized by some academics as well. In the late 1980s a university review committee issued an unfavorable review of Reinisch's research, education, and administrative programs. The committee requested her resignation. However, the institute's board of trustees refused to fire her and supported her tenure as director for five more years. After much heated controversy and a thorough investigation, in January 1993, the president of Indiana University issued a public apology fully exonerating Reinisch and supporting the acccomplishments of her directorship. In mid-1993, she retired with the titles of Director Emerita and Senior Research Fellow and was elected to the institute's board of trustees. Controversy continues to plague The Kinsey Institute as it has from Alfred Kinsey's time. Recently, a new biography, *Alfred C. Kinsey: An American Tragedy* (1997), by James H. Jones, attempted to discredit Kinsey both as a person and a researcher, but the academic and literary reviews have been generally critical of Jones's research, scholarship, and conclusions.

Reinisch is a developmental psychobiologist who is known for her work on the long-term behavioral and physical effects of prenatal exposure to hormones and medications and studies of sex differences and high-risk sexual behavior. She has an eclectic background. She is dyslexic and did not learn to read until she was in the fourth grade. She prepared to be an elementary school teacher, but instead held many other jobs. She helped train dolphins, learned to skydive and obtained a pilot's license, was a singer with a rock band, became a sales representative for a major cosmetics firm, managed a famous Greenwich Village nightclub, and promoted and managed rock groups including Sly and the Family Stone. She returned to school to obtain a master's degree in psychology to enhance her career opportunities in the music business at a time when there were few, if any, women executives. After reading Eleanor Maccoby's *The Development of Sex Differences* (1966), she became fascinated by the discussion of the effects of prenatal hormones on the development of gender and sex differences and decided to pursue advanced studies at Columbia University. After receiving appointments at several universities and several major grants for her research, she was selected to be the third director of The Kinsey Institute and a professor of psychology at Indiana University. She has published scientific articles in many leading journals such as *Nature, Science,* CDC's *Morbidity and Mortality Weekly Report,* and the *Journal of the American Medical Association* as well as *The Kinsey Institute New Report on Sex: What You Must Know to Be Sexually Literate* (1990, 1994). This book for the general public was published in English, French, German, Spanish, Japanese, Taiwanese, and mainland Chinese editions. In addition to a national survey on American sexual knowledge, the volume included an extensive collection of the public's questions that were answered with the most current scientific information. Reinisch donated all her royalties from the column and book to support The Kinsey Institute's library, archives, and research. She now heads her own consulting company, continues her research at the institute and in Denmark, and writes for both scientific journals and the general public.

Among her many awards are the 1976 Morton Prince Award from the American Psychopathological Association, the 1991 Robert Wood Johnson Medical School Dr. Richard J. Cross Award for Outstanding Contributions to the Field of Human Sexuality, the 1992 Teachers College Distinguished Alumni Award from Columbia University, and the 1993 Award for Contributions to Sexology of the Society for the Scientific Study of Sex. She is a fellow of the American Association for the Advancement of Science, American Psychological Association, American Psychological Society, and Society for the Scientific Study of Sex; she is a member of the American Association of Sex Educators, Counselors and Therapists. Her photograph is included in *Psychology Today* (June 1986) and *Science* (April 17, 1992). The information for this entry was provided by June Reinisch in a letter to the author dated May 12, 1998.

***Bibliography:*** *Contemporary Authors* v. 138; *Who's Who in America,* 51st ed., 1997; *Who's Who of American Women,* 20th ed., 1997–1998.

# *Resnik, Judith A.*

(1949–1986)

## *electrical engineer, astronaut*

***Education:*** B.S., Carnegie Mellon University, 1970; Ph.D. in electrical engineering, University of Maryland, 1977

***Professional Experience:*** Electrical engineer, RCA Corporation, c. 1970–1974; biomedical engineer, Laboratory of Neurophysiology, National Institutes of Health, 1974–1977; senior systems engineer, Xerox Corporation, 1977–1978; astronaut, National Aeronautics and Space Administration (NASA), 1978–1986, missions STS 41-D (1984) and STS 51-L (1986)

***Judith (Judy) Resnik*** was one of the first six women to be selected as astronauts by the National Aeronautics and Space Administration (NASA) in 1978. She was the second woman in the United States to fly in space, and she was the first woman astronaut to die—she was a member of the crew on the space orbiter *Challenger* that exploded on January 28, 1986, just after the launch from Cape Canaveral, Florida; no one survived. Earlier, in 1984, she was a member of the crew of the earth orbiter *Discovery* and was responsible for operating the Remote Manipulator System (RMS) on that mission. The RMS is the huge robotic arm that can lift satellites out of the orbiter and bring them back again. The crew was nicknamed "Icebusters" because they were able to use to arm to remove ice particles from the orbiter. However, when the RMS was first tested in space in 1981, Sally Ride assisted from Mission Control.

Resnik was one of the first women to report to NASA after being selected, and the agency used her as a guinea pig for training programs for the whole group of new astronauts. Since she was an engineer, she had a slight advantage over some of the other women in the group because the program was definitely engineering oriented. Although the six women had diverse backgrounds and interests, they shared common experiences as women engineers and scientists.

When one of the male astronauts commented to Resnik that she might find the station unusual to work in, she replied that she had been the only girl in her mathematics class since calculus in her senior year in high school. The women had been pioneers since they were young girls, and they did not see any difference in their present situation. It was the men who felt the difference. Many of the male astronauts and employees of NASA were vehemently opposed to adding women to the program, but most reluctantly admitted that the women were qualified for their jobs. The first men selected had all been military test pilots because they had had experience flying at high altitudes. However, in the late 1970s, the space program was shifting toward developing an orbiting space station, which required more men and women with scientific backgrounds. Some of the physical requirements for the program also changed.

All of the astronauts trained in multiple assignments in order to expand their capabilities to the maximum. Although Resnik was expert on using the shuttle arm, her initial flight assignment on her first flight did not call for that specialty but instead required a great deal of photographic work. Later, when the flight was changed to include the shuttle arm, she had the opportunity to use her expertise. Originally she had not been chosen for the specialty, but she had mastered it quickly.

After her death, people remembered Resnik in different ways. Some remembered her as being rather subdued and difficult to know, but that was how she acted before the media people. Her colleagues called her effusive, knowledgeable, easy to meet, and enthusiastic about her job; the crew members on her first flight said she was just one of the guys. Some of the NASA workers complained that the women stood up to them and would not back down, but those men were not accustomed to working with knowledgeable women who were experienced in working with men as equals. The women astronauts agree that they are women just doing a job; however, it is a very interesting job. People outside NASA have difficulty understanding their work. Resnik said that when people asked her what she did, she told them she was an engineer, for they had difficulty believing she was an astronaut. She and the other five women did not gear their education to space, as some later astronauts were able to, but they were selected on the basis of their expertise and interests. There are numerous photographs of Resnik in the news magazines of the early 1980s and in A.R. Oberg's *Spacefarers of the '80s and '90s,* K. O'Connor's *Sally Ride and the New Astronauts,* and P. Read's *The Book of Women's Firsts.*

***Bibliography:*** Herzenberg, C., *Women Scientists from Antiquity to the Present;* Ireland, N., *Index to Women of the World . . . Suppl.;* Oberg, A. R., *Spacefarers of the '80s and '90s;* O'Connor, K., *Sally Ride and the New Astronauts;* Read, P., *The Book of Women's Firsts.*

# *Richardson, Jane S.*
(1941– )
***biochemist***

***Education:*** B.A., Swarthmore College, 1962; M.A. in natural science, Harvard University, 1966; honorary degrees: D.Sc., Swarthmore College, 1986, and University of North Carolina, 1994

***Professional Experience:*** Technical assistant, Department of Chemistry, Massachusetts Institute of Technology, 1964–1969; general physical scientist, Laboratory of Molecular Biology, National Institute of Arthritis and Metabolic Diseases, 1969; associate, Department of Anatomy, Duke University, 1970–1984, medical research associate professor, Departments of Biochemistry and Anatomy, 1984–1988, medical research associate professor, Department of Biochemistry, 1988–1991, James B. Duke Professor of Biochemistry, Department of Biochemistry, 1991–

***Concurrent Positions:*** MacArthur Foundation grant, 1985–1990; codirector, Molecular Graphics and Modeling Shared Resource, Duke Comprehensive Cancer Center, Duke University, 1988–

***Married:*** David C. Richardson, 1963

***Children:*** 2

***Jane Richardson*** is known as a crystallographer who studies the three-dimensional structures of proteins, emphasizing the underlying principles of their architecture, aesthetics, interrelationships, and folding mechanism. She is an expert on protein folding, and she jokingly compares the protein-folding problem with the paper-folding problems of the Japanese art of origami. However, many of her colleagues and fellow researchers regard her work on protein folding as a unique and completely new style of representing a protein. She was elected to membership in the National Academy of Sciences in 1991.

Her other research interests are protein crystallography, the design of new proteins for synthesis, and the comparison and classification of protein structures. In 1985 she received one of the MacArthur "genius" awards, and in the December issue of that same year, *Science Digest* chose her and her husband's work on the first chemical synthesis of the protein betabellin as one of the year's 100 best inventions. Betabellin is a bell-shaped, beta-pleated-sheet protein whose structural properties were accurately predicated. Creating proteins that do not occur in nature can provide scientists with a better understanding of the structure of natural proteins, and the synthesis of proteins may open the way to designing hormones and drugs and improving myriad industrial products.

Richardson had an early interest in science, and as a teenager in 1958, she won third place in the nation at the Westinghouse Science Talent Search. She studied philosophy, mathematics, and physics at Swarthmore College, married after graduation, and began graduate work at Harvard University after she had worked for several years. After receiving her degree, she worked at the National Institutes of Health in the Laboratory of Molecular Biology for several years before moving to Duke University where she advanced in rank to become the James B. Duke Professor of Biochemistry. She is also codirector of the Molecular Graphics and Modeling Shared Resource at the Duke Comprehensive Cancer Center.

She understands the challenges and barriers that women face as they try to succeed in a male-dominated profession and has commented on the small number of women who are elected to high-profile positions in the National Academy of Sciences. She has been a member of the National Center for Research Resources, National Institutes of Health, since 1990, and she has been an industrial consultant for Upjohn Company,

Hoffman-LaRoche Company, Allied Chemical Corporation, Becton Dickinson, and Nutrasweet. She is a member of the American Academy of Arts and Sciences, Biophysical Society, American Crystallographic Association, and Protein Society Office. Her research includes classification of protein structures, design of new proteins for synthesis, protein crystallography, protein folding, representation of protein structures, conformational details in proteins, and interpretation of electron density maps and evaluation of errors. Her photograph is included in *Notable Women in the Physical Sciences.* Some information was supplied in a letter to the author dated July 27, 1997.

***Bibliography:*** *American Men and Women of Science* 18–19; *Notable Women in the Physical Sciences; Who's Who in Science and Engineering,* 2d ed., 1994–1995.

# *Ride, Sally Kristen*
(1951– )
## *physicist, astronaut*

***Education:*** B.A. in English and B.S. in physics, Stanford University, 1973, M.S., 1975, Ph.D. in physics, 1978

***Professional Experience:*** Researcher, Department of Physics, Stanford University, 1978; trainee, National Aeronautics and Space Administration (NASA), 1978–1979, astronaut, 1979–1987, missions STS-2 (1981), STS-3 (1982), STS-7 (1983), STS 41-G (1984), special assistant for long-range and strategic planning 1987; science fellow, Stanford University Center for International Security and Arms Control, 1987–1989; director, California Space Institute of University of California, San Diego, 1989– , professor of physics, University of California, San Diego, 1989–

***Married:*** Steven A. Hawley, 1982, divorced

***Sally Ride*** was the first American woman to be sent into outer space in 1983. Later she served the National Aeronautics and Space Administration (NASA) in an advisory capacity as the only astronaut chosen for the Rogers Commission investigating the midlaunch explosion of the space shuttle *Challenger* in 1986. She created NASA's Office of Exploration, and she was also the first woman astronaut to leave the space program when she quietly resigned in 1987 and went first to Stanford University and then to the University of California, San Diego.

She was the youngest person sent into orbit at age 32 as well as the first American woman to make two space flights. She was also the first astronaut to marry another astronaut on active duty. During their astronaut training, she and Steven A. Hawley met and married in 1982, but the couple later divorced. Although a Russian textile worker, Valentina Tereskova, had orbited the earth several years before Ride did, that trip was regarded as a mere token flight because she was only a passive passenger. Later, of course, Russian women were allowed to be part of the Russian cosmonaut training. Ride said it was important to her that people did not think she was chosen to go into space just because she was a woman and it was time for NASA to send one on a space flight.

Ride's first flight was in the space shuttle *Challenger* in June 1983. Among the team's missions were deployment of international satellites and numerous research experiments supplied by a number of groups—ranging from a naval research lab to high school students. While operating the shuttle's robot arm she handled the first satellite deployment and retrieval, the first time such an arm had been used in space during flight.

Her second flight was also in the *Challenger* in October 1984. This time the robot arm was used to readjust a radar antenna on the shuttle as well as to deploy and capture a satellite. Objectives on this mission covered scientific observations of the earth and demonstrations of potential satellite refueling techniques. Ride was chosen for a third scheduled flight, but it was called off after the *Challenger* exploded in January 1986. Her response to questions about the safety of the flights was that NASA may have been misleading people into thinking that space flight is a routine operation. One of the recommendations of the Rogers Commission was to include astronauts at management levels to provide needed input on technical aspects at a higher level in NASA. This recommendation was implemented.

After leaving NASA, Ride joined the Stanford University Center for International Security and Arms Control and two years later became director of the California Space Institute and physics professor at the University of California, San Diego. While with NASA, she had regularly gone to high schools and colleges to speak with the students about careers in science and engineering, and one of her goals was to write children's books about space. Although the publishers would have preferred that she write her autobiography, she has written three juvenile books to date: *To Space and Back* (1986), *Voyager: An Adventure to the Edge of the Solar System* (1992), and *The Third Planet: Exploring the Earth from Space* (1994).

Although she was a good student in elementary school she became easily bored, but she began to shine in high school when she was introduced to science in a physiology class. She also ranked eighteenth nationally on the junior tennis circuit and considered turning pro but decided against that career and instead enrolled at Stanford University where she completed all of her academic degrees. She was just completing her doctorate in 1978 when she received a call from NASA. She was one of 35 chosen from an original field of 8,000 for space flight training; she said no one ever knew why they were selected. She was chosen as part of the ground support crew for the STS-2 shuttle flight (1981), and on the third STS-3 (1982), she was an on-orbit capsule communicator.

She was appointed a member of the Presidential Commission of Advisors on Science and Technology in 1994, and she has received the Jefferson Award for Public Service from the American Institute for Public Service (1984) and two National Spaceflight Medals (recognizing her shuttle missions of 1983 and 1984). At the National Air and Space Museum in Washington, D.C., there is a model of Sally Ride in her space uniform honoring her as the first American woman in space; next to her is a model of Guion Bluford, Jr., the first black person in space. Although there are numerous photographs of Ride dating back through the 1980s, the most recent are in *Notable Twentieth-Century Scientists* and *Working Woman* (November–December 1996).

***Bibliography:*** *American Men and Women of Science* 19; *Current Biography 1983;* Herzenberg, C., *Women Scientists from Antiquity to the Present; Notable Twentieth-Century Scientists;* Oberg, A. R., *Spacefarers of the '80s and '90s;* O'Connor, K., *Sally Ride and the New Astronauts; Who's Who in America,* 51st ed., 1997; *Who's Who of American Women,* 20th ed., 1997–1998.

# *Riley, Matilda (White)*
(1911– )
***sociologist***

***Education:*** B.A., Radcliffe College, 1931, M.A. in sociology, 1937; honorary degrees: D.Sc, Bowdoin College, 1972, and Radcliffe College, 1994; LHD, Rutgers University, 1983
***Professional Experience:*** Research assistant, Harvard University, 1932; vice president, Market Research Company of America, 1938–1949; chief consulting economist, War Production Board, 1941–1943; research specialist, Rutgers University, 1950, professor, 1951–1973, director of sociology laboratory, chair of Department of Sociology and Anthropology, 1959–1973, emeritus professor, 1973– ; Daniel B. Fayerweather Professor of political economy and sociology, Bowdoin College, 1974–1978, professor emeritus, 1978– ; associate director, National Institute on Aging, 1976–1991, senior social scientist, 1991–
***Concurrent Positions:*** Staff associate, director of aging and society, Russell Sage Foundation, 1964–1973, staff sociologist, 1974–1977
***Married:*** John W. Riley Jr., 1931
***Children:*** 2

*Matilda Riley* is known as one of the foremost authorities on aging and gerontology. Even as she approached her nineties she continued to work and to write, and she has had a career full of activity. Instead of retiring after spending almost 25 years at Rutgers University, she moved to Bowdoin College and later to the National Institute on Aging. Her election to membership in the National Academy of Sciences in 1994 was a long-delayed recognition of her years of research.

The terms *aging* and *gerontology* have different definitions. Gerontology is the branch of science that deals with aging and the problems of the aged person; aging in the psychological sense is the level of mental, emotional, or educational development of a person, especially a child, as determined by various tests and based on a comparison of the individual's score with the average score for persons of the same chronological age.

In Riley's inaugural address as president of the American Sociological Association in 1986, she outlined her research on age, and in the February 1987 issue of *American Sociological Review* she stated, "I believe that an understanding of age can clarify and specify time-honored sociological propositions, raise new research questions, demand new (as well as the old) methodological approaches, and even enhance the integrative power of our discipline (a power eroded in recent years through pluralism and disputes)." A few years later she developed a theory about the influence exerted by the lives and experiences of sociologists on social and intellectual structure and change, both in sociology and in society as a whole. In the *Annual Review of Sociology* (1990) she uses examples of this influence in four areas of current sociology concern: sociological practice, gender, age, and dynamic social systems.

In her career she was a department chair at Rutgers and an associate director of the National Institute on Aging. Between 1949 and 1960 she was executive secretary of the American Sociological Association, at a time when women rarely were executive secretaries of any associations. She has received numerous awards, such as the Commonwealth Award in Sociology (1984), Distinguished Creative Contribution to Gerontology Award of the Gerontological Society of America (1990), the Kent Award from the same organization (1992), and the Radcliffe Alumnae Award (1982). The Matilda White Riley prize in research and methodology was established in her honor at Rutgers University in 1977, the Matilda White Riley prize was established at Bowdoin College in 1987, and the Matilda White Riley House was dedicated at Bowdoin College in 1996.

In addition to papers published in journals, she wrote eight books over a period of

50 years and edited five more. She coedited *Age and Structural Lag: Society's Failure to Provide Meaningful Opportunities in Work, Family, and Leisure* (1994), in which the authors argue that the current lack of opportunities for work for older people is both unnecessary and modifiable. In view of the fact that America's population is graying quite rapidly, Riley's work is especially pertinent today. She is a fellow of the Center for Advanced Study in the Behavioral Sciences and a member of the Gerontological Society of America, American Association for the Advancement of Science, and American Sociological Association (president, 1986). Her photograph is included in *Annual Review of Sociology* (1990).

***Bibliography:*** *American Men and Women of Science* 16, 19; *Contemporary Authors* v. 114 and 132; Rossiter, M., *Women Scientists in America; Who's Who in America,* 51st ed., 1997; *Who's Who in Science and Engineering,* 3d ed., 1996–1997; *Who's Who of American Women,* 20th ed., 1997–1998.

# *Rissler, Jane Francina*
## (1946– )
### ***botanist***

***Education:*** B.A., Shepherd College, 1966; M.A., West Virginia University, 1968; Ph.D. in plant pathology, Cornell University, 1977

***Professional Experience:*** Fellow, fungal physiology, Boyce Thompson Institute, 1977–1978; assistant professor of plant pathology, University of Maryland, 1978–

***Jane Rissler*** is a plant pathologist who has written on some of the concerns about engineered plants. Although scientists and farmers have practiced plant breeding for centuries, in the past 30 years or so it has become possible to transfer genetic material among plants. As a plant pathologist—that is, a person who researches diseases of plants—she is concerned about the possibility of transferring diseases from plant to plant and about the possibility of introducing diseased plants into food crops. Although her own research centers on ornamental plants and turf grass (such as grass on football fields and golf courses), she is concerned about the entire spectrum of plant diseases.

A genetically altered plant is known as a transgenic plant, and the process leads to some risks that must be examined. Among those risks are the questions, Would the transgenic crop become a weed? Would its transgene move via pollen or soil bacteria into related wild crop plants so they would become more weedy or invasive? Would the transgenic crop invade natural habitats? Might virus-tolerant transgenic plants encourage new and damaging plant viruses?

Rissler is an active member of the Union of Concerned Scientists, and she has coauthored two of the books the group has published. *Perils Amidst the Promise: The Ecological Risk of Transgenic Plants in a Global Market* (1993) was written to try to unclog policy logjams by clarifying the issues that the politics of biotechnology have tended to leave sometimes confused and neglected. The book offers some specific science-based recommendations, and one reviewer recommended it as an introduction to biotechnology environmental issues. That work has been enlarged and revised as *The Ecological Risks of Engineered Crops* (1996), in which the authors acknowledge that applications of biotechnology in crops are already a commercial reality, and they do not oppose genetic engineering as a component of agriculture as a whole. Instead, they discuss a list of hypothetical harmful consequences of transgenic plants and suggest a risk assessment methodology. According to one reviewer, it is unfortunate that even though the purpose of the book is to generate public debate, the authors do not present details of the opposing viewpoints.

She also is coeditor of a newsletter sponsored by the Union of Concerned Scientists and published by the National Biotechnology Center of the National Wildlife Federation. The newsletter, *The Gene Exchange,* started publication in February 1990 and is published quarterly. The primary focus of this alerting service is to provide a reliable source of information for the public. A portion of each issue is devoted to a listing of "applications to field test genetically engineered organisms," and there are short news items to inform readers about pertinent legislation as well as genetically engineered herbicides and other products. Most of the data are presented in nontechnical terms. She was quoted in the February 2, 1998 issue of *Business Week* in an article on genetically altered food, where she criticized chemical companies that promote their own products without concern for safer, more productive agriculture. Rissler is a member of the American Phytopathological Society (phytopathology is another term for plant pathology).

***Bibliography:*** *American Men and Women of Science* 14–19.

# *Rivlin, Alice (Mitchell)*
(1931– )
***economist***

***Education:*** B.A., Bryn Mawr, 1952; M.A., Radcliffe College, 1955, Ph.D. in economics, 1958; honorary degree: LL.D., Hood College, 1970
***Professional Experience:*** Research assistant, economics, Brookings Institution, 1958–1963, senior staff, 1963–1966; deputy assistant secretary of program analysis, Department of Health, Education and Welfare, 1966–1968, assistant secretary of planning and evaluation, 1968–1969; senior fellow, economics, Brookings Institution, 1969–1975; director, Congressional Budget Office, U.S. Congress, 1975–1983; professor of public policy, George Mason University, 1992; deputy director, U.S. Office of Management and Budget, 1993–1994, director, 1994–1996; vice chair, Federal Reserve Board, 1996–
***Married:*** Lewis A. Rivlin, 1955, divorced 1977; Sidney G. Winter, 1989
***Children:*** 3

**Alice Rivlin** is an economist who has spent at least half of her career in the federal government. She was appointed a member of the staff of the Department of Health, Education and Welfare and was the first head of the Congressional Budget Office when it was established in 1975. In 1996 she became vice chair of the Federal Reserve Board.

After completing her doctorate, she obtained a position as an economist with the Brookings Institution in Washington, D.C., a well-known liberal Democratic think tank that is devoted to independent research, education, and publications on social issues. During her time there, she published a large amount of material in economics and related areas, including *Role of the Federal Government in Financing Higher Education* (1961), *Microanalysis of Socioeconomic Systems: Assimilation Study* (1961), *Measure of State and Local Fiscal Capacity and Tax Effort* (1962), and *U.S. Balance of Payments in 1968* (1963). She also acted as a consultant for several government agencies.

In 1966 she joined the Department of Health, Education and Welfare as deputy assistant secretary for program coordination. There she played a prominent role in the reorganization of the agency, and President Lyndon Johnson promoted her to assistant secretary for planning and evaluation. In that position, she implemented a system of budgeting and programming and brought economic analyses to bear on the agency's policy decisions.

On her return to the Brookings Institution, she wrote extensively on many topics, but her papers in the fields of public decision making and the federal budget led to interest in her work. One report consisted of an intensive analysis of the Nixon administration's budget for the subsequent fiscal year and suggested alternatives to the White House's budget priorities.

At the time, there was a controversy in Congress concerning the fact that the members of that body were not receiving sufficient information from the executive branch to determine budget priorities. In 1974, therefore, Congress passed the Congressional Budget and Impoundment Control Act, which provided for a House budget committee, a Senate budget committee, and a Congressional Budget Office (CBO). The last was to be an independent, nonpartisan office that would work with the two congressional committees to assist the members of Congress in analyzing and forming policy on federal spending and income. CBO was responsible also for monitoring the national economy and its impact on the federal budget, for providing budgetary statistics to Congress, and for proposing alternative budgeting policies.

The director of CBO is appointed to a four-year term by the Speaker of the House upon the recommendations of the two congressional budget committees, and Alice Rivlin was selected in 1975. At first she found herself embroiled in controversy because some of the recommendations of CBO stepped on the toes of powerful people in Congress who had pet projects they were promoting. Also, her analyses and recommendations often were more negative than those provided by the executive branch, a factor that annoyed a series of U.S. presidents. However, CBO gradually improved its procedures and began to provide information that was more widely accepted.

After President Carter's election in 1976, she was considered as a possible candidate for secretary of Health, Education and Welfare, but she remained at CBO and served a second term there. After President Reagan was inaugurated, she found herself in conflict with his supply-side economics. She forecast a deficit for 1984 while his office insisted he would balance the budget by 1984. Although her forecast proved to be correct, she was able to keep her job because there was a sharp drop in inflation that diffused the argument.

After completing her second term at CBO, she resigned her office there and returned to teaching, writing, and lecturing; she received a MacArthur fellowship for 1983–1988. In 1993, she returned to federal employment when President Clinton appointed her the deputy director of the U.S. Office of Management and Budget, the budgeting agency for the executive branch and the agency whose data she had disagreed with while head of CBO. She was promoted to director in 1994 but resigned in 1996 to serve as vice chair of the Federal Reserve Board under Alan Greenspan.

Rivlin originally planned on having a diplomatic career and did not become interested in pursuing a career in economics until she was attending college. Her father was a professor of nuclear physics at Indiana University in Bloomington, Indiana, and during a summer course in economics at that university she found that economics seemed less fuzzy than history or political science. She has served on numerous committees and commissions and received the Founders Award from Radcliffe College in 1970. Her photograph is included in *Current Biography* (1982) and *Working Woman* (November–December 1996).

***Bibliography:*** *Contemporary Authors* v. 33–36R; *Current Biography 1982; Who's Who in America,* 51st ed., 1997; *Who's Who of American Women,* 20th ed., 1997–1998.

# Roemer, Elizabeth
(1929– )
**astronomer**

***Education:*** B.A., University of California, Berkeley, 1950, Ph.D. in astronomy, 1955
***Professional Experience:*** Assistant astronomer, University of California, 1950–1952, laboratory technician, Lick Observatory, 1954–1955, research astronomer, 1955–1956; research associate, Yerkes Observatory, University of Chicago, 1956; astronomer, Flagstaff Station, U.S. Naval Observatory, 1957–1966, acting director, 1965; associate professor of astronomy, Department of Astronomy, and member of Lunar and Planetary Laboratory, University of Arizona, 1966–1969, professor, 1969– , astronomer, Steward Observatory, 1980–

***Elizabeth Roemer*** is renowned as the premier recoverer of "lost" comets, that is, comets whose planned rediscovery is based on predictions from previous returns. She calls her profession "astrometry," which is the branch of astronomy that deals with the measurement of the positions and motions of the celestial bodies. In her lifetime study of comets, she has rediscovered at least 79 returning periodic comets and visual and spectroscopic binary stars, plus computing the orbits of comets and minor planets. Her publications have covered many topics, such as comets and minor planets, astronomy and practical astronomy, computation of orbits, astrometric and astrophysical investigations of comets, minor planets and satellites, and dynamical astronomy. She is regarded by her peers as a contributor to many scientific and astronomical discoveries, and her precise photographic observations of comets have led to a great many cometary orbits of importance.

In 1965, a colleague named asteroid 1657 "Roemera" in her honor. Although each comet and asteroid is assigned a number in an international database, not all have names; after the sightings have been verified, it is the privilege of the discoverer to name the item if he or she wishes to. That is the reason that a name is affixed to the comet Shoemaker-Levy 9 and to Roemer's comet. She made her first major rediscoveries while she was working at the U.S. Naval Observatory at Flagstaff, Arizona, and it was at that same time that her photographic records of comets and her notes on their physical characteristics began to earn her national recognition.

She taught adult classes in the local public school system while attending school at the University of California, Berkeley. She also served as an assistant astronomer and later as a laboratory technician at the Lick Observatory. She worked briefly for the university after graduation and was also a research associate at the Yerkes Observatory of the University of Chicago. She then joined the staff of the Flagstaff Station of the U.S. Naval Observatory and later moved to the University of Arizona as an associate professor and a member of the Lunar and Planetary Laboratory before becoming a full professor of astronomy.

She has received numerous prizes such as the B. A. Gould Prize of the National Academy of Sciences (1971), the Donohoe lectureship of the Astronomical Society of the Pacific (1962), the National Aeronautics and Space Administration Special Award (1986), and the Dorothea Klumpke Roberts Prize of the Astronomical Society of the Pacific (1950)—Dorothea Klumpke Roberts (1861–1942) was an American astronomer who was recognized for her work in charting and cataloging stars when she worked for the Paris Observatory during the period 1887–1901. Roemer is a fellow of the American Association for the Advancement of Science and a member of the American Astronomical Society, American Geophysical Union, Astronomical Society of the Pacific, and International Astronomical Union. She has served on numerous committees in these associations, particularly the International Astronomical Union.

***Bibliography:*** *American Men and Women of Science* 11–19; Herzenberg, C., *Women Scien-*

*tists from Antiquity to the Present; Notable Women in the Physical Sciences; Who's Who in America,* 51st ed., 1997; *Who's Who in Science and Engineering,* 3d ed., 1996–1997; *Who's Who of American Women,* 20th ed., 1997–1998.

# Rolf, Ida P.

(1896–1979)

## *biochemist, physical therapist*

***Education:*** Ph.D. in biological chemistry, Barnard College, 1920

***Professional Experience:*** Associate, Department of Chemotherapy, Rockefeller Institute, 1920–1928; developed form of physical therapy called "Structural Integration" or "Rolfing," 1930–1979, organized Rolf Institute of Structural Integration, Boulder, Colorado, 1970

***Married:*** 1920, died 1947

***Children:*** 2

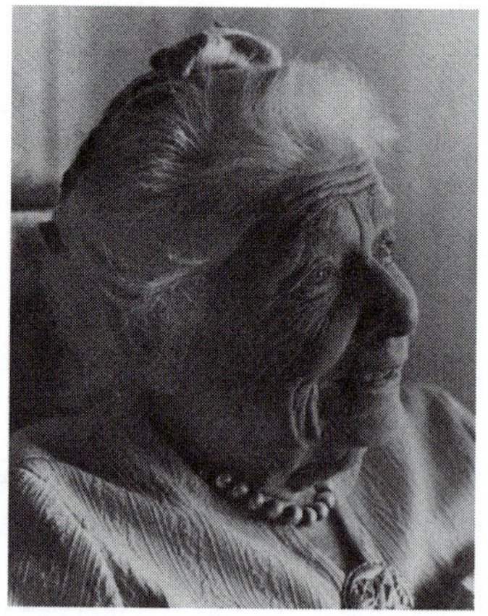

***Ida Rolf*** was a biochemist, but she is known for her research in physical therapy. After receiving her graduate degree she worked for Rockefeller Institute, but in 1920 she inherited some money, quit her job, and started studying various methods of physical therapy. Although she was a very private individual who gave several reasons for this interest, one version is that one of her children required physical therapy. Since she was not satisfied with the type of treatment the child was receiving, she started developing a treatment of her own.

She studied homeopathic medicine in Zurich and chiropractic and osteopathic methods in the United States. Her system is based on the theory that both psychological and physical histories shape, and sometimes deform, people's bodies, thickening connective tissue and tightening muscles in response to psychological as well as physical injury and revealing past tensions and unexpressed angers. These abnormal tightenings and thickenings interfere with the flow of fluids and can sometimes block the free passage of nerves and nerve impulses through the body.

Her treatment was based on a vigorous program of physical manipulations to break up those blocks, release the old angers and tensions, and restore the free flow of fluids, nerve impulses, and energy through the body. It was also based on the belief that the body is plastic and not a fixed unit as medical science would hold. One important feature is that the structure, particularly the alignment, of trouble areas would often be changed, and the patients might look much different because they were standing, moving, and walking in a new way. One person commented that one could always pick out people who had received Rolfing treatments because of the manner in which they stood and walked.

The treatment is still controversial because Ida Rolf did not have a medical degree and the treatment sessions can be quite painful. Some of her colleagues jokingly called her "the Elbow" because, although she was not a large person, she threw her whole body into the treatment, especially her elbows. Rolfing lies outside established medicine, and although many medical personnel will recommend chiropractic treatments and massage for patients, few accept Rolf's method. She did have some success in receiving referrals from osteopaths, however. Another problem with the treatment is that the fears and angers released at a session can be overwhelming for a patient if there is not psychiatric help at hand.

For many years she worked primarily alone, treating patients and training people in various parts of the country in her methods. In the mid 1960s she was invited to give demonstrations at the Esalen Institute in California. Esalen was part of the encounter movement of that period. Communities were established to expand human awareness by intensifying interpersonal and sensory experiences, and in general, the groups tried to integrate elements of Eastern cultures, such as Zen Buddhism, and radical therapy systems, such as Gestalt psychotherapy. Although Rolf did not approve of the Esalen lifestyle, which included nudism and drugs, the institute provided a base of operations for her for a few years. She always insisted that her patients wear underwear during treatment, however, and kept a supply of underwear on hand for anyone who showed up nude for treatment. There were psychiatrists in residence at Esalen to provide treatment also.

In 1970, she organized the Rolf Institute of Structural Integration in Boulder, Colorado, to train Rolf practitioners to carry on her work. After her death, one of her sons continued the business. She wrote a book about Rolfing, *Integration of Human Structure* (1977), and articles were published in several popular magazines in the 1990s describing the treatment. There is a short biography in *Human Relations* (May 1977).

***Bibliography:*** Rossiter, M., *Women Scientists in America;* Stanley, A. *Mothers and Daughters of Invention.*

# *Roman, Nancy Grace*
(1925– )
***astronomer***

***Education:*** B.A., Swarthmore College, 1946; Ph.D. in astronomy, University of Chicago, 1949; honorary degrees: D.Sc., Russell Sage College, 1966, Hood College, 1969, Bates College, 1971, and Swarthmore College, 1976

***Professional Experience:*** Assistant, astronomy and astrophysics, University of Chicago, 1946–1948, research associate in stellar astronomy, Yerkes Observatory, 1949–1952, instructor, Yerkes Observatory, 1952–1954, assistant professor, 1954–1955; astronomer, Radio Astronomy Branch, U.S. Naval Research Laboratory, 1955–1956, head, Microwave Spectroscopy Section, 1956–1957, consultant, 1958–1959; head, observational astronomy program, National Aeronautics and Space Administration (NASA), 1959–1960, chief, astronomy and astrophysics program, 1960–1961, chief, astronomy and solar physics section, 1961–1963, chief astronomer, 1963–1972, chief of astronomy and relativity, 1972–1979, program scientist for space telescope, 1979–1980, principal scientist, Astronomical Data Center, Goddard Space Flight Center, 1980; retired 1980; consultant, Astonomical Data Center, 1980–1990; staff, McDonald Space Systems Division, 1989–

***Nancy Roman*** is renowned for developing satellite observatories to explore the universe from a vantage point that is free from atmospheric interference. She pioneered the use of satellites for gamma ray, x-ray, and radio observations, and she has also used traditional earth-based telescopes to study topics such as stellar motions, photoelectric photometry, and spectroscopy. She is especially noted for the research she conducted at the National Aeronautics and Space Administration (NASA), where for many years she was the highest-ranking woman scientist. NASA's moon program in 1988 greatly expanded opportunities for women scientists, but Roman and others achieved recognition for their work prior to that program. In a 1964 NASA-approved book *Scientists Who Work with Astronauts,* by Lynn and Gray Poole, astronomers Nancy Roman and Jocelyn Gill were the only two women who were profiled.

Roman's association with NASA began in 1959 when she was appointed head of the observational astronomy program. She developed an ambitious plan to observe objects in space by using rocket and satellite observatories, and in the 1960s, she designed instrumentation and made substantial measurements from gamma ray, radio, and visible light satellites, such as the orbiting solar observatories. Her programs provided astronomers with the planetary surface knowledge that led to the successful 1976 *Viking* probes to collect data from Mars. In the 1970s, her papers dealt with new satellite data, but she still did earth-based observation, such as at Kitt Peak Observatory.

She refined the effectiveness of her orbiting observatories in the 1970s and 1980s. She measured x-ray and ultraviolet readings from the successful OAO-3, or *Copernicus,* satellite, which was launched in 1972, and recorded stellar spectra from the U.S. space station *Skylab,* which circled the earth between 1973 and 1979. She was also the NASA program scientist for a projected space telescope during 1979 and 1980, but cost overruns and delays postponed the launching of NASA's Hubble telescope until 1990. Since 1980 she has worked as a consulting astronomer for the Astronomical Data Center where she edits and documents astronomical catalogs for electronic archiving.

While working at the Yerkes Observatory of the University of Chicago in the 1940s and 1950s, she researched stellar astronomy and galactic structure, specializing in radial velocity measurements, photoelectric photometry, and spectral classification. When she moved to the U.S. Naval Research Laboratory, she first worked in radio astronomy and became the head of the microwave spectroscopy laboratory. She studied radio star spectra and the galactic distribution of radio emitters and used radar to measure the distance between the earth and the moon.

She says she wanted to be an astronomer for as long as she can remember. She started an astronomy club among her friends when she was in the fifth grade, and she read every astronomy book she could find in her local library. Although she enjoyed teaching when she worked for the University of Chicago, she did not believe she had a chance for tenure, for at that time, no woman had tenure in a major astronomy department and very few had faculty positions. Therefore, she left Chicago when she had the opportunity to obtain an interesting position in the new field of radio astronomy at the Naval Research Laboratory.

When NASA was formed in 1958, most of the science staff came from the Vanguard project and other groups at the Naval Research Laboratory that were active in rocket astronomy, but even though she was not a member of those groups, she had gained a reputation for her work. She somewhat reluctantly accepted a management position with NASA because doing so meant reducing her time for research, but she felt she could not pass up the opportunity to participate in setting up a new program in space astronomy. She found she even enjoyed administration.

In the history of astronomy there have been a comparatively large number of women working in the field, but most were confined to drudge work that is now handled by computers. Starting with Roman's generation, women astronomers have been able to make significant contributions—as can be seen by the number of astronomers in this volume. Roman is a fellow of the American Astronautical Society and American Association for the Advancement of Science; she is a member of the American Astronomical Society. Her research includes spectral classification, photoelectric photometry, and space research. Her photograph is included in *Notable Women in the Physical Sciences.*

***Bibliography:*** *American Men and Women of Science* 11–19; *Current Biography 1960;* Herzenberg, C., *Women Scientists from Antiquity to the Present;* Hoyt, M., *American Women of the Space Age;* Ireland, N., *Index to Women of the World . . . Suppl.; Notable Twentieth-Century Women; Notable Women in the Physical Sciences.*

# *Rose, Wendy*
## (1948– )
## *anthropologist*

***Education:*** Student, Cabrillo College and Contra Costa College; B.A., University of California, Berkeley, 1976, M.A. in anthropology, 1978

***Professional Experience:*** Lecturer in Native American Studies, University of California, Berkeley, 1979–1983, and California State University, Fresno, 1983–1984; instructor, Fresno City College, 1984– ; visual artist, poet

***Married:*** Arthur Murata, 1976

W***endy Rose*** is an anthropologist who expresses herself in the form of art and poetry instead of printed scientific papers. She was born Bronwen Elizabeth Edwards in Oakland, California, the daughter of a mixed-blood Miwok mother and a Hopi father. Raised in an urban environment just outside San Francisco, her work reflects the experiences of a mixed-blood Indian living apart from the reservation and away from the influence of tribal culture. She became involved in the American Indian movement, participated in the occupation of Alcatraz, and began a writing career under the pen name Chiron Khanshendel. Her accomplishments have helped make Native American writing a legitimate part of the American literature scene as well as reclassifying Native American writers as literary artists rather than literate fossils or anthropological voices.

One of her books, *Going to War with All My Relations: New and Selected Poems* (1993), consists of poems culled from earlier books as well as a large collection of new works. Over a period of some 20 years, her concerns have consistently remained ecology, archaeology, and feminism. More recent poems draw on her experience as a university professor, such as dealing with interminable staff meetings and complacent students, and the book suggests that the ambiguities inherent in the historical interrelationship of Native American and European elements in our culture continue to pose a great problem for American poets. One reviewer commented that while she is grieved and angered by her enforced distance from her people, her poetry does not fall into suicidal bitterness on the one hand or radical excess on the other. It defines a clear line toward her understanding of her position as representing all who are dispossessed.

Rose became interested in anthropology and, after attending two colleges, enrolled in that program at the University of California, Berkeley, where she received her undergraduate and master's degrees. While a student, she worked for the Lowie Museum of Anthropology at Berkeley and served as editor of the *American Indian Quarterly.* After receiving her master's degree, she was a lecturer in Native American Studies at both the University of California, Berkeley, and California State University at Fresno. She is currently an instructor in and coordinator of Native American Studies at Fresno City College.

She is also a visual artist—with occasional exhibits around the country—and a designer of postcards, posters, T-shirts, and bookbags, usually in connection with Indian organizations. She has written a history, *Aboriginal Tattooing in California* (1979) published by the Archaeological Research Facility of the University of California, Berkeley, in addition to ten books of poetry, and she has contributed illustrations and poetry to numerous books and journals.

***Bibliography:*** Bataille, G., *Native American Women; Contemporary Authors* v. 51R; Ireland, N., *Index to Women of the World . . . Suppl.*

# *Rosenblatt, Joan (Raup)*
(1926– )
## *mathematical statistician*

***Education:*** B.A. in mathematics, Barnard College, 1946; Ph.D. in statistics, University of North Carolina, 1956

***Professional Experience:*** Statistical analyst, U.S. Bureau of the Budget, 1948; assistant statistician, University of North Carolina, 1953–1954; mathematician, National Bureau of Standards, 1955–1969, chief statistician, Engineering Laboratory, 1969–1978, deputy director, Computer and Applied Mathematics Laboratory, National Institute of Standards and Technology, 1979–1993, director, 1993–1995; retired 1995

***Married:*** David Rosenblatt, 1950

***Joan Rosenblatt*** is renowned for her research as a mathematical statistician at the National Institute of Standards and Technology, formerly the National Bureau of Standards. At that agency statistics are an integral part of the daily work, and the mission of the institute is to maintain and disseminate the basic units of measurement such as mass, length, temperature, frequency, and electrical units. It also establishes the basis for the uniformity of measurement that makes mass production in industry or air pollution regulations possible. The work of the agency is the key to the ability to compare results in experimental science, and it is also responsible for providing scientific and technical services to other federal agencies and to industry.

The specific role of mathematical statistics in this research-oriented agency is to provide an orderly way to evaluate errors in measurement. For example, the Gaussian distribution, or normal distribution, theory proposed by the eighteenth-century mathematician and astronomer Karl F. Gauss, provides the theoretical frequency distribution represented by a normal curve. The statisticians also use concepts of experimental design and techniques for data analysis that are helpful in achieving sufficiently accurate results. The section that Rosenblatt headed also provides statistical consulting services to all parts of the institute and researches improved statistical methods for applications in the physical and engineering sciences. One of the difficult questions it has received was a request from the Selective Service System to prepare a draft lottery to determine the order in which men born in 1951 would be called for induction into military service in 1970. The result was so successful that the lottery was used again.

The research problems that Rosenblatt was concerned with in the early 1990s arose from the proliferation of new federal regulations that stem from acts of Congress. The regulations are based on physical measurements of such things as water, air, pesticides, noise, radiation, occupational health and safety, and transportation safety. She stresses that measurement is not an absolute fact because there can be measurement errors. One of the most difficult problems is how to measure chemical additives in food that the Food and Drug Administration handles to satisfy regulations that bar the use of known cancer-causing additives in food processing.

Rosenblatt grew up in a family that stressed education, and her mother, a professor of economics at Barnard College, was among the first to promote the study of consumer economics. After receiving her undergraduate degree, Rosenblatt was a National Institute of Public Affairs intern in Washington, D.C., and then obtained a graduate degree from the University of North Carolina. Although she was the only woman in her student group, she did not feel discrimination in her work. Her first job in the National Bureau of Standards was in the Engineering Laboratory, and she later moved to the Computer and Applied Mathematics Laboratory.

Among the awards she has received are the Federal Woman's Award (1971), the

Gold Medal of the Department of Commerce (1976), and the Founders Award of the American Statistical Association in 1991. She was a member of the Committee on Applications and Theoretical Statistics of the National Research Council from 1985 to 1988. She is a fellow of the American Association for the Advancement of Science, American Statistical Association, and Institute of Mathematical Statistics and a member of the American Mathematical Society and International Statistical Institute. Her research includes nonparametric statistical theory, applications of statistical techniques in the physical and engineering sciences, and the reliability of complex systems. Her photograph is included in Alice Fins's *Women in Science.*

***Bibliography:*** *American Men and Women of Science* 11–19; Fins, A., *Women in Science;* Herzenberg, C., *Women Scientists from Antiquity to the Present;* Ireland, N., *Index to Women of the World . . . Suppl.; Who's Who in America,* 51st ed., 1997; *Who's Who of American Women,* 20th ed., 1997–1998.

# *Rowley, Janet Davison*

(1925– )

## *cytogeneticist, geneticist*

***Education:*** Ph.B., University of Chicago, 1944, B.S., 1946, M.D., 1948; honorary degrees: D.Sc., University of Arizona and University of Pennsylvania, 1989, Knox College, 1991, University of Southern California, 1992

***Professional Experience:*** Research assistant, University of Chicago, 1949–1950; intern, Marine Hospital, U.S. Public Health Service, Chicago, 1950–1951; physician, Infant Welfare and Prenatal Clinics, Department of Health, Montgomery County, Maryland, 1953–1954; research fellow, Cook County Hospital, Chicago, 1955–1961; trainee, Radiobiology Laboratory, Churchill Hospital, England, 1961–1962; research associate, Department of Medicine and Argonne Cancer Research Hospital, University of Chicago, 1962–1969, associate professor, Department of Medicine and Franklin McLean Memorial Research Institute, 1969–1977; professor, 1977–1984, Blum-Riese Distinguished Service Professor, Department of Medicine and Department of Molecular Genetics and Cell Biology, 1984–

***Married:*** Donald A. Rowley, 1948

***Children:*** 4

***Janet Rowley*** is a cytogeneticist who is renowned for her research on chromosome abnormalities in a form of leukemia. A cytogeneticist is one who investigates the role of cells in evolution and heredity, and her research has introduced new diagnostic tools for oncologists and has also opened new avenues to possible gene therapies for cancer. She has helped to pinpoint cancer gene locations and correlate them to chromosome aberrations. She was elected to membership in the National Academy of Sciences in 1984.

During her work at the University of Chicago, she developed the use of quinacrine and Giemsa staining to identify chromosomes in cloned cells. Once the chromosomes were easily identifiable, she could study abnormalities that occur in some chromosomes in certain cancers. With the discovery of cancer-inducing genes, or oncogenes, she focused on chromosome rearrangements that occur in a form of blood cancer known as chronic myeloid leukemia (CML), and she was able to show a consistent chromosome translocation, or shifting, of genetic material in CML cells. In 1972, she was the first person to discover the recurring translocation in any species, and since that time, more than 70 such translocations have been detected in human malignant cells. Her research indicates that both translocations and deletions of genetic material occur in malignancy and that cancer is caused by a complex series of events within a single cell, making some genes overactive and eliminating other genes that would normally suppress growth. According to her research, any cell is potentially cancerous.

Starting with her undergraduate studies in the 1940s, Rowley had a long association with the University of Chicago for the majority of her career. She married after she completed her medical degree, and she and her husband had four sons. She has also had an illustrious career. In addition to her numerous scientific papers, she is the author of *Chromosome Changes in Leukemia* (1978) and the editor or coeditor of *Chromosomes and Cancer: From Molecules to Man* (1983), *Genes and Cancer* (1984), *Consistent and Chromosomal Aberrations and Oncogenes in Human Tumors* (1984), and *Advances in Understanding Genetic Changes in Cancer* (1992). She is cofounder and coeditor of the journal *Genes, Chromosomes and Cancer.* Among the awards she received in the 1990s alone are citations from the Sloan-Kettering Cancer Center, GM Cancer Research Foundation, Leukemia Society of America, Academy of Clinical Laboratory Physicians and Scientists, and Gardner Foundation.

She is a member of the American Academy of Arts and Sciences, American Philosophical Society, American Society of Human Genetics (president, 1993), American Society of Hematology, and American Association for Cancer Research. Her research includes human chromosomes, chromosome abnormalities in preleukemia as well as in leukemia and lymphomas, quinacrine and Giemsa stains to identify chromosomes in malignant cells, and molecular genetic analysis of chromosome translocations and deletions.

***Bibliography:*** *American Men and Women of Science* 11–19; Herzenberg, C., *Women Scientists from Antiquity to the Present; Notable Twentieth-Century Scientists; Who's Who in America,* 51st ed., 1997; *Who's Who of American Women,* 20th ed., 1997–1998.

# *Roy, Della Martin*

(1926– )

## *geochemist, materials scientist*

***Education:*** B.S., University of Oregon, 1947; M.S., Pennsylvania State University, 1949, Ph.D. in mineralogy, 1952

***Professional Experience:*** Assistant, mineralogy, Pennsylvania State University, 1949–1952, research associate, geochemistry, 1952–1959, senior research associate, 1959–1969; associate professor of materials science, 1969–1975, professor of materials science, Materials Research Laboratory, 1975–

***Concurrent Positions:*** Senior research associate, Materials Research Laboratory, 1963–1969

***Married:*** Rustum Roy, 1948

***Children:*** 3

***Della Roy*** is known for her research in materials science, which is a relatively new discipline concerned with the uses of new materials and their applications to existing processes and products. The materials scientist may also specify certain hypothetical properties that will allow materials to function better in a given situation and then may try to produce the material to meet those specifications. The materials involved may be metals, ceramics, plastics, biomaterials, or even textiles. Much of the new materials science research arose from the aeronautics program starting in the 1950s when the U.S. Air Force and National Aeronautics and Space Administration (NASA) were developing aircraft and space vehicles that required new components that could withstand the stresses of gravity and extreme heat and cold. Another area of research that contributed to the development of new materials was nuclear science, which required new materials that could come in contact with radioactive materials. She was elected to membership in the National Academy of Engineering in 1987.

Although Roy's background is in mineralogy, she has worked with many types of materials. Minerals are substances that occur in nature; they are composed of inorganic substances of definite chemical composition and usually of definite crystal structure. She also has researched ceramics, which are products made from clay or similar materials, such as brick. One of her specialties is research on concrete, and she has served on a number of national committees in this area as well as on highway commissions. Although her husband is internationally known for his research in ceramics, she has maintained her own research programs, although they have collaborated on a few scientific papers. After receiving her doctorate from Pennsylvania State University, she was appointed as an assistant in mineralogy and progressed through the ranks to senior research associate in the Materials Research Laboratory. She then was appointed to the faculty as an associate professor and became a full professor in 1975.

Roy has been a member of the Highway Research Board of the National Academy of Sciences, was chair of a National Academy of Sciences Research Committee on Concrete (1980–1983), and a member of the Committee on Concrete Durability (1986–1987). She has received numerous awards, including the Jepson Medal (1982) and the Copeland Award (1987) of the American Ceramic Society and the Slag Award of the American Concrete Institute (1989); she was made an honorary fellow of the Institute for Concrete Technology in 1987.

She is also a fellow of the Mineralogical Society of America, American Concrete Society, American Ceramic Society, and American Association for the Advancement of Science and a member of the Materials Research Society, Clay Minerals Society, Concrete Society, American Nuclear Society, American Society for Testing and Materials, and Society of Women Engineers. Her research includes phase equilibria, materials synthesis, crystal chemistry and phase transitions, crystal growth, cement chemistry, hydration and microstructure, concrete durability, biomaterials, special types of glass, radioactive waste management, geological isolation, chemically bonded ceramics, and waste management science.

***Bibliography:*** *American Men and Women of Science* 11–19.

# *Rubin, Vera (Cooper)*

(1928– )

## ***astronomer, cosmologist***

***Education:*** B.A., Vassar College, 1948; M.A., Cornell University, 1951; Ph.D. in astronomy, Georgetown University, 1954; honorary degrees: D.Sc., Creighton University, 1978, Harvard University, 1988, Yale University, 1990, and Williams College, 1993

***Professional Experience:*** Instructor in mathematics and physics, Montgomery County Junior College, 1954–1955; research associate in astronomy, Georgetown University, 1955–1965, lecturer, 1959–1962, assistant professor, 1962–1965; staff member, Department of Terrestrial Magnetism, Carnegie Institution of Washington, 1965–

***Married:*** Robert J. Rubin, 1948

***Children:*** 4

***Vera Rubin*** is one of America's foremost astronomers, and she has spent her life observing galactic structure, rotation, and dynamics. Her pioneering spectroscopic research in the 1970s demonstrated the possible existence of a large percentage of dark matter in the universe that is invisible to the naked eye, and astronomers now estimate that up to 90 percent of the universe may be composed of this dark matter. She is a specialist in the branch of astronomy called "cosmology," which deals with the general structure and origin of the universe. Her work has been honored by her receiving the National Medal of Science in 1993, an honor that is bestowed each year on scientists selected from all disciplines in a White House ceremony presided over by the president. People to receive this medal are selected by a committee of the National Science Foundation. Earlier, in 1981, she was elected to membership in the National Academy of Sciences.

Rubin has always worked outside the mainstream of the astronomy community. She received her master's degree from Cornell University, which at that time had an Astronomy Department that consisted of two people. However, Cornell had a very strong Physics Department, and she studied under Hans Bethe and Richard Feynman. For her master's thesis she analyzed the motion of 108 galaxies and discovered that they shared a large-scale, systematic motion in addition to motion resulting from the expansion of the universe. When she presented her paper at a meeting of the American Astronomical Society in 1950, the scientific community was not prepared to believe in large-scale motions, and although her paper created a great deal of publicity, all of it was negative. She said that at least the astronomers knew who she was. Several years later, she was vindicated when a noted cosmologist agreed with her theory.

When she moved to Georgetown University for her doctorate, she worked under George Gamow, a physicist who was applying nuclear physics to Big Bang cosmology. Her dissertation showed that instead of being randomly distributed, galaxies tend to clump together. She was ahead of her time again, but since the 1970s, the clustering of galaxies has been an important area of research.

She did not start doing observational astronomy until 1963, and in 1965 she joined the Department of Terrestrial Magnetism of the Carnegie Institution. In 1963, she and her husband spent a year at the University of California, San Diego, where she worked with Margaret and Geoffrey Burbidge, who were interested in her theories; the Burbidges had recently helped establish that most chemical elements are made in stars. At the time, the preeminent observatory was Mt. Palomar, operated jointly by the Carnegie Institution and the California Institute of Technology. The facility had been reserved for male astronomers only because there were no restrooms for women, and Vera Rubin was the first woman officially permitted to observe there.

Rubin worked briefly on quasar redshifts with her colleague Kent Ford, but that was a hot topic and very competitive. Since she prefers to work independently, she and Ford returned to the subject of her master's thesis—the systematic motions of galaxies. They found evidence that a large group of galaxies, including the earth's Milky Way, are moving rapidly with respect to the rest of the universe. Although the theory was immediately controversial, this time the astronomy community took the work seriously. The theory is called "the Rubin-Ford effect" and is seen as strong support for the theory that matter is distributed through the universe in clumps, not smoothly. In addition, the gravitational pull of the clumps accelerates groups of galaxies into motion on an immense scale. This theory created controversy because many scientists believe that the expansion of the universe was quiet and smooth. Although some astronomers contended Rubin's results were questionable, her basic idea has been vindicated.

Seeking a less controversial field, Rubin and Ford began to study galaxy rotation and found that stars at the outer margins of galaxies travel as fast as stars closer to the galaxy center. Previously, scientists had believed that stars at the outer margins of a galaxy travel slowly. If this theory is true, it means there must be a large amount of invisible matter even at the fringe of a galaxy where the number of visible stars dwindles, because matter is necessary to accelerate the outer stars in their rapid orbits. The two researchers also found that all the galaxies in a vast region are being gravitationally drawn toward a distant concentration of galaxies called "the Great Attractor."

Rubin then turned to a less-controversial topic, that of the varieties of spiral galaxies. Most galaxies have a luminous central bulge composed of densely packed stars. The spiral disk that surrounds the bulge is very thin, and its brightness falls off steadily toward the edge. Another feature is that stars and gas at a disk's edge travel just as fast as matter closer to the center. Since the stars do not seem to be falling off the edge, they must be held by gravity. Where there is gravity, there is mass. She realized that a huge reservoir of extra material that is invisible to the telescope must be part of each galaxy, and her team has analyzed 200 galaxies on which to base its theories.

Rubin became interested in astronomy as a child from observing the stars at night through her bedroom window. A high school physics teacher tried to dissuade her from a career in science, but her father, an electrical engineer, helped her to build her first telescope when she was 14 and took her to local amateur astronomy meetings. After receiving her undergraduate degree from Vassar, she decided to go to Princeton, but Princeton did not accept women into its graduate astrophysics program until 1971. She ended up accompanying her husband to Cornell, where he received a doctorate in physical chemistry and she a master's in astronomy. They then moved to Washington, D.C., where Robert worked for the National Bureau of Standards and Vera entered the graduate program at Georgetown, the only school in the area with a doctoral program in astronomy. Her parents lived nearby, and they watched the children while her husband drove her to her night classes at Georgetown, eating his dinner in the car while he waited for her.

She is very active in encouraging young women to consider careers in science, but she is keenly aware of the barriers facing them. She wrote a brief history of American women astronomers for *Science* 86 (July–August 1986). She emphasizes how important it has been that her husband supported her career at every step. She also says that when she was in school, she was told continually to find something else to study or told that she would not obtain a job as an astronomer. She did not listen, believing that if there is something you really want to do, you just have to go do it and perhaps have the courage to do it a little differently.

She is a member of the International Astronomical Union, American Astronomical Society, and Astronomical Society of the Pacific. Her research includes external galaxies, galactic dynamics, spectroscopy, and motions of stars in galaxies and motions of galaxies in the universe. There is an interview in *Mercury* (January–February 1992), which includes photos. Her photograph is also included in *Journeys of Women in Science and Engineering,* Alice Fins's *Women in Science,* and *Scientific American* (November 1993). Her work on spiral galaxies was discussed on the public television show "Stephen Hawkings' Universe: On the Dark Side" in 1997.

***Bibliography:*** *American Men and Women of Science* 11–19; Herzenberg, C., *Women Scientists from Antiquity to the Present;* Ireland, N., *Index to the Women of the World . . . Suppl.; Journeys of Women in Science and Engineering; Notable Twentieth-Century Scientists; Notable Women in the Physical Sciences; Who's Who in America,* 51st ed., 1997; *Who's Who in Science and Engineering,* 3d ed., 1996–1997; *Who's Who of American Women,* 20th ed., 1997–1998.

# *Rudin, Mary Ellen (Estill)*
## (1924– )
## *mathematician*

***Education:*** B.A., University of Texas, 1944, Ph.D. in mathematics, 1949
***Professional Experience:*** Instructor in mathematics, Duke University, 1950–1953; assistant professor, University of Rochester, 1953–1957; lecturer, University of Wisconsin, Madison, 1958–1971, professor of mathematics, 1971– , Grace Chisholm Young Professor of Mathematics, 1981–
***Married:*** Walter Rudin, 1953
***Children:*** 4

***Mary Ellen Rudin*** is renowned for her contributions to set-theory topology in mathematics. Topology is the study of those properties of geometric forms that remain invariant under certain transformations, as bending or stretching, and set theory is the branch of mathematics that deals with relations between sets. Her success has come despite the fact that after she received her doctorate she found she was outside the mainstream of mathematics. She had studied under only one person at the University of Texas, R. L. Moore, who was head of the Mathematics Department and taught all of the math classes. He used an archaic language for expressing mathematical concepts, terms that were different from those in general usage. Consequently, when Rudin presented her first papers using Moore's antiquated mathematical language, no one could understand what she was talking about. She had to reteach herself the correct terminology and fill in the gaps in her knowledge of algebra, topology, and analysis.

At the time she completed her course work, Duke University was under pressure to hire women mathematicians, and Moore found her a job as an instructor there. She met and married Walter Rudin, also a mathematician, at Duke, and they moved to the University of Rochester where both taught before moving to the University of Wisconsin, Madison. Since that university had a nepotism rule, she could have an appointment only as a lecturer—which did mean, however, that she was free from committee work. After the nepotism rule was lifted in 1971, she was immediately appointed a full professor and became a distinguished professor in 1981. Her professorship is named for Grace Chisholm Young (1868–1944), a British mathematician. Rudin said she was never concerned about her career; when she arrived in Rochester with her husband, the department found a place for her, and the same thing occurred in Madison.

The center for set-theory topology in the 1970s was the University of Wisconsin. Each summer for several years there were seminars, conferences, and collaborations, and in the summer of 1974, Rudin gave a series of ten lectures in five days at a regional conference; the lectures were later published as *Lectures on Set Theoretic Topology* (1975). About 1969, there had been a notable change in her papers in that she then began citing more of the literature. Prior to that time, her papers had one or two references, but from 1969 on, each of her papers would included citations to ten or more other publications. Instead of just answering questions that someone asked her or that she thought of without reading to see what others were doing, as she had done previously, she had become aware of the work of other mathematicians that impinged on her work.

In 1991, a conference, "The Work of Mary Ellen Rudin," was held in her honor at Madison, and the proceedings were published as volume 705 of the *Annals of the New York Academy of Sciences* (1993). In that volume, several of her colleagues reminisce about their experiences with her, including her absentmindedness. For example, she once admonished a janitor never to lock her office door, and she bought a particular car whose ignition could be turned on and off without using an ignition key.

Her family was committed to the value of education. Both of her parents had college degrees, her father in civil engineering and her mother a bachelor's degree with which she taught high school English. Even both of her grandmothers had college degrees, and they had insisted that their daughters as well as their sons should have the opportunity for further education. Since Rudin did not have a regular professorship until 1971, she never felt she had to prove herself as a mathematician. The pressure was entirely within; she did mathematics because she wanted to and enjoyed the work, not in order to further her career. She accepted a full-time position so she would receive full retirement benefits, although she preferred the freedom of teaching half-time. She and her husband have a Frank Lloyd Wright house. It has a very open design so she can lie on the sofa in the middle of the living room and do her mathematics while checking on everything going on in the house.

Rudin has exhibited outstanding dedication and service to her profession. Between 1969 and 1983 she supervised 11 doctoral students, she is active in professional organizations, and she has written more than 70 research papers on topology—a list of her papers is included in the volume, *The Work of Mary Ellen Rudin* in volume 705 of *Annals of the New York Academy of Sciences* (1993). There is an extensive interview with her in *More Mathematical People,* including photographs of her and her family, and portions of that article were published in *College Math Journal* (1988). She is a member of the American Mathematical Society, Mathematical Association of America, and Association for Symbolic Logic. Her research includes set theoretic topology, particularly the construction of counterexamples.

***Bibliography:*** *American Men and Women of Science* 11–19; *More Mathematical People; Who's Who in Technology Today* v. 5; *Women of Mathematics.*

# Sammet, Jean Elaine
(1928– )
***computer scientist***

***Education:*** B.A., Mount Holyoke College, 1948; M.A. in mathematics, University of Illinois, 1949; honorary degree: D.Sc., Mount Holyoke College, 1978

***Professional Experience:*** Teaching assistant in mathematics, University of Illinois, 1948–1951; dividend technician, Metropolitan Life Insurance Company, 1951; teaching assistant, mathematics, Barnard College, 1952–1953; engineer, Sperry Gyroscope Company, 1953–1958; section head, MOBIDIC Programming, Sylvania Electric Products Company, 1958–1959, staff consultant, program research, 1959–1961; Boston advanced program manager, International Business Machines (IBM) Corporation, 1961–1965, program language technical manager, 1965–1968, program technology planning manager, 1968–1974, program language technology, 1974–1979, division software technical manager, 1979–1983, program language technology manager, 1983–1986; senior technical staff member, 1986–1988; consultant, program languages, 1989–

***Concurrent Positions:*** Lecturer, Adelphi College, 1956–1958, Northeastern University, 1967, University of California, Los Angeles, 1967–1972, Mount Holyoke College, 1974

**Jean Sammet** is renowned for her professional contributions to the use of computers for nonnumerical mathematics and for developments in the theory of high-level programming languages. She is most famous for her work on the design and development of COBOL, the most widely used programming language in the world from the late 1960s through the 1970s, primarily for commercial applications. She was elected to membership in the National Academy of Engineering in 1977.

She organized and supervised the first scientific programming for Sperry Gyroscope Company between 1955 and 1958, she lectured on digital computer programming at Adelphi College between 1956 and 1957, and the following year she taught one of the earliest courses on FORTRAN in the United States. She moved to Sylvania Electric Products in 1958 as the first section head for MOBIDIC programming. During her Sylvania years she was involved in the initial creation of COBOL, being a member of the short-range committee established for the purpose of writing the specifications for COBOL between June and December 1959.

In 1961, she began her long association with International Business Machines Corporation (IBM) to organize and manage the Boston Programming Center to do advanced development work in programming. She initiated the concept, and directed the development of, FORMAC (FORmula MAnipulation Compiler), the first widely used general language and system for manipulating nonnumeric algebraic expression. She also started and directed work on other language projects. In 1965 she became programming language technology manager in the IBM Systems Development Division and moved to the IBM Federal Systems Division in 1968 where she held various positions involving planning, internal consulting, and lecturing on programming languages.

In 1979, she became the divisional program manager for "Ada," with responsibility for coordinating the strategy and actions for the corporation to use that language, the first programming language to be developed for the U.S. Department of Defense (DOD). Ada was named for Augusta Ada King, Lady Lovelace, the daughter of the poet Lord Byron. It was Lady Lovelace who had funded the research of Charles Babbage, the designer of the analytical engine in the late nineteenth century that is credited with being the forerunner of the computer. The names of many of the programming languages are written in uppercase, such as COBOL and FORTRAN, because they are acronyms. Ada was named for a person.

In 1979, Jean Sammet became the software technical manager for the division. In that capacity she continued her general and Ada language responsibilities and also managed a department that assessed and advised on software technology for the division. In 1983, she returned to the position of programming language technology manager to concentrate on programming languages. She continued her involvement with Ada standardization, both internally and externally. In 1986, she was named a senior technical staff member, a title she retained until her formal retirement from IBM in 1988. She continues to consult for the corporation.

She has served on many distinguished committees involving programming languages and standardization. She was a member of the first DOD-organized Ada Distinguished Reviewers group throughout its existence and an original member of DOD's Ada Board, a federal advisory committee, from its inception until her resignation in 1989. She wrote one of the most comprehensive books on programming languages, *Programming Languages: History and Fundamentals* (1969), which contains a description of the histories of many languages as well as significant technical material. One source mentions that she has massive files on programming languages in preparation for a second volume. She was a member of the board of directors of the Computer Museum in Boston from 1983 to 1993 and served on the original executive committee of the Software Patent Institute starting in 1991.

She has received many awards, including IBM's Outstanding Contribution Award (1965), Mount Holyoke College Alumnae Association Centennial Award (1972), Association for Computing Machinery Distinguished Service Award (1985), and Augusta Ada Lovelace Award of the Association for Women in Computing (1989). She is a fellow of the Association for Computing Machinery (president, 1974–1976) and a member of the Mathematical Association of America. Her research includes high-level programming languages, use of computers for nonnumerical mathematics, formula manipulation systems, programming systems, language measurement, practical uses of artificial intelligence, use of natural language on a computer, history of software, and history of programming languages. Her photograph is included J. Lee's *Computer Pioneers.*

***Bibliography:*** *American Men and Women of Science* 11–19; *Journal of Computers in Mathematics and Science Teaching* (winter 1982–spring 1983); Lee, J., *Computer Pioneers;* Stanley, A., *Mothers and Daughters of Invention; Who's Who in Engineering,* 9th ed., 1995; *Who's Who of American Women,* 20th ed., 1997–1998.

# *Sarachik, Myriam Paula*
(1933– )
## *solid-state physicist*

***Education:*** B.A., Barnard College, 1954; M.S., Columbia University, 1957, Ph.D. in physics, 1960

***Professional Experience:*** Research assistant, experimental solid-state physics, IBM Watson Laboratory, Columbia University, 1955–1960, research associate, 1960–1961; member of technical staff, AT&T Bell Laboratories, 1962–1964; assistant professor of physics, City College of New York, 1964–1967, associate professor, 1967–1971, professor, 1971– , distinguished professor, 1995–

***Concurrent Positions:*** Principal investigator, U.S. Air Force research grant, 1965–1972, National Science Foundation grant, 1972–1974; executive officer of Ph.D. program in physics, City College of New York, 1975–1978

***Married:*** Philip E. Sarachik, 1954

***Children:*** 1

***Myriam Sarachik*** is a solid-state physicist who is renowned for her research on semiconductors. Her excellence in research was recognized early in her career when her thesis was published as papers in *Physical Review Letters* and *IBM Journal of Research and Development*, both in 1960. While she was working on her master's degree and doctorate at Columbia University, she worked as a research assistant and then a research associate in the IBM Watson Laboratory at Columbia. After working on the technical staff of AT&T Bell Laboratories for two years, she became an assistant professor of physics at the City College of New York in 1964 and rose through the ranks to become full professor in 1971 and distinguished professor in 1995. She was elected to membership in the National Academy of Sciences in 1994.

In a telephone conversation on June 18, 1997, she said that the highlight of her career was occurring then: beginning the previous year or so, she had been involved in really first-rate research, the best of her career. When asked if membership in the National Academy of Sciences had affected her, she said that membership enhances the way people treat you and listen to you; membership gives you more self-confidence to do greater things. She said she would certainly encourage women to pursue advanced degrees in physics, and they should not be deterred by the hard work involved. At first she found physics incredibly difficult, impossible to handle, and a great challenge. However, once she got the hang of it, she found it great fun. She said she has no problem in balancing career and personal life. She works very hard, but she has family, friends, and a social life.

One honor she has received is the New York City Mayor's Award for excellence in science and technology in 1995. She is a fellow of the American Physical Society and a member of the New York Academy of Sciences. She has published more than 75 scientific papers. Her research includes magnetic and transport properties of semiconductors, the metal insulator transition, and macroscopic quantum tunneling.

***Bibliography:*** *American Men and Women of Science* 11–19; Herzenberg, C., *Women Scientists from Antiquity to the Present; Who's Who in America*, 51st ed., 1997.

# *Savitz, Maxine (Lazarus)*
## (1937– )
## *organic chemist, electrochemist*

***Education:*** B.A., Bryn Mawr College, 1958; Ph.D. in organic chemistry, Massachusetts Institute of Technology, 1961

***Professional Experience:*** National Science Foundation fellow, University of California, Berkeley, 1961–1962; instructor in chemistry, Hunter College, 1962–1963; research chemist, Electric Power Division, U.S. Army Engineering Research and Development Laboratory, Fort Belvoir, 1963–1968; associate professor of chemistry, Federal City College, 1968–1971, professor, 1971–1972; professional manager, Research Applied to National Needs, National Science Foundation, 1972–1973; chief of buildings conservation policy research, Federal Energy Administration, 1973–1975; division director, buildings and industrial conservation, Energy Research and Development Administration, 1975–1976, division director, buildings and community systems, 1976–1979, deputy assistant secretary of conservation, Department of Energy, 1979–1983; president, Lighting Research Institute, 1983–1985; assistant to vice president of engineering, Ceramic Components Division, Garret Corporation, 1985–1987; general manager, Ceramic Components Division, AlliedSignal Aerospace Company, 1987–

***Married:*** S. Alan Savitz, 1961

***Children:*** 2

*Maxine Savitz* is an organic chemist who is recognized for her expertise in research management in both government and industry. Currently she is an executive with an aerospace company, serving as general manager of a division of AlliedSignal Aerospace Company and working on ceramics for turbine engine applications. Earlier she was an executive with the U.S. Department of Energy establishing energy-saving guidelines for buildings during the oil crises of the 1970s. She was elected to membership in the National Academy of Engineering in 1992.

In a telephone conversation with the author on June 5, 1997, she said that the oil embargo hit while she was working at the Energy Research and Development Administration and that she had prepared an energy efficiency study for substituting more efficient methods of energy consumption without changing the quality of life. The study involved the entire area of electricity, such as longer-burning lighting, new batteries, and new technologies, and it involved designing energy-efficient and better methods of transportation including alternate fuels for vehicles and improved public transportation. Such measures were mandated by the Energy Conservation and Production Act of 1976, which called for performance standards designed to achieve the maximum practicable improvements in energy efficiency and increases in the use of nondepletable sources of energy. She feels her work on energy efficiency has been one of her significant contributions.

She said there are good opportunities for women scientists and engineers at the entry level. More women are graduating in engineering each year, and enrollment is still up in most of the top university engineering programs. However, opportunities do not exist at the upper levels of management in industry. There are many women in the upper levels of government agencies, such as Mary Good in the Department of Commerce and Sheila Widnall in the U.S. Air Force; but when Mary Good left AlliedSignal to accept the government position, she was replaced by a man. There are role models for women in government but not in academia, for few women scientists or engineers hold high-level positions in that area.

When the author asked her whether the team approach to research worked against women receiving recognition for their efforts, she said women are much better team members than men but that the old boys' network still hampers advancement. As an executive, she encourages people to recruit women and minorities, and there has been improvement at the recruiting level. Many women are successfully combining careers and family; in fact, husbands are becoming more involved in taking care of the children—a new development.

Among her committee appointments are the Energy and Engineering Board of the National Academy of Engineering (1986–1993), the Office of Technical Assessment of the U.S. Congress Energy Demand Panel (1987–1991), the natural materials advisory board, National Research Council (1993–1994), the advisory committee of the division of ceramics/materials, Oak Ridge National Laboratory (1989–1992), the advisory board for the secretary of Energy (1991– ), and the Defense Science Board (1993–1996). She is a member of the American Association for the Advancement of Science and American Ceramic Society. Her research includes free radical mechanisms, anodic hydrocarbon oxidation, fuel cells, more efficient use of energy in buildings, community systems, appliances, agriculture and industrial processes, transportation, batteries and other storage systems, new materials, and advanced structural ceramic materials.

***Bibliography:*** *American Men and Women of Science* 11–19; Herzenberg, C., *Women Scientists from Antiquity to the Present; Who's Who in America,* 51st ed., 1997; *Who's Who of American Women,* 20th ed., 1997–1998.

# *Scarr, Sandra (Wood)*
## (1936– )
## *psychologist*

***Education:*** B.A., Vassar College, 1958; M.A., Harvard University, 1963, Ph.D. in psychology, 1965

***Professional Experience:*** Instructor, University of Maryland, 1964–1965, assistant professor, psychology, 1965–1966; lecturer, University of Pennsylvania, 1967–1968, assistant professor, 1968–1970, associate professor, 1970–1971; associate professor, University of Minnesota, 1971–1974, professor, 1974–1977; professor, Yale University, 1977–1983; Commonwealth Professor of Psychology, University of Virginia, 1983–1995, chair, Department of Psychology, 1984–1990; chief executive officer (CEO) and chair, Kinder Care Learning Center, Inc., 1995–

***Married:*** Harry A. Scarr, 1961, divorced 1970; Philip H. Salapatek, 1971, divorced c. 1974; James C. Walker, 1982, divorced 1984

***Children:*** 4

*Sandra Scarr* is renowned for her research on how genetics and environment combine to affect human development. She has investigated how the family influences personality development, intelligence, and school achievement and what effects deliberate interventions such as preschool programs have on children. She is considered an expert on day care systems and adoption. She has proposed a theory that people make their own environments, and the theory includes three components: there is a passive correlation between parental characteristics and the child-rearing behavior of parents, the child's individual characteristics elicit responses from others, and individuals choose specific environments for themselves.

She became a minor celebrity when she began her research on racial differences. When Arthur Jensen, who considered blacks inferior in intelligence, disagreed with her findings on race and IQ, his criticism of her work brought her national attention. She then became embroiled in another controversy about the effects of exposure to lead on the IQs of children.

In the 1970s, the scientist Herbert Needleman, a world renowned researcher on lead toxicity, conducted a study for the government on safe levels of lead; his data were used by the government to set the guidelines on what amount of lead in the blood can cause detectable behavioral and medical problems. In a paper in 1979, Needleman stated that children who were exposed to "high" but not necessarily toxic levels of lead did significantly poorer in the classroom and had measurably lower IQs than those exposed to "low" lead levels. When the Environmental Protection Agency (EPA) examined the data and his research methods, it concluded that there were flaws in the data and the procedure; some data were missing. A similar study conducted at Case Western Reserve also contained flaws. The EPA at first refused to allow Scarr and another psychologist to examine the data, and then allowed them only one day to try to decipher the material. In spite of the review and the challenges, the agency is still using Needleman's data in establishing toxicity levels.

One topic on which Scarr has published a great deal of information in the 1990s is that of child care. She states that the concern that child care may have an adverse effect on the emotional development of children is debunked by the fact that not all parents are warm and caring. Moreover, child care services are an important necessity for both children and parents because the service enables women to participate in the labor force to help support their families. In researching the quality of care, she found that day care was a poor indicator of children's behavioral problems and social withdrawal. However, a child's behavior in preschool is the best predictor of individual variation in behavioral adjustment after four years of day care. Another study indicated that both mothers and fathers show similar anxiety levels about separation from their children during working hours. The age of a child has a significant effect on parenting stress, but the sex of the child has no effect.

Scarr is the product of a conservative southern family. From her father she learned that she could be anything she wanted to be, but she shocked her parents by entering graduate school at Harvard to prepare for a career in psychology. When she was an undergraduate, she had become interested in child development at a time when most people considered the subject unworthy of serious intellectual consideration. In 1967 her interest in individual differences led her to examine why black children perform so poorly in school and on intelligence tests. After ten years of research, she concluded such performance was owing to sociocultural disadvantage. As a career woman with four children, she combined her background in child development with research on day care to develop expertise on the subject. Her book *Mother Care/Other Care* (1984) received the National Book Award of the American Psychological Association in 1985, and she has published about 150 articles and reviews and two other books.

She has received awards, such as the Distinguished Contribution to Research on Public Policy of the American Psychological Association (1988) and the James M. Cattell Award of American Psychological Society (1993), and she is a fellow of the American Association for the Advancement of Science, American Psychological Association, and American Psychological Society. She is a member of the American Academy of Arts and Sciences, Behavior Genetics Association (president, 1985–1986), and Society for Research in Child Development (president, 1989–1991). Her research includes genetic variability in human behavior, particularly intelligence and personality, and the effects of variation in the quality of home and child care environments on children's development. Her photograph is included in *American Psychologist* (April 1989) and *Psychology Today* (May 1984).

***Bibliography:*** *American Men and Women of Science* 19; *Contemporary Authors* v. 126; *Who's Who in Science and Engineering,* 3d ed., 1996–1997.

# *Schwarzer, Theresa Flynn*
(1940– )
## *geologist, petroleum geologist*

***Education:*** B.S., Rensselaer Polytechnic Institute, 1963, M.S., 1966, Ph.D. in geology, 1969
***Professional Experience:*** Instructor in geology, State University of New York at Albany, 1969; research fellow in remote sensing, Rice University, 1969–1972; senior research geologist, Exxon Company, 1972–1974, research specialist, 1974–1976, senior research specialist, 1976–1978, senior explorer geologist, Gulf Coast Division, Exxon USA, 1978–1980, project leader, Texas Offshore Division, 1980–1981, district production geologist, East Texas Division, 1981–1983, senior supervisor, Exxon Production Research Company, 1983–1987, geological adviser, Exxon USA, 1987–
***Married:*** Rudy Schwarzer, 1961
***Children:*** 1

*Theresa Schwarzer* is recognized for her expertise in petroleum exploration. For more than 20 years she has worked for Exxon Corporation in increasing levels of responsibility for research in hydrocarbon exploration. Among her achievements are the discovery of commercial oil and gas deposits plus research on and development of unconventional exploration methods. Exploration today requires precise methods of conducting searches, and even a company as large as Exxon cannot afford to start sinking a well on land or in the sea without first conducting an elaborate study of the proposed site. The geologist must have at his or her command detailed maps, soil and rock analyses, soundings, and other details. Remote sensing of an area, such as spectrometric surveys from a helicopter or satellite data, is used to analyze the site.

Historically, women scientists were not welcome in industries such as mining and petroleum, but the Equal Employment Opportunity (EEO) legislation in the 1970s forced all industries to open up many formerly restricted jobs. In order to bid on government contracts now, companies must file statements on their equal access to employment for women and minorities, and many wells are located on government land. Schwarzer says that the projected employment picture for geoscientists in nonacademic jobs is very good and that the demand for qualified women geoscientists is even better. Diminishing energy, mineral, and water resources and increasing environmental concerns have placed a premium on the unique qualifications of geoscientists. In addition, research by both women and men can lead to publications and patents, a standard benefit of research in government, business, and the academy.

She believes that the limits to a woman's advancement will largely be her own limitations. She also feels that industry tends to develop women too rapidly, which can have a deleterious effect because of male backlash and, more important, by undermining a woman's self-confidence if she feels she has not earned an advancement on the basis of true ability and merit. For a successful career, Schwarzer suggests, make sure you are technologically competent; make a positive impression and set career goals early in your career; develop an interest in all aspects of your company's concerns; press for all the special training you can get, even seeking outside education yourself; work at achieving recognition outside your organization by participating in professional organizations; and do not be reluctant to change employers. She also says that women, especially when young and inexperienced, often tend to compete intensely with other women instead of working together with them. She herself served as chair of the women geoscientists committee of the American Geological Institute from 1973 to 1977.

She is a member of the Geological Society of America, American Association of Petroleum Geologists, Society for Exploration Geo-Physicists, and Geochemical Society.

Her research includes inorganic and organic geochemistry; remote sensing; multivariate statistical techniques; and interpretation and integration of geophysical, geological, and geochemical data for hydrocarbon exploration. Her photograph is included in Alice Fins's *Women in Science.*

***Bibliography:*** *American Men and Women of Science* 12–19; Fins, A., *Women in Science;* Herzenberg, C., *Women Scientists from Antiquity to the Present;* Ireland, N., *Index to Women of the World . . . Suppl.; Who's Who in Technology Today* v. 4.

# *Scott, Juanita (Simons)*

(1936– )

***developmental biologist***

***Education:*** A.A., Clinton Junior College, 1956; B.S., Livingston College, 1958; M.S. in biology, Atlanta University, 1962; D.Ed., University of South Carolina, 1979

***Professional Experience:*** High school teacher, 1958–1960; instructor, biological science, Benedict College, 1963–1964; instructor, Morris College, 1965–1967; assistant professor, Benedict College, 1968–1979, associate professor, 1979–1981, professor, 1981–1987, head, Division of Mathematics and Natural Sciences, 1987–1994, head, Department of Biological and Physical Science, 1992–1994, dean, Division of Arts and Sciences, 1994–

***Married:*** Robert Scott, 1959

***Children:*** 3

***Juanita Scott*** is a developmental biologist known for her research on problems of water pollution in the rivers and streams of South Carolina, which is her home. She started her research in the late 1960s on the pollutants being dumped into the waters by industrial firms, and by the mid 1980s, she had become interested in the microscopic characteristics of individual cells. She studied how pollutants, such as lead, cadmium, and mercury, act on different structures within a cell. Her research has indicated that parts of a frog's skin cells are more likely to react to metal contamination than other parts of the skin cells. She and her team of student researchers found that a frog's skin not only repels some toxic compounds but also has some antibiotic properties.

Although she continues her research on pollutants, in the 1990s she became concerned about the quality of science teaching in middle and junior high schools and found that many students arrived at college or university with little knowledge of the sciences and frequently had the attitude that all science courses are too hard. Her first program was to develop a series of hands-on science projects for students in upper elementary and middle school classes. The projects were designed to motivate the students and to show them that science is fun, interesting, and not too difficult. Later she concentrated on working with elementary and high school science teachers under a National Science Foundation grant. Her purpose was to improve the quality of instruction at each level by assuring that teachers understand the basic scientific concepts. For several years she has been involved with directing research, teaching biology, and conducting in-service training classes for teachers. She also has administrative responsibilities as dean of the Division of Arts and Sciences, which is composed of ten academic departments.

When she was a child, she lived on a farm near Columbia, South Carolina, that had no running water or electricity. Although there were 15 children in the family, her parents placed great emphasis on education. She started first grade at the age of 5 and graduated from high school at 16. She did not have any particular ambition to be a scientist, but in junior college, she found she had a good capacity for learning and that she did particularly well in her science courses.

Influenced by her biology teacher, she decided to major in that subject. She continued her education at Livingston College, majoring in biology, but she also completed the courses for a teaching certificate. She then taught in a high school that, although it was relatively new, was segregated and not well funded; for instance, there was no scientific equipment available in the laboratory.

When she decided she wanted to be a research biologist, she enrolled in the graduate program at Atlanta University, which is one of the premier institutions for advanced education for African Americans in the United States. The topic of her master's thesis was the regeneration of lost limbs in amphibians, such as frogs and salamanders. She saw a connection between the ability to regenerate limbs, the process of healing, and the success of skin grafts and organ transplants from one individual to another.

She secured a temporary position teaching at Benedict, but she was expecting a third child and the school did not have a maternity leave policy. The next year she taught at Morris College and later returned to Benedict College. It was at this time that she began to focus on problems of water pollution from toxic industrial waste and to examine the manner and extent to which these materials are harmful to living creatures. In the 1970s, she began her doctoral studies. However, she enrolled in education, not biology, because she felt many college-level science teachers are deeply involved in the details of their subject but have weak teaching skills. After receiving her doctorate, she was promoted to the rank of associate professor and advanced to the rank of full professor. Her photograph can be found in the reference listed below.

***Bibliography:*** *Distinguished African American Scientists of the 20th Century.*

# *Seddon, Margaret Rhea*
## (1947– )
## *physician, astronaut*

***Education:*** B.A. in physiology, University of California, Berkeley; M.D., University of Tennessee

***Professional Experience:*** General surgery resident; medical doctor with a specialty in medical nutrition; astronaut program, National Aeronautics and Space Administration (NASA), 1978–1995, missions STS 51-D (1985), STS-40 (1991), and STS-58 (1993); management position in medicine, 1995–

***Married:*** Robert Gibson, 1981

***Children:*** 1

*Margaret Rhea Seddon,* who uses the name Rhea (pronounced "Ray"), is one of the six women who were first selected for the National Aeronautics and Space Administration (NASA) astronaut program in 1978. She and her husband "Hoot" Gibson, who is also an astronaut, were members of the same training class. She was the first woman to complete her training in 1979, and she had

hopes that she might be the first American woman in space. When plans for the first space shuttle were nearing completion, however, she became pregnant and was thus unable to start the training program; the job was given to Sally Ride. Seddon was afraid she had made a career-killing mistake because most of the NASA administrators were older men whose wives stayed at home, and they might think that her pregnancy was an indication she was not serious about her career. However, she was assigned to later missions. She worked on orbiter and payload software, served as launch and rescue helicopter physician, and worked as technical assistant to the director of flight crew operations. She kept up her medical skills by working weekends in a local hospital emergency room, as the other physician astronauts, Anna and Bill Fisher, did.

Her first mission was STS 51-D aboard *Discovery* in 1985. One task of the mission was to deploy a Leasat-3 satellite; it was deployed but owing to a malfunction, the astronauts could not get it in orbit. Seddon tried to snag the satellite, which was owned by Hughes Aircraft, with the robot arm but without success. Her second flight was STS-40 in *Columbia* in 1991. Among other experiments, this crew explored the response of humans, animals, and cells to microgravity and the return to earth's gravity.

In the 1980s, there was a huge amount of media coverage for the women astronauts, and much attention was paid to Seddon's pregnancy. A photograph of her with her son was included in the December 27, 1982, issue of *People Weekly* among pictures of other celebrities such as movie stars and a baseball player. This intense publicity later dwindled until Shannon Lucid's assignment on *Mir* in 1996. Seddon and Anna Fisher, also a mother and married to an astronaut, were able to continue their careers without experiencing any impact on their job efficiency. Seddon, Fisher, and Lucid just considered themselves working mothers. Seddon and her husband met while members of the same astronaut training class—since Gibson is an experienced navy pilot, he was teaching her to fly a T-38 trainer when the romance blossomed. Although the female astronauts were not expected to be pilots, most of them took flying lessons if they had not already learned, for all of them wanted to be prepared to pilot the shuttle if an emergency arose.

At first the women were not welcomed by the male astronauts or the male employees of NASA. Gradually, though, the men came to realize that the women had scientific skills that complemented their own and that the women just wanted to be treated as equals. Seddon said she thought NASA selected her because she specialized in medical nutrition with an emphasis on diets designed to help mend victims of severe trauma or illness. Another reason was that as a physician, she had a great interest in science. There is a story that on one of her missions, one of the men complimented Seddon when she stitched a makeshift device. He called her an excellent seamstress, but she replied it was the work of a skilled surgeon. There are photographs of her in A. R. Oberg's *Spacefarers of the '80s and '90s,* Karen O'Connor's *Sally Ride and the New Astronauts,* and many news magazines of the period.

***Bibliography:*** Ireland, N., *Index to Women of the World . . . Suppl.;* Oberg, A. R., *Spacefarers of the '80s and '90s;* O'Connor, K., *Sally Ride and the New Astronauts;* Read, P., *The Book of Women's Firsts;* U.S. National Aeronautics and Space Administration, *Astronaut Fact Book.*

# *Sedlak, Bonnie Joy*
(1943– )
## *cell biologist, developmental biologist*

***Education:*** B.A., Northwestern University, 1965; M.A., Case Western Reserve University, 1968; Ph.D. in biology, Northwestern University, 1974

***Professional Experience:*** Instructor in biology, Northwestern University, 1971–1972; research associate, biochemistry, Rush Medical College, 1974–1975; assistant professor, biology, Smith College, 1975–1977; assistant professor, biology, State University of New York at Purchase, 1977–1981; associate research scientist, University of California, Irvine, 1981–1985; sales representative, North American Science Associates, Irvine, 1986–1987; program manager, Microbics Corporation, 1987–1988; sensor analyst, Fritzsche, Pambianchi Associates, 1988–1990; biotechnology consultant, 1990–1991; business development and licensing manager, Becton Dickinson Advanced Cellular Biology, 1991–1992; licensing officer for technical transfer, University of California, Alameda, 1992–

***Bonnie Sedlak*** is a cell biologist who is an expert on using the electron microscope in her research and teaching, but she left that field to work in industry as a business development and licensing manager. This is a burgeoning field for scientists who not only have expertise in science but can also advise companies on new areas of research or the manufacturing of medical or technical products. Much of the research currently done in university research laboratories is funded by corporations, so the corporations need scientists in their employ not only to conduct research but also to oversee the contracts with the universities. Companies also sell licenses to or purchase licenses from other companies for products to be manufactured, which involves paying royalties to or collecting royalties from the other companies. All of these transactions require people who have appropriate scientific and technical knowledge.

She recalls that she made an original discovery even while she was still a student. Biologists have always said that a cell must be a juvenile to divide and that when a cell is fully developed, it will not divide. However, she found a cell that took on adult characteristics and then divided, going against all biological laws. Using an electron microscope gave her the living proof of her discovery. Although another science might show that a process may exist, taking pictures through the microscope day after day shows the process as it is actually happening.

Sedlak has faced some problems in her career. Early in her undergraduate studies, one of her biology professors often tried to discourage her, saying—if she did not do well on a test—that she would be married soon and would not care about biology anymore. She refused to be discouraged, and later the same professor became one of her strongest supporters. After she completed her undergraduate degree, he advised her which colleges might fit her career goals and advised her later on where to find a job in her field.

After teaching and conducting research at several universities, she accepted a position as a sales representative for North American Science Associates, another type of position that demands a strong background in science or technology. She eventually worked as a licensing manager for a company and then became a licensing officer for technical transfer at a university. In that position, she oversees the patents taken out for university-sponsored research and negotiates licenses with companies, government agencies, and other universities. This work is called technical transfer—moving ideas from the research laboratories to useful or marketable products. It is a complex job that requires knowledge of contracts, patent law, and business procedures.

She is a member of the American Society for Cell Biology, American Association for the Advancement of Science, Society for

Developmental Biology, and Electron Microscopy Society of America. Her research includes cellular aspects of development and endocrine control in insects.

***Bibliography:*** Ireland, N., *Index to Women of the World . . . Suppl.; Saturday's Child; Who's Who in Science and Engineering,* 2d ed., 1994–1995.

# *Shalala, Donna Edna*
(1941– )
***political scientist***

***Education:*** B.A., Western College, 1962; M.S., Syracuse University, 1968, Ph.D. in political science, 1970; honorary degrees: 16

***Professional Experience:*** Peace Corps volunteer in Iran, 1962–1964; assistant to director, graduate studies program, Syracuse University, 1965–1969, instructor assistant to dean of Graduate School, 1969–1970; assistant professor of political science, City University of New York, 1972–1979; assistant secretary for policy development and research, Housing and Urban Development (HUD), Washington, D.C., 1977–1980; professor of political science and president, Hunter College, 1980–1988; professor of political science and chancellor, University of Wisconsin, Madison, 1988–1993; secretary, U.S. Department of Health and Human Services, 1993–

*Donna Shalala* occupies one of the most influential offices in Washington, D.C., today, that of secretary of the U.S. Department of Health and Human Services. The agency is one of the largest in government and has one of the largest budgets, much of which includes funds for scientific research. She is a prominent political scientist who has held professorships at several universities and been president of Hunter College and chancellor of the University of Wisconsin, Madison.

After receiving her undergraduate degree, she was a volunteer in the Peace Corps in Iran before attending Syracuse University for her graduate degrees. She obtained a position as an assistant professor of political science at the City University of New York before accepting her first political position as assistant secretary for policy development and research for Housing and Urban Development (HUD). During the early 1970s, she wrote four books: *Neighborhood Governance* (1971), *City and the Constitution* (1972), *Property Tax and the Voters* (1973), and *Decentralization Approach* (1974).

In 1980, she became a professor of political science and president of Hunter College, positions she held for eight years. She then moved to the Midwest when she was chosen to be the first woman to head a Big Ten university, the University of Wisconsin, Madison. Wisconsin is the state's land grant university, and as head of its main campus, she looked at such questions as the professionalism of college athletics, alcoholism, and the roles of business and government in the university. She was selected to be secretary of Health and Human Services in 1993.

In that capacity, she must be concerned with a wide range of topics, for the agencies in her department include the Public Health Service; National Institutes of Health; Centers for Disease Control; Agency for Toxic Substances and Disease Registry; Food and Drug Administration; Alcohol, Drug Abuse, and Mental Health Administration; Social Security Administration; and the Indian Health Service. One of her early actions was to escalate the budgets for cancer prevention at the National Cancer Institute and the Centers for Disease Control, underscoring breast cancer. She is concerned that women feel their issues have been underfunded, underdiagnosed, and undertreated as the system tends to look at issues involving men, not women. Another of her goals is to shield basic research in her department from undue political meddling and excessive bureaucratic burdens. She has questioned the social value of television shows and has been particularly disturbed by the content of the daytime television interview shows—some of which have left the air due to negative feedback from viewers. She has also talked about the violence that appears in cable television programs.

Shalala has been a member of the Committee on Economic Development (1991–1993), a member of the board of directors of the Institute of International Economics (1981–1993), a member of the Children's Defense Fund (1980–1993), and a trustee of the Brookings Institution (1989–1993). She received the Distinguished Service Medal of Teachers College, Columbia University, in 1989. She is a member of the American Political Science Association, American Society for Public Administration, and National Academy of Public Administration.

***Bibliography:*** Ireland, N., *Index to Women of the World . . . Suppl.; Who's Who in America,* 51st ed., 1997; *Who's Who of American Women,* 20th ed., 1997–1998.

# *Shapiro, Lucille (Cohen)*

(1940– )

***molecular biologist***

***Education:*** B.A., Brooklyn College, 1962; Ph.D. in molecular biology, Albert Einstein College of Medicine, 1966

***Professional Experience:*** Assistant professor, Albert Einstein College of Medicine, 1967–1972, associate professor, 1972–1977, Kramer Professor and chair, Department of Molecular Biology, 1977–1986, director, Biological Sciences Division, 1981–1986; Eugene Higgins Professor, and chair, Department of Microbiology, College of Physicians and Surgeons, Columbia University, 1986–1989; Joseph D. Grant Professor and chair, Department of Developmental Biology, School of Medicine, Stanford University, 1989–

***Married:*** Roy Shapiro, 1960, divorced 1977; Harley H. McAdams, 1978

***Children:*** 1

***Lucille Shapiro*** has had a distinguished career as a molecular biologist working on the front line of research. After receiving her doctorate, she was immediately given an appointment as an assistant professor at the Albert Einstein College of Medicine, and within ten years she had become a distinguished professor and chair of the Department of Molecular Biology. She then moved to the College of Physicians and Surgeons at Columbia University as a distinguished professor and chair of the Department of Microbiology and later went to the School of Medicine at Stanford University, again as chair of the Department of Developmental Biology. She was elected a member of the National Academy of Sciences in 1994.

Her papers have been published in the primary journals, such as *Journal of Bacteriology, Journal of Molecular Biology, Cell, Molecular Biology of the Cell, Trends in Genetics,* and *Science,* and she has been a distinguished lecturer at a number of universities. She has served as a member of the board of science advisers for G. D. Searle Company (1984–1986), a member of the science advisory board for Massachusetts General Hospital (1990–1993) and for SmithKline Beecham (1993– ), member of the science board of the Helen Hay Whitney Foundation (1986– ) and of the Whitehead Institute of the Massachusetts Institute of Technology (1988–1993), member of the visiting committee for the board of overseers of Harvard University (1987–1990), member of the science review board for the Howard Hughes Medical Institute (1990–1994), and member of the president's council of the University of California (1993– ). She has also been a member of the board of directors of a company, Silicon Graphics, Inc., since 1993.

She has received several awards, such as the Excellence in Science Award of the Federation of American Societies for Experimental Biology (1994) and the Alumna Award of Honor of Brooklyn College (1983). She is a fellow of the American Association for the Advancement of Science and a member of the American Society of Biochemistry and Molecular Biology, American Society for Microbiology, and New York Academy of Sciences. Her research interests include unicellular differentiation and developmental biology.

**Bibliography:** *American Men and Women of Science* 12–19; *Who's Who in America,* 51st ed., 1997; *Who's Who in Science and Engineering,* 3d ed., 1996–1997; *Who's Who of American Women,* 20th ed., 1997–1998.

# *Shaw, Jane E.*

(1939– )

## *physiologist, clinical pharmacologist*

***Education:*** B.S., University of Birmingham, 1961, Ph.D. in physiology, 1964; honorary degree: D.Sc., Worcester Polytechnic Institute, 1992
***Professional Experience:*** Staff scientist, Worcester Foundation for Experimental Biology, 1964–1970; senior scientist, Alza Research, 1970–1972, principal scientist, 1972– ; president, Alza Research Division, and chair of the board, Alza Ltd., 1985– , executive vice president Alza Corporation, 1985–1987, president and chief operating officer, 1987–
***Married:*** Peter F. Carpenter, 1983
***Children:*** 1

***Jane Shaw*** is renowned for research that led to the development of transdermal drug patches, such as those used for motion sickness. As a graduate student at the University of Birmingham, England, she worked with Peter Ramwell identifying prostaglandins. After graduation, she and about nine other members of the research team followed Ramwell to the Worcester Foundation for Experimental Biology in Massachusetts, part of the much publicized brain drain in England in the 1960s. She accepted the position because she thought a two-year research appointment would be an easy way to see the United States.

In 1970, Alejandro Zaffaroni, already known for his research at Syntex Corporation in Palo Alto, invited the team members to join Alza Corporation (the company's name was probably formed from the first two letters of his names), and Shaw was one of five people who migrated to Alza. Working as a scientist developing the transdermal drug patches that made Alza its fortune, she has seven patents for technology that allows a patient to absorb a prescription drug through the skin from a bandage-like patch. Beginning as senior scientist, she moved quickly through the ranks to become president of the research division, executive vice president of Alza Corporation and board chair of the parent company, Alza Ltd., and then president and chief operating officer of Alza Corporation.

In 1978 she announced an in-vitro test for skin permeability to various drugs and a mathematical model of the permeation process. She and her colleagues determined that the skin behind the ear was the most permeable to the test drug, which was scopolamine, used in treating motion sickness. Other requirements the team had to meet were to find or create a nonirritating adhesive to hold the drug in place but easily release it, a construction that would allow the drug to travel one way only, and a means of suppressing bacterial growth at the site. Their most ingenious development was a drug delivery rate lower than the absorption rate of the least-permeable skin observed from any individual, which meant that the system, not the variable permeability of the patient's skin, determines the actual rate of drug delivery into the bloodstream. Transdermal therapeutic systems for drug delivery are advantageous in chronic conditions such as hypertension because patients may forget to take medication when they have no symptoms. They are also advantageous when medications have to be given very frequently.

Born in England, Shaw started school at the age of three in a two-room Church of England school in her village. She went to a private school at the age of nine, and in her high school years she concentrated on biology, chemistry, and physics. When she took the entrance exam for the University of Birmingham, she was short one point on the physics exam; the headmistress insisted that she retake the exam, which she then passed.

In a profile published in the *Business Journal–San Jose* (February 10, 1992), the reporter said Shaw's most important contribution to Alza is her concern for employees and her willingness to recognize them for their contributions. She knows the first name of almost everyone in the company, which has more than 700 employees. She told the reporter that her biggest fault is she is always right. Alza, a private company that manufactures pharmaceutical products and conducts commercial research and development on drug delivery systems for human and veterinary use, has experienced several mergers and acquisitions in recent years.

Shaw has served on the board of directors of McKesson Corporation and of Intel Corporation. She has published more than 100 professional articles. She is a member of the American Association for the Advancement of Science, New York Academy of Sciences, American Physical Society, American Society of Clinical Pharmacology and Therapeutics, American Association of Pharmaceutical Scientists, and American Pharmaceutical Association. Her research includes elucidation of the physiological role of the prostaglandins, mechanism of action of analeptics, mechanism of gastric secretion, and physiology and pharmacology of the skin.

***Bibliography:*** *American Men and Women of Science* 11–19; Stanley, A., *Mothers and Daughters of Invention.*

# *Shaw, Mary M.*
## (1943– )
## ***computer scientist***

***Education:*** B.A. in mathematics, Rice University, 1965; Ph.D. in computer science, Carnegie-Mellon University, 1972

***Professional Experience:*** From assistant professor to professor of computer science, Carnegie-Mellon University, 1972– , chief scientist, Software Engineering Institute (SEI), 1984–1988, scientist with SEI, 1988–

***Married:*** Roy Weil, 1973

M*ary Shaw* is renowned as a expert in computer software and a leading proponent of developing software engineering as a discipline. She was the first women faculty member in the Computer Science Department at Carnegie-Mellon University when she was appointed in 1972. She has made major contributions to the analysis of computer algorithms as well as to abstraction techniques for advanced programming methodologies, programming language architecture, evaluation methods for software, performance and reliability of software, and software engineering.

One problem she has focused on in improving software design is that large programs are difficult to read or modify. She developed computer programs called "abstract data types" as a method for organizing the data and computations used by a program so that related information is grouped together, and she created a programming language called "Aphard" that implemented those abstract data types. She also made it easier to design programs that are more abstract (here "abstract" means the elements of the program are further removed from the details of how the computer works and closer to the language of the program that a user is trying to understand). She thus made programs more user friendly for the scientists who are using them to manipulate their research data.

She and others realized that the term *software engineering,* which was coined about 1968, was not the name of a discipline but a reminder that one did not exist. She published a paper outlining the components of software engineering in the November 1990 issue of *IEEE Software* entitled, "Prospects for an Engineering Discipline of Software." Carnegie-Mellon had been offering undergraduate courses in computer science for a number of years but did not offer a degree, and she worked with others on revamping the undergraduate curriculum to make it into a degree program. She also worked with the Information Systems Division of International Business Machines Corporation (IBM) to prepare a similar curriculum for that company to offer in-house to its own employees throughout the country. At the same time, her committee revamped the university's graduate program in computer science. Another of her accomplishments is to help create the Software Engineering Institute at Carnegie-Mellon. She was the institute's chief scientist from 1984 to 1988 and now has a joint appointment with the institute and the university.

She credits her parents for treating her and her brother as intelligent human beings and her father for encouraging her interest in science and mathematics. He brought her books and simple electronic kits and encouraged her to collect stamps and participate in science fair projects. This was at the time of Sputnik when the United States was making a concerted effort to bolster science and math education. While she was in high school, a man who worked for IBM started an after-school program to interest students in computers; the students were even permitted to visit a local IBM facility and run a program on an IBM 709 computer. For two summers during high school Shaw worked for the Research Analysis Corporation of the Johns Hopkins University Operation Research Office, which gave her the opportunity to explore fields outside the normal school curriculum.

When she entered Rice University she planned to major in topology, a branch of mathematics, but after looking through the textbook she decided that field was too abstract for her. Although there were no courses in computer science, a small group called the Rice Computer Project had built a computer, the Rice I; when she became acquainted with the group as a sophomore, she joined it permanently. She gained valuable experience working on a programming language, writing subroutines, and studying how to make an operating system run faster.

In her senior year she debated about whether or not to apply to graduate school, and her computing friends encouraged her to apply because she could decide later whether or not to attend. She had met a faculty member from Carnegie-Mellon in a summer session and, impressed with the curriculum, she chose that school. She wrote her thesis on compilers, that is, the programs that translate language a human can easily understand into a language the computer understands. She was invited to join the faculty of the department after she received her degree. One of her first notable accomplishments was to develop what is called "the Shaw-Traub algorithm," an improved method for evaluating a polynomial, which allows computers to compute faster.

She was the first woman faculty member in the department and is currently one of only two tenured women there. She has found that being a woman has never been a serious barrier in her professional life, but she has experienced barriers in the outside world. For example, when she married, she decided to retain her own name, but at that time, credit card companies would not issue cards to married women if they chose to use their own names. She solved the problem by obtaining all the credit cards she needed and then not reporting that she had married.

She has been a member of the Defense Board Task Force on Software (1985–1987), a member of the Working Group on System Implementation Language of the International Federation of Information Processing Society (1985–1994), and a member of the Computer Science and Telecommunications Board of the National Research Council (1985–1993). She is a fellow of the Institute of Electrical and Electronics Engineers and the American Association for the Advancement of Science. She is a member of the Association for Computing Machinery and the New York Academy of Sciences. Her research includes software architecture, programming language design, abstraction techniques for advanced programming, software engineering, and computer science education. Her photograph is included in *Journeys of Women in Science and Engineering* and *Notable Twentieth-Century Scientists.*

***Bibliography:*** *American Men and Women of Science* 18–19; *Journeys of Women in Science and Engineering; Notable Twentieth-Century Scientists; Who's Who in America,* 51st ed., 1997; *Who's Who in Engineering,* 9th ed., 1995.

# *Sheehy, Gail (Henion)*
## (1937– )
## *social and political critic*

***Education:*** B.A. in home economics, University of Vermont, 1958
***Professional Experience:*** Home economist, J. C. Penny Company, 1958–1960; fashion consultant, Rochester, New York, 1960; fashion editor for the *Rochester Democrat & Chronicle,* 1961–1963; feature writer, *New York Herald Tribune,* 1963–1966; fellowship in anthropology, Columbia University, 1970; contributing editor, *New York* magazine, 1968–1977; contributing political editor, *Vanity Fair,* 1988– ; freelance journalist and author, 1968–
***Married:*** Albert F. Sheehy, 1960, divorced 1968; Clay S. Felker, 1984
***Children:*** 2

**Gail Sheehy** is an author and a social and political critic who explores social problems, character development, and adult psychology. When she began working on her fourth nonfiction book, she did not anticipate that it would make her famous. Early in the 1970s, she had signed a contract to write about the ages and stages of couples, but over the next few years her focus shifted to crises in the adult life cycle. When *Passages: Predictable Crises of Adult Life* was published in 1976, it created a sensation, and the critics in general gave it good reviews. More than 5 million copies have been sold, and it is still considered one of the books that has most influenced people.

In the book, she identifies patterns of change in people's lives, basing her conclusions on 115 in-depth interviews with educated, middle-class people between the ages of 18 and 55. Among the crises, or passages, are the pulling-up-roots phase, which begins at age 18; the trying 20s, when people make choices that set certain lifestyle patterns in motion; catch-30, a period of yearning for a change; rooting and extending, when people in their early 30s begin to feel more settled; the deadline decade of the mid 30s, a time of reevaluation; and the renewal or resignation of the mid 40s.

The sequel, *Pathfinders: Overcoming the Crises of Adult Life and Finding your Own Path to Well-Being* (1981), also was a best seller and established her as a writer of popular psychology. For this book, she interviewed women and men who had survived their mid-life crises—including job loss, serious illness, and divorce—with their psyches intact. The third book in her series is *The Silent Passage: Menopause* (1992), an expanded version of an article that she published in *Vanity Fair* in 1991. She found that very little medical research had been conducted on the subject, which had basically been taboo. She concluded that contrary to popular myth, life after menopause can be fulfilling and rewarding. She describes menopause as a normal, temporary transition into possibly the more satisfying half of a woman's adult life. Her endorsement of hormone replacement brought criticism from some sources.

The next book in her series on human behavior and human growth is *New Passages: Mapping Your Life across Time* (1995). Here she turns her attention to the swelling ranks of the country's newly middle-aged and believes that middle age is just not being acknowledged today. For example, 55-year-old women can have babies and 80-year-old people can run marathons. She suggests that people can live not one life but two, with a second adulthood kicking in around the age of 50. Her next book is *Passages for Men: Getting Your Life's Worth out of Every Stage* (1998), which is based on interviews with men conducted as part of her speaking tours around the country. One of her contributions has been to broaden the scope of human development research to include previously ignored subjects such as menopause in both women and men.

Although all of the above books have received generally favorable comments, some critics dismiss her as a tabloid newspaper writer. However, she did have a fellowship in anthropology at Columbia University and there worked under the noted anthropologist Margaret Mead, who became one of her mentors. Sheehy has covered some straight reporting assignments, such as one on Cambodian refugees, during which she found a Cambodian child whom she adopted. She profiled six candidates in the 1988 presidential campaign in *Character: America's Search for Leadership* (1988), and she spent a year and a half in Russia researching the life of Mikhail Gorbachev, whom she profiled in *The Man Who Changed the World: The Lives of Mikhail S. Gorbachev* (1990). Earlier she published a novel, *Lovesounds* (1970) and three nonfiction books, *Panthermania: The Clash of Black Against Black in One American City* (1971), *Speed Is of the Essence* (1971), and *Hustling: Prostitution in Our Wide Open Society* (1973).

When she enrolled in undergraduate school at the University of Vermont, she planned to major in business administration. However, women were not permitted in that curriculum, so she selected home economics because that was the closest program to business she could find. She worked as a traveling home economist for J. C. Penny Company for two years after graduating and was a fashion consultant and a fashion editor for a newspaper in Rochester, New York, while her husband practiced medicine there. She was a feature writer for the *New York Herald Tribune* for a few years and later became a freelance journalist and author. She has received numerous awards for her writings. Her photograph is included in *Current Biography* (1993).

***Bibliography:*** *Contemporary Authors* v. 33R; *Current Biography 1993;* Ireland, N., *Index to Women of the World . . . Suppl.; Who's Who of American Women,* 19th ed., 1995–1996.

# *Shipman, Pat*
(1949– )
## *paleoanthropologist*

***Education:*** B.A., Smith College, 1970; M.A., New York University, 1974, Ph.D. in anthropology, 1977

***Professional Experience:*** Visiting lecturer in anthropology, Jersey City State College, 1974; adjunct instructor, Fordham University, 1975; editor and research associate, American Institutes for Research, 1976–1978; research associate, Johns Hopkins University, 1978–1981, assistant professor, 1981–1984, associate professor of cell biology and anatomy, 1984– , assistant for academic affairs, School of Medicine, 1985–1990; full-time author, 1990–

***Married:*** Alan C. Walker, 1976

***Children:*** 1

***Pat Shipman*** is a paleoanthropologist who spent many years in Kenya as a research scientist. In recent years she has concentrated on explaining scientific subjects to the general public in terms that show the excitement and importance of scientific research without diminishing its accuracy. She has appeared on several television documentaries, such as "In Search of Human Origins" narrated by the anthropologist Don Johnson in 1997. On that program, she talked about whether our ancestors were hunter-gatherers or just scavengers.

For more than 15 years her career was primarily an academic one, and she still maintains an affiliation with Johns Hopkins University. She spent many years conducting research in Kenya, excavating paleontological and archaeological sites and working on fossils stored there, such as the collections from the Olduvai Gorge in Tanzania. She focused on trying to deduce the environmental context in which our earliest ancestors evolved and what their lifestyles and adaptations were like. When she felt herself becoming stale in this pursuit, she turned to scientific research in general. She has published any number of scientific papers and has started publishing popular articles for science magazines. For example, in the December 1987 issue of *Discover,* she wrote that a fossil bed in Germany dating back about 30 million years was being considered by the German government as a garbage dump. An outcry from the scientific community saved the fossils.

She is coauthor of *The Neandertals: Changing the Image of Mankind* (1993), which is primarily about the history of the discovery of Neanderthals and related remains. The book focuses on how the interpretations of these finds have fluctuated through the gradual accumulation of information on both the anatomical characteristics and the geographical distribution of the remains. The central theme is how scientific opinion on the Neanderthals has tended to shift between two extreme positions: the people who see them as being in the main course of human evolution and those who see them as representing a sideline of human population. Reviewers recommended the book for students and the general public

Shipman's book *The Evolution of Racism: Human Differences and the Use and Abuse of Science* (1994) traces the attempts of scientists from the mid nineteenth century to the present to grapple with the issues of race. Beginning with Charles Darwin's explorations of evolution, she talks about Sir Francis Galton's idea of eugenics, which is the theory of advancing the species through careful breeding. From eugenics came intelligence testing, which was used in the early twentieth century to the detriment of immigrants to the United States and prisoners of the Nazis. She continues to track the controversy that started in the 1950s and 1960s about whether to examine or deny racial differences.

In *Taking Wing: Archaeopteryx and the Evolution of Bird Flight* (1998), she draws on diverse scientific fields to give a comprehensive analysis of the ideas that explain how the adaptations needed for animal flight came about. She provides the science and physical evidence for each point of view along with the rebuttals of its critics. Earlier she wrote two other scientifically oriented books: *Life History of a Fossil* (1981) and *The Human Skeleton* (1985).

She is a member of the American Association of Physical Anthropologists, Society for American Archaeology, American Society of Mammalogists, Society of Vertebrate Paleontology, and American Association for the Advancement of Science.

***Bibliography:*** *Contemporary Authors* v. 141.

# *Shockley, Dolores Cooper*
(1930– )
## *pharmacologist*

***Education:*** B.S., Louisiana State University, 1951; M.S., Purdue University, 1953, Ph.D. in pharmacology, 1955
***Professional Experience:*** Assistant in pharmacology, Purdue University, 1951–1953; assistant professor of pharmacology, Meharry Medical College, 1955–1967, associate professor, 1967– , chair, Department of Microbiology 1977–
***Concurrent Position:*** Fulbright fellowship, University of Copenhagen, 1955–1956; visiting assistant professor, Albert Einstein Medical College, 1959–1962
***Married:*** 1957
***Children:*** 4

***Dolores Shockley*** is known for her research in pharmacology, which is the science dealing with research on the preparation, uses, and especially the effects of drugs. When she entered undergraduate school she planned to become a pharmacist (a person who prepares and dispenses drugs and medicines), but during college her interest shifted to research, and she continued her schooling to receive her doctorate. She is the first African American woman to earn a doctorate in pharmacology from Purdue University as well as the first in the United States. The pharmacology curriculum is very intense, and graduates often move on to do research in hospitals, corporate laboratories, and government agencies or to university research and teaching. The pharmaceutical companies, in particular, employ large numbers of graduates.

After completing postdoctoral research at the University of Copenhagen, Shockley returned to the United States as an assistant professor at Meharry Medical College in Nashville, Tennessee. At first she was uncertain that she had made a wise choice because some of the men thought she was just working there temporarily, but she soon proved she was there to stay and became a respected member of the faculty. She was promoted to associate professor in 1967, and in 1977 she was appointed to head the Department of Microbiology.

She is Meharry's foreign student adviser and its liaison for international activities to the Association of American Medical Colleges. Her research interests are the consequences of drug action on stress, the effects of hormones on connective tissue, the relationship between drugs and nutrition, nutrition effects and drug actions, and the measurement of nonnarcotic drugs.

She has received several awards, such as the Lederle faculty award, (1963–1966) and a visiting professorship at the Albert Einstein College of Medicine in New York City (1959–1962). She is a member of the American Pharmaceutical Association and the American Association for the Advancement of Science.

***Bibliography:*** *American Men and Women of Science* 11–19; *Blacks in Science and Medicine; Notable Twentieth-Century Scientists.*

# *Shoemaker, Carolyn (Spellmann)*
(1929– )
***planetary astronomer***

***Education:*** B.A., Chico State College, 1949, M.A., 1950; honorary degree: D.Sc., Northern Arizona University, 1990
***Professional Experience:*** Visiting scientist, astrogeology, U.S. Geological Survey, Flagstaff, 1980– ; research professor of astronomy, Northern Arizona University, 1989– ; member of staff, Lowell Observatory, Flagstaff, 1993–
***Concurrent Positions:*** Research assistant, California Institute of Technology, 1981–1985; guest observer, Mt. Palomar Observatory, 1982–1994
***Married:*** Eugene M. Shoemaker, 1951, died 1997
***Children:*** 3

*Carolyn Shoemaker* became known to the general public when the periodic comet Shoemaker-Levy 9 impacted on Jupiter in July 1994 and she was interviewed on television programs. However, she was already renowned in the scientific community because of the number of comets she had identified. In 1992 she discovered her 27th comet, more than the 26 comets identified by the nineteenth-century French observer Jean-Louis Pons. Since 1992, she has discovered several more—for a total of 32 by July 1997.

Although Pons could only make visual searches with a small telescope, Shoemaker uses the 18-inch Schmidt telescope at Mt. Palomar, ultra-fine-grain film, and a stereomicroscope. She worked with her husband, Eugene Shoemaker, in all of the discoveries except one, but he created the search program for comets and earth-crossing asteroids that they used. She discovered her first comet in 1983. David Levy, of Shoemaker-Levy 9, has identified 21, of which 13 were discovered jointly with the Shoemakers. Eugene Shoemaker died in 1997, and according to a newspaper article in February 1998, Carolyn Shoemaker plans to continue her work in cooperation with Levy, an amateur astronomer.

Another area in which she has worked is in identifying earth-approaching asteroids. For two weeks each month, during the dark of the moon, search teams gather at Mt. Palomar to track asteroids and meteorites that are close enough to impact the earth. Such objects regularly fall to earth throughout the world, and a large one could cause severe damage. For example, Luis and Walter Alvarez theorize that the reason dinosaurs and large mammals disappeared from the earth is that a huge asteroid impacted on the coast in Yucatán. The resulting cloud of debris and gases that circled the earth blotted out the sun, killing the plants on which the animals fed and causing the animals to starve to death.

Eugene Shoemaker was a world expert on impact craters both on earth and on the planets, and he trained the astronauts who landed on the moon in the basics of geology. Carolyn Shoemaker has identified a record 500 asteroids, including 41 earth approachers. She taught school, but after their children were grown she started accompanying her husband as an unpaid assistant on his studies of craters on the earth and then helped with his work surveying the moon. She soon became expert in identifying the tiny dark smudges on the films and continued working on the projects to identify earth approachers. Her discovery ability is unparalleled, and the comet-Jupiter collision is the greatest astronomical event of the twentieth century.

She has received numerous awards, including the National Aeronautics and Space Administration Exceptional Achievement Medal (1996), Woman of Distinction award of the National Association for Women in Education (1996), and Distinguished Alumna of California State University, Chico, (1996). She is the author of the report on Shoemaker-Levy 9 in the U.S. Geological Survey *Yearbook*

(1994), and her work has been featured on such Public Broadcasting System television programs as "The Doomsday Asteroid" in 1997 and "On Jupiter" in 1996. She is a fellow of the American Academy of Arts and Sciences and a member of the Astronomical Society of the Pacific. Her photograph is included in *Scientific American* (August 1996), *Astronomy* (June 1993), and *New Scientist* (July 9, 1994). Some information was supplied in a note to the author May 30, 1997.

***Bibliography:*** *Who's Who in America*, 51st ed., 1997; *Who's Who in Science and Engineering*, 3d ed., 1996–1997.

# *Shreeve, Jean'ne Marie*
(1933– )
***inorganic chemist***

***Education:*** B.A., University of Montana, 1953; M.S. in analytical chemistry, University of Minnesota, 1956; Ph.D. in inorganic chemistry, University of Washington, 1961; honorary degree: D.Sc., University of Montana, 1982

***Professional Experience:*** Teaching assistant in chemistry, University of Minnesota, 1953–1955; assistant, University of Washington, 1957–1961; assistant professor of chemistry, University of Idaho, 1961–1965, associate professor, 1965–1967, professor, 1967–1973, acting chair, Department of Chemistry, 1969–1970 and 1973, head of department and professor, 1973–1987, vice provost of research and graduate studies and professor of chemistry, 1987–

***Jean'ne Shreeve*** is internationally known and nationally recognized for her contributions to the understanding of synthetic fluorine chemistry. The major emphasis of her research has been the synthesis, characterization, and reactions of fluorine compounds that contain nitrogen, sulfur, and phosphorus. She and her students made a significant "find" when they discovered the compound perfluorourea, which is an oxidizer ingredient. She has also developed new synthetic routes to several important compounds, including chlorodifluoroamine and difluoradiazine. These compounds are used in synthesizing rocket oxidizers, but preparation by previously known techniques was hard to accomplish.

Her work as a fluorine chemist earned her the 1972 Garvan Medal of the American Chemical Society, which was one of only two national awards available at that time to recognize outstanding achievements in chemistry by American women chemists. The honor cited her contributions to the fundamental understanding of the behavior of inorganic fluorine compounds and to the synthesis of important new fluorochemicals.

At the time she started her appointment at the University of Idaho, the Chemistry Department was poorly equipped to support research. However, the state had just designated the campus at Moscow as Idaho's research university and had given it permission to grant doctoral degrees; because of her prominence in research, she was able to contribute to the growth of the Chemistry Department and its curriculum. She advanced rapidly through the ranks to full professor, head of the department, and then vice provost for research and graduate studies. She has devoted her life to educating other chemists, and she has drawn many exceptional students into graduate studies. Her own interest in chemistry developed when she was an undergraduate at the University of Montana because of an exceptional teacher.

She has served on numerous committees in the American Chemical Society and the American Association for the Advancement of Science, and she has received numerous awards including the Distinguished Alumni Award, University of Montana (1970); Outstanding Achievement Award, University of

Minnesota (1975); Senior U.S. Scientist Award, Alexander Von Humboldt Foundation (1978); Fluorine Award of the American Chemical Society (1978); and Excellence in Teaching Award, Chemical Manufacturers Association (1980). She began serving on the board of Governors of Argonne National Laboratory in 1992. She is a fellow of the American Association for the Advancement of Science and a member of the American Chemical Society and American Institute of Chemists. Her research includes synthesis of inorganic and organic fluorine-containing compounds. Her photograph is included in *Notable Women in the Physical Sciences* and *Chemical & Engineering News* (September 24, 1990).

***Bibliography:*** *American Men and Women of Science* 11–19; Herzenberg, C., *Women Scientists from Antiquity to the Present; Notable Women in the Physical Sciences; Who's Who in America,* 51st ed., 1997; *Who's Who of American Women,* 20th ed., 1997–1998.

# *Simpson, Joanne Malkus (Gerould)*

(1923– )

***meteorologist***

***Education:*** B.S., University of Chicago, 1943, M.S., 1945, Ph.D. in meteorology, 1949; honorary degree: D.Sc., State University of New York at Albany, 1991

***Professional Experience:*** Instructor in meteorology, New York University, 1943–1944; instructor in physics and meteorology, Illinois Institute of Technology, 1946–1949, assistant professor, 1949–1951; meteorologist, Woods Hole Oceanographic Institution, 1951–1960; professor of meteorology, University of California, Los Angeles, 1960–1965; head, experimental branch, Atmospheric Physics and Chemistry Laboratory, Environmental Science Service Administration, 1965–1971; director, experimental meteorology laboratory, National Oceanic and Atmospheric Administration (NOAA), Department of Commerce, 1971–1974; professor of environmental science and member of Center of Advanced Studies, University of Virginia, 1974–1976, W. W. Corcoran Professor, 1976–1981; head, Severe Storms Branch, Goddard Space Flight Center, National Aeronautics and Space Administration (NASA), 1979–1988, chief scientist for meteorology and earth sciences director and senior fellow, 1988–

***Concurrent Positions:*** Adjunct professor, University of Miami, 1971–1974; project scientist, tropical rainfall measuring mission, Goddard Space Flight Center, 1986– ; member of board of directors, Atmospheric Sciences and Climatology of National Research Council and National Academy of Sciences (NRC/NAS), 1990– ; chief scientist, Simpson Weather Associates, 1974–1979

***Married:*** William Malkus, 1948, divorced; Robert H. Simpson, 1965

***Children:*** 3

***Joanne Simpson*** is a renowned scientist who is the first woman in the world to receive a doctorate in meteorology, and she has had a distinguished career as a meteorologist in academia, government, and private business. In the 1940s she entered a field that was largely dominated by European males who were even less tolerant of female ambition than Americans of that period. She was a pioneer for a generation of women meteorologists and as a pioneer, suffered many hardships and disappointments in trying to secure employment in positions that were commensurate with her abilities. She was elected to membership in the National Academy of Engineering in 1988.

She started college just at the beginning of World War II, and she seized the opportunity to enter the meteorology training program on the University of Chicago campus. Meteorology is the science that deals with the atmosphere and its phenomena, including weather and climate, and after nine months of training, she and the other women in the program trained weather forecasters for the military services. At the end of the war, the women were supposed to return to their families or get married and take care of the children. When a few of the 30 women in the program wanted to continue taking courses toward a master's degree or a doctorate, the faculty members were shocked and some openly hostile. Although she was refused any fellowship support, she would not accept the assertion that her ambition was a lost cause.

Simpson continued her studies and received a doctorate in 1949, but that was just the beginning of her fight for acceptance and respect. She suffered insults and disappointments, including not being taken seriously as a professional by either women or men and being passed over for jobs for which she was better qualified than the male competition. After more than 30 years in the profession, she received an endowed professorship, but even then, many members of the university felt she had received the appointment only to satisfy affirmative action directives. For this and other reasons, she eventually resigned her academic position.

When she started working on her doctoral thesis, none of the faculty at the University of Chicago was willing to supervise her work, so she chose a topic concerning clouds and worked on her own. Eventually a professor agreed to supervise her studies, which proved to be fortuitous because his specialty was tropical meteorology and that topic became a lifelong focus of her research. Since she did not have a scholarship, she needed to find a job to support her research—at a time when thousands of former military personnel were entering college under the GI Bill. She obtained a position teaching physics and meteorology at the Illinois Institute of Technology, and as a faculty member, she was entitled to take courses at that school. She completed most of the course work required for her doctorate there and then transferred the credits to the University of Chicago. During that period she also began working summers at the Woods Hole Oceanographic Institution. She taught at Illinois Institute for two years and then returned to Woods Hole as a full-time research scientist.

When she was director of an experimental meteorology laboratory at Coral Gables, Florida, for the National Oceanic and Atmospheric Administration (NOAA), she was also an adjunct professor at the University of Miami; during that period, she devised and developed a new concept of cloud-seeding experiments aimed at modifying the dynamics of cumulus clouds. When she was a faculty member in the Environmental Sciences Department of the University of Virginia, she and her husband, Robert Simpson, formed a private meteorology consulting service, Simpson Weather Associates. She became head of the Severe Storms Branch of the Goddard Space Flight Center of the National Aeronautics and Space Administration (NASA) in 1979, and she is still affiliated with NASA. She has found the work and attitude at Goddard very stimulating, and she has been allowed to build up a talented group of young researchers doing exciting work.

She said that when she was teaching at the University of Virginia in the 1970s there had been immense progress in accepting women into the meteorology program. At that school about a third of the graduate students were women, and they were completely accepted by the male students. When she was a graduate student, people would not even sit in a chair next to her because they were so embarrassed by her presence, and that was also the experience of women in other professions in the 1940s and 1950s.

Simpson received the highest award of the American Meteorological Society, the Rossby Research Medal, in 1983, plus another medal from the same organization, the Meisinger Award, in 1962. Other awards include Silver Medal (1967) and Gold Medal (1972) of the Department of Commerce, the V. J. Schaefer Award of the Weather Modification Association (1979), and the Exceptional Science Achievement Medal of NASA (1982). She has published more than 100 scientific papers and one book, *Cloud Structure and Distributions over the Tropical Pacific Ocean* (1965). She is a fellow of the American

Meteorological Society (president, 1989), and a member of the American Geophysical Union and the Ocean Society. Her research includes convection in atmosphere, cumulus clouds, tropical meteorology, weather modification, and satellite meteorology. Her photograph is included in *Weatherwise* (August 1984) and *WMO Bulletin* (January 1986). Although she mentions in some sources that she has been married three times, there is no mention of her first husband's name. Some of her publications are listed under "Malkus" and some under "Simpson."

***Bibliography:*** *American Men and Women of Science* 11–19; Ireland, N., *Index to Women of the World . . . Suppl.;* Kundsin, R., "Successful Women in the Sciences"; Noble, I., *Contemporary Women Scientists;* Rossiter, M., *Women Scientists in America; Who's Who in Science and Engineering,* 3d ed., 1996–1997; *Who's Who of American Women,* 20th ed., 1997–1998.

# *Singer, Maxine (Frank)*
## (1931– )
## ***biochemist, geneticist***

***Education:*** B.A., Swarthmore College, 1952; Ph.D. in biochemistry, Yale University, 1957; honorary degrees: 15

***Professional Experience:*** Public Health Service postdoctoral fellow, National Institutes of Health, 1956–1958, research chemist in biochemistry, 1958–1974, head of section on nucleic acid enzymology, 1974–1979, chief of Laboratory of Biochemistry, National Cancer Institute, 1979–1987, research chemist, 1987–1988; emeritus, 1988– ; president, Carnegie Institution of Washington, 1988–

***Married:*** Daniel M. Singer, 1952

***Children:*** 4

***Maxine Singer*** is renowned as a leading scientist in the field of human genetics. Her research laboratory helped to decipher the genetic code, and she is a strong advocate for responsible use of genetics research. During the controversy in the 1970s over the use of recombinant DNA (deoxyribonucleic acid) techniques to alter genetic characteristics, she advocated a cautious approach, and she helped develop guidelines to balance the desire for unfettered research on genetics with designing research programs that make medically valuable discoveries and still meet goals to protect the public from possible harm. In 1992 she received the National Medal of Science. This award is given annually by the National Science Foundation to American scientists representing the spectrum of disciplines, and the medals are awarded by the president in a White House ceremony. She was elected a member of the National Academy of Sciences in 1979.

She spent her career conducting research at the National Institutes of Health (NIH). There scientists learned how to take DNA fragments from one organism in order to insert them into the living cells of another, and the "recombinant DNA" technique had the potential of creating completely new types of organisms. This new research potentially could lead to the discovery of cures for serious diseases, aid in the development of new crops, and otherwise benefit humanity. On the other hand, there is the possibility of creating some as yet unknown life forms, some of them possibly dangerous. In 1972, Singer's colleague Paul Berg of Stanford University was the first to create recombinant DNA molecules. Later he voluntarily stopped conducting studies involving DNA manipulation in the genes of tumor-causing viruses because some scientists feared that a virus with unknown properties might escape from the laboratory and spread into the general population.

In an unprecedented action in 1973, a group of scientists composed a public letter to the president of the National Academy of

Sciences and published it in *Science* magazine. They warned that organisms of an unpredictable nature could result from the new technique and suggested that the academy recommend guidelines. The National Institutes of Health began formulating guidelines for recombinant DNA research, and Singer was instrumental in preparing these guidelines. She also wrote a series of editorials and articles on the topic in *Science* over a period of about five years. She was a strong supporter of the first genetically engineered food, such as "the Flavr Savr tomato," to reach American supermarket shelves in the 1990s.

After a few years at NIH, she accepted the position of chief of the section on nucleic acid enzymology, Division of Cancer Biology and Diagnosis, at the National Cancer Institute, which is where the genetic research started, and she became chief of the Laboratory of Biochemistry in 1980. She was the first person to receive emeritus status from the NIH in 1988 when she became president of the Carnegie Institution, a research organization that conducts high-level biological, earth science, and astronomical research. She still spends two or three days each week at the National Cancer Institute. Some of her other projects are to develop a science program, "First Light," for inner-city children and serving on advisory boards to the pope and science institutes in Israel and Thailand.

Singer and Paul Berg have written two books on genetics, both of which have received positive reviews. The first was *Genes and Genomes: A Changing Perspective* (1990), a graduate-level textbook on molecular genetics. In addition to presenting an in-depth discussion of the topic, the book provides background information for readers who have a limited knowledge of biochemistry, cell biology, and genetics. One reviewer said it captures the sense of discovery, understanding, and anticipation that has followed the recombinant DNA development. The second book is *Dealing with Genes: The Language of Heredity* (1992). Although not a textbook, it is a summary of the mechanisms of heredity and the ways in which biologists study and alter the microscopic structure of organisms. There are chapters on the structure and chemistry of the cell; the mechanisms of replication, development, and evolution; and viruses and cancer.

She has received many awards and served on numerous significant committees. She is a fellow of the American Academy of Arts and Sciences and a member of the American Society of Biological Chemists, American Philosophical Society, and American Association for the Advancement of Science. Her research includes nucleic acid chemistry and metabolism; biochemistry of animal viruses, genome organization, and transposable elements in the human genome. Her photograph is included in *U.S. News & World Report* (August 26–September 2, 1991).

***Bibliography:*** *American Men and Women of Science* 11–19; Herzenberg, C., *Women Scientists from Antiquity to the Present; Notable Twentieth-Century Scientists; Who's Who in America,* 51st ed., 1997; *Who's Who in Science and Engineering,* 3d ed., 1996–1997; *Who's Who of American Women,* 20th ed., 1997–1998.

# *Sinkford, Jeanne Frances (Craig)*
(1933– )
***physiologist***

***Education:*** B.S., Howard University, 1953, DDS, 1958; M.S., Northwestern University, 1962, Ph.D. in physiology, 1963; honorary degree: D.Sc., Georgetown University, 1978
***Professional Experience:*** Research assistant in psychology, U.S. Department of Health, Education and Welfare, 1953; instructor in dentistry, College of Dentistry, Howard University, 1958–1960; clinical instructor, Dental School, Northwestern University, 1963–1964; associate professor and head, Department of Prosthodontics, Howard University, 1964–1968, associate dean, 1967–1974, professor, 1968–1992, dean, College of Dentistry, 1975–1992, professor, Department of Physiology, Graduate School of Arts and Science, 1976–1992; retired 1992
***Concurrent Positions:*** Attending staff, Freedmen's Hospital, Howard University Hospital, 1964– , Children's Hospital, National Medical Center, 1975– , District of Columbia General Hospital, 1975–
***Married:*** Stanley M. Sinkford, 1951
***Children:*** 3

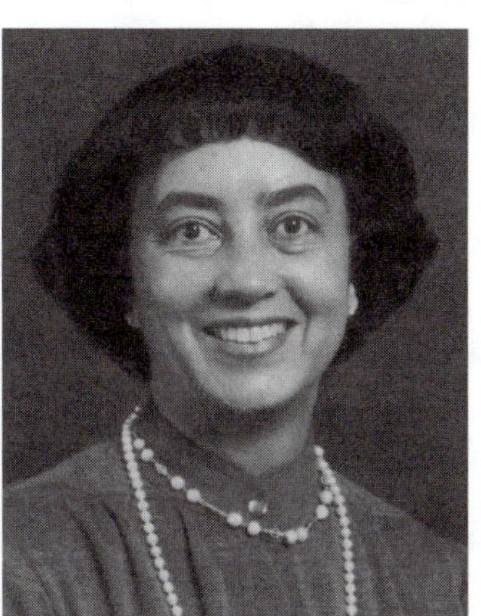

***Jeanne Sinkford*** has the distinction of being the first black woman in the United States to become head of a university department of dentistry. She was born in Washington, D.C., and has spent most of her career at Howard University. She married while she was still in undergraduate school at Howard but continued in school to receive her DDS degree. She moved to the Chicago area to receive her master's degree and doctorate in physiology from Northwestern University and then received an appointment in the Dental School at Northwestern. After she returned to Howard University, she became an associate dean in 1967 and dean of the College of Dentistry in 1975.

At that point she was the first black woman in the United States to head a university department of dentistry, and the next year she took on added responsibilities when she became a professor in the Department of Physiology in the Graduate School of Arts and Science. For many years she also continued her dental practice by serving on the staffs of Howard University Hospital, Children's Hospital of the National Medical Center, and District of Columbia General Hospital.

She has received a number of awards, including the College of Dentistry Alumni Award for Dental Education and Research (1969) and the Alumni Federation Outstanding Achievement Award (1971), both from Howard University; Alumni Achievement Award from Northwestern University (1970); and Certificate of Merit from the American Prosthodontic Society (1971). She has served on review boards for other universities, such as the board of overseers of the University of Pennsylvania Dental School and the Boston University Dental School and the board of advisers for the University of Pittsburgh Dental School. She is also a member of the board of directors for NIH. She is a member of the American Dental Association, International Association for Dental Research, American Association for the Advancement of Science, and New York Academy of Sciences. Her research includes endogenous anti-inflammatory substances, chemical healing agents, gingival retraction agents, hereditary dental defects, oral endocrine defects, and neuromuscular problems. Her photograph was published in *Jet* (July 10, 1958) in a note about her receiving her DDS degree from Howard University.

***Bibliography:*** *Blacks in Science and Medicine; Encyclopedia of Black America;* Ireland, N., *Index to Women of the World . . . Suppl.; Who's Who of American Women*, 20th ed., 1997–1998.

# Smith, Elske (Van Panhuys)

(1929– )

## *astronomer, environmental scientist*

***Education:*** B.A., Radcliffe College, 1950, M.A., 1951, Ph.D. in astronomy, 1956

***Professional Experience:*** Harvard research fellow in solar physics, Sacramento Peak Observatory, 1955–1962; visiting fellow, Joint Institute Laboratory of Astrophysics, Colorado, 1962–1963; associate professor of astronomy, University of Maryland, 1963–1975, assistant provost, Division of Mathematics and Physical Science and Engineering, 1973–1978, acting director, Astronomy Program, 1975, professor, 1975–1980, assistant vice chancellor of academic affairs, 1978–1980; dean, College of Humanities and Science and professor of physics, Virginia Commonwealth University, 1980–1992, interim director, Center for Environmental Studies, 1992–

***Concurrent Positions:*** Research associate, Lowell Observatory, 1956–1957; consultant, Goddard Space Flight Center, National Aeronautics and Space Administration (NASA), 1963–1965

***Married:*** Henry J. Smith, 1950, died 1983

***Children:*** 2

***Elske Smith*** is a solar physicist who has conducted research at several of the prominent observatories in the country and was a member of the faculty at the University of Maryland for more than 15 years. The university has a famous astronomical center that has participated in many noted projects, such as tracking the impact of the comet Shoemaker-Levy 9 on Jupiter in 1994. In addition to her research and teaching responsibilities at Maryland, she was an assistant provost and then an assistant vice chancellor of academic affairs. At Virginia Commonwealth University she has combined her research and teaching responsibilities with an administrative appointment as a dean of the College of Humanities and Science and later as director of the Center for Environmental Studies.

This combination of experiences has given her a slightly different view of the position of women scientists. In 1977 she participated in a symposium on covert discrimination in the sciences at an American Association for the Advancement of Science national meeting—the papers given at the symposium were published as *Covert Discrimination and Women in the Sciences* (1978), edited by Judith A. Ramaley. In Smith's paper, "The Individual and the Institution," she said that her background was in the natural sciences rather than the social sciences like the majority of the other speakers. Therefore, she thought she might have a slightly different viewpoint.

As an administrator at the University of Maryland, she probably gained insight into the factors that are involved in hiring and promoting faculty members. She also interviewed a number of women scientists throughout the country and found that there were three basic types of covert discrimination against women scientists. One type may be conscious discrimination that is deliberately hidden from the oversight of offices or agencies that monitor discrimination. The second is far more general but equally more insidious, unconscious discrimination that is often manifested by attitude rather than acts. The third is the widespread discrimination related to marital status. Although the majority of Smith's respondents were employed in academia, a number worked for government agencies, and the responses were mixed from those who had experience in both areas. Some found more covert discrimination in academia, and others found more in government.

In addition to her numerous scientific papers, she published a book *Solar Flares* (1963), but she comments that the book represents the state of the art in the 1960s and is now sorely out of date. She is a coauthor of *Introductory Astronomy and Astrophysics* (1973; 2d ed., 1992). One reviewer found the new edition to be an excellent textbook for the serious science student at the first-year-undergraduate level.

Smith is a fellow of the American Association for the Advancement of Science and a member of the International Astronomical Union and American Astronomical Society. Her research includes active regions on the sun, especially flares and plages; solar chromosphere; interstellar polarization; and solar physics.

***Bibliography:*** *American Men and Women of Science* 11–19; *Contemporary Authors* v. 77–80; Herzenberg, C., *Women Scientists from Antiquity to the Present;* Ireland, N., *Index to Women of the World . . . Suppl.; Who's Who in America,* 51st ed., 1997; *Who's Who of American Women,* 20th ed., 1997–1998.

# *Solomon, Susan*

(1956– )

***atmospheric chemist***

***Education:*** B.S., Illinois Institute of Technology, 1977; M.S., University of California, Berkeley, 1979, Ph.D. in chemistry, 1981

***Professional Experience:*** Research chemist, National Oceanic and Atmospheric Administration (NOAA), 1981– ; head project scientist, National Ozone Expedition to McMurdo Sound, Antarctica, 1986–1987; adjunct faculty member, University of Colorado, Boulder, 1983–

***Concurrent Positions:*** Member, committee on solar and space physics, National Aeronautics and Space Administration (NASA), 1983–1986, space and earth science advisory committee, 1985–1988

***Married:*** Barry L. Sidwell, 1988

***Susan Solomon*** received recognition as a scientist when she led expeditions to McMurdo Sound, Antarctica, in 1986 and 1987 to examine the "hole" in the ozone layer. Her theory was that chlorofluorocarbons (CFCs) could lead to Antarctic ozone destruction when CFCs encounter large masses of stratospheric clouds. CFCs are human-made gases that were widely used in refrigerators, air conditioners, aerosol spray cans, and the manufacture of semiconductors. The research at McMurdo and elsewhere supported her theory. Her explanation for the cause of the ozone hole is now generally accepted by scientists, and it has led many countries to curtail the production and use of CFCs. She was elected to membership in the National Academy of Sciences in 1992.

In 1985, British scientists reported an ozone hole in the Southern Hemisphere over the South Pole during the pole's spring month of October. The hole was a gap in the atmosphere's ozone layer, located between the altitudes of about 32,000 and 74,000 feet (the stratosphere), which normally shields the earth from the sun's ultraviolet radiation. Scientists suspected the damage had been caused by CFCs but were unable to explain the process; Solomon hit on the solution while attending a lecture on polar stratospheric clouds. She theorized that CFC derivatives react on the cloud surfaces. She volunteered to lead the otherwise all-male expedition to McMurdo Sound in 1986 with a follow-up trip in 1987, and she continues to study the atmospheric chemistry of ozone in Antarctica as well as in the Arctic in the Northern Hemisphere.

As a child she became interested in science through watching natural-science documentaries on television when she was about ten years old, and a project during her senior year of college turned her attention toward atmospheric chemistry. The project involved measuring the reaction of ethylene and hydroxyl radical, a process that occurs in the atmosphere of Jupiter. The summer before entering graduate school, she worked on a study of ozone in the upper atmosphere at the National Center for Atmospheric Research (NCAR) in Boulder, Colorado. At the National Oceanic and Atmospheric Administration (NOAA), she first worked in the Aeronomy Laboratory developing computer models of ozone in the upper atmosphere (aeronomy is the study of the chemistry and physical phenomena in the upper atmosphere). Although she was concentrating on theoretical studies, the McMurdo Sound expeditions provided an opportunity to take up experimental work. Her measurements of chlorine dioxide in Antarctica provided direct evidence that CFCs cause the ozone holes.

In addition to her scientific papers, she is coauthor with Guy Brasseur of the book *Aeronomy of the Middle Atmosphere: Chemistry and Physics of the Stratosphere and Mesosphere* (1984, 2d ed., 1986). She has received several awards, including the J. B. MacElwane Award of the American Geophysical Union (1985) and the Gold Medal for exceptional service of the U.S. Department of Commerce (1989). She was named Scientist of the Year in 1992 by *R&D Magazine.* She is a member of the Royal Meteorological Society, the American Geophysical Union, and the American Meteorological Society. Her research includes photochemistry, transport process in the earth's stratosphere and mesosphere, and polar ozone. Her photograph is included in *Notable Twentieth-Century Scientists* and *Fortune* (October 8, 1990).

***Bibliography:*** *American Men and Women of Science* 17–19; *Notable Twentieth-Century Scientists.*

# *Spaeth, Mary Dietrich*

(1938– )

***physicist***

***Education:*** B.S. in physics and mathematics, Valparaiso University, 1960; M.S. in nuclear physics, Wayne State University, 1962

***Professional Experience:*** Member of technical staff, later senior scientist and project manager, Hughes Aircraft Company, 1962–1974; group leader, later associate program leader, laser development, Lawrence Livermore National Laboratory, 1974–1986, deputy associate director of isotope separation project, 1986–

***Married:*** 1988, divorced

***Children:*** 3

***Mary Spaeth*** is renowned for her work in developing the first tunable dye laser about 1966. The first workable laser was introduced by Theodore Maiman of Hughes Aircraft about 1960, but it was monochromatic; that is, lasers could be built to emit different colors, but once chosen, that color was fixed. There was a clear need for a tunable dye laser, a laser whose color could be changed in midstream. The term *laser* is an acronym for light amplification by stimulated emission of radiation and is the name of a device that produces a nearly parallel, nearly monochromatic, and coherent beam of light by exciting atoms to a higher energy level and causing them to radiate their energy in phase. Lasers are also called "optical masers."

Spaeth did not set out to invent the tunable laser. During a two-week pause in her research while she waited for some equipment to be delivered and since lasers were available to her at Hughes, she started adding saturable dyes to some to see if she could put together one that would switch colors. For a time she did not think she had a laser because it kept changing color, but it was doing what a laser was supposed to do. She said she put it together with glass tubes and Duco cement. Since lasers do not have an on/off switch or a plug to insert in an electrical outlet, she borrowed a large laser to serve as the pump to provide the input energy to drive her laser. It worked the first time. Since Hughes had a contract with the U.S. Army for her research at the time, the patent is owned by the government.

She does have the patent on a component that is important in making ruby range finders work. She actually had a direct order not to work on the idea, but she worked on it anyway, and Hughes has built a great many range finders using that particular component. She says she has not been interested in obtaining patents, just in devising items that work together. She also says she was lucky that lasers were just being invented when she finished her schooling and fortunate to obtain a position at Hughes where she could work with a very creative group of people who were doing pioneering work with lasers.

The next achievement for which she is credited is using the dye laser in isotope separation. The idea began to sound practical in the early 1970s when high-power, high-efficiency lasers were becoming available. The laser is now the primary source for deriving the isotopes used in nuclear reactors, and because different isotopes of the same element absorb light at different frequencies, a properly tuned dye laser can be used to separate isotopes and alter the isotopic composition of many elements. Originally, Lawrence Livermore National Laboratory worked exclusively on refining plutonium for nuclear weaponry, but now most activity is centered on providing a low-cost means of enriching uranium fuel for light-water nuclear power reactors. One of the most promising applications of the tunable dye laser is as part of a guide star project that will allow ground-based stellar observatories to achieve a resolution comparable to that received through the Hubble space telescope, an orbiting observatory that was launched in 1990.

Spaeth is one of very few women who are credited with being an inventor. In the reference work *World of Invention* (1994), she is the only woman listed under "physics" in the index, and she is also the only woman among 16 people profiled in Kenneth Brown's book *Inventors at Work: Interviews with 16 Notable American Inventors* (1988). When she was a child, her father encouraged her to be a tomboy, and he purchased carpentry tools for her, which she learned how to use when she was only two or three years old, and he continued to give her footballs, baseballs, and tools as she grew up. She said she always thought of herself more as a person than as a girl. She became interested in science through a science class in the seventh grade. Although her master's degree was in nuclear physics, she was not interested in nuclear weapons, and it was only when she began to see the potential application of the tunable dye laser that she accepted a job at Lawrence Livermore to research enriching uranium for nuclear power plants.

She has found in her work that once people realize a woman is competent and can contribute to the job at hand, there are no problems being accepted as a part of the group. One reason she left Hughes is that there was a unwritten policy that women could not become a line manager—and she was unable to obtain such a position even though she could sometimes get work done faster than her male colleagues could. Once people realized that a woman can talk about technical problems and understand them, they will go out of their way to be helpful. At Hughes there were particular individuals who discriminated against women and minorities, but that had nothing to do with comparing the working climate of a corporation versus that of a government laboratory. At Lawrence Livermore, she does not feel any discrimination because the manager supports everyone who contributes to the work.

***Bibliography:*** Brown, K., *Inventors at Work; Notable Twentieth-Century Scientists;* Stanley, A., *Mothers and Daughters of Invention; World of Invention.*

# Spurlock, Jeanne
(1921– )
*psychiatrist*

***Education:*** Student, Spelman College, 1940–1942, Roosevelt University, 1942–1943; M.D., Howard University, 1947

***Professional Experience:*** Intern, Provident Hospital, Chicago, 1947–1948; resident in general psychiatry, Cook County Hospital, Chicago, 1948–1950; fellow in child psychiatry, Institute for Juvenile Research, Chicago, 1950–1951, staff psychiatrist, 1951–1953; staff psychiatrist, Women's and Children's Hospital, Chicago, 1951–1953; adult and child psychoanalytic training, Chicago Institute for Psychoanalysis, 1953–1962; director, Children's Psychosomatic Unit, Neuropsychiatric Institute, Chicago, 1953–1959; assistant professor of psychiatry, University of Illinois College of Medicine, 1953–1959; psychiatrist and chief of Child Psychiatry Clinic, Michael Reese Hospital, Chicago, 1960–1968; private practice in psychiatry, 1951–1968; chair, Department of Psychiatry, Meharry Medical College, Nashville, 1968–1973; visiting scientist, National Institute for Mental Health, 1973–1974; deputy medical director, American Psychiatric Association, 1974–

***Concurrent Positions:*** Clinical professor, George Washington University College of Medicine, 1974– and Howard University College of Medicine, 1974–

*Jeanne Spurlock* is a noted psychiatrist who has held many high-level appointments in hospitals and clinics as a specialist in child psychiatry. However, she changed the emphasis of her career in 1974 when she was appointed deputy medical director of the American Psychiatric Association. In that capacity, her work is primarily administrative although she maintains a small private practice and is a clinical professor at two local medical schools. She serves as a lobbyist to policymakers to ensure funding for medical education and postmedical education, particularly for minorities. Much of her work focuses on issues of minority and powerless people who are subject to discrimination—children, minorities, and women. She also has been working with gay people and graduates of foreign medical schools who practice in the United States. She is involved in the recruitment and training efforts of minorities for research and is in charge of a fellowship program for minority psychiatric residents sponsored by the association.

When she was completing her own psychiatric training, it was very difficult for minorities to obtain residencies. In fact, she had difficulties in all of her training. She was inspired to be a physician when, as a child of nine, she suffered a severe leg injury that she felt was mishandled by the Detroit hospital that treated her. She wanted to become a better kind of doctor. She worked full time while she was a scholarship student at Spelman College, but even so, that school was too expensive for her. She studied another two years at Roosevelt University before entering Howard University Medical School on a special accelerated program. She received her M.D. in 1947. She had a series of short-term appointments and training programs until she became director of the Children's Psychosomatic Unit of the Neuropsychiatric Institute in 1953. She then received several high-level appointments in clinics and medical schools until she went to work for the American Psychiatric Association.

She is coeditor of *Black Families in Crisis: The Middle Class* (1988), in which she wrote about stresses in parenting and male-female relationships. She was also coeditor of *Women's Progress: Promises and Problems* (1990), which is focused on various aspects of mothering, including the changing face of adoption in the United States, the problems of working mothers, the special problems of mothers of disabled children, and homosexuality and parenting. Spurlock wrote the chapter on single mothers. She is coauthor of *Culturally Diverse Children and*

*Adolescents* (1994), which addresses the mental health needs of African American, Latino, Asian American, and Amerindian children and adolescents. In this book, the authors explain how the assessment, diagnostic, and treatment phases of clinical work may be modified for cultural relevancy. She is a member of the National Medical Association and the American Academy of Child Psychiatry.

***Bibliography:*** Ireland, N., *Index to Women of the World . . . Suppl.; Notable Black American Women; Who's Who among Black Americans,* 4th ed., 1985.

# *Steitz, Joan (Argetsinger)*
(1941– )
## *biochemist, molecular biologist*

***Education:*** B.S., Antioch College, 1963; M.A., Harvard University, 1967, Ph.D. in biochemistry and molecular biology, 1968; honorary degrees: 6

***Professional Experience:*** Postdoctoral fellow, Laboratory of Molecular Biology, Cambridge University, 1967–1970; assistant professor of molecular biophysics and biochemistry, Yale University, 1970–1974, associate professor, 1974–1978, professor of molecular biophysics and biochemistry, 1978– , investigator, Howard Hughes Medical Institute, 1986– , Henry Ford II Professor of Molecular Biophysics and Biochemistry, 1992–

***Concurrent Positions:*** Director, Jane C. Childs Memorial Fund for Medicine, 1991– ; trustee, Cold Spring Harbor Laboratory, 1992–

***Married:*** Thomas A. Steitz, 1966

***Children:*** 1

***Joan Steitz*** is one of the most prominent scientists in the field of molecular genetics, and one of her most significant contributions is her discovery of small nuclear ribonucleoproteins, or snRNPs, pronounced "snurps." She is working in a field that was not even discovered when she was in high school. While in graduate school at Harvard, her thesis adviser was James D. Watson, who with Francis Crick had demonstrated the double-helix structure of DNA in the 1950s. She pursued postdoctoral studies at Cambridge University where she worked with Crick on how bacterial ribosomes recognize where to start protein synthesis on messenger RNA (mRNA). In 1986, she was awarded the National Medal of Science, one of the highest awards given to an American scientist. These awards are given by the National Science Foundation each year to scientists selected from all disciplines in a ceremony that takes place in the White House with the president presenting the awards. Steitz was elected to membership in the National Academy of Sciences in 1983.

The best known of the snRNPs are involved in the processing of mRNA in the cell nucleus of mammals. By a process called splicing, the double-stranded DNA is first transcribed into single-stranded RNA; then the sections are eventually rejoined in the same order they occurred in on the DNA molecule. The team discovered that some patients with rheumatic diseases made antibodies against their own snRNPs, which resulted in the development of the splicing process. When physicians determine which antibodies patients have, they have additional clues to diagnosing their diseases. Steitz received the 1996 City of Medicine award from Durham, North Carolina for her discovery of snRNPs.

She has said that her father's support of her interest in science was critical in her becoming a scientist. As a child she found it was fun to find out things that no one had ever known before, and she stresses the importance of being interested in what you are doing regardless of what occupation you choose. She advises future scientists to take on the most challenging problems they can find and pursue them to the best of their ability. She mentions the ability to communicate with people and the ability to work with other researchers as important skills for a scientist. Among her honors, she considers the Weizmann Woman and Science Award (1994) from the New York Academy of Sciences as among the most gratifying because it promotes women scientists. Although conditions are improving for women scientists, she felt the need for women role models when she was starting her career in science and believes the presence of women scientists can be an inspiration to women students.

She has received numerous other awards, including the Eli Lilly award in biological chemistry (1976), U.S. Steel Foundation award in molecular biology (1982), the triennial Warren Prize of Massachusetts General Hospital (1989), and the Christopher Columbus Discovery Award from the Christopher Columbus Fellowship Foundation for biomedical research (1992). She is a fellow of the American Association for the Advancement of Science and a member of the American Society of Biological Chemists, American Academy of Arts and Sciences, American Philosophical Society, and New York Academy of Sciences. Her research includes control of transcription and translation, RNA and DNA sequence analysis, structure and function of small ribonucleoproteins from eukaryotes, and RNA processing. Her photograph is included in *Notable Women in the Life Sciences.*

***Bibliography:*** *American Men and Women of Science* 12–19; Herzenberg, C., *Women Scientists from Antiquity to the Present; Notable Women in the Life Sciences; Who's Who in America,* 51st ed., 1997; *Who's Who in Science and Engineering,* 3d ed., 1996–1997.

# *Stubbe, Joanne*
## (1946– )
## *chemist*

***Education:*** B.S., University of Pennsylvania, 1968; Ph.D. in chemistry, University of California, Berkeley, 1971

***Professional Experience:*** Postdoctoral fellowship in chemistry, University of California, Los Angeles, 1971–1972; assistant professor of chemistry, Williams College, 1972–1977; postdoctoral fellowship, Brandeis University, 1975–1977; assistant professor, Department of Pharmacology, Yale University School of Medicine, 1977–1980; from assistant professor to professor, University of Wisconsin, Madison, 1980–1987; professor, Department of Chemistry, Massachusetts Institute of Technology, 1987–1992, John C. Sheehan Professor of Chemistry and Biology, 1992–

***Joanne Stubbe*** has made notable contributions to understanding the mechanisms of enzyme catalysis and has synthesized a broad spectrum of important nucleotide derivatives. Her research has focused on the mechanism of two classes of nucleotide reductases, enzymes that catalyze the key step in DNA biosynthesis, the conversion of nucleotides to deoxynucleotides. She was elected to membership in the National Academy of Sciences in 1992.

Her research has helped scientists understand the ways in which enzymes catalyze, or cause, chemical reactions. She has focused on the mechanism of nucleotide reductases, the enzymes involved in the biosynthesis of DNA (deoxyribonucleic acid), the molecule of heredity. Her work has led to the design and synthesis of nucleotides that have potential antitumor, antivirus, and antiparasite activity. Ribonucleotide reductases are major targets for the design of antitumor and antiviral agents because inhibiting these enzymes interferes with the biosynthesis of DNA and cell growth. She has also explained the mechanism by which the antitumor antibiotic bleomycin degrades DNA (bleomycin is used to kill cancer cells, a function thought to be related to its ability to bind to and degrade DNA). Other research interests include the design of so-called suicide inhibitors and mechanisms of DNA repair enzymes.

In 1986 she received the Pfizer Award in Enzyme Chemistry from the American Chemical Society, a gold medal award given each year to an individual who has done outstanding work in enzyme chemistry and who has not passed his or her fortieth birthday. She has also received the ICI-Stuart Pharmaceutical Award for excellence in chemistry (1989), a teaching award from the Massachusetts Institute of Technology (1990), and the Arthur C. Cope Scholar Award (1993).

After she received her graduate degree, her first two published papers outlined the mechanism of reactions involving the enzymes enolase, which metabolizes carbohydrates, and pyruvate kinase. She had a postdoctoral year in chemistry at the University of California, Los Angeles, and then accepted a second postdoctoral fellowship from the National Institutes of Health, which she spent at Brandeis University while on leave from her faculty position at Williams College. After having appointments at the Yale University School of Medicine and the University of Wisconsin, Madison, she moved to the Massachusetts Institute of Technology as professor of chemistry and was appointed a distinguished professor in 1992.

She is a member of the American Chemical Society, American Society of Biological Chemists, Protein Society, and American Academy of Arts and Sciences. Her photograph is included in *Chemical & Engineering News* (April 28, 1986).

***Bibliography:*** *Notable Twentieth-Century Scientists; Who's Who in Science and Engineering,* 2d ed., 1994–1995.

# *Sudarkasa, Niara*
(1938– )
***anthropologist***

***Education:*** Student, Fisk University, 1953–1956; B.A. in sociology, Oberlin College, 1957; M.A., Columbia University, 1959, Ph.D. in anthropology, 1964; honorary degrees: Fisk University and Oberlin College, 1988, Sojourner-Douglass College, 1989, Franklin and Marshall College, 1990, Susquehanna University, 1990

***Professional Experience:*** Assistant professor of anthropology, New York University, 1964–1967; assistant professor of anthropology and research associate, Center for Research in Economic Development, University of Michigan, 1967–1970, associate professor, 1970–1976, professor, 1976–1987, director, Center for Afro-American and African Studies, 1981–1984, associate vice president for academic affairs, 1984–1987; president, Lincoln University, 1987–

***Married:*** Sudarkasa, divorced; John M. Clark

***Children:*** 1

***Niara Sudarkasa*** is renowned as an authority in the fields of African women, especially Yoruba women traders; West African migration; and the African-American and African family. She has also researched higher-education policies for black Americans and other minorities, and she is an advocate for minority access to education at the university level. She was the first black woman at the University of Michigan to receive tenure and the first woman president of Lincoln University in Pennsylvania.

As a result of her studies of the African continent, she adopted an African name. "Niara" is an adaptation of a Swahili word and means a woman of high purpose; the name "Sudarkasa" was her first husband's name. Her birth name was Gloria Albertha Marshall.

She was an honor student in her childhood, and at age 14 she won a Ford Foundation Early Entrant Scholarship to Fisk University. In her junior year she went to Oberlin College as an exchange student and decided to stay there to receive her undergraduate degree. It was there that she began studying about Africa. Her grandparents came from the Caribbean area, and for the first time she realized black people's cultural ties to Africa. After completing her undergraduate degree at age 18, she went to Columbia University for graduate study. In 1960–1963 she had a Ford Foundation Foreign Area Training fellowship to study the Yoruba language and the role of Yoruba women in the local West African markets, first at the University of London School of Oriental and African Studies and then in Nigeria. She spent 1963–1965 at the University of Chicago as a fellow with a Carnegie Foundation project on a comparative study of new nations.

After receiving her doctorate, she was an assistant professor at New York University. In 1967 she moved to the University of Michigan where she stayed for 20 years. She was the first black woman to be promoted to full professor in the Division of Arts and Sciences as well as being the first tenured black woman. She directed the Center for Afro-American and African Studies and was a research scientist at the Center for Research in Economic Development. She became politically active while she was at Michigan, advocating on behalf of the students for a black studies program and more black and minority students in the university. When she was appointed associate vice president for academic affairs in 1984, she was responsible for academic policy, special academic projects, and minority student affairs.

Sudarkasa has applied her study of West African culture to the African American family structure, with an emphasis on the role of black women within the family and society. She protests the imposition of white middle-class family norms onto the study of black community life. Like the black family, black women have been severely criticized and blamed because of their roles in the family and society, but the imposition of colonial norms in Africa changed those roles. For example, African women traditionally have been active in economic and social activities outside the home, and they have participated equally in family responsibilities; but the introduction of Western technology has eliminated many traditional jobs, and women have been denied access to the necessary education to qualify for the new types of employment. The jobs in which women now dominate are classified as low status and are poorly financed.

Another of her projects is stressing the importance of black colleges because they provide for black students in ways that white colleges cannot. She says that although a large percentage of black students attend predominantly white universities, black colleges have historically produced more leaders; black college graduates are seven times more likely to pursue doctorates than their counterparts in white colleges.

In 1987, she was selected to be the first woman president of Lincoln University, one of the oldest black colleges in the United States. For many years it accepted only male students, but it became a coeducational institution several years ago. The school has a strong science reputation and has an international studies program. Sudarkasa is a member of the American Ethnological Society, American Anthropological Association, African Studies Association, American Association for Higher Education, and Council on Foreign Relations. She is listed in some early references as "Gloria Marshall." Her photograph is included in *Ebony* (February 1988 and July 1996).

***Bibliography:*** *American Men and Women of Science* 11–13; *Black Women in America; Notable Black American Women; Who's Who of American Women,* 20th ed., 1997–1998.

# *Sullivan, Kathryn D.*
(1951– )
## *geologist, astronaut*

***Education:*** B.S. in earth sciences, University of California, Santa Cruz, 1973; Ph.D. in geology, Dalhousie University, 1978; honorary degrees: Dalhousie University, 1985, State University of New York at Utica, 1990, Stevens Institute of Technology, 1992

***Professional Experience:*** Staff member, 1978, National Aeronautics and Space Administration (NASA), astronaut 1979–1993, missions STS 41-G (1984), STS-31 (1990), and STS-45 (1992); chief scientist, National Oceanic and Atmospheric Administration, 1992–1995; director, Ohio Museum of Science and Industry, Columbus, Ohio, 1995–

***Concurrent Positions:*** adjunct professor, Rice University, 1985–1992; commander, U.S. Naval Reserve

***Children:*** 2

***Kathryn D. Sullivan*** was one of the first six women selected to be trained in the astronaut program in 1978, and she was the first American woman to perform a space walk. The first six women were selected for a training program in scientific, engineering, and medical duties, but none was to be trained in piloting the space shuttle. However, most of the women in the program took flying lessons anyway so they would be prepared to land the shuttle in an emergency. Sullivan passed her training tests and became an astronaut in 1979. Prior to completing a doctorate in geology, she had participated in several oceanographic expeditions under the auspices of the U.S. Geological Survey and the Woods Hole Oceanographic Institution.

Her shuttle assignments included software development, lead chase photography of launches and landings, and orbiter and cargo testing. She was a member of the spacesuit monitoring and extravehicular activity (EVA) crew and served as capsule communicator in Mission Control for numerous shuttle missions. Her first space mission was as a mission specialist on STS 41-G in 1984; Sally Ride was also a member of the crew. Sullivan was the first woman to perform an EVA, with orbiter commander David Leetsma, and the two demonstrated the feasibility of in-flight satellite refueling. She said that since her field is marine geophysics, she looked forward to walking in space and that the idea of being able to look back at the earth from orbit was very exciting. She would also like to do more space exploration.

On her second mission, STS-31 in 1990, she was a mission specialist when the crew deployed the Hubble space telescope (the telescope proved to have a defective mirror, and another shuttle crew several years later installed a new mirror). On her third mission, STS-45 in 1992, she was a mission specialist and payload commander.

She resigned from the astronaut corps in 1992 and was selected by President George Bush to be chief scientist of the National Oceanic and Atmospheric Administration (NOAA), replacing Sylvia Earle in that position—Earle is famous for underwater activities while Sullivan is noted for space activities. Although Sullivan enjoyed her work with NASA, she left because she desired new challenges in her career. Of the first eight women astronauts, only Bonnie Dunbar, Anna Fisher, and Shannon Lucid are still active (Judy Resnik died). Sullivan resigned from NOAA in 1995 to become director of the Ohio Museum of Science and Industry.

She has received a number of awards, including the NASA Exceptional Service Medal (1988 and 1991), National Air and Space Museum Trophy (1985), NASA Space Flight Medal (1984 and 1990), Haley Space Flight Award of the American Institute of Aeronautics and Astronautics (1991), Space Achievement Award of the American Aeronautic Society (1991), and NASA Outstanding Leadership Medal (1992). She is a member of the American Institute of Aeronautics and Astronautics, Geological Society of America, American Geophysical Union, and Society of Women Geographers. Post-NASA photographs of her can be found in *Working Woman* (November–December 1996) and *Science* (April 24, 1995).

***Bibliography:*** *American Men and Women of Science* 19; Herzenberg, C., *Women Scientists from Antiquity to the Present;* Ireland, N., *Index to Women of the World . . . Suppl.;* Oberg, A. R., *Spacefarers of the '80s and '90s;* O'Connor, K., *Sally Ride and the New Astronauts;* U.S. National Aeronautics and Space Administration, *Astronaut Fact Book; Who's Who in Science and Engineering,* 2d ed., 1994–1995; *Who's Who of American Women,* 19th ed., 1995–1996.

# T

## *Taylor, Kathleen Christine*
(1942– )
***physical chemist***

***Education:*** B.A., Rutgers University, 1964; Ph.D. in physical chemistry, Northwestern University, 1968

***Professional Experience:*** Fellow, University of Edinburgh, 1968–1970; associate senior research chemist, General Motors Corporation, 1970–1974, senior research chemist, 1974–1975, assistant head, Physical Chemistry Department, 1975–1983, head, Environmental Science Department, Research Laboratories, 1983–1985, head, Physical Chemistry Department, 1985–

***Kathleen Taylor*** is an expert on catalytic converters for automobiles, and in 1988, she was awarded the Garvan Medal of the American Chemical Society, an award sponsored by the Olin Corporation and awarded to an American woman chemist each year. In her early days with the research staff of General Motors, her original research dealt with heterogeneous catalysis, especially with reductive processes involving nitric oxide on ruthenium and noble metal catalysis. Applications of this research by her group led to understanding the catalytic conversion of nitrogen oxides in automobile exhaust, and she published a book on the topic, *Automobile Catalytic Converters* (1984). Her administrative responsibilities in a major corporate research department have involved the following areas: catalysis, surface chemistry, surface coatings, corrosion, combustion, batteries, fuel cells, and chemical processes. She was elected to membership in the National Academy of Engineering in 1995.

She was hired by General Motors in 1970, the year Congress passed the Clean Air Act, which meant that corporations needed new catalysts to meet the stringent limits Congress had set on vehicle exhaust emission of carbon monoxide, hydrocarbons, and nitrogen oxides. Her doctoral thesis had been on catalysis research, and she first worked to develop the appropriate catalysts for oxidizing carbon monoxide and hydrocarbons, then catalysts that would simultaneously reduce nitrogen oxides. She advanced quickly through the research ranks to become head of the Environmental Science Department and then made a lateral move to head the Physical Chemistry Department. A year later, the Electrochemistry Department was merged with her department.

She has published about 30 papers on her research, a fairly good number for a corporate research scientist as corporate legal departments usually attempt to restrict publication of research results until patent protection is in place. She is a member of the American Chemical Society, Catalysis Society (North America), Materials Research Society, and Society of Automotive Engineers. Her research includes surface chemistry, heterogeneous catalysis, and catalytic control of automobile exhaust emissions. Her photograph is included in *Chemical & Engineering News* (November 28, 1988, and April 26, 1993).

***Bibliography:*** *American Men and Women of Science* 12–19; *Who's Who in Science and Engineering,* 3d ed., 1996–1997.

# *Tharp, Marie*
(1920– )
*geologist*

***Education:*** B.A., Ohio University, 1943; M.A. in geology, University of Michigan, 1945; B.S. in mathematics, University of Tulsa, 1948

***Professional Experience:*** Junior geologist, U.S. Geological Survey, 1944; geologist, Stanolind Oil & Gas Company, Oklahoma, 1945–1948; assistant, Lamont-Doherty Geological Observatory, Columbia University, 1949–1952, research geologist, 1952–1960, research scientist, 1961–1963, research associate, 1963–1968; oceanographer, U.S. Naval Oceanographic Office, 1968–1983; owner, map distribution business and consultant, 1983–

***Marie Tharp*** is a geologist who pioneered charting the ocean floor at a time when little was known about undersea geology, and the detailed maps she prepared indicated features that helped other scientists understand the structure and evolution of the bottom of the ocean. Her particular contribution was her discovery of the valley that divides the Mid-Atlantic Ridge, which convinced other geologists that the ocean floor was being created at these ridges in various parts of the world and spreading outward. The confirmation of "seafloor spreading" led to the eventual acceptance of the theory of continental drift, which is now called "plate tectonics."

Scientists were not interested in the seafloor until an earthquake near the Great Banks in the Atlantic Ocean in 1929 broke the transatlantic cables between the United States and Europe. Long before the age of satellites, these cables were the only means of transatlantic telephone communication, and AT&T Bell Laboratories wanted to know where to anticipate future earthquakes before laying new cables. A few studies of the Mid-Atlantic Ridge had been made in the 1870s and between 1925 and 1927, but exploration had stopped during World War II. Working with geologist Bruce C. Heezen at the Lamont-Doherty Geological Observatory, Tharp began preparing a "physiographic" diagram of the Atlantic Ocean floor. The resulting maps show how the floor would look if all the water were drained away—she was unable to prepare three-dimensional maps because such maps were classified by the U.S. Navy between 1952 and 1962. Her first map showed a deep valley dividing the crest of the Mid-Atlantic Ridge. This valley represented the place where newly formed rocks came up from inside the earth, splitting apart the mid-ocean ridge. At the time, Heezen and other scientists thought that continental drift was impossible. Most people believed that the earth was a shrinking globe, cooling and contracting from its initial hot birth.

Another group was studying earthquakes in the Atlantic, and Tharp compared these data to Heezen's, whose team found that the epicenters of the earthquakes fell within the suspected rift valley. For several years only the Lamont scientists knew of the valley's existence until Heezen presented the data at several scientific meetings during 1956. By 1959, most of the skeptics had been convinced the valley existed, because of an underwater movie of the valley made by Jacques Cousteau, who towed a camera across it; today, scientists understand how the rift valley represents the pulling apart of the seafloor as the new rock spreads outward from the ridge. Tharp described the research in an article, "Mappers of the Deep," in the October 1986 issue of *Natural History;* the article includes copies of the maps.

Heezen and Tharp continued working on their North Atlantic map and expanded their work to cover the globe. In 1977, they published the World Ocean Floor Panorama, based on all available geological and geophysical data as well as more than 5 million miles of ocean-floor soundings. For many years, Tharp herself was not able to participate in recording ocean-floor soundings because women were not permitted on U.S.

Navy ships; however, she went on several research cruises in the late 1960s.

She had a very good background for her work. Her father was a soil surveyor for the U.S. Department of Agriculture, and the family frequently moved from one area to another owing to his assignments. He encouraged her to choose a job simply because she liked doing it. Since so many young men were in the armed services during World War II, the University of Michigan opened its program in geology to women for the first time, and she entered the master's program there. That program trained students in basic geology and guaranteed a job in the petroleum industry. At the time, women were not permitted to participate in field research—a restriction that was quite common in mining, petroleum, and other industries. Tharp was therefore assigned to organize the maps and data for the all-male crews.

At Columbia University's Lamont-Doherty Geological Observatory, she was hired as a research assistant for one of the geology professors and assigned to helping graduate students with their data; she never told anyone she had a master's degree in geology. Heezen asked for assistance so often that soon she was working with him exclusively, and their partnership lasted 20 years until his death in 1977. Their work was funded partially by the U.S. Navy. She retired from the observatory and her later appointment with the U.S. Navy in 1983 and operates a map distribution business and consults for oceanographers.

She received the Hubbard Medal of the National Geographic Society in 1978. Her photograph is included in *Notable Twentieth-Century Scientists.*

***Bibliography:*** *American Men and Women of Science* 11–12; *Notable Twentieth-Century Scientists;* Rossiter, M., *Women Scientists in America.*

# *Thomas, Martha Jane (Bergin)*
(1926– )
## ***analytical chemist, physical chemist***

***Education:*** B.A., Radcliffe College, 1945; M.A., Boston University, 1950, Ph.D. in chemistry, 1952; M.B.A., Northeastern University, 1981

***Professional Experience:*** Senior engineer in charge of chemical laboratory, General Telephone and Electronics Corporation (GTE), 1945–1959, group leader, lamp material engineering laboratories, Lighting Products Division, 1959–1966, section head, chemical and phosphor laboratory, Sylvania Lighting Center, 1966–1972, manager of technical assistance laboratories, GTE Sylvania lighting products group, Sylvania Electric Products, Inc., 1972–1981, technical director, Technical Service Laboratories, 1981–1983, director, Technical Quality Control, 1983–1993; retired 1993

***Concurrent Positions:*** Instructor in evening division, Boston University, 1952–1970; adjunct professor of chemistry, University of Rhode Island, 1974–1993

***Married:*** George R. Thomas, 1955

***Children:*** 4

***Martha Thomas*** is renowned for her work in phosphor chemistry at Sylvania Electric Products. In 1983, she was the first woman to be made a director in that division, and she was one of the few women then working in phosphor chemistry. Phosphors are the powdery substances used to coat the inside of fluorescent lighting tubes, and her inventions included developing the phosphors that made possible Sylvania's natural-daylight fluorescent lamps and made mercury lamps 10 percent brighter.

She received at least seven patents in the field, the first being for a method of etching the fine tungsten coils that were designed to improve telephone switchboard lights. She went on to establish two pilot plants for the preparation of phosphors—pilot plants are experimental industrial setups in which processes or techniques planned for use in full-scale operation are tested in advance. She also developed a natural white phosphor that allowed fluorescent lamps to impart daylight hues.

Thomas comments that even as a child she had an intense interest in science, and she pursued that interest as an undergraduate at Radcliffe, graduating from there at 19. She planned to enter medical school but was offered a job at Sylvania, later called GTE, and since it was the first nonteaching job she was offered, she accepted it. Although the changes in the name are somewhat confusing, she actually worked for one company for about 45 years. She attended graduate school part time while working and received her doctorate in 1952. She met her future husband in graduate school, and they married in 1955. She returned to school again in 1980 on a part-time basis to obtain a master's degree in business administration so she could handle her new responsibilities as a manager. Although she had a heavy schedule between family and research, she taught evening chemistry classes at Boston University for about 20 years and served as an adjunct professor of chemistry at the University of Rhode Island.

Even though she was not following the cultural norms of the period to stay at home with her children, she was not tempted to give up her scientific career, explaining that if you were a woman in science at that time, you had to stay with it unequivocally. However, she accorded her family the highest priority in life.

She was named New England Inventor of the Year at a 1991 event sponsored by Boston's Museum of Science, the Inventors Association of New England, and the Boston Patent Law Association. She has also received the National Achievement Award of the Society of Women Engineers (1965), the Gold Plate of the American Academy of Achievement (1966), and distinguished graduate awards from Radcliffe College, Boston University, and Northeastern University. She is a fellow of the American Institute of Chemists and a member of the American Chemical Society, Electrochemical Society, and Society of Women Engineers. Her research includes phosphors, photoconductors, ion exchange membranes, complex ions, and instrumental analysis.

***Bibliography:*** *American Men and Women of Science* 11–19; *Notable Twentieth-Century Scientists;* Stanley, A., *Mothers and Daughters of Invention.*

# *Thornton, Kathryn (Cordell)*
(1952– )
## *physicist, astronaut*

***Education:*** B.S., Auburn University, 1974; M.S., University of Virginia, 1977, Ph.D. in physics, 1979

***Professional Experience:*** NATO fellow, Max Planck Institute for Nuclear Physics, Germany, 1979–1980; physicist, U.S. Army Foreign Science and Technical Center, Charlottesville, Virginia, 1980–1984; staff member, National Aeronautics and Space Administration (NASA), 1984, astronaut 1985– , missions STS-33 (1989), STS-49 (1992), STS-61 (1993), and STS-73 (1995)

***Married:*** Stephen T. Thornton

***Children:*** 3

*Kathryn Thornton* is a physicist who joined the program of the National Aeronautics and Space Administration (NASA) in 1984 and qualified as an astronaut in 1985. The usual assignment schedule was that both men and women handled other roles as mission specialists for four to five years before working in space, and that schedule held for Thornton. [There is some confusion because some people are called mission specialists and some are called astronauts. It appears that once a person in the astronaut program actually goes into space, he or she is designated an astronaut; prior to that, people are called mission specialists. However, other people are called astronauts as soon as they pass their first year of training, but perhaps NASA has changed its categories over the years. There are also payload specialists, defined by NASA's *Astronaut Fact Book* as "career scientists or engineers selected by their employer or country for their expertise in conducting a specific experiment or commercial venture on a space shuttle mission."]

Thornton's first mission was as a mission specialist for STS-33 in 1989, but she did not go into space aboard the space shuttle *Discovery* on that mission. Her second mission was STS-49 (1992) aboard the space shuttle *Endeavour* on its maiden flight, and her third was STS-61 (1993), again in *Endeavour.* Her last flight, STS-73 (1995) aboard the space shuttle *Columbia,* was a memorable one, for on that flight, she had a starring role in the taping of gags for comedian Tim Allen's television show *Home Improvement,* the first footage ever specially shot in space for a television series. In the scene, she was taped using a screwdriver and spinning along with it in the gravity-free environment. That episode was not the first time she was featured in the media, however, for a few years earlier, during the *Endeavour* voyage of 1993, she was featured on the "Chronicles" page of *Time* (December 20, 1993).

In common with other current astronauts, she has a solid scientific background with a doctorate in physics and a postdoctoral appointment at the Max Planck Institute for Nuclear Physics in Germany. Following that appointment, she was a physicist with an army science and technology center before joining NASA. She is a member of the American Association for the Advancement of Science and the American Physical Society.

***Bibliography:*** *American Men and Women of Science* 19; U.S. National Aeronautics and Space Administration, *Astronaut Fact Book; Who's Who in Science and Engineering,* 3d ed., 1996–1997; *Who's Who of American Women,* 19th ed., 1995–1996.

# *Tinsley, Beatrice Muriel (Hill)*
(1941–1981)
***astronomer***

***Education:*** B.Sc., University of Canterbury, New Zealand, 1961, M.Sc. in physics, 1963; Ph.D. in astronomy, University of Texas, Austin, 1967

***Professional Experience:*** Fellow, University of Texas, Austin, 1967–1968; visiting scientist in physics, University of Texas, Dallas, 1969–1973, assistant professor of astronomy, 1973–1974; associate professor in astronomy, Yale University, 1975–1978, professor, 1978–1981

***Married:*** Brian Tinsley, 1961, divorced 1974

***Children:*** 2

***Beatrice Tinsley*** is renowned as the first person to make a realistic, computer-generated model of how the color and brightness of a galaxy change as the stars that make up the galaxy are born, grow old, and die. Before her research, astronomers treated galaxies as static, unchanging objects. Since galaxies are the milestones that astronomers use to measure the universe as a whole, her evolutionary models of galaxies have had a profound impact on cosmology, the branch of astronomy that deals with the general structure and evolution of the universe. Despite her short life she had an extremely prolific and successful career; however, she also encountered most of the striking difficulties that are faced by women scientists.

After receiving her doctorate she found there were no opportunities for her as an astronomer in Dallas, Texas, where she lived with her husband and two adopted children. Frustrated by the situation, she obtained a position as a visiting scientist at the newly formed University of Texas, Dallas, and received part-time National Science Foundation funding. She also kept up communication with other scientists by visits to Mt. Wilson and Mt. Palomar observatories and to the University of Maryland.

In developing her models of galaxies while working on her doctoral dissertation, she added up the colors and luminosities of the evolving stars to find the total color and luminosity of the entire galaxy as it developed, and she continued this work with funding from her grant. Since she was unable to obtain a permanent position at Dallas, she moved to Yale University as an associate professor, and at Yale, she continued her research on models of galaxies. She became increasingly convinced that galaxies evolve so much and in such complex ways that they cannot be used as static fixtures by which to measure the structure of the universe. Her models demonstrated how the results of work in many other areas of astronomy could be synthesized into models of the evolution of galaxies far more accurately than any previous models, and she was largely responsible for establishing the photometric evolution of galaxies as a field of study in astronomy.

She was an extremely disciplined child who organized self-imposed timetables for herself. A brilliant student, she skipped one grade of school and studied mathematics at the boys' high school in her community because the girls' school did not offer upper-level classes in that subject. She studied physics at Canterbury University, and although she was interested in astronomy and cosmology as an undergraduate, there were no facilities available for her to write a master's thesis on the subject.

After she and fellow physicist Brian Tinsley married in 1961, they moved to Dallas where he had a position with the University of Texas in atmospheric physics. There were no opportunities in Dallas for her studies, so she commuted 400 miles round-trip to Austin to work on her dissertation on the evolution of galaxies. After she completed her doctorate, the couple adopted two children; she was a visiting scientist at the University of Texas in Dallas and joined the faculty in 1973. She and her husband divorced before she went to Yale, and while working at that institution in about 1978, she learned that a lesion on her leg was a melanoma, a malignant skin cancer. The cancer later spread to her vital organs, and she died in 1981.

Among the several awards Tinsley received was the Annie Jump Cannon prize in 1974, named for Annie Jump Cannon (1863–1941), an astronomer at the Harvard Observatory who specialized in stellar spectra and the first women to be appointed as a member of the Harvard Corporation. Tinsley is commemorated by a biennial prize awarded by the American Astronomical Society for exceptionally creative or innovative research and by a visiting professorship of astronomy at the University of Texas, Austin. She was a member of the American Astronomical Society, Royal Astronomical Society, and International Astronomical Union. A list of her publications is included in *Women in Chemistry and Physics,* and her obituary and photograph are in *Physics Today* (September 1981).

***Bibliography:*** *American Men and Women of Science* 12–16; *Notable Women in the Physical Sciences; Who's Who in Technology Today* v. 5; *Women in Chemistry and Physics.*

# *Tolbert, Margaret Ellen (Mayo)*
(1943– )
***biochemist***

***Education:*** B.S., Tuskegee University, 1967; M.S., Wayne State University, 1968; Ph.D. in biochemistry, Brown University, 1974

***Professional Experience:*** Research technician in biochemistry, Tuskegee University, 1969, instructor in mathematics, 1969–1970; instructor, Opportunities Industrialization Center, Providence, Rhode Island, 1971–1972; assistant professor of chemistry, Tuskegee University, 1973–1976; associate professor, pharmaceutical chemistry, and associate dean, School of Pharmacy, Florida A&M University, 1977–1978; professor of chemistry and director, Research and Development, Carver Research Foundation, Tuskegee University, 1979–1987; supervisor of budgets, control analyst, and senior planner, BP Research, British Petroleum Corporation, 1987–1989; director, Research Improvement in Minority Institutions Program, National Science Foundation; interim executive secretary, Committee on Education and Training, Federal Coordinated Council on Science, Engineering, and Technology; consulting scientist, Howard Hughes Medical Institute, 1994; director, division of educational programs, Argonne National Laboratories, 1994–

***Children:*** 1

M*argaret Tolbert* had already established herself as a noted researcher on the biochemistry of the liver when she changed her career plans in the late 1980s. At that time, it was apparent that she was particularly adept at science administration, having been able to place the Carver Research Foundation on a sound financial basis and having had an appointment as an associate dean. In 1987, she accepted a position in corporate planning with BP Research, a division of British Petroleum Corporation. At BP she was a member of the team that brought about the merger of the technical interests of British Petroleum and Standard Oil Company of Ohio, and she also involved herself with the development of science education, including programs in science museums. The National Science Foundation then recruited her as program director for the Research Improvement in Minority Institutions Program. She also worked with the Howard Hughes Medical Institute to establish some international research programs in Eastern Europe, and currently she coordinates high school and post high school programs in science education for Argonne National Laboratories.

She realized when she was very young that education was the means for her to achieve a better life, and she was a good student. Her parents separated and then her mother died, leaving the children to be raised by a grandmother. Later the younger children lived with an older sister when the grandmother became too ill to care for them. Margaret worked as a maid and babysitter to help with the family finances all through high school. Her high school teachers arranged for her to take advanced placement courses in mathematics and science, and she enrolled in Tuskegee University.

Her initial goal was to study medicine, but she realized that the cost of medical school was beyond her means and switched to chemistry because there were good prospects for financial aid in basic science. While working as a research assistant, she was involved in the study of how different chemicals, when placed in water solutions, conduct electricity with differing degrees of resistance. One summer she worked at Argonne National Laboratories as a member of a team that was studying the various chemical combinations made by uranium. She enrolled at Wayne State University for her master's degree, which she received in one year. She then returned to Tuskegee as a professional assistant in her old research group and taught a mathematics course.

She was recruited into a minority program in chemistry at Brown University, and she focused her research there on the biochemical reactions that take place in the liver. She also taught basic science to nurses and mathematics to welders in night school at the Opportunities Industrialization Center in Providence, Rhode Island, where adults enrolled to upgrade their employment skills. She returned to Tuskegee as an assistant professor of chemistry after completing her doctorate. Her office was located in the Carver Research Foundation laboratory, where she continued her experiments. She then joined the staff of the College of Pharmacy at Florida A&M University as associate professor and associate dean of the school. She then spent several months in Belgium and back at Brown University conducting research on the liver before returning again to Tuskegee as director of the Carver Research Foundation.

She is a fellow of the American Association for the Advancement of Science and a member of the American Chemical Society and Society for Environmental Toxicology and Chemistry. Her research includes signal transduction in isolated heptocytes. Her photograph is included in *Distinguished African American Scientists of the 20th Century.*

***Bibliography:*** *American Men and Women of Science* 13–19; *Blacks in Science and Medicine; Distinguished African American Scientists of the 20th Century.*

# *Townsend, Marjorie Rhodes*
(1930– )
## *aerospace engineer, electronics engineer*

***Education:*** B.EE., George Washington University, 1951

***Professional Experience:*** Physical science aide, National Bureau of Standards, 1948–1951; electronics engineer, basic and applied sonar research, Naval Research Laboratory, 1951–1959; section head, design and development of electronic instruments, Goddard Space Flight Center, National Aeronautics and Space Administration (NASA), 1959–1965, technical assistant to chief of systems division, 1965–1966, project manager, small astronomical satellites, 1966–1975, project manager, applied explorer mission, 1975–1976, manager, preliminary systems design group of advanced systems design, 1976–1980; consultant, 1980–1990; director, Space Systems Engineering BDM International, 1990–1993; consultant, 1993–

***Married:*** Charles E. Townsend, 1948

***Children:*** 4

***Marjorie Townsend*** is renowned for her work in launching the first astronomical satellites in the Small Astronomy Satellite (SAS) program for the National Aeronautics and Space Administration (NASA) in the 1970s. During her years with NASA she was the only woman in the world who was a project manager for a satellite program, and as such, she was responsible for the origination, design, construction, and testing of the satellites as well as for the actual launches of the instruments.

She joined NASA's Goddard Space Flight Center in 1959, the year after the agency was established. She said that since she worked almost across the street at the Naval Research Laboratory, it was natural that she transfer to the new agency. She had been performing sonar research by developing frequency multiplication systems, an analog logic computer, and new submarine detection and classification techniques; at NASA, her first assignment was to design a ground system for the forerunner of meteorological satellites. The ground system is the part of the system that stays on the ground after a satellite is launched. It is a bank of electronic equipment that filters and sorts out different signals from the Television Infrared Observation Satellite (TIROS), and Townsend and her team designed the computer that helped turn certain of these signals into understandable computer language. TIROS gathered information about the earth's temperature distribution and the heights, outlines, and temperatures of clouds. When the Nimbus, a more advanced meteorological observatory, was put into orbit in 1964, she helped design the beacon for tracking it and the transmitter on which all data came back to earth.

In 1966 she was placed in charge of the SAS program, a joint U.S.-Italian project, and she created quite a controversy when she persuaded NASA administrators to use a launch site owned and operated by the Italian government. Her research indicated that the launch site in the Indian Ocean off the coast of Kenya was the best site because it was located in an area where the satellite could be placed in an equatorial orbit, thereby missing the radiation belt and avoiding a significant amount of background noise. The data received from SAS revolutionized the study of x-ray emitting stars.

The satellites were designed to locate and map sources of x-rays and gamma rays in this and other galaxies. X-ray astronomy has discovered objects unidentifiable by radio or optical astronomy and has furnished new information on objects such as pulsars and black holes. The first launch was SAS-A, later renumbered SAS-1 and also called Uhuru, placed in orbit in December 1970. It was the world's first x-ray astronomy satellite, and with it, scientists discovered 100 stars that emit x-rays, which means high energy. SAS-B, later renumbered SAS-2, was launched in November 1972, but it had a malfunction after six months, and NASA had to abandon retrieving data at that time. SAS-3 was launched in May 1975; also for x-ray detection, it was designed to cover a wider x-ray spectrum.

Townsend continued at Goddard, managing advanced studies, including a preliminary systems design for all future satellite missions, and managing the Explorer Mission until 1980, when she became a consultant until 1990. She then worked for a corporation and continued consulting after 1993.

Engineering was a natural choice of a career for her. She grew up taking for granted that being a female imposed no restrictions on her, largely because her father, a mechanical engineer and an inventor, expected her to do great things. He encouraged her to study engineering, and she found the subject attractive because it offered a combination of science and math. She entered George Washington University at 15, married during her junior year when she was 18, worked at the National Bureau of Standards to support her husband in medical school, and obtained her undergraduate degree in night school. She was the first woman to graduate from George Washington University in engineering.

When an interviewer commented on the difficulties of balancing a career and family, she said that she and her husband did not want to wait until they could "afford" to have children. Her husband was still serving his internship when they had their first child, and she had to continue working. She amazed her bosses by having four babies without ever taking a leave without pay. The first two times her boss did not believe she would return, the third time he began to believe it, and the fourth time he gave her assignments up to the time she actually went to the hospital. She and her husband hired a housekeeper to care for the boys, and after they were older, they took over the chores of cooking and cleaning; they even learned to sew. She said there is a new generation of men and women who share the chores, which makes it possible for a husband to support his wife's having a career. She said that women can have it all, it is possible to give enough time to each aspect of one's life, and young women should not be turned off by all the things they want to do. Everyone has problems, but it is what you do with the problems that matters.

She has received numerous awards, including the Exceptional Service Medal (1971) and Outstanding Leadership Medal (1980) from NASA, Knight of the Italian Republic Order from Italy (1972), Federal Woman's Award from the U.S. Government (1973), and George Washington University Achievement Award. She is a fellow of the American Institute of Aeronautics and Astronautics and of the Institute of Electrical and Electronics Engineers and a member of the American Association for the Advancement of Science, American Geophysical Union, and Society of Women Engineers. She was the coinventor of a digital telemetry system, and her research includes advanced space and ground systems design for a large variety of missions in space and terrestrial applications and in the space sciences, new applications for the use of the space shuttle, and improvements in the data system design of space stations. Her photograph is included in *Working Woman* (May 1980).

***Bibliography:*** *American Men and Women of Science* 14–19; Herzenberg, C., *Women Scientists from Antiquity to the Present;* Ireland, N., *Index to Women of the World . . . Suppl.;* Rossiter, M., *Women Scientists in America;* Stanley, A., *Mothers and Daughters of Invention; Who's Who in America,* 51st ed., 1997; *Who's Who in Engineering,* 9th ed., 1995.

# *Turkle, Sherry*
(1948– )
## *sociologist, clinical psychologist*

***Education:*** B.A., Harvard University, 1970, M.A., 1973, Ph.D. in sociology and personality psychology, 1976; honorary degree: Ph.D., Claremont College, 1990
***Professional Experience:*** Clinical intern in psychology, University Health Services, Harvard University, 1974–1975; assistant professor of sociology, Massachusetts Institute of Technology, 1976–1980, associate professor of sociology, 1980–1989, professor of sociology, 1991–
***Concurrent Positions:*** Member, Laboratory for Computer Science, 1976–
***Married:*** Ralph Willard, 1987
***Children:*** 1

***Sherry Turkle*** is one of the few people who has attracted attention to research on how humans interact with computers, and one of her theories is that computers can change our very identities. The intrusion of computers into more and more aspects of life provokes many questions about the boundaries between computers and humans, and she is especially concerned about a young person's immersion into computer games until the games become more real than reality. Another area of concern is the computer chat rooms on the Internet, in which people may adopt any persona, or several personae, to interact with other people on-line, and she has visited several participants in these chat rooms to interview them in person. She is especially vehement about adults who pretend to be children to prey on children. Some of the people who have interviewed Sherry Turkle refer to her as the Margaret Mead of computer culture or the Margaret Mead of cyberspace for her pioneering work. One called her a pioneer ethnographer of the computer culture.

She entered Radcliffe College, which later merged with Harvard University, in 1965, but in her junior year her mother died. Sherry was so distraught that she dropped out of college and moved to Paris where she supported herself as a live-in cleaning woman. Through contacts at Harvard, she was able to attend seminars of the Parisian intelligentsia, and after the student uprising in 1968, she noticed that the French were accepting the ideas of the German psychoanalyst Sigmund Freud. When she returned to school at Harvard she wrote her doctoral thesis on "Psychoanalysis and Society: The Emergence of French Freud," and her first book, *Psychoanalytic Politics: Freud's French Revolution* (1978), was based on her dissertation.

She first encountered the strange language of computer users when she accepted a position as an assistant professor of sociology at the Massachusetts Institute of Technology (MIT). The university seemed like a foreign country; it was totally different from either Harvard or France. She was fascinated that the students used computer language in their everyday conversations, even when talking about their emotions. They would say they were "debugging their relationships" during difficult times or excuse verbal slips by calling them "information processing errors." She felt she was an anthropologist in a strange land, and she took notes. Her second book was *The Second Self: Computers and the Human Spirit* (1984) in which she theorized that the computer is, not just a tool, but an evocative object with which one can have intense, almost intimate relations, as if it were a person.

For her third book she interviewed more than 1,000 people, 300 of them children. The use of computers had increased dramatically, and in her book *Life on the Screen* (1995), she expressed her concern about the direction the concept of computer literacy has taken. For example, children are taught computer skills but not critical thinking. She suggested that children should be taught that they should not take things at interface value. She talks about the abuses of the multiple user domains (MUDs) on the Internet, where one can assume any identity and act out any fantasy. The Internet encourages people to add facets to their personalities and to create additional identities for themselves. She notes that more men than women use MUDs and many more men than women assume a persona of the opposite sex. Critics have been accusing computer technology of aiding escapist fantasies, but Turkle is not ready to accept that idea. She says that people already think of themselves as having multiple identities, such as mother, wife, career woman, daughter, social activist, etc.

In *Life on the Screen: Identity in the Age of the Internet* (1996), she continues to explore the cultural impact of the digital revolution and looks at how the development of smart machines has affected our idea of what it is to be a human being. In interviews with children of different ages and in different cultures, she asked whether or not an interactive computer program is alive, and she indicates that children quickly learn the difference between simulation and reality.

She is a member of the American Psychological Association, American Sociology Association, and American Association for the Advancement of Science. There are numerous articles in popular magazines about her work, and her photograph is included in *Current Biography* (1997), *Business Week* (May 12, 1997), *Working Woman* (June 1996), and *Technology Review* (February–March 1996).

**Bibliography:** *Contemporary Authors* v. 102; *Current Biography 1997; Who's Who in Science and Engineering,* 2d ed., 1994–1995.

# *Tyson, Laura (D'Andrea)*
(1947– )
***economist***

***Education:*** B.A., Smith College, 1969; Ph.D. in economics, Massachusetts Institute of Technology, 1974
***Professional Experience:*** Staff economist, World Bank, 1974; assistant professor of economics, Princeton University, 1974–1977; assistant professor of economics, University of California, Berkeley, 1977–1979, associate professor of economics, 1979–1988, professor of economics and business administration, 1988–1992; chair, Council of Economic Advisors, 1992–1995; chair, National Economic Council, 1995–1997; professor of economics and business administration, University of California, Berkeley, 1997–
***Concurrent Positions:*** Director, Berkeley Roundtable on International Economics
***Married:*** Erik Tarloff
***Children:*** 1

***Laura Tyson,*** as chair of the National Economic Council (NEC), was considered to be the most powerful woman in President Clinton's inner circle, and she and Alan Greenspan, chair of the Federal Reserve System's Board of Governors, were the nation's most influential economists. Prior to her appointment to the NEC in 1995, she was chair of the president's Council of Economic Advisors (CEA), and in that capacity, she made regular assessments of the nation's economy and in-depth analyses of how government policies affect it. As chair of the NEC, she was responsible for coordinating the economic policies of the administration. Her name was little known outside economic circles when President Clinton selected her for the CEA during his first term. Prior to taking office, he had set up an informal conference with a number of leading economists to solicit their views on economic policy, and although she was invited almost at the last minute, she expressed her views so well that he selected her. She left the NEC to return to the faculty of the University of California at Berkeley in 1997.

She is known for her ability to explain complex economic concepts in an understandable and interesting way in the classroom, in a conference, or in an interview. She has been invaluable in giving interviews to reporters in print and on television about the economic vision of the administration. She has won acclaim for her role in establishing the administration's policies on deficit reduction and trade as well as for her efforts to reduce the cost of health care reform. In February 1995, the president named her chair of the NEC, a coordinating group made up of the president, the vice president, and members of the cabinet. She had the responsibility of managing economic policymaking throughout the executive branch; she also sat on the president's national security and domestic policy councils.

In 1992, she published a book that examined the American trade imbalance problem in-depth, *Who's Bashing Whom: Trade Conflict in High Technology Industries,* in which she advocated aggressive action against foreign traders who close their markets to imports by blocking U.S. markets to the foreign traders. The administration has used that idea in negotiating with several countries. In 1995, after a long series of negotiations with Japan about the trade imbalance, the administration announced that 100 percent tariffs would be placed on 13 models of Japanese luxury cars. Hours before the tariffs were to take effect, the negotiators hammered out a deal.

Another area in which she played a behind-the-scenes role was health care reform during the first year of Clinton's presidency. A task force headed by Hillary Rodham Clinton spent months creating a program that would have provided medical insurance for all Americans, and Laura Tyson was one of the few members of the administration to question the estimated costs of the program. She disagreed with some administration economists that the package would create more jobs than it lost; her opinion was that the plan would not have a major impact one way or the other on employment.

She was born Laura D'Andrea, and the surname of Tyson came from her first husband, whom she divorced in the mid 1970s. When she enrolled in Smith College she planned to major in mathematics and psychology but changed her major to economics after taking an introductory course in that field. In her graduate program at the Massachusetts Institute of Technology, she found the workload daunting because it emphasized the technical and statistical aspects of economics rather than its practical applications. After receiving her doctorate, she taught at Princeton before accepting a position at the University of California, Berkeley, rising through the ranks to professor of economics and business administration. She also was research director of the Berkeley Roundtable on International Economics, which focused on discussions of world trade in high-technology goods, which are products such as semiconductors and computer chips, and the advantages that foreign governments, particularly Japan, give their nationals through financial subsidies and import regulations.

In addition to numerous papers, she has published four more books dealing with international competition, trade, productivity, and politics. She is a member of the American Economic Association and the Association for Comparative Economic Studies. Her photograph was published on the cover of *Working Woman* (August 1993); there are also photographs in *Current Biography* (1996) and *Business Week* (May 24, 1993 and March 9, 1998).

***Bibliography:*** *Current Biography 1996; Who's Who in America,* 51st ed., 1997; *Who's Who in Science and Engineering,* 3d ed., 1996–1997; *Who's Who of American Women,* 20th ed., 1997–1998.

# *Uhlenbeck, Karen (Keskulla)*
(1942– )
## *mathematician*

***Education:*** B.A., University of Michigan, 1964; M.A., Brandeis University, 1966, Ph.D. in mathematics, 1968; honorary degree: D.Sc., Knox College, 1988

***Professional Experience:*** Instructor, mathematics, Massachusetts Institute of Technology, 1968–1969; lecturer, University of California, Berkeley, 1969–1971; assistant professor of mathematics, University of Illinois, 1971–1976; associate professor, University of Illinois, Chicago Circle, 1976–1978, professor, 1978–1983; professor of mathematics, University of Chicago, 1983–1988; Sid Richardson Centennial Chair, University of Texas, Austin, 1988–1992, Sid Richardson Foundation Regent Chairman, 1992–

***Concurrent Positions:*** MacArthur fellow, 1983–1988; chancellor's visiting professor, University of California, Berkeley, 1979; Albert Einstein fellowship, Institute for Advanced Study, Princeton University, 1979–1980

***Married:*** Olke C. Uhlenbeck, 1965, divorced

*Karen Uhlenbeck* is renowned for mathematical research that has applications in theoretical physics and has contributed to much of the current research on instantons, which are models for the behavior of surfaces in four dimensions. In her research, she has used partial differential equations in a much more technical fashion to look at the shapes of space. Mathematicians are looking at imaginary spaces that have been constructed by scientists who are examining other problems. For example, physicists who were studying quantum mechanics had predicted the existence of particle-like elements called instantons. Uhlenbeck and other researchers viewed instantons as somewhat similar to soap films, so they studied soap films to learn about the properties of surfaces. Soap films provide a model for the behavior of surfaces in three dimensions, and instantons provide similar models for the behavior of surfaces in four-dimensional time space. She is the coauthor of a book on this subject, *Instantons and 4-Manifold Topology* (1984). She was elected to membership in the National Academy of Sciences in 1986.

She had intended to major in physics as an undergraduate in an honors program at the University of Michigan, but she later switched to mathematics. After graduating, she spent a year at New York University's Courant Institute; she then married and moved to Boston where her husband was attending Harvard. She received a very generous National Science Foundation graduate fellowship for her graduate work at Brandeis University—as a result of Sputnik, the government had instituted a crash program to increase the number of scientists and engineers. Her graduate thesis was on the calculus of variations. After teaching at the Massachusetts Institute of Technology for a year, she moved to the University of California, Berkeley, as a lecturer in mathematics. There she studied general relativity and the geometry of space-time and worked on elliptic regularity in systems of partial differential equations.

Uhlenbeck and her husband obtained positions at the University of Illinois at Champaign-Urbana, and she later moved to the University of Illinois, Chicago Circle. While at the latter, she received an Albert

Einstein fellowship to work at the Institute for Advanced Study at Princeton University, and between 1983 and 1988, she had a prestigious MacArthur fellowship grant, which she used at the University of Chicago. Both of these fellowships enable scientists, scholars, and artists to pursue research or creative activity. She began a serious study of physics, theorizing that a mathematician's task is to abstract ideas from fields such as physics and streamline them so they can be used in other fields. Her research has included work on partial differential equations, scale-invariant variational problems, gauge field theory, and applications to four manifolds. She later began working in equations with algebraic infinite symmetries.

At the University of Texas, Austin, she has run a relatively new mentoring program for women in mathematics. She is somewhat uneasy being a role model for young women in mathematics, saying one reason she chose mathematics was that she liked to work alone. She was very competitive and a very good mathematician, but she found it difficult to cope with the attitudes of people who lose. However, later in her career she found it stimulating to learn from other people, and she has done collaborative work. Since both of her parents were college graduates, they emphasized the value of education to their children. She was not particularly interested in mathematics, even in high school, because, she said, one cannot understand math until about halfway through college. However, she read a great deal about science, such as books by the astrophysicist Fred Hoyle and the physicist George Gamow.

When she was in college, which was just after Sputnik, women still were being told they could not do math because they were women. However, many faculty members appreciated good students, whether they were men or women, and had no expectations for women just because they were women. While she was teaching at the Massachusetts Institute of Technology and at Berkeley during the Vietnam War, she was not the only woman in her department at either school. The women at both succeeded spectacularly, perhaps because they had decided to do what they chose to do. She said she has mixed feelings about what happened later. Many women were in the midst of successful careers when "there was all this fuss that schools had to hire women." After that, she said she had difficulty finding employment because of often unwritten nepotism rules. Positions gradually opened up again, but she wants to be valued for her work as a mathematician, not because she is a member of a particular group. After seeing the problems that other women scientists have faced, she has had difficulty in coming to grips with her own success as a brilliant female mathematician.

Uhlenbeck has received numerous awards, including Alumna of the Year from the University of Michigan Alumni Association (1984), an Alumni Achievement award from Brandeis University (1988), and the Commonwealth Award for Science and Invention of PNC Bank Corporation (1995). She was named one of America's 100 most important women in 1988 by *Ladies' Home Journal.* She is a member of the American Academy of Arts and Sciences, Association for Women in Mathematics, and American Mathematical Society. Her research includes calculus of variations, global analysis, and gauge theories. Her photograph is included in *Journeys of Women in Science and Engineering.*

***Bibliography:*** *American Men and Women of Science* 11–19; Herzenberg, C., *Women Scientists from Antiquity to the Present; Journeys of Women in Science and Engineering; Notable Twentieth-Century Scientists; Who's Who in America,* 51st ed., 1997; *Who's Who in Science and Engineering,* 3d ed., 1996–1997; *Who's Who of American Women,* 20th ed., 1997–1998.

# *Underhill, Anne Barbara*
(1920– )
## *astrophysicist*

***Education:*** B.A., University of British Columbia, 1942, M.A. in physics and mathematics, 1944; Ph.D. in astrophysics, University of Chicago, 1948; honorary degrees: D.Sc., York University, 1969, and University of British Columbia, 1992

***Professional Experience:*** Physicist, National Research Council of Canada, 1944–1946; National Research Council of Canada fellow, Copenhagen Observatory, 1948–1949; astrophysicist, Dominion Astrophysical Observatory, 1949–1962; professor of astrophysics, State University of Utrecht, 1962–1970; chief, Laboratory for Optical Astronomy, Goddard Space Flight Center, National Aeronautics and Space Administration (NASA), 1970–1977, senior scientist, Astronomical and Solar Physics Laboratory, 1977–1985; retired 1985; honorary professor, Department of Geophysics and Astronomy, University of British Columbia, 1985–

***Concurrent Positions:*** Visiting lecturer, Harvard University, 1955–1956; visiting professor, University of Colorado, 1967

***Anne Underhill*** is renowned as an astrophysicist who helped develop a research area on the theory and observation of stars that is done at the level of ultraviolet wavelengths. These are not accessible from ground-based observatories because the wavelengths are blocked from the ground by the atmosphere. While she was a fellow at the Copenhagen Observatory, she began work on the development of numerical methods for the interpretation of high-resolution spectra of young, hot stars (spectral types O and B), and she expanded this work while at the Dominion Astrophysical Observatory to include computing model atmospheres for these hot stars in order to predict theoretical spectra from them. She had difficulty obtaining high-resolution photographic spectrograms while using the telescopes, for the weather conditions in Victoria, British Columbia, where the observatory is located, are not ideal for this type of work. She based her interpretations of the spectra of the hot stars on basic physics. At this point, the local thermodynamic equilibrium (LTE) theory of model atmospheres proved to be inadequate to predict what is actually observed in the young, hot stars as well as the Wolf-Rayet stars.

Since she did not have access to modern, powerful computing equipment in Canada, she accepted the 1970 invitation from the National Aeronautics and Space Administration (NASA) to become chief of the Laboratory for Optical Astronomy at the Goddard Space Flight Center. Probably she was recommended for this position by Nancy Roman, a fellow student at the University of Chicago who already worked for NASA.

When Underhill joined the laboratory, NASA was just launching the Orbiting Astronomical Observatory (OAO-2) satellite, but unfortunately, the protective shroud did not fully disengage from the spacecraft, and it fell into the ocean. However, the International Ultraviolet Explorer (IUE) was launched successfully in 1978, and the ultraviolet spectral data obtained from the IUE and the Copernicus (OAO-C) spacecraft provided a new basis for the analysis of early-type stars at ultraviolet wavelengths. Underhill computed the effective temperatures of approximately 200 early-type stars utilizing space-based and ground-based data, and she pursued independent research on solar, stellar, and galactic astronomy during this period. She continues to be active as an astrophysicist.

She has published more than 200 papers during her career; a partial list is included in *Women in Chemistry and Physics.* She describes the design of the IUE satellite, which was launched successfully in 1978, in an article in *Sky and Telescope* (December 1973). In 1960, the International Astronomical Union named an asteroid after her, "Asteroid Underhill." She is a member of the American Astronomical Society, Astronomical Society of the Pacific, and International Astronomical Union. Her research includes atmospheres of hot stars, Wolf-Rayet stars, models of atmospheres, and the ultraviolet spectra of stars.

***Bibliography:*** *American Men and Women of Science* 11–19; Herzenberg, C., *Women Scientists from Antiquity to the Present; Who's Who in America,* 51st ed., 1997; *Who's Who of American Women,* 19th ed., 1995–1996; *Women in Chemistry and Physics; World Who's Who in Science.*

# *Vaughan, Martha*
(1926– )
***biochemist***

***Education:*** Ph.B., University of Chicago, 1944; M.D., Yale University, 1949
***Professional Experience:*** Research fellow, University of Pennsylvania, 1951–1952; National Research Council fellow, National Heart Institute, 1952–1954, member of research staff, 1954–1968, head, metabolism section, National Heart and Lung Institute, 1968–1974, acting chief, molecular disease branch, National Heart, Lung, and Blood Institute, 1974–1976, chief, cell metabolism laboratory, 1974–1994, deputy chief, pulmonary and critical care medical branch, 1994–
***Concurrent Position:*** Senior assistant surgeon to medical director, U.S. Public Health Service, 1954–1989
***Married:*** Jack Orloff, 1951, died 1988
***Children:*** 3

***Martha Vaughan*** is renowned for her research at the National Institutes of Health (NIH) on the mechanism of hormone action. She has worked for the same institute during her long career with the agency, but the name has changed from National Heart Institute, to National Heart and Lung Institute, to National Heart, Lung, and Blood Institute. After serving on the research staff, she was appointed head of the metabolism section in 1968, acting chief of the molecular disease branch in 1974, chief of the cell metabolism laboratory in 1974, and deputy chief of the pulmonary and critical care medical branch in 1994. She also was senior assistant surgeon to the medical director of the U.S. Public Health Service from 1954 to 1989. She was elected to membership in the National Academy of Sciences in 1985.

She is among the many women scientists who have been appointed to administrative positions in government agencies over the years. Although the prospects for advancement have varied from agency to agency, some women listed in this volume voiced the opinion that they have had better chances for advancement in government than in academia. In earlier years, many women could find jobs only in women's colleges or state universities where there were few or inadequate opportunities for research funding. Since many women scientists are in biomedical fields, the competition for the few good jobs in that area has been fierce at times. She also held other positions within the U.S. Public Health Service, including being a member of the metabolism study section, Division of Research Grants (1965–1968), on the review committee for the Fogarty International Center (1973–1974 and 1977–1978), and a member of the board of science counselors for the National Institute of Alcohol Abuse and Alcoholism (1988–1991). She was also a member of the board of directors of the Foundation for Advanced Education in Science, Inc. (1979–1992; president, 1988–1990) and a member of the Yale University Council on medical affairs (1974–1980).

She has received numerous awards, including Harvey Society Lecturer (1982); G. Burroughs Mider Lecturer, National Institutes of Health (1979); Meritorious Service Medal (1974) and Distinguished Service Medal (1979), Department of Health, Education and Welfare; and Command Officer Award (1982) and Superior Service Award (1993), Public Health Service. She is a coeditor of the book *ADP-Ribosylating Toxins and G Proteins: Insights into Signal Transduction* (1990) published by the American Society for Microbiology and has written many scientific papers.

Vaughan is a member of the American Society of Biochemistry and Molecular Biology, American Society of Clinical Investigation, Association of American Physicians, American Academy of Arts and Sciences, and American Society of Biological Chemists.

***Bibliography:*** *American Men and Women of Science* 11–19; Herzenberg, C., *Women Scientists from Antiquity to the Present; Who's Who in America,* 51st ed., 1997; *Who's Who in Science and Engineering,* 3d ed., 1996–1997; *Who's Who of American Women,* 20th ed., 1997–1998.

# *Villa-Komaroff, Lydia*
(1947– )
## *molecular biologist, neurobiologist*

***Education:*** Student, University of Washington, Seattle; B.A., Goucher College, 1970; Ph.D. in cell biology, Massachusetts Institute of Technology, 1975

***Professional Experience:*** Research fellow in biology, Harvard University, 1975–1978; assistant professor of microbiology, Medical School, University of Massachusetts, 1975–1981, associate professor, 1982–1985; senior research associate, Department of Neurology, Division of Neuroscience, Children's Hospital, Boston, and associate professor, Department of Neurology, Harvard Medical School, 1985–1994; associate vice president for research administration and professor of neurology, Northwestern University, 1994–

***Concurrent Positions:*** Associate director, Mental Retardation Center, 1987–1994

***Married:*** Anthony L. Komaroff, 1970

*Lydia Villa-Komaroff* is renowned for her theory of brain development. She is concentrating on the role of a protein called insulin-like growth factor II (IGF-II) in brain development, and members of her team are studying what they believe will help determine how many cells an organism has—the number of cells affects how big and how tall people will be when they become adults. In 1995, her work was featured on a public television program called "Discovering Women," a three-part, six-hour miniseries chronicling six contemporary women scientists.

Her particular focus is the flow of information in the cell. DNA in the cell nucleus has all the information needed to specify all the parts of the organism, and the flow of information from DNA to RNA to protein and the biochemistry of those molecules is what molecular biologists study. The team uses mice for its studies because mice are remarkably similar to humans in the way their brains are put together.

Both of Villa-Komaroff's parents were the first in their respective families to attend college, and she comes from a long line of strong and professional women. Her father bought the children books that her mother read to the children, and both parents encouraged each of their six children to do whatever it was he or she thought would be satisfying. It was critically important in her development that her father supported her mother in her career. Even as a little girl, Lydia wanted to be a scientist, although she probably did not know what scientists actually do. However, she always wanted to find things out, and she knew that is what scientists do. Her parents even accepted and supported her decision to go far from her home in New Mexico to attend college, first to the University of Washington, Seattle, and then to Goucher College in Maryland. Many Mexican-American families discourage their children from attending college because they are afraid they will drift away from the family, and there is special pressure on daughters to stay close.

Villa-Komaroff initially was a chemistry major at the University of Washington until her adviser told her that women did not belong in chemistry. After switching majors several times, she selected biology and became interested in developmental and molecular biology. She moved to Goucher College to complete her degree because her fiancé was doing his public health service there. Since Johns Hopkins University was not accepting women at the time, she went to its sister college, Goucher.

After their marriage the couple moved to Boston for Anthony's internship and residency, and Lydia selected the Massachusetts Institute of Technology (MIT) for graduate school. Although she wanted to conduct research in developmental biology, she did not want to work with the people who were in charge of that program at MIT. Since the best work in molecular biology was being done on viruses, she focused on poliovirus. Her department at MIT was very supportive of the women students, and although some people thought women did not belong at MIT or in science, she and the other women graduate students simply avoided them. She said she was pretty oblivious to the attitudes of others about being a woman in science because she was pursuing something that she loved.

In her postdoctoral study at Harvard, she first worked on the development of the silk moth eggshell and then on making proteins in bacteria. In 1976, a controversy arose in Cambridge, Massachusetts, where Harvard is located, about recombinant DNA technology. Some people feared that if one took genes from one organism, such as a human, and put them into bacteria, one might somehow create a supergerm or a new disease. Since the city council banned certain experiments, Villa-Komaroff's team had to move to a laboratory in Cold Spring Harbor on Long Island for a year. In 1977, the Cambridge city council rescinded the ban. After receiving her doctorate, she taught and conducted research at the University of Massachusetts Children's Hospital in Boston and Harvard Medical School and later became a professor of neurology at Northwestern University and an associate vice president of the university.

In addition to writing scientific papers, she has also received several patents. She has received awards, including the Hispanic Engineer National Achievement Award (1992) and the Helen Hay Whitney Foundation fellowship (1975–1978). She was associate director of a mental retardation research center (1987–1994), a member of the mammalian genetics study section of the National Institutes of Health (1982–1984), and member of the Neurological Disease Program Project Review Committee (1989–1994).

She is a member of the American Society for Microbiology, American Society of Cell Biology, American Association for the Advancement of Science, Federation of American Scientists, and Society for Neuroscience. Her research includes growth factors in brain development, structure and function of insulin-like growth factors in brain development, and the structure and function of genes expressed in central and peripheral nervous systems. Her photograph is included in *Journeys of Women in Science and Engineering* and in *Chemical & Engineering News* (March 20, 1995).

***Bibliography:*** *American Men and Women of Science* 14–19; Herzenberg, C., *Women Scientists from Antiquity to the Present; Journeys of Women in Science and Engineering; Who's Who of American Women,* 20th ed., 1997–1998.

# *Vitetta, Ellen Shapiro*
(ca. 1942– )
## *microbiologist, immunologist*

***Education:*** B.A., Connecticut College, 1964; M.S., New York University, 1966, Ph.D. in microbiology and M.D., 1968

***Professional Experience:*** Research assistant, Biology Department, New York University, 1964–1968; postdoctoral fellow, New York University School of Medicine, 1968–1970, assistant research scientist, 1970–1971, assistant professor of microbiology and associate research scientist, Department of Medicine, 1971–1974; associate professor of microbiology, University of Texas Southwestern Medical Center, 1974–1976, professor of microbiology 1976– , chair of immunology graduate program, 1984–1988, director, Cancer Immunobiology Center, 1988– , S. S. Patigan Distinguished Chair in Cancer Immunobiology, 1989–

***Ellen S. Vitetta*** is renowned for her research on monoclonal antibodies and in microbiology. After receiving her master's, doctoral, and M.D. degrees from New York University, she conducted research in the Medical School and Department of Medicine at that university for more than ten years. She then moved to the University of Texas Southwestern Medical Center where, in addition to being director of the Cancer Immunobiology Center, she holds the S. S. Patigan Distinguished Chair in Cancer Immunobiology. She was elected to membership in the National Academy of Sciences in 1994.

She is a member of many distinguished committees and commissions, including member of the science board of the Ludwig Institute (1983– ), member of the Task Force on Immunology of the National Institute of Allergy and Infectious Diseases of the National Institutes of Health (1989–1990), member of the science advisory board of the Howard Hughes Medical Institute (1992– ), member of the board, science council, National Cancer Institute's Cancer Treatment Board (1993– ), member of Kettering Selection Committee, General Motors Cancer Research Foundation (1987–1988), member of the task force in immunology, National Institute of Allergy and Infectious Diseases (1989–1990), member of Board of Scientific Counselors, National Cancer Institute's Division of Cancer Treatment (1993–1994), and consultant for Eli Lilly, Inc. (1982–1985), Abbott, Inc. (1987–1989), and Genetics Institute (1988–1990). She has also served on the editorial boards of numerous journals in the field.

Vitetta has received a merit grant award from the National Institutes of Health every year since 1987, and she is the recipient of the Women's Excellence in Science award from the Federation of the American Societies in Experimental Biology (1991), the Tattinger Breast Cancer Research Award from the Komen Foundation (1983), Pierce Immunotoxin Award (1988), Immunology Award of the American Society for Microbiologists (1992), and the Rosenthal Foundation Award of the American Association for Cancer Research (1995).

She is a member of the American Association of Immunologists (president, 1993) and the American Association for Cancer Research. Her research includes development and identification of immunotoxins on murine boron cells. Some information was supplied in a letter to the author dated May 23, 1997.

***Bibliography:*** *American Men and Women of Science* 19; *Who's Who in Science and Engineering,* 3d ed., 1996–1997; *Who's Who of American Women,* 20th ed., 1997–1998.

# *Walbot, Virginia Elizabeth*
(ca. 1945– )
***biologist, plant geneticist***

***Education:*** B.A., Stanford University, 1967; M.Phil., Yale University, 1969, Ph.D. in biology, 1972

***Professional Experience:*** National Institutes of Health fellow, University of Georgia, 1972–1975; assistant professor of biology, Washington University, St. Louis, 1975–1980; professor of biological sciences, Stanford University, 1980–

***Virginia Walbot*** is a plant geneticist whose focus in research is corn genetics. She and other scientists have found corn to be the ideal organism for studying fundamental questions about genetics and development because so much work has been done with corn and maize over the years that scientists are very familiar with the organism. The plant geneticist Barbara McClintock (1902–1992) received the Nobel Prize in Physiology or Medicine in 1983 for her fundamental research on corn, and Walbot was able to confer with her while McClintock still was active in research. In the late 1970s, Virginia Walbot met Barbara McClintock through friends, and after long telephone conversations, worked with her in her laboratory at Cold Spring Harbor.

Walbot's research is involved with the molecular biology of the expression of corn genes, especially in the details of how individual genes are regulated during plant development. One method is to isolate genes and then study them in the lab; another is to make mutations, or let the plant make mutations, that alter the expression of the gene. Transposable genetic elements, or transposons, which were discovered by McClintock more than 40 years ago, figure prominently in Walbot's research. She defines a transposable element as a segment of DNA that can cut itself out of the chromosome and reinsert itself elsewhere. That is the reason they are called "jumping genes," or mobile DNA. She is particularly interested in developmental timing, and some transposons she studies are active only after an organ such as a leaf has already begun to form. Plants have continuous development, that is, they are continuously making organs from scratch. For example, if one places a plant with dark leaves in sunlight, the dark leaves will fall off to be replaced by light-colored leaves to filter the sunlight.

Scientists are using recombinant DNA methods in plant research to clone genes that produce specific proteins that may be associated with certain stages of development. These methods have made new biotechnologies possible, and work is being done to manipulate plant genomes to breed for resistance to disease. She says that with biotechnology, just like with normal breeding, scientists need to ensure that there is a diversity of varieties that have any new trait. If only a few genetic variants are developed, it means the food sources are more susceptible to a new disease or environmental conditions that are fatal to that one type.

Walbot says that teaching helps with her research because it forces her to think about how to explain ideas clearly and completely. Especially when teaching introductory biology classes, every year is the first time the students hear an idea or concept, and the instructor has another chance to make it more fundamental, more clear, and more precise. She advises undergraduates to try out a career in science by being a summer intern in someone's lab or to participate in what is called "directed reading" at Stanford, which means meeting with a faculty member each week to discuss a topic of mutual interest.

While she was on the faculty of Washington University, St. Louis, she developed, in cooperation with a team of University of Missouri researchers and commercial corn breeders, a corn that is genetically incapable of losing its sweetness and turning starchy. She did not start her research on corn until she began working with the people at the University of Missouri, and it was after she had presented one of her first papers on the subject that she met Barbara McClintock. In addition to Walbot's numerous scientific publications, she is coeditor of *The Maize Handbook* (1993), a compendium for the maize research community of the standard procedures and protocols for maize research. The book may also be used when working with higher plants to which the procedures may be applicable. The preface mentions the *Maize Genetics Cooperation Newsletter* and suggests books that can be consulted.

Walbot is a member of the American Association for the Advancement of Science, Botanical Society of America, Society for Developmental Biology, and American Society of Plant Physiologists. Her research includes plant molecular biology and development, genetics, and botany. Her photograph is included in *American Biology Teacher (*February 1993).

***Bibliography:*** *American Men and Women of Science* 12–19; Stanley, A., *Mothers and Daughters of Invention.*

# *Wallace, Joan (Scott)*
## (1930– )
## ***psychologist, sociologist***

***Education:*** B.A., Bradley University, 1952; M.S. in social work, Columbia University, 1954; Ph.D. in social psychology, Northwestern University, 1973; honorary degrees: HHD, University of Maryland, 1979; LHD, Bowie State College, 1981; LL.D., Alabama A&M University, 1990

***Professional Experience:*** Assistant professor then associate professor, University of Illinois, Chicago Circle, 1967–1973; associate dean and professor, Howard University, 1973–1976; vice president of administration, Morgan State University, 1976–1977; assistant secretary for administration, U.S. Department of Agriculture (USDA), 1977–1981, administrator, Office of International Cooperation and Development, 1981–1989; representative to Trinidad and Tobago, Inter American Institute for Cooperation in Agriculture, USDA, 1989–1992; international consultant, U.S. Partnerships International, 1993–

***Concurrent Positions:*** Vice president of programs, National Urban League, 1975–1976

***Married:*** John Wallace, 1954, divorced 1976; Maurice A. Dawkins, 1979

***Children:*** 3

***Joan Wallace*** is the first black and the third woman to serve as assistant secretary for administration in the U.S. Department of Agriculture (USDA), one of the oldest federal departments in the United States. Her appointment to the position is significant because it marked a change in the pattern of appointing blacks to high-level federal positions. From that point on, many blacks were placed in top positions in the entire range of government, not just the cluster of federal agencies primarily concerned with minority, poverty, or civil rights issues.

Her accomplishments in that position were extensive. There was improved productivity among managers, professionals, and white-collar workers. She created an equal employment opportunity evaluation and planning system to document employment practices, to provide statistics on minority employment, and to provide a mechanism for drawing up realistic affirmative action plans. She engaged in major efforts to publicize programs and opportunities for blacks. She also publicized that agriculture is not just farming; it also includes forestry, consumer affairs, foreign agriculture, science, and education.

In talks around the nation, she emphasized what the Department of Agriculture can do for minorities and what it contributes to the welfare of minorities. Although the food stamp program, the Women, Infants and Children (WIC) nutrition program, and the school lunch program are well known, there are many other services such as business aid and development programs as well as foreign agriculture trade programs. Probably many people did or do not know all the services that are available to black farmers, such as grants to upgrade housing on farms and in rural areas, business and industry loan guarantees available to minority businesspeople, grants to local governments to upgrade local public facilities, and information about energy technologies that involve agricultural products, such as gasohol.

In 1981, Wallace was named administrator of the Office of International Cooperation and Development, USDA, which is responsible for coordinating and implementing international policies and programs. She oversaw foreign technical assistance, international research, scientific and technical exchanges, international research, and the relationships between the USDA and international food and agricultural organizations and negotiated scientific exchange and research agreements with developing countries.

She was an outstanding student in high school, and she entered college as a premedical student, later changing her major to sociology. Her parents had instilled in her a strong commitment to racial equality, an appreciation for hard work, and the importance of a good education. She continued in school to receive a doctorate in social psychology in 1973. After a successful career in administration and teaching in several colleges, she was appointed to the USDA where she held two significant administrative positions. She continues to work as an international consultant and as a public speaker.

Wallace has received numerous awards for her work both in government and education. These include the Udall/Derwinsky Award for leadership in implementing the Civil Service Reform Act in the USDA (1979), the presidential rank of Meritorious Executive, given to senior government executives (1980), the Distinguished Alumni Award of Bradley University (1978), the achievement award from the Links in Washington, D.C., a civic and social welfare organization (1979), and a presidential award for outstanding public service from Florida A&M University (1990). She is a member of the American Psychological Association and the American Association for the Advancement of Science.

***Bibliography:*** Ireland, N., *Index to Women of the World . . . Suppl.; Notable Black American Women; Who's Who in America,* 51st ed., 1997; *Who's Who in Science and Engineering,* 3d ed., 1996–1997; *Who's Who of American Women,* 20th ed., 1997–1998.

# Wallace, Phyllis Ann
(1923–1993)
***economist***

***Education:*** B.A., New York University, 1943; M.A., Yale University, 1944, Ph.D. in economics, 1948; honorary degrees: Valparaiso University, 1977, Mount Holyoke, 1983, Brown University, 1986, Northeastern University, 1987
***Professional Experience:*** Economic statistician, National Bureau of Economic Research, 1948–1952; associate professor of economics, Atlanta University, 1953–1957; senior economist, U.S. government, 1957–1965; chief of technical studies, U.S. Equal Employment Opportunity Commission, 1966–1969; vice president for research, Metropolitan Research Center, New York City, 1969–1972; visiting professor, Sloan School of Management, Massachusetts Institute of Technology, 1973–1975, professor 1975–
***Concurrent Positions:*** Lecturer, New York University, 1948–1951

***Phyllis Wallace*** is known as a pioneer in research on the economics of discrimination. She was the first black woman to receive a doctorate in economics from Yale University (1948) and the first black woman on the faculty to be tenured at the Massachusetts Institute of Technology (1975). She was also the first African American and first woman president of the Industrial Relations Research Association. One author describes her as a woman who refused to be defined by her race, gender, or occupation. She said she chose economics as a major because it allowed her to leave Maryland at a time when segregation policies there prevented her from attending the all-white University of Maryland, for the state provided out-of-state educational funds for those black students whose chosen major was not offered at the all-black Morgan State College in Baltimore, Maryland. As a professor and researcher she had difficulty attending those meetings of the American Economics Association that were held in cities in which African Americans' access to public accommodations was restricted, but those who knew her said that she lacked racial bitterness.

Early in her career she concentrated her research on issues dealing with international trade. She had written her dissertation on commodity trade relationships, concentrating on international sugar agreements. She first had a non-tenure-track position at New York University and, at the same time, did research for the National Bureau of Economic Research. She then moved to Atlanta University, where she was an associate professor, before working as a senior economist for an elusive government agency. Many people speculated she worked for the Central Intelligence Agency (CIA), and much later she admitted that was so.

She then became chief of technical operations for the Equal Employment Opportunity Commission (EEOC) a few months after it started operations in 1965. She was a pioneer in research on the economics of discrimination, and she distinguished herself in stretching scarce resources to obtain research results by farming out government data to academicians for analysis. She also worked to coordinate hearings for the EEOC about racial employment patterns in many industries, including the textile and drug industries. Her research focused on the status of African Americans in urban poverty neighborhoods and on patterns of employment in private industry. Another of her key contributions was developing interdisciplinary teams that focused on issues of discrimination and employment testing.

She left the EEOC still fully committed to continuing research on racial employment discrimination and equal employment opportunity. At the Metropolitan Applied Research Center, she worked on issues affecting urban youth in labor markets and on issues affecting young black women, which had not been explored at that point. She published extensively on race and gender discrimination in the labor market. She joined the faculty of the Massachusetts Institute of Technology (MIT) and continued her research on employment discrimination.

Wallace was a scholar activist who studied some of the most important and intractable problems of our time, such as alleviating poverty and the damage done by racial and sexual discrimination. One of her books is *Black Women in the Labor Force* (1980), in which she presented data on the work patterns of black, urban teenage girls, which contrast significantly from the patterns of white, urban teenage girls. She concluded that black girls have the highest unemployment rate and the lowest economic status of any group—and that there is the possibility that a disproportionate number will become impoverished single parents. She was a member of the American Economic Association and the Industrial Relations Research Association (president).

***Bibliography:*** *Blacks in Science and Medicine; Contemporary Authors* v. 105; *Notable Black American Women.*

# *Watson, Patty Jo (Anderson)*

(1932– )

## ***anthropologist, archaeologist***

***Education:*** B.A., University of Chicago, M.A., 1956, Ph.D. in anthropology, 1959
***Professional Experience:*** National Science Foundation fellow, University of Michigan, 1957–1958, and University of Minnesota, 1958–1959; archaeologist and ethnographer, Oriental Institute, University of Chicago, 1954–1960, research associate, archaeology, 1964–1970; instructor in anthropology, University of Southern California, University of California, Los Angeles, and Los Angeles State University, 1961; assistant professor of anthropology, Washington University, St. Louis, 1969–1970, associate professor, 1970–1973, professor, 1973–1993, department chair, 1982–1984, Edward Mallinckrodt Distinguished University Professor, 1993–
***Concurrent Positions:*** Project associate, anthropology curriculum study project, American Anthropological Association, 1965–1967
***Married:*** Richard A. Watson, 1955
***Children:*** 1

***Patty Jo Watson*** is a distinguished anthropologist and archaeologist who has conducted research in such diverse areas as Iraq, Iran, Turkey, Kentucky, and Tennessee. Her subjects range from the prehistory of Iran to the archaeology of the Mammoth Cave area in Kentucky to method and theory in shipwreck archaeology. Early in her career she was an archaeological field assistant for the Oriental Institute of the University of Chicago, and as such, she was involved in the Iraq-Jarmo project of 1954–1955 and was an archaeologist and ethnographer on an Iranian prehistory project in 1959–1960. Her dissertation project was an investigation of early village farming in the Levant. She was elected to membership in the National Academy of Sciences in 1988.

At one symposium, one of the speakers summarized the personal characteristics that have shaped Watson's professional career: her complete commitment to archaeology, the thoroughness with which she approaches her work, her remarkable ability to remain friends with colleagues in all philosophical areas and of all professional statures, her willingness to do more than her share, and her zeal for knowledge and openness to new ideas. She has been instrumental in training a large number of archaeologists in the basics of geology, botany, and zoology because archaeological problems require investigation using all types of knowledge.

In North America, she has conducted studies in Kentucky, New Mexico, and Tennessee. One of her books is *Of Caves and Shell Mounds* (1996), and another, *Girkihaciyan: A Halafan Site in Southeastern Turkey* (1990), describes a small mound principally occupied about 5000–4500 B.C.E. She directed the excavation of the site in Turkey in 1968 and 1970 on behalf of the Istanbul-Chicago Joint Prehistoric Project. She and her coauthor characterize the site as a rural village with a mixed agricultural/pastoral economy representing the expansion of the Halafian culture far to the north of its heartland in northern Syria. She is also coeditor of *The Origins of Agriculture: An International Perspective* (1992), which is a collection of papers originally presented at a symposium of the American Association for the Advancement of Science in 1985. All of the speakers were experts in crop evolution or on the archaeological record for early plant cultivation, and their papers point out the increased awareness of a need for standardized sampling and analytical techniques.

Watson received the Fryxell Award for interdisciplinary research given by the Society for American Archaeology at a symposium held in her honor in 1990 entitled, "The State of Interdisciplinary Research in Archaeology." She is a fellow of the American Anthropological Association and a member of the American Association for the Advancement of Science, Society for American Archaeology, and Cave Research Foundation. Her photograph is included in *American Antiquity* (October 1990). She was featured in a three-part miniseries on women scientists called "Discovering Women" produced for public television in 1995.

***Bibliography:*** *Contemporary Authors* v. 77–80 and CANR-13; *Who's Who of American Women*, 20th ed., 1997–1998.

# *Wattleton (Alyce) Faye*
## (1943– )
## ***biologist***

***Education:*** B.S. in nursing, Ohio State University, 1964; M.S. in maternal and infant health care, Columbia University, 1967; certification as nurse-midwife, Columbia University; honorary degrees: 6

***Professional Experience:*** Instructor, Miami Valley School of Nursing, 1964–1966; assistant director of nursing, Dayton Public Health Nursing Association, 1967–1970; executive director, Planned Parenthood Association of Miami Valley, Dayton, Ohio, 1970–1978; president, Planned Parenthood Federation of America, 1978–1992; host, syndicated television show, Chicago, 1992– ; president and founder, Center for Gender Equality, 1995–

***Married:*** Franklin Gordon, 1973, divorced 1981

***Children:*** 1

***Faye Wattleton*** is known for her work to bring the Planned Parenthood Federation of America (PPFA) to the forefront during her presidency of that organization. She led the nation's oldest and largest voluntary family planning organization in a crusade to guarantee every person's right to decide if and when to have a child. She became president in 1978 believing that family planning is the best solution to a host of problems that are intensified by the high rate of unintended pregnancies. These problems include child abuse, teenage pregnancy, and sexually transmitted diseases as well as poverty, hunger, and an estimated 200,000 deaths per year from illegal, often self-induced abortions. She was inspired to work with Planned Parenthood on the local level in Dayton, Ohio, after seeing the number of girls and women who suffered or died from illegal or self-induced abortions. When she was selected as president of the national organization, she was the first black woman, the first black person, and the youngest president of the organization.

Margaret Sanger (1883–1966), the foremother of the birth control movement, opened America's first birth control clinic, the forerunner of PPFA, in 1916. All family planning programs have had to overcome entrenched and powerful resistance to their efforts to provide educational, medical, and counseling services in the highly controversial areas of sexuality and reproductive health. PPFA offers pregnancy diagnosis, prenatal care, infertility counseling, AIDS testing, and contraceptive services. On the international scene, Family Planning International Assistance provides similar services in developing countries.

In the 1960s and early 1970s, some black activists and some feminists criticized Planned Parenthood as being racist and anti-women. In the view of the former, the organization was a white-managed agency whose mission was to reduce the black birthrate through population control, and the latter viewed the organization as a male-directed effort to control women's reproductive rights at the expense of their health. The selection of Wattleton as president greatly allayed the fears of both groups. Opposition to Planned Parenthood escalated during the 1980s, and there are continuing attempts to restrict abortion rights through legal decisions. However, Wattleton could not know that the fire-bombing of abortion clinics would begin during her first year as president or that she would receive death threats. Her position previously had been held only by white men, and many people in the organization feared that her decision to change the organization's image would drive away corporate sponsors. She kept emphasizing that Planned Parenthood is pro-choice, not pro-abortion.

The largest setback for the pro-choice movement since Medicaid funding was abolished in two-thirds of the states was the Supreme Court's Webster decision in July 1989. Although the Webster ruling did not overturn *Roe v. Wade,* it did refer the abortion issue back to the state legislatures. The Webster decision not only invigorated the pro-choice movement but also caused the National Organization for Women and other groups to form a coalition with Planned Parenthood. Wattleton resigned as president in 1992 for a well-deserved rest. Since that time she has hosted a syndicated television show, and in 1995 she founded the Center for Gender Equality, a think tank on women's issues.

Her family was very poor, but her parents stressed the importance of helping people who were less fortunate. Her mother became an itinerant preacher in the Church of God, and Faye herself originally planned to become a missionary in Africa. She entered the School of Nursing at Ohio State University at age 16 and was the first person in her family to receive a college degree. In her first position, as a maternity nursing instructor, she saw the physical and emotional complications of women who had had illegal abortions, and during her training at Columbia University as a nurse-midwife, she saw even more examples of botched abortions. After she accepted a position in Dayton, Ohio, she was asked to head the local Planned Parenthood group and was later chosen to serve as president of the national group.

She has received numerous awards, including the Claude Pepper Humanitarian Award (1990), Boy Scouts of America Award (1990), Spirit of Achievement Award of the Albert Einstein College of Medicine, Yeshiva University (1991), Margaret Sanger Award (1992), Jefferson Public Service Award (1991), and Dean's Distinguished Service Award of the Columbia School of Public Health (1992). In addition to her scientific papers, she has written a book, *How to Talk to Your Child about Sexuality* (1986), and her autobiography, *Life on the Line* (1996). Her photograph is included in *Current Biography* (1990) and *Business Week* (March 26, 1990).

***Bibliography:*** *Blacks in Science and Medicine; Current Biography 1990; Notable Black American Women; Who's Who in America,* 51st ed., 1997; *Who's Who of American Women,* 20th ed., 1997–1998.

# Weertman, Julia (Randall)
(1926– )
## solid-state physicist, metallurgist

***Education:*** B.S., Carnegie-Mellon University, 1946, M.S., 1947, D.Sc. in physics, 1951
***Professional Experience:*** Rotary International fellow, École Normale Supérieure, University of Paris, 1951–1952; physicist, U.S. Naval Research Laboratory, 1952–1958; visiting assistant professor, Northwestern University, 1972–1973, assistant professor, 1973–1978, associate professor of materials science, 1978–1982, professor, 1982–1988, department chair, 1987–1992, Walter P. Murphy Professor of Materials Science, 1988–
***Married:*** Johannes Weertman, 1950
***Children:*** 2

***Julia Weertman*** is renowned for her research on high-temperature metal failure and the nanocrystalline structures of metals. She has also contributed to the understanding of the basic characteristics of different materials in her research on small angle neutron scattering. She was elected to membership in the National Academy of Engineering in 1988, just 15 years after returning full-time to research, which she had interrupted to devote time to her children.

After she completed her postdoctoral studies at the École Normale Supérieure, she was appointed to a position as a physicist at the U.S. Naval Research Laboratory. Her work there centered around ferromagnetic spin resonance and the study of the basic concepts of magnetism. She interrupted her formal research to accompany her husband to London where he worked for the Naval Research Laboratory. She and her husband collaborated on a textbook during this period, *Elementary Dislocation Theory* (1964). When they returned to the United States, her husband accepted a position at Northwestern University, and she stayed at home with their children.

Weertman returned to research formally when she joined Northwestern University as a visiting assistant professor and then joined the faculty full time, rising through the ranks to full professor and then a distinguished professorship, the Walter P. Murphy Professor of Materials Science. Much of her work has centered not only on dislocation, which allows metals to be controlled more easily, but also on an examination of the effects of very high temperatures on pure metals and alloys with respect to their fatigue and failure. She has researched the mechanical effects of extremely high temperatures on such properties as tensile strength and brittleness, and her research on small angle neutron scattering has aided in characterizing material so that scientists can more easily understand boundary interactions and mechanical properties.

As a child, she was fascinated with airplanes and flying. Her parents told her she would have to become an aeronautical engineer before they would allow her to learn to fly; she studied diligently but eventually decided she preferred physics. She received all of her collegiate schooling at the Carnegie Institute of Technology, which is now Carnegie-Mellon University.

In addition to her scientific papers, she has been coauthor of six books. She was a member of the Evanston Environmental Control Board (1972–1979)—Northwestern University is located in Evanston, Illinois. She has received a number of awards, including the Creativity Award of the National Science Foundation (1981 and 1986), Achievement Award of the Society of Women Engineers (1991), and Environmental Award of the City of Evanston, Illinois (1979). She is a fellow of the American Society for Metals International and the Minerals, Metals, and Materials Society. She is a member of the American Institute of Physics, American Crystallographic Association, American Society for Testing and Materials, Materials Research Society, and American Physical Society. Her research includes dislocation theory, high-temperature fatigue, small angle neutron scattering, and nanocrystalline material.

***Bibliography:*** *American Men and Women of Science* 12–19; *Notable Twentieth-Century Scientists; Who's Who in America*, 51st ed., 1997; *Who's Who in Technology Today* v. 4; *Who's Who of American Women*, 20th ed., 1997–1998.

# *Weisburger, Elizabeth Amy (Kreiser)*
(1924– )
## *chemical carcinogenesist, toxicologist*

***Education:*** B.S., Lebanon Valley College, 1944; Ph.D. in organic chemistry, University of Cincinnati, 1947; honorary degrees: D.Sc. University of Cincinnati, 1981, and Lebanon Valley College, 1989

***Professional Experience:*** Research associate, University of Cincinnati, 1947–1949; research fellow, National Cancer Institute, 1949–1951, research organic chemist, Biochemical Laboratory, 1951–1961, carcinogen screening section, 1961–1972, chief, Carcinogen Metabolism and Toxicology Branch, 1973–1978, chief, Laboratory of Carcinogen Metabolism, 1978–1981, assistant director of chemical carcinogens, Division of Cancer Etiology, 1981–1989; consultant, 1989–

***Married:*** John H. Weisburger, 1947, divorced 1970

***Children:*** 3

***Elizabeth Weisburger*** is renowned for her pioneering research in chemical carcinogenesis, a field that explores the mechanisms by which environmental chemicals cause mutations and cancer. The field came into existence in the 1920s and just recently became important in studies of cancer. Her most important contributions to the areas of carcinogenesis and toxicology are the application of chemistry to synthesize reference metabolites and the relationships of structure and activity in selecting compounds for testing as possible carcinogens. She has also studied specific biochemical pathways of malignant growths and inhibitory effects of chemicals in the prevention of carcinogenesis.

Her research has aided in providing insight at the molecular level of carcinogenesis, which is vital in developing methods for the treatment and prevention of cancer. Among the compounds that she has studied are fluorenes, nitrosamines, aromatic amines, halogenated hydrocarbons, fumigants, and food preservatives. She has also investigated the relationship between mutagens and cancers and emphasized developing improved test systems for evaluating carcinogenic risk. She was also among the first scientists to test some of the drugs used in clinical cancer chemotherapy and to point out their potential dangers. These medicinals, like many known chemical carcinogens, are alkylating agents and mutagens.

Both of her parents were college graduates, and both had taught school. She was schooled at home by her mother until she was eight, and later she was a good student in elementary and high school. She originally was interested in biology when she began undergraduate school, but she was stalled when a professor said that one had to be able to draw well to work in that field. She therefore shifted her major to chemistry and studied mathematics and physics as well. During World War II, graduate assistantships in chemistry were readily available to women because so many of the men were in the military service. Weisburger received an assistantship at the University of Cincinnati where she began work in cancer research and continued working as a research associate after graduation. She and her husband then joined the National Cancer Institute, and they both worked there for a number of years. She became a commissioned officer in the U.S. Public Health Service in

1951 and retired with the rank of captain in 1989. She has continued to work as a consultant, review grants and proposals, and write.

Although biomedical research is a competitive field, she says that competition is constructive, for if one has an open mind, one can find the competition inspiring instead of threatening. She encourages young people to start science careers but says they should learn as much as they can, especially about research techniques. Understanding computer science is a necessary part of biomedical research.

Weisburger has been a member of the Chemical Substances Committee of the American Conference of Government Industrial Hygienists since 1978. She has received numerous awards, including the Meritorious Service Medal (1973) and Distinguished Service Medal (1985) of the U.S. Public Health Service, the Garvan Medal of the American Chemical Society (1981), and the Hillebrand Prize (1981). The Garvan Medal was awarded each year to an American women chemist for outstanding work in the field. She is a member of the American Association for the Advancement of Science, American Association for Cancer Research, American Chemical Society, Society of Toxicology, and American Society of Biochemistry and Molecular Biology. Her research includes metabolism of chemical carcinogens, carcinogen testing and chemical carcinogenesis, and toxicology.

***Bibliography:*** *American Men and Women of Science* 11–19; *Notable Women in the Physical Sciences; Who's Who in America,* 51st ed., 1997; *Who's Who in Technology Today* v. 6; *Who's Who of American Women,* 20th ed., 1997–1998; *Women in Chemistry and Physics.*

## *Weisstein, Naomi*

(1939– )

***psychologist***

***Education:*** B.A., Wellesley College, 1961; Ph.D. in psychology, Harvard University, 1964
***Professional Experience:*** Lecturer, University of Chicago, 1965; from assistant professor to associate professor, Loyola University, Chicago, 1966–1973; professor of psychology, State University of New York at Buffalo, 1973–
***Concurrent Position:*** Consultant, Xerox Corporation, 1973–1974
***Married:*** Jesse Lemisch, 1965

***Naomi Weisstein*** is an experimental psychologist who is known for her research in vision, perception, and cognition. She is also known for her activity in civil rights feminist causes starting in the 1960s. She has participated in several civil rights protest groups, first as a graduate student at Harvard and then as a postdoctoral lecturer at the University of Chicago, and she is one of the few women to speak out about employment practices in academia. In addition to her scientific publications, she has written several papers concerning the difficulties of entering the scientific profession and staying there if one is a women. These difficulties reflect the experience of many of the other women scientists who are profiled in this volume, but Weisstein has provided one of the most complete descriptions of the problems.

Since she attended Wellesley College as an undergraduate, she did not experience discrimination. At the time, she did not realize that her brilliant and dedicated female professors who had received degrees from first-class universities were teaching at a women's college because they were unable to secure positions at the first-class universities. As a result, they had heavy teaching loads and little time, equipment, or funds to conduct research. On her first day at Harvard, the department chair told the assembled graduate students that women did not belong in graduate school, and she was not permitted to use the equipment she needed for her research because she might break it—although the male students regularly broke equipment. She solved the problem by going to Yale University to use their equipment and transferring her credits and work back to Harvard in order to receive her doctorate.

Weisstein was promised a position at the University of Chicago, but about ten days before classes started the department suddenly invoked the unwritten nepotism rule to deny her a position on the faculty. She was hired as a lecturer to teach in areas outside her research interest because her husband was a faculty member. Her classrooms constantly were changed without prior notice, she was unable to borrow a library book for an extended period without permission from the department, and she was not notified that her contract was not being renewed for the following year. However, when the department suddenly found she had obtained a grant it wanted her to stay—because the department could claim part of the grant funds for overhead expenses.

Instead, she and her grant moved to Loyola University, Chicago, where she became an assistant professor. Unfortunately, that school did not have all of the support services that research universities such as Chicago have, not even such mundane services that experimental scientists need as machine shops, electrical engineering departments, and a large computer. The next year the department head promised her she could share the new computer that the department was purchasing, but one of her male colleagues refused to allow her to use it, and the department head supported him. At that time, in the late 1960s and early 1970s, there were no computer service companies such as Kinko's to sell computer time to outsiders, and personal computers were just being developed. She was thus forced to do her calculations and projections by hand, which stalled her research and her possibilities for publication. She later moved to the State University of New York at Buffalo.

One subject that concerns her is that the field of psychology has persevered in describing male personalities and female personalities even though psychologists have been unable to agree on how to identify people as schizophrenics or homosexuals or heterosexuals. In addition, clinical psychologists have never been able to show that psychotherapy is an effective means of changing behavior. In an article published in *Federation Proceedings* (September 1976) she states, "What all this means for women is that personality theory has given us no idea of what our true 'natures' are; whether we were intended from the start to be scientists and engineers, and thwarted by a society that has other plans for us, or whether we were intended, as claimed by some of the learned men in the field, only to be mothers."

Weisstein is a member of the Association for Research in Vision and Ophthalmology, Optical Society of America, and American Psychological Association. Her research focuses on vision, perception, and cognition.

***Bibliography:*** Ireland, N., *Index to Women of the World . . . Suppl.;* Rossiter, M., *Women Scientists in America; Working It Out.*

# West-Eberhard, Mary Jane
(1941– )
***entomologist***

***Education:*** B.A., University of Michigan, 1963, M.S., 1964, Ph.D. in zoology, 1967
***Professional Experience:*** Teaching fellow, Department of Zoology, University of Michigan, 1963–1965; fellow, Biology Department, Harvard University, 1967–1969; associate, Department of Entomology, Smithsonian Tropical Research Institute, 1973–1975, entomologist, 1975–
***Concurrent Positions:*** Staff member, Department of Biology, University of Valle, Colombia, 1972–1978; distinguished visiting scientist, Museum of Zoology, University of Michigan, 1982
***Married:*** 1967
***Children:*** 3

*Mary Jane West-Eberhard* is a renowned entomologist who has studied insects of all types, primarily in Central and South America. She has published papers on the insect world, including insects' chemical communication, scent trails, social behavior, and diversity. Much of her work has treated the evolution of some species. She was elected to membership in the National Academy of Sciences in 1988.

One area of her research has been the evolution of worker behavior, or eusociality, which is characterized by a reproductive division of labor. The topic has interested biologists from the time of Darwin, and her theory is that evolved traits such as cyclic reproductive behavior, aggressiveness, and group life presumably reflect the genetic makeup of the individuals performing them. It seems that even caste determination, according to which some individuals end up as helpers and others as egg-laying queens, depends to some degree on heritable differences in aggressiveness, for example, especially in relatively simple societies in which there is no extensive manipulation of the brood, which can overwhelm heritable variation.

She is the coeditor of *Natural History and Evolution of Paper-Wasps* (1996), which is based on a workshop held in Italy in 1993 to celebrate the fiftieth anniversary of Leo Pardi's original description of dominance hierarchies in *Polistes*. In her chapter in the volume, she discusses how the differentiation of paper-wasp behavior and physiology may provide an illuminating model for some of the largest questions concerning the interface between development and evolution. One reviewer noted that the volume includes a strong historical perspective, and it also includes a previously unpublished lecture by Leo Pardi.

West-Eberhard is one of several women listed in this volume who seem to have had gaps in their formal employment for several years, according to the listings in reference books. However, she apparently continued her research during those periods because she was elected to the National Academy of Sciences at a comparatively young age. She has been a member of several distinguished committees and commissions, including the International Committee for the International Union Study of Social Insects in the 1980s, the board of directors of the Organization for Tropical Studies (1985–1987), and the advisory committee of the Monteverde Conservation League Committee on Human Rights of the National Academy of Sciences (1990– ). She is a member of the American Society of Naturalists, International Union for the Study of Social Insects, and Society for the Study of Evolution (president, 1992). Her research includes the evolution of social behavior and the social behavior of polistine wasps.

***Bibliography:*** *American Men and Women of Science* 11–14, 18–19.

# *Westheimer, (Karola) Ruth (Siegel)*
(1928– )
***psychologist***

***Education:*** Degree in psychology, University of Paris, Sorbonne; M.S., New School for Social Research, 1959; Ed.D., Columbia University, 1970
***Professional Experience:*** Research assistant, Columbia University School of Public Health, 1967–1970; associate professor, Department of Sex Counseling, Lehman College, 1970–1977; counselor, radio talk show hostess, television show hostess, writer, private practice in psychology, c. 1980–1997, retired 1997
***Married:*** Manfred Westheimer, 1961, died 1997
***Children:*** 2

***Ruth Westheimer*** is known as a popular psychologist primarily because of her television and radio shows, appearances on talk shows, and books written for the general public. She has solid credentials as a counselor and has maintained a private practice for a number of years. She is popularly known as "Dr. Ruth." She says she is able to talk about controversial subjects concerning sex because of her German accent—that people would not accept her if she spoke an unaccented English and that people expect European women to talk about unmentionable things such as sex. She also says that people find her commentary to be entertaining and they appreciate her calling the parts of the body by their proper names. She still travels, gives talks, makes talk show appearances, writes, and appears in documentaries and commercials, although she is "retired."

She was born Karola Ruth Siegel in Frankfurt, Germany. In 1939 her parents decided to flee Germany, but her grandmother refused to leave. Her parents sent Ruth to Switzerland with a group of 100 other Jewish girls for safety, intending to join her later. However, her father was arrested before she left, and she presumes all of her family died in the concentration camps. Since the school considered her a welfare case, she was trained only as a maid. After the war, she emigrated to Palestine where she dropped her first name "Karola" because it sounded too German. By the time she was 20, she was a member of the Haganah, the Jewish underground movement fighting for creation of a Jewish homeland. She dreamed of becoming a physician, but without family support and money, it was an impossible dream. She married her first husband, an Israeli, and accompanied him to Paris where he studied medicine and she received a degree in psychology from the Sorbonne. However, they divorced, and he returned to Israel.

She married her second husband, a Frenchman, and they moved to New York in 1956 with their daughter. However, this marriage broke up also, and she supported herself and her daughter by working as a housemaid, the skill she had learned in the Swiss school. She learned English and attended evening classes for a master's degree at the New School for Social Research. She later worked as a research assistant at the School of Public Health at Columbia University. She married her third husband, Manfred Westheimer, in 1961; they had a son, and he adopted her daughter. Ruth continued working toward her doctorate at Columbia University in night school and took courses in sex counseling. Her thesis was on the interdisciplinary study of the family. She had a position at Lehman College in the Department of Sex Counseling for a time and then worked for Brooklyn College and a few other schools.

After giving a lecture to a group of New York broadcasters about the need for sex education programming, she was invited in 1980 to tape a 15-minute radio show, "Sexually Speaking," which was broadcast just before midnight on Sundays. This was the first of a series of radio shows, some of which featured calls from the listening audience.

Her career as an author for the general public started with *Dr. Ruth's Guide to Good Sex* (1983), and she has now written about a dozen additional titles, including *Sex for Dummies* (1996). Her autobiography is *All in a Lifetime* (1987). She is a firm believer in marriage and the family and believes that just about any nonviolent sexual activity between consenting adults is a normal, healthy part of life. There are numerous articles about her in popular magazines; most include a photograph, such as *People Weekly* (October 20, 1997).

***Bibliography:*** *Current Biography 1987;* Ireland, N., *Index to Women of the World . . . Suppl.; Who's Who of American Women,* 20th ed., 1997–1998.

# *Wexler, Nancy Sabin*
(1945– )
### *neuropsychologist*

***Education:*** B.A., Radcliffe College, 1967; Ph.D. in clinical psychology, University of Michigan, 1974; honorary degrees: DHL, New York Medical College, 1991; D.Sc., University of Michigan, 1991

***Professional Experience:*** Intern and teaching fellow, University of Michigan, 1968–1974; assistant professor of psychology, graduate faculty, New School of Social Research, and private practice in psychology, 1974–1976; health science administrator, National Institute of Neurological Communicable Disorders and Stroke, National Institutes of Health, 1978–1983; associate professor of clinical neuropsychology, College of Physicians and Surgeons, Columbia University, 1985–1992, professor of clinical neuropsychology, 1992–

***Concurrent Positions:*** President, Hereditary Disease Foundation, Santa Monica, California, 1983–

N*ancy* ***Wexler*** is renowned as one of the primary leaders in the fight to discover the cause of and cure for the hereditary Huntington's Disease, which is also called Huntington's Chorea, named for George Huntington, a physician who identified the disease in 1872. The disease appears in middle age and slowly kills nerve cells in the brain, causing dementia and rapid, uncontrollable movements of the joints and limbs. Patients live an average of 15 years after the symptoms first appear. The most-well-known person to have had the disease is the musician Woody Guthrie, and the Guthrie and Wexler families have become leaders in the fight to find a cure.

In 1968, when she was in graduate school at the University of Michigan, Nancy Wexler learned that her mother had developed symptoms of the disease, which had killed her grandfather and three of her uncles. Her mother's illness meant that both Nancy and her sister had a 50 percent chance to have inherited the defective gene that causes the disease—and that they might pass it on if they ever had children. Her father, a psychoanalyst, founded the Hereditary Disease Foundation in order to support research; Nancy assumed the presidency in 1983.

Wexler received her doctorate and wrote her dissertation on the neuropsychological and emotional consequences of being at risk for Huntington's Disease—the term *neuropsychological* refers to the brain and nervous system. Several families joined in lobbying Congress to establish the Commission for the Control of Huntington's Disease and Its Consequences to draw up the first comprehensive national plan for battling the disease; she was head of the commission.

When the commission found there was a village in Maracaibo, Venezuela, that had a high incidence of the disease, it funded a study starting in 1981 to identify the defective gene. She was in charge of visiting the village to gather blood samples that the geneticists hoped would lead to a DNA (deoxyribonucleic acid) marker for the gene itself. The villagers were wary of the procedure and suspected black magic until she showed them the scar on her arm where she had been tested and told them that her mother had died from the disease. After several trips to Venezuela to gather samples to bring back to the United States for testing, the geneticists were able in 1983 to trace the disease to one woman who had lived in the area in the early 1800s. This woman's father had been an English sailor. Since families in the village usually consisted of 10 or 12 children, the incidence of the disease was very high.

Wexler also helped to organize the Huntington's Disease Collaborative Research Group in 1984, an international consortium of scientists whose mandate was to track down the gene. The gene was isolated in 1993, but unfortunately, there is not yet a treatment for the disease. Wexler has decided that she will not have children because they, too, would have a 50 percent chance of inheriting the defective gene. In several families, siblings have refused to be tested because if one child does not have the gene, that means at least one of the siblings does. Such knowledge can create emotional trauma within a family.

She was awarded the Albert Lasker Public Service Award, the highest honor in American medicine, in 1993 for her efforts connected with Huntington's Disease, and since 1991, she has served as an adviser on social and medical ethics issues to the Human Genome Project, an international effort to map and identify the approximately 100,000 genes in the human body. She has received several other awards, including an award from the Alumnae Council, University of Michigan (1989), Venezuelan Presidential Award (1991), Distinguished Service Award, National Association of Biology Teachers (1993), and National Medical Research Award of the National Health Council (1993). She is a member of the American Psychological Society, American Society for Human Genetics, and American Neurological Association. Her photograph is included in *Current Biography* (1994), *Time* (February 10, 1992), and *American Biology Teacher* (February 1990).

***Bibliography:*** *Current Biography 1994; Notable Twentieth-Century Scientists; Who's Who of American Women,* 19th ed., 1995–1996.

# *Whitman, Marina (von Neumann)*
(1935– )
***economist***

***Education:*** B.A., Radcliffe College, 1956; M.A., Columbia University, 1959, Ph.D. in economics, 1962; honorary degrees: 20
***Professional Experience:*** Administrative assistant, Educational Testing Service, 1956–1957; consultant, Pittsburgh Regional Planning Association, 1961, staff economist, 1962; lecturer in economics, University of Pittsburgh, 1963, assistant professor of economics, 1963–1966, associate professor, 1966–1971, professor, 1971–1973, Distinguished Public Service Professor of Economics, 1973–1979; chief economist, General Motors Corporation, 1979–1985, group executive vice president for public affairs, 1985–1992; distinguished visiting professor of business administration and public policy, University of Michigan, 1992–1994, professor of business administration and public policy, 1994–
***Concurrent Positions:*** Senior staff economist, Council of Economic Advisers, Office of the President, 1970–1973; member, National Price Commission, 1971–1972
***Married:*** Robert F. Whitman, 1956
***Children:*** 2

*Marina Whitman* is renowned as an international economist in a field that is dominated by males. She has served as a senior staff economist for the Council of Economic Advisers, its first woman member, and she was the only woman member of the National Price Commission. She was also one of only three women top executives at General Motors Corporation during the late 1980s and early 1990s.

As the only daughter of the eminent mathematician John van Neumann and his first wife, she grew up in an atmosphere of stimulating people. Many famous people visited her family home because her father was a member of the Institute for Advanced Study at Princeton University, and she was 15 before she realized that this was not the norm. She had tremendous intellectual drive and intense pressure to produce while she was an undergraduate. She married after graduation, and since her husband obtained a teaching position at Princeton, she worked as an administrative assistant for the Educational Testing Service, a nonprofit organization specializing in educational measurement and research. She then enrolled in Columbia University, planning to receive a master's degree in economics and journalism with the idea of pursuing a career in financial writing. Instead, she concentrated on the economics. As part of her graduate studies, she prepared an economic development plan for the greater Pittsburgh area for the Pittsburgh Regional Planning Association.

She accepted an appointment as a lecturer in economics at the University of Pittsburgh, advancing through the ranks to professor and then distinguished professor. She wrote four books on international economics on topics such as government risk sharing in foreign investment, international and interregional payment adjustments, economic goals and policy instruments, and interdependence issues for economic theory and U.S. policy. She also was selected for membership on the prestigious Council of Economic Advisers, Office of the President, for a three-year term. In that capacity, she advised other members on the need for a realignment of currency exchange rates and helped to formulate President Nixon's 1971 directive that temporarily suspended the convertibility of U.S. currency into gold in an attempt to stabilize the dollar. She also served as the only woman member and the youngest member on the National Price Commission where she followed a flexible approach to price controls. A commission colleague praised her ability to cut through all the words and statistics to get to the heart of a problem.

In 1979, Whitman left academe to join General Motors Corporation (GM) as chief economist. Her experience in both international economics and government administration was a great asset to the company, which faced great competition from the Japanese automobile manufacturers. She pushed GM to adopt a global perspective. She linked international exchange rates to the company's market share and convinced GM executives that the Japanese did have a cost advantage, partially owing to subsidies from the Japanese government. When she was appointed group executive vice president for public affairs in 1985, she was in charge of the public affairs and marketing staff groups. When she resigned in 1992 during a corporation reorganization, she was the highest-ranking woman executive at GM. She then accepted a position as a visiting professor of economics at the University of Michigan and was later appointed to the faculty as professor of business administration and public policy.

She probably has been in the right place at the right time, coming of age professionally just as the women's movement began to gain credibility. Although she is not known as an activist, she has been able to exert influence on women's salaries. While a member of the Council of Economic Advisers, she was able to insert in the 1973 Economic Report to the President a chapter on women in the American economy, the first time such a chapter had appeared. The report stated that despite ten years of civil rights legislation, women had made little progress toward job equality with men—in 1971, the average full-time female employee earned 59.5 percent as much as the average male worker. In her own family life, Whitman gives credit to her husband for the support he has given to her career. She says he had the unusual idea that the husband should share in caring for the children, and the couple also shared cooking and household responsibilities.

She has been a member of several committees, including the President's Advisory Committee on Trade Policy and Negotiations (1987–1993), the technical assessment advisory council of the U.S. Congress Office of Technical Assessment (1990– ), trustee of the National Bureau of Economic Research (1993– ), member of the visiting committee for the Kennedy School 1992– ), and trustee of Princeton University (1980–1990). She is a member of the American Economic Association, American Academy of Arts and Sciences, and Council on Foreign Relations. Her photograph is included in *Working Woman* (November 1988).

***Bibliography:*** *Contemporary Authors* v. 17–20R; *Current Biography 1973;* Ireland, N., *Index to Women of the World . . . Suppl.; Who's Who in America,* 51st ed., 1997; *Who's Who of American Women,* 20th ed., 1997–1998.

# *Widnall, Sheila (Evans)*

(1938– )

## *aeronautical engineer*

***Education:*** B.S., Massachusetts Institute of Technology, 1960, M.S., 1961, D.Sc. in aeronautical engineering, 1964; honorary degrees: D.Sc., New England College, 1975, Lawrence University, 1987, Cedar Crest College, 1988, and Smith College, 1990

***Professional Experience:*** Research assistant, aerodynamics, Massachusetts Institute of Technology, 1961–1964, Ford fellow, 1964–1966, assistant professor of aeronautics, 1964–1970, associate professor 1970–1974, professor 1974–1992, head, Dynamics Division, Department of Aeronautics and Astronautics, 1978–1979, Abby Rockefeller Mauze Chair, 1986– , associate provost, 1992–1993; secretary of U.S. Air Force, 1993–

***Concurrent Position:*** Director of university research, U.S. Department of Transportation, 1974–1975

***Married:*** William S. Widnall, 1960

***Children:*** 2

*Sheila Widnall* became the first woman to head a branch of the U.S. military when she was selected to be secretary of the U.S. Air Force in 1993. She brought to the position a solid background in aeronautical engineering, which is recognized by her peers, plus some experience in administering a government agency, from her appointment as director of university research for the U.S. Department of Transportation in the 1970s. She was a member of the board of governors for the Air Force Academy from 1978 to 1993, and she has served on numerous national committees and commissions plus a term as president of the American Association for the Advancement of Science, the largest science association in the United States. She was elected to membership in the National Academy of Engineering in 1985.

She was the first woman graduate to be appointed to the engineering faculty of the Massachusetts Institute of Technology (MIT) in 1964, and there she specializes in the theories and applications of fluid dynamics. Her doctoral thesis dealt with wing theory; complex wing structure, both unsteady and steady; and cavitating hydrofoils. Her research has centered particularly on problems associated with the air turbulence created by rotating helicopter blades, examining the vortices, or eddies, of air created at the ends and at the trailing edge of the helicopter blades as they swirl through the air. The vortices are the source of noise, vibration, and instability that affect the soundness of the blades and the stability of the aircraft. Another area of research is the vortices of aircraft that make vertical, short takeoffs and landings and the noise associated with them (the aircraft are called V/STOL, vertical/short takeoff and landing, aircraft). One of her projects was to design an anechoic wind tunnel at MIT to study V/STOL aircraft—a wind tunnel that has a low degree of reverberation and is echo-free. The theme of her research has been unsteady flow, whether it concerns turbulence, stability, or acoustics.

As secretary, Widnall is responsible for all U.S. Air Force matters, including recruiting, organizing, training, administration, logistical support, maintenance, and welfare of personnel plus research and development. She very carefully explains to people that she does not have the authority to order an air strike. The military operations are controlled by a chain of command through the secretary of defense to the commanders of each service, in this case, the chief of staff of the air force. She always jokes that whenever she flies on Air Force One everyone else tries to sit next to the president but she wants to go up front and fly the plane. She has been able to fly other aircraft on at least two operational missions. The first was a routine AWACS flight from Turkey over northern Iraq and the second was in the Adriatic aboard a RC-135 aircraft.

She states she was fortunate that MIT hired her fairly soon after universities began accepting women for faculty positions. Prior to that, no matter how good you were, if you were a woman you would not be considered for a faculty position. When people ask her why she stayed so long at MIT, she replies that since both she and her husband are aeronautical engineers at that institution, it would be difficult to time a move that would be beneficial to both of them. She stayed in academia instead of moving to industry because she loves teaching and she enjoys the autonomy of faculty life.

Widnall considers both science and engineering to be wonderful careers for women. The engineering fields are very interesting, and usually they pay pretty well. What is important for women is that contributions can be measured; there is not much subjectivity in evaluating work in many areas of science and engineering. She also believes that engineering is a good career choice for women because it offers a wide range of opportunities in industry, academe, and government and at different levels depending on whether one has a bachelor's, master's, or doctoral degree. She has published papers and presented talks about the changing attitudes and trends in education for prospective engineers and scientists. In her inaugural address as president of the American Association for the Advancement of Science, she spoke about seeing that more women become scientists and engineers and outlined the problems they face in attaining their degrees and achieving professional goals. In 1986, MIT awarded her the Abby Rockefeller Mauze Chair, an endowed professorship given to people who promote the advancement of women in industry or in the arts and professions.

She credits her father with fostering her interest in science and math and her mother for showing her that women can manage both a career and a family. All through elementary and high school, no one discouraged her interest in science and math. There were 20 women in her class of about 900 at MIT, but she decided to pursue a doctorate when she was a junior in college because many of her teachers encouraged her. She married in her senior year in college, and the couple had their first child before she completed her doctorate. Fortunately, there was a large number of wives of graduate students on campus who were available for child care during the day, but she says she could not have done it all without a supportive husband.

She has received numerous awards, including the Lawrence Sperry Award of the American Institute of Aeronautics and Astronautics (1972) and the Outstanding Achievement Award of the Society of

Women Engineers (1975). She is a fellow of the American Institute of Aeronautics and Astronautics, American Physical Society, and American Association for the Advancement of Science. She is a member of the Society of Women Engineers and American Society of Mechanical Engineers. Her research includes unsteady aerodynamics, aeroelasticity, aerodynamic noise, turbulence, applied mathematics, vortex flows, numerical analysis, aerospace, transportation, aerodynamics and fluid mechanics, acoustics, and noise and vibration. Her photograph is included in *Notable Twentieth-Century Scientists, Working Woman* (November–December 1996), and *People Weekly* (October 6, 1997).

**Bibliography:** *American Men and Women of Science* 11–19; Herzenberg, C., *Women Scientists from Antiquity to the Present;* Ireland, N., *Index to Women of the World . . . Suppl.; Journeys of Women in Science and Engineering; Notable Twentieth-Century Scientists; Who's Who in America,* 51st ed., 1997; *Who's Who in Engineering,* 9th ed., 1995; *Who's Who of American Women,* 19th ed., 1995–1996.

# *Williams, Roberta*

(1952– )

## *computer games designer*

***Education:*** High school

***Professional Experience:*** Part-time programmer; designer of computer action games, 1979–1980; cofounder and chief game designer, Sierra On-Line, Inc., 1980–1996; chief game designer, Sierra On-Line subsidiary of CUC International, Inc., 1996–

***Married:*** Kenneth A. Williams, 1971

***Children:*** 2

***Roberta Williams*** is considered the queen of the adventure computer game. Although she considers herself only an average programmer, she is expert at designing multimedia games. Her career started when her husband, a programmer, brought home a computer game that she found was easy to solve. After she had criticized it, she felt she could do a better job. She invented the first home-computer adventure game to use graphics, called "Mystery House," and her husband programmed it on an Apple computer. When they marketed the game through a computer magazine, they had sales of $8,000 the first month. They formed their own company in 1980, Sierra On-Line, with Roberta as chief designer and Ken as chief operating officer. By 1983, they were earning $10 million a year in sales. After they sold the company to CUC International, Inc. in 1996 for about $1 billion, she stayed on as chief designer. She says she does not feel there is competition from the video games in the malls; they are so fast and flashy, they do not compare with her action games in content or design.

When the Williamses sold their first game, buyers would telephone when they became frustrated with attempting to solve it. It was much more complicated than any previous game. The couple therefore built up a following for Roberta's second game, "The Wizard and the Princess," which was programmed on a disk rather than on a cassette. This new format revolutionized the microcomputer game industry by making possible much longer games. Although most games then used only 6 colors, Roberta's used 21. Her most complex and interesting adventure game in the 1980s was called "Time Zone," which occupies both sides of six disks, making it ten times as long as most games; usually it requires months to complete. The programming for this game took a team of programmers two years. One of the most complicated projects the couple has worked on is the Jim Henson movie *Dark Crystal.* They designed a computer game by the same name, which was released at the same time as the movie, and Roberta also advised on some of the layouts for the movie.

She designed a third-generation computer game for the IBM-PC, "King's Quest," which offers animation, enhanced graphics and sound, and simulated 3-D screens. There are two ways to solve each puzzle. She also has designed a range of other computer products. Some early software products were "Homeword," for the IBM-PCjr, "Homeword Speller," and "Homeword Tax."

In 1997, Sierra On-Line, Inc. released the "Roberta Williams Anthology," which is a collection of 14 of her games. Most of the early ones are primitive by today's standards, but the anthology is a compact history of the form. Although she still composes games by drawing them on large sheets of paper, the preparation of one of her new ones, "Phantasmagoria," involved almost 200 people, including animators, programmers, musicians, and composers. However, she still has as much control over the product that she always has. "Phantasmagoria" is the first game to include some violence, but the boxes are marked "Adults Only." She feels it is the parents' responsibility to monitor the games their children are playing.

Earlier, she was one of the first designers to use a female protagonist in an adventure game. The men at Sierra On-Line told her that men would not want to play it, but she felt there were many women who would and probably the men would not care. After it had sold extremely well, she asked buyers how they liked it. Both men and women replied they did not mind playing a game with a female protagonist as long as the game was fun. When an interviewer asked her what she thought people would remember about her work, she replied that the adventure-game genre was hers because she has been able to define where the genre would go next.

She says that as a child, she had a big imagination and loved to read. She is a born storyteller and loves solving problems. She was too restless to go to college, but she had had some technical training in computers, so in 1979, she just sat down at her kitchen table and designed the first game. She is still designing games and other software. Her photograph is included in *Newsweek* (March 31, 1997) and *Fortune* (August 5, 1996).

***Bibliography:*** Stanley, A., *Mothers and Daughters of Invention.*

# Woods, Geraldine (Pittman)
## (1921– )
## *embryologist*

***Education:*** Student, Talladega College, 1938–1940; B.S., Howard University, 1942; M.A., Radcliffe College, 1943, Ph.D. in neuroembryology, 1945; honorary degrees: D.Sc., Benedict College, 1977, and Talladega College, 1980, Fisk University, 1991, Bennett College, 1993; LHD, Meharry Medical College, 1988, and Howard University, 1989

***Professional Experience:*** Instructor in biology, Howard University, 1945–1946; special consultant, National Institute of General Medical Sciences, National Institutes of Health, 1969–1987, retired 1987

***Married:*** Robert Woods, 1945

***Children:*** 3

***Geraldine Woods*** in known for her many years of effort to gain federal government support for improving access to higher education for minorities. She developed programs to provide scholarships and financial aid for minority students to obtain doctorates, financial support to minority schools to purchase needed equipment and provide research funds, and support for minority faculty to work with researchers at universities that have superior research facilities, serving as a consultant to the National Institute of General Medical Sciences in implementing these programs. She was only the third black woman in the United States to receive a doctorate in biological science.

Although her family was not wealthy, she attended a private elementary school; however, she graduated from the black high school in segregated West Palm Beach. She did have an early interest in science, but she received little encouragement from her teachers and family. In those days, black women rarely became professional scientists. While she was attending Talladega College, her mother became seriously ill. The physicians recommended she take treatments at Johns Hopkins University, so Geraldine transferred to nearby Howard University. She became a very good student in science, and several of her teachers assisted her in gaining admittance to the graduate program in biology at Harvard University.

At that time, the women enrolled in Radcliffe College took all of their science classes at Harvard. When she attended her first laboratory session, she was amazed to see students working with equipment she had never seen before. The experience inspired her to excel in her work, and she earned two graduate degrees in three years. Her doctoral research involved the early development of nerves in the spinal cord. While still in the early embryo stage, nerve cells are barely distinguishable from other kinds of cells, but as the fetus matures, the nerve cells become specialized and begin transmitting messages. She studied whether this specialization process was governed by the cell's heredity or by stimulation from nearby cells.

After receiving her doctorate, she taught for one semester at Howard University before marrying a dental student. After he received his degree from Meharry Medical School, they moved to California where he set up practice. When their children were teenagers, she began her long years as a volunteer for social services, equality of opportunity, and civil rights efforts. She began in her local Los Angeles community, then became active in statewide activities. Her work was beginning to attract national attention when Lady Bird Johnson, wife of President Lyndon Johnson, invited her to the White House in 1965 to help launch Project Head Start, a federal program to help children from low-income families attend preschool. In 1968, President Johnson appointed her chair of the Defense Advisory Committee on Women in the Services.

Probably her best known efforts were centered on developing minority access to research careers and biomedical research support. In 1969, she was appointed as a special consultant to the National Institute of General Medical Sciences of the National Institutes of Health, and one of her primary concerns was the seeming inability of scientists from minority institutions of higher education to compete successfully for research grants from various government agencies and philanthropic organizations. A second problem was that the minority institutions lacked adequate equipment to do noteworthy research in biology, chemistry, and physics, and her third concern was to improve educational opportunities for students in the sciences. The minority students faced problems stemming from the debilitating effects of financial worries, a lack of encouragement on the part of elementary and high school counselors, and difficulty in mastering standardized tests.

The National Institutes of Health installed two programs under her guidance. The first was the Minority Biomedical Research Support (MBRS) program to help grant applicants win funding by holding seminars and tutorials at minority institutions to coach faculty members on how to apply for grants that included funds to purchase equipment for their research. The second program, Minority Access to Research Careers (MARC), was established to provide scholarships and counseling to students interested in a science career. In addition, fellowships were made available to faculty members at minority schools to allow them to work with colleagues at some of the prestigious universities in the country. Although Woods's own career as a scientist was brief, she has been instrumental in guiding the actions of the federal government to the educational needs of minority science students and the research capabilities of minority schools.

She is a member of the American Association for the Advancement of Science and the New York Academy of Sciences. Her research includes continuing to assist colleges with minority students to move into research and research training to encourage more participation in health and scientific careers. Her photograph is included in *Distinguished African American Scientists of the 20th Century.*

***Bibliography:*** *American Men and Women of Science* 13–19; *Blacks in Science and Medicine; Distinguished African American Scientists of the 20th Century; Notable Black American Women; Who's Who in America,* 51st ed., 1997.

# *Wu, Ying-Chu (Lin) Susan*

(1932– )

## *aerospace engineer*

***Education:*** B.S., mechanical engineering, National Taiwan University, 1955; M.S. in aerospace engineering, Ohio State University, 1959; Ph.D. in aeronautics, California Institute of Technology, 1963

***Professional Experience:*** Engineer, Taiwan Highway Bureau, 1955–1956; senior engineer, Electro-Optical Systems, 1963–1965; assistant professor, University of Tennessee, 1965–1967, associate professor, 1967–1973, professor of aerospace engineering, University of Tennessee Space Institute (UTSI), 1973–1988; president and chief executive officer, Engineering Research Consulting, Inc., 1988–

***Concurrent Positions:*** Laboratory manager, research and development laboratory, University of Tennessee, 1977–1981, administrator, Energy Conversion Research and Development Program, University of Tennessee, 1981–1988

***Married:*** Jain-Ming (James) Wu, 1959

***Children:*** 3

***Susan Wu*** is renowned for her research on the potential for cleaner and more efficient methods of coal-fired power generation in the United States through the use of magnetohydrodynamics (MHD). Coal-fired power plants are used to generate electricity in cities for industrial as well as domestic use, and some large manufacturing plants have their own power plants to generate electricity for their production and office facilities. Wu's field of research is an important one primarily because of more and more mandates from the federal government to reduce emissions from coal-fired power plants and to reduce the use of fossil fuels, such as coal, to preserve them for future generations.

MHD generation is the production of electric power without the use of rotating machinery by passing a plasma through a magnetic field. The conventional power generators use steam, coal, or oil power to turn an armature on which a continuous wire is wrapped. A magnetic field surrounds the armature, and as the wires cut through the magnetic field, a current is induced in the wire, thereby producing electricity. In using MHD, the armature is replaced by plasma, a very hot gas on the order of 5,000 degrees Fahrenheit. At times, elements such as cesium or potassium ions are introduced into the gas to increase its conductivity. As the electrically conductive plasma cuts through the magnetic field, an electric current is generated. This method of power generation is cleaner and more efficient than the traditional power plant, and MHD generation is also used as a power source for aircraft.

After she received her undergraduate degree, Susan Wu found that engineering jobs for women were scarce in China because employers viewed jobs as a lifetime commitment for employees and concentrated on hiring men. She moved to the United States where she received her graduate degrees in aerospace aeronautics and engineering. She was appointed an assistant professor at the University of Tennessee and advanced through the ranks to become a professor in only eight years. She left the university after 23 years to found Engineering Research Consulting, Inc., in Tullahoma, Tennessee, an aerospace engineering and MHD consulting firm that consults for such agencies as the National Aeronautics and Space Administration, the Department of Energy, and Argonne National Laboratory plus companies such as Boeing and McDonnell Douglas.

She has been a member of the advisory board of the National Air and Space Museum of the Smithsonian Institution since 1993 and has received several awards, including the University of Tennessee's Chancellor's Research Scholar Award (1978), Outstanding Educators of America Award (1973 and 1975), Society of Women Engineers Achievement Award (1985), and Plasmadynamics and Lasers Award of the American Institute of Aeronautics and Astronautics (1994). She is a fellow of the American Institute of Aeronautics and Astronautics and the American Society of Mechanical Engineers; she is a member of the Society of Women Engineers. Her research is magnetohydrodynamic power generation.

***Bibliography:*** *American Men and Women of Science* 11–19; *Notable Twentieth-Century Scientists; Who's Who in America,* 51st ed., 1997; *Who's Who in Science and Engineering,* 3d ed., 1996–1997; *Who's Who in Technology Today* v. 6; *Who's Who of American Women,* 20th ed., 1997–1998.

# BIBLIOGRAPHY


*American Men and Women of Science.* New York: Bowker, 1906– .

"America's Top 100 Young Scientists." *Science Digest* 92:12 (December 1984): 40–73.

Bataille, Gretchen M. *Native American Women: A Biographical Dictionary.* New York: Garland, 1993.

*Black Women in America: An Historical Encyclopedia.* Edited by Darlene Clark Hine. 2 volumes. Brooklyn, NY: Carlson Publishing, 1993.

*Blacks in Science: Ancient and Modern.* Edited by Ivan Van Sertimea. New Brunswick, NY: Transaction Books, 1984.

*Blacks in Science and Medicine.* Edited by Vivian O. Sammons. New York: Hemisphere Publishing, 1990.

Blashfield, Jean F. *Hellraisers, Heroines, and Holy Women: Women's Most Remarkable Contributions to History.* New York: St. Martins Press, 1981.

Brown, Kenneth. *Inventors at Work: Interviews with 16 Notable American Inventors.* Redmond, WA: Microsoft Press, 1988.

Bylinsky, G. "America's Hot Young Scientists." *Fortune* 122 (October 8, 1990): 56–69.

*Contemporary Authors,* v. 1–150; *Contemporary Authors New Revision Series* v. 1– Detroit: Gale Research, 1962– .

*Current Biography.* Detroit: Gale Research, 1956– .

*Distinguished African American Scientists of the 20th Century.* Edited by James H. Kessler and others. Phoenix, AZ: Oryx Press, 1996.

Dobson, A. K., and K. Bracher. "A Historical Introduction to Women in Astronomy." *Mercury* 21 (January–February 1992): 4–15.

Ehrhart-Morrison, Dorothy. *No Mountain High Enough: Secrets of Successful African American Women.* Berkeley, CA: Conari Press, 1997.

*Encyclopedia of Black America.* Edited by Augustus Low and Virgil Clift. New York: McGraw-Hill, 1984.

Felder, Deborah G. *The 100 Most Influential Women of All Time: A Ranking Past and Present.* New London, CT: Citadel Press, 1996.

Fins, Alice. *Women in Science.* Skokie, IL: VGM Career Horizons, 1979.

Golemba, Beverly E. *Lesser-Known Women: A Biographical Dictionary.* Boulder, CO: Lynne Rienner Publishers, 1992.

*Good Housekeeping Woman's Almanac.* New York: Newspaper Enterprise Association, 1977.

Hanauer, M. "A Friendly Frontier for Female Pioneers." *Fortune* 109 (June 25, 1984): 78–85.

Herzenberg, Caroline L. *Women Scientists from Antiquity to the Present.* West Cornwall, CT.: Locust Hill Press, 1986.

*Hidden Scholars: Women Anthropologists and the Native American Southwest.* Edited by Nancy J. Perez. Albuquerque: University of New Mexico Press, 1993.

*History of Programming Languages.* Edited by Richard L. Wexelblat. New York: Academic Press, 1981.

Holden, C. "Model Systems." *Science* 252 (May 24, 1991): 1110–1132.

Holloway, M. " A Lab of Her Own." *Scientific American* 269:5 (November 1993): 94–101.

Howard, H. "The Year's Top 100 Innovations and the Men and Women Behind Them." *Science Digest* 93:12 (December 1985): 27–63.

Hoyt, Mary F. *American Women of the Space Age.* New York: Atheneum, 1966.

*Indians of Today.* 4th ed. Edited by Marion Gridley. Chicago: I.C.F.P., 1971.

*International Dictionary of Anthropologists.* Christopher Winters, general editor. New York: Garland, 1991.

*International Dictionary of Women's Biography.* Edited by J. S. Uglow and F. Hinton. New York: Continuum Publications, 1982, reprinted 1985.

Ireland, Norma O. *Index to Women of the World from Ancient to Modern Times: Biographies and Portraits.* New York: Faxon, 1970.

_____. *Index to Women of the World from Ancient to Modern Times, a Supplement.* Metuchen, NJ: Scarecrow Press, 1988.

*Journeys of Women in Science and Engineering: No Universal Constants.* Edited by Susan A. Ambrose and others. Philadelphia: Temple University Press, 1997.

Kundsin, Ruth B. "Successful Women in the Sciences: An Analysis of Determinants." *Annals of the New York Academy of Sciences,* v. 208, 1973. Reprinted as *Women & Success: The Anatomy of Achievement.* Edited by Ruth B. Kundsin. New York: Morrow, 1974.

Lamson, Peggy. *In the Vanguard: Six American Women in Public Life.* Boston: Houghton Mifflin, 1979.

Land, Barbara. *The New Explorers: Women in Antarctica.* New York: Dodd, Mead, 1981.

LeBihan, J. "Gorilla Girls and Chimpanzee Mothers: Sexual and Cultural Identity in the Primatologist's Field." *Journal of Commonwealth Literature* 27:1 (1992): 139–148.

Lee, J. A. N. *Computer Pioneers.* Los Alamitos, CA: IEEE Computer Society Press, 1995.

Levin, Beatrice S. *Women and Medicine.* Metuchen, NJ: Scarecrow Press, 1980.

Lichtenstein, Grace. *Machisma: Women and Daring.* Garden City, NY: Doubleday, 1981.

Longstreet, Stephen. *The Queen Bees: The Women Who Shaped America.* Indianapolis: Bobbs-Merrill, 1979.

McKinney, R. E. "Sister Presidents." *Ebony* 43:4 (February 1988): 82, 84– .

Macksey, Joan. *Book of Women's Achievements.* New York: Stein & Day, 1976.

*Mathematical People: Profiles and Interviews.* Edited by Donald J. Albers and G. L. Alexanderson. Boston: Birkhauser, 1985.

May, Charles P. *Women in Aeronautics.* New York: Nelson, 1962.

Merrill, S. "Women in Engineering." *Cosmopolitan* (April 1976): 162, 164– .

*More Mathematical People: Contemporary Conversations.* Edited by Donald J. Albers and others. Boston: Harcourt Brace Jovanovich, 1990.

Morell, Virginia. "Called 'Trimates': Three Bold Women Shaped Their Field." *Science* 260 (April 16, 1993): 420–425.

Mount, Ellis, and Barbara A. List. *Milestones in Science and Technology: The Ready Reference Guide to Discoveries, Inventions, and Facts.* 2d ed. Phoenix, AZ: Oryx Press, 1994.

National Academy of Sciences. *Biographical Memoirs.* Washington, DC, vol. 63, 1994.

National Academy of Sciences and National Academy of Engineering. *Organization and Members, June 30, 1995.* Washington, DC, 1995.

*The Native North American Almanac.* Edited by D. Champagne. Detroit: Gale Research, 1994.

*The Negro in Science.* Edited by J. H. Taylor. Baltimore: Morgan State College Press, 1955.

Noble, Iris. *Contemporary Women Scientists in America.* New York: Messner, 1979.

*Notable Black American Women.* Edited by J. C. Smith. Detroit: Gale Research, 1992.

*Notable Hispanic American Women.* Edited by D. Telgen and J. Kamp. Detroit: Gale Research, 1993.

*Notable Native Americans.* Edited by S. Malinowsky. Detroit: Gale Research, 1995.

*Notable Twentieth-Century Scientists.* Edited by E. J. McMurray. Detroit: Gale Research, 1995.

*Notable Women in the Life Sciences: A Biographical Dictionary.* Edited by Benjamin J. and Barbara S. Shearer. Westport, CT: Greenwood Press, 1996.

*Notable Women in the Physical Sciences: A Biographical Dictionary.* Edited by Benjamin J. and Barbara S. Shearer. Westport, CT: Greenwood Press, 1997.

Obert, Alcestis R. *Spacefarers of the '80s and '90s: The Next Thousand People in Space.* New York: Columbia University Press, 1985.

O'Connor, Karen. *Sally Ride and the New Astronauts.* New York: Franklin Watts, 1983.

*The Omni Interviews.* Edited by Pamela Weintraub. New York: Ticknor & Fields, 1984.

*The 100 Greatest American Women.* Edited by R. C. Hirsch. New York: Lexington Library, 1976.

O'Neill, Lois D. *The Women's Book of World Records and Achievements.* Garden City, NY: Anchor Press/Doubleday, 1979.

*Particular Passions: Talks with Women Who Have Shaped Our Times.* Edited by Lynn Gilbert and G. Moore. New York: Clarkson Potter, 1981.

"The Power of Women." *Working Woman* 16:11 (November 1991): 87–97.

"Profiles in Leadership." *Hispanic Engineer* (fall 1989): 22–24.

Purl, M. "One Giant Step for Womankind: Equal Opportunity Gets off the Ground." *Working Woman* 5 (May 1980): 32–58.

Rayner, William P. *Wise Women.* New York: St. Martin's Press, 1983.

Read, Phyllis J., and Bernard L. Witlieb. *The Book of Women's Firsts.* New York: Random House, 1992.

Rossiter, Margaret W. *Women Scientists in America: Before Affirmative Action, 1940–1972.* Baltimore: Johns Hopkins University Press, 1995.

_____. *Women Scientists in America: Struggles and Strategies to 1940.* Baltimore: Johns Hopkins University Press, 1982.

*Saturday's Child: 36 Women Talk about Their Jobs.* Edited by Suzanne Seed. Chicago: J. Philip O'Hara, 1973.

Schanstra, C. "Women in Infosystems: Climbing the Corporate Ladder." *Infosystems* (May 1980): 72, 74– .

Schneider, Dorothy, and Carl F. *The ABC-CLIO Companion to Women in the Workplace.* Santa Barbara, CA : ABC-CLIO, 1993.

Sherr, Lynn. "Remembering Judy." *Ms Magazine* 14:12 (June 1986): 56–58.

Silver, Lily J. *Profiles in Success: Forty Lives of Achievement.* New York: Fountainhead Publishers, 1965.

Smith, C. H. "Black Female Achievers in Academe." *Journal of Negro Education* 51:3 (1982): 318–335.

Sochen, June. *Movers and Shakers: American Women Thinkers and Activists 1900–1970.* New York: Quadrangle, 1973.

Stanley, Autumn. *Mothers and Daughters of Invention: Notes for a Revised History of Technology.* Metuchen, NJ: Scarecrow Press, 1993.

Teitz, Joyce. *What's a Nice Girl Like You Doing in a Place Like This?* New York: Coward, McCann & Geoghegan, 1972.

"350 Women Who Changed the World 1976–1996." *Working Woman* 21:11 (November–December 1996): 32–50.

Townsel, L. J. "Husbands of Powerful Women." *Ebony* 51:9 (July 1996): 115–118.

U.S. National Aeronautics and Space Administration. *Astronaut Fact Book.* Washington, DC: NASA, May 5, 1996.

Vare, Ethlie Ann, and Greg Ptacek. *Mothers of Invention: From the Bra to the Bomb; Forgotten Women & Their Unforgettable Ideas.* New York: Morrow, 1988.

*Who's Who among Black Americans.* Detroit: Gale Research, 1975–1976– .

*Who's Who in America.* Chicago: Marquis Who's Who. 51st ed. 1997.

*Who's Who in Engineering.* Washington, DC: American Association of Engineering Societies. 8th ed., 1991; 9th ed., 1995.

*Who's Who in Science and Engineering.* Chicago: Marquis Who's Who, 2d ed., 1994–1995; 3d ed., 1996–1997.

*Who's Who in Technology Today.* 2d ed. 6 vols. Pittsburgh: Technology Recognition Corporation, 1981.

*Who's Who of American Women.* Chicago: Marquis Who's Who. 19th ed., 1995–1996; 20th ed., 1997–1998.

*Women Anthropologists: A Biographical Dictionary.* Edited by Ute Gacs and others. New York: Greenwood Press, 1988.

*Women in Chemistry and Physics: A Biobibliographic Sourcebook.* Edited by E. S. Grinstein and others. Westport, CT: Greenwood Press, 1993.

*Women in Psychology: A Bio-Bibliographic Sourcebook.* Edited by Agnes O'Connell and Nancy F. Russo. Westport, CT: Greenwood Press, 1990.

*Women of Mathematics: A Biobibliographic Sourcebook.* Edited by L. S. Grinstein and P. J. Campbell. New York: Greenwood Press, 1987.

*Working It Out: 23 Women Writers, Artists, Scientists, and Scholars Talk about Their Lives and Work.* Edited by Sara Ruddick and Pamela Daniels. New York: Pantheon Books, 1977.

*World of Invention.* New York: Gale Research, 1994.

*World Who's Who in Science: A Biographical Dictionary of Notable Scientists from Antiquity to the Present.* Edited by A. G. Debus. Chicago: Marquis Who's Who, 1968.

Yarmish, R. J., and L. S. Grinstein. "Brief Notes on Six Women in Computer Development." *Journal of Computers in Mathematics and Science Teaching* 2 (winter 1982): 38–39; (spring 1983): 26–27.

Yount, Lisa. *Twentieth-Century Women Scientists.* New York: Facts on File, 1996.

# CREDITS

1 AP/Wide World Photos
7 Courtesy of Morris Brown College
16 Courtesy of Cynthia Beall
21 Courtesy of May Berenbaum
33 UPI/Corbis-Bettmann
37 Courtesy of University of California, San Diego
43 Courtesy of Marjorie Caserio
48 AP/Wide World Photos
50 Courtesy of Jewell Plummer Cobb
54 Courtesy of Rita Colwell
62 AP/Wide World Photos
73 Courtesy of Cecile DeWitt-Morette
80 Courtesy of Mildred Dresselhaus
89 Courtesy of Fermilab Photography
91 AP/Wide World Photos
103 Courtesy of Anne Fausto-Sterling
112 Yann Arthus-Bertrand/Corbis
129 Courtesy of Elsa Garmire
133 Courtesy of Keith Warnack/Puget Sound Blood Center
136 Courtesy of Adele Goldberg
138 AP/Wide World Photos
142 AP/Wide World Photos
149 Courtesy of Sheila Greibach
156 Reuters/Corbis-Bettmann
166 AP/Wide World Photos
174 Courtesy of Darleane Hoffman
182 Courtesy of Alice Huang
192 AP/Wide World Photos
194 UPI/Corbis-Bettmann
203 Courtesy of Harvard Business School
210 Courtesy of Margaret Kidwell
218 AP/Wide World Photos
231 Courtesy of Tamara Ledley
242 Courtesy of Oregon State University
246 NASA
259 Courtesy of Lynn Margulis
267 Courtesy of Jane Menkin
289 AP/Wide World Photos
292 AP/Wide World Photos
299 L.A. Cicero/Stanford News Service
314 NASA
321 Rob Fraser
325 NASA
332 Courtesy of the Rolf Institute
353 NASA
361 AP/Wide World Photos
371 Courtesy of Jeanne Sinkford
392 Louis Fabian Bachrach
402 Courtesy of Lydia Villa-Komaroff
411 AP/J. Scott Applewhite
417 AP/Wide World Photos
421 AP/Wide World Photos

# *INDEX*